EAST ASIAN ECONOMIC ISSUES

VOLUME III

EAST ASIAN ECONOMIC ISSUES

VOLUME III

Editorial Advisers

Tan Teck Meng
Lim Chong Yah
Chew Soon Beng

Nanyang Business School

Edited by

Jon D Kendall
Park Donghyun
Randolph Tan

Nanyang Business School

World Scientific

Published by

World Scientific Publishing Co. Pte. Ltd.
P O Box 128, Farrer Road, Singapore 912805
USA office: Suite 1B, 1060 Main Street, River Edge, NJ 07661
UK office: 57 Shelton Street, Covent Garden, London WC2H 9HE

British Library Cataloguing-in-Publication Data
A catalogue record for this book is available from the British Library.

The electronic version of this document is available at web site:
http://www.ntu.edu.sg/nbs/publications/regional_issues_in_economics/

EAST ASIAN ECONOMIC ISSUES — Volume III
Copyright © 1997 by World Scientific Publishing Co. Pte. Ltd.
          and
          School of Accountancy and Business, Nanyang Technological University

ISBN 981-02-3298-5

This book is printed on acid-free paper.

Printed in Singapore by Uto-Print

FOREWORD

It gives me great personal pleasure to introduce Volume III of the Applied Economics Research Series published by the Nanyang Business School. This volume, which is entitled *East Asian Economic Issues* rather than *Regional Issues in Economics* as the first two volumes were, epitomises our school's constant pursuit of excellence in both teaching and research in economics. As the title suggests, its primary focus is on economic issues in East Asia. All the papers contained here embody one-on-one interaction and cooperation between staff and students. We believe such close working relationships are of immeasurable value in helping Applied Economics graduates develop the many skills needed for sound economic analysis.

THE BACHELOR OF BUSINESS PROGRAMME

The Bachelor of Business (B. Bus) is an undergraduate programme normally completed in six semesters over three years. Honours may be awarded depending on performance in the examinations. The classes of honours conferred are first-class Honours, second-class Honours (Upper Division) and second-class Honours (Lower Division).

All Business students read a common curriculum in their first two semesters comprising subjects in Accounting, Business Statistics, Principles of Economics, Information Technology, Management, Marketing, Principles of Law and Business Communications. Students opt for one of the following specialised areas of study for the remainder of the course to enable them to work in their area of interest:

Actuarial Science	Human Resource Management
Applied Economics	Industrial Management
Banking	Insurance
Financial Analysis	Marketing
Hospitality & Tourism Management	Quality Management

Students specialising in one area, wishing to obtain additional exposure, may undertake to read for a Minor comprising of four core subjects in another area of specialisation. In addition, students are also able to read a minor in Business Law, Entrepreneurship, Information Technology, or Research.

In step with the philosophy of providing professional, business and industry-oriented training, the School requires students to undergo an eight-week structured Professional Attachment programme during their course of study. During this time, they are placed in business organisations for exposure to the business environment. It provides an opportunity for the students to gain some practical experience and observe the complex working of an organisation so that they may be productive almost immediately upon assuming a full-time appointment after graduation.

Students also undertake a supervised Applied Research Project over their final two semesters of study. They are required to develop and effectively implement a research proposal and write up a report. This project provides the opportunity for them to apply the material and techniques learnt during their coursework.

THE APPLIED ECONOMICS SPECIALISATION

The strength and uniqueness of the University's Business Programme lies in the specialisation of its undergraduates in the above disciplines. The Applied Economics specialisation was introduced in academic year 1993/94 to complement the drive to further develop the Business programme to serve the needs of both the private and public sectors. The B. Bus (Applied Economics) degree will enable our graduates to play a decisive role in the top ranks of large corporations as well as the public sector.

Specifically, we aim:

- to inculcate in our students the analytical tools and statistical methods used in economic analysis

- to equip students with specialised training that is useful and effective in a business environment or in the public sector, through a strong emphasis on applications of economic analysis for solving issues and analysing policies.

- to orientate our students towards global developments (especially those in the East-Asian region) so that their implications and impact on the Singapore economy are better understood.

THE CURRICULUM

After the first two semesters, students who specialise in Applied Economics normally read a total of 12 core and 2 prescribed elective subjects and 8 AUs of general electives. The core subjects are:

Economic Theory I	Economic Theory II
Mathematical Economics	Econometrics
Applied Econometrics	Management Accounting
Economics of Money and Banking	Public Sector Economics
International Economics I	Economic Development and Growth

Contemporary Economic and Business Issues, Policies and Trends

Applied Research Project	Research Methodology

In addition to the above subjects, students must also complete their Professional Attachment and Applied Research Project.

Depending on their interests, students may use their prescribed elective slots to read Economics Electives which include:

Industrial Economics	Computing and Simulation
Financial Economics	Urban and Transport Economics

Economic Modelling and Forecasting Practices

Alternatively, they may opt to read for a Minor in any of the other Business specialisations or in Business Law, Entrepreneurship, Information Technology, Business Research or Accountancy. The four subjects constituting a Minor in Accountancy are Corporate Accounting and Reporting, Auditing, Income Tax Law and Practice and Advanced Management Accounting.

All Applied Economics students are expected to develop good research and writing abilities. As part of their training, they are required to submit at least one research paper for each subject in each semester. In addition, they are required to pursue their Applied Research Projects individually and independently.

The structure of the Bachelor of Business (Applied Economics) curriculum ensures that the Applied Economics graduate will have obtained definitive training in business, applied economics and (because of the strong emphasis on quantitative methods) research.

APPLIED ECONOMICS RESEARCH SERIES

This series is a collective volume of joint staff-student working papers that are based on students' Applied Research Projects and published annually by Nanyang Business School since 1995. The papers usually cover a wide spectrum of issues. In this particular volume, for example, there are works on Islamic banking and global income convergence as well as public transportation and private property prices in Singapore. All of the papers are products of rigorous economic analysis, with many of them involving sophisticated econometric modelling.

Some articles in previous volumes have been published in refereed international journals. We believe and hope that this will continue to be the case in the future. Be that as it may, the basic aim of the Applied Economics Research Series is to produce quality research relevant to Singapore and the region. I would like to emphasise that the collective volumes represent an important integral element of both research and teaching efforts at our school.

I am more than confident that this third volume of the Applied Economics Research Series, *East Asian Economic Issues*, will make significant contributions toward the tradition of excellence at our Nanyang Business School.

*Professor **Tan** Teck Meng*
Dean, Nanyang Business School
Nanyang Technological University, Singapore
(tmtan@ntu.edu.sg)

PREFACE

I am both honored and delighted to serve as an editorial advisor for East Asian Economic Issues, which represents the third volume of the Applied Economics Research Series published by Nanyang Business School.

I am presently the head of the Applied Economics Division at Nanyang Business School. All the works included in this collective volume are the products of research collaboration between the staff and students of our division. At the outset, I would like to draw your attention to the change in the name of the Applied Economics Research Series. The previous two volumes had been entitled Regional Issues in Economics. This change does not reflect any fundamental re-direction of substance or content but rather our desire to clarify the basic aim and scope of the series, which is to examine economic issues which are relevant to East Asia and, in particular, Singapore and Southeast Asia.

Our division strives to provide students with solid training in as well as sound knowledge of economics. In particular, we focus our teaching efforts on imparting to our students not only the quantitative, analytical and problem-solving skills required of an economist but perhaps just as importantly, the ability and confidence to apply those skills to real-world issues in a real-world environment. We have built our rigorous yet practical curriculum of courses on the basis of this guiding philosophy. The Applied Economics Research Series represents the culmination of our efforts to enable students to effectively apply and use the knowledge they acquire and absorb. I am especially proud of the fact that the staff-student joint papers are joint papers in the true sense of the term, with staff and students working together as research partners.

I hope that you will find the volume both interesting and useful. Thank you.

*Associate Professor **Chew** Soon Beng*
Head, Applied Economics Division
Nanyang Business School
Nanyang Technological University, Singapore
(asbchew@ntu.edu.sg)

CONTENTS

---

[1]   An author whose name is underlined is a staff member of the Division of Applied Economics; bold denotes an author's surname.

PART III   ASEAN AND EAST ASIAN ECONOMIC ISSUES

PART IV   GLOBAL AND THEORETICAL ECONOMIC ISSUES

INTRODUCTION

East Asian Economic Issues is the third volume of the Applied Economics Research Series at Nanyang Business School. The papers provide a comprehensive summary of the students' final year research projects, which average around fifty pages. They represent the commitment of both staff and students here at NTU to produce quality research of relevance to Singapore and the entire region.

The focus of Part I is on microeconomic issues in Singapore. Chee and Cao analyse the price structure of the private real estate market in Singapore from a hedonic perspective. Chow and Chew examine economic factors that affect fringe benefits in the banking sector. Goh and Sakellariou use the Almost Ideal Demand Systems (AIDS) model to forecast Singapore's share of Japanese tourist arrivals in ASEAN. Ho and Yao address the issues of rates of return to education and effectiveness of worker training programs. Kwan and Das-Gupta attempt to measure compliance with the personal income tax and the effects of various factors on compliance. Lee and Wu use panel data to study the wage-output relationship across occupational groups. Neo and Li perform an analysis of Area Licensing Scheme (ALS), focusing on its impact on commuters' travel patterns. Seah and Li evaluate the economic viability of the proposed extension of Mass Rapid Transit (MRT) to the northeast region. Wong and Park assess whether the Central Provident Fund (CPF) will be able to adequately provide for Singaporeans who are expected to retire in the near future.

Part II addresses the macroeconomic aspects of the Singaporean economy. Chan and Rahman study the effects of foreign direct investment on growth, exports, imports and domestic investment. Foo and Cao look into factors that account for the total factor productivity growth of the manufacturing sector between 1980 and 1994, in particular the effects of the 1979 industrial restructuring program. Foo and Rahman test a model of exchange rate determination which takes into account the effects of both monetary variables and the current account. Foong and Rahman explore the role of the exchange rate on inward and outward foreign direct investment. Foong and Liu evaluate the impact of asset inflation on production costs for both the economy as a whole and various sectors within the economy. Goh and Wu derive the demand and supply functions for the commercial loan market under both equilibrium and disequilibrium conditions. Loh and Tan tackle the issue of identifying performance differentials across manufacturing industries and provide some estimates of productivity growth in doing so. Soh and Maysami examine whether exchange rate objectives or monetary stability is of greater concern to the Monetary Authority of Singapore. Tan and Soon analyse the effect of Singapore's ageing population on its aggregate private savings and consumption.

Part III concerns ASEAN and East Asian economic issues. Chua and Lee look into the impact of financial development on economic growth in 5 ASEAN countries. Lau and Chen build an econometric model to study certain features of three sectors in China's Sichuan Province. Lau and Kendall compare three different forecasting models that predict the daily movement of the Thai baht. Lee and Tan attempt to estimate Malaysia's natural rate of unemployment and sustainable growth by employing the Lucas-Sargent aggregate supply function. Lim and Leu use revealed comparative advantage indices to examine the extent of trade competition between China and 5 ASEAN economies. Ng and Wang perform a quantitative analysis of the economic links between China and Hong Kong. Poa and Leu analyse the evidence on trade competition between the NIEs and 4 ASEAN economies in the US market. Poh and Chen construct an econometric model to assess the economy of China's Shandong Province, in particular foreign investment and rural industry.

Part IV deals with global and theoretical economic issues. Goh and Yao use regression analysis to identify the importance of education as a determinant of a country's competitiveness. Mong and Maysami empirically examine the stability of Islamic financial systems that are based on interest-free assets. In a theoretical paper, Poh and Tan assess the relative power and performance of Johansen's trace test. Finally, Tan and Park address the issue of whether international economic inequality has been decreasing during the period 1960-1990.

An important foundation of Nanyang Business School and Nanyang Technological University is close cooperation between industry and academia. We hope that this volume will contribute towards further solidifying those ties by providing our partners in both sectors with relevant, useful knowledge in applied economics.

*Jon D **Kendall** (kendall@pacific.net.sg)*
***Park** Donghyun (adpark@ntu.edu.sg)*
*Randolph **Tan** (arandolph@ntu.edu.sg)*
Nanyang Business School
Nanyang Technological University, Singapore

PART I

SINGAPOREAN MICROECONOMIC ISSUES

SINGAPORE'S MACROECONOMIC ISSUES

The Price Structure of Private Property in Singapore: A Hedonic Approach

Cao Yong
&
Chee Meng On

Nanyang Business School, Nanyang Technological University, Nanyang Avenue, Singapore 639798
Fax: +(65) 792.4217, Tel: +(65) 799.1322, Email: aycao@ntu.edu.sg

Abstract This paper analyses the price structure of the private real estate market in Singapore. The objective is two-fold: (I) To identify periods of stable consumption behaviour and determine the amount of pure inflation over such periods; and (II) To gain insight into the consumers' buying of condominiums, and how the valuations of their qualities have changed over the period considered. We found 3 short periods of stable consumption behaviour. The marginal prices for condominium qualities generally exhibited an upward trend. Furthermore, the convenience of having more facilities inside the estate is becoming more valuable than accessibility. The May 15 policy is found neither to have had a deflationary effect in the third quarter nor did it alter buying behaviour.

1. INTRODUCTION

Being a small open economy and a price taker in the international arena, conventional wisdom has it that most of Singapore's inflation is imported from abroad. However the MAS annual report shows years of negative imported inflation. Asset inflationary expectation, caused by the rapid appreciation of domestic assets, especially real estate, is believed to have fuelled domestic inflation, causing significant total inflation. It is therefore important to have an understanding of the real estate market.

The housing market of Singapore has come a long way from providing relief to the homeless to meeting aspirations of upgraders and improving the quality of life. The private residential market is believed to have started in the '70s with the introduction of the first condominium in Singapore - Pandan Valley. Since then, the market appears to have completed only 1 full cycle, peaking in 1981 and falling to a trough during the recession year of 1985. Prices for condominiums generally exhibited an upward trend, with the average transaction price reaching new heights almost every quarter. However, casual observation alone will reveal that the quality of the new offerings is also improving, reflecting the higher expectations of an increasingly affluent customer base.

2. BUYERS' PREFERENCES FOR PRIVATE PROPERTY IN SINGAPORE

According to KFCB Research (1987), the 5 most important selection criteria for the purchase of a condominium unit are accessibility to work, design & layout, title, main-gate security, and privacy, in descending order of importance. CBD is the primary workplace area, especially for the high budget group who consequently prefer units near to the CBD or those located near major access routes to CBD. The vast majority of those surveyed (82.4 percent) stated preferences for units with freehold titles. The lower budget group, however, are less concerned with the type of title.

A later study by KFCB Research (1993), revealed that the 4 factors most sought after are locational factors, factors that affect the quality of the development and facilities, factors concerning individual housing units, and pricing. Accessibility to shops and markets are ranked high as buyers value the convenience of shopping for daily necessities. However, proximity to means of transport is a good substitute for proximity to residential amenities. Therefore, nearness to the main transport routes and especially the MRT, is much sought after by house buyers. Among facilities, a swimming pool, children's playground and security features are deemed to be important. The qualities of furnishing and a good interior design & layout are also highly valued.

According to a study by JLW Research (1994) on expatriate housing accommodation, although the expatriates consider the availability of recreational facilities important, they are generally satisfied with basic facilities such as a swimming pool, 24 hour security, tennis courts and a children's playground. While posh recreational facilities may be redundant, we believe that buyers in general will welcome the convenience of having more facilities such as a minimart or a crèche to be located inside their estate.

A more recent study by Ngee Ann Poly Building Dept (1994), indicates that the 5 most important criteria for the selection of private housing are, in decreasing order of importance, price, floor area, design & layout, proximity to workplace & schools, and peacefulness. It is also noteworthy that out of the 1223 respondents interviewed, 10 percent bought their properties as an investment, and to them, the important considerations are good investment returns or capital gain, price, design & layout, prestige of location, and tenure.

3. HEDONIC PRICE ANALYSIS[1]

Due to differences in the quality of housing units, comparison of prices becomes a problem. Where prices are substantially different across consecutive quarters, the implicit quality of the property transacted may itself be substantially different. That is, when consumers are paying a higher price for properties, they may in fact be buying better properties. The amount of pure price change may actually be very little or even negative.

Hedonic Price analysis is a type of regression analysis that is particularly useful in dealing with quality changes over time. It utilises dummy variables to capture the amount of pure inflation over the base year, which is represented by the constant term. Quality characteristics, captured by the explanatory variables, are held fixed in the interpretation of the dummy variables in the regression equation. The simple linear functional form is chosen so that the implicit price for the characteristics is directly given by the estimated parameter coefficients. Moreover, as the supply of such characteristics is fairly price inelastic, and relatively fixed in the short-run, the demand curves for these characteristics will intersect with the vertical supply curves of such. In this case, changes in implicit prices will reflect changes in buyers' valuations of these quality characteristics. The identification of such trends will enable the alert developer to construct an optimal product that will satisfy consumers and increase in value over time.

---

[1] For better exposition on the methodology, see Ernst R. Berndt (1991).

4. CHOICE & SPECIFICATION OF VARIABLES

Consolidating the findings of the above studies, we consider 5 factors to be the most important. They are accessibility, location, tenure, facilities, and living space.

4.1 ACCESSIBILITY

It has been said that an MRT station is what really convinces the housebuyer to put down a deposit on a condominium unit. MRT, being the life-line of the island, links the major employment areas and residential centres. It is especially favoured by HDB-upgraders (the back-bone of the market) and those willing to live outside prime districts. However, as most of the buyers are car-owners, proximity to the expressway, highway, or other major roads is certainly important. This is especially true for those residing in the new waterfront developments.

For a measure of accessibility, distance of the condominium to the nearest MRT station (Dmrt) and distance to the nearest highway or expressway (Dexpw) are taken (both in terms of metres). However, as both these measures are defined in terms of air-space, they are likely to be downward biased. To get a single measure of accessibility, Dmrt and Dexpw are weighted equally in the variable **Access**[2].

4.2 LOCATION

While the promise of a newly completed condominium in pristine condition is enough to trigger buyers' interest, the price a development can fetch is significantly affected by its location. In the local context, people are very concerned about social status. That is, people prefer properties located in prestigious locations. District 9, 10 & 11 has always been the choicest residential spot in Singapore. The underlying demand for prime units is reflected in the higher collective sale prices for prime land relative to non-prime land.

In order to represent location within the prime area, a dummy variable **PA** is created. Although some studies have included District 15 as prime area due to its proximity to beach front recreational facilities, this conventional study will only consider District 9, 10 & 11 as prime land.

4.3 TENURE

Due to the limited supply of freehold land, 99 year leasehold land is fast becoming the source of development land. However, consultants generally agree that when property prices soften, the 99 year leasehold market will be worst hit. Its weakness lies in the fact that its value would be affected long before expiry, especially when the development runs into its second decade. Such weakness has its roots in the uncertainty over the fate of expired leases. One proposed remedy is redevelopment-cum-lease-renewal. However, we must consider the fact that sites are sold on 99 year leases so as to allow redevelopment to meet needs prevailing in the future. Therefore it is highly unlikely that the Land Office will allow renewal or topping up of the 99 year lease. Although it seems that leasehold properties rank a second poor, the bullish property market over the past 8 years has seen leasehold developments doing as well, if not better than their freehold counterparts. However, in a bear market, these properties will slide with greater momentum.

---

[2] Access = $(1/2)$Dmrt + $(1/2)$Dexpw.

The variable **Ten** is created to represent properties of the freehold, 999 year leasehold or Statutory Land Grant type.

4.4 FACILITIES

Although facilities offered in newer developments are becoming more innovative, consumers are generally satisfied with the generic product. However, the offering of more facilities will certainly be welcomed. While the existence of a minimart or crèche is desired by tenants, their provision is only feasible within a large estate. Smaller developments, such as those with less than 50 units, are usually seen to offer only the core facilities. While having more households inside the estate may mean the loss of privacy and exclusivity (maximum privacy & exclusivity requires the development to be no more than 200 units), we believe that the convenience of having more facilities should be of over-riding concern to the occupiers, although this remains an empirical question.

Therefore the variable **Units**, representing the number of households within the development, is created as a proxy for the amount of facilities offered.

4.5 LIVING SPACE

While people are upgrading from HDB estates to private dwellings, they are really down-sizing as units offered in the condominium market are usually of a smaller size. Apart from its price, floor area is also a chief consideration to the buyers. We believe that this consideration has a fair measure of privacy factored into it. That is to say, more privacy is better enjoyed in bigger dwellings.

Living space is directly measured by floor area (in terms of square metres), represented by the variable **Area**.

4.6 THE VARIABLES

In as much as buyers' preferences can be represented by these variables, it must be remembered that in any country, demand patterns do not remain static. Buyers' preferences are expected to change over time as the market matures, the level of consumer affluence increases, or as the family size varies. Many forces, be it economic, environmental, rational or even irrational, are always around and constantly shaping consumers' perceptions. It is therefore unlikely that the implicit prices for these quality characteristics will remain stable for a long time.

5. THE DATA

Data for price and floor area for condominiums is obtained from the quarterly publication of URA Real Estate Statistical Series: Prices & Rental Indices, which records caveats lodged within each quarter. A caveat is lodged with the Registry of Titles & Deeds soon after a buy/sell agreement is signed or after an option to purchase a property is exercised, to protect the buyer's interest. These data are then matched with information from published sources[3] on tenure, the number of units in the development and its location to form the database. Altogether 9 quarters are considered stretching from 3Qtr 94 to 3Qtr 96.

---

[3] These sources include Sim(1992), URA *"Supplement on Private Residential Development"*, Times Periodicals *"Singapore Business"*.

The dummy variables D44, D15, D25, D35, D45, D16, D26 and D36 represent observations for each quarter (excluding that for 3Qtr 94) respectively.

A cross-sectional analysis reveals the relationship between price and quality at a given point in time. A pooled regression, however, requires the parameter estimates to remain stable over the period the data is pooled.

6. ESTIMATION & EMPIRICAL FINDINGS

A Hedonic price regression equation in its simple linear form is typically specified as

$$\text{Price} = \alpha_0 + \alpha_1 PA + \alpha_2 Ten + \alpha_3 Area + \alpha_4 Units + \alpha_5 Access. \tag{1}$$

Dummy variables may be added into the equation when a pooled regression is run, to segregate the observations for each quarter. The coefficients for these dummy variables will then reflect the amount of pure price change for the respective quarters over the base quarter that is represented by the constant term. However, a prerequisite for running a pooled regression in that the parameter coefficients remain constant throughout the pooled period. Therefore, to identify periods of stable consumption behaviour, data for every consecutive quarter are pooled to form one Part. That is, data for 3Qtr 94 and 4Qtr 94 forms Part1, 4Qtr 94 and 1Qtr 95 forms Part2, 1Qtr 95 and 2Qtr 95 forms Part 3 and so on, until 2Qtr 96 and 3Qtr 96 which forms Part 8. For each pooled data Part, the simple linear equation is estimated. A stability test is then performed on each Part with the break-point at the last observation of the earlier quarter data. That is, for Part1 the Break-point is at the last observation for 3Qtr 94; that for Part2 is at the last observation for 4Qtr 94; that for Part3 is at the last observation for 1Qtr 95, and so on. The null hypothesis postulates stability at the 10 percent level of significance. Results of the stability analysis are shown in Table 1. The methodology is this: If only Part1 is stable, a stable consumption pattern will occur from 3Qtr 94 to 4Qtr 94 only. However, if both Part1 & Part2 are stable, the stable period will stretch from 3Qtr 94 to 1Qtr 95, and so forth. When stable periods are identified, the data for these periods are pooled and a hedonic regression is performed to identify the amount of pure inflation for the respective quarters over the base quarter, i.e., the first quarter for the stable period, represented by the constant. Dummy variables are utilised here to represent observations for the subsequent quarters within the stable period. For example, if Part3, Part4 and Part5 are found to be stable, this would mean that for the period 1Qtr 95 to 4Qtr 95, consumers have exhibited a stable consumption pattern and the regression equation

$$\text{Price} = \alpha_0 + \beta_1 D25 + \beta_2 D35 + \beta_3 D45 + \alpha_1 PA + \alpha_2 Ten + \alpha_3 Area + \alpha_4 Units + \alpha_5 Access \tag{2}$$

will have to be estimated. Here, the dummies D25, D35 & D45 represents observations for 2Qtr 95, 3Qtr 95 and 4Qtr 95 respectively. The coefficient for these dummies (β_is) will then represent the respective amount of pure price change over 1Qtr 95. A cross-sectional analysis is also performed individually for each of the 9 quarters. The simple linear equation is estimated. These results are shown in Table 5. Changes in consumers' valuations of these quality characteristics over the 9 quarters will be reflected by the changes in these coefficient estimates.

With reference to Table 1, 4 Parts are found to be stable. They are in sequence, Part 1, Part 3, Part 4 and Part 8. This means that we have 3 periods of stable consumption behaviour: 3Qtr 94 to 4Qtr 94, 1Qtr 95 to 3Qtr 95, and 2Qtr 96 to 3Qtr 96 respectively. Therefore 3 pooled regressions are run:

$$\text{Price} = \alpha_0 + \beta_1 D44 + \alpha_1 PA + \alpha_2 Ten + \alpha_3 Area + \alpha_4 Units + \alpha_5 Access$$

$$\text{Price} = \alpha_0 + \beta_2 D25 + \beta_3 D35 + \alpha_1 PA + \alpha_2 Ten + \alpha_3 Area + \alpha_4 Units + \alpha_5 Access$$

$$\text{Price} = \alpha_0 + \beta_4 D36 + \alpha_1 PA + \alpha_2 Ten + \alpha_3 Area + \alpha_4 Units + \alpha_5 Access \qquad (3)$$

The results are shown in Tables 2 to 4.

Despite expectations of a softening market and warnings of an impending correction in property prices, the euphoria which ruled the market in 1993 and the earlier quarters of 1994 continues to rule. Table 2 bears out this finding with a positive and significant estimate (22851, the T-ratio being 1.890) for the variable D44. This means that asset inflation is significant, at about 13.94 percent[4] in 4Qtr 94, from the 3Qtr 94 level. Further examination of the Table reveals that the coefficients for Tenure and Accessibility, represented by Ten & Access (which also measures the implicit prices for these qualities), are insignificant. We attribute this to the distortions due to speculative buying. These speculators may not have considered the qualities of the units thoroughly upon buying. Many may have bought out of a gut feeling, in anticipation of a price rise to sell the units off a few days later to reap a quick profit, due to the availability of an "ever-absorbing" market.

Market sentiments changed in 1995. The F-Statistic of 3.087 for Part2 testifies to this. The instability of the pooled regression for 4Qtr 94 and 1Qtr 95 implies a transition in buyer behaviour between the 2 quarters. The stable period from 1Qtr 95 to 3Qtr 95 marks the emergence of a new consumption pattern. Market fundamentals have changed in 1995 with many developments not achieving sales as quickly as they used to. The number of caveats lodged (for condominiums only) fell from 228 in 4Qtr 94 to 152 in 1Qtr 95. The market is seeing more owner-occupiers than speculators, evidenced by fewer resale of new properties. Buyers are starting to rule. They are less pressurised to commit quickly, due in part to the realisation that there will be many units for sale. Moreover, as their HDB flats are appreciating noticeably and more importantly, as they wait for the downward revision in condominium prices, buyers are not rushing into the market. This possibly explains (referring to Table 3) why asset inflation has not been significant for both 2Qtr 95 and 3Qtr 95, over that for 1Qtr 95[5]. Furthermore, buyers are getting more selective when searching for a dwelling. They are more rational than earlier buyers (the coefficients for qualities are significant and have their expected signs) and they focus on developments with better characteristics. Apart from prime area, buyers are willing to pay more for better qualities (contrast the coefficients for qualities in Table 3 with those in Table 2).

Resilience of the market is perhaps best demonstrated in 4Qtr 95. Contrary to what many analysts and consultants have predicted, prices of condominiums did not come down. 4Qtr 95 is another transition period for the buyers. They realise that the much anticipated correction of the market will not materialise. According to analysts, the gravity-defying act are due mainly to 3 factors[6]: (i) The strong holders and eager-buyers for top-end condominiums and those located in the prime area; (ii) Developers cutting down on the marketing of new projects so that the looming over-supply situation that was

---

[4] Calculated by [22851/163880] * 100 percent.

[5] Notice that the coefficients of both D25 and D35 are insignificant.

[6] See Times Periodicals Publications, *Singapore Business*, Dec 95 issue.

expected to cause the down-turn was averted; and (iii) The active HDB segment. Perceptions changed. Buyers are no longer exhibiting the same behaviour in 4Qtr 95 as they did in the previous 3 quarters. The high F-Statistic for Part 5 in Table 1 testifies to this. Those who were once adopting a wait-and-see attitude are now entering the market. Table 5 shows the cross-sectional regression results for each quarter. For 4Qtr 95, the coefficient for tenure (Ten), is again insignificant. Buyers do not mind the 99 year tenure as the market is buoyant and ready buyers are always available to absorb such units once they are put for sale. Furthermore, the coefficient for Units shows a negative sign for the first time. Consumer preferences are markedly different this quarter. They are willing to pay more to live in a smaller estate to better enjoy more privacy.

In 1Qtr 96, URA announced that it has set aside enough land to build up to 100000 homes in a 5 year period starting from 1997. In addition, URA also published take-up rates for residential projects and developments for the first time These details are revealed to reassure buyers of a steady supply of new homes and an abundance of unsold units, in a view to cool the market. However, the announcement effect does not seem to have much impact as the number of caveats lodged in 1Qtr 96 climbed up to 278 (the highest in the period of the study) from the previous 232. The market is consolidating. Buyers are exhibiting new buying patterns, different from those in 4Qtr 95, as evidenced by the instability of Part6 in Table 1. The cross-sectional regression for 1Qtr 96 in Table 5 shows a more than 200 percent leap in the implicit price for tenure[7], from the 4Qtr 95 level. Buyers now value the ownership of a freehold unit and are willing to pay much more for it than they previously do. The parameter for Units has become insignificant and its coefficient has fallen by almost 10-fold. This means that buyers are indifferent to the size of the development. Such drastic shifts in consumption behaviour between the 2 quarters have contributed to the unstable result of Part6.

While perceptions have undergone many adjustments in the previous quarters, the market arrived at a stable consumption behaviour in the period of 2Qtr 96 and 3Qtr 96. Part8 of Table 1 bears this result[8]. However, many disturbances have affected the market. The government, being concerned with escalation of property prices, introduced policies to clamp down on speculative activities which have sent property prices sky-rocketing. The May 15 Policy, as many have called it, comprises many comprehensive measures. These includes: (i) Various taxes on the gains from sale of property within 3 years of purchase, depending on the year the property is resold; (ii) Stamp duty to be paid on the full value of the property, on every sale and sub-sale of all properties, regardless of whether it is completed or not; (iii) Housing loans being limited to 80 percent of purchaser price or valuation, whichever is lower, including funds to be withdrawn from borrowers' CPF account. Permanent residents are limited to 1 Singapore dollar loan each to buy properties for owner occupation. Foreigners are not eligible for any Singapore dollar loans for the purchase of properties. A disquieting calm descended on the property market following the new rules of May 15. Effects of the policy are fairly immediate, as prospective buyers hold out in anticipation of a drop in prices. Therefore, although there are 188 observations in 2Qtr 96, most of these are transactions which occurred before the announcement. The observations for 3Qtr 96 should reflect the policy effects. Table 2 gives the results of the

---

[7] The coefficient for Ten is significant in contrast to that in 4Qtr 95.

[8] Notice the very low F-Statistic for Part 8 of Table 1.

pooled regression for 2Qtr 96 and 3Qtr 96 (the stable period). The coefficient for D36, observations for 3Qtr 96, is found to be insignificant although it is negative. This means that the May 15 Policy has not been effective in bringing down the amount of pure inflation from the 2Qtr 96 level. Although the policy has cooled the market, as evidenced by the drop in caveats lodged (by more than half), it has not been effective in correcting consumption behaviour either. This is evidenced by stability in the coefficient estimates for Part8, which implies that the way buyers value the qualities (the implicit prices) do not change. The market appears to have attained some level of maturity with much rigour in its behaviour.

6.1 CHARACTERISTIC TRENDS

Results of the cross-sectional analysis are produced in Table 5. Such analysis is useful for identifying trends in the way consumers value the qualities of a condominium.

6.1.1 Prime Location

The coefficient for PA has always been positive and significant. Apart from the dip in 1Qtr 95 and a slight drop in 3Qtr 96, the implicit price for prime area has exhibited a continuous upward trend. Developments within district 9, 10 & 11 are known to be the favourite for buyers from Indonesia, Hong Kong, and especially those working in high-prestigious posts Prime units, which have the reputation for being "blue chip" investment properties, are also much in demand by speculators since such units generally hold out better in a soft market. It therefore comes to no surprise that the coefficient for PA dropped in 1Qtr 95 when speculative buying decreases. In the period of rational consumption during the first 3 quarters of 95, this implicit price has remained below the $200 000 level. However, bullish buying in the period of consumption adjustment (4Qtr 95 to 2Qtr 96) has sent the price soaring past the $200 000 mark, overtaking the $300 000 level (in 2Qtr 96) as buyers' appetite for prime units increases.

The implicit price for prime area is likely to continue rising, as such units become more exclusive due to the scarcity of prime land. However, the Bukit Timah and Upper Bukit Timah areas, which already have the reputation for being a high class residential area, may be transformed into another prime district as they are expected to be the focus of residential development for the next 2 years (Ellis (1996)).

6.1.2 Tenure

It has been said that freehold land is worth a king's ransom. However, this may not hold true in general for freehold units. Result of the cross-sectional analysis shows that more than half of the time the coefficient for Ten is insignificant and there are even negative signs in 4Qtr 94 and 1Qtr 95, although this is corrected in the subsequent quarters when buyer behaviour became more rational. The buoyant market witnesses positive responses to 99 year leasehold developments, which indicates that such properties have become quite well accepted by the public. Moreover, as the time span of 99 years is enough to see through at least 2 generations and buyers from Hong Kong, China and Thailand are not averse to leasehold properties as they are used to such at home, there are all the more reasons for the good performance of such properties. The owner-occupier market of 1Qtr 95 to 3Qtr 95 has seen a steady increase in the implicit price for this characteristic. However, when perceptions changed in 4Qtr 95, the market saw a drastic drop in its valuation. As the market consolidates and new perceptions develop and mature, the craving for freehold units re-ignites.

The contention that the combination of freehold and prime area is a sure winner certainly has much basis. Stability in their parameters in Part8 of Table 1 testifies to this. The implicit price for these qualities holds out well even in the face of government interventions to temper demand. The demand for freehold units is likely to remain strong as the 99 year leasehold condominiums face direct competition from the 99 year Executive Condominiums[9].

6.1.3 Floor Area

Except for PA, the variable Area is perhaps the only other parameter that is always positive and significant. Generally, the implicit price has hovered around the $7 000 psm level, for the period 3Qtr 94 to 2Qtr 95. A slight drop is observed in 3Qtr 95, although the price has picked up, and in fact took a big leap past the $8 000 psm level in 4Qtr 95. Since then, this price rose steadily to reach $9 977.50 in 3Qtr 96.

The demand for bigger living space is unambiguous from the increase in its implicit price. This demand should persist as new offerings are expected to be smaller.

6.1.4 Units & Access

The coefficient for the variable Units has, like for Ten, insignificant estimates for more than half the time, with a negative sign in 4Qtr 95. However, unlike Ten, the negative estimate has a logical explanation - people refer the privacy and exclusivity associated with smaller estates (i.e. having less neighbours in the development). The variable has a positive and significant estimate in 3Qtr 94. That is, buyers are willing to pay $49.54 more for every additional household to be located within the estate, as more households can mean the provision of more facilities. However, it becomes insignificant in 4Qtr 94 and 1Qtr 95. The demand revived in 2Qtr 95 with a significant estimate of 67.47, fell in 3Qtr 95, turned negative in 4Qtr 95 and thereafter becomes insignificant.

The variable Access has a counter-intuitive positive estimate of 3.764 in 3Qtr 94. However, this estimate is insignificant. Subsequent estimates produce the expected sign, but they remain insignificant until 3Qtr 95. Henceforth, the coefficient estimates exhibited an upward trend, showing greater rationality in consumption behaviour. A marked jump in this price (about 300 percent) is observed in 3Qtr 96.

We hold the view that buyers have undertook a process of substitution in their consumption behaviour. When market is consolidating in the period 4Qtr 95 to 2Qtr 96, buyers' preferences change. In 4Qtr 95, buyers are seen to be preferring smaller developments. This means they are willing to forego the convenience of having more facilities inside their estate. Such behaviour becomes more prominent subsequently as buyers become unwilling to pay more for a bigger estate (from 1Qtr 96 onwards, the variable for Units has remained insignificant). On the other hand, the price for Access rises during the same period. Buyers are increasingly willing to pay more for better accessibility. They are substituting better linkages for the convenience of having more residential

---

[9] At the end of June this year, details of the first batch of Executive Condos is announced at an irresistible price of $400 psf. However, only 400 out of the 2100 units launched this year is opened to the public. The rest are allotted to those already in the queue for executive flats.

amenities within their estates. Therefore we feel that when the core facilities[10] are in place, additional ones[11] are not so important after all. The developer should instead focus on bidding for a better site(one with better accessibility) for the development.

7. CONCLUSION

The real estate market sees the interplay of a large number of factors. Demand patterns for the product do not remain static but instead, is constantly evolving. Although certain trends may be particularly prominent in a certain period, a measure of caution must be exercised when trying to ride on such trends. This is because a reversal is always possible. However, although some irrationality is observed initially, the study indicates that the market is becoming more mature, with more rational buying behaviour, especially for the later part of the study.

While a pooled regression over the entire period of study is not feasible due to the lack of stability in the estimates, we believe that much of the increase in prices is due to better quality condominiums being transacted. Results of cross sectional regression reveal that buyers value the quality characteristics increasingly more each quarter, reflecting a higher underlying demand for better dwellings. They are paying more for better condominiums. Pure asset inflation may not be so significant after all. Furthermore, the market is seen to have undergone a period of adjustment (4Qtr 95 to 2Qtr 96) during which buyers correct their behaviour. The result, as already mentioned above, is more rationality in buying behaviour[12]. Therefore, the May 15 Policy may not have come at the right time because behaviour has already been corrected by 2Qtr 96[13] by the market itself. Although the policy is effective in cooling the market, the increase in the supply of land for housing developments may lead to an increase in the transaction volume in the future. This is because demand is likely to remain strong due to good economic fundamentals and factors such as a large pool of HDB upgraders, favourable demographics[14], a sound financing environment[15], and strong foreign demand.

---

[10] These include 24-hour security, a swimming pool, tennis courts and a playground.

[11] These may include facilities like wake-up call, a green house or other posh facilities.

[12] This is because the estimated coefficients are significant and have their expected (logical) signs. Contrast this with estimates from the earlier quarters.

[13] Therefore there are no statistically significant differences between the coefficient estimates for 2Qtr 96 and 3Qtr 96. Hence stability is achieved in Part 8.

[14] The baby boom people of 1960s are in their late 30s now, with family, and are in the peak of their earning capacity.

[15] Stiff competition among the banks makes financing convenient and cheap. Under the Approved Residential Properties Scheme, CPF members are allowed to draw on their CPF balance for repayment of mortgage loans.

REFERENCES

Ellis, R. (1996): *Market Report 1 Qtr 96.*

Ernst R. Berndt (1991): *The Practice of Econometrics*, Addison Wesley.

KFCB Research (1987): "Condominiums in Singapore - Buyers' Preferences".

KFCB Research (1993): "A Survey of Buyers' Preferences".

Lim, S. L. (1992): "Guide to Condominium Housing in Singapore, District 10".

Lim, S. L. (1992): "Guide to Condominium Housing in Singapore, District 9, 11".

Lim, S. L. (1992): "Guide to Condominium Housing in Singapore, Eastern".

Lim, S. L. (1992): "Guide to Condominium Housing in Singapore, Western".

Ngee Ann Poly Building Dept (1994): "A Survey of Property Owners & Investors in Singapore".

Official Publication of Redas: "Property Review", Various Issues.

Times Periodical Publication: "Singapore Business", Various Issues.

URA Real Estate Statistical Series: Prices & Rental Indices, Various issues.

URA Real Estate Statistical Series: Prices & Rental Indices, 3/94 - 3/96.

URA Real Estate Statistical Series: Potential Supply, Supplement on Private Residential Development, 2/94 - 3/96.

URA Real Estate Statistical Series: Stock & Occupancy, 2/94 - 2/96.

Wooton, J.L. (1995): Property Research Paper.

Wooton, J.L. (Sept 1992): Property Research Paper Financial Series "Residential Real Estate - An Inflation Hedging Perspective".

Wooton, J.L. (Feb 1994): Property Research Paper Market Analysis Series "Expatriate Housing Accommodation in Singapore".

TABLE 1

Results of Stability Analysis

	F-Statistic	P-Value
Part1 (3/94 - 4/94)	1.455	0.190
Part2 (4/94 - 1/95)	3.087	0.006*
Part3 (1/95 - 2/95)	0.458	0.839
Part4 (2/95 - 3/95)	2.557	0.019
Part5 (3/95 - 4/95)	13.63	0.000*
Part6 (4/95 - 1/96)	23.97	0.000*
Part7 (1/96 - 2/96)	31.59	0.000*
Part8 (2/96 - 3/96)	1.421	0.207

    *   Represents instability at the 10 percent level of significance.

TABLE 2

Pooled Regression for Period 3Qtr 94 to 4Qtr 94
(Dependent variable is price)

Variable Name	Estimated Coefficients	T-Ratio
D44	22851	1.890
PA	231680	17.23
Ten	5729.7	0.366*
Area	7184	53.31
Units	38.023	1.799
Access	-12.864	-1.059*
Constant	-163880	-6.051

a.   R-Square = 0.897.

b.   D44 is the dummy created for the observations for 4Qtr 94 observations.
*   Represents insignificance at the 10 percent level.

TABLE 3

Pooled Regression for period 1Qtr 95 to 3Qtr 95
(Dependent variable is price)

Variable Name	Estimated Coefficients	T-Ratio
D25	-4541.9	-0.474[*]
D35	3466.4	0.351[*]
PA	175640	22.46
Ten	19059	2.123
Area	7482	80.940
Units	42.5	2.807
Access	-17.796	-2.211
Constant	-124880	-6.428

a.   R-Square = 0.937.

b.   D25 and D35 are the dummies created for 2Qtr 95 and 3Qtr 95 observations respectively.

*   Represents insignificance at the 10 percent level.

TABLE 4

Pooled Regression for period 2Qtr 96 to 3Qtr 96
(Dependent variable is Price)

Variable Name	Estimated Coefficients	T-Ratio
D36	-28470	-0.984[*]
PA	345260	12.170
Ten	113630	3.678
Area	9524.5	34.170
Units	43.799	0.926[*]
Access	-124.12	-4.236
Constant	-167030	-2.868

a.   R-Square = 0.887.

b.   D36 is the dummy created for 3Qtr 96 observations.

*   Represents insignificance at the 10 percent level.

TABLE 5
Cross Sectional Regression for period 3Qtr 94 to 3 Qtr 96
(Dependent variable is price)

Variable Name	3Qtr 94	4Qtr 94	1Qtr 95	2Qtr 95	3Qtr 95	4Qtr 95	1Qtr 96	2Qtr 96	3Qtr 96
PA	211500	249510	153650	167170	185530	200330	261110	341960	311760
	(12.70)	(11.71)	(9.543)	(12.17)	(15.95)	(14.35)	(18.03)	(15.21)	(3.712)
Ten	14587*	-1439*	-12501*	28838	34095	16603*	45105	111480	109190
	(0.734)	(-0.060)	(-0.627)	(1.793)	(2.685)	(1.088)	(3.088)	(4.609)	(1.178)*
Area	7265.4	7126.7	7782.6	7706.1	6948.4	8047.5	8252.6	9407.2	9977.5
	(39.53)	(36.58)	(46.83)	(47.14)	(46.34)	(50.98)	(54.19)	(41.89)	(12.76)
Units	49.54	35.251	31.557	67.472	35.605	-53.332	5.807	45.626	36.869
	(1.906)	(1.036)*	(0.892)*	(2.499)	(1.713)	(-2.912)	(0.298)*	(1.215)*	(0.267)*
Access	3.768	-27.324	-7.043	-11.382	-29.006	-58.496	-73.022	-80.35	-245.15
	(0.241)*	(-1.502)*	(-0.362)*	(-0.891)*	(-2.437)	(-3.628)	(-5.323)	(-3.465)	(-2.848)
Constant	-189730	-123930	-143960	-175810	-55169	-70108	-71349	-198740	-116500
	(-5.626)	(-3.060)	(-3.807)	(-5.806)	(-2.198)	(-2.448)	(-2.453)	(-4.329)	(0.721)*
R-Square	0.908	0.891	0.952	0.933	0.930	0.939	0.943	0.941	0.820

a.   Figures in parenthesis are the respective T-Ratios.
*   Represents insignificance at the 10 percent level of significance.

Relationship between Performance and Fringe Benefits in the Banking Sector

Juliet **Chow**

&

Rosalind **Chew**

Nanyang Business School, Nanyang Technological University, Nanyang Avenue, Singapore 639798
Fax: +(65) 792.4217, Tel: +(65) 799.4762, Email: archew@ntu.edu.sg

Abstract As part of the total compensation package, fringe benefits in the past were assigned only a marginal degree of importance. Over the years, however, as employee aspirations advanced to a higher level, employee benefits have gained greater prominence in attracting, retaining and motivating employees. This is especially so in Singapore in the light of the tight labour market situation. The purpose of this paper is to enable a better understanding of the economic factors that affect fringe benefits. An attempt is made to establish a relationship between the performance of the firm and the fringe benefits provided. The banking sector is chosen for this study because it has always offered the highest employee benefits. The study indicates that there is a positive relationship between firm performance and fringe benefits.

1 INTRODUCTION

It is widely accepted that fringe benefits, as part of the total compensation package, is an important human resource policy tool for attracting, retaining and motivating employees. In view of the tight labour market condition in Singapore, an understanding of what may affect the provision of employee benefits is crucial to strategic human resource management. While most surveys and studies carried out by human resource consultants and other organisations focus on the motivational factors from a psychological perspective, this paper looks at the determinants of fringe benefits from an economic point of view.

Many researchers hold that the performance of the firm would not affect the provision of non-monetary benefits. Adherents of this view argue that regardless of how well the firm performs, the provision of fringe benefits would remain fixed; the variable component is the money wage. This means that there is absolutely no relationship between the performance of the firm and the fringe benefits it provides. In this paper, an attempt is made to establish that such a relationship does in fact exist.

The banking sector is selected for this study as it appears to be the sector that offers the highest employee benefits. This could be due to the significant presence of foreign banks in Singapore, which often provide relatively more and better employee benefits than local banks. However, this is not an issue for this paper. This paper looks at the banking sector as a whole, and uses data from both local and foreign banks.

The rest of the paper is set out as follows. Section 2 provides a brief discussion of the variables employed and data limitations. Section 3 details the proposed model and the methodology adopted in assessing the data on the basis of the model. Section 4 analyses the results obtained in the study. Lastly, Section 5 presents the concluding remarks.

2   VARIABLES EMPLOYED AND DATA LIMITATIONS

2.1   *FRINGE BENEFITS INDEX*

The fringe benefits index (FBI) is the dependent variable in this study. This variable is used to represent the fringe benefits provided. It is computed for each bank in the study based on a rating system covering all types of fringe benefits. For each benefit offered by the bank, the rating system gives a score corresponding to the level of·generosity. The scores of all the benefits provided by the bank are then added up to yield a FBI for the bank for a particular year. A higher FBI indicates that the bank is relatively more generous in the provision of employee benefits.

The average of the fringe benefits indices of the collective agreements for all the banks in the study is used to represent the fringe benefit index for the entire banking sector for a particular year. Data (extracted from *Employee Benefits and Industry Performance, 1995*) are collected for a total of 30 banks for the years from 1980 to 1992.

2.2   *NET RETURNS INDEX*

The net returns of a bank is used as a measure of the bank's performance. The net returns index (NRI) is calculated using the following formula:

(Net Profit After Tax / Total Assets) x 100

This is our most important independent variable as we want to see whether there is a relationship between firm performance and fringe benefits. The main hypothesis which we test in this study is that net returns would have a positive impact on fringe benefits provision. Annual data (extracted from the *Survey of Financial Institutions, Various Years*) for the net profit after tax are collected for the 30 banks for the period of study.

2.3   *GDP GROWTH RATE*

The GDP growth rate of the country (RGDP), is included as a determinant of fringe benefits since the general economic performance of the country is likely to have an impact on all compensation packages. For a small country like Singapore, the GDP growth rate would have considerable influence on the various sectors of the economy. The hypothesis is that the GDP growth rate would have a positive impact on fringe benefits provision. Annual data (extracted from the *Yearbook of Statistics, Various Years*) for the years from 1980 to 1992 are used.

2.4   *CHANGES IN PRODUCTIVITY*

Productivity levels achieved can indicate to human resource managers and union leaders the stragtegic amount of employee benefits to negotiate for. Union leaders, in particular, may use productivity levels as an argument for better rewards. That is, they may request for more and/or better benefits as a reward to employees for high productivity levels achieved. Thus, changes in productivity level (PDTY) is included as one of the determinants. Such an argument would be acceptable to management if the latter believes that higher productivity is due to the effort of the employees. The hypothesis therefore is that changes in productivity would have a positive impact on fringe benefits provision. Unfortunately, data specific to the banking sector are not available; hence changes in productivity of the financial and business services sector are used instead. Annual data (extracted from the *Yearbook of Statistics, Various Years*) for the period of study are used.

2.5   CHANGES IN WAGES

Changes in wages, as proxied by data on changes in average monthly earnings (AME), may also help to explain changes in the provision of fringe benefits. A decline in the FBI for a firm could be due to an increase in its money wages; which may act as a substitute for reduced benefits. Thus a wage change could have some impact on the FBI. The hypothesis is that money wage increases would have a negative impact on fringe benefits provision. Again, unfortunately, data specific to the banking sector is not available so changes in wages of the financial and business services sector are used instead. Again, annual data (extracted from the *Yearbook of Statistics, Various Years*) for the years from 1980 to 1992 are used.

2.6   DATA LIMITATIONS

The major limitation of this paper is the small number of observations, both in the number of years and the number of banks included in the study. This is due to the unavailability of data as many of the banks are unwilling to provide information on their employee benefits scheme. Secondly, we have had to omit 1991 from our study period because the data for Fringe Benefits Index are not available for that year. Nevertheless, we proceeded with this small sample size since we feel that the existing data set can still throw some light on the relationship between firm performance and the provision of fringe benefits.

At this juncture, we would like to note that the variables included in our study are not exhaustive. There are likely to be other variables which also influence the provision of fringe benefits, such as firm size. However, due to the problem of degrees of freedom, only the more important variables are included.

3 METHODOLOGY

Having defined our variables, we adopt a general vector autoregressive (VAR) model. for our equation specification. This involves regressing the current value of fringe benefits index (FBI) on lagged values of the independent variables. The VAR model has the advantages of requiring no prior restrictions from economic theory (within which the model is grounded), as well as no assumptions regarding the endogeneity/exogeneity of the variables. The general model is given by equation (1).

$$FBI_t = C + \sum\alpha_i NRI_{t-i} + \sum\beta_i RGDP_{t-i} + \sum\delta_i PDTY_{t-i} + \sum\gamma_i AME_{t-i} + \varepsilon_t \qquad (1)$$

$$(+) \qquad (+) \qquad (+) \qquad (-)$$

where

FBI_t = Fringe Benefits Index

C = Constant

NRI_{t-i} = Lagged Net Returns Index

$RGDP_{t-i}$ = Lagged Growth Rate of Real GDP

$PDTY_{t-i}$ = Lagged Changes in Productivity

AME_{t-i} = Lagged Changes in Average Monthly Earnings

The expected signs of the coefficients are given in parenthesis.

To estimate Equation (1), we apply Akaike's Information Criterion (AIC) to determine the number of lags to use for each variable. We therefore choose the number of lags that minimises the value of AIC, such that

$\text{AIC} = k \ln(\text{residual sum of squares}) + 2n$

where k is the number of parameters and n is the sample size.

Since we employ annual time series data, we need to check for stationarity of the data series. Regressions involving non-stationary time series data will lead to spurious findings, with the regression results appearing to be statistically significant even if there is actually no relationship between the variables. This problem arises if the time series variables exhibit strong trends (sustained upward or downward movements), since any observed relationship could reflect the presence of a trend rather than a true relationship between the variables.

To test for stationarity, one can apply the Augmented Dickey-Fuller (ADF) unit roots test or the Phillips-Perron (PP) unit roots test to the data series. This determines whether the data series contain unit roots, which indicate non-stationarity.

Engle and Granger (1987) proposed the concept of cointegration to overcome the problem of non-stationarity in time series data: If a series of data are non-stationary but a linear combination of these series is stationary, then they are said to be cointegrated. This means there exists a meaningful relationship between them. The Engle and Granger approach to testing for cointegration is to determine whether the residuals of the equilibrium relationship are stationary. This amounts to testing for unit roots in the residuals of the regression equation. We apply both the ADF and the PP unit roots test to the residuals of our regression equation.

4   RESULTS & ANALYSIS

4.1   REGRESSION RESULTS

The results that we obtain by estimating Equation (1) are presented in Table (1). The most notable finding is that the variable NRI_{t-1} is rather insignificant, even though it has the correct sign. We also observe that the coefficients of two of the variables, RGDP_{t-1} and RGDP_{t-3}, have the wrong signs. However, the coefficient of RGDP_{t-2} has the correct sign.

At the same time, the variable PDTY_{t-1} is highly insignificant, even though it does have the correct sign. As such, we suspect that changes in productivity actually does not have an effect on the provision of fringe benefits, and is thus an irrelevant variable. The inclusion of an irrelevant variable would lead to inefficient, even though unbiased, estimates. We therefore omit the variable from the model and estimate Equation (2) instead:

$$\text{FBI}_t = C + \sum \alpha_i \text{NRI}_{t-i} + \sum \beta_i \text{RGDP}_{t-i} + \sum \gamma_i \text{AME}_{t-i} + \varepsilon_t \qquad (2)$$

The results from estimating Equation (2) are presented in Table (2). There is an overall improvement in the significance of all the variables after dropping the variable PDTY_{t-1}. This confirms our suspicion that changes in productivity are indeed irrelevant to the determination of fringe benefits provision. More importantly, the variable NRI_{t-1} is now found to be highly significant. The wrong signs for RGDP_{t-1} and RGDP_{t-3} remain, however.

The Durbin-Watson (DW) statistic of 1.94 permits us to reject serial correlation. The adjusted R^2 value of 0.97 represents a fairly good fit.

4.2 IMPLICATIONS OF THE RESULTS

Given the results presented in Table (2), we can write out the following equation:

$$FBI_t = 40.05 + 2.77NRI_{t-1} - 0.48RGDP_{t-1} + 1.12RGDP_{t-2}$$
$$- 0.42RGDP_{t-3} - 0.68AME_{t-1} \tag{3}$$

4.2.1 GDP Growth Rate

First, we analyse the two wrong signs for the coefficients of $RGDP_{t-1}$ and $RGDP_{t-3}$. A close examination of the estimated coefficients for these two variables shows that they add up to -0.9, which is very close to one. Notice, too, that the coefficient for $RGDP_{t-2}$ is 1.12 which is also very close to one and that it has a positive sign. We can conclude from these two observations that, rather than the coefficents of $RGDP_{t-1}$ and $RGDP_{t-3}$ having the 'wrong' signs, Equation (3) shows that the appropriate way to compute the total effects of $RGDP_{t-i}$ on FBI is to take the weighted average of the $RGDP_{t-i}$ values for the past three years to derive the total effect, using the values of the coefficients as the respective weights. The proportions (the coefficient values) are such that the effects would almost cancel out each other if the $RGDP_{t-i}$ values remain constant. This means if all the $RGDP_{t-i}$ values were the same, then they would have almost no effect on FBI. Intuitively, this makes sense: if the growth rate of GDP remains constant, then the generosity in providing fringe benefits would not change.

Note that we cannot isolate the effect of each $RGDP_{t-i}$ variable and should consider them simultaneously.[1] We conducted a Wald Test of Coefficient Restrictions to see if the group of $RGDP_{t-i}$ variables do have a joint effect on FBI. The restriction is given as :

$$H_0 : \beta_1 = \beta_2 = \beta_3 = 0$$

where β_i is the coefficient for $RGDP_{t-i}$

The null hypothesis is that the three variables do not have a joint effect on the dependent variable. The result of the Wald Test gives a F-statistic of 80.08 and the p-value for rejecting the null hypothesis is 0.002. This means that we can reject the null hypothesis and conclude that the $RGDP_{t-i}$ variables do have a joint effect on FBI and thus should be

---

[1] Alternatively, it may be that the variable is more appropriately defined as a 3-year moving average. We therefore regress and obtain the following equation:

$$FBI = 36.7434 - 6.1362NRI_{t-1} - 0.4060RGDPMA + 0.3298PDTY_{t-1} + 0.0402AME_{t-1}$$
$$(6.90) \quad\quad (-1.99) \quad\quad\quad (-0.91) \quad\quad\quad\quad (1.38) \quad\quad\quad\quad (0.11)$$

$R^2 = 0.60$ Adjusted $R^2 = 0.3395$ DW = 1.76
where   RGDPMA = the three-year moving average of RGDP
and   figures within parentheses represent the t-statistics.

The regression equation shows that, by replacing RGDP with RGDPMA, only NRI is now significant, and then only at the 10 percent level of significance. Moreover, its coefficient has the wrong sign. Furthermore, both Adjusted R^2 and DW are lower and less acceptable. We therefore stay with equation (3).

considered simultaneously. Again, this is intuitively plausible because each Collective Agreement (CA)[2] between unions and firms is valid for three years.

If the growth rate of GDP is not constant, then the total effects of $RGDP_{t-i}$ on FBI could be positive or negative. Does this contradict our hypothesis that the growth rate of real GDP has a positive impact on the provision of fringe benefits? Our hypothesis is a generalisation that each past value of the growth rate of GDP would have a positive effect on FBI. Since we cannot consider the effect of each $RGDP_{t-i}$ variable independently, and should view them as a result of some interactions, then our hypothesis no longer holds.

4.2.2   Net Returns Index

The coefficient of NRI_{t-1} is given as 2.77 in Equation (3). This is in line with our hypothesis that the net returns of the firm has a positive impact on the provision of fringe benefits. Thus, contrary to conventional beliefs, we manage to establish a relationship between firm performance and fringe benefits.

Notice that only one lagged variable of NRI appears in Equation (3). This implies that only a lag of one year is important for the fringe benefits index. Perhaps this is because the NRI is specific to the firm, so that just looking at the past year's net returns is sufficient to determine how generous the firm will be in providing fringe benefits.

4.2.3   Changes in Productivity

As mentioned earlier, we find that changes in productivity is actually not important in the provision of fringe benefits. This probably means that management does not believe that fringe benefits are an important means of bringing about improvements in productivity levels and hence productivity levels would have no impact on the provision of fringe benefits. This is not surprising, since changes in productivity levels in the banking sector can be the result of many other factors such as windfall gains, technology advancement, strategic management decisions, etc. This finding has a very important and rather interesting implication: Unions in the banking sector cannot actually use productivity levels to negotiate for better employee benefits since management does not believe that better fringe benefits would help to increase productivity in this sector!

4.2.4   Changes in Average Monthly Earnings

Equation (3) also reveals that the coefficient for AME_{t-1} is -0.68 and the variable is lagged only once. This finding supports our hypothesis that money wage changes have a negative impact on the provision of fringe benefits. It confirms that some substitutability exists between money and fringe benefits. For example, a firm may convert some existing fringe benefits into wages.

The significance of this variable in the model implies that in analysing the provision of fringe benefits, we cannot ignore the effects of wages. We expect wages to play a rather significant role in the provision of fringe benefits since wages constitute the bigger part of the total compensation package. Management and unions need to consider the interactions of wages and fringe benefits so as to achieve a mutually satisfying total compensation package.

---

[2] A Collective Agreement represents the results of negotiations between unions and management concerning the types and quantity of employee benefits. As such, it determines the fringe benefits index (FBI).

4.3   UNIT ROOT TESTS

As discussed above, we need to determine whether a cointegrating relationship exists among the variables. The results of using the ADF test and the PP test on the residuals obtained from Equation (2) are presented in Table (3). Both the ADF test and the PP test show that we can reject the null hypothesis of a unit root at the 5 percent level. Thus we can conclude that a meaningful relationship exists among the variables.

5 CONCLUSION

The primary motive of this paper is to explore the economic determinants of the provision of fringe benefits. To determine the existence of a positive relationship between performance of the firm and its fringe benefits, we specify a simple linear relationship and include other determinants so as to gain deeper insight into the provision of fringe benefits. The results of our study show that a positive relationship between firm performance and fringe benefits does exist, as well as between general economic performance over the past three years and fringe benefits. It also confirms the substitutability between fringe benefits and money wages. Most interestingly, it implies that management in the banking sector does not believe that improving fringe benefits provision would lead to higher productivity growth in the sector. We believe that these findings have important implications for human resource managers and union leaders in their negotiations on a Collective Agreement.

REFERENCES

Berndt, E.R. (1991): *The Practice of Econometrics: Classic and Contemporary,* Addison-Wesley.

Chew, S.B. and Chew, R., "Employee Benefits and Industry Performance" paper presented at the *Inaugural Assembly of Chief Executives and Employers in Singapore*, Shangri-la hotel, 28-29 June, 1995.

Department of Statistics : *Yearbook of Statistics, (1980-1990),* Singapore.

Engle, R.F. and Granger, C.W.J. (1987): "Cointegration and Error Correction Representation, Estimation, and Testing," *Econometrica*, March, 55, 251-276.

Harris, R.I.D. (1995): *Using Cointegration Analysis in Econometric Modelling.* Harvester Wheatsheaf: Prentice Hall.

KPMG Peat Marwick : *Survey of Financial Institutions In Singapore, (1980-1992),* Singapore.

Maddala, G.S. (1992): *Introduction to Econometrics*, Maxwell Macmillan International.

TABLE 1

Results on Estimation of Equation (1)

Variable	Coefficient	t-Statistic	p-Value
Constant	38.92	19.42	0.003
NRI_{t-1}	2.24	2.09	0.17
$RGDP_{t-1}$	-0.44	-5.01	0.04
$RGDP_{t-2}$	1.04	6.40	0.02
$RGDP_{t-3}$	-0.35	-2.61	0.12
$PDTY_{t-1}$	0.05	0.59	0.61
AME_{t-1}	-0.61	-3.77	0.06
	adjusted R^2 = 0.96		DW = 1.95

Note : Definitions of all variables are given in Section 3.

TABLE 2

Results on Estimation of Equation (2)

Variable	Coefficient	t-Statistic	p-Value
Constant	40.05	73.68	0.000
NRI_{t-1}	2.77	5.37	0.013
$RGDP_{t-1}$	-0.48	-9.99	0.002
$RGDP_{t-2}$	1.12	14.17	0.000
$RGDP_{t-3}$	-0.42	-8.97	0.003
AME_{t-1}	-0.68	-7.30	0.005
	adjusted R^2 = 0.97		DW = 1.94

Note : Definitions of all variables are given in Section 3.

TABLE 3

Results of Unit Roots Tests on Residuals, ε_t

Unit Roots Test	Test Statistic	Critical Values
Augmented Dickey-Fuller (ADF)	-2.39	-3.05 (1%)
		-1.99 (5%)
		-1.64 (10%)
Phillips-Perron (PP)	-2.95	-2.97 (1%)
		-1.98 (5%)
		-1.63 (10%)

TABLE 4

Key Variables of the Banking Sector

Year	FBI	NRI	RGDP	PDTY	AME
1980	29.83	0.8086	9.694679	8.8	11.7
1981	29.07	0.9102	9.604664	4.7	16.7
1982	26.00	1.085	6.874236	-0.1	12.4
1983	35.43	0.4952	8.179281	4.3	8.1
1984	34.21	0.3498	8.311655	7.7	11.6
1985	36.00	0.0819	-1.620248	12	7.3
1986	41.00	-0.1344	2.300369	1.4	1.1
1987	32.59	0.2845	9.726438	17.7	3.8
1988	37.00	0.5865	11.63303	6	7.8
1989	37.27	0.6417	9.622658	7.4	8.8
1990	39.33	0.522	8.974487	5.3	8.8
1992	37.05	0.3915	6.221307	1	4

Forecasting Singapore's Share of
Japanese Tourist Arrivals in ASEAN

*Chris **Sakellariou***

&

***Goh** Hong Cheng*

Nanyang Business School, Nanyang Technological University, Nanyang Avenue, Singapore 639798
Fax: +(65) 792.4217, Tel: +(65) 799.4809, Email: acsake@ntu.edu.sg

Abstract The fact that there are relatively few studies of tourism inspired us to apply the Almost Ideal Demand System Model to the demand for ASEAN destinations by Japanese tourists. Because of the unique nature of tourism demand, modelling this dynamic industry is not a straightforward exercise. Our results indicate that the model is applicable. We categorised the destinations on the basis of their elasticities. We then used the model to forecast the market shares of the ASEAN destinations.

1. INTRODUCTION

Econometric studies on tourism are relatively few compared to Financial Economics, International Finance, Development Economics and other areas. There are mainly two reasons for this. Firstly, the unique nature of tourism demand and secondly, the lack of both quantitative and qualitative data.

To address the issue, one would have to look carefully into the unique form of tourism demand and examine the underlying problems. The first problem is that tourism represents a demand for a 'bundle of goods and services'; however, there is no unique sector that 'produces tourism'. Thus, tourism is not well-defined as an economic concept.

The next difficulty is that tourism is not 'transported' to the consumers. Rather, it is the other way round (i.e. consumers travel to the desired destination). This poses a major problem in the estimation of tourist arrivals since tourist flows are highly vulnerable to external influences such as political instability, natural disasters or major events.

These reasons not only explain the lack of economic tourism studies. More importantly, they point to the reason why studies on tourism demand are on an *ad-hoc* basis i.e. there is no widely accepted theory of tourism demand. The studies available include O'Hagan and Harrison (1984), Fiji, Khaled and Mak and Syriopoulos and Sinclair (1993) [who used the Almost Ideal Demand System (AIDS) model] and Smeral, Witt and Witt (1992) [who used the Linear Expenditure System (LES) model to forecast tourism imports and exports for various major geographical areas from 1991 to 2000].

1.1 STUDY OF JAPAN'S TOURISM DEMAND IN ASEAN

The main reason for selecting Japan is that Japan sends the largest number of tourists to ASEAN than any other single country. In 1992, Japan send the most tourists to Indonesia, Malaysia and Singapore, and second most to Philippines and Thailand.

Moreover, one of the three objectives of the ASEAN Promotion Centre is to increase the number of tourist arrivals from Japan to ASEAN. Brunei has recently joined the ASEAN Centre.

1.2 OBJECTIVES OF THE PAPER

The objectives of this paper are to examine the applicability of the Almost Ideal Demand System model to Japan's tourism demand for ASEAN[1] destinations and to forecast the market share of tourist arrivals from Japan for Singapore and the rest of ASEAN countries.

2. CHOICE OF FUNCTIONAL FORM

Economic theory assumes that a rational consumer allocates his expenditure (budget) among a basket of goods and services to maximise utility. By using a system of equations to estimate the share of tourist arrivals, we are able to measure the elasticities of budget shares with respect to changes in the explanatory variables.

The advantages of the AIDS model are : it allows a first-order approximation to any demand system, it is easy to estimate, it can be estimated linearly and it can be used to test for homogeneity and symmetry restrictions. In addition, the AIDS model provides a framework for calculating and interpreting the restrictions on cross-prices effects.

2.1 THE ALMOST IDEAL DEMAND SYSTEMS (AIDS) MODEL

As mentioned earlier, the Almost Ideal Demand System model is based in consumer theory which states that the rational consumer chooses from a bundle of goods and services subject to a given level of budget w. On the other hand, the problem can be formulated in such a way that the consumer has to minimise his expenditure to attain a specific utility level U. This is the principle of *duality* in consumer theory. The minimum expenditure is the cost function, and the first derivative of the cost function with respect to individual commodity prices is the demand function for that particular commodity.

The cost function specified by Deaton and Muellbauer (1980) is as follows:

$$\log C\,(p,u) = \alpha_0 + \sum_{i=1}^{n} \alpha_{ij} \, \log p_i + \frac{1}{2} \sum_{i=1}^{n} \sum_{j=1}^{n} \gamma_{ij}{}^* \log p_i \log p_j + u\beta_o \prod_{i=1}^{n} p_i{}^{\beta i} \qquad (1)$$

where C denotes the cost function, i denotes the particular commodity, p_i denotes the price of the *ith* commodity, p_j denotes the prices of the other commodities u denotes the utility level, and α_0, α_{ij}, $\gamma_{ij}{}^*$ *and* β_i are parameters.

Since we can differentiate the cost function with respect to the price of the *ith* commodity to derive the quantity demanded for that particular commodity, the following must be true:

$$\partial \log C\,(u,p) \,/\, \partial p_i \,=\, q_i \qquad (2)$$

where q_i denotes the quantity demanded of a particular commodity, and

$$\partial \log C\,(u,p) \,/\, \partial \log p_i \,=\, p_i\,q_i \,/\, C\,(u,p) = w_i \qquad (3)$$

where w_i denotes the budget share.

---

[1] ASEAN destinations refer to Indonesia, Malaysia, Philippines, Singapore and Thailand. The other countries in ASEAN are not included due to lack of data.

Therefore, by differentiating Equation 1 with respect to $\log p_i$ and taking account of Equation 2, we would obtain a system of budget share equations for every commodity as follows:

$$w_i = \alpha_i + \sum_{j=1}^{n} \gamma_{ij} \log p_j + \beta_i \log (y/P) \tag{4}$$

where the restrictions

$$\gamma_{ij} = \frac{1}{2} (\gamma_{ij}^{*} + \gamma_{ji}^{*}) = \gamma_{ji} \tag{5}$$

are imposed. Y denotes the total expenditure on the bundle of goods and services, and P is the aggregate price index expressed as:

$$\log P = \alpha_0 + \sum_{j=1}^{n} \alpha_j \log p_j + \frac{1}{2} \sum_{i=1}^{n} \sum_{j=1}^{n} \gamma_{ij} \log p_i \log p_j \tag{6}$$

2.1.1 Restrictions Imposed on the Almost Ideal Demand System Model

Consumer theory requires the demand system to satisfy the restrictions of homogeneity, adding up, symmetry and negativity.

Homogeneity is satisfied when

$$\sum_{j=1}^{n} \gamma_{ij} = 0 \tag{7}$$

Symmetry is satisfied when

$$\gamma_{ij} = \gamma_{ji} \tag{8}$$

Adding up is satisfied when

$$\sum_{i=1}^{n} \alpha_i = 1, \ \sum_{i=1}^{n} \beta_i = 0, \ \sum_{i=1}^{n} \gamma_{ij} = 0, \ \sum_{i=1}^{n} \delta_{1i} = \sum_{i=1}^{n} \delta_{2i} = \sum_{i=1}^{n} T_i = 0 \tag{9}$$

where δ_i denotes the dummy variables and T_i denotes the time trend variable.

The negativity conditions cannot be imposed by simple parametric restrictions, but as Fiji, Khaled and Mak (1985) pointed out, the conditions are likely to be satisfied automatically by any data set generated by utility maximising behaviour.

2.1.2 Multicollinearity Problem

There is a high probability that there is multicollinearity among the price variables. A possible solution is to use a single relative price index for each commodity (or for each country in this case) [see Bond (1979) and Schulmeister (1979)]. The price index is expressed as follows:

$$p_i^{*} = p_i \ / \ (\prod_{i \neq j} p_j^{s}{}_j)^{1/\Sigma w}{}_i \tag{10}$$

The use of the above price index is equivalent to imposing the following restriction:

$$\gamma_{ij} = - (\gamma_{ij} \, w_j \, / \Sigma \, w_j \,) \quad \text{for all } i \neq j \tag{11}$$

and the symmetry condition of $\gamma_{ij} = \gamma_{ji}$ is reduced to

$$\gamma_{ii} \, / \, \gamma_{jj} = w_i \, (\, 1\text{-}w_j \,) \, / \, w_j \, (\, 1\text{-}w_j \,) \tag{12}$$

The equation to be estimated is therefore expressed in the following form:

$$w_i = \alpha_i + \gamma_i \, \log p^*_j + \beta_i \, \log (y / P) \tag{13}$$

2.2 APPLICATION OF THE ALMOST IDEAL DEMAND SYSTEM MODEL TO JAPAN'S TOURISM DEMAND FOR ASEAN DESTINATIONS

In order to apply the Almost Ideal Demand System model, we have to bring in the concept of *separability* in consumer theory. Separability is a property whereby the different types of consumption expenditure can be divided into groups. This requires that the demand for goods and services within one group be independent of the demand for goods and services in other groups.

The concept of *separability* assumes that consumption expenditures are allocated in stages. In the first stage, the consumer allocates between broad groups of goods and services. It is at the first stage that the consumer divides his expenditure between tourism and other goods and services. In the second stage, the consumer allocates tourism expenditure between geographical areas or regions (e.g. ASEAN, Europe, and Latin America). In the third stage, the consumer allocates his expenditure between the different countries in ASEAN.

Now that the model has been specified, we look at how the variables fit into the model. In equation 13, the symbols represents the following:

w_i = share of Japanese tourist arrivals in country i

y = total number of Japanese tourists

P = aggregate price index

p^*_i = single relative price variable for each country

i = particular country

With the coefficients γ_i and β_i , the following elasticities can be calculated:

Own-Price (uncompensated), ε_i $(\gamma_i / w_i) - (\beta_i / 100) - 1$

Own-Price (compensated), ε^*_i $(\gamma_i / w_i) + (w_i / 100) - 1$

Arrival, η_i $(\beta_i / w_i) + 1$

$$\tag{14}$$

3. VARIABLES USED

3.1 DEPENDENT VARIABLES

The dependent variable is the market share of each ASEAN country with respect to Japanese tourist arrivals, where the market share is expressed as the total number of Japanese tourist arrivals in that particular country divided by the total number of Japanese visitor arrivals to all the ASEAN countries. The data is obtained from the Pacific Asia Travel Association (PATA) Annual Statistical Report.

Ideally, the dependent variable should reflect the expenditure of Japanese tourists in ASEAN destinations. The dependent variable depends on three factors: the number of tourist arrivals, the average length of stay of each tourist and the average tourist expenditure. Only data on the first is available. The period of estimation is from 1967 to 1995.

3.2 INDEPENDENT VARIABLES

As Crouch (1992) pointed out, the role of prices in determining international tourism is a complex issue. O'Hagan and Harrison (1984) suggested three determinants of price in tourism are: the price of travel, the prices of goods and services that the tourist buys in the country of destination and the exchange rate between the country of origin and destination.

The price of travel encompasses the cost of transportation in the various modes of transport. However, given that the ASEAN destinations are close to one another, and that travel by air is by far the most dominant[2] mode of transport, the cost of travel to the different ASEAN destinations for a Japanese tourist would not differ significantly. Therefore, the cost of transportation is not included. Prices of goods and services in the country of destination and the exchange rate form the major part of the price index.

The unavailability of a tourism price index means that a price index has to be constructed. The next best price index to be used in the computation would be the Consumer Price Index (CPI). Crouch (1992) pointed out that the price index to be used for tourism studies is rather complex, and a number of different definitions[3] have been used in the various studies of tourism demand.

Taking the different issues into consideration, an effective price index was constructed using the country of destination consumer price index and the exchange rate, adjusted for the other destinations' consumer price indices and exchange rates. The base year is 1985. The exchange rates are all expressed as the number of country i's currency per one US dollar.

As mentioned earlier, the number of tourists can be easily affected by external events. Two dummy variables were included to reflect such major changes in Malaysia and Philippines. In addition, a time trend variable was included to account for trends in the pattern of travel.

The data are collected from the International Monetary Fund's (IMF) International Financial Statistics, from 1967 to 1995.

4. METHODS OF ESTIMATION AND EMPIRICAL RESULTS

The SUR method of estimation is, theoretically, asymptotically more efficient than OLS method of estimation. This is because the disturbances of the different equations are not independent, and the reduced form coincides with the structural form, causing the OLS estimator to be consistent but not asymptotically efficient. The results using Zellner's method of Seemingly Unrelated Regression are shown in Table 1.

---

[2] The figures can be found in Pacific Asia Travel Association Annual Statistical Report

[3] The various definitions are found in Crouch, Geoffrey I. (1992) : " Effect of Income and Price on International Tourism," *Annals of Tourism Research*, 19, 643-664

An inspection of the results shows that with exception to the price variable for Singapore and the dummy variable for Philippines, the rest of the coefficents have a higher *t*-ratios under SUR estimation. Under SUR estimation, there were four coefficents that were statistically insignificant at the 5 percent significance level, of which two are statistically significant at the 10 percent significance level. Under the OLS estimation, there were six coefficents that were statistically insignificant at both the 5 percent and 10 percent significance level.

The coefficents for the dummy variables and the trend variables are all statistically significant at the 5 percent significance level under both estimations. The R^2 (goodness of fit) vary from 0.6 to 0.8. However, as Syriopoulous and Sinclair (1993) pointed out, the results are not surprising since the equations explain shares rather than levels, and market share equations typically fit the data only loosely.

The DW-statistics are all less than 1. This shows that there could be serial correlation. Deaton and Muellbauer (1980) pointed out that this serial correlation may be associated with the imposition of homogeneity. No attempt was made to correct for serial correlation as this would probably increase the number of parameters, thus further complicating the estimation procedure.

5. TOURIST ARRIVAL AND EFFECTIVE PRICE ELASTICITIES

The expenditure elasticity η_i , and the uncompensated and compensated own-price elasticity, denoted by ε_i and ε^*_i respectively are all shown in Table 3. In the calculation of the respective elasticities, three compensated own-price elasticities were statistically insignificant at the 5 percent significance level, of which two were statistically significant at the 10 percent significance level. There were three uncompensated own-price elasticity that were inconclusive as they each have a significant and an insignificant coefficient. All the arrival elasticities are statistically significant at the 5 percent significance level. Since out of a total of fifteen elasticities, only three are statistically insignificant, we can argue that the Almost Ideal Demand System model is applicable to the Japanese tourists' demand for ASEAN destinations.

5.1 ARRIVAL ELASTICITY

From table 3, the absence of any negative arrival elasticity indicates that no destination is considered an inferior 'good'. The total arrival elasticity η_i , is less than 1 for Singapore and Thailand. This means that for any 1 percent change in the total arrivals, the corresponding change in the market share of tourist arrivals is less than 1. These countries with an *inelastic total arrival elasticity of demand* are interpreted as 'necessities'. On the other hand, Indonesia Malaysia and Philippines have an *elastic total arrival elasticity of demand* since their values of η_i are greater than 1. They are interpreted as 'luxuries'.

5.2 OWN-PRICE ELASTICITY OF DEMAND

The negative compensated and uncompensated price elasticities of demand imply that the demand for tourist destinations is consistent with consumer theory, in that a rise in the relative price of 'country i' will lead to a fall in the market share of tourist arrivals i.e. fall in quantity demanded.

Malaysia, Singapore and Thailand have an *inelastic own-price elasticity of demand* (i.e. ε_i and ε^*_i are all less than 1) while Indonesia and Philippines have an *elastic own-price elasticity of demand* (i.e. ε_i and ε^*_i are all greater than 1).

5.3 OVERALL

Singapore and Thailand belong to the '*inelastic*' or more '*stable*' countries in the sense the market share of tourist arrivals are not affected by the changes in relative price and arrival levels. This is because both countries have *inelastic price* and *arrival elasticities*. An inspection of Table 5 shows that at 1995, Singapore attracted 38 percent while Thailand attracted 26 percent of the market share of Japanese tourists to ASEAN. The findings should not be a surprise since both countries have well-developed tourism sectors.

Malaysia belong to the '*inconclusive zone*'. Malaysia has an *inelastic own-price elasticity* and an *elastic arrival elasticity*. This would mean although a change in the price variable may not have any effect on Malaysia's market share, arrivals have a direct impact. Therefore, the resulting change in the market share of tourist arrivals will depend on the relative magnitude of the changes in the price and total arrivals.

Indonesia and Philippines each have an *elastic own-price elasticity of demand* and *expenditure elasticity of demand*. Therefore, it belongs to the '*unstable zone*' since an increase in the market share due to a favourable change in one of the variables can be offset by an unfavourable change in the other variable. On the other hand, the resulting change in the market share can be 'reinforced', depending on the direction of change of the variables.

We are now going to make use of this model to forecast the market shares of the ASEAN destinations from 1996 to 2005.

6. FORECAST OF MARKET SHARES

The forecast equations for the market share of Japanese tourist arrivals are shown on Table 3. Note that we are forecasting market shares and not tourist arrivals. The market shares of Japanese tourist arrivals from 1967 to 1995 are shown in Table 5 while the forecasted market shares are shown in Table 8.

6.1 EX-POST FORECAST

In arriving at the forecasting model, the AIDS Model was extended to include other variables (usually lags of the dependent variables). Stepwise regressions were used to indentify the variables to be included. The ex-post forecast was performed for the year 1994 and 1995. The statistics of fit are shown in Table 4.

6.2 EX-ANTE FORECAST

In deriving ex-ante forecasts of tourist shares, expected future values of Consumer Price Indexes, Exchange Rates and arrivals of Japanese tourists in ASEAN had to be fed into the model. A forecast of the Consumer Price Indexes and Exchange Rates for the ASEAN destinations is shown in Table 6 and 7 respectively. The forecasting of the Consumer Price Index and total number of Japanese tourists is based on a simple extrapolation . The general trend for the respective variables was observed, and the forecast was done based on the average change of the variables from 1985 to 1995. The forecasted Singapore exchange rate was done by assuming a constant rate of appreciation against the US dollars to a predetermined level by the year 2005. The Exchange Rates were forecasted using the exponential smoothing method.

The forecasted market shares of the various ASEAN destinations are shown in Table 8.

6.3 EVALUATION

From Table 4, we can see that the *root-mean-square percentage error* (RMS %) is the lowest for Indonesia and the highest for Thailand. Thus, we would expect the forecast accuracy to fall as we move down the table.

Table 7 shows that the market shares of Japanese tourist arrivals remain relatively constant for Singapore, Malaysia and Thailand. The market share for Indonesia and Philippines are expected to increase, from 15 percent to 21 percent for Indonesia, and from 11 percent to 16 percent for Philippines. The share of Singapore is expected to remain approximately constant throughout the period.

The intercepts in the forecasting equations are positive for all the ASEAN destinations except Malaysia. Recalling from section 5.3 that Singapore and Thailand belong to the *'stable destinations'* , the forecast reconfirms the inelasticities of demand for the two destinations. For the *'inconclusive destination'* (i.e. Malaysia), the combination of forces produce an unfavourable result. As for the *'unstable destinations'* (i.e. Indonesia and Philippines), an increase in their market shares is expected.

7. POLICY IMPLICATIONS AND CONCLUSION

There are two important implications for policy makers. Firstly, the forecast allow us to see that because Singapore and Thailand have well-developed tourism sectors, their market shares remain relatively stable, while the remaining destinations are affected by relative changes in real prices to different degrees. Secondly, the governments of the other three ASEAN destinations should take a more active role in the development of their tourism industries.

The promotion and development of the tourism industry does not mean an automatic increase in market shares; rather, development and promotion will bring about an increase in competition for market shares. This increase in competition is beneficial for ASEAN as a whole because a vibrant tourism sector in ASEAN will attract more tourists to the entire region. This strategy is clearly spelt out in the report by the Singapore Tourist Promotion Board (STPB)[4]. Singapore should not view her ASEAN partners as competitors. Rather, there should be a coexistence of co-operation and competition.

Thus, ASEAN countries should continue their efforts to promote tourism in their respective countries. With the emergence Brunei, Vietnam, Myanmar and Cambodia, the future of the tourism sector in ASEAN certainly looks promising.

---

[4] The report can be found in the publication entitled 'TOURISM 21: Vision of a Tourism Capital'.

REFERENCES

Brenton, P.A. (1994): "Negativity in an Almost Ideal Import Demand System," *Applied Economics*, 26, 627-633

Crouch, G.I. (1992): "Effect of Income and Price on International Tourism," *Annals of Tourism Research*, 19, 643-664

Crouch, G.I. (1995): "A Meta-Analysis of Tourism Demand," *Annals of Tourism Research*, 22, 103-118 Deaton, A. And Muelbauer, J. (1980): "An Almost Ideal Demand System," *American Economic Review*, 70, 312-326

Fujii, E.T., Khaled, M. And Mak, J. (1985): "An Almost Ideal Demand System for Visitor Expenditures," *Journal of Transport Economics and Policy*, 19, 161-171

O'Hagan, J.W. and Harrison, M.J. (1984): "Market Shares of US Tourist Expenditure in Europe: An Econometric Analysis," *Applied Economics*, 16,919-931

Pindyck, Robert S. And Rubinfeld, Daniel L. (1991): *Econometric Models & Economic Forecasts*, McGraw-Hill International Editions, third edition

Parikh, A. (1988): "An Econometric Study on Estimation of Trade Shares Using the Almost Ideal Demand System in the World Link," *Applied Economics*, 20, 1017-1039

Smeral, E., Witt, S.F. and Witt, C.A. (1992): "Econometric Forecasts: Tourism Trends to 2000," *Annals of Tourism Research*, 19, 450-466 Syriopoulos, Theodore C. And Sinclair, M. Thea (1993): " An Economic Study of Tourism Demand: The Almost Ideal Demand System model of US and European Tourism in Mediterranean Countries," *Applied Economics*, 25, 1541-1552

Thomas, R. L. (1993): *Introductory Econometrics*, Longman, second edition

Table 1

Japanese Tourist Demand Estimates by SUR, 1967-1995

(t-statistics in parenthesis)

Country i	Intercept α_i	Price γ_i	Arrivals β_i	DUM1 Malaysia (1990-1991) δ_{1i}	DUM2 Philippines (1977-1980) δ_{2i}	Time-Trend T	R^2	F Statistics	D-W
Indonesia	-0.328	-0.038	0.020				0.681	27.808	0.721
	(-5.103)	(-3.904)	(2.822)						
Malaysia	-0.260	0.044	0.024	0.077			0.653	30.404	0.909
	(-2.596)	(1.961)	(3.503)	(6.448)					
Philippines	-0.390	-0.057	0.060		0.049	-0.009	0.602	11.747	0.808
	(-1.463)	(-1.667)	(2.353)		(2.711)	(-5.300)			
Singapore	0.807	0.023	-0.062			0.010	0.788	31.102	0.515
	(3.846)	(0.928)	(-3.188)			(6.425)			
Thailand	1.484	0.099	-0.094				0.718	33.459	0.718
	(10.681)	(2.663)	(-8.22)						

Source: Author's calculation

Table 2

Ex-Post Forecast Equations for Market Shares of Japanese Tourists Arrivals using Stepwise Regression

(t-statistics in parenthesis)

1. $IND = 0.25 - 0.023*\log (y/P)_t + 0.002*T + 0.762*IND_{t-1}$
   (2.76) (-2.571) (3.002) (5.905)
   $R^2 = 0.82$ D-W = 1.867

2. $MAL = -0.049*\log (y/P)_t + 0.058*\log (y/P)_{t-1} + 0.085*DUM1$
   (-1.678) (1.961) (6.143)
   $R^2 = 0.686$ D-W = 0.895

3. $PHI = 0.042 - 0.106*\log P_{PHI,t-1} + 0.125*\log P_{PHI,t-2} + 0.035*DUM2 + 0.777*PHI_{t-1}$
   (1.477) (-2.151) (2.48) (1.32) (6.53)
   $R^2 = 0.801$ D-W = 1.482

4. $SING = 0.097 + 0.051*\log P_{SING,t} - 0.078*\log P_{SING,t-1} + 0.921*SING_{t-1}$
   (2.664) (2.766) (-3.889) (11.758)
   $R^2 = 0.918$ D-W = 1.576

5. $THAI = 0.431 + 0.064*\log (y/P)_t - 0.093*\log (y/P)_{t-1} + 0.615*THAI_{t-1}$
   (2.587) (1.714) (-2.508) (6.147)
   $R^2 = 0.926$ D-W = 2.183

Source: Author's calculation

Table 3

Arrival Elasticity and Own-Price Elasticity by SUR

Country i	Average Japanese Tourists Share w_i	Uncompensated Own-Price Elasticity of Demand ε_i	Compensated Own-Price Elasticity of Demand ε_i^*	Arrival Elasticity of Demand η_i
Indonesia	0.089614	-1.420	-1.419	1.228
Malaysia	0.102953	-0.568	-0.567	1.235
Philippines	0.182410	-1.311	-1.309	1.329
Singapore	0.319971	-0.927	-0.924	0.805
Thailand	0.305052	-0.676	-0.674	0.692

Source: Author's calculation

Table 4

Statistics of Fit for Forecasted Model

Variable	Mean Abs % Error	RMS % Error
Indonesia	7.0409	7.3631
Malaysia	7.1564	7.3760
Singapore	8.1923	8.6833
Thailand	11.9573	13.6474
Philippines	13.9802	15.1876

Source: Author's calculation

TABLE 5

Market Share of Japanese Tourist Arrivals by Destination

Year	Indonesia	Malaysia	Philippines	Singapore	Thailand
1967	0.03	0.08	0.22	0.22	0.44
1968	0.06	0.07	0.20	0.22	0.45
1969	0.08	0.05	0.17	0.26	0.44
1970	0.08	0.06	0.15	0.30	0.42
1971	0.11	0.03	0.17	0.31	0.38
1972	0.10	0.08	0.12	0.30	0.40
1973	0.09	0.14	0.14	0.27	0.36
1974	0.08	0.13	0.30	0.22	0.27
1975	0.07	0.11	0.35	0.21	0.26
1976	0.09	0.13	0.28	0.24	0.26
1977	0.07	0.20	0.27	0.24	0.22
1978	0.07	0.09	0.30	0.28	0.26
1979	0.06	0.09	0.31	0.30	0.24
1980	0.07	0.08	0.28	0.31	0.26
1981	0.07	0.09	0.20	0.38	0.26
1982	0.08	0.10	0.17	0.40	0.26
1983	0.09	0.10	0.18	0.38	0.24
1984	0.10	0.11	0.17	0.39	0.24
1985	0.10	0.12	0.16	0.39	0.23
1986	0.11	0.12	0.13	0.39	0.25
1987	0.12	0.10	0.10	0.41	0.27
1988	0.10	0.09	0.11	0.42	0.28
1989	0.09	0.10	0.11	0.42	0.28
1990	0.10	0.19	0.08	0.38	0.25
1991	0.13	0.17	0.09	0.38	0.24
1992	0.16	0.10	0.09	0.41	0.23
1993	0.16	0.10	0.10	0.41	0.24
1994	0.17	0.10	0.10	0.39	0.24
1995	0.16	0.10	0.10	0.38	0.26

Source: Pacific Asia Travel Association Annual Statistical Report

Table 6

Forecasted Consumer Price Indexes for ASEAN Destinations

Year	Indonesia	Malaysia	Philippines	Singapore	Thailand
1996	245.5	140.2	262.0	123.6	159.7
1997	262.6	145.5	287.5	126.1	166.8
1998	280.3	150.9	315.2	128.7	174.2
1999	298.5	156.6	345.5	131.2	181.9
2000	317.2	162.5	378.5	133.8	189.8
2001	336.4	168.6	414.6	136.3	198.0
2002	356.0	175.0	453.9	138.8	206.5
2003	376.1	181.6	496.8	141.4	215.3
2004	396.5	188.4	543.6	143.9	224.4
2005	417.4	195.5	594.7	146.4	233.9

Source: Author's calculation

Table 7

Forecasted Exchange Rates for ASEAN Destinations

Year	Indonesia	Malaysia	Philippines	Singapore	Thailand
1996	2337.895	2.491	26.058	1.411	25.098
1997	2427.19	2.479	26.402	1.394	25.282
1998	2516.484	2.466	26.747	1.382	25.465
1999	2605.779	2.45	27.091	1.371	25.648
2000	2695.074	2.44	27.436	1.359	25.832
2001	2784.369	2.427	27.78	1.347	26.015
2002	2873.664	2.414	28.124	1.335	26.198
2003	2962.958	2.401	28.468	1.324	26.382
2004	3052.253	2.388	28.813	1.312	26.565
2005	3141.548	2.375	29.157	1.3	26.748

Source: Author's calculation

Table 8

Forecasted Market Share of Japanese Tourists Arrivals in ASEAN by Destination

Year	Indonesia	Malaysia	Philippines	Singapore	Thailand
1996	0.154	0.113	0.107	0.352	0.236
1997	0.157	0.11	0.12	0.341	0.225
1998	0.161	0.11	0.127	0.34	0.217
1999	0.167	0.11	0.133	0.341	0.212
2000	0.173	0.11	0.139	0.343	0.209
2001	0.181	0.11	0.144	0.347	0.208
2002	0.189	0.11	0.149	0.352	0.207
2003	0.198	0.11	0.153	0.358	0.206
2004	0.207	0.11	0.157	0.362	0.207
2005	0.217	0.11	0.158	0.363	0.207

Source: Author's calculation

The Rates of Return to Education and Effectiveness of Training Programmes for Singaporean Workers

Ho Yuet Yen
&
Yao Hong

Nanyang Business School, Nanyang Technological University, Nanyang Avenue, Singapore 639798
Fax: +(65) 792.4217, Tel: +(65) 799.5725, Email: ahyao@ntu.edu.sg

Abstract It has always been said that Singapore has only one 'natural' resource - human resources. This explains the policy makers' strong commitment to develop its citizens to their fullest potential via formal as well as informal education. In this paper, we explore whether scarce resources are efficiently invested in education by examining the rates of return to education for the Singapore labour force, in particular for those with only primary and secondary education. In addition, we analyse the effects of training programmes on an individual's stock of human capital.

1. INTRODUCTION

Since human resources are Singapore's only 'natural resource', it is extremely important that its labour force be developed to its fullest potential via formal education as well as post-employment training and re-training geared towards job requirements.

In this paper, we would like to examine and compare the rates of return to human capital among Singaporean workers possessing different human capital levels, which are captured by formal education and post-employment training. These, in turn, are empirically proxied by years of schooling and length of training programmes respectively.

It is important for policy makers to know whether scarce resources are efficiently allocated in education. We hope that this paper would provide some information to policy makers when they evaluate earlier policies on education expansion and manpower development.

The remainder of this paper is organised as follows: In section two, we discuss some issues regarding the rates of return to education and the effectiveness of post-employment training on wage growth. In section three, we provide some descriptive statistics on the data sample, and explain the methodology used in this paper. In section four, we present the major findings. And lastly, in section five, we summarise and conclude this paper.

2. LITERATURE REVIEW

2.1 HUMAN CAPITAL THEORY

Education is typically regarded as an investment in human capital, and the return to this investment is the increase in expected earnings discounted over a lifetime. Therefore, an appropriate proxy for the returns to education will be wages.

According to the human capital school, variations in labour income are due mainly to differences in labour productivity, which are, in turn, the consequence of differences in the amount of human capital acquired by workers via formal education, and informal education in the form of post-school investments, such as post-employment training. Education is thus viewed as a form of investment in human potential, and the more education an individual receives, the more productive he is assumed to become. And, higher productivity is purportedly reflected in the higher earnings he receives.

However, although there is a positive correlation between education and earnings, critics have questioned the strength of the relationship, and whether the existence of earnings differentials truly reflects differences in the productivity of workers, as a result of differing amounts of education received. Apart from the differences in education of workers, worker's natural ability, family background, and other personal characteristics have also determined the pattern of earnings differentials. The failure to take into consideration of differences in other factors besides the amount of education received, has been the major criticism against the human capital theory.

In terms of empirical studies, multivariate regression analysis and earnings functions have been used to analyse the determinants of earnings. A discussion on the results of these studies are beyond the scope of this paper (see Woodhall (1987)); hence, it will be enough to point out that education remains to be the most powerful determinant of earnings although sex, race, family background and natural ability may also be significantly influence the earnings.

On the other hand, it has been argued that education does not increase productivity of workers but simply acts as a filter or "screening device," which enables employers to identify individuals who have superior abilities or attitudes or personal qualities that make them more productive. The argument put forth by the screening hypothesis had been refuted by Layard and Psacharopoulous (1974)[1]. If education is only useful as a screening device, this device would have been too expensive, and employers would have sought to replace the education system with a quicker and cheaper screening device instead. In addition, it has been observed that the age-earnings profiles by level of education diverge rather than converge over time. This observation indicates that even employers have direct evidence about the workers' productivity, they still continue to pay educated workers more. Besides the formal education, on-the-job training is also an investment in human capital and will bring a higher earnings for the workers.

2.2 EFFECTS OF POST-EMPLOYMENT TRAINING ON WAGE GROWTH

According to human capital theory, post-employment training refers to both formal training programmes, and informal on-the-job training and "learning by doing".

Although much has been said about the role that informal on-the-job training plays in augmenting one's stock of human capital, little research has been done to distinguish the effect of on-the-job training on wages from those of ageing. The primary reason is that it is difficult to observe or even define in some appropriate way the amount of on-the-job training an individual possesses.

It was only in 1976 that Edward Lazear derived a model whereby one could compare the effects of work experience to those of ageing per se. The difference is then attributed to on-the-job training.

---

[1] The author draws this section from Woodhall (1987).

This paper will focus on the effects of the post-employment training, in particular, formal training programmes, on wage growth.

3. RESEARCH METHODOLOGY

3.1 DATA

The data used in this paper is obtained from an informal survey undertaken by a local private non-profitable organisation in 1996. The sample consists of 156 workers aged between 21 and 55. Two alternate decompositions of the sample were used, differing by either gender or educational level[2].

From the first subsample, there are 124 working males and 32 working females. From the second subsample, there are 61 workers with partial or full primary education, and the remaining 95 of them had partial or full secondary education.

3.2 THE RATES OF RETURN TO EDUCATION

Three methods had been developed for estimating the rates of return to education. They are the complete method, reverse method and earnings function method.

3.2.1 The Complete Method - Constructing Age-Earnings Profiles

The complete method for estimating the rates of return to education involves two steps. The first step requires one to construct average net earnings profiles for working individuals at different levels of educational attainment. After this first step, one then proceed on to the second step of estimating the pure internal rate of return as expressed in the formula below:

$$\sum_{t=0}^{n}[(B_t - C_t)^t / (1+r)^t] = 0 \tag{1}$$

where

B_t is the benefits of the particular educational investment (For example, completing secondary education following the completion of primary education) in year t;

C_t is the costs of the particular education investment in year t;

n is the expected life of the investment, calculated as retirement age less age in year t;

r is the discount rate which makes the present value of the net benefit stream equal to zero.

In this method, the benefits of an educational investment is measured as the average additional earnings received by (for example) the graduates of secondary school, over and above the graduates of primary school, controlling for other determinants of earnings.

On the other hand, the costs of the investment on education comprise of the direct costs and indirect costs. Direct costs for individual would include all expenditures related to school attendance; and for society, the full resource costs of providing the educational

---

[2] The 156 workers in the sample, either received a (partial or full) primary or (partial or full) secondary education. This means that the analysis on the rates of return to education for the Singapore labour force in this paper does NOT include those with higher education.

service, including any subsidised costs not borne by the individual or the individual's family. Indirect costs includes the average earnings forgone by the individual as a result of the particular educational investment; and for society, the opportunity costs of devoting the resources to investments in education, rather than investments in some other activities.

As the data set used in this paper does not satisfy the stringent data criteria demanded by this method, we are not able to estimate the rates of return to education by using this technique.

3.2.2 The Reverse Method - Estimating Switching Values

A simple but useful application of switching values[3] to education is the "reverse cost-benefit analysis." This method consists of finding the minimum productivity differential which could imply an acceptable social rate of return for investments in education.

For instance, given the cost of producing a student with secondary education, what productivity differential is required to make the investment worthwhile for the society? Assuming that the discount rate is 10 percent, we can estimate the required differential using the reverse cost-benefit method, as expressed in Equation 2:

$$D_{s/s-1} = 0.10 \, [t_s(C_s + W_{s-1})] \tag{2}$$

where

$D_{s/s-1}$ is the required productivity differential between an individual who has graduated from schooling level S and one who has graduated from level S-1;

t_s is the number of years required to complete level S (that is, six years for primary education, assuming no grade repetition);

C_s is the annual direct cost of investment per student;

W_{s-1} is the earnings forgone during each year of investment.

According to this method, the closer the actual earnings differentials are to the required differentials at a 10 percent discount rate, the more socially desirable the education investment is.

As the data sample lacks the detailed cost information required by this method, we are not able to estimate the rates of return education using the reverse method too.

3.2.3 The Earnings Function Method

The human capital earnings function (HCEF), has been the dominant methodology for estimating the rate of return to education in recent years. This is because unlike the two models mentioned above, this model does not require detailed information about the direct costs of education. It can be estimated with earnings information alone!

This function, formally derived by Jacob Mincer (1974), is:

$$\text{Ln } Y = \alpha + \beta_1 \, \text{SCHOOL} + \beta_2 \, \text{EXP} + \beta_3 \, \text{EXPSQ} \tag{3}$$

where

---

[3] In the language of project appraisal, a switching value is the value that an element of an investment project with an acceptable rate of return must reach in order to push the project below the minimum level of acceptability and switch the appraisal decision from a "go" to a "no go".

Ln Y^4 is the natural logarithm of average gross annual earnings across number of years of schooling;

α is the intercept;

SCHOOL is the number of years of schooling;

EXP is the number of years of potential labour market experience, calculated as age less years of schooling less 6;

EXPSQ is the square of the number of years of potential labour market experience.

In Mincer's semi-log specification, the coefficient on SCHOOL (β_1) is interpreted to be the average private rate of return or rate of growth of earnings due to an additional year of schooling.

3.3 THE EFFECTS OF TRAINING PROGRAMMES ON WAGE GROWTH

3.3.1 The Proposed Wage Growth Model
The proposed wage growth is specified as follows:

$$\text{Ln } Y_1 - \text{Ln } Y_0 = \alpha + \beta_1 \text{ TRG} + \beta_2 \text{ EXPSQ} \tag{4}$$

where

Ln Y_1 is the natural logarithm of average gross annual earnings across number of years of schooling for an individual, after he takes up the training programme;

Ln Y_0 is the natural logarithm of average gross annual earnings across number of years of schooling for an individual before he takes up the training programme;

TRG is the length of the training programme undertaken, expressed in years;

EXPSQ is the square of the number of years of potential labour market experience.

4. MAJOR FINDINGS

4.1 RATES OF RETURNS TO EDUCATION
Table 1 presents the results of estimating the standard Mincerian earnings equation where Ln Y is the dependent variable and SCHOOL, EXP and EXPSQ are the explanatory variables.

Column 1 of Table 1 gives estimates of the returns to education in Singapore for the overall sample of workers, while columns 2 and 3 show the estimates of the returns to education for the working males and females. The regression analysis was repeated with the other subsample group with differing amounts of education received. Columns 4 and 5 show the estimates of the returns to education for those with partial or full primary education, and partial or full secondary education respectively.

Some interesting results emerge when we examine the regression results. When the schooling variable used is years of schooling received, the coefficient of this variable is actually insignificant for the overall sample as well as for both subsamples. However the experience is significantly influence worker's earnings for overall sample and for working

---

[4] For a more extensive discussion on the variable specification for this dependent variable, see Appendix.

males. This means that the amount of education does not have a significant impact on a person's earnings. Hence, even though worker A might have received more education than worker B, worker A may earn less than worker B.

This finding indicates that education does **not** always generate positive returns for all groups of workers. This is so because if a person does not fully utilise his human capital, investment on education is likely to be wasted since it will not guarantee him a higher level of earnings.

A possible reason for such results is that the sample we use is a group of low skilled labour with non-professional jobs. Since these non-professional jobs do not require employees to posses special knowledge or skills, the employers are most likely indifferent between employing a worker with primary education or hiring someone with secondary education. Rather, they would like to pay more for the workers with more experience. Therefore, as a result, the earnings differentials between a worker with primary education and another one with secondary education may be minimal.

Here, owing to the small sample size of the working females in our data, we should interpret the results for the working females with caution. Thus, even though column 3 shows that the estimates for all the variables, including the intercept, are statistically insignificant for the working females, we should **not** jump to the conclusion that educational investments for female workers are unproductive! In fact, studies by Psacharopoulos (1985) had shown that females obtain higher rates of return to education than males in many countries.

4.2 EFFECTS OF TRAINING PROGRAMMES ON WAGE GROWTH

Table 2 presents the results of estimating the wage growth model proposed in Equation 4 in subsection 3.3.1. The dependent variable is $Ln\ Y_1 - Ln\ Y_0$, which is the wage growth, and the explanatory variables are TRG and EXPSQ.

Column 1 of Table 2 gives estimates of the effectiveness of training programmes for the overall sample of workers, while columns 2 and 3 show the estimates of the effectiveness of training programmes for working males and working females. Columns 4 and 5 show the estimates of the effectiveness of training programmes for those with partial or full primary education and partial or full secondary education respectively.

Table 2 shows a number of interesting results. Firstly, the coefficient of training programmes is significant at the 10 percent level of confidence for the overall sample, working males sample and the sample with 7 - 10 years of schooling (that is, those who received partial or full secondary education). This indicates that the length of the training programmes has a positive impact on earnings on these three sample groups. The longer the training programme, the more the remuneration. In fact, the effects of formal training programmes on wage growth is the greatest for the sample with 7 - 10 years of schooling.

However, we do not obtain the same results for the female sample and the sample with 1- 6 years of schooling (that is, those who received either partial or full primary education). At face value, the results imply that formal training programmes do not have a significant effect on the wage growth for these two groups. However, caution should be used when interpreting these results, in particular, the female sample, owing to the limited number of observations in this sample.

Although the coefficient of training programmes is insignificant at the 10 percent level of confidence for workers with partial or full primary education, the result should **not** be taken to imply that post-employment training is unimportant for these workers. Since majority (about 60 percent) of this group of workers in our sample are aged above 40, owing to their incompetence in the level of school education, they may not be able to successfully accomplish formal training programmes. Therefore, the post-employment training in the form of informal on-the-job training may have a greater impact on their wage growth than formal training programmes.

5. SUMMARY AND CONCLUSIONS

In this study, we try to estimate and compare the impact of education and training programmes on earnings by analysing the data obtained from an informal survey undertaken by a local private non-profitable organisation in 1996. The data set includes 156 workers who are holding low-professional positions in Singapore. The major findings are as the followings.

Firstly, years of schooling do not have a significant impact on earnings. This means that there is no positive return to education for our sample. This result gives us an indication of the efficiency of resource allocation - if a person receives a relatively high level of education but holds a low professional position (an indication that he may be under-employed), the additional years of education he or she receives is wasted because they do not generate any extra earnings. As a result, finding an appropriate job for those workers will be essential to bring about a positive return to their education.

Secondly, with the exception of female workers and workers with primary schooling, post-employment training in the form of formal training programmes has a positive effect on the workers' incremental earnings in our sample. The longer training programmes they received, the higher earning they obtained.   This is because the formal training programmes provide them with skills which can directly help them to do their jobs more effectively and productively.

Therefore, for a better allocation of scarce resources and more efficient investment in human capital, people with a higher level of education should be encouraged to take up more challenging and professional jobs. In addition, post-employment training should be given more attention. Longer and continuous training should be encouraged and more training programmes, especially appropriate programmes for older and less educated workers, should be implemented.

REFERENCES

Lazear, E. (1976): "Age, Experience, and Wage Growth," *American Economic Review*, 66(4), 548-558

Mincer, J. (1974): *Schooling, Experience and Earnings*. New York: National Bureau of Economic Research

Psacharopoulous, G. (1985): Returns to education: a further international update and implications," *The Journal of Human Resources*, 20(4), 583-611

Psacharopoulous, G. (1987): "Earnings Functions," in Psacharopoulous, G. (1987) ed., *Economics of Education: Research and Studies*. New York: Pergamon Press, 218-223

Woodhall, M. (1987): "Earnings and Education," in Psacharopoulous, G. (1987) ed., *Economics of Education: Research and Studies*. New York: Pergamon Press, 209-217

TABLE 1

Coefficient Estimates for the Standard Mincerian Earnings Equation

	All workers	Males	Females	1 - 6 years of schooling	7 - 10 years of schooling
Constant, α	8.633# (12.040)	7.914# (10.490)	47.010** (3.880)	39.943# (6.295)	9.487# (26.538)
SCHOOL, β_1	0.007** (0.198)	0.035** (0.955)	-0.085** (-1.140)	0.289** (3.554)	-0.050** (-3.172)
EXP, β_2	0.086# (2.051)	0.121# (2.594)	-2.723** (-3.019)	-2.131** (-4.693)	0.070** (2.314)
EXPSQ, β_3	-0.002# (-2.536)	-0.003# (-2.740)	0.049** (2.913)	0.035** (4.577)	-0.002** (-2.798)
R^2	0.833	0.837	0.935	0.982	0.942
Adjusted R^2	0.732	0.740	0.739	0.930	0.769

a.   t-statistics are indicated in parentheses.

b.   # indicates that the coefficient estimates are significant at the 10 percent level of even better.

c.   ** indicates that the coefficient estimates are not statistically significant at the 10 percent level.

TABLE 2

Coefficient Estimates for the Proposed Wage Growth Model

	All workers	Males	Females	1 - 6 years of schooling	7 - 10 years of schooling
Constant, α	0.230# (2.347)	0.193# (4.431)	1.650** (0.933)	0.207** (2.588)	0.463# (6.478)
TRG, β_1	0.248# (2.910)	0.229# (6.016)	-0.855** (-0.593)	0.233** (2.400)	0.453# (6.392)
EXPSQ, β_2	-0.0002# (-2.009)	-0.0001# (-3.607)	-0.001** (-0.400)	-0.0001** (-2.146)	-0.001# (-6.596)
R^2	0.864	0.950	0.170	0.962	0.984
Adjusted R^2	0.819	0.934	-0.660	0.885	0.952

a.   t-statistics are indicated in parentheses.

b.   # indicates that the coefficient estimates are significant at the 10 percent level of even better.

c.   ** indicates that the coefficient estimates are not statistically significant at the 10 percent level..

APPENDIX

One important distinction in earnings functions analyses is whether the data refer to individuals (that is, the dependent variable ranges over the earnings of A to earnings of Z) or to groups of individuals. In the latter case, the average earnings of a group of people is treated as one observation in the earnings function.

The dependent variable, Ln Y, used in this paper is an example of averaging of annual gross earnings across the number of years of schooling received.

Here, the distinction between individual and average data is important because in the latter case, a major part of the variation earnings is removed before the dependent variable enters the regression. This explains for the high R^2 in this paper, as compared with the R^2 of other empirical studies that had used individual data.

Income Tax Compliance in Singapore

Arindam ***Das-Gupta***
&
Kwan *Chang Yew*

Nanyang Business School, Nanyang Technological University, Nanyang Avenue, Singapore 639798
Fax: +(65) 792.4217, Tel: +(65) 799.4825, Email: aadasgupta@ntu.edu.sg

Abstract Income tax compliance is measured by an index of the ratio of gross assessed tax to GDP times the average effective tax rate. Besides national income, inflation , tax structure and tax enforcement activity were important determinants of income tax compliance and revenue in Singapore during 1965-1993. Unlike earlier studies for other countries, there is a positive association between tax revenue and marginal tax rates, suggesting that Singapore's tax rates are moderate. Even so, marginal tax rates exert a negative effect on compliance. Inflation has a negative effect on both compliance and revenue, especially the former. Tax collection lags have negligible revenue effects so that a move to PAYE taxation and withholding may not have any net benefit.

1. INTRODUCTION

The paper extends methods developed in earlier studies to measure compliance with the personal income tax in Singapore and examine the effects of different determinants of compliance and revenues suggested by economic theory. The study focuses on resident individual taxpayers. The contribution of the income tax to total tax revenues has been growing in Singapore, from an average of around 20 percent in the years following independence to over 30 percent in recent years. The study of the determinants of revenue and compliance is nevertheless important for the purpose of assessing actual revenue performance relative to potential and to identify causes of any shortfall that may exist. Improved performance will enable further revenue neutral reduction in either marginal income tax rates or other taxes. As is well known, substantial economic efficiency losses and decreased international competitiveness are caused by high marginal personal tax rates and such taxes as the corporation tax and stamp duties. More directly, a study of compliance and revenue determinants can provide answers to important tax policy questions, including: (i) Are tax rates still inefficiently high, despite their being lowered in recent years, causing Singapore to operate beyond the peak of the Laffer curve? (ii) What is the extent of loss, if any, due to inflation? (iii) Are administrative procedures for tax collection capable of improvement? (iv) Have efforts by the tax administration to enforce compliance with the income tax been effective? (v) Do Singapore's extreme openness and unique institutions such as the CPF affect tax revenue and compliance?

The main findings are, firstly, that Singapore's income tax rate structure is not such that it is beyond the peak of the Laffer curve. Nevertheless, the rising burden of the income tax, due to per capita income growth and despite a few reductions in tax rates since 1975, has caused a fall in compliance. Second, despite low inflation rates, revenues and compliance have a surprisingly large and significant elasticity with respect to the measure of inflation used, testifying to the importance of the Tanzi-Olivera effect in Singapore. Third, compliance has fallen in Singapore despite the sustained efficiency of tax administration. Fourth, an unexpected finding was that Singapore's "old-fashioned" system of subsequent year official assessment which leads to revenue collection lags, has little effect on compliance and revenues other than possible inflationary costs. This vindicates Singapore not switching over to broad-based withholding and pay-as-you earn (PAYE) and imposes large compliance costs on taxpayers and withholders [Vaillancourt (1987)]. Finally, Singapore's openness and CPF have no discernible effect on tax compliance and revenue.

After a brief review of relevant theory and earlier empirical work for other countries, data sources and methods of analysis are described in Section 2. In the third section, empirical estimates are reported. In Section 4, we report policy simulations performed to obtain quantitative estimates of revenue and compliance effects of enforcement policy, tax structure and inflation during the past 3 decades. Concluding comments are in Section 5.

1.1 DETERMINANTS OF REVENUES AND COMPLIANCE: THEORY

Traditionally, the performance of most broad-based taxes has been studied by estimating tax buoyancies and elasticities. These studies have as their theoretical underpinning the identity

Tax Revenue ≡ Average Effective Tax Rate. Tax Base.   (1)

As discussed, for example, in the review by King (1995), the *buoyancy* of a broad based tax is the elasticity of tax revenue with respect to a proxy measure of the tax base, usually GDP. Since this procedure is only justified if the tax code is constant over time, the *tax elasticity* adjusts buoyancy estimates for year-to-year discretionary changes in tax rates and exclusions. Recent examples of buoyancy and elasticity studies for Singapore's personal income tax are Asher and Booth (1980), Asher (1989) and Low (1996). Buoyancy estimates are obtained, in these studies, by employing double log regressions of tax revenue on GDP. Implicitly, these studies do not allow for possible determinants of the tax base itself, such as variations in tax compliance and the effectiveness of tax enforcement. Furthermore, the methods of adjusting for discretionary changes in the tax code are relatively crude and the Average Effective Tax Rate (AETR) is seldom independently calculated.

The economic theory of taxpayer compliance (or its mirror image in the absence of tax avoidance - tax evasion) stems from a pioneering paper by Allingham and Sandmo (1972). This paper drew attention to the trade-off between the cost to individuals of complying with tax laws, in terms of taxes paid, and the cost of non-compliance in the form of the penalty for tax evasion imposed in the event of detection by the tax administration. They studied the case of a risk averse taxpayer whose Von Neumann-Morgenstern utility (U) depends on (after tax) income. After-tax income depends on pre-tax income (W), the proportional income tax rate (θ) and the amount of income the taxpayer chooses to declare (X). If underreporting is detected (with probability p) then, in addition, the taxpayer would pay a proportional penalty $\pi > \theta$ on undeclared income, (W-X). The resulting decision problem of the taxpayer is to choose X to maximise:

$$E(u) = (1 - p)U(W - \theta X) + pU(W - \theta X - \pi(W - X))$$ (2)

The theory predicts that evasion will be negatively affected by p and π, provided these policy variables are low enough to make evasion worthwhile in the first place. The effect of a tax rate change is ambiguous due to opposing income and substitution effects. Finally, the impact of income changes depends on whether relative risk aversion of the taxpayer is increasing (evasion would decrease), constant or decreasing.

Yitzhaki (1974) modified equation (2) to take account of the fact that most countries - including Singapore - assess monetary penalties or fines on evaded taxes rather than on underreported income. This implies that $\pi=F\theta$, $F>1$, in (2). He found that the substitution effect of higher taxes disappeared under this penalty regime. Contrary to a priori expectations and empirical evidence, however, the model now predicts a negative response of tax evasion to tax rate changes because the penalty rate rises along with the tax rate. The failure of the model to allow for a positive response of evasion to tax changes shows that it is incomplete in some respect.

A large literature has since developed attempting to extend the basic Allingham-Sandmo-Yitzhaki (ASY) model and this defect by providing taxpayers with alternative means of escaping taxation such as the labour-leisure choice. This literature, along with other theoretical developments, is surveyed by Cowell (1990) and Das-Gupta and Mookherjee (1997). We focus on one relevant extension. Das-Gupta, Lahiri and Mookherjee (1995) (hereafter DLM) extend ASY to allow for two sources of income, income from black and white assets, with income from black assets being harder for the tax administration to observe than income from white assets. They show that this leads to a Laffer curve relation between tax rates and tax revenue or compliance. DLM also consider a generalised tax function, which allows for an exemption limit (or tax threshold) and either constant or rising marginal tax rates. The find that the exemption limit, besides having an adverse direct effect on revenue, also has an indirect negative effect by causing falling compliance. In using this model to examine compliance in Singapore, black to white capital flows can be reinterpreted as international capital movements.

1.2 DETERMINANTS OF REVENUES AND COMPLIANCE: EMPIRICAL EVIDENCE

Several empirical studies of compliance, mainly in OECD countries, have been carried out. A recent survey is in De Juan, Lasheras and Mayo (1994). Nine of the papers surveyed examined the relation between tax rates and revenues or compliance. All found these variables to be negatively associated. A similar result is reported in DLM (1995). Other determinants of compliance found to be important include the perceived severity of tax enforcement, compliance costs and a number of cultural and sociological variables. Of these, variables other than enforcement (and the tax structure) are likely to affect the level of compliance across different countries or socio-economic groups, but not the year-to-year fluctuations that form the focus of time-series studies, especially if the data series is relatively short.

Cross-section studies are made possible by taxpayer surveys, such as under the periodic Taxpayer Compliance Monitoring Program (TCMP) of the US Internal Revenue Service. For example, an early study by Clotfelter (1983) uses data from the 1969 TCMP. Besides an effect of tax rates on compliance, he found significant variation in compliance by source of income. He attributed this to differences in tax withholding and external information across income sources. He also found the efficiency of tax audits and tax compliance costs (via simplified tax forms) to be important determinants of compliance. A second important study by Witte and Woodbury (1985) found significant differences in the impact of different enforcement activities such as auditing and prosecutions or, more accurately, the audit probability, and civil and criminal penalties. This alerts researchers to the need to distinguish between different types of administration or enforcement activity. For Singapore, no TCMP has yet been conducted, so any study of compliance must rely on less accurate time series data.

There appear to be only two studies conducted to date with time series data, Crane and Nourzad (1986) for the US and DLM for India. An important contribution of the Crane and Nourzad paper was their finding that tax evasion was positively related to the inflation rate. This showed that the negative Tanzi-Olivera effect of inflation on tax revenue was not merely due to the revenue collection lags emphasized, for example, by Tanzi (1987) but also due to compliance effects. DLM suggest that these compliance effects are due to the negative effect of inflation on nominally fixed asset returns, causing a substitution to inflation proof assets (such as black assets in India or, in open economies, foreign assets). DLM also examine the effect of different enforcement activities, the exemption limit and tax amnesties on compliance and tax revenue. They find that the exemption limit had a significant effect other than the tax rate and the inflation rate. The DLM specification of tax structure does not include a measure of tax progressivity and the direct incorporation of the impact of tax concessions.

Both Crane and Nourzad and DLM worked with data which had significant deficiencies. In consequence, a useful contribution of DLM was to devise an aggregate measure of tax compliance that can be estimated for broad-based taxes in most countries. The measure modifies the tax revenue identity given earlier to:

Tax Revenue ≡ Average Effective Tax Rate.**True** Tax Base.Compliance.

Rearrangement of this gives a measure of compliance. This definition of compliance reflects both illegal tax evasion and legal tax avoidance through the use of tax loopholes. Using the traditional proxy for the base of broad based taxes, GDP, and noting that the base will be proportional to GDP if (1) tax structure effects are controlled for and (2) capital gains are not a part of the tax base, we obtain a compliance measure that is empirically observable for most countries even if they do not have data available from a TCMP type survey. That is:

$$\text{Compliance} \equiv \frac{\text{Tax Revenue}}{\text{AETR.True Tax Base}} = \frac{\text{Proportionality factor.Tax Revenue}}{\text{AETR.GDP}} \tag{3}$$

The denominator of this compliance measure provides an estimate (up to a proportionality constant) of potential tax revenue in the absence of evasion. Empirical estimation of the AETR, and therefore the compliance measure, has two inherent limitations. First, the AETR cannot be measured using actual revenue and assessed income data as this will lead to contamination from existing tax evasion. Instead, it must be estimated from statutory tax rates and exogenous estimates of income distribution. Secondly, if the distribution of tax concessions across taxpayers is not proportional to taxes paid and if data on the distribution of tax concessions are not available (as in India and Singapore), the AETR will be biased in an unknown way. Even so, the measure is likely to track changes in tax compliance behaviour from year to year fairly accurately unless the structure of concessions changes drastically over time.

1.3 EXTENDING THE FRAMEWORK: THE SINGAPORE CASE

To sum up the discussion above, the following model for either compliance or revenue determinants is suggested:

Dependent = f(GDP, inflation rate, tax structure, enforcement; long run effects) (4)

(+) (-) (?) (+) (in constant term)

These are essentially the models studied by DLM. The impact of GDP on compliance is related to whether, on average, risk aversion is increasing or decreasing in the population. Furthermore, the tax structure (through tax rates and exemption limits) can have Laffer curve effects. The model also provides a check on the reasonableness of the compliance estimates: Since revenue and compliance are linked by an identity, the revenue elasticity with respect to GDP and the AETR will be one plus the corresponding compliance elasticity if the compliance estimate is unbiased.

In the Singapore case, at least four additional determinants appear relevant on a priori grounds. *Openness* should affect compliance and revenue if the ease with which foreign source income of residents can be taxed differs from domestic source income or if there are significant differences in the nature of available tax concessions. Secondly, the ASY model implies that the availability of tax concessions can affect compliance and expected revenues. Since a major tax concession in Singapore is the deductibility of employee and employer contributions to the CPF, variations in the *permissible rate of tax deductible contributions to the CPF* should be a determinant. Inclusion of this variable will also provide a check on how seriously the omission of tax concessions from the AETR biases measured compliance.

Third, besides inflationary losses, delayed tax collection also causes a decrease in the present value of tax revenues. From the taxpayer's point of view, this means a lower effective tax rate in present value terms. This will have a direct effect on revenue and also an indirect effect through compliance changes. Thus, the *decrease in the effective tax rate due to collection lags* could possibly be an additional determinant of tax revenue and compliance. Delayed tax collection also has, in the ASY model, a second effect because of the fact that current tax liability must be paid from future income. *Expected future income* and the *riskiness of future income* can be shown to affect compliance, the former negatively and the latter positively.[1] The study of these administrative effects can then be used to assess if it is worthwhile for Singapore to consider switching to broad-based withholding and PAYE taxation.

2. METHODOLOGY AND DATA

Raw data for the study are time-series for the years 1965 to 1993, obtained from Inland Revenue Department (IRD) and Inland Revenue Authority of Singapore (IRAS) Annual Reports and the Singapore Yearbooks of Statistics. The IRAS is the statutory board that took over the functions of the IRD in 1991. Our choice of period is dictated, firstly, by the fact that 1965 is the year of independence. Second, data for the revenue effect of an income tax credit for the GST, introduced in 1994, are not available.

---

[1] This can be shown by extending the ASY model to allow for income to be W+a with probability q and W-b with probability (1-q). Taxes, however are legally imposed on W alone. Then an increase qa+(1-q)b with no change in its variance reflects the effect of higher expected future income while an increase in its variance holding the mean constant reflects higher future income risk.

2.1 EQUATIONS AND ESTIMATION PROCEDURES

All revenue and compliance equations reported are estimated using double log specifications or their first differences and ordinary least squares estimation. The use of these functional forms is as in earlier work and has the advantage that the estimated coefficients are elasticities. All monetary variables are adjusted for inflation using the Consumer Price Index (CPI).

Tests using the Augmented Dickey-Fuller test for unit roots failed to reject the hypothesis of non-stationarity for most variables at the 10 percent significance level. However, all regressions reported are cointegrated at the 10 percent significance level upon testing for the stationarity of the first step residuals of the Engel-Granger 2-step procedure (EG). This suggests that the estimated equations reflect stable long-run relationships. To choose between alternative theoretically acceptable specifications, the first model selection criterion was absence of serial correlation. Given no serial correlation, a simple average of the ranks according to the 3-period within sample forecast error, Akaike's information criterion and the Durbin-Watson statistic was used.

Simplicity is considered a virtue if no oversimplification is involved. So, before proceeding to more complex models of revenue, we re-examined the traditional buoyancy model to find out if an improved estimation technique, namely the Engle-Granger-Yoo 3-step procedure, would lead to a satisfactory model. The estimated equation is

$$\log (GAT_t) = a + b \log (GDP_{t-1}), \tag{5}$$

Lagged GDP is used since, under Singapore's administrative system, tax collection is on previous year's income. Nevertheless, we may point out that estimated coefficients are not very different with current year GDP. It is also worth noting that buoyancy estimates previously obtained by Asher (1989) and Low (1996) are very close to ours - new estimation techniques (Table 1) do not overturn their conclusions about tax buoyancy. The residuals of this equation are, however, serially correlated. This suggests the possibility of additional determinants of revenue.

Additional determinants, for the inflation rate, the tax structure and enforcement variables, are described in section 2.2. Extensions based on the discussion in section 1.3 lead to additional variables in these regressions. However, we incorporate the modification in the measurement of the AETR suggested by our discussion directly into the AETR. Variables and their construction are now discussed.

2.2 CONSTRUCTION AND SELECTION OF VARIABLES

2.2.1 Dependent Variables

Real Gross Assessed Tax (GAT): This series is obtained from IRD/IRAS Annual Reports. It gives the final tax assessment figures for resident individual taxpayers for each year of assessment. The years of assessment corresponds, for individuals, to the calendar year following the year in which income is earned. Penalties and arrears are not included in GAT, making it approximately equal to voluntarily declared income after official correction of prima facie reporting errors.

The Compliance Index (COM): GAT is the numerator of the expression in equation (3), while lagged instead of current GDP is used as the proxy for the tax base for the reason given earlier. The construction of the AETR is explained below.

2.2.2 Economic Variables

Lagged Real Gross Domestic Product (GDP): This is the proxy used for true economic income, since the income tax is broad-based and capital gains are exempt from the income tax in Singapore. This choice follows previous studies.

The Inflation Rate (INF): This is measured by the proportionate change in the CPI (1987=100). However, since there are years in which the inflation rate was negative, the gross inflation rate, INF=(1+the inflation rate), is used.

2.2.3 Tax Structure Variables

The Average Effective Tax Rate (AETR): Total tax paid in year t can be written as $\Sigma ETR_{it}Y_{it}$, where ETR_{it} is the effective tax rate of taxpayers with income Y_{it} in year t. We get the AETR by dividing through by $Y_t=\Sigma Y_{it}$. To ensure that evasion does not affect the calculations, fixed income proportions are used as the weights applied to the ETRs. The weights correspond to the income proportions of individual taxpayers in a base year, 1987. The distribution corresponds to the assessed income distribution from the relevant annual report of the IRD. Furthermore, for each year, assessed incomes are adjusted using the CPI to hold their distribution constant at the 1987 level. Third, taxes due are computed using the statutory tax schedule and personal allowance of that year. That is $T_{it}=T_t(Y_{i0}[P_t/P_0])$, for each year t, where 0 corresponds to the year 1987, and T_t is the tax liability calculated using the year t tax schedule and personal allowance. The effective tax rate is then the ratio of the tax payable to assessed income $Y_{i0}[P_i/P_0]$.

While removing bias due to evasion, this procedure neglects changes in the income distribution due to changing inequality and per capita incomes. Bhanoji Rao (1996) has argued that inequality apparently changed little over our sample period. To adjust for rising per capita income, we replace the income adjustment factor $[P_t/P_0]$ by $[P_tZ_t/P_0Z_0]$, where P_tZ_t is the nominal per capita GDP in year t. This modified AETR is called the MAETR. The MAETR is the series used in the denominator of the compliance index. Finally, to take account of the decrease in the real present value of tax liability due to the collection we further adjust the MAETR to make it reflect the real present value of taxes due. The CPI and the interest rate on one year bank deposits are used and the possibility of up to 12 monthly tax payment instalments is taken account of. The revised series is called the RMAETR. The three series are plotted in Figure 1.

The Average Marginal Tax Rate (AMTR): the procedures used to compute effective tax rates area also used for the AMTR, MAMTR and RMAMTR, except that marginal tax rates and not ETRs are used. Marginal tax rates are theoretically important in determining compliance in addition to average tax rates. Only marginal tax rates are used in regressions as they are highly correlated with effective rates (the correlation coefficient of the RMAETR and RMAMTR is 0.978).

Both effective and marginal rate indices are biased upward because exclusions are not taken account of except for personal allowances, due to lack of data. What is of importance, however, is not the average level of bias - this will only effect the constant term in regressions - but any variation over time. An attempt to correct for the trend, using information on the CPF, tends to suggest that trend bias is not serious.

Tax Rebates: Tax rebates were introduced as a substitute for frequent tax rate changes in 1981. Due to lack of data on their revenue effect a dummy variable with the value 1 for 1981 to 1993 is used to capture the effects of the switch to rebates on taxpayer behaviour.

2.2.3.1 Enforcement Efforts

Enforcement variables are the empirical counterparts of the probability of detection and penalty variables in theoretical models. Following Witte and Woodbury and DLM, we try to include indicators of different enforcement activities. Data are available on two types of enforcement activity, actions against taxpayers who fail to file returns and tax investigations. Field audits of taxpayers did not commence in Singapore till 1992 according to the Singapore Master Tax Guide, 1995. Data are not separately available for resident individual taxpayers. As such, we assume that the enforcement effort is uniform across all categories of taxpayers. After trying out both current and lagged variables in regressions, we selected the current variable specification. All but one of the variables are expected to have positive effects on compliance and, via compliance, revenue. The variables, which reflect both volume and intensity of enforcement, are as follows.

Non-filing ratio: This is the ratio of the number of taxpayers who failed to file tax returns to the total number of taxpayers. The effect on compliance and revenue is expected to be negative.

Penalty for failure to file returns: The ratio of total fines and penalties imposed to the total income tax collected.

Tax investigation cases: The ratio of the number of tax investigations to total taxpayers.

Additional revenue from investigations: The ratio of additional tax and penalties levied to total tax.

Effective penalty rate in tax investigation cases: The penalty rate is calculated by the following formula:

$$P0 = \frac{\text{Additional tax \& penalties}}{\text{tax rate.additional income revealed}} \qquad (6)$$

3. EMPIRICAL RESULTS

3.1 DATA PLOTS

The most important feature of the AETR (Figure 1) is that it has been declining from a peak reached in 1973-76, reflecting tax schedule changes introduced by the government. Nevertheless, the plot of the MAETR suggests that the tax burden is actually increasing due to growing per capita income. We emphasize that this may be partly due to data bias from the omission of most tax concessions, if concessions have been becoming more liberal over the years. Comparing the MAETR with the RMAETR, we see that collection lags do lower effective tax rates, but only marginally. This suggests that collection lags do not have a significant direct real cost in terms of revenue foregone.

Time plots of the logarithms of real gross assessed income (LGAT) and the compliance index (LMCOM) are presented in Figure 2. Strikingly, the two variables show opposite time trends. The decreasing trend of COM reflects any upward bias in the MAETR.

3.2 *ESTIMATED COMPLIANCE AND REVENUE EQUATIONS*

All regressions reported are, as stated earlier, co-integrated. The equations reported in Table 2 are those with RMAMTR as the tax variable. First-step estimates from the EG procedure are reported in the levels columns and second step results are reported in the first differences columns. The levels coefficients reflect long run equilibrium effects of variables while the first difference results capture the relationship during short run adjustment. We do not report regressions results with the AMTR and the MAMTR here since they are broadly similar. The main inferences that can be drawn from any differences that do exist are discussed below. To test for the effects of groups of variables, additional regressions were run without economic variables or tax structure variables or enforcement variables. The F-tests for the joint significance of each of these groups of variables are reported in Table 3.

The coefficient of lagged GDP in the revenue equation is significantly below the expected value of one, the value that would obtain if compliance was unrelated to GDP. In contrast, the corresponding coefficient in the alternative regression with the AETR is 1.26: Results are sensitive to the tax variable used. If the bias in the RMAMTR is not significant, then this suggests that rising income is associated with rising avoidance or evasion. This would confirm the common perception that there are greater opportunities for the rich to escape taxation.

Although inflation has been historically low in Singapore, the inflation elasticity of revenue is surprisingly large (-0.98), showing that the Tanzi-Olivera effect is present in Singapore. This finding is true for all tax proxies. This could possibly be due to collection lags. However, the major effect appears to be through the indirect effect of falling compliance rather than the direct effect. This is unexpected in the Singapore context but tends to confirm the findings of Crane and Nourzad and DLM.

The revenue coefficient of the RMAMTR is positive in contrast to all studies surveyed earlier. This is welcome since it confirms that tax rates are not inefficiently high in Singapore. That is, Singapore is operating to the left of the Laffer Curve peak. Even so, in all revenue regressions the elasticity was significantly below one, confirming the importance of negative compliance effects. This is caused by tax progressivity and per capita income growth, which have resulted in rising tax burdens over time. The effect of tax rebates appears to be insignificant in the long run.

The coefficients and R^2s of the RMAMTR and MAMTR regressions are only marginally different in all cases. This suggests that indirect effects of collection lags are also absent.

Regression coefficients reflect the impact of variation in regressors and not their average level. The latter, along with other variables, merely affects the constant term and cannot be econometrically identified. Available anecdotal information suggests that IRAS enforcement has continued to be strict while its efficiency has been increasing. This is consistent with regression results and confirmed by simulations reported below. There is an unexpected wrong sign for the coefficient of tax investigation cases. The coefficient remains significant and negative in alternative regressions. We have ruled out the possibility of this being due to multicollinearity. Thus, if the wrong sign is not the result of data deficiencies, the following hypothesis is suggested. Tax investigations draw resources away from other administration and enforcement activities, causing compliance and revenue to be adversely affected. This hypothesis can be tested when additional data become available. Table 3 shows that enforcement efforts are significant, but only at the 11 percent level.

Overall, the diagnostics tell us that revenue regression is reasonably satisfactory, though Durbin-Watson statistics are in the inconclusive region, a problem absent from the regressions with the unadjusted AMTR. The forecast error of the compliance equation is also fairly large. The results tend to confirm the importance of inflation, tax structure and enforcement effects on revenue and compliance.

3.3 ADDITIONAL VARIABLES FOR SINGAPORE

The impact of including additional Singapore-specific variables is as follows. Openness was measured by a standard indicator, the ratio of exports plus imports to GDP. It was found to be insignificant in all specifications. This suggests that, despite increased opportunities to escape tax, compliance by Singapore residents has not been affected by openness. The finding with respect to the statutory rate of CPF deductions is similar, which is encouraging as it suggests that unavailability of data on concessions does not seriously affect our results.

The indirect impact of taxpayers paying taxes on current income out of subsequent year income is studied as follows. Income expectations and risk for, say, year t were measured by a 5-year moving average of real per capita GDP for the years t-2 to t+2 and the associated 5-year variance. The expectations indicator proved to be of the right sign (negative) and significant while the risk indicator proved to be insignificant. These results are not reported due to the possibility that the expectations variable is correlated with GDP and the RMAMTR. Regressions with these variables also perform worse than the ones reported. On the basis of this finding we tentatively conclude that this channel of influence of collection lags on compliance is also absent, though further work is needed.

4. POLICY ANALYSIS

What do our results imply about the quantitative importance of determinants of revenue and compliance? To study this we examine the decrease in revenue or compliance due to variables differing from their sample average values. For inflation, however, we examine the decrease caused by non-zero inflation. These results are reported for four different time periods in Table 4. The table shows, first, that inflation has had a large negative effect on both compliance and revenue given the low rates of inflation in Singapore. Second, enforcement and administration have made a fairly large contribution to improving revenue and compliance, especially in recent years. The negative effect of tax progressivity is thus the major reason for falling compliance, though the effect on revenue is beneficial.

The second major conclusion is on the impact of collection lags. The insignificant direct and indirect effects of lags on revenue and compliance vindicates Singapore's persisting with official assessment and subsequent year tax collection instead of jumping on the bandwagon of broad-based withholding and PAYE taxes. The compliance costs of taxpayers and withholders, if these are similar to costs in countries surveyed by Vaillaincourt (1987), will outweigh the current cost borne by the government.

The government may wish to consider reducing the number of tax brackets, since tax progressivity appears to negatively affect compliance. However, lowering average tax rates is not necessary as Singapore is not beyond the Laffer curve peak. Second, while its tax administration strategy is largely vindicated, the IRAS may wish to examine internal manpower allocation between activities to ensure that this is not reducing efficiency.

5. CONCLUSION

We reiterate that all our conclusions, especially the limited revenue effect of changing concessions, are tentative due to possible data deficiencies. Besides data on concessions, information on enforcement activity, other than actions against non-filers and tax investigations, is also deficient. Most important, a TCMP type taxpayer survey would greatly facilitate research on determinants of compliance.

Other economic variables may also affect taxpayer behaviour. As a regional financial hub with minimal restrictions on money flows, financial market effects may also be important in Singapore. Our failure to take account of this possibility reflects the lack of progress in this area of economic theory.

We conclude from our study that it is important to go beyond the traditional tax buoyancy models in examining income tax performance in order to fully capture taxpayer's behaviour and administrative actions. Important determinants in Singapore, as in other countries, include inflation, tax structure, and variations in enforcement levels.

REFERENCES

Allingham, M. G. and A. Sandmo (1972): "Income Tax Evasion: A Theoretical Analysis," *Journal of Public Economics*, 1, 323-388.

Asher, M. G. (1989*): Fiscal Systems and Practices in ASEAN: Trends, Impact and Evaluation*, Singapore: Institute of Southeast Asian Studies.

Asher, M. G. and S. Osborne (1980): *Issues in Public Finance in Singapore*, Singapore: Singapore University Press.

Bhanoji Rao, V.V. (1996): "Singapore Household Income Distribution Data from the 1990 Census: Analysis, Results and Implications," in Kapur, B. K., E. T. E. Quah and H. T. Hoon (eds), *Development Trade and the Asia-Pacific: Essays in Honour of Professor Lim Chong Yah*, Singapore: Prentice-Hall

Crane, S. E. and F. Nourzad (1986): "Inflation and Tax Evasion: An Empirical Analysis," *Review of Economics and Statistics*, 68, 217-223.

Clotfelter, C. T. (1983): "Tax Evasion and Tax Rates: An Analysis of Individual Returns," *Review of Economics and Statistics*, 65, 363-373.

Cowell, F. A. (1990): *Cheating the Government: The Economics of Evasion*, Cambridge, Mass.: MIT Press.

Das-Gupta, A., R. Lahiri and D. Mookherjee (1995): "Income Tax Compliance in India: An Empirical Analysis," *World Development*, 23, 2051-2068.

Das-Gupta, A. and D. Mookherjee (1997): "Design and Enforcement of Personal Income Taxes in India," in Mundle, Sudipto (ed) *Public Finance - Policy Issues for India*, New Delhi: Oxford University Press.

De Juan, A., M. Lasheras and R. Mayo (1994): "Voluntary Compliance Behaviour of Spanish Taxpayers," *Public Finance/Finances Publiques*, 49(Supplement), 90-105.

Inland Revenue Authority of Singapore, *Annual Reports*, various years.

King, J. R. (1995): "Alternative Methods of Revenue Forecasting and Estimating," in Shome P. (ed) *Tax Policy Handbook*, Washington D. C.: International Monetary Fund.

Low, L. (1996): "Personal Income Taxes: Structure, Performance and Issues," in Asher, M.G. and Amina Tyabji (eds*) Fiscal System of Singapore: Trends Issues and Future Directions*, Singapore, Centre for Advanced Studies, NUS.

Tanzi, V. (1977): "Inflation, Lags in Collection, and the Real Value of Tax Revenue", *IMF Staff Papers*, 24, 154-167.

Vaillancourt, Francois (1987): "The Compliance Costs of Taxes on Business and Individuals: A Review of the Evidence" *Public Finance/Finances Publiques*, 42. 395-413.

Yitzhaki, S. (1974): "A note on Income Tax Evasion: A Theoretical Analysis*," Journal of Public Economics*, 3, 201-202.

TABLE 1

Buoyancy Estimates

Period	β from previous work	Ordinary Least Squares	R^2	Durbin-Watson Statistic	EGY Estimate[a]
log $GAT_t = \alpha + \beta\ GDP_t$					
1966 - 1985	1.39[b]	1.44	0.968	0.859	1.44
1975 - 1987	1.0665[c]	1.14	0.812	1.009	1.17
1965 - 1993	NA	1.26	0.967	0.576	1.26
log $GAT_t = \alpha + \beta\ GDP_{t-1}$					
1966 - 1985	NA	1.40	0.973	1.355	1.40
1975 - 1987	1.0348[c]	1.10	0.853	1.421	1.11
1965 - 1993	NA	1.26	0.974	0.803	1.27

a. Engle-Granger-Yoo third step estimates. All equations are co-integrated.
b. Estimates by Asher (1989).
c. Estimate by Low (1996).

TABLE 2
Regression Results with RMAMTR as the Marginal Tax Rate Variable

	Revenue Equation				Compliance Equation			
	Levels		Engel-Granger		Levels		Engel-Granger	
	Coefficient	t-ratios	Coefficient	t-ratios	Coefficient	t-ratios	Coefficient	t-ratios
Constant	6.94	1.33	NA	NA	6.69	1.26	NA	NA
Lagged GDP	0.54	2.32[b]	0.67	3.39[a]	-0.45	-1.91[b]	-0.32	-1.60
Inflation Rate	-0.98	-2.53[b]	-0.63	-2.58[b]	-1.36	-3.46[a]	-1.01	-4.08[a]
Ave. Marginal Tax Rate	0.54	3.27[a]	0.39	3.07[a]	-0.46	-2.75[a]	-0.62	-4.83[a]
Tax Rebates	0.03	0.29	-0.23	-2.68[b]	0.02	0.18	-0.25	-2.82[b]
Non filing Ratio	-0.09	-1.83[b]	-0.07	-2.37[b]	-0.09	-1.83[b]	-0.07	-2.36[b]
Penalty for failure to file return	0.14	1.45	0.06	0.98[a]	0.14	1.45	0.06	0.95
Tax investigation Cases	-0.10	-2.47[b]	-0.11	-3.52[a]	-0.10	-2.47[b]	-0.11	-3.52[a]
Addl. revenue from investigations (%)	0.06	1.66	0.05	2.50	0.06	1.65	0.05	2.48[b]
Penalty rate for tax investigation cases	0.08	1.31	0.07	1.65	0.08	1.36	0.07	1.73[b]
Error-Correction	NA		-1.28	-6.45[a]	NA		-1.28	-6.44[a]
R²	0.9937		0.7761		0.9797		0.9032	
Durbin-Watson Statistic	2.4457		1.2232		2.4328		1.2296	
3-period Forecast Error (%)	0.09%		NA		17.20%			
Akaike's Information Criterion	-4.68		NA		-4.65			

a. Significant at the 1 percent level.
b. Significant at the 10 percent level.

TABLE 3

Joint F-Tests of Significance: Economic, Tax Structure and Enforcement Variables

Null Hypothesis	Revenue Equation		Compliance Equation	
	F-statistic	P-value	F-statistic	P-value
Economic variables.	5.52	0.0135	8.28	0.0028
Tax structure.	6.19	0.0089	5.02	0.0185
Enforcement variables	2.18	0.1018	2.17	0.1032

TABLE 4

Revenue or Compliance Increase (+) or Decrease (-) Due to Deviation of Key Determinants from their Average Values[a]

Period	Revenue Equation			Compliance Equation		
	Enforcement	Tax Structure	Inflation	Enforcement	Tax Structure	Inflation
1965 - 71	-8.09%	-89.25%	-1.14%	-8.36%	38.11%	-1.59%
1972 - 78	-4.02%	-6.69%	-7.30%	-4.12%	3.30%	-10.47%
1979 - 85	9.09%	14.81%	-4.06%	9.24%	-14.71%	-5.70%
1986 - 93	23.39%	15.27%	-1.78%	23.85%	-15.81%	-2.49%

a. Deviation from zero in the case of inflation.

FIGURE 1

Time-plots of Average Effective Tax Rates (AETR), Income-modified AETR (MAETR) and Revenue-loss-adjusted MAETR (RMAETR)

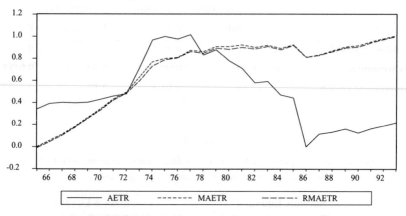

Source: Computations by authors.

FIGURE 2

Time-plots of Compliance Index and the Gross Assessed Tax (Logarithms)

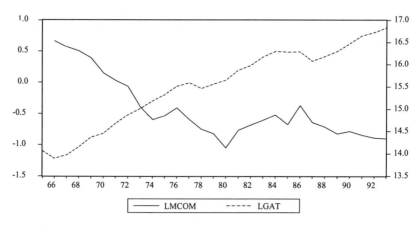

Source: *IRAS Annual Reports*, various years and computations by authors.

Wages and Output across Occupational Groups in Singapore

Lee Gek Lan

&

Wu Ying

Nanyang Business School, Nanyang Technological University, Nanyang Avenue, Singapore 639798
Fax: +(65) 792.4217, Tel: +(65) 799.6293, Email: awuying@ntu.edu.sg

Abstract This paper studies panel-data on the wage-output relationship across occupational groups in Singapore. We find that, unlike other groups, managers' (the group mainly representing entrepreneurial human capital) wages are negatively related to the output level, which indirectly suggests that manager's effective labour supply is backward-bending. In addition, the wages of managers increase with those of professionals and are significantly unit-elastic. We also further test an optimality condition in a theoretical growth model, concluding that, for all sectors considered, the productivity of entrepreneurial human capital uniformly grows faster than the counterpart of professional human capital.

1. INTRODUCTION

The past decades have seen increasing studies on the independent contributions by human capital to economic growth. It is a non-debatable fact that human capital plays an important role in economic advances today. [see Romer (1996)] The measurements of human capital is rather inharmonious, due to the wide range of definitions of human capital. In general, an investment in human capital takes the form of education, on-the-job training, accumulating work experience and, simply, learning-by-doing. [see Thirlwall (1994)] Human capital investment is expected to yield its returns to the labour force.

In this paper, we use wage rate as a measurement of the returns to an investment in human capital. In Singapore, wage rate plays a vital role in the economic development. On the one hand, it is a main ingredient in costs of production which in turn influence prices of output, hence, the competitiveness of Singapore's output in the world market. On the other hand, wages have been the main sources of income for the majority of Singaporeans.

Comparing the input level with the output level of different occupations in Singapore will give us an idea of the value added of the occupations. Considering various human capital as inputs, we measure output using sectors' output data published in government statistics. Investigating a relationship between them will allow us to have an overview of whether the human investors earn what they deserve for their endeavour.

2. WAGES VERSUS OUTPUT : AN OCCUPATIONAL VIEW

2.1 OBJECTIVE

Part I of this paper will investigate the relationship underlying real output and real wage rate of various occupations in Singapore. With output being an indispensable measurement of growth, the relationship will then reveal the contributions made by human capital, via its returns, to economic growth. As argued in the introduction, an investment in human capital refers to factors such as education, training, work experience and learning which could be reflected in the wage rate since it is the measure of the monetary and quantitative reward for any human capital invested. Any investment in human capital will boost the personal efficiency of labour, thus enhancing productivity of labour and increasing output. [see Grossman and Helpman (1994)]

2.2 METHODOLOGY

Following the objective stated above, we anticipate a positive relationship between human capital investment and growth, thereby a positive relationship between real wage rate and real output.

The data set used in our analysis is from the *Report on Wages in Singapore, 1986 - 1995, Profile of the Labour Force of Singapore, 1983 - 1994* and *Singapore System of National Accounts, 1995*. Specifically, we collect the data of *Mean Monthly Basic Wage of Selected Occupations* in five major sectors of Singapore. Among these sectors are manufacturing; construction; commerce; transport, storage and communications; financial, insurance, real estate and business services. We also have the data of the number of employees and real output level in various sectors. The six occupations covered are managers*(m)*; professionals*(p)*; technicians and associate technicians*(t)*; clerical workers*(c)*; service workers and shop and market sales workers*(s)*; production craftsman and related workers, plant and machine operators and assemblers, cleaners, labourers and related workers*(l)*. The regression will be run for a period of 10 years from 1986 to 1995.

2.3 MODEL

To start off, we first conduct Granger Causality tests [see Granger (1990)] to test the two-way causality between the real wage rate and output. Results of the test is summarised in Table 1 and would be discussed later. We initially used three models to evaluate the contribution of human capital to output of various occupations. All the three models regress GDP on real wages; the differences lie in the form in which the variables are expressed: one uses growth rates, another uses logarithm and the other uses the level form.

Below is a modified regression -

$$\text{Routput}_{t,j} = \alpha + \beta \text{Rwage}_{t,j} + \gamma N_{t,j} + \delta \text{Rwage}_{t-1,j} + \phi N_{t-1,j} + \varepsilon \qquad (1)$$

where Routput is the real gross domestic product, Rwage is the real wage rate, N is the number of employees; t = time trend for year (1986, 1987......1995) and j = sectors (manufacturing, construction......)

Real values, adjusted for the inflation effects, are obtained from dividing the nominal values by the industry deflators. We include the lagged values of the independent variables since output this period is likely to be influenced by the wage rate and number of employees the period before. That is, with an increase in the wage rate and number of employees last year, there is a time lag for output to react. We also run the regression with Routput as the explanatory variable and Rwage as the explained variable:

$$\text{Rwage}_{t,j} = \lambda + \mu \text{Routput}_{t,j} + \theta N_{t,j} + \varphi \text{Routput}_{t-1,j} + \sigma N_{t-1,j} + \varepsilon \qquad (2)$$

2.4 EMPIRICAL RESULTS AND IMPLICATIONS

Table 1 summarises the results of Granger Causality tests. The null hypothesis of Granger Causality test is that A does not Granger Cause B. Taking the pair of the real wage rate of managers and real sector GDP as an example, the values reported are the p-values when the null hypothesis is true. The smaller the probabilities, the stronger the evidence of

Granger Causality. Table 1 reads that the probability value that W_m (real wage rate of managers) does not Granger Cause G (real output level) is 0.28680; the probability value that G does not Granger Cause W_m is 0.40181. In both cases, statistical evidence is not significant to reject the null hypothesis. The test, in most cases, does not seem to be conclusive with respect to the bi-variate causal relations. However, the test significantly supports a causal relationship running from the wages of professionals to output, and a causal relation from output to the wages of service and sales workers.

Tables 2 and 3 show a tabulation of models 1 and 2 respectively. Lagged variables do not play an important role in both models, except for occupation s (service workers and shop and market sales workers). We will first discuss the results of Table 2, followed by Table 3. For occupation m, W_m has a negative relationship with G. When the real wage rate of managers increase by 1 unit, *ceteris paribus*, output level of all sectors considered will fall by 7.3 units. A positive relationship exists between the real wage rate and output for other occupations, with occupation p having a coefficient of 8.7 and occupation t, a coefficient of 11.2. For occupations c and l, the presence of a constant term results in a much larger coefficient: 1 unit increase in the real wage rate of clerical workers leads to a 174.8 units of rise in output and 452.5 units in occupation l. Although occupation s shows a positive sign as well, the t-statistic for W_s is only 1.213, which implies that W_s is statistically insignificant at 90 percent confidence interval.

Table 3 represents a summary of the regression results of model 2. Occupation m has a negative relationship between W_m and G, with the coefficient being -0.04. Likewise, occupation s also has a negative relationship between W_s and G. When G increase by 1 unit, W_s decrease by 0.015 unit. But this variable is rejected at 10 percent level of significance. Small coefficients are observed by other occupations too. Occupation p and t have coefficients of 0.004 and 0.007 respectively, however are both rejected at 10 percent level of significance. The remaining two occupations are statistically significant at 90 percent confidence interval, however coefficients remained small at 0.004 for occupation c and 0.002 for occupation l. This seems to be consistent with the Granger Causality results in Table 1, which shows that simultaneity only exists in occupations c and l. Nevertheless, G is statistically significant in occupation m which is not suggested by the causality results. We observe that the influence of output on the real wage rate is mild (because of the small coefficients) compared to the effect that wage rate has on output. This could suggest that Singapore is cost-driven rather than output-driven.

In contrast to our prior anticipation that there is a positive relationship between the real wage rate and output, the regression results suggest the opposite for occupations m and s. In fact, variables in occupation s are statistically insignificant at 90 percent confidence level. The reason for this could be traced to the data. Those in occupation s rely more on commission and other variable components of salary, which is not reflected in our data set of mean monthly basic wage of various occupations. A mean monthly gross wage would be more appropriate but is not available due to the constraint on data availability. The negative sign between wage rate and output in occupation m could be explained by the backward bending labour supply curve.

Figure 1 shows a backward bending labour supply curve. It shows that labour supplied increases as wage rate rises from 0 to W_1. However, after W_1, any increase in wage rate will actually decrease the labour supplied. This is because income effects outweigh the substitution effects. For highly-paid managers, we speculated that they could be lying on the negative slope of the labour supply curve. This could be because the managers have comparatively less leisure time than those with other occupations. For managers, the marginal utility of one additional unit of leisure is more than the marginal utility of one additional unit of wage income, therefore they are willing to substitute leisure for income and decrease the labour supplied. A reduction in the labour supplied could cause a decrease in the output produced by managers. This explains a negative relationship between wage rate and output for managers.

3. OCCUPATIONAL COMPARISON ON CROSS ELASTICITIES OF WAGES AND ON PRODUCTIVITY GROWTH

3.1 OBJECTIVES

The second half of the paper will explore the relationship between wages among occupations, specifically occupations m, p and t. Narrowing the exploration to only these three occupations is due to the belief that they have the highest value-added to their jobs. An analysis of their relationship in wage rate will allow us to observe how the wage rates of high earning occupations are correlated with one another. A theoretical framework suggests that, in a standard one-sector growth model with both entrepreneurial and professional human capital, the wage elasticity of one occupational group should be unity with respect to the other occupational group. [see Wu and Yao (1996)] This is to say that if the wage rate of occupation m increases by 1 percent, the wage rates of occupations p and t will follow suit and rise by exactly 1 percent as well.

3.2 METHODOLOGY

As in Part I, we will continue to use the mean monthly basic wage rate of various occupations from *Report on Wages in Singapore, 1986 - 1995*. We consider a simple model of regressing real wage rate of one occupation on the real wage rate of another occupation. Then we will carry out further tests on the coefficients to determine the empirical relevance of the theoretical framework mentioned above.

3.3 MODEL

The simple double logarithm model we will consider is as follows.

$$\text{Log}(Rwage_{t,j}) = \tau + \eta \text{Log}(Rwage_{t,j}) + \varepsilon \tag{3}$$

where the symbols are applied in the same way as in the previous part of the paper. However, a change now is that we run the regression for only three occupational groups, the managers, professionals, technicians and associate professionals. As far as equation (3) is concerned, Table 4 reports all the possible results when combining any two of the three occupational groups.

3.4 EMPIRICAL RESULTS AND IMPLICATIONS

When W_p increases by 1 percent, we find that W_m increases by 0.76 percent, which is close to the hypothesis of unit cross elasticity of wages between groups. A similar positive relationship also exists between logarithm of W_m and logarithm of W_t. That is, a 1 percent increase in the real wage rate of technicians and associate professionals leads to an 0.82 percent increase in the counterpart of managers, which supports the unit-elasticity hypothesis too. However, the wage rate of professionals tends to be less responsive to the wage rate of managers as well as of technicians and associate professionals. (the latter estimate being insignificant) In contrast, wage rate of technicians and associate professionals is "well tied" with that of managers, their cross elasticity is almost unity.

We observe that the R-squared statistics are uniformly small, lying between a value of 0.2 to 0.3 for 4 of the regressions. However, this does not pose a major problem as we are now finding a simple relationship between two variables, not attempting to explain the determination of a dependent variables by independent variables.

To test the hypothesis of unit cross wage-elasticity between occupational groups(η=1), we perform the Wald-Coefficient Restrictions Test to all the regressions. A Wald-Coefficient test deals with hypotheses involving restrictions on the coefficients of the explanatory variables. Testing $\eta = 1$ is to test the immediacy of reaction of wage rate of one occupational group with respect to another. If $\eta < 1$, it would mean that there requires some time lag for the wage rates to react. The outcome of this test is summarised in Table 5. We found that when W_p is the dependent variable, the Wald-Coefficient restriction test leads to a rejection to the null hypothesis of η=1 in both cases of W_m and W_t being the regressors. This phenomenon could be explained by the definition of specific jobs in the professional group. This group includes lawyers, teachers, accountants and so on. The group seems to have a higher percentage of civil servants than other groups. Unlike the private sector, the public sector is more stringent in the annual adjustments of wages, so that the wage rate elasticities of this group with respect to managers and associate professionals are significantly less than 1. This means that the wage rate of professionals are not responding as readily as compared to the managers and technicians and associate professionals. The wage rate of professionals will respond relatively sluggishly when the government realises that a review of the wage rate is necessary to improve the efficiency of labour in this occupational group.

3.5 RELATIVE GROWTH RATE OF HUMAN-CAPITAL PRODUCTIVITIES

According to Wu and Yao (1996), one of the testable dynamic optimality conditions in a one-sector growth model with entrepreneurial and professional human capital is the following:

$$\text{Log}(\text{Rwage}_e) = \beta_0 + \beta_1 \text{Log}(\text{Rwage}_p) + \beta_2 T + \varepsilon \qquad (4)$$

where Rwage_e is the real wage rate of entrepreneurs, Rwage_p is the real wage rate of professionals and T is the time trend. In the original model-setting, β_0 is determined by the shadow prices associated with the growth rates of total entrepreneurial human capital and professional human capital, and β_1 represents the relative sensitivity of the wage of entrepreneurs with respect to the wage of professionals. β_2 measures the difference in the growth rates of productivity between entrepreneurial human capital and professional human capital. Structurally, we have $\beta_2 = \lambda_e - \lambda_p$, where λ_e and λ_p are productivity-growth rates of entrepreneurial and professional human capital respectively.

Equation (3) discussed earlier is a variation of (4) without including time trend. In retrospect, the estimation of (3) with panel data across production sectors suggests that, as far as the aggregate economy is concerned, the wage of entrepreneurs is unit-elastic with respect to the wage of professionals and their relationship is positive. To compare between sectors, we expand the data set for each production sector by including sub-categories in the group of managers (entrepreneurs) and the group of professionals. The main results of regression (4) for each of the five production sectors are summarised in Table 6. A common feature is that the estimated β_2 is uniformly positive for the five regression equations; moreover, they are all individually significant except for the equation for the commerce sector. This empirical result implies that the productivity of entrepreneurial human capital grows faster than its counterpart for professional human capital for the five main production sectors in Singapore. In addition, our estimation results also suggest that there exists differences in the relative sensitivity of two human-capital groups across sectors. More specifically, 1 percent increase in the real wage rate of professionals reduces the real wage rate of managers by 36 percent in the manufacturing sector and by 45 percent in the construction sector; however, 1 percent increase in the real wage rate of professionals raises the real wage rate of managers by 36 percent in the commerce sector.

4. CONCLUSION

With the caveat that only basic wages are used to measure remuneration of various occupational groups, we have found in this empirical study that the group of managers has probably a negatively-sloped wage schedule for its effective labour supply while all the other occupational groups exhibit a positive wage-output relationship. The traditional wage theory of income-substitution effect could be used to explain the finding. Our findings also indicate that manager's real wages do increase proportionally with the real wages of professionals, technicians and associate professionals respectively. On the other hand, if we include efforts, experience, education and training into the measure of unit labour productivity or effective labour, our comparative study across sectors suggests that unit productivity of managers grows faster than that of professionals for all five sectors concerned.

According to our research, it seems that entrepreneurial human capital has played a rather important role in Singapore's economic growth. This implies that it would be worthwhile to invest in the promotion of entrepreneurship. In fact, in recent years, the government has helped quite a number of entrepreneurs in the scratch of their businesses and encouraged their investment overseas. At the same time, we should place more emphasis on the deepening of professional human capital in order to maintain long-term economic growth. As our economy keeps growing, the relatively important role of professional human capital will become increasingly indispensable.

REFERENCES

Department of Statistics (1996): *Singapore System of National Accounts*, Department of Statistics.

Granger, C. W. J. (1990): *Modelling Economic Series*, Oxford University Press.

Grossman, G. M. and Helpman, E. (1994): "Endogenous Innovation in the Theory of Growth," *Journal of Economic Perspectives - Vol. 8*, American Economic Association.

Pindyck, R. S. and Rubinfeld, D. L. (1992): *Microeconomics*, Macmillan Publishing Company.

Ministry of Labour, Research and Statistics (1995): *Profile of the Labour Force of Singapore, 1983-1994*, Ministry of Labour.

Ministry of Labour, Research and Statistics (various years): *Report on Wages in Singapore*, Ministry of Labour.

Romer, D. (1996): *Advanced Macroeconomics*, McGraw Hill.

Thirlwall, A. P. (1994): *Growth and Development with Special Reference to Developing Economies*, Macmillan Press Ltd.

Wu, Y. and Yao, H. (1996): "A Growth Model with Entrepreneurial and Professional Human Capital," *Mimeo*, Nanyang Technological University.

TABLE 1

Granger Causality Tests

Null Hypothesis	Prob-Value
Wm does not Granger Cause G	0.28680
Wp does not Granger Cause G	0.09126
Wt does not Granger Cause G	0.23041
Wc does not Granger Cause G	0.45234
Ws does not Granger Cause G	0.15305
Wl does not Granger Cause G	0.27816
G does not Granger Cause Wm	0.40181
G does not Granger Cause Wp	0.45445
G does not Granger Cause Wt	0.42091
G does not Granger Cause Wc	0.19954
G does not Granger Cause Ws	0.94629
G does not Granger Cause Wl	0.02830

TABLE 2

Estimation of the Occupational Effects of Wages on Output

Dependent Variable	Regressors	R^2	DW
G	$31613.44 - 7.349Wm + 0.399Nm$ (2.155) (-1.695) (14.115)	0.982	2.249
G	$8.740Wp + 0.701Np$ (6.186) (11.890)	0.952	1.387
G	$11.230Wt + 0.311Nt$ (4.159) (11.135)	0.964	1.641
G	$-186543.7 + 174.792Wc + 0.508Nc$ (-4.969) (4.121) (8.503)	0.933	1.171
G	$35.478Ws - 1.154Ns - 40.279Ws(-1) + 1.517Ns(-1)$ (1.213) (-2.899) (-1.506) (4.167)	0.824	1.374
G	$-341714.0 + 452.475Wl + 0.138Nl$ (-6.850) (8.513) (2.474)	0.914	1.603

Figures in parentheses are t-statistics

TABLE 3

Estimation of the Occupational Effects of Output on Wages

Dependent Variable	Regressors	R^2	DW
Wm	3614.045 - 0.0396G + 0.0193Nm (14.411) (-1.695) (2.242)	0.689	2.345
Wp	2194.204 + 0.00439G - 0.00109Np (7.630) (0.333) (-0.113)	0.132	1.387
Wt	1105.859 + 0.000735G + 0.00178Nt (10.822) (0.110) (0.786)	0.762	2.119
Wc	891.605 + 0.00413G - 0.00146Nc - 0.963MA(2) (31.498) (16.166) (-6.984) (-42.623)	0.978	2.197
Ws	-0.0146G + 0.0135Ns + 0.0216G(-1) - 0.0108Ns(-1) (-0.485) (2.649) (0.665) (-1.762)	0.576	1.515
Wl	758.636 + 0.00202G - 0.00029Nl (13.484) (8.513) (-2.452)	0.913	1.811

Figures in parentheses are t-statistics

TABLE 4

Estimation of Cross Wage-Elasticities between Occupational Groups

Dependent Variable	Regressors	R^2	DW
Log(Wm)	2.390 + 0.758Log(Wp) (0.803) (1.981)	0.329	1.290
Log(Wm)	2.358 + 0.821Log(Wt) (2.267) (5.699)	0.802	2.039
Log(Wp)	5.628 + 0.297Log(Wt) (3.519) (1.343)	0.184	1.365
Log(Wp)	4.178 + 0.434Log(Wm) (2.302) (1.981)	0.329	1.398
Log(Wt)	-0.878 + 0.978Log(Wm) (-0.618) (5.699)	0.802	1.493
Log(Wt)	3.103 + 0.530Log(Wp) + 0.393MA(1) (0.773) (1.028) (0.953)	0.341	1.329

Figures in parentheses are t-statistics

TABLE 5

Wald-Coefficient Restriction Test ($H_0 : \eta = 1$)

Dependent Variable	Independent Variable	F-statistic	Probability
Wm	Wp	0.3985	0.5455
Wm	Wt	1.5486	0.2486
Wp	Wt	10.0726	0.01312
Wp	Wm	6.6732	0.03245
Wt	Wm	0.01711	0.8992
Wt	Wp	6.8294	0.3927

TABLE 6

Estimation of the Relative Growth Rates of Productivity

Dependent Variable	Regressors	R^2	DW
Log(W1m)	11.024 - 0.365Log(W1p) + 0.0104T	0.242	1.971
	(7.368) (-1.878) (3.8454)		
Log(W2m)	11.603 - 0.449Log(W2p) + 0.00940T	0.188	1.665
	(7.216) (-2.129) (3.297)		
Log(W3m)	5.492 + 0.366Log(W3p) + 0.00304T	0.188	2.612
	(5.285) (2.458) (0.731)		
Log(W4m)	7.901 + 0.0216Log(W4p) + 0.0136T	0.411	1.513
	(6.164) (0.135) (5.560)		
Log(W5m)	9.162 - 0.0992Log(W5p) + 0.00819T	0.143	1.898
	(11.457) (-0.996) (2.429)		

1 - Manufacturing sector

2 - Construction sector

3 - Commerce sector

4 - Transport, storage and communications sector

5 - Financial, insurance, real estate and business services sector

Figures in parentheses are t-statistics

FIGURE 1

A Backward Bending Curve of Effective Labour Supply

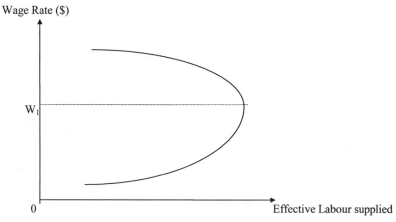

Source : Pindyck R. S. and Rubinfeld D. L. (1992): *Microeconomics*

An Evaluation of the Impact of the
Area Licensing Scheme on Commuters

Neo Yi-Min
&
*Michael **Li** Zhi-Feng*

Nanyang Business School, Nanyang Technological University, Nanyang Avenue, Singapore 639798
Fax: +(65) 792.4217, Tel: +(65) 799.1461, Email: zfli@ntu.edu.sg

Abstract This paper studies the impact of the Area Licensing Scheme (ALS) on commuters in Singapore. The ALS was a pioneer road-pricing scheme in Singapore introduced in June 1975 to curb congestion in the Central Business District (CBD) area. The objective of this study is to perform an analysis of the ALS, focusing on the impact of the scheme on changes in travel patterns of commuters. It is found that the scheme has effectively alleviated congestion problems within the Restricted Zone and has contributed significantly to the improvement of traffic conditions by encouraging the use of high-occupancy public and private transport. Classified vehicle counts were analysed to see the effect of the ALS on inbound traffic flows to the Restricted Zone. Private cars formed the majority of the inbound traffic to the Restricted Zone both during and beyond the Restricted Hours. Estimates of the values of travel time to different groups of commuters were used to compute the time savings/losses due to the scheme. The value of travel time was assumed to be 60 percent of average hourly wage rates. This study found the annual net savings of the ALS to commuters to be about $87,137 per kilometre.

1. INTRODUCTION

1.1 BACKGROUND

The Area Licensing Scheme (ALS) is a pioneer road pricing scheme in Singapore. Inaugurated on 2nd June 1975, the aims of the scheme are as follows: (a) to alleviate congestion problems in the Central Business District (CBD) Area by limiting non-essential categories of motorists (those who do not need their cars during the course of their work and those who can change their time of travel to off-peak hours); (b) to encourage commuters to use high-occupancy public transport instead of private automobiles when travelling to and from the CBD area; (c) to reduce congestion in the Restricted Zone (RZ) with minimal disruption to economic activity; (d) to provide an element of choice (i.e. commuters are still allowed to drive into the RZ except that they have to pay a certain fee); and (e) to lay the foundation for more sophisticated and extensive road pricing schemes in the future.

The CBD area is the core and heart of Singapore's financial and commercial activities. The concentration of many major firms and large-scale MNCs in the area has resulted in many Singaporeans travelling to and from the RZ for work.[1] To improve the efficiency of business activities in the area and the quality of the environment within the city, traffic congestion has to be controlled. In contrast to the cities in the United States, Western Europe and Canada where only 3 percent to 26 percent of all trips in urban areas are made

---

[1] Employment in the CBD had increased from 200,000 in 1975 to 270,000 in 1983 (Singapore Yearbook of Statistics, various issues).

by public transport, its share of modal split in Singapore is as high as 51 percent. By 1975, traffic was moving at a speed of 12 miles per hour during peak hours. After the implementation of the ALS, the total volume of traffic entering the RZ fell by a phenomenal 44 percent by the end of 1975.

While the ALS has been an effective means of significantly reducing urban congestion within the restricted zone during its operation hours, congestion has emerged in the ring roads and expressways. Moreover, new peak hours emerged just before and after the start and end times of the ALS. The volume of cars entering the RZ half an hour before the ALS increased by 23 percent by the end of 1975. The congestion problems were not eliminated but shifted as commuters rescheduled their travelling times and routes to avoid paying the fee.

Changes were made to the times and hours of operation and the area of the RZ was extended to address the changing traffic conditions throughout the years. Many complementary transport policies were also introduced to further enhance and improve the effectiveness and efficiency of the ALS in controlling vehicle growth and curbing congestion problems. The Whole-Day ALS, a full-fledged manual road pricing scheme, was implemented in January 1994 to facilitate the flow of traffic throughout the day in the RZ and to pave the way for the introduction of the Electronic Road Pricing system in late 1997.

1.2 MOTIVATION/OBJECTIVES

Studies on the effects of traffic management policies are useful to policy-makers in their assessment of the effectiveness of such systems and provide useful information for the design and implementation of future policies. Since the implementation of the ALS two decades ago, several changes have been made to achieve the desired goal of reducing urban congestion without serious disruptions of economic activities within the Central Area. Some of these changes have had long-lasting effects while others have had only short-lived ones. The ALS has affected certain groups of people more directly and others indirectly. The extent and intensity of effects also differ between different groups of commuters and in different time periods.

Given the controversy regarding the net benefits of the scheme, we are very much interested to provide a fair and thorough analysis of the impacts of the scheme on commuters, after allowing for the initial shocks and implementation lags, and taking into account its complementarity with other related transport policies and strategies. We attempt to use the estimates of the value of travel time savings/losses of commuters in order to evaluate the impact of the ALS.

1.3 SCOPE AND ORGANISATION OF PAPER

The scope of this study is limited to the impact on commuters and the period from 1975 to 1989. We do not assess the effects of the Whole-Day ALS here.

Section two provides an overview of the ALS in Singapore, explores its unique characteristics and examines the factors which have contributed to success. Section three explains the methodology adopted in this study; Section four presents the analysis of the scheme. Lastly, Section five provides a conclusion.

2. EFFECTS OF THE AREA LICENSING SCHEME (ALS)

2.1 AN OVERVIEW

The ALS had immediate effects on the modal distribution of journeys to the RZ; the proportion of home to work journeys made by car fell from 56 percent to 46 percent and 45 percent of the motorists gave up driving cars to become car-pool or bus passengers. Percentage changes in the modal distribution of home-work journeys to the RZ are shown in Table 1 and the effects of ALS on vehicle-owning families are shown in Table 2. The number of shopping trips to the zone declined but by no more than 5 percent.

2.2 VOLUME AND SPEED-FLOW EFFECTS

The number of cars entering the RZ between 7:30AM and 10:15AM fell by 73 percent but the volume rose by 23 percent before 7:30AM and car-pooling increased by about 60 percent during the restricted hours.[2] The net result was a 44 percent reduction in total traffic during the restricted period, which was much higher than the initial target of 25 percent to 30 percent. However, after conditions have stabilised over past years, there has been a gradual increase in the number of vehicles entering the RZ and the figure of 41,514 in October 1975 had increased to 51,054 in 1988 (Refer to Table 3), which was about 31 percent lower than the pre-ALS conditions. Mean speeds rose 22 percent higher during the restricted hours than previously. The proportion of commuting trips by car decreased from 56 percent to 46 percent while the share of bus trips increased from 33 percent to 46 percent.

Table 4 shows the number of average trips made per license for different categories of vehicles. Taxis top the list, making an average of about 4 trips into the RZ during the restricted hours. This is expected because taxi drivers will make full use of the ALS charge by ferrying passengers to and from the CBD.

The flow rate of total inbound traffic varies with different time periods of the day, as shown in Table 5. The highest flow rate of 25,580 vehicles per hour occurred during the period from 8:45AM to 9:00AM.

2.3 DISTRIBUTION EFFECTS

The ALS has different effects on different groups of commuters and in different time periods. The incidence of its effects is very important in determining the overall impact. The comparisons between the welfare of these groups involve much interpersonal judgement rather than traditional value free economic comparisons. This study attempts to model a broader range of demand responses as it is known that these responses might vary with the type of commuter.

On the demand side, travel decisions into the Restricted Zone are examined, given the generalised costs of all alternatives. The travel decisions include the choice of time travel, the route taken, the mode of transport chosen, the type of commuter, the destination of the traveller and the frequency of the trip. The supply side reflects how the transport system respond to a given level of demand. The effect of reduced congestion in the CBD on highway and peripheral speeds, the effects of congestion on public buses, and parking problems both within and outside the Restricted Zone are taken into account.

---

[2] The hours of operation during the morning peak was extended to 10:15AM on 23rd June 1975.

For the purpose of this research, more emphasis will be placed on the demand characteristics of commuters.

2.3.1 Types of Commuters

The sensitivities of impacts on commuters depend not only on journey purposes, but also on the commuter types, which allow for different reactions according to income levels and the proportion of transport costs relative to total expenditure.

Table 6 shows that leisure commuters have the greatest flexibility to avoid the ALS charging and their demand to enter the RZ is the most price elastic. This is the group the ALS hopes to discourage from driving into the RZ especially during peak hours. The number of shopping trips made to destinations in the RZ fell by 34 percent shortly after its implementation, however this was also partly due to the decentralisation of jobs and increased parking charges. The retail businesses within the RZ area have created a niche for themselves and most target primarily the working class who do their purchasing during lunch-time or after work, hence they are not adversely affected by the ALS. Shopping malls located in the residential areas can serve the needs of the rest of the majority.

On the other hand, the ALS is thought to have a great impact on transportation companies whose transportation costs constitute the bulk of its operating expense. However, many wholesalers and retailers have reported that they have benefited very much from the easier movement of goods in the Central Area in the morning when most of their deliveries are made, and have also benefited from customers' more favourable responses as a result of more timely and reliable deliveries.

Business, work commuters and students travelling to schools in the central area have the most inelastic demand for entering the RZ. Employees on employer-assisted motoring are even more inelastic. Companies incur additional expenses to buy licenses for company cars but many have reflected that the time saved on travelling along the less congested roads and reduced search time for parking spaces within the RZ have more than offset the fees of the licenses. Those who are most greatly affected by the ALS will be businesses for which the local transport represents a high proportion of the total costs, but they do not have the ability to pass on the costs or make offsetting gains. Educational institutions are being relocated to areas outside the RZ and nearer to housing estates and residential areas to minimise the travelling time of students and to avoid cars from congesting the roads near the schools. As to date, there are very few schools located within the RZ, therefore this group of commuters will not be affected greatly by the ALS.

The ALS attempts to discriminate commuters not so much by their income-levels but by the mode of transport they take to work. Insistent drivers can still drive to work but they must incur additional cost, however they are normally the ones who can more than afford the $3/$2 charge and also benefit from enjoying quicker and less congested car travel. The majority of the masses who are public transport users also gain from more reliable public buses and less congested roads. Hence, the ALS cannot be said to benefit the rich at the expense of the masses.

2.3.2 Allocation Equity

One fundamental issue of the distribution impact is whether the allocation by congestion charging is equitable. The revenue collected by the ALS has been used to upgrade the public transport system and facilities as well as the roads. The masses who are frequent users of public transport will inevitably gain from such a scheme in terms of travelling time and comfort. Hence, Foster (1974) sees road pricing as likely to be progressive in impact. In addition, with the heavier use of road pricing schemes and usage policies, the government will be able to release more Certificates of Entitlement (COEs).

2.4 IMPROVEMENTS IN PUBLIC TRANSPORT

The waiting, boarding and alighting time of buses may have increased and overcrowding may occur as a result of more bus commuters after the ALS, but these costs have been offset by an increase in the fleet size of public buses from 5,299 in 1977 to 9,000 in 1989, and also by an increase in the capacity of each bus (an average increase of 7.2 passengers). Frequency of buses have also increased from an average of 7 minutes to 5 minutes during peak hours. Total waiting time may have increased but total travelling time has declined despite the fact that the number of buses entering the RZ rose after ALS. This is primarily due to a significant fall in overall traffic flow into the RZ from 74,014 in March 1975 to 51,054 in 1988 as shown in Table 3.

The Land Transport Authority aims to increase the percentage of city trips made on public transport from 50 percent to 75 percent. The ALS has resulted in more city commuters switching to public transport and this higher demand has justified the upgrading and improvements of the public transport system. Many improvements have been made in the bus service standards, for example : for direct routes, bus journeys are no more than 30 percent longer than by car; during peak periods, the headways of 70 percent of all trunk bus services are not to exceed 10 minutes and 85 percent are not to exceed 12 minutes. Public transport fares have also been kept at an affordable level. The basic bus service standards dictate that only a maximum of 60 percent of the bus fleet be air-conditioned. A Straits Times survey showed that 87 percent of the respondents felt that bus fares were reasonable. The average annual increase in bus fare is 2.9 percent while the annual average wage increase is 8.2 percent.

Public transport users and private car commuters will both gain from ALS only when the reduction in congestion that comes about from congestion pricing lowers the line-haul travel (transit) times sufficiently so as to offset the additional boarding and alighting costs. Singapore is likely to benefit from such a situation since the bus share of the car/bus modal split is high.

3. THE METHODOLOGY

The period studied will be from 1974 to 1989. Emphasis will be placed in evaluating the morning peak hour. The concept of the value of travel time is used to assess the impact of the ALS on commuters.

3.1 CONCEPT OF THE VALUE OF TRAVEL TIME

The supply of time is finite and is a scarce commodity with a value. The valuation of travel time is basically differentiated between time spent travelling in paid and unpaid (leisure) time. An individual derives utility not from travel time itself, but from goods and leisure time left after travel expenses and travel time are deducted from the money and time budgets. Travel cost involves disutility of foregone consumption of goods. Travel time involves disutility of foregone leisure.

In the economic analysis of the impact of traffic management schemes on travel behaviour of commuters, the concept of time plays a significant role. Time for travel has a value which depends on the motorists' perception of time. The definition of the value of time is often translated into dollar value.

3.2 COMPUTATION OF THE AVERAGE VALUES OF TRAVEL TIME

In this study, time savings and losses are measured, valued and used together with speed-flow relationships, to calculate time benefits from reduced traffic congestion and and time losses from changes in travel patterns. Changes in travel patterns include changes in mode, route or speed or a combination of these. The average value of travel time is assumed to be 60 percent of the gross hourly wage rates of commuters.

Gross hourly wage rates of commuters are obtained from dividing their respective monthly incomes from work by the average number of working hours per month which is assumed to be at 189.2 [Ng and Li (1996)]. The monthly income, hourly wage rates and average values of travel time of classified commuters are shown in Table 7.

We will make the following assumptions :

1) Car drivers who give up driving into the Restricted Zone either switch to public transport or change their routes

2) Average value of travel time is calculated as 60 percent of the gross hourly wage rates

3) Public transport commuters refer to bus passengers only

4) Private car users who switch to public transport account for fifty percent of the increment in the number of buses going into the CBD after ALS

4. THE ANALYSIS

4.1 PRIVATE AUTOMOBILES USERS

It is reported that the travelling speed of a car within the Restricted Zone is 27km/h before ALS and is 33km/h after the ALS [Watson and Holland (1978)]. The average value of travel time to car drivers is $10.20 per hour.[3] The time savings per car per km is 0.4 min, and savings per car per km in monetary terms is $10.20×0.4/60 = $0.068.

The restricted morning hours last from 7:30AM to 10:15AM, a total of 165 minutes. From Menon and Lam (Sept.1992), the total number of private cars entering the RZ during the restricted morning hours is 11,459 after the ALS. Therefore, the flow of private cars per hour into the RZ is 4,167 cars per hour.

Total savings per km is $0.068×4,167 = $283.356. After ALS, total time savings of car drivers per km per day amount to $283.356×165/60 = $779.229. Hence, the annual time savings per km is $779.229×300 = $233,772 (assume 300 operating days in 1 year).

The $3 ALS fee is incorporated to find the cost (in per km terms) to private car drivers. Assume that the RZ has 60 km of roads and an average of 3 lanes, the total lane-km within the RZ is 180 (60×3). The annual revenue from sale of licenses is $10,785,714 [Menon

---

[3] 60% of gross hourly wage of $17 (Refer to Table 7).

and Lam (1992)]. Therefore, the annual cost per km is $10,785,714/180 = $59,920, and the annual net savings of car drivers per km amount to $233,772-$59,920 = $173,852.

4.2 PUBLIC TRANSPORT COMMUTERS

Commuters who were bus riders both before and after the implementation of ALS also benefited from the scheme in terms of time savings. The speed of buses within the RZ was 19km/h before the ALS and was 22km/h after the ALS. According to Watson and Holland (1978), bus riders from non-vehicle owning families spent on the average 1 minute less commuting after ALS. The number of buses entering the RZ from 7:30AM to 10:15AM before ALS is 3980, and the total capacity of each bus (assuming full capacity) is 81.

Savings per bus per km is 0.46 min. Hence, the total time savings of all passengers per km per day is given by 0.0057×81×3980 = 1837.57min = 30.6 hr.

Since the average value of travel time to each bus commuter entering the CBD for work is $3.60 per hour,[4] the total amount saved as a result of travel time savings per km per day is $3.60×30.6 = $110.16. Therefore, the annual savings per km of bus commuters is equal to $110.16×300 = $33,048.

4.3 CAR-POOL PASSENGERS

Car-Pool passengers are the biggest gainers because they enjoy shorter travelling time and greater comfort without having to pay the ALS fee. The average value of travel time to Car-Pool passengers is $7.20 per hour[5] and the average car occupancy rate is 2.17 during morning restricted hours [Menon and Lam (1992)].

Total number of passengers benefiting from the ALS is (2.17-1)×11,459 = 13,407 and total savings per car per km is 0.4 min. The total time savings of all passengers per km per day is calculated as (13,407×0.4)/60 = 89.38 hours, total savings in monetary terms per day is given by 89.38×$7.20 = $643.54. Therefore, annual time savings per km for Car-Pool passengers amounts to $643.54×300 = $193,062.

4.4 DELIVERY DRIVERS

Delivery and transportation drivers benefit from the lighter and smoother traffic within the RZ after ALS because they are able to make more frequent and timely deliveries. These drivers are usually paid according to the number of deliveries made. Therefore, with less heavy traffic within the RZ (where many of the deliveries are made in the morning), these drivers will be able to make more deliveries and thus earn more. More efficient deliveries also lower the cost of stocks in transit. The greatest increase in the type of vehicles entering the RZ between 7:30AM and 10:15AM after ALS is the goods vehicles, from 4,597 in March 1975 to 13,478 in 1988, a 116 percent increase. Both retailers and wholesalers benefited from the more reliable and timely delivery of goods, especially during the morning periods. Loading and unloading is also made easier with lighter traffic within the CBD.

The average value of travel time is $3 per hour for delivery drivers. The number. of goods vehicles delivering goods inside the RZ between 7:30AM and 10:15AM is

---

[4] 60% of the gross hourly wage of $6

[5] 60% of the gross hourly wage of $12

calculated as 50%×9,941 = 4,970.[6] The speed of goods vehicles is 19km/h before ALS and 22km/h after ALS.

The savings in travelling time per vehicle per km (time) equals to 3.16-2.73 = 0.43min, and savings in travelling time per vehicle per km ($) equals to $0.02. The number of goods vehicles (excluding bypassing) entering the RZ per hour is given by 4,970/165×60 = 1,807.

The total time savings per km per hour amounts to $0.02×1,807 = $36.14, hence, total time savings per km in 1 day is $36.14×165/60 = $99.40. Therefore, annual savings per km of goods vehicles is totalled to $99.40×300 = $29,820.[7]

4.5 PRIVATE CAR DRIVERS WHO CHANGE ROUTES TO AVOID ALS

According to Menon and Lam (1992), the number of private cars entering the RZ between 7:30AM and 10:15AM fell from 42,790 to 11,459. Assume that 20 percent of the car drivers who previously drove into the RZ but turned to alternative routes after the ALS are trans-zonal drivers. These commuters are forced to bypass the RZ and switch to less convenient routes after ALS.

Due to these diverted drivers, the ring roads outside the RZ became more congested. Assuming original speed on the ring roads to have been 27km/h before the ALS, with a 20 percent reduction in speed (Watson and Holland, 1978), the post ALS speed is 22km/h.

Loss in travelling time per km equals to (60/27)-(60/22) = 0.51min. The total number of diverted drivers becomes 20%×(42,790-11459) = 6,266, and the total loss in travel time per km due to diversion is calculated as (6,266×0.51)/60 = 53.261 hours. The average value of travel time to diverted car drivers is $10.20 per hour. Loss in time savings per km per day is $10.20×53.26 = $543.25. Therefore, annual loss per km of diverted car drivers is given by $543.25×300 = $162,975.

4.6 CAR DRIVERS WHO SWITCH TO PUBLIC TRANSPORT

Assume that car drivers who switch to public transport account for 50 percent of the increase in the number of new public transport commuters after ALS, the number of new public bus users is equal to 50%(4,154-3,980)×81 = 7,047. According to Watson and Holland (1978), car drivers who switched to bus spent on average 9 minutes longer to commute. The average value of travel time is assumed to be $10.20 per hour.

The time loss per km per person is (60/22 - 60/27) = 0.5 min, and the total cost of increased travel time per km per person becomes $10.20×0.5/60 = $0.085. Total cost of longer travelling time per km per day is $0.085×7,047 = $598.90. Therefore, annual loss per km of car drivers who switch to public transport amounts to $598.90×300 = $179,670.

---

[6] According to Menon and Lam (1992), 50% of goods vehicles was just using the RZ as a by-pass route.

[7] The annual savings is exclusive of savings in loading and unloading time. Goods vehicles were exempted from the ALS fee from 1975-1989.

5. CONCLUSION

5.1 ANALYSIS OF RESULTS

The above analysis shows that the annual benefit of the scheme in terms of net time savings is about $87,137 per km (Refer to Table 8). The ALS has effectively reduced congestion in the downtown area and the benefits of the scheme are expected to increase over time as the average value of travel time savings and the growth of vehicles increases. The amount of investment which would have been required to keep pace with the growth in traffic if the ALS had not been implemented is $1,500 million.

From the analysis results, car-pool passengers enjoy the highest annual savings per km ($193,062) as a result of the ALS. These passengers enjoy the benefits of private transport without having to pay the ALS fee. The percentage of car-pools peaked to 54 percent in the early 80's, and the number of car-pools in November 1988 amounted to the carrying of about 22,484 or approximately 175 bus loads in the morning peak period [Menon and Lam (September 1992)]. Table 9 shows the number of car-pools entering the RZ during the restricted hours. Private car users generally found the benefit of less crowded traffic in the CBD after ALS to outweigh the cost of the fee. Furthermore, licenses were easily available at Post Offices, petrol stations and more recently, drive-through booths were also set up along convenient roads leading to the entry points of the RZ, making it less time consuming and more convenient for car drivers to purchase them. Bus commuters on the whole also benefited from the scheme, mainly from the various improvements in public transport. They were also able to enjoy the intangible benefits of journey-time reliability and predictability. Delivery drivers and companies benefited from more efficient and reliable deliveries. They found it much easier to load and unload the goods with less heavy traffic. Driving within the RZ was so much easier for these big vehicles as compared to driving through the small roads, so much so that, a number plate survey done at the cordon points of the RZ showed that about 50 percent of the goods vehicle traffic was just using the RZ as a by-pass route. As a result of the large numbers of trans-zonal goods vehicle traffic, these vehicles were also required to pay the ALS fee from 1 June 1989. The composition share of total traffic entering the RZ is shown in Table 10. It shows the largest percentage increase for goods vehicles.

The annual loss of car drivers who switch to public transport is a conservative amount because public transport excludes MRT for our analysis. The loss is expected to be smaller because the MRT is able to transport a much larger passenger load in a shorter amount of time, without being subjected to traffic conditions. The loss incurred by trans-zonal drivers will also be reduced with more convenient ring roads and expressways being constructed.

5.2 CONCLUDING REMARKS

For the past two decades, the ALS has no doubt alleviated the serious problems of congestion within the RZ by keeping traffic in the CBD free-flowing but congestion seems to have shifted to the expressways. The Central Expressway (CTE) and Pan-Island Expressway (PIE) have become more congested and wasted time on both expressways is estimated to cost $45 million a year. Electronic Road Pricing, when implemented, will allow for the optimal pricing of roads and the correction of such distortions. The ALS has successfully paved the way for more sophisticated road pricing schemes to be introduced in Singapore by increasing the awareness of the general public to the detrimental economic effects of congestion. For car-owning households, the mode choice in Singapore is elastic with respect to income but inelastic with respect to car operating and parking costs. The increased emphasis on road pricing charges will increase the ratio of car usage to ownership costs and thus raise the elasticity of mode choice with respect to operating and parking expenses.

While the ALS has met many of the objectives of demand management, it is not perfect and its implementation would involve complications; it was unpopular with the public at least in the initial stage, but if policy-makers want to reduce congestion and traffic levels in the CBD, ALS has to be assessed in relation to other possibilities, including doing nothing, none of which is perfect or risk-free.

5.3 LIMITATIONS OF RESEARCH

There are many less direct effects of the ALS which are not covered in this study. The scheme also has far-reaching effects on the welfare and social and financial aspects of the economy. On the plus side, there is the increase in rent revenue to the economy due to conversion of parking spaces within the RZ into commercial buildings; the annual revenue in excess of operating costs of $403,571 goes toward the provision of new transportation infrastructure and the upgrading of the public transport system;[8] there is a considerable reduction in the costs of road maintenance within the RZ and finally, there is a significant reduction in the number of accidents and the level of pollution within the RZ. On the minus side, statistics show that there is an increase in trans-zonal goods vehicles; there is also believed to be an increase in the operating costs of public transport. Many of these indirect effects have significant policy implications for the Singapore economy.

5.4 AREAS OF FUTURE RESEARCH

A detailed Cost-Benefit-Analysis can be performed for ALS to cover welfare as well as social considerations. Further research can also evaluate the effects of the ALS after 1989, in particular the effects of the Whole-Day ALS. The feasibility of replicating the scheme in other countries can also be examined.

REFERENCES

Ang and Tan (1993/94), "The Effect of ALS on Motorists' Behaviour", *Final Year Project (1993/94)*, School of Civil and Structural Engineering, Nanyang Technological University.

Button, K. J. and Pearman, A. D. (1985): *Applied Transport Economics: A Practical Case Studies Approach*, Gordon and Breach Science Publishers, 25-54.

Department of Statistics (1991): *Singapore Census of Population 1990*, SNP Publishers Pte Ltd.

Evans, Andrew W. (1992), "Road Congestion Pricing: when is it a good policy?" *Journal of Transport Economics and Policy*, vol. 26, p213-224.

Foster, C. D. (1974), "The Regressiveness of Road Pricing: A Further Note", *International Journal of Transport Economics*, vol. 1, pp. 273-275.

---

[8] For a detailed breakdown of the capital and operating costs and revenue of the ALS, refer to Menon and Lam (1992, pg. 23-24)

Gomez-Ibanez, J. A. and G. R. Fauth, (1980), "Downtown Auto Restraint Policies: the costs and benefits for Boston", *Journal of Transport Economics and Policy*, vol. 14, pp. 133-153.

Land Transport Authority's White Paper (1996): *The Straits Times*, Singapore Press Holdings, 3 January.

Menon, A. P. G. and Lam, S. H. (1992): *Singapore's Road Pricing System 1975-1989*, Research Report CTS/NTU/92-2, Centre For Transportation Studies, Nanyang Technological University, September.

Menon, A. P. G. and Lam, S. H. (1993): *Singapore's Road Pricing System 1989-1993*, Research Report CTS/NTU/93-2, Centre For Transportation Studies, Nanyang Technological University, November.

Menon, A. P. G. and P. A. Seddon (1990): "Traffic in the Central Area Part I: Volume Characteristics," *Journal of the Institution of Engineers*, Singapore. 15-19.

Ng, G. S. and Li, Z. F. (1996): "Singapore Road Pricing Scheme: Is $3 Really Too High?", *Regional Issues in Economics*, vol. II, Applied Economics Research Series:1996.

Pigou, AC. 1920, *The Economic of Welfare*, London: McMillan and Company.

Png, G. H., Olszewski, P. and A. P. G., Menon (March 1994): "Estimation of the Value of Travel Time of Motorists," *Journal of The Institution of Engineers, Singapore*, vol. 34, no. 2, pp. 9-13.

Toh, R. (1977): "Road Congestion Pricing: The Singapore Experience," *Malayan Economic Review*, vol. 22, pp. 52-61.

Watson, P. L. and E. P. Holland (1978): "Relieving Traffic Congestion: The Singapore Area Licensing Scheme," *World Bank Staff Working Paper No. 281*, World Bank.

Wilson, P. W. (1988): "Welfare Effects of Congestion Pricing on Singapore," *Transportation*, vol. 5, Kluwar Academic Publishers.

Yee, J. (1980): "Area Licensing Scheme in Singapore", *Public Works Publications*, Singapore.

TABLE 1

Changes in Modal Distribution of Home-Work Journeys to the RZ between 7:30am to 10:15am

Mode	Before ALS	1976	1983	1988
Private car	56%	46%	23%	23%
- driver	- 47%	- 28%	- 15%	N/A.
- passenger	- 9%	- 18%	- 8%	N/A.
Bus	33%	46%	23%	55%
Motorcycle	7%	6%	6%	8%
Others	4%	2%	2%	3%

Source : Menon and Lam (1992) and Watson and Holland (1978, pg. 103)

TABLE 2

Effect of ALS on Vehicle-Owning Families (Mar 1975--May 1976) (%)

Trips	Car		Bus		Car Pools	
	1975	1976	1975	1976	1975	1976
To Work	56	46	33	46	8	19
From Work	53	43	36	48	5	12
Across Zone	52	50	32	40	5	14

Source: Yee, 1980

TABLE 3

Vehicles Entering the RZ during Restricted Hours 7:30am-10:15am

	March 1975 (pre-ALS)	October 1975 (post-ALS)	1988
Private cars	42790	11459	16637
Taxis	10923	3902	5235
Goods Vehicles	4597	9941	13478
Motorcycles	11724	12058	11094
Buses	3980	4154	4610
Total	74014	41154	51054

Source : Menon and Lam (1992)

TABLE 4

Number of Trips (Per License) Made during Restricted Hours

Transport Mode	Number of Trips
Company Cars	1.09
Private Cars	1.03
Taxis	4.03
Non-scheduled Buses	2.33
Goods Vehicles	1.88
Motorcycles	1.16
Total	1.44

Source : Ang and Tan, 1993/94

TABLE 5

Total Inbound at Gantry Points (Veh/Hr)

Time	Private Cars	Company Cars	Buses	Taxis	Goods Vehicles	M/cycles	Total
0715-0730	11064	740	1032	1788	2080	2368	19072
0730-0745	4272	460	1120	1628	1056	1016	9552
0745-0800	4980	456	1228	1820	1192	1640	11316
0800-0815	7712	952	1436	1972	1704	1848	15624
0815-0830	9596	1044	1244	2548	1732	2228	18392
0830-0845	12392	1252	1620	3124	2520	2488	23396
0845-0900	13256	1108	1748	4340	2508	2620	25580
0900-0915	9504	908	1244	5412	2584	2880	22532
0915-0930	6300	612	1280	4716	2540	1980	17428
0930-0945	5644	592	1072	4644	2384	2172	16508
0945-1000	4088	448	872	4416	2060	1916	13800
1000-1015	5588	504	808	5044	2952	2364	17260

TABLE 6

Responses of Commuters to Changes in Travel Patterns

Category of travel	Change route?	Change time?	Change destination?	Change mode?	Change frequency?
Education	yes	no	no	yes	no
Work	yes	no	no	yes	no
Business (own)	yes	no	no	yes	no
Leisure	yes	yes	yes	yes	yes
Goods Delivery	yes	no	no	no	no

TABLE 7

Average Value of Travel Time of Classified Commuters

Transport Mode	Average Monthly Income ($)	Average Hourly Wage Rate ($)	Average Value of Travel Time ($)
Private Car Owners	3,094	17	10.20
Car-Pool Passengers	2,255	12	7.20
Public Bus Commuters	1,119	6	3.60
Deliver Truck Drivers	914	5	3

TABLE 8

Results of Analysis

	BENEFITS	COSTS
Annual savings per km for private car users who drive into the RZ during Restricted Hours	$ 173,852	
Annual savings per km for car-pool passengers	$ 193,062	
Annual savings per km for public transport commuters[9]	$ 33,048	
Annual savings per km for delivery drivers	$ 29,820	
Annual loss per km of previous car drivers who switch to public transport after ALS		$ 179,670
Annual loss per km incurred by drivers who diverted routes to avoid ALS fee		$ 162,975
Annual Net Savings per km	**$ 87,137**	

TABLE 9

Car Pools Entering the Rz during Morning Restricted Hours

Month	Number of Car-Pools
October 1975	4,179 (36.5%)
November 1980	7,460 (52%)
May 1983	6,783 (43.8%)
November 1988	5,621 (34%)

Source : Menon and Lam, 1992

TABLE 10

Composition Share of Total Traffic Entering the RZ between 7:30am and 10:15am

Mode	March 1975 (pre-ALS)	1988
Goods vehicles	6.2%	26.4%
Private cars	57.8%	32.6%
Buses	5.4%	9%
Taxis	14.8%	10.3%
Motorcycles	15.8%	21.7%

[9] Refer only to public-bus commuters.

The North-East MRT Line:
Financial and Economic Appraisal

Seah Wei Ming Daniel
&
Michael Li Zhi-Feng

Nanyang Business School, Nanyang Technological University, Nanyang Avenue, Singapore 639798
Fax: +(65) 792.4217, Tel: +(65) 799.1461, Email: zfli@ntu.edu.sg

Abstract It is the government's aspiration to achieve a target whereby 75 percent of all trips are made by public transport. The extension of the MRT to the north-east is one of the ways in which the government hopes to attain this objective. However, the government has always taken a prudent and conservative approach to all public transport projects. Public transport projects are only carried out if all the financing principles are satisfied. This paper attempts to provide an insight on the financial appraisal of the North-East Line (NEL). The revision of the financing framework will expedite the construction of the North-East Line. A simple economic appraisal will also be done in the later part of this paper, which shows that despite constraining ourselves to only two intangible benefits - time savings and comfort, the NEL is still economically viable.

1. INTRODUCTION

The green light for the LTA to build the North-East line (NEL) is given on the 16th January 1996. Spanning a distance of 20 km, the NEL will comprise 16 stations and a 40 ha depot. A predominantly underground line, the construction of the NEL is estimated to cost $5 billion. This decision to build the NEL in 1996 was found to be financially viable only after the financing framework on which major transport projects are based was revised [LTA (1996)].

The objectives of this paper are to examine the impact of this revision of the financing framework on the financial and the economic viability of the NEL. The paper will attempt to accomplish this by first discussing the impact of the financing framework on the financial viability of the NEL. Section 3 will provide the economic analysis for the NEL. Section 4 will examine some of the unmonetised costs and benefits that accrues to the construction of the MRT. Finally, the conclusion is presented in Section 5.

2. FINANCING FRAMEWORK

2.1 TERMINOLOGY

If the existing arrangement with Singapore Mass Rapid Transit (SMRT) is taken as the precedent, the licence to operate the NEL will be leased to an operator. Operating revenue refers to only the fare revenue. Advertising and other sources of income are ignored. The expenses incurred refer to the costs of running the NEL. Expenses also include the provision for maintenance. The net of these two items will give us the operating surplus.

The investment costs are separated into two main categories: the rolling stock and the rail plant. These two are separated due to the differences in the periods over which they are annualised. The rolling stock are annualised over 30 years [LTA (1996)]. The rail plant is annualised over the composite service life of its components and is estimated to be 34.5 years.[1] The planning horizon of the NEL operations is 30 years. By then, a second capital outlay will then be required to replace the operating assets.[2]

The operator is expected to set aside an asset reserve fund for the replacement of the operating assets. Operating surplus after asset replacement reserve is obtained by deducting the operating expenses and the annualised investment in the rolling stock from the operating revenue. This is in accordance with the principle in the LTA's financing framework that operating expenses should include both the operating expenses and the replacement costs of the operating assets.

2.2 NEED FOR A FINANCING FRAMEWORK

The NEL requires massive investment and is unlikely to break-even in the strictest financial sense of recovering both the capital and operating costs. Use of financial analysis disregards any intangible benefits that arise due to the NEL. Thus, financial analysis is unlikely to support the construction of a rail system in most cases.

The question of whether to build the NEL is not an issue. The main issue is when to build it [ST (17/10/95)]. In a compact city like Singapore, an efficient and comprehensive bus system would not be able to serve the heavier traffic corridors without a deterioration of service levels. Only rail can meet the expectations of our increasing affluent society. In fact, preliminary studies have indicated that Singapore could have a rail network comprising as much as 160 km of MRT and LRT in the long run [LTA (1996)].[3]

The government believes that the burden of constructing the NEL is ultimately borne by the people. The main challenge is, therefore, to set up a system that best encourages fiscal prudence, individual discipline and efficient operations. This would ensure that cross-subsidies on operations would be kept to a minimum and the system would be self-sustainable. The financing framework was set up with these considerations in mind.

2.3 THE OLD FINANCING FRAMEWORK

2.3.1 The Financing Principles behind the Old Framework

The financing framework as set out in the LTA's White Paper is based on three sound and tested principles. The first principle is that the fares have to be realistic and regularly adjusted to account for justifiable cost increases. This is especially important in the context of Singapore where major productivity gains in public transport are already exhausted and a higher standard of transport is expected.

The second principle states that public transport projects must at least recover operating costs. The capital costs will be funded by the government, but the operating costs must at least be covered by the operating revenue. Only projects that pass this market test will be implemented. This helps prevent the need for cross-subsidies.

---

[1] This is taken from the Mass Transit Studies done by Wilbur Smith and Associates (1978). It is based on the assumption that the composition of the rail plant does not differ much between that of the initial line and that of the NEL.

[2] The operating assets refer to the fleet of trains and the computer equipment.

[3] The current MRT network spans 83 km.

Under the third principle, fare collection is expected to cover not only the operating costs but also the replacement cost of the second set of operating assets. This principle helps ensure that only self-sustainable systems are built. The costs of the operating assets at the end of the thirty years will depend on the asset inflation rate. The historical asset inflation rate is around 5 percent [LTA (1996)].

2.3.2 Impact of the Old Financing Framework on the NEL

Under this old financing framework, the NEL is expected to incur an annual loss of $250 million during the first 4 years of operation if construction is to start in 1996. This includes operating losses, asset depreciation and opportunity costs of investing in the NEL. This is despite the fact that the NEL is expected to attract an initial traffic of about 240,000 passengers per day when it starts operating in 2002. The NEL is expected to break-even only after 4 years of operation (*i.e.*, in 2006).[4]

Table 1 attempts to emulate the financial viability test on the NEL (assuming that construction commences in 1996) based on the old financing framework. The NEL is expected to be completed before 2002 and start operations from then.[5] The average fare paid by a passenger is about $0.93.[6] The estimated revenue collected from the NEL in the first year of operation if construction is to commence in 1996 is hence about $81 million.[7] The annual operating cost for the NEL is estimated to be about $90 million.[8]

The historical cost of the operating assets is assumed to be at about $1 billion. Applying the historical asset inflation rate of 5 percent, the cost of the second set of operating assets that would be required by 2031 would be about $4.3 billion. The operating assets are written off over a period of 30 years. The investment on the operating assets is annualised at $144 million dollars.

Applying the first principle in the financing framework, it is assumed that any justified increase in operating costs is exactly offset by a fare adjustment. As such, any increase in the operating costs and operating revenue (that occurs as a result of fare adjustment) is irrelevant to the financial viability. The fare revenue will therefore be affected only by the increase in ridership. The ridership for NEL is expected to increase by 30 percent annually from 2002 to 2006.[9]

---

[4] Break-even in the sense that the operating revenue must cover both the operating costs and the replacement costs of the operating assets.

[5] This is based on a 6 year construction period, commencing in 1996.

[6] This is obtained by dividing the total fare revenue of the SMRT in 1995 by the total number of passengers [SMRT (1995)].

[7] Since the initial traffic is forecasted to be 240,000.

[8] The NEL is assumed to operate at the same frequency and in the same operating environment as the entire network. By taking proportionality of the expenditure of the backbone MRT using the length of the network, the operating cost of the NEL in the first year of operation is obtained [SMRT (1995)]. The figure obtained is then increased by 70 percent to reflect the higher operating cost due to most of it being underground [ST (1996 March 5)].

[9] Under the assumptions made, the NEL has to enjoy about 30 percent growth in ridership in the first five years of operation if it is to breakeven in the fifth year of operation. It would be interesting to note that the ridership on the initial MRT system (without the Woodlands extension) also grew at an annual rate of about 30 percent in the first five years of operations [SMRT (various years)].

From Table 1, one can see that by 2003, the operating expenditure can be recovered. Thus, the second financing principle is not breached. The NEL, however, fails to meet the third condition in the first four years. The operating revenue is not able to cover the replacement costs of the operating assets for this period. It will only marginally break-even from the fifth year onwards. Hence, the argument for the delay in the construction of the NEL is justified under the old financing framework.

2.4 THE REVISED FINANCING FRAMEWORK

2.4.1 Changes to the Third Principle

Under the revised framework, the SMRT needs only cover the historical cost of the operating assets. The government will pay for the difference that is due to the asset inflation. In this case, it is the historical cost of $1 billion (revised framework) versus the future cost of $4.3 billion (under the old framework). The contrasts between the old and the revised financing scheme are shown in Table 2.

Under this new scheme, the government grant not only has to bear the initial capital cost but also any subsequent increases in the cost of the operating assets. Hence, the excess amount that the government has to provide as subsidy is dependent on the actual rate of asset inflation.

2.4.2 Impact of the Revised Principle

The decision to go-ahead with the NEL is only possible with the revised financing framework and the adoption of a separate fare structure from the existing line for the NEL. These developments will enable the NEL to break-even in 2003, instead of the forecasted 2006. The construction of 3 stations will also be delayed to improve the financial viability of the NEL. Due to data limitations, it shall be assumed that the entire NEL will be constructed.

An attempt is now made to illustrate the decision making on the NEL after the above changes. Refer to Table 3. In accordance with the revised financing framework, the operator needs only set aside an amount equivalent to that of the historical cost of the operating assets. Assuming that this historical cost is annualised over the thirty years, SMRT needs only put aside an average sum of $33 million per year for 30 years.[10]

The government has assured the public that the fare on the NEL will not exceed the fare charged on the initial MRT system by more than 20 percent[ST (02/11/95)]. If fares on the NEL is jacked up by 20 percent, the average fare of the NEL users will be about $1.12.[11] The increase in the fare of the NEL may result in a lower growth in the ridership. To be conservative, we shall assume a reduced growth rate of 25 percent for the first five years. All the other parameters remaining unchanged.

The NEL is very close to breaking even in 2003, with a deficit of only $1million. One of the reasons for the discrepancy of these results against that of the government's forecast may be due to the decision of the government to delay the construction of three stations.

---

[10] The assumed $1 billion divided by the estimated operating life of the first set of equipment which is 30 years.

[11] This is obtained by raising the initial average fare (as mentioned in section 2.3.2) of $0.93 by 20 percent

By requiring the transport operator to pay only the historical cost, the government is actually subsidising the operating cost of the SMRT. Under this scheme, the government not only have to bear the initial capital investment of $5 billion, but also the asset inflation of $3.3 billion if historical asset inflation of 5 percent holds.

3. ECONOMIC EVALUATION FRAMEWORK

In this paper, the construction of the NEL network is assumed to start in 1996 and complete by 2001. The annual benefits accruing to the NEL will start flowing in from 2002 and end in 2031. All costs and benefits would be estimated in 1995 prices and expressed in Singapore dollars. All impacts are measured relative to a no-NEL base case.

This paper proposes to find the annual benefits accruing to the NEL under the new fare structure in 2002. The annual benefits after the first five years of operations are then maintained at the 2006 level. This paper attempts to present a simplified version of the economic evaluation by focusing on only two of the more major benefits. They are time savings and increase in comfort. These two benefits shall be constructed based on certain assumptions and available information from published sources.

We will then quantify the present values of the costs and benefits. The internal rate of return (IRR) for the MRT is also be computed.

3.1 CAPITAL COST CALCULATION

3.1.1 NEL Capital Outlays

The capital cost of the NEL system includes the land, buildings and structures, viaducts and tunnels, rolling stock and operating equipment. The entire NEL line is to be completed at a total cost of $5 billion.

The entire cost of the MRT is annualised over the period of 6 years from 1996 to 2001. During this period, an annual capital outlay of $833 million is required. No more massive investments is required until 30 years later, when the operating assets has to be replaced.

3.1.2 Salvage Value of The MRT System

The train fleet is completely written off within the analysis period. Land, viaducts, tunnels, permanent ways, buildings and structures are estimated to have a composite life of 34.5 years [Smith et al (1978)]. The depreciation of these assets are calculated on a straight line basis. Based on the assumed costs of $4 billion for the rail plant, the salvage value of the NEL at the end of the 30 year period will be $520 million. This is represented by a very large negative value in 2031. See Table 4.

3.2 BENEFITS

3.2.1 Reduced Travel Time and Relief of Traffic Congestion

3.2.1.1 Private Transport Users

Most of the time saved by the private vehicles is likely to be during the peak hours. In fact, a Public Works Department (PWD) survey in 1994 actually finds that traffic along the north-east corridor moves at a slow 18.8 km/hr during the morning peak hours. The evening peak hours is not spared either [ST (25/10/1995)]. To estimate the time savings by the private vehicles, one would need to approximate the number of trips made during the peak hours.

It has been estimated by LTA that the daily number of vehicular trips in 1995 is 7 million. This is expected to reach a high of 10 million in 2010. 23 percent of the daily vehicular trips are made in the peak hours [LTA (1996)]. By interpolation, 8.32 million trips will be made in 2002. Approximately, 1.92 million trips are made daily during the peak hours in 2002. To be conservative, we shall use this figure to estimate the number of trips made by people staying in the north-east region.

In 1990, the number of people staying in the north-east region is 16.8 percent of the population [Census (1990)] . With much development plans to be carried out in the north-east region, the population density there is expected to increase. Development plans revealed by Urban Redevelopment Authority [URA (1991)] shows that the northeast area is likely to be a matured region by the year 2010. The population is also expected to be more evenly distributed in the year 2002. This paper assumes that the north-east region contains about 18 percent of the population in the year 2002. If the number of trips made daily are proportional to the population density in each of the region, the number of peak hour trips made by the people staying in the north-east region is about 345,600.

From LTA (1996) estimates, trips made by MRT, bus and private transport are in the following percentages: 10 percent, 41 percent and 49 percent.[12] Trips made by private transport include those made by taxis, scooters and all other privately owned motorised vehicles. The completion of NEL is likely to result in a modal shift from private transport to public transport. With government policies geared towards achieving a higher level of public transport usage, it is likely that there will be a shift from private to public transport usage. (Singapore is using Zurich where 75 percent of all trips are made by public transport as the benchmark.) Hence, it is assumed that in the year 2002, the modal split into MRT, bus and private transport will be 15 percent, 40 percent and 45 percent respectively. Using this proportion, the percentage of private transport trips made by northeast residents during the peak hours is 155,520.

At a speed of 18.8 km/hr, a vehicle would take 32 minutes to cover 10 km. In contrast, it would take only 20 minutes if it is travelling at 30 km/hr. By providing an alternative transport mode, the NEL would be able to relieve the congestion on the affected corridor. If each private transport user is able to save 5 minutes in the peak hour, the annual savings in time is 3.42 million hours.[13]

According to the 1990 Census, the average monthly wage rate of those who travel by private vehicles is $2,931. Based on a 8 hour work day for 22 days in a month, this is about $16 per hour. Therefore, the total savings in the time by private car owners is about $32.8 million a year.[14] This benefit is assumed to be constant over the years.[15]

---

[12] This is based on the fact that out of the 7 million daily trips made in 1995, the number of daily vehicular trips made by bus and MRT are 3 million and 0.7 million respectively. 500 thousand trips are made by taxis daily. Although taxi is a form of public transport, this paper will classify it as a mode of private transport.

[13] The total time savings by private transport users in 2002 is annualised over 264 days. This is to account for the non-working days during which there is a lower probability of traffic congestion.

[14] In this paper, time is valued at 60 percent of the wage rate. This is based on a study in 1987 that estimate value of time savings by bus commuting to be between 60 percent and 129 percent [Button (1993)]. Studies have also shown that there is a positive correlation between the value of time and the wage rate. While the average wage rate of the private transport users is higher than that of the public transport users, 60 percent is employed so as to maintain a conservative stance.

3.2.1.2 Public Transport Users

The provision of the NEL offers an alternative mode of transport. This mode is especially efficient in regions whereby the transportation demand has exceeded its threshold. Time savings do not accrue only to peak hours but throughout the day.

The total number of daily vehicular trips in 2002 is expected to be around 8.3 million. The total number of trips made by the public transport users in the northeast region is estimated at 821,700.[16] The amount of time savings per transit user depends on the 'door to door' travel time saved and not just the time saved on the vehicular journey. Assuming that an average of two transfers are required before one can reach his destination, the number of 'door to door' trips made in the north-eastern region is about 410,850.

If each traveller is able to save 10 minutes, the total amount of hours saved is 25 million hours per year.[17] The hourly wage rate of a public transport user is about $6.75.[18] The annual value of time saved by public transport users is thus $101 million.

The annual savings in time increases in tandem with the ridership on the NEL. With the ridership expected to increase by 25 percent under the revised scheme, this paper assumes that the annual savings in time by the public transport users increases at a conservative rate of 15 percent in the first five years and remains constant from 2007 onwards.

3.2.2 Comfort

Increasing affluence of Singaporeans has resulted in not only increase in the demand for transport but also rising expectations for quality transport. Only rail can provide services with reliability, high frequency, speed and comfort. A bus system will not be able to meet the needs of a densely populated city like Singapore.

Most commuters tend to favour rail over bus due to its greater comfort. To model this choice correctly, a penalty of four to six minutes is attached to bus travel to reflect the relative discomfort of buses [Abelson (1995)]. Because the NEL is less packed than buses and provide a smoother ride than that of the bus, this paper adopts the equivalence of a five minute saving per rail trip to proxy for a comfort premium.

With initial ridership expected to be about 240,000, the annual comfort premium equivalence is expected to be 5.3 million hours in the year 2002.[19] Since the hourly rate of a public transport user is $6.75, the total annual comfort premium due to the rail is $21.5

---

[15] The diversion of traffic from the roads to the rail will reduce the traffic on the road. Smaller benefits will accrue to the road users as the number of vehicles on the road decreases. But the higher travelling speed is a compensating factor. Unable to identify which is the greater, this paper assumes that the two effects balances out.

[16] This figure is derived by taking proportionality of the total number of daily public transport trips. It should be noted that public transport trips are expected to make up 55 percent of the total number of daily trips made and that the northeast region is assumed to contain 18 percent of the population in 2002.

[17] The construction of the NEL will reduce the travelling time regardless of the period of the day. As such, the total number of daily trips made by public transport in the northeast region is taken into account.

[18] This is obtained by getting the mean monthly wage rate of all the public users and then basing the hourly wage rate on a 8-hour 22 workday month. [Census (1990)].

[19] For consistency ,this is also annualised over a period of 264 days.

million[20] in monetary terms. The total annual comfort premium is expected to increase at a rate of 25 percent[21] in first five years under the revised financing scheme and remains constant thereafter.

3.3 ECONOMIC EVALUATION

Table 5 provides the economic spreadsheet under the new fare structure. The estimated internal rate of return of the NEL is about 7 percent. According to Gaikheimer (1990), typical values around 12 or 13 percent is a reasonable estimate of the alternative productive uses of the project capital. However, as in the Mass Transit Studies [Smith et al (1978)], 6 percent is adopted as the discount rate in this paper.[22] The NPV obtained is $706 million 1995- dollars .

Table 5 shows how the benefit cost ratio is computed. As indicated, the ratio is 1.02. This implies that the social benefits exceed the social costs of the NEL. Hence, it is economically viable to build the NEL now.

As seen, the capital costs of the NEL is annualised over a period of 6 years. This ignores the staging programme of the NEL. While the staging programme will have an impact on the NPV and the IRR, lack of information at this stage prevents us from being able to annualise the capital cost as in the staging programme.

The utilisation of 34.5 years as the composite life of the rail plant [Smith (1978)] for the NEL may have underestimated the life of these assets. In contrast with the initial MRT network where only 35 percent of the stations are underground, the NEL is predominantly underground. As such, a much higher portion of the capital costs will go to the permanent ways and tunnels which will be written off over a longer period of 99 years. Thus, the salvage value period is underestimated.

3.4 EVALUATION SENSITIVITIES

The above economic evaluation is based on a 30 year horizon and a 6 percent discount rate. The asset life of the operating assets is assumed to be 30 years while the composite life of the rail plant is 34.5 years. This section attempts to examine the impacts of some of the parameters on the benefit-cost ratio if the assumptions on them are altered.

From Table 6, it can be seen that the benefit-cost ratio decreases as the discount rate increases. This is because the use of a high discount rate means that the benefits tend to nearly zero in twenty years time. Increasing the analysis horizon results in an increase in the benefit-cost ratio. The ratio increases from 1.02 to 1.14 as the analysis period is extended from 30 to 50 years.

---

[20] This is based on the valuation of time at 60 percent of the wage rate.

[21] This is in tandem with the increase in ridership of 25 percent in the first five years of the NEL under the revised financing scheme which has been covered in section 2.

[22] Interest rates reflect two components: a rent on the pure time value of money and an allowance for any dilution of the value (due to inflation). The 12 percent discount rate which is desirable as a criterion for economic merit is inappropriate when using constant cost models. This is because the use of 12 percent discount rate recognises the dilution of money through inflation. To prevent the imposition of an arbitrary standard from beclouding relative benefits of transport proposals, Smith (1978) advocates the use of 6 percent as the discount rate if costs and benefits are fixed at the price level of a particular year. Note that in this paper, all are valued in 1995 Singapore dollars.

4. OTHER NON- MONETISED BENEFITS AND COSTS

In this section, we will look at the benefits and costs that are not monetised in the economic evaluation. This is one of the limitations faced in this paper.

4.1 NON-MONETISED BENEFITS

4.1.1 Vehicle Operating Costs

The construction of the NEL will result in a diversion of trips from private modes of transport to mass rapid transit. The reduction of traffic flow on the road will imply that vehicles are now able to travel at a higher speed. Vehicle operating cost is a function of speed and will fall as speed increases until a minimum cost speed is reached. Research in the UK has found that the minimum cost speed is higher than the average speed in most urban areas [Tyson (1991)]. Besides stop-and-go traffic condition is especially wasteful of fuel.

4.1.2 Regional Development

Major transport system can assist cities in achieving 'urban efficiency'. This helps to break up the vicious cycle of declining accessibility, outward migration and greater demand for mobility [Tyson (1991)].

4.1.3 Environmental Benefits

Prolonged exposure to noise levels above 85 decibels over an 8 hour period may result in induced hearing loss and our health will be affected. This is becoming an increasingly important issue as Singaporeans begin to put a high premium on aural peace due to increased affluence.

Emission from vehicles is a major source of air pollution. The reduction of the number of trips made by private modes due to the NEL will reduce the level of air pollution. However, the impact is not expected to be great. The main impact will come from the empowerment of the government by the Road Traffic Act and the Motor Vehicles Act to regulate the emission of pollutants by vehicles. This is evident by the fact that both the lead and the carbon monoxide levels are quite stable despite the fact that the number of vehicles has been increasing by 3 percent annually [LTA (1996)].

4.1.4 Government Tax Revenue

Tax revenue from the diesel tax will decrease due to a reduction of traffic on the roads as some of the trips are diverted to the rail. But this may be offset by the increase in the development charges and property taxes. The government may also benefit from an increase in the value of state land.

4.1.5 Reduction in the Number of Accidents

The usage of mass rapid transit will also tend to reduce the number of accidents on the road. This is due to the lower accident rates associated with trains as compared to the road vehicles.

4.2 NON-MONETISED COSTS

4.2.1 Relocation Costs

To build and develop the areas around the stations, the government will be acquiring 20 ha of private land, including apartments, landed homes and shophouses. Besides this, 26 blocks of Housing Development Board (HDB) flats and 43 hectares of land belonging to the statutory boards and government linked companies will also be acquired [ST (05/03/96)]. Relocation cost is incurred due to the involuntary sale and relocation of the affected parties.

4.2.2 Social Costs Incurred During the Period of Construction

The NEL spans 20 km. Major disturbance impacts will be associated with the construction of the NEL. During the six years of construction, people will have to tolerate the noise pollution, air pollution and traffic disruptions along affected roads. This will also inflict a social cost on the people.

5. CONCLUSION

The revision of the financing framework marks a turning point in the history of mass rail transport in Singapore. The government has always been prudent and conservative in approving transport projects as they regard themselves as the custodians of the people's money [ST (23/10/95)]. To ensure that the reserves are not squandered away, the government imposed upon itself a set of criteria and only those projects that satisfy these criteria will be carried out.

Faced with the immediate problems of traffic congestion along the north-east corridor and the rising expectations of the people, the government decide to relent on the third principle of the financing framework. This will enable us to bring forward some rail projects that are just short of being viable under the existing terms. The NEL is one of the projects that is now financially viable. The government will now undertake not only the initial capital costs of the project but also the inflation component of the operating assets. This increases the burden of the government.

But if the results from the economic analysis in section 3.3 is anything to go by, the NEL is definitely viable in the economic sense. This is especially so as many more benefits are not considered. The validity of the results may also be constrained by data limitations. With forecasts of the conditions in the early 21st century not forthcoming, the computation of the benefits are actually based on present conditions and whatever scarce forecasts available in the published sources. While this may not be desirable, this paper hopes to provide an insight into one of the reasons which may have persuaded the government to revise its financing policies for transport projects.

REFERENCES

Abelson, P. (1995): "Cost benefit analysis of proposed major rail development in Lagos, Nigeria," *Transport Reviews*, 15(3), 265-289.

Black, A. (1995): *Urban Mass Transportation Planning*, McGraw Hill.

Button, K. (1993): *Transport Economics* (Second Edition), Cambridge.

Fouracre, P. (1988): "Assessing mass transit railway viability in developing countries," *UITP City Transport in Asia*, Singapore Conference 11-13th October 1988.

Gaikheimer, R. (1990): "The two analytic cultures of rail transit planning," *Rail Mass Transit Systems for Developing Countries*, 1-21, The Institution of Civil Engineers.

Hansen, K.R. (1980): *Singapore's Transport and Urban Development Options*, Singapore.

Land Transport Authority (1996): *White Paper: A World Class Land Transport System*, LTA.

Mohring, H. (1996): " The Singapore MRT: Closed-economy Vs open-economy cost benefit analysis," *Development, Trade and the Asia Pacific: Essays in Honour of Professor Lim Chong Yah*, 105-121, Prentice Hall.

Mass Rapid Transit Corporation (various years): *Annual Reports*.

Republic of Singapore (1981): *Comprehensive Traffic Study: Phase A*, Singapore.

Singapore Population Census 1990.

Singapore Mass Rapid Transit (various years): *Annual Reports*.

Smith, W. and Associates. (1974): *"Final Report: Singapore Mass Transit Study: Phase 1,"* Singapore.

Smith, W. and Associates. (1977): *"Republic of Singapore: Singapore Mass Transit Study: Phase II,"* Singapore.

Straits Times (1995): "Mah's poser: Will users pay more to get it faster?" October 9.

Straits Times (1995): "New four tier traffic system coming up," October 14.

Straits Times (1995): "Mah comes face to face with jam," October 18.

Straits Times (1995): "North-east line: Issue is when to build it," October 17.

Straits Times (1996): "16 MRT stations for the North-East line," March 5.

Straits Times (1996): "Government spells out its vision of top transport system," January 3.

Thomson, J.M., Allport, R.J. and Fouracre, P. R. (1990): "Rail mass transit in developing cities," *Rail Mass Transit Systems for Developing Countries*, 21-41, The Institution of Civil Engineers.

Tyson, W.J. (1991): "Non-user benefits from public Transport," *49th UITP Congress - Stockholm 1991*, Report 4.

Urban Redevelopment Authority (1991): *Living the next lap*, Singapore.

TABLE 1
Financial Viability under the Old Financing Framework 2002 to 2012
(in Millions of 1995 $)

Year	Revenue	Expenses	Operating Surplus	Rolling Stock	Surplus After Asset Reserve[23]
2002	$81	$90	($9)	$144	($153)
2003	$105	$90	$15	$144	($129)
2004	$137	$90	$47	$144	($97)
2005	$178	$90	$88	$144	($56)
2006	$231	$90	$141	$144	($3)
2007	$231	$90	$141	$144	($3)
.	.	.	.	.	.
.	.	.	.	.	.
.	.	.	.	.	.
2030	$231	$90	$141	$144	($3)
2031	$231	$90	$141	$144	($3)

TABLE 2

Old vs. Revised Financing Scheme

Cost	Old Financing Scheme	Revised Scheme
Infrastructure	$4b (Government)	$4b (Government)
Operating Costs	$90m (Commuters)	$90m (Commuters)
Replacement of Operating Assets:		
Original Costs	$1b (Commuters)	$1b (Commuters)
+ Asset Inflation (5%)	$3.3b (Commuters)	$3.3b (Government)
Break-even[24] Year	2006	2003

---

[23] This is obtained by deducting the operating expenses and the annualised replacement cost of the second set of operating assets from its operating revenue.

[24] Break-even in the sense that the operating revenue can cover both the operating costs and the replacement costs of the operating assets. The replacement costs of the operating assets under the old and new financing scheme refers to the historical and 2031 price respectively.

TABLE 3

Financial Viability under the New Financing Framework 2002 to 2031
(in Millions of 1995 $)

Year	Revenue	Expenses	Surplus	Rolling Stock	Surplus After Asset Reserve
2002	$98	$90	$8	$33	($25)
2003	$122	$90	$32	$33	($1)
2004	$ 153	$90	$63	$33	$30
2005	$ 191	$90	$101	$33	$68
2006	$ 239	$90	$149	$33	$116
2007	$ 239	$90	$149	$33	$116
.	.	.	.	.	.
.	.	.	.	.	.
.	.	.	.	.	.
2030	$239	$90	$149	$33	$116
2031	$239	$90	$149	$33	$116

TABLE 4

Economic Spreadsheet under the Revised Financing Scheme (Millions of 1995 S$)

Year	Capital Costs	Revenue	Expenses	Operating Surplus	Total Time Savings	Comfort	Net Project Benefits
1996	$833	$0	$0	$0	$0	$0	($833)
1997	$833	$0	$0	$0	$0	$0	($833)
1998	$833	$0	$0	$0	$0	$0	($833)
1999	$833	$0	$0	$0	$0	$0	($833)
2000	$833	$0	$0	$0	$0	$0	($833)
2001	$833	$0	$0	$0	$0	$0	($833)
2002		$98	$90	$8	$134	$49	$191
2003		$122	$90	$32	$149	$61	$242
2004		$153	$90	$63	$166	$77	$306
2005		$191	$90	$101	$186	$96	$383
2006		$239	$90	$149	$209	$120	$478
.		.	.	.	.	.	.
2030		$239	$90	$149	$209	$120	$478
2031	($520)	$239	$90	$149	$209	$120	$998
Present Value, 6%	$4032	$2072	$873	$1198	$1906	$1038	$110

TABLE 5

NEL Benefit-Cost Ratio (Revised Financing Scheme)

Benefits / Costs	Present Value (1995) S$ m
Passenger Benefits	
Time Savings	1588
Comfort	1038
Road Users	
Congestion Relief	318
Revenue	
Operating Revenue	2072
Total Benefits	5016
Costs	
Capital Costs	4032
Operating Costs	873
Total Costs	4905
Benefits Cost Ratio	1.02

TABLE 6

Economic Evaluation Sensitivities

Assumptions	Benefit PV (1994) S$	Costs PV (1994) S$	Benefit Cost Ratio
Analysis horizon:			
30 year	5016	4905	1.02
40 year *	5529	5051	1.09
50 year *	5815	5096	1.14
Discount rate:			
5 %	5980	5171	1.16
6 %	5016	4905	1.02
7 %	4237	4669	0.91

Note: *Assume that the salvage value of the NEL is zero at the end of 40 and 50 year period.

The Adequacy of CPF for Old-Age Support

*Daniel **Wong** Chi Hoong*
&
***Park** Donghyun*

Nanyang Business School, Nanyang Technological University, Nanyang Avenue, Singapore 639798
Fax: +(65) 792.4217, Tel: +(65) 799.6130, Email: adpark@ntu.edu.sg

Abstract The population of Singapore is fast-ageing, rendering old-age support for retirees an increasingly important issue. This paper investigates the adequacy of CPF (Central Provident Fund), Singapore's fully-funded social security system based on mandatory contributions from both employers and employees, as a source of financial security for future retirees. Finally, we discuss the policy implications of our findings.

1. INTRODUCTION

Singapore has experienced rapid economic growth over the past thirty years. A decline in birth rates has accompanied the resulting increase in real income and living standard. At the same time, life expectancy has increased due to better health conditions. This phenomenon of falling fertility and mortality levels follows the experiences of developed nations like Japan, the United States and the United Kingdom. A consequence of these demographic changes is an ageing population. In a study of Singapore's demographic trends, Shantakumar (1994) has pointed out that the rate at which Singapore's population is ageing is among the three fastest in the world, along with that of Japan and Hong Kong. In only 17 years, the proportion of the aged[1] would double from the present 10 percent to 20 percent of the population. Shantakumar shows that the growth of the youthful population (i.e. population below 15 years old) is stabilising while the older population (i.e. population aged 60 and above) continues to grow in both absolute and relative terms.

An ageing population throws up new challenges which policy makers will have to grapple with for decades to come. One such challenge is the issue of old-age support for future retirees. According to Bauer (1996), at present the CPF (Central Provident Fund), Singapore's social security system based on mandatory contributions from both employers and employees, is not the primary source of old-age support for retirees. Most of them rely instead on children and relatives as well as voluntary savings. Given the government's aversion to welfare programs, such programs do not constitute a major source of support. It is expected that the role of the CPF will increasingly become more significant as the population ages and the dependency burden increases. The ODR[2] (Old-age Dependency Ratio) is projected to rise from about 13 percent in 1990 to 50 percent by 2030. The trend towards smaller families implies that the elderly will have fewer children who may support them in old-age.

In view of the continuous increase in life expectancy and the increasing liberalisation of the CPF, which now allows withdrawals before the age of 55 for the purchase of homes,

---

[1] Persons aged 60 and above, according to UN conventions.

[2] ODR = Number of people aged 60+ per 100 people aged 15-59.

investments and other purposes, the adequacy of CPF savings as a source of post-retirement financial security is an issue of growing concern.

The 1988 Household Expenditure Survey revealed that voluntary savings comprised 11 percent of total household savings. However, in the 1993 survey, this proportion has declined to 5 percent. In this connection, Prime Minister Goh Chok Tong has said that 'many Singaporeans do not save anything beyond what was in their Central Provident Fund accounts' [see *The Sunday Times* (6 October 1996)]. The purpose of this paper is to study the adequacy of CPF as a source of financing one's retirement needs, especially for Singaporeans in the 45 to 54 age group. Section two summarises Singapore's recent demographic trends and prospects. Section three takes a brief look into the history of the CPF and provides a description of the CPF system. Section four reviews the various schemes offered by the CPF. Section five presents the results of simulations concerning the adequacy of CPF as a means of old-age support. Section six discusses the policy implications of our findings in section five. Section seven concludes with a summary.

2. SINGAPORE'S DEMOGRAPHIC TRENDS AND PROSPECTS

Singapore is undergoing a rapid demographic transition from a relatively youthful to an increasingly older population. This is largely due to two main factors; declining fertility rate and increasing life expectancy[3]. In 1970, the fertility rate was 3.3, but this has fallen to 1.6 in 1994 [*SILS Information Series No. 8* (1995)]. On the other hand, life expectancy has risen from 67 in 1970 to 76 by 1995. In terms of the 'demographic transition theory' which summarises the different stages in the demographic transition of a country, Singapore is now at the end of stage three, characterised by falling mortality and fertility levels, declining population growth and the greying of the population. Singapore is expected to reach stage four, in which population growth is negligible, and the population structure is stable with a high proportion of the aged, in 30 to 40 years' time [Shantakumar (1994)].

An issue arising from an ageing population is the heavier old-age dependency burden on the economically active population. Shantakumar has noted that there is a significant shift of the economic burden from the young to the old. Calculations based on Table 1 show that the Economic Dependency Ratio (EDR)[4] of persons below 15 has declined from 1.185 in 1970 to 0.495 in 1990. On the other hand, EDR of the aged population has increased from 0.175 to 0.195. In addition, the EDR of non-active dependents between 15 and 59 has declined from 0.669 to 0.448. All these factors have led to a decline in EDR of the total resident population[5] from 3.029 to 2.138 during the same period. In 1990, there were 7.5 working persons for every aged person. By the year 2030, there will only be 2 working persons for every aged person.

---

[3] Fertility rate is defined as number of resident live-births per 1,000 resident females. Resident live-births refer to babies with at least one parent who is a Singapore citizen or permanent resident.
Life expectancy is defined as the mean number of years a newly-born resident can expect to live, assuming the resident population is subject to a fixed pattern of age specific mortality rates.

[4] EDR = Number of persons per economically active persons aged 15-59.

[5] EDR of total resident population = 1 + EDR of persons aged below 15 + EDR of persons aged 60 and above + EDR of economically inactive persons aged 15-59.
For example, from Table 1, EDR of persons aged below 15 = 787.8 ÷ 664.9 = 1.185.

3. A BRIEF HISTORY OF THE CPF AND THE CPF SYSTEM

3.1 THE HISTORY OF THE CPF

In 1951, the British colonial government set up a Retirement Benefits commission to study the need for old-age insurance. Before that, only employees of the colonial government and some private firms received pensions.

On 27 February 1952, the commission recommended a mandatory social insurance scheme for workers. They made the recommendation after having considered two alternative schemes, a social pension scheme and a provident fund. The commission felt that the mandatory social insurance scheme would be more appropriate as it better suited the circumstances prevailing in Singapore.

However, the government favoured the provident fund scheme instead since the Federation of Malaya had already set up a provident fund in that same year and large numbers of workers were employed in both Singapore and Malaya.

On 1 July 1955, the CPF Ordinance came into force. Later that year, two other commissions were set up to study the feasibility of a social insurance scheme. They recommended that the CPF scheme be abolished and be replaced by a comprehensive social insurance scheme.

When Singapore gained self-rule in June 1959, the new government placed a higher priority on economic growth than on social policy in its development agenda. The CPF was adopted and remains the social security system of Singapore to this day.

3.1.1 An overview of some developments in the CPF

Over the years, the CPF has expanded its role. The first step towards the liberalisation of the CPF took place in April 1968. Mr Lee Kuan Yew, then Prime Minister, revealed that the feasibility of permitting CPF members to use their CPF funds to purchase HDB flats and private residential homes was under study. Six months later, the policy change came into effect.

From 1968 to 1977, various other home-ownership schemes were introduced. Amid concerns that the primary objective of the CPF had been compromised, the Special Account was introduced in July 1977. This was to serve as a safeguard against members using up all their CPF savings and leaving nothing for retirement. A member can withdraw funds accumulated in his Special Account only when he turns 55, or if he is disabled or permanently leaves Singapore and West Malaysia. In contrast, a member can withdraw his Ordinary Account balances before he reaches the age of 55 for various purposes such as home purchase, investment and education.

The home-ownership scheme was further expanded in 1981 with the introduction of the Approved Residential Properties Scheme. This enabled CPF members to use their Ordinary Account balances to buy private residential homes. However, under the same scheme, should the purchaser sell his property before the age of 55, he must deposit the amount withdrawn plus interest back into his CPF account.

In April 1984, the Medisave scheme was introduced. According to this scheme, a CPF member could use funds from the newly created Medisave Account to help pay his or his immediate family's hospitalisation expenses. Medisave is designed to take care of one's medical expenses even after retirement.

To ensure a comfortable retirement for members, the Minimum Sum scheme was launched in 1987 (later revised in 1995). Under this scheme, a member would have to set aside a certain sum in his Retirement Account for basic retirement needs.

In 1990, Medishield, an insurance scheme, started operations. This was meant to supplement the existing Medisave scheme. Medishield, unlike Medisave, provides insurance against catastrophic illnesses.

3.2 THE CPF SYSTEM

When the CPF was conceived in 1955, it was basically a forced savings scheme to provide a degree of financial security for workers in their old age. CPF is not a PAYG (Pay-As-You-Go) scheme, which is partially-funded. In a PAYG scheme, the contributions of the present working generation are paid out to the present old-age population. In contrast, CPF is a fully-funded system in which contributions and benefits are closely linked. Upon turning 55, participants receive what they put in plus a return on their savings. There is no cross-subsidisation among account holders.

Today the CPF has evolved into a comprehensive social security system which takes care of a member's needs in retirement, healthcare, home-ownership, family protection and asset enhancement. Membership is compulsory for all employed Singaporeans and Permanent Residents except pensionable civil servants and employees who contribute to approved provident funds. In terms of coverage, contributors have comprised about 67 percent of the labour force since 1990. Currently, the total contribution rate is 40 percent of the employee's salary, with the employer and the employee contributing 20 percent each, subject to a wage limit of $6000. This formula applies to members up to the age of 55. For those between 55 to 60 years of age, the employer contributes 7.5 percent and the employee 12.5 percent. The self-employed need only contribute 5 percent of their net trade income to their Medisave account, if they earn more than $2400 a year. Unpaid family workers, contract workers and hawkers are not covered by the CPF.

The contribution of each member goes into his own account and accumulates tax-exempt interest. The interest rate is the average of the 12-month fixed deposit and the month-end savings rate of the big four local banks. The rate is revised twice yearly in January and July. Interest accrues monthly and is then credited and compounded annually. Members are guaranteed a statutory minimum interest rate of 2.5 percent. Furthermore, should a member hold funds in his Special and Retirement Account for an extended period of time, he would enjoy an additional interest of 1.25 percent. After adjusting for inflation, the real rate of return on CPF balances has generally been relatively low. In 1994, for example, the rate of return was in fact negative.

Each member's account is divided into three separate accounts: (1) the Ordinary Account, which is available for withdrawals under approved schemes (e.g. for home purchase, investment and education), (2) the Medisave Account (which can be used to pay for hospitalisation expenses and approved medical insurance) and (3) the Special Account (which is available only for old age and contingencies).

A member can withdraw his CPF savings upon turning 55. To ensure that he has a steady monthly income from the age of 60, he has to set aside a minimum sum in his Retirement Account. These savings in the Retirement Account need not be held by the CPF board. The member may deposit them instead in an approved bank or use them to buy an approved life annuity. If a member becomes permanently disabled, dies or leaves

Singapore and West Malaysia permanently, he can withdraw funds before the age of 55.

4. SOME CPF SCHEMES

4.1 *MINIMUM SUM SCHEME*

As of 1 July 1996, a CPF member has to set aside a minimum sum of $45,000 in his Retirement Account. This sum will be increased by $5000 annually until it reaches $80,000 in the year 2003. A member must hold a part of this sum in cash but he may hold the remainder in pledged property.

A member can begin receiving monthly payments from the Minimum Sum upon reaching the retirement age of 60 although this minimum age may be revised upwards later. If he leaves the sum with the CPF or approved banks, he will get a monthly income until the sum plus interest is exhausted. Alternatively, a member could use the Minimum Sum to purchase a life annuity from an approved insurance company.

Should a member use up all his Ordinary Account balances for housing, he can use his Special Account balances to satisfy the cash requirement of the Minimum Sum.

4.2 *MEDISAVE*

This scheme was introduced in 1984 to cover the hospital expenses of the CPF member and his immediate family. Medisave Account balances have to be at least $13,000 even after the withdrawal age of 55. A member who uses his Medisave balances has to reimburse Medisave for any amount that he receives from his employer or insurance company. The maximum balance in the account is currently set at $17,000—any surplus will be transferred automatically into the Ordinary Account.

4.3 *MEDISHIELD*

Medisave, which is sufficient only for basic healthcare needs, was supplemented by Medishield, a voluntary sickness insurance scheme, on 1 July 1990. Medishield helps the insured pay for his hospitalisation expenses if he is struck with "catastrophic illnesses". Co-payment is a key feature of Medishield. Medishield covers 80 percent of the hospitalisation expenses and the claimant the remaining 20 percent. From 1 July 1996, the maximum eligible age for coverage has been revised to 75 years. This means that persons up to the age of 75 can apply for Medishield insurance. However, the premiums for people in older age groups will be higher.

4.4 *PUBLIC HOUSING SCHEME*

Introduced in 1968, it enables members to use their CPF savings to purchase HDB flats. If a member purchases a flat from the HDB, he can use 100 percent of his Ordinary Account balance to pay the initial 20 percent deposit as well as the remainder of the purchase price. If a member takes up a HDB housing loan, he can use his future CPF contributions to service his monthly installment payments.

Similarly, if a member buys a resale flat in the open market, he can use up his entire Ordinary Account balance and his monthly CPF contributions to pay for the flat or to service his HDB housing loans subject to two withdrawal limits—the Valuation Limit and the Available Housing Withdrawal Limit.

5. THE ADEQUACY OF CPF AS A SOURCE OF OLD-AGE SUPPORT

We now turn to the central topic of this paper. Considering the increase in average life expectancy, which has now reached 76 years, as well as the multiplicity of schemes within the CPF, how effective is the CPF in providing for one's retirement needs?

Asher (1993) has noted that the problem of no or small balances will become acute over the next 3 to 4 decades. While CPF members are becoming asset rich, they tend to be cash poor. In particular, there is a concern about the ability of those between the ages of 45 to 55 to finance their retirement needs.

According to the 1994 CPF annual report, about 35 percent of active CPF members between the ages of 45 to 55 had balances below $60,000 (see Table 2). However, this percentage understates the potential problem since these balances include amounts withdrawn for various purposes. According to Beckerling (1996), it is estimated that 'more than 60 percent of active members may have balances below $30,000' after taking into account withdrawals for housing.

For a 45 year old who started contributing at the age of 25, the average rate of return on his CPF balances would have been a low 1.5 percent. Most of these people would also have faced low wages and low CPF contribution rates for most of their working lives. From 1955 to 1973, the average CPF contribution rate was below 30 percent. From 1974 onwards, the rate rose steadily until it reached a high of 50 percent in 1984 [see Asher (1993), p. 36-37].

Table 3 shows the distribution of active CPF members by monthly wage level and age group for 1994. We can see that 45.4 percent of members in the 46 to 50 years age group and 51.9 percent of members in the 51 to 55 years age group had monthly wages of below $1500.

In order to perform a meaningful assessment of the adequacy of CPF as a source of financial security in one's twilight years, we have to consider factors such as real wage growth rate and the rate at which CPF balances have been withdrawn for other purposes. In the next section, we report the results of simulations which take into account these factors.

5.1 SIMULATIONS

Table 4 shows the real wage growth rate for each year from 1985 to 1994. Over a period of 10 years up to 1994, the average annual real wage growth rate is about 5.2 percent. The real annual rate of return on CPF balances has averaged 2.1 percent over the same period. The third column of Table 5 shows the real rate of return on CPF balances in recent years.

The ratio of total CPF withdrawals to contributions has fluctuated over the years, as can be seen in Table 6. On average, the withdrawal rate has been about 58 percent. It should be noted that withdrawals under Section 15 of the CPF Act have been excluded as they pertain to withdrawals on the grounds of reaching the age of 55, leaving Singapore and West Malaysia permanently, physical incapacity, unsound mind or death.

The simulations are based on the following formula:

$$EBAL = IBAL(1+ROR)+(CR+CE-WD)(1+ROR)^{0.5} \qquad (1)$$

where EBAL = end of year CPF balance;

        IBAL = initial CPF balance;

ROR = real annual rate of return on CPF balances;

CR = contribution by employer, equal to 20 percent of annual remuneration;

CE = contribution by employee, equal to 20 percent of annual remuneration; and

WD = withdrawals.

Consider a 45 year old starting off with a certain amount of initial CPF balance (*IBAL*). A real rate of return (*ROR*) on these balances would yield a sum of *IBAL(1+ROR)* at the end of the year. Adding up CPF contributions by both the employer (*CR*) and the employee (*CE*) and then subtracting withdrawals (*WD*) gives us the net CPF contribution (*CR+CE-WD*). The annual real rate of return on the net contribution is also *ROR*. However, the net contribution in January would earn much more interest than the net contribution in December. Using a compounding factor of $(1+ROR)^{0.5}$ gives a very close approximation to fully adjusting for such differences. Then the end of year balance due to net contributions during the year is $(CR+CE-WD)(1+ROR)^{0.5}$. Therefore, the total CPF balance at the end of the year, *EBAL*, would be $[IBAL(1+ROR)+(CR+CE-WD)(1+ROR)^{0.5}]$. We can apply the same formula for subsequent years after adjusting for real wage growth. The initial CPF balance for the current year would be the ending balance of the previous year.

Tables 7 shows the simulation results.

5.1.1   Simulation 1 (Baseline Simulation)

As stated earlier, in recent years, the average real rate of return on CPF balances, the average real wage growth rate and the average withdrawal rate is 2.1 percent, 5.2 percent and 58 percent, respectively. Simulation 1, our baseline simulation, assumes those numbers for a 45 year old whose initial annual wage is $18,000 and initial CPF balance is $30,000. Such an individual would have a CPF balance of $85,971 when he turns 55.

5.1.2   Simulation 2

In our second simulation, we assume the initial wage to be $24,000 and withdrawal rate to be 60 percent. The CPF balance would be $98,995 at the age of 55.

5.1.3   Simulation3

The starting wage is $36,000 and the withdrawal rate 65 percent. The rest of the assumptions remain unchanged. This yields a CPF balance of $118,148 at the age of 55.

5.1.4   Simulation 4

Simulation 4 is similar to Simulation 1 except that we assume a higher real rate of return on CPF balances—2.5 percent. With a higher rate of return, we obtain a balance of $88,623 at the age of 55.

5.1.5   Simulation 5

We use a real rate of return of 2.5 percent, a wage of $36,000 and real wage growth rate of 5.2 percent. A 45 year old with an initial CPF balance of $30,000 and a withdrawal rate of 65 percent. can expect to have a CPF balance of $121,464 when he turns 55.

5.2   IMPLICATIONS OF SIMULATION RESULTS

Table 8 shows the monthly payment a person can expect to receive if he chooses to buy an immediate annuity using his CPF lump sum, assuming he retires at age 55 and lives until

75. An immediate annuity provides for payments to commence shortly after the purchase date according to an agreed upon schedule of payments. This annuity will provide the annuitant with immediate, regular income for a specified number of years. The interest rate paid on annuities will never be lower than a particular rate specified in the contract, which is usually 4 percent [see *Annuities, Mutual Funds and Life Insurance as Investment Products* (1988) p. 57]. The monthly annuity can be calculated by dividing the final CPF balance at the age of 55 by the present value interest factor for a 20 year (or 240 period) annuity, assuming 4 percent annual interest rate compounded monthly. The interest factor is found to be 165.02[7].

In Simulation 1, the monthly annuity would be about $521. This is 35 percent of the last-drawn salary of $1,500.

For Simulation 2, the annuity would be about $600 or 30 percent of the last-drawn salary of $2,000. For simulations 3, 4 and 5, the annuities would be $716, $537 and $736 respectively. These represent 24 percent, 36 percent and 25 percent of last-drawn salary respectively.

However, actuarial studies show that most people will need a monthly retirement income equal to at least 60 to 70 percent of their last-drawn salary to maintain their standard of living [see, for example, Wiatrowski (1993)]. This is only a rough rule of thumb since workers at higher income levels may require a higher percentage of their monthly salary. Nevertheless, we can see that regardless of the simulation assumptions, relying on CPF savings alone will not be enough for a comfortable retirement.

6. POLICY IMPLICATIONS AND RECOMENDATIONS

The simulation analysis suggests that a person in the 45 to 54 year age group should not rely solely on his CPF savings if he is to enjoy a comfortable retirement. The CPF board has always maintained that 'CPF was never meant to be the only source of old-age income' [see, for example, *The Straits Times* (25 September 1996)]. With the lump sum withdrawal age currently set at 55 and the life expectancy rising, a member will have to draw on his CPF savings for a longer period of time.

As our simulation results show, the majority of those aged between 45 and above would need sources of financial support other than their CPF savings when they retire. Family support would be one of them. As the majority of the aged live with their children, this form of support for the elderly must be preserved by stressing the importance of family ties and filial piety. In this connection, the passing of the Maintenance of Parents Act in November 1995 is an unfortunate but necessary piece of legislation since it provides neglected parents a legal recourse against lack of filial piety.

Wherever possible, the elderly should be encouraged to live with their children. An alternative would be to have the elderly live in smaller homes close to their children's homes. The benefits of such an arrangement is two-fold—the elderly not only gain resources by moving from larger to smaller homes but they also enjoy greater proximity to their children. This kind of arrangement already exists in Japan.

---

[7] The formula for computing the present value interest factor for an n period annuity at monthly interest rate i is given by $[1-(1+i)^{-n}]/i$. In our case $n = 240$ (or 20*12) and $i = 4/100 \div 12$.

According to Beckerling (1996), at the end of March 1995, '90 percent of HDB flats were owned rather than rented'. In 1994, purchases of public housing accounted for 50 percent of all CPF withdrawals. For many people, HDB flats are their most valuable assets. Many Singaporeans who are expected to retire in the near future tend to be cash poor but asset rich. With property prices rising in Singapore over the years, the sale of properties holds out the promise of substantial capital gains.

One of the recommendations of the Cost Review Committee Report 1996 was that the government take steps to facilitate reverse mortgages, first mooted in the Howe Report of 1984. Under a reverse mortgage scheme, home-owners can sell their homes to a bank in return for monthly payments based on the value of their homes. To facilitate reverse mortgages, administrative procedures could be streamlined and banking and housing regulations modified. Some form of indexation could help prevent the erosion of the annuity's value.

The Singapore government plays a decisive role in the market for HDB flats. At the same time, as we have seen, those properties are likely to play an increasingly important role in providing much needed retirement income for the elderly. This suggests the possibility of a policy conflict in the future. On one hand, the government seeks to provide affordable housing for all Singaporeans but on the other hand, it has an obligation to look after the elderly. Any sensible future housing policies must take this potential trade-off into account.

In response to the tight labour market, the government raised the retirement age to 60 in April 1993. This will be raised further to 67 by the year 2003. In addition, the government has attempted to move away from a seniority-wage system to a base-up wage system. It is believed that this new system would help reduce labour turnover and solve the problem of "over-priced" older workers.

For some future retirees, an alternative would be to continue working past the withdrawal age of 55. However, employers are concerned about the productivity of older workers and the cost of hiring them. One possible solution to the high cost of hiring older workers is to implement a system of flexible wages. The turnover rates are expected to be lower for older workers under such a system. Research on U.K. workers shows that older workers have lower turnover rates and are more likely to remain with the same employer [Dibden and Hibbett (1993)]. Many studies in industrial countries indicate that concerns about older workers being less productive are unfounded. Older workers can be productive in many jobs. It seems that there is a need to change the attitude of employers toward older workers. In Finland there is a nationwide campaign to promote the hiring of such workers. It encompasses research, training and public information campaigns. In the U.K., the Advisory Group on Older Workers persuades employers to tap the skills and experience which older workers can offer.

In this connection, encouraging the employment of older workers as temporary employees is a possible option. Older workers themselves are likely to prefer part-time employment for physical reasons. In developed countries, particularly the U.S. and Europe, the need for a more flexible labour force is rendering part-time employment increasingly important. We can expect a similar trend here in Singapore as the economy matures further. Thus, promoting the employment of retirees as temporary employees may not only help solve the problem of old-age financial security but also the need for a more flexible labour force.

7. CONCLUSION

As Singapore's population ages rapidly, old-age financial security is becoming an increasingly important issue. In light of this, we have investigated the adequacy of CPF as a source of old-age financial security for those in the 45 to 54 year age group. Not only will those people retire in the near future but they are also likely to have low CPF balances due to the low contribution rates and wages they faced for most of their working lives.

Although our simulation results suggest that CPF savings alone may not ensure a comfortable retirement, we should not view this in isolation since there are other possible additional sources of financial support such as reverse mortgages and other means of obtaining income from properties, family support and continued employment. In this connection, we made a number of policy recommendations.

REFERENCES

Asher, M.G., (1985): "Forced Saving to Finance Merit Goods: An Economic Analysis of the Central Provident Fund Scheme of Singapore," Centre for Research on Federal Financial Relations, Occasional Paper No. 36, Australian National University, Canberra.

Asher, M.G., (1993): *Social Security in Malaysia and Singapore: Practices, Issues and Reform Direction.* Malaysia: Institute of Strategic and International Studies.

Bauer, J., (1996): "Responses to Labour Scarcity and Ageing in Singapore," in Lim, C.Y. (ed.), *Economic Policy Management in Singapore*, Singapore: Addison-Wesley.

Beckerling, L., (1996): "Too Small a Nest Egg?" *Singapore Business*, Singapore, March, 18-22.

CPF Board (1994): *CPF Board Annual Report*, various issues.

_ (1995): *CPF Member's Handbook.*

_ (1995): *The CPF Story: 40 years serving Singapore.*

CPF Study Group (1985): *Report of the CPF Study Group*, Department of Economics and Statistics, National University of Singapore.

Dibden, Jennifer and Hibbett, Angelika, (1993): "Older Workers—an overview of recent research," Employment Gazette, Britain, June 1993.

International Social Security Review, (1994): Vol. 44, 1-2/91.

Lo, Y.L., (1995): "Managing an Ageing Workforce," SILS Information Series, No. 8, Singapore Institute of Labour Studies.

_ (1996): "Preparing for Retirement," SILS Information Series, No. 9, Singapore Institute of Labour Studies.

Republic of Singapore, Department of Statistics: *Yearbook of Statistics*, various issues.

Shantakumar, G., (1994): *The Aged Population of Singapore*, Singapore: Singapore National Printers Publishers Pte Ltd.

Singapore Press Holdings (1996): *The Straits Times*, Singapore, 11 June, 3 August, 4 September, 2 ,4 November.

Singapore Press Holdings (1996): *The Sunday Times*, Singapore, 2 June, 6 October.

The Institute of Financial Education (1988): *Annuities, Mutual Funds and Life Insurance as Investment Products.*

Tok, A., (1981/1982): "Social Security System of Singapore since 1970: Public and Private Support for the Aged," Academic Exercise, Department of Economics and Statistics, National University of Singapore.

Wiatrowski, William J., (1993): "Factors Affecting Retirement Income," Monthly Labour Review, March 1993.

TABLE 1

Resident Population Composition by Economic Status and Broad Age Group, 1970-1990

(Thousand)

Category of Population	1970	1980	1990
Total Population	2,013.6	2,282.1	2,705.1
Persons (Inactive)			
Aged < 15	787.8	630.6	626.3
Aged ≥ 60	116.1	170.4	246.9
Persons aged 15-59			
Economically Active	664.9	995.1	1,265.2
Economically Inactive	444.8	486.0	566.7

a.   Active = Working + Unemployed.

b.   Adapted from *The Aged Population of Singapore* by Dr G. Shantakumar.

TABLE 2

CPF Members by Size of Accounts (>45-55 years)

Year	<$5,000	$5,000-9,999	$10,000-59,999	>$60,000	Total
1994	6,072 (3.8%)	6,284 (4.0%)	43,447 (27.3%)	103,134 (64.9%)	158,937 (100%)

Source: Calculated from data in *CPF Annual Report 1994*, CPF Board, Singapore.

TABLE 3

Distribution of Active Members by Monthly Wage Level & Age Group, 1994

Age Group	Monthly Wage Level ($)					
	<1,500	1,500-1,999	2,000-2,499	2,500-3,999	>3,999	Total
>45-50	45,900	13,350	9,637	17,072	15,079	101,038
	(45.4%)	(13.2%)	(9.5%)	(16.9%)	(15.0%)	(100%)
>50-55	29,806	7,177	4,583	8,353	7,517	57,436
	(51.9%)	(12.5%)	(8.0%)	(14.5%)	(13.1%)	(100%)

Source: Calculated from data in *CPF Annual Report 1994*, CPF Board, Singapore.

TABLE 4

Real Wage[a] Growth Rate, 1985-1994

Year	1985	1986	1987	1988	1989	1990	1991	1992	1993	1994
Real Wage Growth Rate (%)	7.4	2.2	2.6	6.7	7.4	5.9	5.7	5.2	3.9	5.2

a. Real wages refer to average monthly earnings deflated by the consumer price index.

b. Source: *Productivity and Related Statistics for Singapore Productivity in Brief (1995)*, National Productivity Board.

TABLE 5

Real Interest Rate Paid on CPF Balances

Year	Nominal Interest Rate Paid on CPF Balances (%)	Rate of Change in CPI (%)	Real Interest Rate Paid on CPF Balances (%)
1985	6.5	0.5	6.0
1986	5.7	-1.4	7.1
1987	3.8	0.5	3.3
1988	3.1	2.4	0.7
1989	3.2	3.4	-0.2

TABLE 5 (CONT)

Real Interest Rate Paid on CPF Balances

Year	Nominal Interest Rate Paid on CPF Balances (%)	Rate of Change in CPI (%)	Real Interest Rate Paid on CPF Balances (%)
1990	3.8	3.4	0.4
1991	4.7	2.3	2.4
1992	4.0	2.3	1.7
1993	2.5	2.3	0.2
1994	2.5	3.1	-0.6

Source: *CPF Annual Report*, CPF Board, Singapore, various issues.
Yearbook of Statistics, Department of Statistics, Singapore, various issues.

TABLE 6

CPF Contributions and Withdrawals, 1985-1994

Year	Amount Contributed ($)	Amount Withdrawn[a] ($)	Withdrawals as Percentage of Amount Contributed
1985	5,993,413	2,658,927	44.4
1986	4,777,837	2,946,880	61.7
1987	4,446,800	3,549,923	79.8
1988	4,985,091	3,225,912	64.7
1989	6,107,529	2,822,262	46.2
1990	7,174,210	2,973,687	41.4
1991	8,101,376	3,697,951	45.6
1992	9,028,203	4,398,027	48.7
1993	10,427,035	9,756,907[b]	93.6
1994	11,278,556	5,919,111	52.5

a. Excludes Section 15 of the CPF Act.
b. Amounts withdrawn in 1993 increased largely because of Singapore Telecom Shares offer.
c. Source: Calculated from data in *CPF Annual Report*, CPF Board, Singapore, various issues.

TABLE 7

Simulation Results

	Simulation 1	Simulation 2	Simulation 3	Simulation 4	Simulation 5
Initial CPF Balance	$30,000	$30,000	$30,000	$30,000	$30,000
Initial Wage	$18,000	$24,000	$36,000	$18,000	$36,000
Real Wage Growth Rate	5.2%	5.2%	5.2%	5.2%	5.2%
CPF Real Rate of Return	2.1%	2.1%	2.1%	2.5%	2.5%
Withdraw Rate	58%	60%	65%	58%	65%
Final CPF Balance at Age 55	$85,971	$98,995	$118,148	$88,623	$121,464

TABLE 8

Expected Monthly Annuity

Simulation	Last-drawn Salary ($)	Monthly Annuity ($)	Monthly Annuity as Proportion of Last-drawn Salary
1	1,500	521	35 %
2	2,000	600	30%
3	3,000	716	24%
4	1,500	537	36%
5	3,000	736	25%

PART II

SINGAPOREAN MACROECONOMIC ISSUES

Effects of Inward Foreign Direct Investment on the Singapore Economy

***Chan** Boon How*
&
*Shahidur **Rahman***

Nanyang Business School, Nanyang Technological University, Nanyang Avenue, Singapore 639798
Fax: +(65) 792.4217, Tel: +(65) 799.6404, Email: asrahman@ntu.edu.sg

Abstract   Inward Foreign direct investment (FDI) has been important for Singapore's economic growth. Since independence in 1965, Singapore has been able to induce foreign multi-national corporations (MNCs) to set up their bases in Singapore. We analyse the impact of FDI on Singapore's economy using four main economic variables: gross domestic product, exports, imports and domestic investment. Our analysis shows that the effects of FDI on these four variables are significant.

1. INTRODUCTION

Singapore has transformed from an economy dependent on entrepot trade in the 1960s to the present one with a dynamic manufacturing sector as well as a sophisticated services sector involving finance, business, tourism, telecommunication and consultancy services. Though Singapore lacks resource endowment and is vulnerable to exogenous shocks, she has managed to turn adversities into opportunities and to foresee weaknesses and threats beforehand to forge corrective or compensating strategies.

Singapore has been one of the most dynamic and robust economies in the world with a high real growth rate and low inflation.   An outward-looking policy and reliance on foreign direct investment for industrialisation has played a great role in shaping the Singapore economy.

In the early sixties and seventies, Singapore has adopted a free enterprise, open-door policy to attract foreign investors from all types of industries such as garments, textiles, toys, wood products and electronics. This was the only route to fast industrialisation through tapping both the MNCs' capital and expertise and to solve the immediate mass unemployment problem. After the 1985-1986 recession, there was continuing expansion of the world economy, notably United States.   Vigorous growth was seen throughout East Asia too.   Singapore continue to seek enhancement in its industrial and technological base through greater focus on research and development in niche areas. The foreign investment promotion was directed at high value added industries, high technology industries as well as the financial and services sector. To date, this has continued to be pursued.

Hence, FDI seems to be a very important determinant of Singapore economy. This has prompted us to embark on this project to give an insight on the effects of FDI on gross domestic product (GDP), exports, imports and domestic investment, i.e. how and to what extent FDI has helped to propel Singapore's economy.

The objectives of this project are to specify theoretical models of how FDI affects the various economic variables and to provide an empirical analysis of the models using Singapore data sets.

The structure of this paper is as follows. Section two summarises the trends of FDI in Singapore and the policies the government undertook to attract FDI. Previous studies on the subject of FDI is presented in section three. Section four provides the specification of the models and their variables. Section five gives an analysis of the empirical results of the models. Finally, section six concludes with a summary, policy implications and limitations of the studies.

2. TRENDS OF FDI IN SINGAPORE

FDI is said to occur when an investor in a foreign country retains at least partial ownership and substantial control over an investment[1]. Currently, the foreign investment stands at nearly S$86 billion by the end of 1994, up S$12.6 billion or 17 percent from 1993[2].

FDI has played a crucial role through the years in accelerating the economic development in Singapore. Being a small country with no natural resources, Singapore had depended on leading international companies not only in bringing in capital funds to broaden her economic base, but also in upgrading the technology and skill content of her industries.

The importance of FDI can be seen in Table 1 as the increase in the number of foreign-controlled companies from 7,417 in 1988 to 11,243 in 1993. The number of such companies is the highest in the commerce industry. Both the commerce and transportation and storage industries exhibit an increasing trend. The number of foreign-controlled companies is set to increase further.

The importance of FDI can be further seen in Table 2. The table shows that the United States is the top host economy for FDI with US$477.5 billion while Singapore is ranked eleventh with US$40.8 billion. However, the leading FDI host economy in per capita terms is Singapore with US$13,650 while the United States is ranked thirteenth.

Figure 1 shows the stock of FDI in Singapore by country. The number one foreign investor in Singapore is Japan, followed by the United States and United Kingdom as at 1993. From the period 1971 to 1982, the United Kingdom is the top foreign investor in Singapore, while the United States is second and Hong Kong is third. However, from 1983 to 1989, the United States has become the top foreign investor. Since 1989, Japan has been the top foreign investor in Singapore, followed by the United States and the United Kingdom.

Referring to the graph of stock of FDI by sectors as shown by Figure 2, the total FDI received by Singapore has been increasing over the years. The two sectors that has received the majority of the FDI is the manufacturing sector and the financial/business services sector. Traditionally, from 1971 to 1989, the majority of the FDI has been in the manufacturing. However, there seems to be a switch of FDI into financial/business services sector from 1990 onwards. This could be due to the government policy in

---

[1] Hall, C. P. and Ronald MacDonald (1994), *International Money and Finance*, Blackwell p. 316.

[2] *The Straits Times*, (21 December 1996), p. 46.

promoting Singapore to be the international financial centre. Furthermore, with such an increment of FDI into this sector, it can help to cushion the economy from any cyclical downturn in the manufacturing sector. This could be seen in the drop of economic growth to 6.5 percent in 1996 due to the cyclical electronics sector downturn as the electronics sector is the backbone of the manufacturing sector.

FDI is attracted to Singapore mainly due to Singapore favourable investment climate and strategic geographical location. Some other reasons include political and social stability, good infrastructure, and a foreign investment policy that is liberal, comprehensive and well co-ordinated.

With a population of just about three million, the government has adopted the following measures to alleviate manpower shortages: immigration restrictions were relaxed, women were encouraged to enter the workforce in a bid to boost the female labour force participation rate, accelerated education and industrial training programmes were initiated and corporate industrial training received financial support.

The government liberal attitude on tax incentives also plays a significant role in attracting FDI into Singapore. A range of tax incentives which was first introduced in 1959 has played key role in promoting new investments in both the industrial and services sector. It has also encouraged existing companies to further upgrade through either mechanisation and automation or through the introduction of new products and services. The corporate income tax has been reduced from 27 to 26 percent, with effect from Year of Assessment 1997. This will help to maintain Singapore attractiveness to foreign investors. Other added assistance revealed in Budget 1996[3] includes the development and expansion incentive for firms investing in high-tech projects and major upgrading, tax deduction for general provisions of finance companies, trimming of the withholding tax rate from 27 to 15 percent, investment allowance incentive for water recycling plants, and tax concessions for pollution control and energy conservation.

3. PREVIOUS RESEARCH

This section of the paper gives a brief review of past literature done on FDI in this economic region of Asia and Singapore. In particular, we will review the analysis taken by Lim, *et. al* (1988), Fry (1993) and SEACEN C (1995).

On the role of FDI in Singapore economy, Lim, *et. al* (1988) explains the reasons why Singapore is so dependent on FDI and why the domestic entrepreneurs failed to emerge in significant numbers. The paper also discusses whether Singapore can continue to attract FDI and whether local enterprises can play a larger role in the future. The analysis has revealed that Singapore is very dependent on the FDI. The active investment promotion efforts of the government has been successful in attracting FDI. The FDI has increased and improved the quality of Singapore's entrepreneurial, managerial, marketing, technological and manpower resources. FDI has contributed considerably a higher economic growth and higher exports. The analysis also points out that continuing large inflows of FDI may not be fully absorbed by the economy due to the scarcity of land and shortage of labour. This may lead to crowding out of domestic entrepreneurs. A reduction

---

[3] *The Straits Times Budget 1996 Special*, (29 February 1996), p. VI-VII.

in reliance on FDI is only possible if more domestic entrepreneurs emerged and invest outward to overcome the limitations of a small domestic market.

Fry (1993) analysed FDI in a macro-economic setting in order to shed new light on the various channels through which FDI can have an influence on the economy. In the case of Southeast Asian countries, FDI raises domestic investment by the full extent. According to him, FDI has not crowded out domestic investment, rather increasing domestic investment to raise the growth rate. On exports FDI has a positive but insignificant impact. An inflow of FDI is closely associated with a higher import ratio. This implies that FDI is used to finance a larger import bill. Finally, in the absence of financial repression and trade distortion FDI has a favourable impact on the rate of economic growth.

In another study by the SEACEN C (1995), it shows the trends and patterns of capital inflow in the SEACEN countries: Indonesia, Korea, Malaysia, Nepal, Philippines, Singapore, Sri Lanka, Taipei and Thailand. The study reviews major policy implementation and measure empirically the impact of foreign capital on growth and savings. The study also shows that the empirical tests are more significant in countries which have macro-economic stability and a good track record of economic growth.

In our paper we will extend Lim, *et. al* (1988) study by doing an empirical analysis on the effects of FDI on Singapore's economy for the period 1971 to 1993. In addition, our paper will concentrate solely on Singapore, a slight departure from Fry (1993) study which focus on Southeast Asian countries as a whole. As a supplement to SEACEN C (1995) study , we will consider three more economic variables: exports, imports and domestic investment.

4. THE MODELS

The models that will be discussed below is based on the model presented by Fry (1993). The specification of the four models used transformed variables, keeping non-stationarity, heteroscedasticity and autocorrelated problems in mind. All the models will be estimated using secondary data from various issues of *Yearbook of Statistics* Singapore, *International Financial Statistics*, *Economic Survey of Singapore* and the *World Investment Directory*. All variables are in real terms.

4.1   THE MODEL OF FDI EFFECT ON GDP

Singapore is a small country lacking in natural resources. Her technological ability is somehow limited, FDI is one way that Singapore can tap foreign technology. Therefore a substantial amount of capital is required to help generate GDP. Hence FDI is a determinant of GDP. Exports has an impact on the GDP and this is expected to be positive. Imports will thus have a negative impact on GDP. Furthermore, exchange rate will also play a role in determining GDP. Here the exchange rate is defined as the amount of Singapore dollar per United States dollar. A slow appreciation of the currency will increase the confidence of those who are investing in Singapore and helps to attract more investment. The Singapore dollar appreciation will also curb imported inflation. Domestic investment will also have a positive effect on GDP, as an increase in domestic investment will help to generate more output. The model for GDP using the FDI effect can be specified as follows:

$$DLGY_t = \alpha_0 + \alpha_1 DLGFDI_t + \alpha_2 DLGEX_t + \alpha_3 DLGIM_t + \alpha_4 DLGER_t +$$
$$\alpha_5 DLGDI_t + e_t \tag{1}$$

where

Y	=	GDP;
FDI	=	foreign direct investment;
EX	=	total exports;
IM	=	total imports;
ER	=	exchange rate;
DI	=	domestic investment;
DLG	=	first-order difference of logarithms;
α_i	=	parameters of the model;
e_t	=	the disturbance term assuming normally distributed with zero mean and constant variance.

4.2   THE MODEL OF FDI EFFECT ON EXPORTS

FDI usually has a positive impact on exports. This means that when there is an increase in FDI, in general, we can expect exports to increase as well. FDI contributes to the expansion of exports since most FDI is concentrated on the production of exports. The previous year imports could also play a part in determining exports. The impact of imports on exports is expected to be positive. The exchange rate may be a determinant of exports. The coefficient of the exchange rate is expected to be positive, as an increase indicates a real depreciation of the Singapore dollar making exports cheaper to foreigners. Thus the export model using the FDI effects takes the following form:

$$LGEX_t = \beta_0 + \beta_1 LGFDI_t + \beta_2 LGIM_{t-1} + \beta_3 DLGER_t + u_t \tag{2}$$

where

LGEX	=	logarithms of total exports;
LGFDI	=	logarithms of foreign direct investment;
LGIM	=	logarithms of total imports;
DLGER	=	first-order difference of logarithms of exchange rate;
β_i	=	parameters of the model;
u_t	=	the disturbance term assuming normally distributed with zero mean and constant variance.

4.3   THE MODEL OF FDI EFFECT ON IMPORTS

FDI has a positive impact on imports. When there are FDI inflows, it reflects the ability to import raw materials, machinery and capital equipment. Hence, the imports is explained by the FDI and the exchange rate. The coefficient of the exchange rate should be opposite to that under the section 4.2. An increase in domestic investment may increase the amount of imports. Hence, the imports model is given by:

$$DLGIM_t = \gamma_0 + \gamma_1 DLGFDI_t + \gamma_2 LGER_t + \gamma_3 DLGDI_t + \nu_t \qquad (3)$$

where

IM	=	total imports;
FDI	=	foreign direct investment;
ER	=	exchange rate;
DI	=	domestic investment;
DLG	=	first-order difference of logarithms;
LG	=	logarithms;
γ_i	=	parameters of the model;
ν_t	=	the disturbance term assuming normally distributed with zero mean and constant variance.

4.4   THE MODEL OF FDI EFFECT ON DOMESTIC INVESTMENT

The effect of FDI on domestic investment will depend on the economic climate and the structure of the host country involved. The domestic investment is a measure of capital formation. The relationship between FDI and domestic investment is the focus of this equation. In certain countries, domestic investment may be crowded out by FDI.

GDP is one of the factors that has a positive impact on domestic investment, since an increase in GDP will increase domestic investment. The domestic investment model using the FDI effects can be given by:

$$LGDI_t = \varphi_0 + \varphi_1 LGFDI_t + \varphi_2 LGDI_{t-1} + \varphi_3 LGY_t + \varepsilon_t \qquad (4)$$

where

LGDI	=	logarithms of domestic investment;
LGFDI	=	logarithms of foreign direct investment;
LGY	=	logarithms of GDP;
φ_i	=	parameters of the model;
ε_t	=	the disturbance term assuming normally distributed with zero mean and constant variance.

5. EMPIRICAL RESULTS AND ANALYSIS

All equations are estimated using Ordinary Least Squares (OLS) method. For all the models, the Durbin-Watson, Phillips Perron and Augmented Dickey Fuller test statistics show that there are stationarity in the residuals. The estimated empirical results are shown in Table 3.

5.1   GDP MODEL

From the results given in Table 3, the variable FDI is significant with a coefficient of 0.19, which means 100 point increase in the FDI will result in 19 point increase in the GDP.

Exports has a positive relationship with GDP as expected earlier, but it is insignificant with a coefficient of 0.08. Imports is also insignificant with a negative coefficient of 0.12. Exchange rate is insignificant with a negative coefficient of 0.09 implying that a 100 point increase in exchange rate (depreciation) will have a 9 point decrease in the GDP. Lastly, the domestic investment is significant with a coefficient of 0.23. This indicates that a 100 point increase in domestic investment will have a 23 point increase in the GDP.

5.2   EXPORTS MODEL

FDI does have a positive impact on total exports. Every 100 percent increase in FDI will result in 40 percent increase in the total exports.

The previous year imports is positively linked to exports. This suggests a 'spillover' effect of last year imports on the present year exports. This may be due to imports of raw materials and semi-processed goods used in the production of exports. The results show that 100 percent increase in previous year imports has a 55 percent increase in current year exports.

The coefficient of the exchange rate is positive as expected. An increase in the exchange rate (depreciation) will lead to an increase in total exports due to cheaper exports. However, the exchange rate does not seem to play a significant role in determining exports.

5.3   IMPORTS MODEL

FDI has a role to play in imports. From the results, it can be seen that a 100 point increase in FDI will cause the imports to increase by 59 point, which is a substantial amount. This could be due to the import of raw materials by the MNCs for manufacturing products as FDI has been quite dominant in the economy.

The exchange rate has a negative coefficient as expected. However, the variable is found to be insignificant. This could be due to the lack of natural resources in Singapore. Since Singapore is not self-sufficient, the exchange rate may play an insignificant role towards imports.

The sign for domestic investment to imports is also positive as expected. From the results, a 100 point increase in the domestic investment result in an increase of imports by 50 point. This is because domestic investment needs to import raw materials for manufacturing output.

5.4   DOMESTIC INVESTMENT MODEL

FDI crowds out domestic investment as indicated by a negative coefficient of 0.45, implying that a 100 percent increase in FDI will cause the domestic investment to decrease by 45 percent. This is in line with the findings of Lim (1988) that FDI has a negative impact on domestic investment in Singapore. This explains why Singapore lacks domestic entrepreneurs.

The lagged domestic investment is significant with a coefficient of 0.66. The coefficient of the previous period domestic investment indicates that the adjustment to changes in the domestic investment is relatively slow and the variable domestic investment is heavily dependent on previous year domestic investment. Lastly, the GDP has a positive impact on domestic investment. An 1 point increase in the GDP will cause 1.08 point increase in domestic investment.

6. CONCLUSION

The empirical results presented in Section 5 has shown that FDI favourably affects the economic growth. With the government continuing their efforts to attract FDI, Singapore should be able to sustain her economic growth for the next few years.

FDI affects the economic growth of Singapore through foreign trade. FDI has a positive effect on exports and imports. Most of the foreign invested firms are export-oriented and have used Singapore as a regional hub to export to this Asia-Pacific region. Although Singapore is a high wage nation and the cost of doing business here is high when compared to the neighbouring countries, the foreign firms still invest in Singapore. This could be due to our political stability, reliable and efficient governmental set-up, geographical location advantage, skilled and productive workforce as well as our high level of technology. In order to achieve a higher rate of economic growth, the government can introduce more incentives to the export-oriented companies.

The foreign invested firms have brought in their technology, managerial skills and capital. This has helped our domestic entrepreneurs to move up the ladder to become more competitive and efficient entrepreneurs. However, FDI crowds out domestic investment for the case of Singapore. There still seems to be a shortage of local MNCs due to over-reliance on foreign MNCs. Therefore there is still a need for more incentives and policies to be drawn up to encourage domestic investment, in order to reduce the reliance on foreign direct investment. This is precisely what the government is doing as revealed in the Budget 1996. In this way, the government can help our local entrepreneurs move into the international arena and this will be beneficial to Singapore.

Hence, to conclude, the impact of FDI on Singapore economy is beneficial. In general, Singapore has been quite successful in attracting FDI to promote economic growth and foreign trade.

Referring to Figure 2 again, we can see that there is a majority of FDI in the manufacturing sector and the financial/business sector. The limitation here is if there is any change in sectoral compositions of the FDI, there could be some effects on the regression results.

As the current paper takes the form of single equation linear regression model, future research can be done by using a system of simultaneous equations. Thus more consistent estimates will be obtained after eliminating the possibility of simultaneity bias. Further research can also be carried out in the area of analysing the effect of FDI on the various sectors, and the different effects of any change in the sectoral composition of the FDI on the Singapore's economy.

REFERENCES

Asian and Pacific Development Centre (1987): *Business and Investment Environment in Singapore*, South Pacific Bureau for Economic Co-operation.

Department of Statistics Singapore (1980-1995): *Yearbook of Statistics*, Singapore National Printers Ltd.

Department of Statistics Singapore (1984): *Economic Survey of Singapore*, First Quarter, Singapore National Printers Ltd.

Fry, M. J., (1993): *Foreign Direct Investment in Southeast Asia: Differential Impact*, Institute of South East Asia Studies Singapore.

Grosse, R. and Trevino, L. J., (1996): "Foreign Direct Investment in the U.S.: An Analysis by Country of Origin", *Journal of International Business Studies*, First Quarter 1996, 139-155.

Lansbury M., Pain N. and Smidkova K., (1996): "Foreign Direct Investment in Central Europe Since 1990: An Econometric Study", *National Institute Economic Review*, May 1996, 104-114.

Lim, C. Y. and Associates, (1988): *Policy Options for the Singapore Economy*: McGraw Hill.

Pfaffermayr, M., (1994): "Foreign Direct Investment and Exports: A Time Series Approach", *Applied Economics*, 26, 337-351.

Ramesh, C. C., (1994): *Foreign Investment and Technology Transfer in Developing Countries*, England: Avebury.

Singapore Press Holdings (1996): *The Straits Times Budget Special*, Singapore, 29 February.

Singapore Press Holdings (1996): *The Straits Times*, Singapore, 17 October, 21 December.

South East Asian Central Banks (SEACEN) (1995): *International Capital Movements in the SEACEN Countries*, Kuala Lumpur, Malaysia.

TABLE 1

Foreign-controlled Companies by Industry

	1988	1989	1990	1991	1992	1993
Agriculture & Fishing	7	8	8	5	9	5
Mining & Quarrying	6	5	8	10	30	4
Manufacturing	1014	1059	1180	1328	1170	1323
Construction	303	322	185	188	215	435
Commerce	3113	3249	3650	3835	4553	5043
Transportation & Storage	566	625	797	644	827	889
Financial/Business Services	2312	2539	2775	2649	3447	3400
Social & Personal Services	96	107	83	120	167	144
Total	7417	7914	8686	8779	10418	11243

Source: *Yearbook of Statistics* 1995, Singapore.

TABLE 2

Leading Host Economies for Foreign Direct Investment
(based on cumulative inflows, 1985-1995)

Rank	Country	FDI (US$ billion)	Rank	Country	FDI per capita (US$)
1	US	477.5	1	Singapore	13650
2	Britain	199.6	2	Belgium-Luxembourg	6900
3	France	138.0	3	Netherlands	4410
4	China	130.2	4	Sweden	4270
5	Spain	90.9	5	Switzerland	3580
6	Belgium-Luxembourg	72.4	6	Australia	3470
7	Netherlands	68.1	7	Britain	3410
8	Australia	62.6	8	Denmark	3000
9	Canada	60.9	9	Hong Kong	2890
10	Mexico	44.1	10	France	2380
11	Singapore	40.8	11	Spain	2320
12	Sweden	37.7	12	Canada	2060
13	Italy	36.3	13	US	1820
14	Malaysia	30.7	14	Malaysia	1520
15	Germany	25.9	15	Argentina	680
16	Switzerland	25.2	16	Italy	630
17	Argentina	23.5	17	Mexico	470
18	Brazil	20.3	18	Germany	320
19	Hong Kong	17.9	19	Brazil	130
20	Denmark	15.7	20	China	110

Source: *The Straits Times*, 17 October 1996, p. 54.

TABLE 3

Estimates for the Four Equations

GDP		Exports	
Independent Variable	**Estimates**	**Independent Variable**	**Estimates**
Intercept	0.0376*	Intercept	0.8175
	(3.3183)		(0.8205)
FDI	0.1891*	FDI	0.3999*
	(2.1152)		(2.4574)
Exports	0.0801	Imports Lagged	0.5458*
	(0.7308)		(2.3625)
Imports	-0.1227	Exchange Rate	0.0515
	(-0.9624)		(0.1186)
Exchange Rate	-0.0917		
	(-1.2905)		
Domestic Investment	0.2261*		
	(3.7101)		
R-squared	0.6478	R-squared	0.9675
R-squared adjusted	0.5378	R-squared adjusted	0.9621
D-W statistics	1.8949	D-W statistics	1.2701
PP test statistics	-4.2590**	PP test statistics	-3.5460**
ADF test statistics	-3.6686**	ADF test statistics	-3.1862**

TABLE 3 (CONT)

Estimates for the Four Equations

Imports		Domestic Investment	
Independent Variable	**Estimates**	**Independent Variable**	**Estimates**
Intercept	0.1200	Intercept	-3.5276*
	(1.0103)		(-2.0054)
FDI	0.5933*	FDI	-0.4518*
	(1.8438)		(-2.0963)
Exchange Rate	-0.2585	Domestic Investment Lagged	0.6556*
	(-1.2928)		(4.8380)
Domestic Investment	0.4957*	GDP	1.0795*
	(2.4725)		(2.9174)
R-squared	0.4479	R-squared	0.9718
R-squared adjusted	0.3558	R-squared adjusted	0.9671
D-W statistics	1.5612	D-W statistics	1.6819
PP test statistics	-3.7994**	PP test statistics	-3.8515**
ADF test statistics	-3.2853**	ADF test statistics	-2.1865**

a.   t-statistics are given in parentheses.

b.   * Significant variables at the 10 percent level.

c.   **Rejection of the null hypothesis of non-stationarity at the 10 percent level.

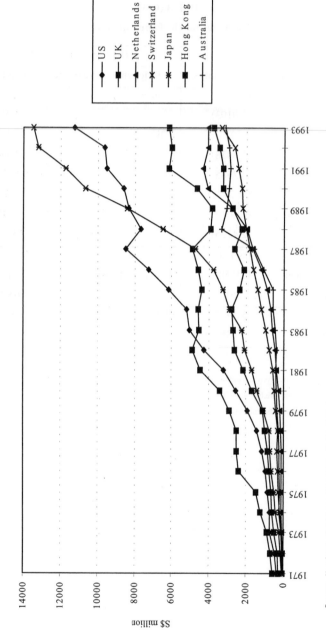

FIGURE 1

Stock of Foreign Direct Investment by Country

Source: *Yearbook of Statistics* Singapore, Various Issues.
        Economic Survey of Singapore, First Quarter 1984.

FIGURE 2

Stock of Foreign Direct Investment by Sector

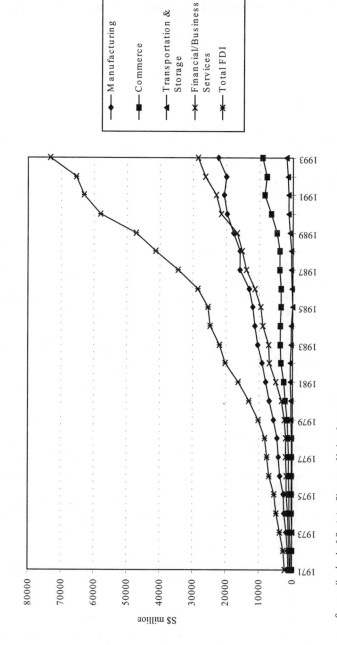

Source: *Yearbook of Statistics* Singapore, Various Issues.
Economic Survey of Singapore, First Quarter 1984.

Singapore's Industrial Restructuring and Evolution

Cao Yong
&
Foo *Sey Yuen*

Nanyang Business School, Nanyang Technological University, Nanyang Avenue, Singapore 639798
Fax: +(65) 792.4217, Tel: +(65) 799.1322, Email: aycao@ntu.edu.sg

Abstract Singapore's manufacturing sector experienced negligible total factor productivity growth in the 1970s and early 1980s. This paper first looks into the factors that account for the TFP growth of the domestic manufacturing sector between 1980 and 1994; in particular the policy effects of the 1979 industrial restructuring program. We find evidence that Singapore's manufacturing sector fits Alwyn Young's model of 'invention and bounded learning by doing'. In addition, the manufacturing industries are further categorised into different capital intensity groups. We then perform a cross-sectional analysis to look into the differences in their performances.

1. INTRODUCTION

Owing to its smallness and openness, Singapore's manufacturing sector constantly faces challenges, both internal and external. Given her high degree of export content[1] (61.5% in 1994), maintaining her international export competitiveness is crucial. This is done primarily through capital deepening and remaining technologically on par with her major competitors.

Since the beginning of the 1970s, Singapore has begun to enjoy full employment. However during the early period of industrialisation, most industries were still labour-intensive in nature despite the growing pressures of rising labour costs. To prevent an overheated economy and to retain competitiveness, the National Wages Council (NWC) recommended moderate wage increases between 1972 and 1978.

In 1979, with a view to enhance long term competitiveness, the 'industrial restructuring program' was enacted to upgrade the domestic industrial structure. Under this scheme, the Economic Development Board (EDB) handed out generous fiscal and financial incentives to manufacturers who embarked on automation plans and capital investments. Another facet of this program is the 'three-year wage correction' policy. This, coupled with the tight labour market, resulted in real unit labour costs[2] in the manufacturing sector rising at an average of 13.4% per annum between the period 1980 to 1985. As labour costs constituted a major portion of overall business operating costs, manufacturers were thus induced to substitute capital for labour. The consequence was that capital inputs grew at a phenomenal rate of 8.9% per annum during the same period.

The objective of this paper is to look into the factors that account for TFP changes in Singapore's manufacturing sector between 1980 and 1994. In particular, we look at the

---

[1] Export content is total direct exports divided by total output of the manufacturing sector.

[2] Real unit labour cost is remuneration divided by number of workers, where remuneration include wages, CPF contributions, allowances, etc.; all figures are deflated using CPI deflators (base year 1985).

impacts of the 1979 industrial restructuring program, which had a major impact on subsequent growths in labour productivity, unit labour cost, capital input, R&D expenditures and exports. In addition, the industries are further categorised into different capital-intensity groups. We aim to study the causes of the differences in their performances.

The next section provides an overview of the main sources of growth in the Singapore manufacturing sector between 1980 and 1994. This is followed by a description of the research methodology in section 3. We then present the empirical findings and analysis of those findings in section 4. Last but not least, we provide some policy recommendations in section 5 before concluding.

2. AN OVERVIEW OF THE MAIN SOURCES OF GROWTH, 1980-1994

The growth of an economy is governed primarily by the growths of capital input, labour input and total factor productivity (TFP). TFP growth refers to the growth of output less the growth of a composite of all factor inputs. In this respect, it reflects the efficiency with which an economy's productive inputs are jointly put to use.

The notion that TFP growth is especially important to Singapore's economic growth cannot be overstated. With a trend decline in the growth of labour input, the only impetus left are capital and TFP growth. But as Wong and Gan (1994) pointed out, a rise in capital input without a commensurate rise in labour input is unsustainable. The outcome is a decline in marginal productivity of capital, and hence the rate of return.

In his model of 'invention and bounded learning by doing', Alwyn Young (1991a)[3] propounded the existence of a linkage between the productivity of new technologies and a society's learning maturity. Earlier studies[4] have shown that newly developed technologies usually do not attain their full productive potential in the beginning. In fact, it is experience accumulated through the utilisation of such new techniques at the factory floor that results in gradual productivity gains. In other words, only close interaction between research and development (R&D) in the laboratory, and technical experience gained at the factory floor will allow for significant productivity growth to take place.

Young (1992) reported that Singapore's growth in the 1970s and 1980s was mainly attributable to the accumulation of factors (especially that of capital), while the contribution of TFP growth was negligible. He believed this phenomenon was due to the lack of indigenous R&D activities, which meant there was little scope for improvements in home technologies. Using the technological frontier analogy, our manufacturing sector is gradually moving towards the boundary; however the frontier itself does not move much.

Nevertheless, starting from the late 1980s, there seems to be an improvement in TFP growth. Using conventional growth accounting techniques, Rao and Lee (1995)[5] estimated

---

[3] See ----.(1991a). Invention and Bounded Learning by Doing. NBER Working Paper No. 3712.

[4] Examples are Head's (1991) empirical study on productivity growth in the U.S. steel rail industry, and Mak and Watson's (1972) research on the introduction of steamboats to Western inland rivers.

[5] This paper was presented at the 20th Federation of ASEAN Economic Associations Conference, December 7-8, 1995.

the TFP growth of the manufacturing sector (1987-94) to be as high as 32 percent. If this were true, it would be useful to find out the causes of the improvement.

3. RESEARCH METHODOLOGY

At this juncture, it should be noted that the crux of this paper does not lie in TFP measurement, but in accounting for the factors that influence TFP growth. Hence, there are essentially two methodologies in this section: The first deals with TFP measurement. This subsequently provides the framework for our analysis on the determinants of TFP growth under the second methodology.

3.1 MEASURING TOTAL FACTOR PRODUCTIVITY GROWTH

Basically, there are two general approaches to computing TFP growth. One is the parametric form used by Kim and Lau (1994) which involves flexible parametric specification of a meta-production function. The advantage of this is its flexibility, or absence of any a priori restrictions on the production technology. The second method is the non-parametric form (also known as the index number approach) that has been used before by Tsao (1982) and Young (1992). We choose the latter approach because it is more widely accepted and used by academics, hence allowing us to compare results.

As we all know, different approaches to measuring TFP growth yield different results. Nonetheless, the estimated pattern of TFP growth remains largely similar under either method. And, what we are using in section 3.2 is the pattern of TFP growth and not TFP growth itself.

3.1.1 The Translog Index of Total Factor Productivity

Our framework is based on the neo-classical model formulated by Solow (1956)[6]. It has also previously been used by Gollop and Jorgenson (1980), as well as Young (1994). Consider the following translogarithmic value added production function :

$$Q = \exp\left[\alpha_0 + \alpha_K \ln K + \alpha_L \ln L + \alpha_t t + \frac{1}{2}\alpha_{KK}(\ln K)^2 + \alpha_{KL}(\ln K)(\ln L) + \alpha_{Kt}\ln K \cdot t + \right.$$
$$\left. \frac{1}{2}\alpha_{LL}(\ln L)^2 + \alpha_{Lt}\ln L \cdot t + \frac{1}{2}\alpha_{tt}t^2\right] \tag{1}$$

The assumption of constant returns to scale imply that the parameters satisfy the following:

$$\alpha_K + \alpha_L = 1 \tag{2}$$

$$\alpha_{KK} + \alpha_{KL} = \alpha_{LL} + \alpha_{KL} = \alpha_{Kt} + \alpha_{Lt} = 0 \tag{3}$$

Further assuming that the aggregate labour and capital inputs are subject to constant returns to scale, the translog indices of subinputs are:

$$K = \exp\left[\beta_1 \ln K_1 + \beta_2 \ln K_2 + \ldots + \beta_n \ln K_n + \frac{1}{2}\Phi_{11}(\ln K_1)^2 + \Phi_{12}(\ln K_1)(\ln K_2) + \ldots + \right.$$
$$\left. \frac{1}{2}\Phi_{nn}(\ln K_n)^2\right] \tag{4}$$

---

[6] Solow, R.M. (1956). A Contribution to the Theory of Economic Growth, Quarterly Journal of Economics 70, pp.65-94

$$L = \exp [\chi_1 \ln L_1 + \chi_2 \ln L_2 + \ldots + \chi_n \ln L_n + \frac{1}{2} \Gamma_{11} (\ln L_1)^2 + \Gamma_{12} (\ln L_1)(\ln L_2) + \ldots +$$

$$\frac{1}{2} \Gamma_{nn}(\ln L_n)^2] \qquad (5)$$

First differencing the above functions yields:

$$\ln \frac{Q(t)}{Q(t-1)} = \varphi_K \ln \frac{K(t)}{K(t-1)} + \varphi_L \ln \frac{L(t)}{L(t-1)} + TFP_{t,t-1} \qquad (6)$$

where

$$\ln \frac{K(t)}{K(t-1)} = \sum \theta_{Ki} \ln \frac{k(t)}{k(t-1)} \qquad (7)$$

$$\ln \frac{L(t)}{L(t-1)} = \sum \theta_{Lj} \ln \frac{l(t)}{l(t-1)} \qquad (8)$$

φ_i's represent the share of each aggregate factor in total factor payments and θ_i's the share of each subfactor in payments to the aggregate factor. They are the indices of the aggregate input constructed on the basis of the 'Tornqvist index'. The latter is the discrete approximation of the continuous 'Divisia index'. The primary advantage of this method is that it takes into account quality changes in factors of production over time.

The last term on the right-hand side of equation 6, $TFP_{t,t-1}$, is the translog index of TFP growth, which is also known as the 'Solow Residual'. It measures the amount by which the log of output would have increased had all inputs remained constant between the two time periods. The economic intuition is that output can be increased either by utilizing more inputs, or by combining existing quantities of inputs more efficiently. Typically, TFP growth is represented by an upward movement of isoquants for any fixed amount of input combination.

3.2 ACCOUNTING FOR FACTORS INFLUENCING TFP - USING THE FOUR-TIER SYSTEM

A system of four equations is constructed. The purpose is to analyse the effects of growth in capital, unit labour cost, direct exports, labour productivity and R&D expenditures on TFP growth. Besides, we can also infer from the system the inter-relationships among the various variables.

$$TFP_t = \beta_1 + \beta_2 LAB_t + \beta_3 ULC_t + \beta_4 CAP_t + \beta_5 EXP_t + \beta_6 R\&D_{t-1} \qquad (9)$$

$$LAB_t = \beta_7 + \beta_8 CAP_t + \beta_9 EXP_t + \beta_{10} R\&D_{t-1} \qquad (10)$$

$$CAP_t = \beta_{11} + \beta_{12} ULC_t + \beta_{13} EXP_t \qquad (11)$$

$$ULC_t = \beta_{14} + \beta_{15} EXP_t + \beta_{16} LAB_t \qquad (12)$$

where   TFP$_t$ is total factor productivity growth between year (t-1) and t

           LAB$_t$ is labour productivity growth between year (t-1) and t

           ULC$_t$ is unit labour cost growth between year (t-1) and t

           EXP$_t$ is export growth between year (t-1) and t

           R&D$_t$ is R&D expenditure growth between year (t-1) and t

The rationale for using a system of equations instead of running separate ones is that the variables are interrelated with one another. Take for instance CAP$_t$, which can simultaneously affect both TFP$_t$ and LAB$_t$. Simply ignoring the nested multi-relationships would produce biased results.

3.3 DATA

The primary source of data for this study is derived from 1980-1994 issues of 'The Report on the Census of Industrial Production'. We obtained the data on 'R&D expenditures by industry'with the assistance of the Research and Statistics Unit of Economic Development Board (EDB). The 29 types of manufacturing industries covered are categorised according to the 3-digit Singapore Standard Industrial Classification Codes (SSIC). This study encompasses all manufacturing establishments with 10 or more workers, spanning the period from 1980 to 1994. We are not able to cover the period prior to 1980 due to incompatibility arising out of classification differences. For instance, the 'electrical appliances' and 'electronic components' industries used to be under the same classification code before 1980, but were subsequently segregated.

As the raw data are in current market prices, they are deflated to avoid spurious correlation. Figures for gross output, net value added, net capital stock, direct exports and R&D expenditures are deflated using the GDP deflators[7]; workers' remuneration are deflated by CPI deflators[8]. Please refer to Table 1 for definitions of the various variables.

4. EMPIRICAL ANALYSIS

This section presents the empirical results and analysis according to the methodology discussed in section 3.2. Each equation is critically examined, followed by explanations and comments.

4.1 OVERALL MANUFACTURING SECTOR

Please refer to Table 2 for empirical results on the overall manufacturing sector.

4.1.1 Equation (9)

Two out of the five independent variables are positively correlated with TFP growth.

(a)   The main determinant of TFP$_t$ is LAB$_t$, which has a coefficient of 0.999 (with a high t-statistic of 80.974). The interpretation is that for every one percent rise in LAB$_t$, TFP$_t$ rises by 0.999 percent.

---

[7] GDP deflators are available from the 1980-1995 issues of "Singapore Yearbook of Statistics".

[8] CPI deflator is chosen to deflate remuneration upon the advice of Ms. Kok Y.H, Head of Research & Statistics Unit, EDB.

(b)Since ULC_t is a form of business operating cost (and a major one in the case of Singapore), it is only natural that it is negatively correlated with TFP_t .

(c)   The coefficient of CAP_t is the most significantly negative one (at -0.764). This is attributable to the accelerated capital deepening from the late 1970s right through to mid 1980s. Capital growth outpaced the learning capability of the workforce, hence adversely affecting TFP growth.

(d)EXP_t captures the effects of external market demand. If the coefficient is negative, it implies that TFP growth suffers from the unpredictable swings in world demand. On the contrary, a positive coefficient means that the economy is highly adaptive to external conditions; in other words, it is export-competitive. Our results show that Singapore's export growth negatively affects TFP growth, even though the coefficient is rather small (at -0.01).

(e)   The coefficient of $R\&D_{t-1}$ takes into account the impact of research and development (R&D) activities on TFP growth. The first lag is chosen because R&D normally reaps returns at least a year later. As a matter of fact, R&D expenditure growth has been phenomenal in recent years. Between 1980 and 1994, the real rate of growth stood at an average of 38% per annum. Results indicate that $R\&D_{t-1}$ is statistically insignificant. This is consistent with Young's model mentioned earlier on, which suggests that the domestic workforce have not accumulated enough experience to make optimal use of the R&D investments.

4.1.2 Equation (10)

(a)   The coefficient of Cap_t is positive (i.e. 0.075). This is in line with economic intuition, since increasing capital intensity means that each worker has more resources to work with, thereby raising labour productivity.

(b)EXP_t is also found to be positively correlated with LAB_t with high statistical significance. It seems to imply that the domestic labour force is highly adaptive to fluctuating external demand.

(c)   The coefficient of $R\&D_{t-1}$ is negative, albeit a low one (of -0.01). Once again, it reflects that the workforce has not yet been able to fully utilise the improvements in technology. In any case, such a phenomenon is to be expected in the short run.

4.1.3 Equation (11) : $CAP_t = \beta_{11} + \beta_{12} ULC_t + \beta_{13} EXP_t$

This equation seeks to answer the following question : To what extent is capital intensity growth determined by the growths in unit labour cost and exports?

(a) ULC_t shows a highly significant coefficient of 0.703. It appears to be the main determinant of capital intensity - that is, the substitution of capital for labour. This is exactly what policy-makers hoped to achieve in the 1979 industrial restructuring. Nevertheless, later years saw labour costs rise more as a result of labour shortage rather than due to government policies.

(b)The coefficient of EXP_t is also positive at 0.061. We reckon that as the demand for Singapore's exports grows, Singapore's production capacity must increase accordingly. Therefore capital inputs, which constitute a major portion of any production facility, will also rise.

4.1.4 Equation (12)

As mentioned , labour shortage (i.e. supply side) is the main reason behind the surge in labour costs in Singapore. However, this study focuses on another facet - the demand-pull side.

More specifically, we want to find out the extent to which unit labour costs in Singapore are determined by export and labour productivity growths.

(a)   Our regression results show that on the whole, EXP_t has a weak positive impact on ULC_t . Every 1 percent increase in exports accounts for 0.014 % increase in unit labour costs.

(b)On the other hand, labour productivity growth appears to affect labour cost growth quite substantially with a coefficient of 0.167. Given that our labour productivity has grown at an average of 4.8% per annum between 1980-94, its contribution to labour cost growth must be significant as well.

4.2 COMPARISON BETWEEN THREE CATEGORIES OF INDUSTRIES - BASED ON CAPITAL INTENSITIES

In this section, the 29 types of manufacturing industries are grouped into three categories, namely low, medium and high capital intensity industries. They are ranked on the basis of their capital intensities in 1994, with 10 industries in both the 'high' and 'medium' categories, and 9 industries in the 'low' one. Please refer to Table 3 for a list of the three classifications of industries. The share of value-added of each industry is also shown to highlight the relative importance of each industry.

The regression system in Section 3.2 is once again applied here. Please refer to Table 4 for the empirical results. Due to space constraint, we choose to compare only the two extreme groups, i.e. high vis-à-vis low categories.

4.2.1 Equation (9)

For the high capital intensity group, all the variables are statistically significant. Other than LAB_t , the coefficients for all regressors are negative. On the other hand, for the 'low' group, export and R&D growths are found to be insignificant.

Incidentally, the 'low' group belongs to the family of 'sunset industries' which are declining in terms of their share of total output of the manufacturing sector. One of the characteristics of this group is that they are generally not export-based, and therefore do not face the same level of competition as export-oriented ones. This explains part of the reason why they have made little investments in R&D in the last decade. In short, exports and R&D play a very small role in the TFP growths of the 'low capital intensity' industries.

4.2.2 Equation (10)

In the high capital intensity group, LAB_t is significantly correlated only with EXP_t. Why has capital growth not contributed much to labour productivity growth in this category?

One plausible explanation is that human capital is unable to develop as fast as physical capital, especially since the physical capital growth of this group is the highest. The result is that the returns to physical capital are marginal. We believe that period corresponded to the initial 'capital set-up' phase. Over time, as the speed of capital formation slows down[9] (which is exactly what is happening now), we should gradually move out of this 'low-level adjustment trap' to fully tap into the benefits of our capital investments.

4.2.3 Equation (11)

In the case of high capital intensity industries, capital intensity growth is very much affected by growth in unit labour costs and exports, with coefficients of 0.522 and 0.210 respectively. It thus follows that labour costs are pushing up capital intensities, and that capital formation moves very much in tandem with external demand for our manufactures.

On the contrary, the other group's capital intensity growth is strongly affected only by growth in unit labour costs (with a high coefficient of 0.609), but not export growth (which is expected due to the reasons mentioned in section 4.2.1).

4.2.4 Equation (12)

The last equation deals with the rise in unit labour costs. Both the increase in labour productivity and exports account significantly for labour cost increase in the high capital intensity industries, especially labour productivity (with a coefficient of 0.147).

This augers well for our manufacturing sector in the sense that our labour productivity growth does in fact keep up with labour cost increase. Foreign investors would be more willing to make their investments here if they know that the remuneration they pay are worth it.

In the other case, labour productivity growth, but not export growth, explains a large portion of the increase in labour cost.

5. POLICY IMPLICATIONS

Singapore's policy makers have been encouraging technological improvement and capital-intensive processes since the industrial restructuring program in 1979. To a large extent, the 'industrial targeting' policies have been successful. Many industries answer to the calls of the authorities (namely EDB and the then NPB) to voluntarily upgrade the quality of their workforce, as evident in the increase in enrolment in NPB upgrading courses from 7480 in 1982 to 26949 in 1994. The growth in membership of Quality Control Circles is even more phenomenal, i.e. from 2682 in 1982 to 117363 in 1994.

Furthermore, there has also been a sharp increase in R&D expenditures in the overall manufacturing sector. In 1980, it was 18,625,000 dollars; but in 1992, it reached a high of 876,842,000 dollars[10].

While the industrial policies have generally been set in the right path, more caution is needed on timing and co-ordination. For instance, the 1979 industrial restructuring was implemented before our human resources were skilled enough to handle the sophisticated processes. That explains the unfavourable TFP growth of the manufacturing sector for a few years right after the restructuring program.

---

[9] The average real growth rate (deflated to 1985 figures) of capital per head was 8.1% per annum between 1980-87; this slowed down to 1.7% per annum between 1988-94.

[10] R&D expenditure figures are kindly provided by Ms. Kok Y.H., Senior Officer, Research & Statistics Unit, EDB.

At this juncture, we would like to offer some suggestions based on our observations.

(1) The R&D expenditures increased quite substantially in the early 1990s. For example, there was a jump of 228% from 267,163,000 dollars in 1991 to 876,842,000 dollars in 1992. We have no doubt that R&D investments should increase over time so as to help close up our technological gaps with the OECD countries. Nevertheless, there is a need to look into whether such a rapid rise is justifiable. Otherwise, the industries may suffer from 'side-effects' akin to the effects of accelerated capital deepening after 1979.

In this connection, we feel that the pace of increase should be set such that the increased R&D resources are efficiently utilised by the available R&D manpower. That is, the rise in R&D expenditures must be co-ordinated with the growth of R&D personnel in Singapore.

(2) Since the inception of the 'growth triangle concept[11], Singapore has intensified its regionalisation efforts. With the advent of high technological tools like video-conferencing and Internet, there exist enormous opportunities for international R&D collaborations. The potential benefits for a small country like Singapore is especially great, since we can tap into the large pool of expertise abroad (which is the one thing that we always lack).

Following on this, we recommend closer interactions between local and foreign institutions (in particular, tertiary educational ones) , as well as with international commercial R&D firms.

(3) After peaking in the early 1980s, the growth in capital has gradually slowed down. It is widely believed that the poor TFP growth back then was due to the incompatibility of imported foreign capital with domestic workforce. The former embodied mature technologies (developed in their home countries) which the locals could not adapt to successfully.

With regard to this, the relevant authorities can provide assistance in identifying and arranging for the appropriate capital goods to be imported here. Perhaps one such way is through setting up a one-stop agency to perform the functions of technological-procurement research and information dissemination.

6. CONCLUSION

In retrospect, Singapore's manufacturing sector displays a clear pattern of improved performance (based on TFP growth) in recent years. This is indeed an encouraging sign since TFP growth is the major source of long term economic growth. As a matter of fact, the stated .objective of the Singapore Productivity and Standards Board (SPSB) is to "sustain TFP growth at 2 percent a year or more in order to achieve 4 percent productivity growth and 7 percent annual economic growth".

We find evidence in the domestic manufacturing sector that support Alwyn Young's model of "invention and bounded learning by doing". This sector suffered from unhealthy TFP growth in the early stages of industrialisation (i.e. 1970s and early 1980s) due to the lack of indigenous R&D and excessively rapid rise in foreign capital goods. However, in

---

[11] The 'growth triangle' , initiated by Prime Minister Goh, covers Singapore, Johor and Batam.

subsequent years, technical experience gained by the workforce and the heavy investments in R&D eventually translated themselves into substantial productivity gains.

Yet another contributing factor is that the high mobility of capital and labour inputs (which is the case for Singapore) has led to optimal resource-allocations. That is, the domestic industrial structure has, over time, adjusted itself dynamically to achieve the ideal capital-labour ratio, hence maximising returns.

With respect to the entire manufacturing sector, our empirical results show that gains in labour productivity is the major determinant of TFP growth, while the rapid increase in capital and unit labour costs are found to negatively affect it. In addition, growth in capital is very much affected by the rise in unit labour costs (i.e. labour-capital substitution) and exports. Also, other than the tight labour market, labour productivity and exports growth play important roles in pushing up unit labour costs in Singapore.

As for the various capital intensity categories of industries, export growth has relatively more impact on the high capital intensity group than on the low capital intensity group. It significantly affects capital intensity and unit labour cost growths in the former, but not the latter. This group of 'sunset industries' (i.e. the low capital intensity ones) faces two options. One is for them to intensify their efforts to upgrade their industrial structure so they can compete in the global market. This can be achieved through selective capital investments and comprehensive skill upgrading of the workers. The second is to accept the total collapse of those industries. To name a few, the 'wearing apparel' and 'footwear' industries are exactly in that predicament now.

REFERENCES

Chng, M. K., Low, L. and Toh, M. H. (1988): Industrial Restructuring in Singapore : For ASEAN-Japan Investment and Trade Expansion . Chopmen Publishers.

Hobday, M. (1994). Technological Learning in Singapore: A Test Case of Leapfrogging, The Journal of Development Studies 30(4), July, pp. 831-858.

Kim, J. and Lau, L.J. (1994): "The Sources of Economic Growth of the East Asian Newly Industrialised Countries," Journal of the Japanese and International Economies, 8(3), 235-371.

Lall, A., R. Tan and Chew, S.B. (1996): "Total Factor Productivity Growth Experience of Singapore: An Interpretative Survey," Economic Management Policy in Singapore, ed. by Lim, C. H. Singapore: Addison Wesley Publishing Company.

Rao, V. V. Bhanoji and Lee, C. (1995): "Sources of Growth in the Singapore Manufacturing Economy and its Manufacturing and Service Sectors," Paper presented at the 20th Federation of ASEAN Economic Associations Conference, Singapore.

Saito, M. and I. Tokutsu (1992): "Technological Trends in the Pacific Basin," Economic Development of ROC and the Pacific Rim in the 1990s and Beyond, ed. by Klein, L. R. and Yu, C. T. World Scientific Publishing Company.

Solow, R.M. (1994). "Perspectives on Growth Theory," Journal of Economic Perspectives 8(1), pp. 45-54.

Tsao, Y. (1982): Growth and Productivity in Singapore: A Supply Side Analysis, Unpublished Ph.D. dissertation, Harvard University, Cambridge MA.

Tsao, Y. (1985): "Growth Without Productivity: The Case of Singapore Manufacturing, 1970-79," Journal of Development economics, 19: 25-38.

Wong, F. C. and Gan, W. B. (1994): "Total Factor Productivity Growth in Singapore Manufacturing Industries During the 1980s," Journal of Asian Economics, 5(2), 117-196.

Young, A. (1992): "A Tale of Two Cities: Factor Accumulation and Technical Change in Hong Kong and Singapore," NBER Macroeconomics Annual, ed. by Oliver J. Blanchard and Stanley Fischer. Cambridge, MA: The MIT Press.

Young, A. (1994b). The Tyranny of Numbers: Confronting the Statistical Realities of the East Asian Growth Experience, Unpublished Manuscript, Cambridge, MA: MIT.

TABLE 1

Definitions and Profiles of Variables

Average Labour Productivity Growth (LPG) Profile

Definition :	The change in net value added per worker head, where net value added is calculated as gross output less materials, utilities, fuel, transportation costs and work given out.	
Industry with Highest LPG	Pottery, China, Earthware & Glass Products	29.7%
Industry with Lowest LPG	Iron & Steel	-8.0%
Industrial Mean LPG		5.7%

Average Unit Labour Cost Growth (ULCG) Profile

Definition :	The change in net remuneration per worker head, where net remuneration includes wages, salaries, bonuses, CPF contributions, pensions, benefits and other costs such as lodging.	
Industry with Highest ULGC	Pottery, China, Earthware & Glass Products	14.3%
Industry with Lowest ULGC	Transport Equipment	2.1%
Industrial Mean ULGC		5.6%

Average Capital Intensity Growth (CIG) Profile

Definition :	The change in net capital stock per worker head, where net capital stock includes building & structures, machinery & equipment, office equipment and transportation equipment.	
Industry with Highest CIG	Leather & Leather Products	12.4%
Industry with Lowest CIG	Cement	-14.0%
Industrial Mean LPG		3.7%

Average Exports Growth (EG) Profile

Definition :	The change in net direct exports per worker head.	
Industry with Highest EG	Structural Cement & Concrete Products	21.8%
Industry with Lowest EG	Petroleum Refineries & Petroleum Products	-26.9%
Industrial Mean EG		3.72%

a) All figures are based on five-year moving averages from 1990 to 1994.

TABLE 2

Regression Results for System of Equations

Dependent Variable : TFP Growth

Independent Variable	Coefficient	t-statistics	
Constant	0.004	2.406	
Labour Productivity Growth	0.999	80.974	
Unit Labour Cost Growth	-0.312	-14.247	
Capital Intensity Growth	-0.764	-101.951	
Export Growth	-0.010	-1.829	$R^2 = 0.987$
R&D Expenditure Growth	0.0003	0.297	DW=1.941

Dependent Variable : Labour Productivity Growth

Independent Variable	Coefficient	t-statistics	
Constant	0.039	5.043	
Capital Intensity Growth	0.075	1.888	
Export Growth	0.070	2.415	$R^2 = 0.058$
R&D Expenditure Growth	-0.010	-1.706	DW=1.604

Dependent Variable : Capital Intensity Growth

Independent Variable	Coefficient	t-statistics	
Constant	0.018	1.529	
Unit Labour Cost Growth	0.703	5.358	$R^2 = 0.093$
Export Growth	0.061	3.008	DW=1.907

Dependent Variable : Unit Labour Cost Growth

Independent Variable	Coefficient	t-statistics	
Constant	0.046	13.485	
Labour Productivity Growth	0.010	1.393	$R^2 = 0.133$
Export Growth	0.167	7.600	DW=1.833

TABLE 3

Classification of Industries by Capital Intensity (in Descending Order of Ranking[b])

High Capital Intensity Industries

Rank	SSIC Code	Industries	% of Value-Added[b]
1	353/54	Petroleum Refineries & Petroleum Products	6.17
2	351	Industrial Chemicals & Gases	3.69
3	361/62	Pottery, China, Earthware & Glass Products	0.39
4	314	Cigarettes & Other Tobacco Products	0.67
5	364	Cement	0.58
6	313	Beverage	0.98
7	371	Iron & Steel	0.48
8	372	Non-Ferrous Metal	0.25
9	352	Paints, Pharmaceuticals & other Chemical Products	5.03
10	341	Paper & Paper Products	1.48
		Total % Contribution to Value-Added	**19.72**

Medium Capital Intensity Industries

Rank	SSIC Code	Industries	% of Value-Added
11	363	Bricks, Tiles & other Structural Clay Products	0.07
12	311/12	Food	2.50
13	381	Fabricated Metal Products except Machinery & Equip.	6.51
14	385	Transport Equipment	7.30
15	386	Instrumentation Equip., Photographic & Optical Goods	1.87
16	365	Structural Cement & Concrete Products	0.71
17	355/56	Rubber Products, Jelutong & Gum Damar	0.30
18	342	Printing & Publishing	4.76
19	382	Machinery except Electrical & Electronic	5.66
20	384	Electronic Products & Components	41.36
		Total % Contribution to Value-Added	**71.04**

Low Capital Intensity Industries

Ran	SSIC Code	Industries	% of Value-Added
21	357	Plastic Products	2.71
22	383	Electrical Machinery, Apparatus, Appliances & Supplies	3.68
23	331	Sawn Timber & other Wood Products except Furniture	0.25
24	321	Textile & Textile Manufactures	0.35
25	369	Non-Metallic Mineral Products	0.26
26	323	Leather & Leather Products	0.11
27	332	Furniture & Fixtures Except Primarily of Metal, Stone & Plastics	0.65
28	324	Footwear	0.05
29	322	Wearing Apparel Except Footwear	1.18
		Total % Contribution to Value-Added	**9.24**

a) All configurations are based on 1994 figures extracted from "Report on Census of Industrial Production".

b) Each industry's % contribution to overall manufacturing value-added is presented to indicate the relative importance of that industry's output to the sector.

TABLE 4

Regression Results for 3 Categories of Industries by Order of Capital Intensity

	High Capital Intensity Group	Medium Capital Intensity Group	Low Capital Intensity Group
Dependent Variable : TFP Growth			
Independent Variable	**Coefficient**	**Coefficient**	**Coefficient**
Constant	0.010 *(3.308)*	0.001 *(1.759)*	0.0002 *(0.090)*
Labour Productivity Growth	1.002 *(50.702)*	1.004 *(153.041)*	1.020 *(47.990)*
Unit Labour Cost Growth	-0.299 *(-7.758)*	-0.382 *(-33.579)*	-0.396 *(-15.283)*
Capital Intensity Growth	-0.800 *(-79.330)*	-0.644 *(-108.712)*	-0.628 *(-53.949)*
Export Growth	-0.020 *(-2.206)*	-0.003 *(-0.926)*	0.021 *(1.417)*
R&D Expenditure Growth	-0.004 *(-1.736)*	0.0004 *(0.912)*	0.002 *(1.413)*
Dependent Variable : Labour Productivity Growth			
Independent Variable	**Coefficient**	**Coefficient**	**Coefficient**
Constant	0.026 *(1.434)*	0.038 *(3.568)*	0.038 *(3.816)*
Capital Intensity Growth	0.057 *(0.895)*	0.099 *(1.180)*	-0.006 *(-0.082)*
Export Growth	0.120 *(2.192)*	0.0645 *(1.332)*	0.302 *(3.620)*
R&D Expenditure Growth	-0.0002 *(-0.016)*	-0.009 *(-1.400)*	-0.017 *(-1.798)*
Dependent Variable : Capital Intensity Growth			
Independent Variable	**Coefficient**	**Coefficient**	**Coefficient**
Constant	0.043 *(1.697)*	0.010 *(0.690)*	0.004 *(0.260)*
Unit Labour Cost Growth	0.522 *(1.980)*	0.788 *(4.390)*	0.609 *(3.347)*
Export Growth	0.210 *(4.100)*	0.008 *(0.430)*	-0.023 *(-0.356)*
Dependent Variable : Unit Labour Cost Growth			
Independent Variable	**Coefficient**	**Coefficient**	**Coefficient**
Constant	0.045 *(6.803)*	0.048 *(8.887)*	0.042 *(7.643)*
Labour Productivity Growth	0.147 *(4.603)*	0.118 *(2.758)*	0.331 *(5.793)*
Export Growth	0.039 *(2.552)*	-0.0003 *(-0.038)*	0.029 *(1.007)*

a) The critical value at 10% significance level is ± 1.640

b) The coefficients are in the form of percentages, i.e. 1.00 means 100%

Portfolio Balance Approach to
Exchange Rate Determination in Singapore

Foo Tee Sing
&
Shahidur **Rahman**

Nanyang Business School, Nanyang Technological University, Nanyang Avenue, Singapore 639798
Fax: +(65) 792.4217, Tel: +(65) 799 6404, Email: asrahman@ntu.edu.sg

Abstract Neither the monetary approach nor the portfolio balance approach has led to robust estimates of models explaining changes in the market values of most currencies. Earlier tests of the monetary models have usually not performed well. On the other hand, recent tests of the portfolio balance model have performed well. The purpose of this study is to test a model that can incorporate monetary as well as current account effects on exchange rates using the bilateral (SGD/USD) rate. This study analyses the performance of reduced-form exchange rate models of the portfolio balance approach in the context of a Singapore database. Various past empirical models are tested and compared. A number of tests are carried out to determine whether these models provide useful information about recent movements in exchange rates. The strongest results are highlighted.

1. INTRODUCTION

The empirical performance of exchange rate models has been widely criticised in recent years. The concerns derive partly from studies that have found certain models to fit poorly within the sample over which they were estimated or to predict poorly out of sample. The former being the main part of this paper.

Much of the literature on exchange rate determination has been done on the basic theoretical models such as the Purchasing Power Parity (PPP) approach, the monetary approach as well as the asset market approach. Underlying all these approaches are fundamental forces that economists believed affects the exchange rate. Amongst the three, the PPP or a classical monetary approach, received the earliest attention. As far back as the early 20th century, pronounced economists like Cassel (1928), Hawtrey (1919), and Pigou (1920) has liken to the notion of a law of one price.

The modern monetary approach has included the existence of a domestic and foreign bond market. They are assumed to be perfect substitutes and that these markets clear instantaneously. The law of one price holds in the securities market. As a result, the condition of uncovered interest parity holds. Unfortunately, the monetary approach only offers a partial picture of the forces determining exchange rates. Exchange rates are determined in a broad general equilibrium framework where not only the supplies of and demands for national money are important but also the supply of and demand for goods and securities are important. The econometric evidence shows that the monetary approach has failed to provide an adequate explanation of exchange rate movements since the beginning of the floating exchange rates. Cao and Ong (1994) has found a similar lack of explanation for the (SGD/USD) bilateral exchange rate. Although this approach has been widely acknowledged to be an incomplete theory of exchange rate determination, it serves as the foundation for more sophisticated and complex models of exchange rate determination. Therefore, it goes to show that knowledge of the monetary model properties are of great importance. Indeed the monetary approach can be integrated with other approaches to arrive at a clearer picture of the path that currencies may take.

Therefore the authors decided to examine the portfolio balance approach (P-B) to exchange rate determination. It has been recognised that this approach is an extension of the modern monetary approach. This is especially evident when one looks at the restrictive assumption inherent in the monetary models and the relaxing of them under the P-B approach. The P-B approach has been a rather recent concept. Compared to the monetary approach of exchange rate the portfolio balance approach has not been extensively tested. This is probably due to the fact that it is very difficult to find data on domestic resident's foreign currency assets, broken down by the currency denomination of the assets. Thus most empirical studies begin from the stock of foreign currency assets held by domestic residents and add the cumulated current account balances for each country. This method therefore ignores any capital gains earned on foreign assets and assumes that only domestic residents hold domestic assets. A fair amount of literature has been associated with the approach and perhaps the reason for it is due to the greater financial innovation and advancement globally that has increasing cast light on the role of financial assets and their impact on the exchange rates. The basic premise of this approach has been to estimate the asset demand function of various financial assets and incorporating the wealth variable into the exchange rate equation. The method we adopted in handling the models has been to estimate the reduced form equations whereby we bypass the problems associated with data insufficiency. There is however a study by Nguyen and Yao (1989) which attempted to estimate the various structural equations[1] with some measure of success.

The outline of this paper is as follows. The next section gives a brief account of the history of the approach. Section three provides an understanding of the economics of the exchange rate in the portfolio balance model. The analyses of the various models are presented in section four. The final section sums up the paper and gives some comments and outline of future research.

2. HISTORY OF PORTFOLIO BALANCE MODEL

In the second half of the 1960s, the analysis of exchange rates and the balance of payments was entering a new stage. Critics of the Mundell-Fleming model has argued that the capital account balance should be conceptualised not as an ongoing flow, but rather as a reflection of efforts to adjust asset stocks to the levels that economic participants desired.

This new conceptualisation of the capital account was reflected in two different classes of asset equilibrium models: the monetary approach to the balance of payments and the portfolio-balance approach. The former approach extends to contributions by Polak (1959) and Hahn (1959), and was subsequently popularised by Johnson (1972) and others.[2]

---

[1] See Sarantis (1987) for a comprehensive overview of the structural equations estimated as the model used by them is modelled after his study.

[2] Kenen (1985, pp.669-71). Frankel and Johnson (1976) for a collection of theoretical and empirical contributions.

In order to understand the portfolio balance model further, it is necessary to briefly review the modern monetary models. Perhaps it is more important to recognise that the most serious deficiency of the monetary model was its inability to take into account of changes in external trade imbalances and what impact such changes would have on the exchange rates.[3] Correcting for this fault is the Hooper-Morton model. They postulated that the current account does not influence exchange rate directly but only indirectly through its impact on exchange rate expectations. Hooper and Morton assume that the exchange rate is expected to equilibrate the current account in the long run. At any point in time, it is assumed that the equilibrium real exchange rate is determined by the cumulative sum of past and present current account balances. If there is an unexpected permanent rise in the cumulative current account surplus, an upward revision in the currency's equilibrium real long-term value would be required if current account balance is to be restored. An upward revision to the equilibrium long-run real exchange rate would drive up the nominal exchange rate higher according to the extended PPP model. One can derive a model that incorporates both monetary and current account influences in the determination of exchange rates in the following form :

$$E = M_t - \beta_1 Y_t + \beta_2(p_t - p_t^*) - \beta_3 i_t - \beta_4 \Sigma CAB + \beta_5 \Sigma CAB^* \tag{1}$$

where the E is the exchange rate, M_t is the relative money supply of the domestic and the foreign country, Y_t is the relative income levels of the two countries, P_t is the relative price differential, i_t is the interest rate differential, ΣCAB and ΣCAB^* are the domestic and foreign cumulative current account balances respectively.

Changes in the cumulative current account balances give rise to changes in market expectations of the equilibrium long-run real exchange rate. This in turn give rise to market expectations of changes in the equilibrium long-run nominal exchange rate. The market adjustment to the new nominal long-run equilibrium rate is depicted by a gradual process with the speed of adjustment.

This improvement and many more others still does not suffice to validating the monetary models. The usual causes of the failure of the monetary model include (i) the failure of purchasing power parity and uncovered interest parity to hold in the short-run and possibly in the medium-run also, (ii) the assumption of a stable demand for money, when evidence suggests that the money supply and level of output are exogenously, rather than endogenously, determined, and (iii) the overly simplified equations describing how exchange rate expectations are formed.

Indeed the monetary models in various forms have been tested. However, most evidence suggests that this approach does not suffice for a very satisfactory explanation. James Boughton. (1988) acknowledged that the monetary approach has clearly failed to provide an adequate explanation of the movements in major currency values during the floating period that began in 1973. Cao and Ong (1994) found disappointing results in the popular monetary models for the within sample estimation of the (SGD/USD) bilateral rate. Reduced form testing of the monetary model have found substantial problems with the parameter estimates.

---

[3] In Hooper and Morton (1982) they identified that introducing the effects of trade imbalances served to better explain the movements of the exchange rate. To remedy the deficiency, they explicitly introduced the current account balance into the monetary model.

The second class of models, which originated from Metzler (1951) in its treatment of savings and wealth, was formulated along the lines of the theory of portfolio selection developed by Markowitz (1959) and Tobin (1967).[4] It is here where our interest lies. The second class of models of asset stock equilibrium has been named the P-B approach. Like the monetary approach, the P-B approach focuses on the links between balance-of-payments flows and adjustments in asset stocks. It emphasises that models of the capital account should be rooted in behavioural models of the supplies of and demand for portfolio stocks. The main difference between the monetary approach and the P-B approach is that the monetary approach regards home-currency securities (which represents asset other than money) as perfect substitutes for foreign-currency securities, while the P-B approach regards them as imperfect substitutes. Among other things, in the absence of perfect substitutability the larger set of distinct assets under the P-B approach implies that the equilibrium condition for at least one of the securities markets must be modelled explicitly. That is to say, since the uncovered interest parity condition does not hold when the assets are imperfect substitutes, the interest rates on home country securities cannot be equated to the foreign interest rate plus the expected rate of change in the exchange rate.

The P-B approach emerged during the late 1960s but did not mature until the late 1970s , after the Bretton Woods system had collapsed. In its early developments, the approach received nourishment from econometric efforts to explain the empirically-observed behaviour of capital flows. Branson (1968) was one of the first to put stock-adjustment terms into capital flow equations. Mackinnon and Oates (1966) and Mackinnon (1969) were early contributors to the conceptual framework, although their model included only one financial asset other than money. Also, by not treating the case of imperfect capital mobility, they did not move as far as subsequent contributions in breaking away from the monetary approach. Argy and Porter (1972) were among the first to focus explicitly on how the nature of exchange rate expectations influenced the effects of changes in the monetary and fiscal policies and various other internal and external shocks. Girton and Henderson (1973, 1976) extensively explored the effects of central bank policies on financial capital movements in a two-country model. The specification of the portfolio-balance models was reviewed by Branson and Henderson (1985), who distinguished between models in asset demand functions and postulated models in which asset demand functions are derived from microeconomic foundations.[5]

In order to fully understand the many variations to the way that the portfolio balance approach can be modelled and verified, we need to know the fundamentals behind it.

3. PORTFOLIO BALANCE EXCHANGE RATE ECONOMICS

3.1 MONETARY POLICY AND EXCHANGE RATE DETERMINATION

A once and for all rise in money supply represents a net increase to domestic wealth. Assuming that portfolio were balanced prior to the rise in reserve money, asset holders will

---

[4] Allen and Kenen (1980, p.4).

[5] See also Allen and Kenen (1980), who developed and extensively analyse a portfolio balance model of an open economy in which the markets for three financial assets (money, domestic bonds and foreign bonds) are fully integrated with markets for labour, traded goods, and nontraded goods.

try to rebalance their portfolio because their net wealth has increased. With their net wealth having risen and the share of reserve money in net wealth larger than before, asset holders will find themselves with an excess supply of money and a corresponding excess demand for both domestic and foreign bonds. The supplies of domestic and foreign bonds are assumed to be fixed in the short run. Excess demand for domestic bonds can only be eliminated by a decline in domestic interest rates; excess demand for foreign bonds can only be eliminated by a decline in both the currency's value and the domestic interest rate.

When a central bank engages in an open market purchase of domestic bonds, there is no net addition to domestic wealth. Instead, the central bank merely exchanges reserve money for domestic bonds with the private sector. Following that, private resident asset holders find themselves with excess supply of reserve money and excess demand for domestic bonds. Both the excess supply of reserve money and the excess demand for bonds can be eliminated by a decline in domestic interest rates. The decline in domestic interest rates then induces resident asset holders to switch from domestic to foreign bonds. Since the supply of foreign bonds is assumed to be fixed in the short run, the increased demand for foreign bonds puts a downwards pressure on the domestic currency's value. Although the domestic currency's value and the domestic interest rate both decline, the magnitude of change differs from the previous section. Similar to the previous section, there is a substitution effect arising from lower domestic interest rates that induces resident asset holders to acquire more foreign bonds. However, there is no wealth effect at work in this case that contributes to a further rise in the demand for foreign bonds that pushes the domestic currency lower.

3.2 FISCAL POLICY AND EXCHANGE RATE DETERMINATION

In this section expansionary fiscal policy is generated by an increase in the supply of domestic bonds. This increase represents a net addition to domestic wealth. Assuming portfolios were balanced prior to the rise in bonds, asset holders will attempt to rebalance their portfolios because their net wealth has increased. With net wealth having risen and the share of domestic bonds in net wealth larger than before, resident asset holders will find themselves with an excess supply of domestic bonds and an excess demand for reserve and foreign bonds. The increased supply of domestic bonds may be willingly held only if domestic interest rates rise. Since the supply of reserve money is assumed to be fixed in the short-run, a rise in domestic interest rates is also required to eliminate the excess demand for money.

Although it is clear that domestic interest rates must rise following an increase in the supply of domestic bonds, it is less clear which direction the exchange rate will take. There exists two forms of pressure on the exchange rate. One causes it to rise and the other causes the exchange rate to fall. The excess demand for foreign bonds caused by the initial rise in net wealth tends to place downward pressure on the domestic currency value. The rise in domestic interest rates that is necessary to clear the domestic bond and money markets tends to induce asset holders to switch from foreign to domestic bonds, Such switching will tend to place upward pressure on the domestic currency's value. The force which dominates is ambiguous. If the wealth-induced rise in the demand for foreign bonds dominated the interest rate induced decline, the exchange rate will fall in value and vice versa.

3.3 MONETARY/FISCAL POLICY AND EXCHANGE RATE DETERMINATION

It can be shown that an expansionary fiscal policy coupled with a tight monetary policy has a clear unambiguous impact on the exchange rate. If an expansionary fiscal policy is accompanied by a move toward a tighter monetary policy, the expansionary fiscal policy will result in an increase in the supply of domestic bonds, which adds to net wealth. While the restrictive monetary policy decreases the supply of reserve money, it also reduces net wealth. The mix of the two policies, assuming the magnitudes of changes in the two policies are identical, will result in an unchanged level of domestic wealth. With no increase in net wealth, there is no wealth effect to influence the exchange rate. Instead, the expansionary fiscal and tight monetary policy mix acts to push domestic interest rates upward, which induces resident asset holders to switch from foreign to domestic bonds. This places unambiguous upward pressure on the domestic currency's value.

If the fiscal policy and monetary policy mix is an important determinant of exchange rate changes, one would expect to find a close relationship between changes in the ratio of domestic bonds to reserve money and the trend in exchange rates.

3.4 CURRENT ACCOUNT IMBALANCES AND EXCHANGE RATE DETERMINATION

The current account balance plays no role in the determination of exchange rates. However, the current account plays an important role in the P-B approach in terms of both the short-and long-run determination of exchange rates. A current account surplus will generated an increase the supply of foreign bonds in the hands of resident asset holders. The increase in the supply of foreign bonds temporarily increases the net wealth of resident asset holders. Assuming that portfolios were again balanced prior to the increase in foreign bond supply, asset holders will attempt to rebalance their portfolios because their net wealth has increased. Due to this, they will find themselves with an excess supply of foreign bonds. An excess supply of foreign bonds will be willingly held only if the foreign currency falls ie. the domestic currency rises in value.

4. MODELS AND ANALYSIS

Broadly three kinds of empirical approach of the portfolio balance model have been carried out. Assuming static expectations[6], the first approach concentrates on solving the short-run portfolio balance model as a reduced form for the exchange rate. The second approach involves estimating a structural system of equations as attempted by Kearney and Macdonald (1985, 1987) and Boughton (1984, 1987). The third approach involves an indirect testing of the existence of a risk premium. In this section, we examine the second approach but we by-pass the problems of data unavailability in structural asset equations by looking at the reduced form ones.

4.1 MODELS

4.1.1 Boughton's Model

This model introduced by Boughton (1984), also called a preferred-habitat model is with imperfect substitutability between securities denominated in different currencies. Expectations are asymptotically but not continuously rational. The structural model avoids

---

[6] See Branson et al. (1977, 1979)

the problems of estimating asset demand functions by specifying both asset demand and supply functions and then estimating equations for asset prices. Specifically, the money supply function depends upon the target level of the money supply and the levels of domestic and foreign interest rates. Combining this with the standard demand for money functions through a stock adjustment equation, Boughton. derives an equation for the interest rate which depends upon the foreign real interest rate, the domestic level of output, expected inflation and the monetary target. The proportionate change in the exchange rate depends on the excess demand for foreign assets plus expected inflation differential between the home and the foreign country. Specifying equations for the demand and supply of foreign assets and postulating a stock adjustment process, inter alia, the change in the exchange rate can be expressed as a function of the nominal interest rate differential, the expected inflation differential and the change of the cumulated balance of private capital flows, Δkw. Since the nominal interest rate differential is replaced by the estimates obtained from direct estimation of the interest rate equation, the model may be expressed by the following reduced-form equation:

$$\log RE_t = c_0 - \beta_1 i_t + \beta_2 \Pi_t + \beta_3 \Delta kw + \beta_4 \log RE_{t-1} + e_t \tag{2}$$

where RE_t is the real exchange rate, i_t is the domestic and foreign nominal interest rate differential. Π_t is the expected inflation differential.

4.1.2 Frankel's Model

Frankel (1983) model has been subjected to extensive testing in recent years. The model is a reduced form equation that incorporates the Frankel (1976) and the Dornbusch (1976) monetary models. Hooper and Morton (1982) has also described the model in a different form. The principal difference between the monetary and portfolio balance approaches is the assumption made about the substitutability of domestic and foreign bonds. In the monetary approach, domestic and foreign bonds are viewed as perfect substitutes. That means that asset holders will be indifferent to the currency composition of their bond portfolios, which implies that there is no scope for relative shifts in bond supplies or in asset preferences to influence exchange rates. Alternatively, in the portfolio balance approach, because domestic and foreign bonds are viewed as imperfect substitutes, the exchange rate can be influenced by changes in bond supplies and asset preferences. An attempt is made to integrate the two approaches to arrive at a more robust and comprehensive model. This is done through the relaxing of the monetary approach assumption to perfect asset substitutability. Frankel use the basic flexible-price model of exchange rate (FLPM) as

$$\log E_t = \log M - \beta_1 \log Y_t + \beta_2 P_t \tag{3}$$

in whaich M_t is the domestic and foreign money supply differential, Y_t is the domestic and foreign income differential and P_t is the expected inflation differential.

This equation describes that the long-run equilibrium value of the exchange rate, E_t between two currencies is determined by the relative supply of and demand for the two countries monies. All variables are expressed in logarithm form. For more details, please see Cao and Ong (1994).

The basic properties of the monetary model plus the impact of relative bond supplies that is incorporated in the P-B model. This can be represented :

$$logE_t = logM_t - \beta_1 Y_t + \beta_2 P_t - \beta_3 i_t + \beta_4(b-f) \tag{4}$$

where b is the domestic bonds and f is the foreign value bonds. Equation (4) synthesizes the two approaches to exchange rate determination. The integrated model states that a domestic currency will (i) fall in value if domestic monetary growth exceeds foreign monetary growth, (ii) rise in value if domestic economic growth exceeds foreign economic growth, (iii) fall in value if expectations of domestic inflation exceed expectations of foreign inflation, and (iv) fall in value if the increase in the supply of domestic bonds exceeds the increase in the supply of foreign bonds.

The general representation of this model is :

$$logE_t = c_0 + \beta_1 logY_t - \beta_2 i_t + \beta_3 logM_t\ \beta_4 kw_t + \beta_5 \Pi_t + e_t \tag{5}$$

where E_t is the nominal exchange rate, i_t is the nominal interest rate differential, Π_t is the inflation rate differential, and M_t and Y_t are the ratio of domestic to foreign money stocks and domestic to foreign real income, respectively. The variable kw_t is the cumulative external capital balance scaled down by the wealth variable (GNP). It is defined as the cumulated deficit in the home country's current account balance. An increase in its net foreign liabilities gives a positive value.

4.1.3 Artus's Model

This model builds on the stock-flow models of Kouri and Porter (1974). This model may be reduced to :

$$\Delta logRE_t = c_0 - \Delta i_t + \Delta kw_t + \Delta^2 kw_t + e_t \tag{6}$$

where Δkw is the external capital balance and $\Delta^2 kw$ is the first differnce of that flow, and $\Delta logRE_t$ is the difference of the real exchange rate. The Δi_t variable is the difference of the interest rate differential between the domestic and the foreign country.

4.2 METHODOLOGY

The main method of testing of the models is using latest econometric techniques. OLS regression is run for each of the different models. First, the stationary test on the variables are performed. Then, standard diagnostic checks were done on the equations such as the 'Breusch Godfrey' serial correlation LM test, 'White Heteroskedasticity' test. The domestic interest rate is assumed to be endogenously determined and is estimated by instrumental variables.[7] Results are shown in tables1-4.

4.3 ANALYSIS

All variables in the boughton model are significant and the signs are correct. The interest rate is negatively related to the real exchange rate. The external capital balance is assumed to be proportionately related to the real exchange rate such that the real exchange rate will depreciate until the capital account weakens enough to restore equilibrium. The Hooper and Frankel model is likewise treated. The variables yielded wrong signs and some of them are statistically insignificant. The relative money supply differential is predicted to be positively signed but results showed it to be negative. An analysis of the correlation matrix

---

[7] The instruments are domestic and foreign values of real income and inflation, and current and lagged values of the money stock. See Boughton (1984)

of the variables revealed the variable to be inversely related to the exchange rate. The inflation rate differential is not statistically significant. Although R^2 is high, there is serious correlation problem. Artus's stock flow adjustment model appears to be less able to explain the changes in the dependent variable. However, there is no serial correlation problem and the residuals are stationary when tested. The correlation matrix revealed that the interest rate differential is not of the proper sign. Therefore, the Boughton model is chosen over the other two models.

Following that, a unit root test is undertaken for the Boughton model. The reason is simply because if the time series variables are not stationary there can be no meaningful relationship between the variables which might cause spurious regression. The dependent variable, Δkw and the lag of the dependent variable are found to be integrated in the first order at the 5 percent level of significance. Relative interest rates and inflation differential are $I(0)$ at 5 percent level of significance. The variables are all integrated of order one and there exists a stationary relationship between all the variables. Therefore a unit root test is done on the residuals of the equation and it is found to be stationary at the 1 percent level of significance. This means that the equation is cointegrated and the regressors can be deemed to be weakly exogenous. Further testing may be done since we managed to verify that the relationship between the variables is meaningful.

The error correction for the Boughton model is constructed to capture the short-run adjustment process. This is performed by using the Engle-Granger-Yoo three step methodology. At first step using the level model, we have already found that the variables are cointegrated. In the second step the short-run error correction model obtained by regressing the first difference of the regressors and regressands with an additional variable : the lagged residual form the first step. The coefficient of the lagged of the residuals will be the speed of adjustment of the dependent variable in the event of a disequilibrium. The coefficient value obtained is -0.38. (Refer to table 4). Using the speed of adjustment value and a set of residuals from the second step the third stage regression can be estimated where the long-run variable coefficient is adjusted. (See table 5). Finally we arrived at the long-run model depicting the relationship between the variables.

5. CONCLUSION

We have managed to examine a wide variety of P-B models to exchange rate determination applied to the Singapore database. The model adopted from Boughton (1987) showed the most promising among the few reduced form equations tested. A long-run equilibrium relationship between the various fundamental variables is established. Using this relation, a short-run model was ran to capture the temporal effects and the adjustment process. An error correction model was constructed and the speed of adjustment coefficient showed that the exchange rate adjusted in over 38 percent in a period. The external capital balance variable that we have considered in the Boughton model is actually the net foreign liabilities obtained as the cumulative current account balance. This means that we have included in the process a wide variety of non-monetary assets. It is worthwhile to note separate effects perhaps will provide a more insightful picture of the portfolio balance models which is essentially the clearing of the interest-bearing asset market. Essentially the significancce of the coefficients of this variable served only to support sterilised intervention have strong effects on the exchange rate. An alternative model which is the synthesised monetary and portfolio balance approach, has weaker statistical properties. However it makes it clear, between the two, that the role of monetary policy is only indirect.

The adapted model is a valid long-run equilibrium model that has faired more than satisfactorily using a battery of diagnostic tests. Only the Boughton model showed consistently displays coefficient estimates that conform to prior expectations. Other areas of future research include testing for the seasonality of the exchange rate using seasonal cointegration. An indirect test of the portfolio balance approach using the risk premia can also be done but is beyond the scope of this paper.

REFERENCES

Allen, P. R. and Peter B. K., (1980): "Asset Markets, Exchange Rates, and Economic Integration: A Synthesis", Cambridge: Cambridge University Press.

Artus, J. R., (1981): "Monetary stabilisation and government credibility", Staff papers, International Monetary Fund 28, pp.495-533.

Argy, V. and Michael, G. P., (1972): "The Forward Exchange Market and the Effects of Domestic and External Disturbances Under Alternative Exchange Rate Systems", International Monetary Fund Staff Papers 19, pp.503-32.

Boughton, J. M.,(1984): "Exchange rate movements and adjustment in financial markets", Staff papers, International Monetary Fund 31, pp. 445-468.

Boughton, J. M., (1987): "Tests of the performance of reduced form exchange rate models", Journal of International Economics 23, pp. 41-56, North-Holland.

Boughton, J. M., (1988): "The Monetary Approach to Exchange Rates: What Now Remains?", Essays in International Finance Vol. 171, Princeton University.

Branson et. al., (1979): "Exchange Rates in the Short-Run: Some Further Results", European Economic Review 12, pp.395-402.

(1977): "Exchange Rates in the Short-Run: The Dollar Deutsche Mark Rate", European Economic Review 10, pp.303-24.

Branson, W. H., (1968): "Financial Capital Flows in the U.S. Balance of Payments", Amsterdam, North-Holland.

Branson, W. H. and Dale W. H., (1985): "The Specification and Influence of Asset Markets", in Jones and Kenen (eds.): pp.749-805.

Cassel, G., (1928): Post-war Monetary Stabilisation, New York: Colombia University.

Cao Y. and Ong W L, (1994): "PPP and the Monetary Model of Exchange Rate Determination", Regional Issues in Economics Vol 1, pp. 131-150.

Dornbusch, R., (1976): "Expectations and Exchange Rate Dynamics", Journal of Political Economics Vol 84, pp.1161-76.

Frankel, J. A., (1983): "Monetary and portfolio-balance models of exchange rate determination, in: Jagdeep S. B. and Bluford H. P., eds., Economic interdependence and flexible exchange rates (MIT Press, Cambridge, MA).

Girton, L., Dale W. H., (1976): "Financial Movements and Central Bank Behaviour in a Two Country, Short-Run Portfolio Balance Model". Journal of Monetary Economics, Vol. 2, , pp.33-61.

Hahn, F. H., (1959): "The Balance of Payments in a Monetary Economy", Review of Economic Studies 26, pp.110-25.

Haldrup, N., (1994): "The asymptotics of single-equation cointegration regressions with I(1) and I(2) variables", Journal of Econometrics Vol. 63, pp.153-81.

Hooper, P. and John M., (1982): "Fluctuations in the Dollar: A Model of Nominal and Real Exchange Rate Determination", Journal of International Money and Finance 1, pp. 39-56.

Johnson, H. G., (1977): "The Monetary Approach to the Balance of Payments: A Nontechnical Guide", Journal of International Economics 7, pp.251-68.

Kouri, P. J. K. and Michael G. P., (1974): "International Capital Flows and Portfolio Equilibrium", Journal of Political Economy 82, pp.443-67.

Kearney, C. and Macdonald, R., (1986) "A Structural Portfolio Balance Model of the Sterling-Dollar Rate 1972-82", Journal of Economic Studies 12, pp.3-60.

Macdonald, R. and Mark P. T., (1993): "The Monetary Approach to the Exchange Rate: Rational Expectations, Long-Run Equilibrium, and Forecasting", IMF Staff Papers 40, pp. 89-107.

Markowitz, H. M, (1959): Portfolio Selection, New York: Wiley.

McKinnon R. I., (1969): Portfolio balance and international payments adjustment, in : Mundell R.A. and Swoboda A.K., eds., Monetary problems of the international economy, University of Chicago Press, Chicago, pp. 199-234.

McKinnon, R. I. and Oates, W. E., (1966): The implications of international economic integration for monetary, fiscal and exchange-rate policy, Studies in International Finance no. 16 (International Finance Section, Princeton University, Princeton).

Metzler, L. A., (1951): "Wealth, Saving and the Rate of Interest", Journal of Political Economy 59, pp.930-46.

Nguyen, D. and Yao C. C. (1989): "Exchange Rate Determination : The Case of Singapore", University of Adelaide.

Pigou, A. C., (1920): "Some Problems of Foreign Exchanges", Economic Journal 30, pp.460-72.

Sarantis, N., (1987): "A Dynamic Asset Market Model for the Exchange Rate of the Pound Sterling", Weltswirtsiscaftliches archiv. 123, pp. 24-38.

Tobin, J., (1967): "Liquidity Preference as Behaviour Toward Risk", New York: Wiley.

TABLE 1

Estimates of Exchange Rate Equations (1975-95)

Models	Dependent variable	Coefficient and t-statistics on :										$R^2/$ DW
		c	$logY_t$	i_t	Δi_t	$logM_t$	kw_t	Δkw_t	$\Delta^2 kw_t$	Π_t	$logRE_{t-1}$	
(1) Frankel	$logE_t$	-1.068	-0.366	-0.005		-0.011	0.304			0.001		0.97/
		$(2.92)^5$	$(-2.30)^5$	(-1.032)		(-0.135)	$(3.36)^1$			(0.204)		0.85*
(2) Boughton	$logRE_t$			-0.011				0.493		-0.012	-0.970	0.93/
				$(-2.96)^1$				$(2.66)^5$		$(-3.20)^1$	$(40.86)^1$	1.53
(3) Artus	$\Delta logRE_t$	0.009			0.001			0.667	-0.06			0.57/
		(1.22)			(-0.13)			$(4.04)^1$	(-0.18)			1.68

[1] denotes significance at the 1 percent level.

[5] denotes significance at the 5 percent level.

[10] denotes significance at the 10 percent level.

* shows that autocorrelation is present.

TABLE 2

Representation

Variable	Description
C	= constant term.
Y	= gross domestic product at market prices.
E	= exchange rate.
RE	= real exchange rates.
I	= short term interest rates.
M	= broad money supply (M2).
Π	= expected level of inflation differential
kw	= cumulative external capital balance (scaled down by GNP).
Resid	= residuals of the regression.

a.   variables with the * denotes foreign ones

TABLE 3

Regression Results
(Dependent variable: LOGRE$_t$)

Variable	Coefficient	t-statistics	Proper sign
i_t	-0.012	-2.96	-
$logRE_{t-1}$	0.970	40.86	+
Π_t	-0.012	-3.20	-
Δkw	0.493	2.66	+

$R^2 = 0.93$ DW = 1.60

ADF Statistic = -4.16***

TABLE 4

Error Correction Model (Step 2)
(Dependent variable: D(LOGRE$_t$))

Variable	Coefficient	t-statistics
C	-0.028	-1.81
i_t	-0.009	-2.10
D(logRE$_{t-1}$)	0.356	1.14
Π_t	-0.011	-2.24
Resid $_{t-1}$	-0.383	-0.847
D(kw$_{t-1}$)	-0.24	0.245

$R^2 = 0.641$ DW = 1.90

α = speed of adjustment coefficient = -0.383

TABLE 5

Error Correction Model (Step 3)
(Dependent variable: RESID)

Variable	Coefficient (c)	δ (c/α)	β
i_{t-1}	-0.001	0.0026	-0.0152
(logRE$_{t-1}$)$_{t-1}$	0.004	-0.01	0.960
Π_{t-1}	0.0005	-0.0013	-0.0135
D(kw$_{t-1}$)	0.029	-0.076	0.417

DW = 1.96

The Singapore Dollar in Inward and Outward Foreign Direct Investment: An Econometric Analysis

Foong Chee Weng
&
Shahidur **Rahman**

Nanyang Business School, Nanyang Technological University, Nanyang Avenue, Singapore 639798
Fax: +(65) 792.4217, Tel: +(65) 799.6404, Email: asrhaman@ntu.edu.sg

Abstract Inward and outward foreign direct investment play significant roles in Singapore's economy. Since the exchange rate will affect these two factors of growth, the current strong Singapore dollar has caused concern. In this paper, we explore the effect of the exchange rate on inward and outward foreign direct investment. The individual country models suggest that the real exchange rate is a significant determinant of the source and host countries for Singapore's inward and outward foreign direct investment, respectively. In pooled models, the results suggest that the real exchange rate has a significant negative effect on inward foreign direct investment and no significant effect on outward foreign direct investment. Finally, we consider some of the policy implications of these findings.

1. INTRODUCTION

As it is widely accepted, inward foreign direct investment (IFDI) has been a cornerstone in Singapore's rapid ascent from post war ruin to its current economic status. Many had regarded her IFDI strategy as highly and exceptionally successful. Throughout 1961-1990, Singapore attracted 42.7 percent of the total net IFDI flows into ASEAN, making her the most favoured nation by foreign investors in the region (Chia,1992). And further in 1996, World Trade Organisation (WTO)[1] has ranked Singapore top in the world for receiving highest IFDI per capita totalling US$13650 and ASEAN's top investment spot for receiving a total of US$40.8 billion over the period of 1985-1995.

Needless to say, IFDI had provided Singapore with abundance of benefits. They had brought in financial capital, foreign exchange, new technologies and management, marketing know-how and market access which is significant in the development of Singapore economy. Being such an important catalyst for economic growth in the past, IFDI will therefore continue to contribute significantly to Singapore growth in the future.

Nevertheless, Singapore could not depend solely on IFDI. The country had to diversify and develop its external economy in order to maintain current economic growth in the future. As such, over the past few years, Singapore has begun to focus on outward foreign direct investment (OFDI). Many companies have set up operations abroad and invested in low cost production area. Thus, as at the end of 1995, Singapore OFDI has increased tremendously to S$46.24 billion[2] from a mere S$1.7 billion in 1981. Singapore has also been one of the largest investors in Malaysia over the period 1981-1991. In addition, she

---

[1] The Straits Times, 10 of October 1996.

[2] The Straits Times, 14 of March 1997.

was also China's sixth largest investors over the first nine months of 1992 and ninth largest investors in Vietnam [Toh (1996)].

The reason is mainly because of her limitation on resources and space. The ever rising cost of doing business has forced local companies to look abroad so as to remain competitive both at home and abroad. Further, venturing abroad will enable Singapore companies to capitalise on the fast growing economy in the region. As the regional economic growth continue to be spectacular coupled with the current resource constrain, Singapore OFDI is definitely a factor of growth to be reckoned in the future.

However, the ever appreciating Singapore Dollar (SGD) had sparked off some debates as to whether it will significantly erode Singapore attractiveness and also affect Singapore position in her regionalisation drive. Even Singapore Prime Minister, Mr Goh Chok Tong, himself had requested for a re-evaluation on Singapore economic competitiveness base on the current strong SGD and high wage cost[3].

In this paper, we explore the role of exchange rate in Singapore IFDI and OFDI. As IFDI continues to be a major factor of growth and regionalisation drive gaining importance in the near future, it is significant to examine the effect of Singapore exchange rate on IFDI and OFDI and how various other factors complement each other to drive higher economic growth. Section 2 will provide an overview on IFDI, OFDI and exchange rate policies in Singapore. Next, we will examine the role of exchange rate in determining IFDI and OFDI. This will lead to an empirical study in Section 4. Lastly, a summary and some policy implications are put forward in the final section.

2. INWARD AND OUTWARD FOREIGN DIRECT INVESTMENT AND EXCHANGE RATE IN SINGAPORE

2.1 INWARD FOREIGN DIRECT INVESTMENT[4]

The separation from Malaysia in 1965 had been the turnover point for Singapore development. As Singapore could no longer rely on Malaysia for her survival after the separation, she had to find a quick solution to her serious unemployment problems. Constrained by her lack of resources, a small market, no paralled pool of domestic entrepreneurs and the inability to penetrate the world market, the only quick and sure way to solve the unemployment problem and diversify the economy at that moment was to embark on attracting foreign investors especially multinational companies (MNCs).

Singapore has consistently adopted an open and liberal policy towards IFDI even though foreign investment was not welcome in other developing countries in the early 1960s. There are no restriction and regulations on both the entry and operation of foreign companies, no control on repatriation of profits, no foreign exchange rate control, no limits on equity ownership, no rules on technology transfer and no performance requirements while imposing only minimal restrictions on foreign workers employment.

The government has also adopted a tax policy to facilitate efforts to attract foreign investors. They have granted tax incentives for pioneer operations, export promotions,

---

[3] The Strait Times, 26 of November 1996.

[4] The discussion is kept brief here. For a more detail discussion, please refer Chia (1986) and Lim et al (1988).

research and development activities and industrial upgradings. The first, introduced in 1959, was the tax holiday provided to pioneer firms. During this period, tax incentives were also provided for industrial expansion.

When Singapore adopted the export-led industrialisation strategy in 1965, the government has further introduced incentives to export based industries. These include accelerated depreciation allowances and double tax deductions for expenses on export promotion and concessionary tax rates on profits from new exports. In 1979, when Singapore attempted to restructure the economy, a new tax incentive was undertaken to promote higher technology skilled projects and to emphasise on research and development (R & D).

The government has also put in tremendous efforts to build an efficient infrastructure in an attempt to attract foreign investments to Singapore. Realising the danger of bottlenecks, they have set up industrial parks and an efficient network of telecommunications, public utilities and transportation in order to facilitate smooth transactions. This will enhance cost competitiveness which is important to make Singapore attractive to foreign investors.

Manpower has also been a major pull factor for Singapore IFDI policy in the initial stage of implementation. However, as more and more foreign investments coming in, the labour market became tight. As this could lead to high operation costs, the government has then taken numerous measures to alleviate this problem. They have taken a bold step to relax the immigration restrictions so as to increase Singapore labour force. In addition, they have encouraged higher female labour involvement, organised training programmes and at the same time provide financial support for corporate training through various schemes.

As IFDI is still an important factor to Singapore economic growth, her policies to attract IFDI are not expected to change in the future. She has yet to prove herself to be self sufficient without MNCs. Nevertheless, the nature and the type of investments sought after will be different. The emphasis will now be on high technology value added activities.

The reason for the switch is because Singapore is facing keen competition from the Third World countries in attracting IFDI. Many of them have switched their import substitution policies to export oriented policies which have caused intensive competition in attracting foreign MNCs. As such, in order to stay ahead of her competitors, Singapore has to attract higher technology and value added investment.

2.2 OUTWARD FOREIGN DIRECT INVESTMENT

Singapore companies have been investing in abroad as early as in the late seventies when the government implemented a high wage policy in order to restructure the economy. At that moment, OFDI had not been given much attention. Emphasis was then given to IFDI since foreign investors had brought tremendous growth to Singapore economy. Nevertheless, as OFDI gets more important in the later years, goverment has then started to focus on this factor.

Over the last 30 years IFDI has a key role in transforming Singapore from a poor developing country to a newly industrialising economy. IFDI has brought in capital, skills, technology and market access to Singapore. The challenge now is to sustain and build on this success for the next 30-40 years and transformed Singapore into a developed nation in terms of standard of living and quality of life and also into a global city of distinction.

However, given the resource limitation Singapore has to enhance the domestic productivity capacity to attract higher technological base activities and at the same time develop an external economy which is to encourage local companies to invest abroad and Singaporean to live and work overseas. The objective is This is needed to transform Singapore to a developed nation and to stay ahead in the competition as well as to overcome the resource limitation.

The development of Singapore external economy has to be linked to the domestic economy. This is because the ultimate goal of investing overseas is to strengthen the domestic economy and to build up Singapore reputation as the international business hub and a global city. If OFDI is at the expense of the domestic economy, it will then hollow out the latter and thus will result in structural unemployment.

The shift of a more emphasis on the external economy started when Senior Minister Lee Kuan Yew launched the regionalisation policy in 1993. This policy focus on promoting overseas investment in the Asia-Pacific region and at the same time encouraging investment in other regions where opportunity exists especially in the niche sectors in OECD countries.

Singapore government commitment was clearly reflected when it set up the Committee to Promote Enterprise Overseas (CPEO) in 1993. The objective of this committee is to recommend measures that would assist and encourage Singapore companies and businesspersons to venture overseas[5]. Later in the year, Economic Development Board had organised the first Regionalisation Forum to provide platform for comprehensive discussions on issues relevant to the regionalisation thrust.[6]

The government has also helped in providing financial assistance such as Local Enterprise Finance (overseas) Scheme (LEFS) to help Small and Medium Enterprises (SMEs) and large consortia. In response to the views and recommendation by the CPEO, the 1993 Budget had incorporated several major incentives to promote overseas investment. Some of them are unilateral tax credit for dividend income, unilateral tax credit for service income, sole tax deduction for expenses for export services and double tax deduction for expenses for overseas investment development. In addition, tax exemption for venture capital and regional funds, overseas enterprise incentive unilateral tax credit for overseas employment income and directors' fees were also introduced.

Singapore government has also participated in setting up industrial parks in host countries such as the Suzhou Industrial Park in China. They have acted as a facilitator to create the necessary environment, removed obstacles and paved the way for private sector investment. Such leadership is needed and will lead to the development of a new relationship between government and the private sector companies which is significant to the philosophy of Singapore Inc., a co-operation between the public and private sector.

With the region's spectacular economic growth expected to persist until the next decade, the prospect of outward foreign direct investment is therefore very good. This is because the development of the external economy is of paramount importance to

---

[5] In the presentation of Interim Report of the Committee to Promote Enterprise Overseas (CPEO) by Commodore Teo Chee Hean

[6] Keynote Address by Singapore's Prime Minister, Mr. Goh Chok Tong in the Regionalisation Forum Proceedings, 21-22 May 1993

Singapore goal to become a developed nation. It will provide a high standard of living and quality of life, and also make Singapore into a global city of distinction. As such, Singapore government will continue to encourage overseas investment, providing the capital, expertise and capabilities and other facilities.

2.3 EXCHANGE RATE POLICY

When Singapore gained independence in 1965, she had chosen to pegged the SGD to pound sterling. With pound sterling devalued in 1967, the authority then decided to peg SGD to gold and the US dollar. In 1972, when the pound went floating, Monetary Authority of Singapore (MAS) decided to replace it with US dollar as the intervention currency.

Following the depreciation of the US dollar which will significantly caused SGD to devalue, MAS then decided to replace the fixed exchange rate regime with a managed floating regime in June 1973. And from the September 1975 onwards, the SGD has then been managed by relating it to an undisclosed basket of trade-weighted currencies (with weights varying from time to time). In June 1978, Singapore exchange rate was "completely liberalised". This move was sparked off by the devaluation of the pound and Singapore's exclusion from the Sterling Area Countries.

Singapore's exchange rate policy has been influenced by the structure and circumstances of the economy. The small size and high degree of openness have limited the effectiveness of the conventional policies adopted by the large and closed economy where independent monetary and interest rate policies are used to achieve non-inflationary growth. The excerpts in MAS Annual Report in 1981/82 and 1984/1985 clearly reflect Singapore policy to focus on exchange rate as the intermediate target for intervention while leaving the money supply and interest rate be determined by the international market.

Teh and Shanmugaratham (1992) have pointed out two rationales for targeting exchange rate. Firstly, Singapore small size had made her a price taker in the international market. As her economy is characterised by a high degree of openness in trade, targeting the exchange rate is the most effective policy to control inflation. Secondly, as there is high capital mobility in Singapore, targeting interest rate and money supply will lead to enormous capital flows. As such, it will significantly affect the stability of the exchange rate.

In addition, Yip (1996) has also emphasised that targeting monetary growth rate is extremely difficult. This is because the development of the financial sector in the 1970s and 1980s had caused significant growth in money supply thus making it difficult to choose the appropriate growth rate to target. Further, she had also explained that a small error in interest rate targeting will have significant impact on the capital flows, causing changes in exchange rate and money supply.

3. ROLE OF EXCHANGE RATE IN INWARD AND OUTWARD FOREIGN DIRECT INVESTMENT

There are several channels through which exchange rate affects the IFDI and OFDI[7]. Some of the related researches done on this relationship are in Chunanuntatham and Sachchamarga (1982), Cushman (1987),. Froot and Stein (1991), Campa and Goldberg (1993), (Soon, 1996).

Chunanuntatham and Sachchamarga (1982) has demonstrated the role of exchange rate in affecting the present value of investment. A devaluation will lead to a positive present value and thus increasing the foreign investment and the opposite is true when there is an appreciation.

An alternative explanation focuses on the effect of currency movement on relative labour costs This is the relative wage effect cited in Cushman (1987). Relative labour costs among major industrial countries have been heavily influenced during the floating exchange rate system. A depreciation will lower the foreign currency price of its wages resulting in labour cost savings for the foreign investors. As such, a depreciation of a country's currency is associated with an increase in its IFDI

In Froot and Stein (1991), they had emphasised the effect of currency movements on relative wealth across countries and the consequences of this for IFDI when the capital market is subject to informational imperfections. A real depreciation of the currency will encourage the purchases of domestic asset by foreigners and this is associated with the increase in host countries IFDI and the opposite is true when there is a real appreciation.

Nevertheless, whether a depreciation of the host currency will lead to an influx of foreign investment, will have to depend on the import exposure of the inputs used in production. According to Campa and Goldberg (1993), a host country's currency depreciation will decrease foreign investment if there is a high percentage share of the import contents in the foreign production. In Singapore, export and import exposures are high. As such, whether a depreciation SGD will increase or decrease IFDI will have to depend on which effect dominates. If a strong SGD lowers input cost rather than increases the export price, IFDI will accelerate. Then there is a positive relationship between the exchange rate and foreign investment. On the other hand, a negative relationship is expected when the increase in export price is not completely offset by a lower imported input cost (Soon, 1996).

4. MODELLING INWARD AND OUTWARD FOREIGN DIRECT INVESTMENT WITH SINGAPORE EXCHANGE RATE

4.1 MODEL SPECIFICATION

Studies that illustrate modelling exchange rate with IFDI are found, among others in Chunanuntatham and Sachchamarga (1982), Klein and Rosengren (1990), Froot and Stein (1991) and Soon (1996).

Chunanuntatham and Sachchamarga (1982), has examined the direct theoretical relationship between the change in an exchange rate and IFDI. The paper has regressed IFDI on exchange rate, real GDP, relative prices and time trend. The methodology used

---

[7] In this section, even though the various articles only refer to IFDI, it does apply to OFDI as well.

were Ordinary Least Square and Cochrane-Orcutt iterative procedure for correcting autocorrelation. In their result, they find that exchange rate is significant in affecting IFDI.

Klein and Rosengren (1990) have explored the effect of real exchange rate on IFDI base on the relative wealth and relative wage effects. Their independent variables are real exchange rate, relative wages, relative stock which represents the wealth effect and time trend. The results obtained confirmed the relationship between the real exchange rate and IFDI and also support the relative wealth effect.

In another study, Froot and Stein (1991) have regressed different forms of capital inflows into the United States (e.g. foreign official assets, IFDI and US Treasury securities) on the real value of the dollar and a time trend. The paper has used Ordinary Least Square and find that only IFDI is statistically correlated with value of dollar. To further confirm their findings, regressions were also run on different industries and types of direct investments and on different data frequencies using the same method and similar results were obtained. Nevertheless, there were some limitations as the data were found to be autocorrelated and the model could not explain the upward trend in IFDI experienced by US in the study period.

Soon (1996) has examined the effect of wages and exchange rate in determining IFDI in Singapore. She has included IFDI stock, bilateral real exchange rate, lagged real bilateral exchange rate, cumulative effects of exchange rate and foreign and domestic unit labour cost, lagged unit labour cost and cumulative effects of unit labour cost as her independent variables. The methodology used is Ordinary Least Square and she finds that the bilateral real exchange rate and cumulative exchange rate effect have significant impact on IFDI.

Base on the above discussions, we can see that exchange rate does affect IFDI. The common variable used are real exchange rate and they have used time series model. In our paper, we will consider the model studying the impact of exchange rate on IFDI and OFDI respectively in Singapore. The model will consider individual source and host countries data as well as pooled (time series cross sectional) data[8]. The reason for performing individual regressions is to see the individual countries exchange rate effect on their investment in Singapore. On the other hand, the pooled regression will enable us to see the overall impact of exchange rate on IFDI and OFDI. Further, the rationale for considering the pooled data, unlike previous study is because it will not be able to provide us a more accurate parameter estimate. In addition, pooled model will contain the information necessary to deal with the characteristics of both the time series and cross sectional data.

Since our research is to find the role of exchange rate over IFDI and OFDI, the common explanatory variable used will be the real exchange rate while the dependent variable will be the IFDI and OFDI respectively. There are other explanatory variables that influence IFDI and OFDI, but their inclusion may complicate the model in detail but not in substance, and so, for simplicity, those are ignored. In line with Soon (1996), we use real exchange rate instead of nominal to adjust for different inflation rates. Thus, the regression models for individual countries are specified as:

$$IFDI_t = \alpha_0 + \alpha_1 RER_t + \varepsilon_t \tag{1}$$

---

[8] Please refer to any econometric textbook for a more detail theoretical discussion on time series cross sectional model

$$OFDI_t = \beta_0 + \beta_1 RER_t + \mu_t \tag{2}$$

and combining the time series and cross sectional data together, the pooled regression models are specified as:

$$IFDI_{it} = \alpha_{0i} + \alpha_1 RER_{it} + \varepsilon_{it} \tag{3}$$

$$OFDI_{kt} = \beta_{0k} + \beta_1 RER_{kt} + \mu_{kt} \tag{4}$$

> i =1 to 9 for USA, Japan, UK, Australia, Germany, Hong Kong, Malaysia, Switzerland, Netherlands respectively,
>
> k =1 to 9 for Malaysia, Indonesia, Thailand, Hong Kong, Taiwan, USA, Australia, Netherlands and UK respectively;
>
> t = 1981-1993 for IFDI and 1982-1994 for OFDI respectively.

In this specification, IFDI and OFDI represent annual inward and outward foreign direct investment respectively. RER denotes the bilateral real exchange rate which is the amount of foreign currencies per unit of SGD. An increase means that SGD appreciate with respect to the nominator foreign currency. α and β are intercepts and slope coefficients respectively. μ and ε are the stochastic disturbance term

As explain in the previous section, the sign of the parameter α_1 in equation (1) and (3) could be either positive or negative depending on whether the increase in cost could be offset by profit gained investing here or whether export or import exposure dominates. On the other hand, in equation (2) and (4), β_1 is expected to be negative as an increase in RER means a depreciation in SGD. This will result in higher cost of capital for local investors to invest abroad, thus depressing overseas investment.

Countries chosen for the first model are the major investors in Singapore during 1981-1993. In the second model, we have chosen the three major hosts ASEAN countries throughout 1982-1994 and two major East Asian economies due to the current emphasis on regionalisation. We have also included USA, Australia, Netherlands and UK as there will also be opportunities fro profitable investment in these industrial countries.

4.2 METHODOLOGY

We have used Ordinary Least Square method to estimate the individual country regressions. In pooled regressions, we have employed the Ordinary Least Square with dummy variable estimation technique. In this technique, α_{0i} and α_{0k} are assumed to be fixed parameters and ε_{it} and μ_{it} are assumed to be independently and identically distributed random variables respectively. The above two pooled models using specific country dummy variables D's are re-specified as

$$IFDI_{it} = \sum_{j=1}^{9} \alpha_{0j} D_{jt} + \alpha_1 RER_{it} + \varepsilon_{it} \tag{5}$$

$$OFDI_{kt} = \sum_{j=1}^{9} \beta_{0j} D_{jt} + \beta_1 RER_{kt} + \mu_{kt} \tag{6}$$

For equation (5) the dummy variable is $D_{jt} = 1$, if $j = i$ and 0 otherwise. For equation (6) $D_{jt} = 1$, if $j = k$ and 0 otherwise.

Thus the dummy variable that corresponds to individual country j will take the value unity for observations on individual country j but will be zero for observations on other countries.

4.3 DATA SOURCES

Singapore inward and outward foreign direct investment model are estimated by using data from Foreign Equity Investment in Singapore, Singapore Investment Abroad and Singapore Yearbook of Statistics[9]. The bilateral real exchange rate is generated from the bilateral nominal exchange rate adjusted for CPI inflation. Data for the nominal exchange rate and consumer price indices at base year 1990 are abstracted from International Financial Statistics.

4.4 REGRESSION RESULTS

4.4.1 Inward Foreign Direct Investment and Econometric Interpretation

The regressions for individual country are presented in Table 1. Majority of the estimated coefficients are negatively signed except for USA, Malaysia and Switzerland. The results show that real exchange rate is significant in affecting investment flows from Japan, United Kingdom and Netherlands. The R^2 for each of these individual country models is between 25 percent and 37 percent, indicating a good fit for IFDI, explaining 25 percent to 37 percent of the latter. The results also show that the estimated coefficients are negatively signed indicating that an appreciation of SGD will lead to a depression in IFDI from these countries. This is because a strong SGD will imply a higher amount of foreign currencies needed to invest. As all of them are the top investors in Singapore, any changes in the real exchange rate will lead to a huge change in their cost of capital and subsequently their production cost.

Nevertheless, RER does not have a significant impact on the investment flows from other countries. They will invest in Singapore even though SGD appreciates against their home currencies or their home currencies depreciate against SGD. For countries like Australia, Germany and Switzerland, the rationale for investing in Singapore may be because of her strategic locational advantage, political stability and the large market surrounding her. With Singapore's strategic situation in the heart of South East Asia and the huge regional market mostly not penetrated, the foreign investors will find it profitable to invest here even though the strong SGD will incur additional costs to them. Further, the amount invested is not as much as compare to Japan, United Kingdom and Netherlands which implied that the movement of RER will not lead to a huge variation in their capital and production costs. For USA, which is the top investor over the last decade, the appreciation of SGD will significantly affect their production and capital costs as the amount invested is large. However, the strategic location of Singapore and the profits from penetrating the huge regional market will be large enough to cover the loss due to the increase in these costs. In addition, many of the USA companies invested here were large multinationals. They would have enough capital to deal with the appreciating SGD.

---

[9] The IFDI and OFDI data are computed by first differencing the year end equity data and then deflated by Gross Fixed Capital Formation deflator base at 1990.

Besides the locational advantage and large regional market, the reason for increasing investment from Hong Kong despite the strong SGD, may be because of the uncertainty in Hong Kong future. Furthermore, the culture and the environment in Singapore is similar to Hong Kong which enable the Hong Kong investors to adapt to the local working life, easily. For Malaysia, the major attractive point may be due to opportunities in some businesses which are not available there. The cultural similarity in Singapore will also be an attractive point as it will not pose any problems for Malaysian to adapt to the working life here. In addition, Singapore is very near to Malaysia which will enable easy communication with their headquarters in Kuala Lumpur.

The pooled regression result is shown in Table 3. From this table, we can see that the R^2 is closed to 40 percent indicating a good explanation of the model by using RER alone. The estimated coefficients of the RER are highly significant and positively signed. These suggest that an appreciating SGD against the major investors country has an overall negative impact on IFDI in Singapore. Mathematically, one unit increase in RER (i.e. one unit of appreciation in SGD), will lead to a 571.62 units decrease in IFDI. This evidence suggests that the profits gained may not be able to cover up the loss incurred due to a higher initial cost of capital. In addition, despite the high exposure of imported inputs, the decrease in cost of production due to the strong SGD has not be able to offset the increase in the highly competitive export price. As such, the strong SGD has affected Singapore's export competitiveness.

The coefficients of dummy variables are all positive and significant. This simply means that each of these countries will have a significant different positive intercept.

4.4.2 Outward Foreign Direct Investment and Econometric Interpretation

Table 2 presents the results for individual host country regressions. Majority of the estimated coefficients are negatively signed except for Hong Kong, Taiwan, Netherlands and UK. The results also show that RER does significantly affect Singapore investment abroad particularly in Malaysia, Indonesia and Hong Kong. The R^2 of each of these countries range from 29 percent to 67 percent indicating a good explanation of OFDI by using RER. The estimated coefficient for Malaysia and Indonesia are also negatively signed which are consistent with prior expectation as it indicates that a stronger SGD will lead to an initial lower cost of capital, thus ncouraging more overseas investment. However, Hong Kong estimated coefficient is negatively signed. This may be due to the uncertainty in Hong Kong future when the British colony is returned back to China.

Nevertheless, the RER does not have a significant impact on Singapore OFDI to other countries. For Thailand, this may be because of her large domestic market and low cost of production which are attractive enough for local companies to invest there. Even though, Baht is to appreciate against SGD slightly, the benefits gain from the large domestic market and low production cost are good enough to cover the lost incurred. For Taiwan, the major plus point may be due to her large domestic market which might outweigh the impact of real exchange rate on the investment flows. Furthermore, her position as one of the Newly Industrialised Economies (NIEs) will enable Singapore companies to ride on her success. In USA, Australia, Netherlands and UK, local investors are targeting the niche industries. They will only invest if there is an opportunity to secure a quick and substantial profits from the industries. In this case, even though SGD depreciates, the profit gained will be sufficient to cover the loss sue to the depreciation. As such, exchange rate considerations will be minimal in their decision making.

Table 3 presents the pooled regression results. Even though the R^2 is not as high as in the pooled regressions for IFDI, it indicates a reasonably good fit for the model, explaining about 20 percent of the total variation in OFDI especially when one is considering only RER as an independent variable in the model. Nevertheless, the estimated coefficient for RER is insignificant even though it is correctly signed. These suggest that even if SGD is to depreciate, local investors will not be attracted to spread out their operations overseas given that there are other determining factors such as the large host country markets, the low production costs and beneficial local and foreign tax incentives.

Table 3 also shows that all the coefficients of dummy variables are positively signed except for Indonesia and Thailand. However, only dummy variable for Malaysia is significant which indicates that there will be a different intercept for this country.

5. POLICY IMPLICATIONS AND CONCLUSION

IFDI and OFDI play an important role in Singapore goal to achieve a developed nation status in terms of standard of living and become a global city of distinction. A critical factor to consider is whether the current strong SGD has any impact on these important source of growth to Singapore.

The discussion earlier has given us some insight on the exchange rate impact on inward and outward foreign direct investment in Singapore. We have done an exchange rate analysis on IFDI and OFDI. The results obtained suggest that a RER has a significant impact on IFDI but not so on OFDI. In IFDI context, the overall significance of RER implies that exchange rate policy management has a high influence on the IFDI policy and other policies such as the wage, manpower and tax policy. This is because a strong exchange rate policy which increases the capital and production costs will need a low wage and tax rate policy in order to compensate for the loss of cost competitiveness. In order to have a low wage rate, the government then have to relax the intake of foreign labours so as to increase the supply the labour and thus lowering the wage rate. As such, to stay ahead in international competition, Singapore has to continue to depend, even more heavily than in the past, on other factors that made her attractive such as a highly skilled labour force, an efficient network of telecommunication and infrastructure, a stable political environment and a responsive government. In OFDI context, the insignificance of RER implies that exchange rate should not be used as a tool to boost overseas investment. To become an international business hub, Singapore will has to coordinate the OFDI policy with other policies such as tax and manpower policies so as to encourage local investors to invest overseas.

For the future research, more rigorous analysis of the model can be done by using error component and random coefficient framework. The model may be further extended by considering other explanatory variables that relate to IFDI and OFDI. In addition, the concern of whether IFDI (OFDI) cause the movement of exchange rate or exchange rate causes the changes of IFDI (OFDI) may also be another future research.

REFERENCES

Campa, J. and Goldberg, L. (1993): "Investment in Manufacturing, Exchange Rate and External Exposure," NBER working paper series no. 4378.

Chia, S. Y. (1986): "Direct foreign investment and the Industrialization process in Singapore," In Lim, C.Y. and Lloyd, P.J. eds., Singapore: Resources and Growth, Singapore: Singapore University Press, pp79-117.

Chia, S.Y. (1992): Foreign Direct Investment in ASEAN economies. Asian Development Review, 5(1), pp. 60-102.

Department of Statistics: Yearbook Of Statistics, various years, Singapore.

Department of Statistics: Foreign Equity Investment in Singapore 1980-1989, Singapore.

Department of Statistics: Foreign Equity Investment in Singapore 1990-1992, Singapore.

Department of Statistics: Singapore Investment Abroad 1976-1989, Singapore.

Department of Statistics: Singapore Investment Abroad 1990-1993, Singapore.

Judge G. G. et all (1988): "The Theory and Practice of Econometrics," Canada: John Wiley & Sons, Inc. .

Cushman, D. O. (1987): "The effects of real wages and labour productivity on foreign direct investment," Southern Economic Journal, 54, pp. 174-185.

Economic Development Board: Regionalisation Forum Proceedings, 21-22 May 1993

Economic Development Board: Singapore Unlimited: Singapore Forum Proceedings, 19th April 1994, Queen Elizabeth II Conference Centre - London.

Froot, K. A. and Stein, J.C. (1991): "Exchange rates and foreign direct investment: An imperfect capital markets approach," Quarterly Journal of Economics, 55(4), pp.1191-1217.

Klein, M. W. and Rosengren, E. (1992): "The Real Exchange Rate and Foreign Direct Investment in the United States: Relative Wealth vs Relative Wage Effects," NBER working paper series no. 4192.

Lim, C. Y. and Associates (1988): "Policy Options for Singapore Economy," Chapter 9 and 11, Singapore: McGraw Hill.

Ministry of Finance: Final Report of the Committee to Promote Enterprise Overseas. Singapore National Printers Publishers Pte Ltd. August 1993.

Ministry of Finance: Interim Report of the Committee to Promote Enterprise Overseas. Singapore National Printers Publishers Pte Ltd. May 1993

Soon L.Y. (1996): "Economic Restructuring through Foreign Direct Investment: The Role of Wages and Exchange Rates," Economic Policy Management in Singapore, Singapore: Addison Wesley.

Teh K.P. and Shanmugaratnam, T. (1992): "Exchange rate policy: Philosophy and conduct over the past decade," In Low, L. and Toh M. H. eds., Public Policies in Singapore: Changes in the 1980s and Future Signpost, Singapore: Times Academic Press.

The Straits Times, 10 October 1996

The Straits Times, 26 November 1996

The Straits Times,14 March 1997

Toh T. S. (1996): "Regionalism, Sub-regionalism and Regionalisation," Economic Policy Management in Singapore, Singapore: Addison Wesley.

Yip. S. L.(1996): "Exchange Rate Management in Singapore," Economic Policy Management in Singapore, Singapore: Addison Wesley.

TABLE 1

Individual Country Regression Results for IFDI

(Sample size 13)

COUNTRIES	CONSTANT	RER	R^2
USA	58.997	1181.60	0.0068
	(0.0248)	(0.2749)	
JAPAN	2913.6	-2205.90	0.3687
	(3.718)***	(-2.535)**	
UK	2217.10	-5379.10	0.2953
	(2.399)**	(-2.147)*	
AUSTRALIA	741.52	-653.25	0.0093
	(0.466)	(-0.3209)	
GERMANY	104.41	-48.623	0.0308
	(1.195)	(-0.591)	
HONG KONG	1495.9	-290.92	0.1146
	(1.365)	(0.258)	
MALAYSIA	-30.721	132.37	0.0059
	(-0.045)	(0.2545)	
SWITZERLAND	182.44	49.511	0.0042
	(0.8669)	(0.2153)	
NETHERLANDS	1336.7	-903.03	0.2575
	(2.507)**	(-1.953)*	

Notes: Figures in parenthesis are t-statistics

*** significant at 1 percent level

** significant at 5 percent level

* significant at 10 percent level

TABLE 2

Individual Country Regression Results for OFDI

(Sample size 13)

COUNTRIES	CONSTANT	RER	R^2
MALAYSIA	-2881.9	2454.3	0.6630
	(-4.048)***	(4.652)***	
INDONESIA	-241.89	33.843	0.3702
	(-1.944)*	(2.543)**	
THAILAND	-342.51	28.686	0.1445
	(1.174)	(1.363)	
HONG KONG	2949.7	-588.86	0.2980
	(2.428)**	(-2.161)*	
TAIWAN	319.71	-1708.6	0.0781
	(1.085)	(-0.9653)	
USA	-637.76	1399.6	0.1035
	(-0.9197)	(1.127)	
AUSTRALIA	55.278	13.269	0.0001
	(0.1925)	(0.0369)	
NETHERLANDS	283.94	-220.24	0.0478
	(0.8349)	(-0.743)	
UK	-29.204	247.70	0.0272
	(-0.09)	(0.2862)	

Notes: Figures in parenthesis are t-statistics

*** significant at 1 percent level

** significant at 5 percent level

* significant at 10 percent level

TABLE 3

Pooled Regression Results for IFDI and OFDI

REGRESSORS:	ESTIMATED COEFFICIENT	REGRESSORS:	ESTIMATED COEFFICIENT
RER	-571.62	RER	28.189
	(-2.684)**		(0.8172)
CONSTANT		CONSTANT	
USA	1027.6	MALAYSIA	362.05
	(6.150)***		(4.108)***
JAPAN	1477.7	INDONESIA	-190.12
	(6.670)***		(-0.5857)
UK	459.72	THAILAND	-335.63
	(3.239)***		(-0..6948)
AUSTRALIA	678.03	HONG KONG	209.13
	(3.328)***		(1.226)*
GERMANY	652.81	TAIWAN	32.349
	(2.582)**		(0.4295)
HONG KONG	2753.8	USA	125.74
	(2.863)***		(1.622)*
MALAYSIA	886.15	AUSTRALIA	43.427
	(2.938)***		(0.5433)
SWITZERLAND	739.18	NETHERLANDS	4.1598
	(3.289)***		(0.0492)
NETHERLAND	961.55	UK	52.3347
	(3.759)***		(0.6870)
R^2	0.3523	R^2	0.2034

Notes: Figures in parenthesis are t-statistics

*** significant at 1 percent level

** significant at 5 percent level

* significant at 10 percent level

Impact of Asset Inflation on Production Cost in Singapore

Foong Yat Leng
&
Liu *Yunhua*

Nanyang Business School, Nanyang Technological University, Nanyang Avenue, Singapore 639798
Fax: +(65) 792.4217, Tel: +(65) 799.4949, Email: ayuliu@ntu.edu.sg

Abstract Asset inflation may result in high production cost. However, the impact may differ across industries due to differing relative importance of fixed asset expenditure. This study analyses the trends in share of land and buildings costs in total production costs for different industries over time. Results show moderate increases of land and buildings cost share in all economic sectors except manufacturing. The study also finds that asset inflation has a negative impact on the share of both manufacturing and commerce in total output, but not t for the shares of transport and communications, and finance and business services.

1. INTRODUCTION

Reports of multinational companies (MNCs) moving out of Singapore to neighbours have increased in recent years. High production cost could be one reason. Asset inflation may result in high production cost. However, the impact may be different to industries due to various weightings in fixed asset expenditure. Over the years, the different industries have either grown or shrunk in their share of Singapore's Gross Domestic Product (GDP). This study analyses the possible impact of asset price changes on production cost and the structural change of Singapore's economy.

Two questions that may be asked are:
Question 1: What is the trend of cost share of land in total production cost for each economic sector?
Question 2: Has the rising land cost affected Singapore's economic structure?

The paper is organised as follows. The current development of asset market in Singapore is briefed in Section 2. Methodology and data management are explained in Section 3. Sections 4 and 5 analyse the results and attempts to answer the two questions as posed. Finally, Section 6 concludes the report.

2. THE CURRENT DEVELOPMENT OF ASSET MARKET IN SINGAPORE

Figure 1 plots the various property price indices and the GDP deflator over the time period of 1980-1994. Property price index, the price ratio of current price per square meter (psm) of floor space compared with that of the base year 1990, is used to monitor the price movement of private property in Singapore. 'Commercial' refers to the property price index for the commercial sector, while 'Industrial' refers to the property price index for the industrial sector. 'All Properties' refers to the weighted property price index for all sectors. 'GDP deflator' is the aggregate price index of the GDP of the economy. It measures implicitly the price level of the current GDP relative to the base year set at 100. The deflators are derived as ratios of current price estimates of the year in question to corresponding estimates of the base year price.

This is an attempt to compare the various property inflation rates with that of the overall economy's. Property prices fell sharply in the recession years, before they picked up and rose rapidly in the 1990s. In sectoral analysis, prices for the commercial sector rose higher than the industrial sector under years 1986-1990 and reflected the higher demand for, or the lower supply of commercial space. In the 1990s however, the industrial property price index rose higher.

According to Ho and Sim (1992), rentals and sale prices of office space in the Central Area (Central Business District and Orchard Road) soared to unprecedented high from about $25psm and $2,500psm in 1978 to over $70psm and $15,000psm respectively by 1981 due to speculative activities and economic boom in the period 1979-1981. The real impact of boom was felt in 1986-1987 when several large office complexes were completed. Unfortunately, Singapore was then facing recession and this created a glut situation and occupancy rate dropped to a low of 78 percent in 1986. From 1987 to the present, the occupancy rate has been increasing steadily, rising from 85.8 percent in 1988 to over 90 percent in 1990. Rentals and sale prices have also been on the upward trend in response to the higher demand as the economy recovers and the slow increase in supply of new office space.

3. METHODOLOGY AND DATA MANAGEMENT

The industries studied in this paper are classified according to the Singapore Standard Industrial Classifications as at 1990. The four economic sectors studied are: manufacturing; commerce; transport, storage and communications, and finance, insurance, real estate and business services. The period observed is 1980-1993.

Cost share of land and buildings in total production cost for different economic sectors is calculated. Rent and expenditure on land and buildings are used for the asset expenditure in this study. Department of Statistics (1990) defines expenditure on land and buildings, a capital expenditure, as purchases of land and buildings, cost of alteration and major repairs to land and buildings during the year, valued at actual costs incurred. Total operating expenditure and total capital expenditure make up total cost of production. The cost share of land and buildings expresses the sum of rent and expenditure on land and buildings as a percentage of the total cost of production for the year. Results are collected for all the four sectors to determine any possible trend movements.

In order to see whether the change in Singapore's economic structure is affected by asset inflation, a linear regression model is constructed. The change in Singapore's economic structure represented by the share of GDP contributed by economic sector i, is denoted by Q_i, which is used as the dependent variable. The regressor is the cost share of land and buildings for economic sector i, CR_i. The model is:

$$Q_i = a + bCR_I \tag{1}$$

where a and b are parameters. The significance of parameter b is that it can provide us information on whether the change in output share of a specific sector to the total output is affected by the change in the land cost share of its total production cost.

4. LAND COST IN DIFFERENT INDUSTRIES

Table 1 tabulates the cost share of land and buildings for all sectors by expressing the rent and expenditure on land and buildings of all four sectors as a percentage of total cost of production by all four sectors. The respective cost share of land and buildings for each sector is achieved by dividing its rent and expenditure on land and buildings with its total cost of production for the year.

A rise in the cost share of land and buildings implies that asset price increases faster than that of other production factors. A higher cost share of land and buildings means that rent and expenditure on land and buildings carries a greater cost burden on companies. The rise can also imply an expansion in real asset expenditure.

All Sectors. Cost share of land and buildings for all sectors has increased from 5.81 percent in 1980 to 11.31 percent in 1993. Asset inflation has almost doubled the share of rent and expenditure on land and buildings in total production cost for the past 13 years. There is no sharp reduction in the cost share of land and buildings in 1986, despite the slowdown in economy. Closer inspection shows rapid rise in the cost share by the finance and business services sector being the reason.

Manufacturing. The manufacturing sector is the only sector that records no change in the cost share of land and buildings over the years. Rent and expenditure on land and buildings remains at around 7 percent of total production cost in both 1980 and 1993. Since the economic boom in 1982, the cost share has remained stable at 5 percent-7 percent. Asset inflation appears to have no impact on cost share of land and buildings for manufacturing. This can imply lower real asset expenditure by the companies in the recent years. The fall in the years 1985-1988 reflects companies' unwillingness to invest so much in land and buildings given low economic growth rates and business confidence, hence the lower asset prices and real asset expansion.

Commerce. Rent and expenditure on land and buildings contributes a large 15.25 percent of total production cost for the commerce sector in 1993. The sector's share of rent and expenditure on land and buildings has been the largest among the 4 since 1980. The cost share has increased from 13.18 percent in 1980 to 15.25 percent in 1993. The fall in cost share in years 1985-1986 reflects the lower demand for commercial space during the recession period.

Transport, Storage and Communications. Cost share of rent and expenditure on land and buildings is 5.88 percent in 1993, a rise from 3.41 percent in 1980. 1984 stands out with a high 20.50 percent due to the construction of Mass Rapid Transit (MRT), hence the higher asset prices. Cost share of land and buildings has increased due to higher asset prices. Asset inflation does have some impact on production cost for the transport and communications sector.

Finance, Insurance, Real Estate and Business. While asset expenditure for finance and business services makes up 4.66 percent in 1980, the cost share rises to 15.60 percent in 1993. This is a 10.94 percent increase for the period. Higher rentals and land prices especially in the Central Area is seen to have a huge impact on total production cost of the sector.

With regard to escalating business cost since the cost-cutting period of 1986-87, the Cost Review Committee (1993) noted that businessmen are most concerned with the increasing labour cost, rising rentals and appreciating Singapore currency. Table 2 records the cost share of remuneration and the impact on various sectors. Remuneration, comprises of wages and salaries, employers' contribution to CPF/pension funds and other benefits, is used as a measure of labour cost.

During the period, the share of remuneration to total production cost for all sectors has increased by 6.79 percent. Remuneration contributes 33.41 percent to total production cost for manufacturing in 1993. The cost share of remuneration for manufacturing is the largest among the four sectors. Remuneration, rather than rent and expenditure on land and buildings, carries a greater cost burden to the manufacturing companies. To them, increasing labour cost may be of greater concern than rising rentals and land prices. Cost share of remuneration for commerce falls by 3.49 percent to 26.12 percent in 1993, while that of transport and communications, and finance and business services increase to 13.43 percent and 13.07 percent respectively.

5. LAND COST AND STRUCTURAL CHANGE

In Table 3, finance and business services sector records an impressive 28.37 percent of GDP in 1993. In contrast, the manufacturing sector have shrunk from contributing the highest share in 1980 to a lower 26.02 percent in 1993. Both commerce, and transport and communications have also reduced their share of Singapore's GDP.

This section examines the impact of asset inflation on the economic structure of Singapore. Estimation is based on Ordinary Least Square (OLS) method. Lags of CR_i are used in the models since it is reasonable to assume that the impact on the economic structure will not appear in the same year. The following model is used, after CR_{i-1} is seen the most significant for the model, hence:

$$Q_i = a + bCR_{i-1} \tag{2}$$

where CR_{i-1} is the first lag of CR_i .

Manufacturing

$$Q_m = 0.37 + (-1.59)CR_{m-1} \tag{3}$$
$$(15.435) \quad (-4.430)$$

R-square = 0.6856   n = 12

It is a reasonably good fit with R-square of 0.6856. At 90 percent level of confidence, CR_{m-1} is significant with the t-value at -4.430 and proves that the rise in cost share of land and buildings is negatively related to the economic contribution of the manufacturing sector. That is, that high rent and land cost do have a direct impact on the shrinking of the manufacturing sector.

Commerce

$$Q_c = 0.24 + (-0.40)CR_{c-1} \tag{4}$$
$$(14.877) \quad (-3.713)$$

R-square = 0.5796   n = 12

As in the manufacturing sector, CR_{c-1} is again significant at 90 percent level of confidence with t-value of -3.713. Asset inflation has a negative impact on commerce's economic performance. However, the impact is not as significant as that in manufacturing. This is best reflected by the relatively poor fit of the model at R-square of 0.5796 and a smaller b at -0.40 compared to those of manufacturing.

Transport, Storage and Communications

$$Q_t = 0.13 + 0.02CR_{t-1} \tag{5}$$
$$(50.356) \quad (0.768)$$

R-square = 0.0557   n = 12

A relatively poor fit of R-square at 0.0557 and insignificant CR_{t-1} at 90 percent level of confidence indicate that the change in cost share of rent and expenditure on land and buildings, hence asset inflation, have no impact on the sector's economic performance during the period.

Finance, Insurance, Real Estate and Business Services

$$Q_f = 0.24 + 0.10CR_{f-1} \qquad\qquad\qquad\qquad (6)$$
$$\text{(16.769)} \quad \text{(0.889)}$$

R-square = 0.0733   n = 12

Similarly for finance and business services, with R-square at 0.0733 and insignificant CR_{t-i} at 90 percent level of confidence, there is no evidence that rising asset cost has any impact on the growth of the finance and business services sector. There is a problem of causality. The expansion of the sector may have led to greater demand for land and this in turn jack up the land and property prices.

6. CONCLUSION

This study analyses the impact of asset inflation on the cost share of land and buildings, and on the Singapore's economic structure. All sectors are observed to have moderate increases in the cost share of land and buildings, except manufacturing. Commerce has the highest percentage of rent and expenditure on land and buildings in total production cost, while the finance and business services sector experiences the greatest increase in the cost share for the period. Regression analysis in section 5 finds that asset inflation has a negative impact on the percentage of output of manufacturing and commerce sectors to the total output respectively. On the other hand, transport and communications, and finance and business services prove that higher rentals and land prices have no such impact on theirs.

REFERENCES

Cost Review Committee, Singapore (1993): "Business Costs and Competitiveness" in *Report of the Cost Review Committee*, Ministry of Trade and Industry, Singapore.

Department of Statistics, Singapore (1990-93): *Economic Survey Series:Hotels and Catering*, Singapore.

_____ (1990-93): *Economic Survey Series:The Service Secto*, Singapore.

_____ (1990-93): *Economic Survey Series: Wholesale and Retail*, Singapore.

_____ (1980-89): *Report on the Survey of Services*, Singapore.

_____ (1979-89): *Report on the Survey of Wholesale trade, Retail trade, Restaurants and Hotels*, Singapore.

_____ (1990-94): *Yearbook of Statistics*, Singapore.

Economic Development Board, Singapore (1980-1993): *Report on the Census of Industrial Production*, Singapore.

Ho, C.W. and Sim L.L. (1992): *Studies on the Property Market*, Singapore University Press, Singapore.

TABLE 1

Cost Share of Land and Buildings by Industry (1980-1993)

(%)

Year	All Sectors	Manufacturing	Commerce	Transport and Communications	Finance and Business Services
1980	5.81	7.29	13.18	3.41	4.66
1982	6.41	9.00	16.52	5.74	4.34
1984	8.68	8.24	17.40	20.50	3.64
1985	6.77	6.13	16.88	5.13	5.54
1986	10.64	5.92	14.88	3.25	17.74
1987	9.88	5.52	14.48	3.65	17.38
1988	8.24	5.34	13.25	3.15	11.87
1989	10.66	6.72	14.45	3.24	18.14
1990	11.48	6.58	15.69	7.57	15.85
1991	9.79	6.50	16.59	5.77	10.25
1992	10.44	6.51	15.65	5.45	13.77
1993	11.31	7.29	15.25	5.88	15.60
Increase	*5.49*	*0.00*	*2.08*	*2.48*	*10.94*

a. Source: *Economic Survey Series, 1990-1993, Report on the Survey of Services, 1980-1989, Report on the Survey of Wholesale trade, Retail trade, Restaurants and Hotels, 1979-1989.* Department of Statistics, Singapore. *Report on the Census of Industrial Production, 1980-1993.* Economic Development Board, Singapore.

b. Rent is adjusted for cost share of land and buildings in table 1.

TABLE 2

Cost Share of Remuneration by Industry (1980, 1993)

(%)

Year	All Sectors	Manufacturing	Commerce	Transport and Communications	Finance and Business Services
1980	14.63	32.80	29.61	11.98	5.58
1993	21.41	33.41	26.12	13.43	13.07
Increase	*6.79*	*0.61*	*-3.49*	*1.44*	*7.22*

Source: Refer to Table 1.

TABLE 3
GDP by Industry (1980-1993)

Year	Total (million dollars)	Manufacturing (million dollars)	(%)	Commerce (million dollars)	(%)	Transport and Communications (million dollars)	(%)	Finance and Business Services (million dollars)	(%)
1980	25,090.7	7,312.7	29.15	5,435.1	21.66	3,522.2	14.04	4,944.0	19.70
1982	32,669.9	8,153.5	24.96	6,387.5	19.55	4,435.8	13.58	7,756.6	23.74
1984	40,047.9	9,863.4	24.63	6,885.5	17.19	5,222.3	13.04	9,962.7	24.88
1985	38,923.5	9,184.3	23.60	6,636.3	17.05	5,234.5	13.45	1,0652	27.37
1986	38,962.0	10,305.0	26.45	6,516.0	16.72	5,333.0	13.69	9,798.0	25.15
1987	43,145.0	12,209.0	28.30	7,369.0	17.08	5,941.0	13.77	10,945.0	25.37
1988	51,082.0	15,461.0	30.27	8,877.0	17.38	6,899.0	13.51	12,315.0	24.11
1989	58,943.0	17,346.0	29.43	10,142.0	17.21	7,987.0	13.55	14,731.0	24.99
1990	67,878.9	19,393.1	28.57	12,764.2	18.80	8,715.6	12.84	17,835.1	26.27
1991	75,320.9	21,191.4	28.13	14,081.9	18.70	9,991.3	13.26	19,857.8	26.36
1992	80,997.5	21,236.7	26.22	15,093.9	18.64	10,168.7	12.55	22,235.5	27.45
1993	94,258.7	24,524.3	26.02	17,933.9	19.03	11,494.5	12.19	26,738.6	28.37

a.   Source: *Yearbook of Statistics, 1990-1994.* Department of Statistics, Singapore.

FIGURE 1

Property Price Index by Sector and GDP Deflator (1980-1994)

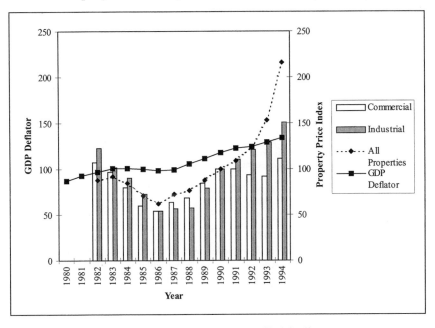

a.   Source: *Yearbook of Statistics, 1990-1994*. Department of Statistics, Singapore.

b.   1980, 1981 figures not available for property price indices.

A Model of the Commercial Loan Market in Singapore

Goh Kuang Hui
&
Wu Ying

Nanyang Business School, Nanyang Technological University, Nanyang Avenue, Singapore 639798
Fax: +(65) 792.4217, Tel: +(65) 799.6293, Email: awuying@ntu.edu.sg

Abstract We set ourselves the task of deriving both the demand and supply functions for the commercial loan market. The model is estimated under both equilibrium and disequilibrium conditions. The former is estimated using the Two Stage Least Squares method, and Directional Method I is used for the latter. The Directional Method I helps us to separate the loan market into credit slack or credit rationing regime for the period from 1985-1995. We do not find evidence that the loan market is either predominantly in excess demand or excess supply. The results from the Granger Causality test also show that the growth of commercial loan aggregates does not help explain real GDP growth.

1. INTRODUCTION

1.1 MOTIVATION FOR OUR STUDY

For years, Singapore has committed to maintaining a managed floating exchange-rate policy as a way to ensure macro-economic stability, particularly price stability. Monetary policy is not suitable due to its ineffectiveness in a small open economy. This argument is based on the IS-LM approach, which disregards bank credit and implicitly assumes that bank loans are perfect substitutes for bonds. However, recent theoretical work on corporate finance indicates that capital market imperfections could result from asymmetries of information between borrowers and lenders. In contrast, banks may have comparative advantage over securities markets. Fama (1985) noted that banks had informational advantage attributed to the ongoing credit relationships and established knowledge of borrowers' deposit history. This comparative advantage suggests a sort of imperfect substitutability between indirect finance and direct finance. It follows that banking relationships and the availability of bank loans may become a conduit to transmit monetary shocks to real sectors of the economy.

The aim of our study is to construct a model of demand and supply for commercial loans in Singapore. We hope that it will deepen our understanding of the loan market and in particular, its macroeconomic implications for the real effect of bank credit channel in Singapore.

1.2 THE MARKET FOR COMMERCIAL LOANS IN SINGAPORE

Commercial banks provide the necessary funds for loans to the various industries in Singapore. The types of loans and advances include overdrafts, term loans, bill discounting and trust receipts. About 70 percent of the total assets of banks are in the form of loans and advances which include bill financing.

Commercial lending is largely influenced by the economic development and growth of the various sectors in the economy. In the period from 1985 to 1995, the general commerce sector and building and construction sector absorbed on average about 50 percent of the total amount of loans in nominal values. Their contribution to the growth in loans and advances averaged 54 percent for the period from 1987 to 1995, excluding the years when these two sectors were badly hit by the 1985 recession. (see Table 1). Both sectors are likely to continue to dominate the loans market in the future. Term loans with one year or less to maturity accounted for more than half of total loans and advances. The rest is made up of overdrafts followed by bill discounting and trust receipts.

2. SPECIFICATION OF THE MODEL

Our objective is to construct a quarterly model of demand and supply for commercial loans in Singapore. The period of our study is from 1985 to 1995. Information originates from official publications such as the Monthly Digest of Statistics. Commercial loans refer to loans and advances to all non-bank customers. In the absence of direct information on the quantity of loans demanded and supplied, explicit demand and supply equations for commercial loans must be specified. The model used in this paper is specified along the lines of the model developed by Melitz and Pardue (1973).

2.1   DEMAND EQUATION

As mentioned, the demand for loans is largely influenced by the sectoral performance. Both the construction and commerce sectors' real GDP have been included as explanatory variables since these two sectors account for nearly half of total loans. In addition, as Singapore is highly dependent on trade, manufacturing firms will require loans for their production of goods for exports. Real exports is also included as a regressor. These output variables can be viewed as indices of the level of production which in turn determine the desired demand for commercial bank loans. Lags are included to take into account the fact that borrowers form adaptive expectations about the future output level and thus the amount of loans demanded are based on past performance. Due to the non-availability of the various loan rates charged for each sector, the prime lending rate has been used as the price variable. The specification of the demand equation is as follows:

$$LR_d = \alpha_1 + \alpha_2(r_L)_t + \sum\gamma_i(GDPCON)_{t-i} + \sum\delta_i(GDPCOM)_{t-i} + \sum\eta_i(EXP)_{t-i} + \mu_t \tag{1}$$

where LR_d = Loans and advances demanded by non-bank customers in real terms

r_{Lt} = Real prime lending rate

GDPCON = Real GDP for construction sector

GDPCOM = Real GDP for commerce sector

EXP   = Exports in real terms

μ = Error term, with zero mean and constant variance

Prior expectations indicate α_2 to be negative and the coefficients of the remaining regressors to be positive.

2.2   SUPPLY EQUATION

The commercial loan supply function uses portfolio theory as its theoretical basis as mentioned by Melitz and Pardue (1973). It takes into account 4 factors namely: (1) a scale constraint; (2) the yield on commercial bank loans; (3) the yield on alternative commercial bank earning assets; and (4) the cost per dollar of bank deposits liabilities.

The scale constraint takes into account the fact that the banking sector is subjected to significant control by the Monetary Authority of Singapore (MAS). Banks have to maintain 6 percent of their liabilities base with the MAS as the minimum cash balance and another 18 percent in various prescribed papers such as Treasury Bills, Government Bonds and Trade Bills. This scale constraint is expressed as the total commercial bank assets in excess of legally required reserves less commercial bank loans. The latter must be deducted to avoid regressing commercial bank loans against itself. It is termed as adjusted assets (AA). Thus,

AA = Total assets - Required reserves - Bank loans

The yield on commercial loans is measured by the prime lending rate. Our measure of the yield on alternative commercial bank earning assets is the 3-month Treasury Bills rate in real terms. The cost variable is measured by taking the total interest costs paid on both savings and fixed deposits divided by total deposits which include current deposits.

The supply equation is specified as follows:

$$LR_s = \beta_1 + \beta_2(r_L)_t + \beta_3(r_T)_t + \beta_4(AA)_t + \beta_5(CD)_t + \beta_6(GDP1990)_t + v_t \qquad (2)$$

where LR_s = Loans and advances supplied by commercial banks in real terms

     r_{Lt} = Real prime lending rate

     r_{Tt} = 3-month Treasury Bills rate in real terms

     AA_t = Adjusted assets of commercial banks

     CD_t = Cost per dollar of bank deposits

     GDP1990   = Real GDP with 1990 as the base year

     v_t = Error term, with zero mean and constant variance

Real GDP is included because if the economy performs well, people will increase their deposits and banks will in turn be able to increase their loans supply. Prior expectations indicate that β_2, β_4 and β_6 are positive. β_3 is expected to be negative and β_5 can be either positive or negative [Sealey (1990)].

3. METHODOLOGY

3.1 DATA

To obtain parameter estimates of the model, we use a sample that covers the period from the 1st quarter of 1985 to the 4th quarter of 1995. Altogether, 44 observations are used for each variable. Data sources comprise published data from MAS monthly bulletin, Monthly Digest of Statistics, Singapore System of National Accounts and the International Financial Statistic year books.

3.2 EQUILIBRIUM HYPOTHESIS

Following the traditional Walrasian economic principle, we first assume that the lending rate is flexible enough to equate supply and demand each period, i.e., the exchanged quantity Q_t is such that:

$$Q_t = LR_d = LR_s \qquad (3)$$

The model presented in Equations (1) through (3) is estimated using two stage least squares (2SLS). The instrumental variables specified in the first stage include all the other exogenous variables except for the real loans and prime lending rate. After estimating the demand and supply equations, we use the Augmented Dickey-Fuller (ADF) test to check whether the residuals from these equations are stationary. If they are, the linear combination of the variables in each equation forms a stationary cointegration relationship. Thus, there exist meaningful long run relationships as specified by the equation forms.

3.3 DISEQUILIBRIUM HYPOTHESIS

Next, we assume that the lending rate is not perfectly flexible and that rationing occurs. D.G. Harris (1974) had provided empirical evidence on the existence of credit rationing at commercial banks. We know that it is not true all borrowers can obtain loans even if they are willing to pay the lending rates. The commercial banks will conduct a credit analysis on the borrowers and grant approval only to those loan applicants with low credit risk. The presence of non-price credit rationing per se means that disequilibrium regime substitutes equilibrium regime.

In the absence of the market clearing condition, Equation (3) would be inapplicable. This requires us to make an additional hypothesis:

$$Q_t = \min (LR_d, LR_s) \tag{4}$$

This assumption was used by Fair and Jaffee (1972). It means that the quantity exchanged in the market is either on the demand or supply equation, whichever is less. For instance, if the quantity demanded exceeds the quantity supplied, demanders will go unsatisfied. The rationale for the assumption is that, in markets with voluntary exchange, the short side of the market must prevail.

Under this circumstance, the change in the lending rate could be used as an indicator of the amount of excess demand (or supply) in the market. The lending rate adjustment process is postulated as:

$$\Delta r_{Lt} = f (LR_d - LR_s), \quad f'(LR_d - LR_s) > 0 \tag{5}$$

In other words, if there is excess demand, the change in lending rate will be positive. Conversely, if there is excess supply, the change will be negative. In periods when there is no change in the lending rate, the market is assumed to clear.

Following Fair and Jaffee (1972), we use the Directional Method I to estimate the model represented by Equations (1), (2) and (4).

3.3.1 Directional Method I

Directional Method I can be illustrated by graphing the demand and supply Equations (1) and (2) against the lending rate as shown in Figure 1. The market clearing rate is indicated as R*. Whenever the quoted rate is less than R*, there is excess demand. Based on Equation (5), the lending rate will be increasing. When there is excess demand, we know from Equation (4) that supply will be the observed quantity. Conversely, whenever the quoted rate is greater than R*, excess supply prevails. Demand will then be the observed quantity. In summary, in periods of rising lending rate, only the supply schedule will be observed. In periods of falling lending rate, the demand schedule will be observed.

3.3.1.1 Implementation of Directional Method I

A plot of the lending rate over time allows the sample to be separated into periods of excess demand or supply based on the direction of change. Subsequently, the supply equation is estimated over periods of excess demand (or when $\Delta r_{Lt} > 0$), and the demand function can be estimated over periods of excess supply (when $\Delta r_{Lt}<0$). Periods of temporary equilibrium ($\Delta\ r_{Lt} = 0$) are included in both samples since both schedules are observed at such times. The darkened portions of the two functions in figure 1 will be estimated with this method. The 2SLS approach[1] is used for the estimation. Subsequently, the Augmented Dickey Fuller test is used to check if the residuals from the equations are stationary.

4. EMPIRICAL RESULTS

4.1   DETERMINATION OF THE ORDER OF INTEGRATION

As time series variables are used in the regression, it is important to find out the order of integration for each variable. The order of integration is the number of times a series needs to be difference before it becomes stationary. If the variables in a regression are all integrated of the same order, and the residuals exhibit stationarity, we can confidently say that the variables are cointegrated and the regression provides a meaningful economic relationship.

The Phillips-Perron test procedure[2] is applied to each variable. The observed test-statistics fail to reject the null hypothesis of a unit root for all variables. All the variables are found to be random walks and thus integrated of order 1.

4.2   RESULTS FOR EQUILIBRIUM MODEL

Table 2 presents the results for the model under equilibrium conditions.

4.2.1   Demand Equation

The lags as shown in the demand equation are found to be significant after allowing up to 4 lags to each variable. The signs for the coefficients are as expected except for the prime lending rate which is supposed to be negative. One possible explanation is that it did not reflect the true price of loans which can be better captured by a weighted average of the different types of loan rates. The t-statistic also shows the prime lending rate to be insignificant. The AR(1) is included to correct for serial-correlation, after an examination of the correlogram of the residuals from the equation.

The Augmented Dickey-Fuller unit root test is then conducted on the residuals to check for stationarity. The residuals are found to be stationary at 1 percent significance level and thus the variables in the demand equation are cointegrated.

4.2.2   Supply Equation

From the regression results for the supply equation, all the coefficients are found to be significant at the 5 percent level. In addition, the signs are within expectations. The coefficient of CD or cost per dollar of deposits has a negative sign which shows that an increase in the interest costs on deposits will cause the commercial banks to substitute

---

[1] As noted by Fair and Jaffee (1972), the addition of Equation (5) makes the lending rate an endogenous variable. This will result in simultaneous bias and OLS cannot be used.

[2] The Phillips-Perron test procedure allows us to test for the presence of an intercept term and trend in the data generation process (d.g.p) of the variables. It comprises seven steps, each step allows us to test for the presence of a unit root under a different d.g.p. See Cointegration Analysis in Econometric Modelling by Harris (1995), pg. 31, Table 3.2.

other interests earning assets for loans.

When the Augmented Dickey-Fuller Unit Root Test is carried out on the residuals, we can reject the null hypothesis of non-stationary residuals at 1 percent significance level, which implies that the supply equation is also cointegrated.

4.3   RESULTS FOR DISEQUILIBRIUM MODEL

The results for the disequilibrium model are presented in Table 3.

4.3.1   Demand Equation

The adjusted sample period used for estimating the demand equation includes the following: 1986:2-1988:2; 1989:2-1989:4; 1990:3-1991:1; 1991:3-1993:4; 1995:1-1995:4. Altogether, 29 observations for each variable are included after adjusting endpoints.

After the separation of the sample into credit slack regime (excess supply) and using the resultant observations to estimate the demand equation, the coefficients are all of the correct signs. However, just as in the case of 2SLS estimation under equilibrium conditions, the lending rate variable is found not to be significant. The AR(1) is included to correct for serial correlation.

The residuals obtained from the estimated equation is tested for stationarity. The ADF test statistic is -1.89 as against a 10 percent critical value of -1.63, showing that there is a cointegrating relationship among the variables in the demand equation at 90 percent confidence level.

4.3.2   Supply Equation

For the supply equation, the sample periods include 32 observations after adjusting endpoints. They are as follows: 1986:1-1986:2; 1986:4-1987:4; 1988:1-1990:3; 1991:1-1991:3; 1993:1-1995:1; 1995:3-1995:4.

Table 3 gives the results for the equation. All coefficients are of the expected signs. The 3-month treasury bill rates which is a measure of opportunity cost, is negatively related to loan supply; so is the cost per dollar of deposit variable. All coefficients are significant at 10 percent level except for adjusted assets.

The result from the Augmented Dickey-Fuller Test shows the residuals from the supply equation are stationary. Again, there is a cointegrating relationship among the variables in the supply equation at 99 percent confidence level.

5. RESULTS AND IMPLICATIONS

5.1   ANALYSIS OF REGRESSION RESULTS

The results obtained for the model of commercial loan market in Singapore enabled us to make the following observations:

Firstly, the demand for loans is largely determined by the performance of the construction, commerce as well as the manufacturing (exports) sector. These 3 variables are significant in explaining the change in total commercial loans to non-bank customers overtime. Furthermore, the real GDP for commerce has a greater impact on real loans as compared to the remaining two sectors. The lending rate is not important in affecting loan demanded.

Secondly, the amount of loans commercial banks can supply depends to a certain extent on how much excess assets they hold as proxied by the variable AA. Also, as the cost of deposits increases, banks will channel their resources to other interest earning assets. The increase in the return to 3-month treasury bills encourages banks to direct their resources away from loans into buying this asset. In addition, as the economy performs well, this has a significant effect on the supply of bank loans. This is due to the increase in savings which in turn increase the ability of the banks to make loans. The lending rate is found to be significant in affecting loan supply decisions.

Thirdly, when separating the sample into periods of excess demand or supply under the disequilibrium hypothesis, it is found that 21 observations supports the credit slack regime (Excess supply) as compared to 17 observations in support of the credit rationing regime (Excess demand). This excludes the observations when the lending rate is relatively stable. There is thus no strong indication of whether the loan market is predominantly in excess demand or supply.

In order to see how well the estimated model of demand and supply equations under each hypothesis fit actual observations, the forecasted real loans are compared with the actual values. Figures 2 to 5 provide the graphical illustrations. The forecasted demand gives a reasonably good fit as compared to the forecasted supply.

5.2   EFFECT OF BANK LOANS ON REAL GDP

From our estimation of the commercial loan demand function, we know that sectoral performance will affect loan demand. In turn, industrial borrowers who are able to obtain loans will be able to carry out their investment or production plans that subsequently affect the GDP. It is therefore of interest to see if commercial loan aggregates can help in the prediction of future GDP.

We use the Granger Casualty test to find out if the past growth of 4 financial aggregates aid the prediction of GDP growth, each taken separately. These financial aggregates are: (1) Demand deposits (DD), (2) Commerce and other industrial loans which include manufacturing, construction and transport and communication (LC&I), (3) Other loans besides those to the industrial sectors (LOTH), and (4) Total loans (Loans). The test is carried out by regressing GDP growth against a constant, 4 lagged values of GDP growth and four lagged growth rates of the financial aggregate selected.

Table 4 shows the results of the test which is carried out using 3 different time periods. The first period is the full sample period from 1st quarter of 1985 to last quarter of 1995, the second period is from 1st quarter of 1985 to last quarter of 1990 and the last period is from 1st quarter of 1991 to the last quarter of 1995. The values shown are P-values for the test of the null-hypothesis that GDP is not "Granger caused" by the financial aggregate concerned. Hence, a number smaller than 0.05 leads to the rejection of the null-hypothesis.

As observed, none of the four financial aggregates aid in the prediction of GDP growth in either the whole sample or the two sub-periods. However, the commercial and industrial loans growth rates have a stronger relationship with GDP growth as compared to the rest using the full sample period. On a closer look, in the first sub-period from 1st quarter of 1985 to last quarter of 1990, the commercial and other industrial loans have a relatively stronger contribution to the growth in GDP. From the beginning of 1991 to 1995, growth rates of other loans begin to have a stronger casual relation with GDP growth. This can be attributed to increasing loans going into non-bank financial institutions as well as professionals and private individuals.

6. CONCLUSIONS

6.1   SUMMARY OF STUDY

We have estimated the model of commercial loan market in Singapore under equilibrium and disequilibrium conditions. Demand for loans is found to be highly dependent upon sectoral performance especially the construction, commerce and exports sector. On the supply side, portfolio theory provides a good explanation of the factors that banks will take into account when they supply loans. These include: (1) amount of assets in excess of legally required reserves, (2) cost per dollar of deposits, (3) yield from loans, (4) yield from alternative interest earning assets.

The Directional Method I approach allows the sample period to be separated into periods of excess demand and excess supply. We find no evidence to show whether the loan market is either predominantly in excess demand or supply.

Finally, we proceed to test whether bank asset aggregates help in the prediction of GDP growth. We found none of the financial aggregates to have a significant relationship with GDP growth. However, the growth of the commercial and industrial loans has a relatively stronger impact on real GDP growth. We conclude from this preliminary study that bank credit aggregates do not have a significant impact on real GDP and thus is not useful in predicting future real GDP.

6.2   LIMITATIONS OF STUDY

In this study, we faced a number of difficulties which are worth mentioning in this section.

Firstly, the commercial loan figure is a stock variable. No information is available on the transacted amount of loans for each period. It would definitely be more accurate to use the transacted amount as the dependent variable rather than the observed variable at the end of the period.

The prime lending rate is not a good indicator of the price of loans. If data are available, a better indicator may be an average of all the rates charged for the different loans weighted by the proportions of each type of loans.

As mentioned by Fair and Jaffee (1972), the sample separation implied by Directional Method I is correct but there is a source of inconsistency in the estimation. A better approach will be to use the Maximum Likelihood estimation.

REFERENCES

Amemiya, T. (1974): "A Note on a Fair and Jaffee Model," *Econometrica*, 42, 759-762.

Davis, E. P. (1994): "Banking, Corporate Finance, and Monetary Policy: An Empirical Perspective," *Oxford Review of Economic Policy*, 10, 49-64.

Fair, R. C., and D. M. Jaffee (1972): "Methods of Estimation for Markets in Disequilibrium," *Econometrica*, 40, 497-514.

Fair, R. C., and H. Kelejian (1974): "Methods of Estimation for Markets in Disequilibrium: A Further Study," *Econometrica*, 42, 177-190.

Harris, R. D. (1995): "Testing for Unit Roots," in *Using Cointegration Analysis in Econometric Modelling*, New York: Prentice Hall/Harvester Wheatsheaf.

Laffont, J. J., and R. Garcia (1977): "Disequilibrium Econometrics For Business Loans," *Econometrica*, 45, 1187-1204.

Maddala, G. S., and F. D. Nelson (1974): "Maximum Likelihood Methods for Models of Markets in Disequilibrium," *Econometrica*, 42, 1013-1030.

Melitz, J., and M. Pardue (1973): "The Demand and Supply of Commercial Bank Loans," *Journal of Money, Credit and Banking*, 5, 669-692.

Sealey, C. W. JR. (1979): "Credit Rationing in the Commercial Loan Market: Estimates of a Structural Model Under Conditions of Disequilibrium," *The Journal of Finance*, 34, 689-702.

Stephen, R. K. (1986): "Monetary Transmission: Through Bank Loans or Bank Liabilities?" *Journal of Money, Credit and Banking*, 18, 290-303.

Tan, C. H. (1996): "Commercial Banks," in *Financial Markets and Institutions in Singapore (8th Edition)*, Singapore University Press.

Yam, W. L., and P. Gerrard (1996): "Bank Services," in *Commercial Banking in Singapore*, ed. by K. H. Ng, Singapore: Addison-Wesley.

TABLE 1

Contribution to Growth (%) in Banks' Loans and Advances by Industrial Classification: 1984 - 1995

Year	Building & Construction	General Commerce	Total
84-85	119.17	-188.37	-69.20
85-86	-0.26	-14.00	-14.26
86-87	-16.02	19.18	3.16
87-88	8.57	21.67	30.24
88-89	32.37	8.89	41.26
89-90	28.38	18.82	47.20
90-91	42.99	31.82	74.81
91-92	45.48	29.13	74.61
92-93	55.84	5.84	61.68
93-94	40.74	13.66	54.40
94-95	33.13	12.23	45.36

Note: Growth rate for each period is computed by taking the absolute change in loans and advances in each sector as a ratio of the absolute change in total loans and advances.

TABLE 2

Regression Results for the Model under Equilibrium Hypothesis

1) **Demand Equation (2SLS):**

LR_d = -10334.88 + 186.05$(r_L)_t$ + 4.63$(GDPCON)_{t-4}$ + 5.47$(GDPCOM)_t$
          (-1.46)   (0.47)   (1.36)   (3.22)

          + 10.40$(GDPCOM)_{t-2}$ + 0.47$(EXP)_{t-1}$ + 0.86[AR(1)]
             (6.51)   (2.81)   (8.59)

R^2 = 0.99, DW = 1.67

Augmented Dickey-Fuller Test on Residuals

Null Hypothesis H_0 = Residuals are non-stationary

F-test statistic = -3.10   Critical value at 1% significance level = -2.63

continuation of table 2

2) **Supply Equation (2SLS):**

LR_s = -21787.46 + 3685.65$(r_L)_t$ - 676.72$(r_T)_t$ + 0.13$(AA)_t$ -1857.78$(CD)_t$
          (-5.65)   (6.08)   (-2.16)   (2.24)   (-3.14)

          + 3.15$(GDP1990)_t$
             (13.56)

R^2 = 0.99, DW = 1.30

Augmented Dickey-Fuller Test on Residuals

Null Hypothesis H_0 = Residuals are non-stationary

F-test statistic = -4.12   Critical value at 1% significance level = -2.62

Note: The values in parentheses are t-statistics.

TABLE 3

Regression Results for the Model under Disequilibrium Hypothesis

1) **Demand Equation (Directional Method I):**

$LR_d = -10681.43 - 248.09(r_L)_t + 4.29(GDPCON)_{t-4} + 3.61(GDPCOM)_t$
  (-1.34)   (-0.50)   (1.11)   (1.59)

  $+ 11.48(GDPCOM)_{t-2} + 0.47(EXP)_{t-1} + 0.86[AR(1)]$
    (6.09)   (2.81)   (8.59)

$R^2 = \underline{0.99}$, DW = $\underline{1.10}$

Augmented Dickey-Fuller Test on Residuals

Null Hypothesis H_0 = Residuals are non-stationary

F-test statistic = $\underline{-1.89}$ Critical value at 1% significance level = $\underline{-1.63}$

2) **Supply Equation (Directional Method I):**

$LR_s = -20319.02 + 3392.28(r_L)_t - 881.14(r_T)_t + 0.10(AA)_t -1336.79(CD)_t$
  (-5.79)   (5.18)   (-2.06)   (1.44)   (-1.70)

  $+ 3.22(GDP1990)_t$
    (11.72)

$R^2 = \underline{0.99}$, DW = $\underline{1.31}$

Augmented Dickey-Fuller Test on Residuals

Null Hypothesis H_0 = Residuals are non-stationary

F-test statistics = $\underline{-3.32}$ Critical value at 1% significance level = $\underline{-2.68}$

Note: The values in parentheses are t-statistics.

TABLE 4

Bivariate Tests of Predictive Content for GDP

Period	DD	LC&I	LOTH	Loans
1985:1 - 1995:4	0.91	0.22	0.70	0.77
1985:1 - 1990:4	0.42	0.18	0.53	0.42
1991:1 - 1995:4	0.31	0.66	0.32	0.80

a. DD stands for demand deposits, LC&I for commercial and other industrial loans (Manufacturing, Construction, Transport & Communication). LOTH for other (Agriculture, Professional & Private individual) loans and Loans for the total commercial loans to non-bank customers.

b. 4 lags of each variable are included in the Granger Casualty test.

c. The values in the table are P-values for testing the null-hypothesis that GDP is not "Granger caused" by the variable. At 5 percent significance level, any value below 0.05 will lead to the rejection of the null-hypothesis.

FIGURE 1

Markets in Disequilibrium

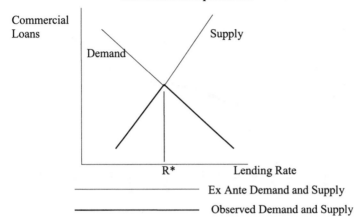

Commercial Loans

Demand

Supply

R*   Lending Rate

——————————— Ex Ante Demand and Supply

——————————— Observed Demand and Supply

FIGURE 2

Actual Demand against Forecasted Demand under 2SLS Estimation

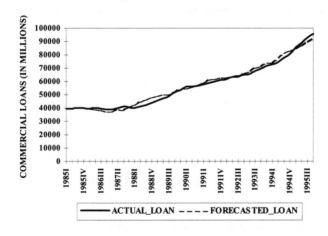

COMMERCIAL LOANS (IN MILLIONS)

——— ACTUAL_LOAN ‑ ‑ ‑ ‑ FORECASTED_LOAN

FIGURE 3

Actual Supply against Forecasted Supply under 2SLS Estimation

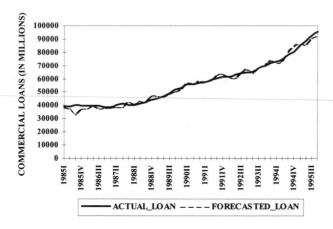

FIGURE 4

Actual Demand against Forecasted Demand under DMI* Estimation

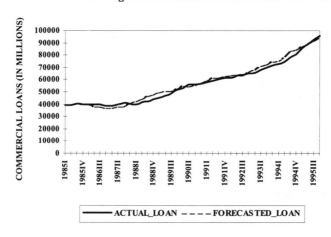

DMI stands for Directional Method I

FIGURE 5

Actual Supply against Forecasted Supply under DMI Estimation

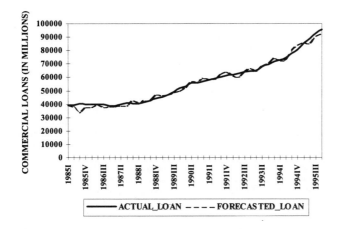

Productivity Analysis for the Singapore Economy[1]

*Simon **Loh** Kai Hong*

&

*Randolph **Tan***

Nanyang Business School, Nanyang Technological University, Nanyang Avenue, Singapore 639798
Fax: +(65) 792.4217, Tel: +(65) 799.4895, Email: arandolph2@ntu.edu.sg

Abstract This study provides some estimates of productivity growth, which may serve as benchmarks for assessing more detailed studies. In of studies of this nature, the availability of data has been a crucial factor in determining if sector-specific comparisons can be made. In this paper, we consider the problem of identifying performance differentials across manufacturing industries at the three-digit level of the Singapore Standard Industrial Classification (SSIC). We employ only published sources for our computations. The major step in this direction is to use a published version of manufacturing value-added as the output measure. The results we have obtained are compared with previous papers. They indicated that while comparison across sectors is not possible due to the lack of sector-specific data, the overall manufacturing results are close to those obtained by previous studies. An indication of the robustness of our result is obtained by re-computing the productivity figures with an alternative measure of capital input.

1. INTRODUCTION

1.1   ECONOMIC DEVELOPMENT, LABOUR PRODUCTIVITY AND IMPROVING TECHNOLOGY IN SINGAPORE

In the late 1950s, Singapore's economic outlook was grim. Singapore's prosperity since its founding as a British settlement in 1819 seemed to be faltering in the face of rising unemployment. To solve the unemployment problem, Singapore adopted an industrialisation programme. This programme emphasised diversification and in the initial stage, the development of import-substituting industries in the early 1960s to stimulate the domestic market [see Lim (1988)]. When Singapore separated from Malaysia in 1965, Singapore chose an export-oriented industrialisation strategy. The success of this strategy lay in its ability to attract many foreign firms into Singapore that in turn made her into a booming world economy.

Though there is rapid growth in the economy, the unemployment rate ballooned to more than 10 percent in the early 1960s because job creation failed to keep pace with the growing number of job seekers and the inflow of people from Peninsula Malaysia. Fortunately, job opportunities began to expand faster than the growth in the labour supply in the late 1960s. By the early 1970s, Singapore was able to achieve full employment and this situation continued to prevail, aided by the declining rate of population and domestic labour force growth, and continued rapid growth in all sectors of the economy.

---

[1] The initial discussion of this paper is an exposition on the Jorgensen approach to growth accounting. In the context of Singapore data, two major studies are our important secondary references for this method, namely Tsao (1982) and recently, Seow and Lall (1996). Our exposition parallels very closely these two sources. Of course, we bear responsibility for any inadvertent misinterpretation of their discussions of the Jorgensen approach.

In such a labour-driven economy, the effects of new capital investment are amplified through its infusion into a workforce that is eager for new technological experiences. However, this type of framework is precisely the same one used to argue that sufficient time must be provided for the absorption of new technologies. The amount of time required would increase with the weight of new technologies, which is when capital accumulation also takes on a questionable face.

The concepts of labour productivity – which determines the possibility that the rate of wage growth and total factor productivity (TFP) are intrinsically linked. In 1989, for example, better TFP, rather than higher capital intensity, was the major source of Singapore's good labour productivity performance in the past three years (Annual Bulletin of Productivity Statistics, 1989).

1.2   ORGANISATION OF REPORT

This paper will be organised as follows. In Section 2, we consider the special institutional characteristics of the Singapore economy, which have evolved by design of the years to encourage output and productivity growth. Section 3 will present a brief description of the trends of the electronics sector as a special case of manufacturing. In Section 4, we describe some previous work in the area of productivity measurement. Next, Section 5 provides the methodology used in this paper and it will be followed by Section 6 that presents the data and variables used to measure TFP. At the same time, we also summarise some issues relating to the data. Some concluding remarks can be found in Section 7.

2. INVESTMENT IN CAPITAL AND HUMAN RESOURCE

To assess the value of improving technologies in Singapore, it is useful to begin by considering the full extent of the economic commitment to investment. This commitment occurs at all levels and may be regarded as one of the institutional characteristics of the manufacturing sector.

Since independence, the Singapore government has been implementing a variety of policies and institutions to upgrade and restructure the economy, especially the manufacturing sector. The aim is to phase out low-wage, low skill, labour intensive industries, and to encourage the establishment of high value-added, skill and capital-intensive industries.

The Economic Development Board (EDB), the main government agency overlooking economic development in Singapore, provides many *investment incentives* to foreign and local manufacturing firms. These include granting exemption from the 40 percent corporate income tax for 5 to 10 years; allowing about 90 percent tax exemption on profits derived from exports for 3 to 5 years and an investment allowance granting tax exemption based on the size of fixed investment. At the same time, various measures that have been implemented to encourage research and development (R & D). These include providing allowances of up to 50 percent of the capital investment in R & D and initial allowance of 25 percent and annual allowance of 3 percent for R & D buildings. Moreover, a Product Development Assistance Scheme (PDAS) has been established for local firms [see Lim (1988)].

Some of the initiatives are also labour-specific. The Ministries of Trade and Industry, Labour, and Education have introduced many innovations in the area of *manpower policy*. In order to curb the growth of unskilled jobs and maintain competitiveness in labour-intensive export industries, the National Wages Council (NWC) was set up in 1972 to ensure orderly wage changes. It embarked on a wage correction policy in 1979 to maintain wages at the 'proper market level' [Lim (1988)].

There are also plans to provide continued education and training programmes for workers. To upgrade the skilled of the labour force, EDB provides grants to finance on-the-job and formal training of workers locally and overseas. Moreover, the Vocational and Industrial Training Board (VITB) with some training centres and companies also offer courses that provide specialised training to improve the manpower for the industry. To further encourage training of workers' skill, a Skills Development Fund (SDF) was set up in 1979 and grants are awarded to firms to defray their training costs incurred in upgrading workers.

As can be seen from the above, the government is trying increase the demand for skilled labour by providing some investment incentives to attract more investors and on the other hand, increase its supply through its manpower policies. This appears to be very crucial for Singapore as the government is aiming to attract more capital-intensive, high-technology industry to invest in its manufacturing sector. Changes in manufacturing can be interpreted in this light. One important area of change is electronics.

3. PRODUCTIVITY IN THE MANUFACTURING SECTOR

3.1   AN EXAMPLE OF MANUFACTURING: THE ELECTRONICS INDUSTRY

The ·rapid and often evolutionary changes of manufacturing are best illustrated by the electronics sector.

Electronics has been an important industry to the Singapore government since the late 1960s. Due to its dynamic technological and market characteristics, it fits peculiarly well with the changes in the Singapore manufacturing sector. Moreover, it also makes a good example of changing 'appropriate technology' and employment creation in a rapidly industrialisation developing country [Lim and Pang (1981)].

Technology in all sectors is characterised by short product life cycles, constant innovation, and rapid obsolescence. Innovations over the past 30-odd years have been both capital-saving and labour-saving. Miniaturisation and better design have progressive reduced the number of components and amount of materials used, while dramatically improving product performance and capabilities, and contributed to better product quality. However, many processes and assemblies remain labour-intensive because some products are either too complex or too costly to merchandise.

Electronics manufacturers developed an international division of labour, in which labour-intensive products and processes were located in low-wage developing countries, while R & D, and more skill- and capital-intensive production were retained in the developed countries which were the home markets of the parent companies.

The electronics multinational enterprises (MNEs) from North America, Western Europe, Australia and Japan had chosen the developing countries of the East and Southeast Asia as their offshore manufacturing locations. Over the years, changes in the international division of labour within the vertically integrated MNE and between the different host and home countries reflect changing in comparative advantages. Therefore, those in complex, skill- and capital-intensive stages of production are being moved offshore to countries like

Hong Kong, Singapore, South Korea and Taiwan. On the other hand, those in simple and more labour-intensive stages are being phased out from these countries and moved to Indonesia, the Philippines, India, Sri Lanka and Bangladesh.

As technology increasing becomes the major determinant of production costs and quality, market success in the 1980s, R & D activities become more crucial for industry leadership. The capital- and skill-intensity of R & D, together with the intensifying political struggle for access to developed country markets, firmly established the electronics industry's 'centre of gravity' in the developed countries. For example, Japan has been the industry leader in semiconductors as well as in the consumer products market, which they have dominated for over a decade.

3.2   THE LOCAL ELECTRONICS SECTOR

The electronics industry in Singapore consisted of only one local firm assembling television sets and radio kits for the small, protected domestic market in the year 1965. However, attracted by plentiful, low-cost, disciplines labour available and tax incentives offered to labour-intensive export manufacturers, American semiconductor multinationals began establishing offshore plants in Singapore. With the Japanese and European consumer and component electronics multinationals following the lead of the Americans, this triggered the start of a period of phenomenally rapid growth up to early 1974. Most major electronics multinationals in the world established a subsidiary in Singapore to produce for the world market—from the US came Texas Instruments, Hewlett Packard and General Electric of the USA; from Japan came Hitachi, Toshiba and Matsushita; from Europe came Philips, Siemens and Thomson [Lin and Pang (1981)].

From the period between 1965 and 1979, the electronics industry created over 55,000 new jobs which was around one-third of the employment expansion in Singapore's manufacturing sector. In addition, employment creation in the electronics industry in Singapore also contributed to the rapid increase in the female labour force, around 80 percent of the new jobs created were for unskilled or semi-skilled female production operators.

Other than direct employment creation, the electronics industry has also generated many new jobs indirectly through the purchase of inputs from both local and foreign-owned supporting industries. The number of indirectly new manufacturing jobs created by the electronics industry in supporting firms that sell mainly to it is around 12,000, while if firms in both the manufacturing and service sectors that depend partly on the industry for their sales are estimated at least 20,000 new jobs indirectly created since 1968.

In summary, the electronics industry plays an important role not just with the respect to technology, and also employment creation in Singapore. This is the natural setting for a measure like TFP to be used as an overall performance indicator. Moreover, the measurement of total factor productivity growth and technical change has been the focus of attention in empirical studies concerning industrial productivity. With the computed estimates, planning and forecasting can be carried.

4. MEASUREMENT OF TFP FOR SINGAPORE: PREVIOUS STUDIES

Tsao (1982) is the first thorough study of TFP growth in Singapore. In her study, she highlights that TFP growth rates were 0.6 percent and -0.9 percent for 1966-72 and 1972-80 respectively. Moreover, she finds that the contribution of capital for both the periods, which more than three times greater to labour, mainly due to high growth rate of capital [Tsao (1982), p. 149].

Wong and Gan (1994) evaluates the TFP growth of the manufacturing industries in Singapore to determine whether the negative TFP growth found in the 1970's by Tsao (1985) persisted during the 1980's. Their results show that the TFP growth of the manufacturing sector has been estimated to be 1.6 percent between 1981 and 1990, which accounted for around a quarter of the output growth. And this signifies an improvement in the TFP as compared to Tsao [Wong and Gan (1994), p. 180.]

The data they used for computation in the estimates of TFP is also from published sources and the data support from the Economics Development Board of Singapore. This indicates that their paper also obtained data from private sources in help for their computations.

In Young (1994), he disputes a common premise that underlies productivity growth in the East Asian NICs have been extraordinary high by showing that the productivity growth in the manufacturing sector of the NICs, ranges from a low of -1.0 percent in Singapore to a high of 2.9 percent in South Korea between 1966 and 1990. The reasons he gives for the result of the low productivity growth in Singapore are slow growth of output per weighted worker and rapid fall in output per unit of capital input [Young (1994), p. 19 and 33]. As Wong and Gan pointed out, his comments are more relevant to manufacturing.

In his computing of TFP for Singapore, Young uses published sources for his primary data and qualifies his data using thousands of pages of unpublished census tabulations obtained from the government of Singapore. This is another paper that uses private sources for his computations. The reason he gives for not using only published tabulations alone is that it might pollute one's estimates of the returns to different types of labour input with non-labour capital income.

5. MEASURING PRODUCTIVITY IN THE MANUFACTURING SECTOR

In this chapter and the next, we assemble a suitable database and use that to compute TFP for the manufacturing. The methodology that I used to calculate *total factor productivity growth* in one or more sectors follows that of Gollop and Jorgenson (1980).[2]

5.1   THE AGGREGATE PRODUCTION FUNCTION

To analyse the sources of growth of value added at the aggregate level, we first have to assume that an aggregate production function, Q is made up of aggregate inputs like labour input L, capital input K and time T:

$$Q=F(L,K,T) \tag{1}$$

where $L=L(L_1, L_2, ... L_P)$ and $K=K(K_1, K_2, ..., K_q)$

Here, we assume that the aggregate production function, Q and the aggregate input functions of individuals components are characterised by constant returns to scale. This is important because the conditions for an aggregate production function to exist are [Tsao (1982)]:

---

[2] Using the study from Tsao (1982) during the 1970s.

1. The sectoral production function Q_z has to be identical up to a constant of proportionality A_z:

$$Q_z = F_z(L_z, K_z, T) = A_z F (L_z, K_z, T) \text{ for } (z = 1,2, \ldots, n) \tag{2}$$

2. The sectoral inputs are has to be each identical functions of their individual components:

$$L_z = L (L_1, L_2, \ldots, L_P)$$

$$K_z = K (K_1, K_2, \ldots, K_q) \text{ for } (z = 1,2, \ldots, n) \tag{3}$$

Then, by selecting the units of measurement of sectoral value added, we therefore are able to maintain the constant of proportionality, A_z to equal to unity.

5.2 DIVISIA INDEX OF TOTAL FACTOR PRODUCTIVITY

To derive the Divisia index of total factor productivity, we first have to define the value shares of labour and capital as

$$V_L = \left(\frac{P_L * L}{P_V * V} \right), \ V_K = \left(\frac{P_K * K}{P_V * V} \right) \tag{4}$$

where P_K is the price of capital inputs, P_L is the price of labour inputs, and P_V is the price of value added.

Given that producer in equilibrium, the above mentioned value shares of inputs will each be equal to the elasticity of output with respect to the input:

$$V_L = \left(\frac{d \ln V}{d \ln K} \right)(L,K,T) , \ V_K = \left(\frac{d \ln V}{d \ln L} \right)(L,K,T). \tag{5}$$

and under constant returns to scale, $V_L + V_K = 1$.

For differentiated inputs, the value shares of each aggregate input, under producer equilibrium, can be expressed as,

$$V_L = \left(\frac{P_{Ll} * L_l}{\sum P_{Ll} * L_l} \right) = \left(\frac{d \ln L}{d \ln L_l} \right)(L_1, L_2, \ldots, L_p), \ (l = 1,2, \ldots, q), \tag{6}$$

$$V_K = \left(\frac{P_{Kk} * K_k}{\sum P_{Kk} * K_k} \right) = \left(\frac{d \ln K}{d \ln K_K} \right)(K_1, K_2, \ldots, K_q), \ (k = 1,2, \ldots, p). \tag{7}$$

Therefore, the growth rates of the aggregate inputs and value added are:

$$\left(\frac{d \ln L}{d T} \right) = \sum V_{Ll} \left(\frac{d \ln L_l}{d T} \right), \ (l = 1,2, \ldots, q), \tag{8}$$

$$\left(\frac{d \ln K}{d T} \right) = \sum V_{Kk} \left(\frac{d \ln K_k}{d T} \right), (k = 1,2, \ldots, p), \tag{9}$$

$$\left(\frac{d \ln V}{d T} \right) = \left(\frac{d \ln V}{d \ln L} \right) * \left(\frac{d \ln L}{d T} \right) + \left(\frac{d \ln V}{d K} \right) * \left(\frac{d \ln K}{d T} \right) + \left(\frac{d \ln V}{d T} \right)$$

$$= V_K * \left(\frac{d \ln L}{d T} \right) + \left(\frac{d \ln K}{d T} \right) + V_T \tag{10}$$

The expression of the Divisia index of total factor productivity in continuous time, V_T is given above. It is equal to the subtraction of the weighted sum of the growth rates of labour and capital input with respect to their weighted values shares, from the growth rate of value added.

5.3   THE TRANSLOG INDEX OF TOTAL FACTOR PRODUCTIVITY

The Divisia index of total factor productivity is meant to be for continuous time.

$$Q = \exp[\alpha_0 + \alpha_K \ln K + \alpha_L \ln L + \alpha_t\, t + \frac{1}{2}\, B_{KK}\, (\ln K)^2$$

$$+ B_{KL}\, (\ln K)\, (\ln L) + B_{Kt} \ln K \cdot t + \frac{1}{2}\, B_{LL}\, (\ln L) \cdot t + \frac{1}{2}\, B_{tt}\, t^2\,] \tag{11}$$

where its assumption of constant returns to scale implies that the parameters must satisfy the conditions $\alpha_K + \alpha_L = 1 B_{KK} + B_{KL} = B_{LL} + B_{KL} = B_{Kt} + B_{Lt} = 0$. The translog index of technical change, $TFP_{T-1,\,T}$, is defined by the translog production function given by :

$$\ln\left(\frac{Q(T)}{Q(T-1)}\right) = \Theta_K \ln\left(\frac{K(T)}{K(T-1)}\right) + \Theta_L \ln\left(\frac{L(T)}{L(T-1)}\right) + TFP_T \tag{12}$$

where $\Theta_K = \frac{1}{2}\, [\, Q_K\, (T) + Q_K\, (T-1)\,]$, $\Theta_L \quad = \quad \frac{1}{2}\, [\, Q_L\, (T) + Q_L\, (T-1)\,]$, and $TFP_T = \frac{1}{2}\, [\, Q_T\, (T) + Q_T\, (T-1)\,]$.

Therefore, the translog index of technical change for the time (T-1) and time T is the growth rate of aggregate value added less the weighted sum of the growth rates of aggregate capital and labour inputs, and the weights being their average value shares over the two time periods.

For more finely differentiated inputs, one must assume that the aggregate capital and labour inputs are constant returns to scale translog indices of sub-inputs :

$$K = \exp[\, \alpha_1^K \ln K_1 + \alpha_1^K \ln K_2 + \ldots\ldots + \alpha_q^K \ln K_q$$

$$+ \frac{1}{2}\, B_{11}^K\, (\ln K_1)^2 + B_{12}^K\, (\ln K_1)\, (\ln K_2) + \ldots\ldots + \frac{1}{2}\, B_{qq}^K\, (\ln K_q)^2\,] \tag{13}$$

$$L = \exp[\, \alpha_1^L \ln L_1 + \alpha_1^L \ln L_2 + \ldots\ldots + \alpha_p^L \ln L_p$$

$$+ \frac{1}{2}\, B_{11}^L\, (\ln L_1)^2 + B_{12}^L\, (\ln L_1)\, (\ln L_2) + \ldots\ldots + \frac{1}{2}\, B_{pp}^L\, (\ln L_p)^2\,] \tag{14}$$

Differencing the logarithms of these translog production functions can provide a measure of the causes of growth across discrete time period. Therefore, the translog quantity indexes of aggregate capital and labour for the period between time (T-1) and time T are :

$$\ln\left(\frac{K(T)}{K(T-1)}\right) = \Sigma\, \Theta_{Kk} \ln\left(\frac{K_k(T)}{K_k(T-1)}\right), \tag{15}$$

$$\ln\left(\frac{L(T)}{L(T-1)}\right) = \Sigma \; \Theta_{LI} \ln\left(\frac{L_I(T)}{L_I(T-1)}\right), \tag{16}$$

where $\Theta_{Kk} = \frac{1}{2}$ [Q_{Kk} (T) + Q_{Kk} (T-1)], (k=1,2,..... ,q) and Θ_{LI} $= \frac{1}{2}$ [Q_{LI} (T) + Q_{LI} (T-1)], (l=1,2,..... ,p). In this case, the translog index of technical change is then computed as :

$$\ln\left(\frac{Q(T)}{Q(T-1)}\right) = \Theta_K \; \Sigma \; \Theta_{Kk} \ln\left(\frac{K_k(T)}{K_k(T-1)}\right) + \Theta_L \; \Sigma \; \Theta_{LI} \ln\left(\frac{L_I(T)}{L_I(T-1)}\right) + TFP_T \tag{17}$$

The translog index of TFP growth (TFP_T) gives an exact measure of the amount the log of output would have increased had all inputs remained constant between the two discrete periods. The main reasons for preferring the translog model of production is that it is able to provide a second-order approximation to an arbitrary twice-continuously-differentiable linear homogenous function. Furthermore, the translog quantity index is exact for the translog function; and as the translog function provides a local second-order approximation to any production frontier, the translog quantity index is also the superlative index. The purpose of econometric modelling is indeed shown by an exact correspondence between the use of translog indexes and the translog model of production.

6. DATA AND VARIABLES USED

To estimate industry specific cost function based on time series data, it is preferable to use as long a time series as possible as though data are available from 1960s onwards. The construction of the inputs will depend on the availability of the published data.

6.1 DATA SOURCE

Most of primary data obtained for this paper are from the various annual issues of the *Report of the Census of Industrial Production* (CIP) and the *Yearbook of Statistics Singapore*. As our paper focusses on calculating the TFP on the manufactured industries based on the availability of publications, any changes in those publications where we extract time series data between 1970 and 1994 may pose problems to our computations.

In the process of data collections, we have observed that the Singapore Standard Industrial Classification Code (SSIC) in CIP, with reference to the tables of Principal Statistics, Capital Expenditure and Net Value of Fixed Assets, was revised three times for the period between 1970 to 1994. The first change occurred in the year 1975 where the industrial code of 361 & 362 are combined. Therefore the manufactured industries, which are classified into 30 types of industries in prior, shrink into 29 SSIC. In 1980, there were major revisions to SSIC 383, 384 and 385 and a new SSIC 386 was added to the list. Some assumptions are made to accommodate these changes like assuming that the old SSIC 383, 384 and 385 correspond to the new SSIC 383, 385 and 386. The last change happened in 1993 where the SSIC 355 and 356 are merged into a single SSIC. This change maintains the number of sectors at 29.

For sectors that merge in the later year, we combine them right from the beginning of the sample period in 1971. And finally, we will compute TFP based on the 29 industries.

6.2 LABOUR

6.2.1   Labour Input

Young (1994) cross-classified the working population into seven categories, including gender, age, education, hours of work and others. Tsao (1982) classified the labour force data into four occupational status groups. They are:

1. Workmen

2. Other employees

3. Working proprietors

4. Unpaid family workers

As the remuneration of parts (3) and (4) are not available, Tsao (1982) assumes that the average remuneration of working proprietors is equal to the average remuneration of other employees and the average remuneration of unpaid family workers is equal to the average remuneration of workmen in order to compute the labour input [Tsao (1982), p. 71].

Young has said that the labour surveys on the countries (including Singapore) which he had worked in his paper are subjected to an enormous margin of error and that he has had to constrain himself to an appropriate 'population'. Given the lack of detailed data in the publications, most studies like his acquire unpublished data to improve the accuracy of their estimates.

In this paper, we obtained the data in the CIP for the number of workers and remuneration for each SSIC to compute the average remuneration for the working population. The data on the remuneration in the CIP comprise wages and salaries (which include bonuses), contributions to the Central Provident Fund and pension paid by employers, as well as the value of other benefits provided such as food, lodging and medical care.[3]

As there are no data on the hours worked by education and sex is not available, we assume that the series on weekly hours worked for manufactured sector to be the same for all the manufactured industries. The *Yearbook of Labour Statistics* and the *Yearbook of Labour Singapore* only provide the series for the basic hours worked from 1972 onwards. Since our data series start from 1971, we have to make assumption that the hours-worked in 1971 were similar to those in 1972. The data on average weekly hours are shown in Table 2.[4]

By multiplying employment the number of weeks in a year (assuming that there are 52 weeks in a year) with the average number of hours worked and the number of workers, we then obtained the series on worker hours worked per year.

Before we compute the value shares for the labour input so as to reflect the price of the labour input to the producer, there are three factors to consider whether to include into the labour compensation. The first factor is the employers' contribution to the Central

---

[3] Definition is extracted from the CIP.

[4] The data are obtained from various issues of the *Yearbook of Labour Statistics*.

Provident Fund (CPF).[5] The CPF was first set up in 1955 and then, an employee only contributed 5 per cent of his monthly salary, matched by another 5 per cent from his employer, subject to a maximum amount of $50. The rate of contribution has been adjusted over the years, to ensure sufficient funds for employee retirement. In order to compute the employer's contribution, we make use the rates of contribution and the contributors by age level to calculate.

The second factor that would affect the labour compensation is the payroll tax. The employers in Singapore had to pay a two per cent payroll tax on all the wages and salaries including bonuses and commissions paid. This would indicate that the remuneration of each employee must multiply by 1.02. However, payroll tax was suspended with effect from April 1985 and we can thereby exclude it from the labour compensation.

The last factor is the Skill Development levy that is instituted by the government to help companies to defray their training costs incurred in upgrading workers. In April 1986, the levy was reduced from 2 percent to 1 percent. From 1991 onwards, the National Productivity Board took over the administration and enforcement from Inland Revenue Authority of Singapore. This levy also constituted a cost to the producer.

The three above-mentioned factors do represent some costs to the producer in term of remuneration payment and do need to include them in the labour compensation. As there is no publication on the breakdown the CPF contribution, payroll tax and Skill Development levy on the manufacturing industry, Tsao thereby assumes that the three factors are distributed in proportion to the total remuneration. This would mean that the three factors will not be included and the income data that will be used for the calculation for the value shares remain unchanged.

6.2.2   *Laspeyres Index to Compute the Price of Labour*

The Laspeyres index number for the nth period is obtained using the following equation:

$$L_{n:0} = 100 \times \frac{\sum p_{in} q_{i0}}{\sum p_{i0} q_{i0}} \tag{18}$$

In the equation above, n is referred to as the sample size, which ranges from 1971 to 1994. The price in period n is p_{in}, and the quantity is q_{in}. The amount spent in the base period is $p_{i0} q_{i0}$, and the grand total of $\sum p_{i0} q_{i0}$.

6.3   CAPITAL

To construct the index of capital input, according to Tsao (1982)[6], the capital stock is classified into seven asset categories:

1. Land

2. Buildings and structures

3. Machinery and equipment

---

[5] The CPF was set up on 1July 1955 as a statutory authority to implement saving scheme to provide workers with retirement benefits. It is a compulsory savings fund to which both the employees and their employers contribute.

[6] Tsao adopted her methodology from Gollop and Jorgenson (1979).

4. Office equipment

5. Transport Equipment

6. Stocks of output

7. Stocks of materials.

The details to compute the total capital stock for all the above mentioned categories are explained below.

6.3.1   Owned Capital

The capital stocks for the first five categories are constructed using the perpetual inventory method. According to Tsao (1982), the replacement requirements follow a declining balance pattern for each asset and its relationship between investment and capital stock at the beginning of the year is

$$A (T_{i-1}) = I (T_i) + (1-d)*A(T_i) \tag{19}$$

Where $A(T_i)$ is the capital stock at time T_i (beginning of the year i), $I(T_i)$ if the investment at time T_I, and d is the rate of replacement.

To construct the owned capital stock, first we must obtain the capital stock benchmarks for the five categories. Then we used the perpetual inventory method mentioned above. However, there is not yet been a survey of wealth in Singapore and a benchmark for the capital stock is not easy to come by. By using the net value of fixed assets at the beginning of the year 1970, they can serve as benchmarks for the construction of the capital stock prices by asset category and industry.

In order to obtain the gross investment series, the value of the fixed assets sold should be subtracted from the capital expenditures. But the data for the value of fixed assets sold were no longer available in the year 1991 and onwards, therefore, we decide to use the difference of the net value of the capital assets between two periods, $t - 1$ and t, to replace the gross investment in the period t. And the asset price deflators are derived from the *National Accounts 1995* using data report on nominal and real (1990 prices) gross fixed capital formation[7] for:

I.   Non-residential buildings

II. Machinery and equipment, office equipment and transport equipment

The first deflator obtained for non-residential buildings is used to deflate for the categories in land and buildings structures; whereas the second deflator for machinery, office and transport equipment is for the categories in machinery and equipment, office equipment and transport equipment.

The data of the net value of fixed assets, obtained from CIP, are referring to their cost net off accumulated depreciation. The capital stocks for the two categories, land, buildings and structures & machinery and equipment, office equipment and transport equipment, are computed as follows:

---

[7] Data are from the *Singapore System of National Accounts 1995, Department of Statistics Singapore.*

$$A\ (T_{i-1}) = I\ (T_i) + (\ 1 - d\ )*A(T_i)$$

$$= \left(\frac{A\ (T_{i-1}) - A(T_i)}{A_i}\right) \tag{20}$$

6.3.2   Stocks of Output and Materials

In Jorgenson's definition, where Tsao adopts the capital that includes the stocks of materials and output, the value of the two inputs are then obtained by taking their beginning year stocks of materials and output respectively. For their respective deflators, the GDP deflator is used for the stocks of material and domestic supply price index is then for the stocks of output. However, the data for the beginning year stocks of both inputs are no longer available from the year 1991 onwards. Thus, these two inputs are not included in my paper.

6.3.3   Price of Capital

The formula of the user cost of capital used is extracted from Boadway, Bruce and Mintz (1987). It differs from the formula used by previous studies, which use the approach from Jorgenson (1967).

$$\left(\frac{(1 - U.Z_i)}{(1 - U)*(1 - T_p)}\right) * [\ r + d_i - \left(\frac{(q_{it} - q_{it-1})}{(q_{it-1})}\right)]$$

where U is the corporate income tax rate; Z is the present value of capital consumption allowances (CCA) deductions on a dollar's worth of investment; T_p is the property tax rate; r is the prime lending rate for the marginal opportunity cost of capital; q_i is the investment price deflator for capital input i; d_i is the depreciation rate for capital input i.

The corporate income tax rates used are from 1971 to 1994. Z is computed using the straight-line method of depreciation. The capital gains used for the formula are realised instead of expected. A nine-year moving average of realised capital gains was used to reduce volatility. For property taxes, it is set at 23 percent and is only applicable to non-residential buildings and q_i is the investment price deflator for capital type i. The depreciation rates for the formula is explained in the following paragraph.

The depreciation rates for each asset category used in Tsao (1982) and Wong and Gan (1994) are:[8]

- Non-residential buildings   0.0361
- Machinery and Equipment   0.1047
- Office Equipment   0.2729
- Transport Equipment   0.2935

As we have combined machinery and equipment, office equipment and transport equipment into one category to compute the gross investment series, we use the geometric mean, the number calculable as the nth root of a product of n numbers, of the last three as the rate of replacement for the combined asset category

---

[8] Wong and Gan use the depreciation rates reported in Jorgenson (1990).

6.3.4   Rented Capital

The data in the CIP only provide the sum of the net rental cost for all the capital categories. The ratios of the net value of the owned capital are used to apportion the total sum of the rental capital into the following two categories:

1. Building and structures

2. Machinery and Equipment, Office Equipment and Transportation Equipment.

To derive the total value of each category, we have to add the net rental cost of each category to the value of the owned capital of each category. Using the data computed, we can proceed to compute the price and value share of the capital inputs.

6.3.5   Indexes of Capital

For capital stock, A_k, to transform into capital services, K_k, it should be multiply with a constant of proportionality X_k to get,

$$K_k = A_k . X_k, \ (k=1,2,\ldots, p) \tag{21}$$

The translog index of capital input is then calculated as

$$\ln K(T) - \ln K(T-1) = \sum V_{kk} [\ln K_k(T) - \ln K_k(T-1)]$$
$$= \sum V_{kk} [\ln A_k(T) - \ln A_k(T-1)] \tag{22}$$

where $V_{kk} = \dfrac{1}{2} [V_{kk}(T) - V_{kk}(T-1)]$, $(k=1,2,\ldots, p)$.

Here, the aggregate capital stock is defined as

$$A = \sum A_k, \ (k=1,2,\ldots, p) \tag{23}$$

In this context, an index of capital quality, X_k, would be defined by

$$K = X_k . A, \tag{24}$$

$$\ln X_k(T) - \ln X_k(T-1) = [\ln K(T) - \ln K(T-1)] - [\ln A(T) - \ln A(T-1)]. \tag{25}$$

6.4   MATERIALS AND ENERGY

In constructing the translog quantity index for materials (referred to as non-energy intermediate inputs and energy inputs), Tsao (1982) first classified materials into three categories:

1. materials and work given out;

2. water;

3. transport;

and the factor input of energy into the four categories:

1. electricity;

2. fuel oil;

3. gas;

4. other fuels.

Then, the quantities for the materials and energy required are obtained from various issues of the Census of Industrial Production, while the values of both two inputs are obtained using the methodology of Gollop and Jorgenson in the construction of composite material input price deflators. By having the quantities and values of the materials, we can use the translog of materials to reflect changes within the industries.

However, the data for the beginning year stocks of both inputs are no longer available from CIP in 1991 onwards. Therefore, we decide to use the data on the census of value added instead. Detail of how these two inputs are accounted in the computation for TFP growth will be discussed under output section.

6.5   OUTPUT

The output measure here is referring to the real gross output. In order to compensate for the two inputs of material and energy, we decide to use the data of census value added in CIP for our output measure. Census value added is computed by minus materials, utilities, fuel, transportation charges and work given from gross output. By assuming that the amount of transport charges are proportional throughout the industries over our time series, the change in the census value added between two periods, $t - 1$ and t, is used to represent the nominal value for the output in the period t. Using the GDP deflator for manufacturing sector, we get our real gross output.

6.6   BIAS IN THE USE OF THE VALUE ADDED SPECIFICATION

It has been a common practice to calculate the rate of technical change by subtracting a weighted sum of the rates of growth of the factor inputs like capital and labour from the rate of growth of value added in constant prices. The validity of this approach depends on certain conditions: the prices of the output and intermediate inputs (material and energy) must always move in fixed proportions; the ratios of the quantities of materials to output and energy to output must also move in fixed proportions; finally, the three variables like capital, labour and time can be easily separable from the intermediate inputs. All of these conditions mentioned above that involved the usage of the value-added approach. must be met, otherwise, there will be bias in the measurement of technical change [Tsao (1982) p.98-99]. To measure the extent of bias, we can subtract the weighted sum of the growth rate of the capital and labour from the residual of the rate of growth of value added. It is expressed as follows:

$$V^{*i}_{vt} = \ln V_i(T) - \ln V_i(T-1) - V^*_{vk} [\ln K_i(T) - \ln K_i(T-1)]$$

$$- V^*_{vl} [\ln L_i(T) - \ln L_i(T-1)], (i = 1,2,.....,n) \qquad (26)$$

where V_i is value added in constant prices; V^{*i}_{vk} is the shares of capital compensation in nominal value added; and V^{*i}_{vl} is the shares of labour compensation in nominal value added.

To obtain the value added in constant prices, we have to use the output prices to deflate the nominal value added.

Tsao (1982) showed that the discrepancy between the two average values of $V*^i_{vk}$,

$V*^i_{vl}$ is quite large and believes it is difficult to predict the extent of bias *a priori* without recourse to the prices or quantities of intermediate goods. Therefore, she concludes that the results found are against the use of the value-added specification in prior to the verification of the sufficient conditions mentioned above being met.

7. EMPIRICAL RESULTS AND CONCLUSION

Here I describe whether the calculated measures of the productivity source is comparable to TFP measures obtained from other writers and concluded the advantages of having the study for usage for planning and forecasting.

7.1   RESULT ON THE COMPUTATIONS

Figure 1 summarises our main result, which is that for the period between 1970-79, the TFP growth of the manufacturing sector is 1.86 percent. This estimate appears optimistic when compared to the findings by Tsao. Out of the twenty-nine industries, seven industries or 20 percent of the sample experienced negative growth rate per annum.

Between 1980-91, the TFP growth of the manufacturing sector is estimated at 1.39 percent. In Figure 2, the estimate turns out to be positively close to the finding by Wong and Gan. It also turns out to be optimistic to the finding by Young[9]. Out of the twenty-nine industries, 28 percent of the sample shows negative growth per annum.

From 1971-90, the average rate of TFP growth in Figure 3 summarises the result for individual 3-digit industries. These should be interpreted with caution: the lack of industry specific data is one main reason for the lack of variation across industries. However, some results are close to expectations. Thus, we find that the electronics industry is a star performer.

7.2   SENSITIVITY TEST

Tsao (1982), p. 153-156, in her thesis, states that the results depend on the reliability of the data. Therefore, she conducts some tests to justify the shortcomings in her database used and it turns out that the 'so-called' problems did not appear to have significant effect as compared to the original results generated.

In our paper, we consider the following issue to be 'so-called' problems and conduct a test to find out whether they would affect results. The issue, in this case, is the use in the changes of net values of fixed assets in replacement for capital stock computed by the perpetual inventory method followed by other studies. The reason for this usage is due to data on the sales of fixed assets is no longer available in the CIP. In the sensitivity test, we conducted a computation of TFP from 1971-90 using the perpetual inventory method.[10] The result turns out to be quite good as most of the sectors in Figure 3 do not deviate differently to our initial computations. This shows that our assumption is justifiable.

---

[9] The estimate computed is used to compute with Young (1994).

[10] The data for the sales of fixed capital was available until 1990.

7.3 CONCLUSION

The primary motive in this paper is to compute TFP using only published data. This method provides an alternative towards calculation based on the traditional Jorgensen methodology of detailed input construction. The results obtained tend to support the robustness of the growth accounting method to reduced detail in the inputs data. Our recommendation is that this method may serve as the benchmark for the future estimation of TFP, especially when comparing studies that construct their inputs data independently.

REFERENCES

Annual Bulletin of Productivity Statistics (1989): Singapore: National Productivity Board, 1988-89.

Boadway, R. W., Bruce, N., and Mintz, J. M. (1987): "Taxes on Capital Income in Canada: Analysis and Policy," Canadian Tax Paper #80, Canadian Tax Foundation, Toronto.

Central Provident Fund, Annual Reports.

Diewert, W.E. (1976): "Exact and Superlative Index Numbers," *Journal of Econometrics*, 4, 115-145.

Jorgenson, D.W. and Gollop, F. and Barbara Fraumeni (1987): *Productivity and U.S. Economic Growth,* Amsterdam: Elsevier Science Publishers.

Lall, A., R. Tan and Chew S.B. (1996): "Total Factor Productivity Growth Experience of Singapore: An Interpretative Survey," *Economic Management Policy in Singapore*, ed. By Lim Chong Yah, Singapore: Addison Wesley Publishing Company.

Lim C.Y. *et al* (1986). *Policy Options for the Singapore Economy.* Singapore: McGraw Hill.

Loh Kai Hong, Simon (1997) Final Year Project submitted to School of Accountancy and Business, Nanyang Technological University.

Rao, V. V. Bhanoji and Lee, C. (1995): "Sources of Growth in the Singapore Manufacturing Economy and its Manufacturing and Services Sectors," Paper presented at the 20th Federation of ASEAN Economic Associations Conference, Singapore.

Seow, Elaine L. H. and Lall, A. (1996): " Technical Change in Manufacturing Industries in Singapore: 1980-91," *Regional Issues in Economics,* Volume II, 68-87.

Tsao,Y. (1982): *Growth and Productivity in Singapore: A Supply Side Analysis,* Unpublished PH.D. dissertation, Harvard University, Cambridge MA.

Tsao, Y. (1985): "Growth without Productivity: Singapore Manufacturing in the 1970s." *Journal of Development Economics,* 19: 25-38.

Wong, F. C. and Gan, W. B. (1994): "Total Factor Productivity Growth in Singapore Manufacturing Industries During the !980s," *Journal of Asian Economics,* 5(2), 117-196.

Young, A. (1992): "A Tale of Two Cities : Factor Accumulation and Technical Change in Hong Kong and Singapore,". *NBER Macroeconomics Annual*, ed. by Oliver J. Blanchard and Stanley Fischer. Cambridge, MA: The MIT Press.

Young, A. (1994): "the Tyranny of Numbers: Confronting the Statistical Realities of the East Asian Growth Experience," Unpublished Manuscript, Cambridge, MA:MIT

FIGURE 1

Comparing TFP Estimates - Tsao (1985)

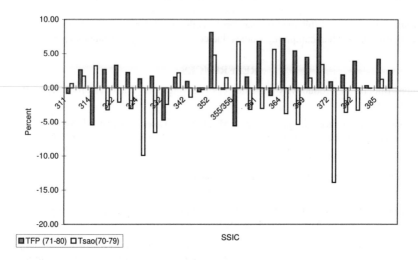

FIGURE 2

Comparing TFP Estimates - Wong and Gan (1994)

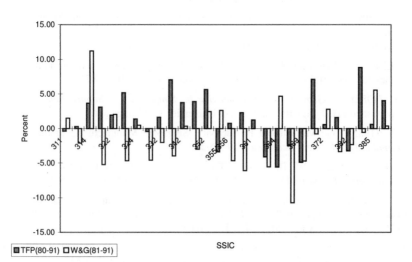

FIGURE 3

Effect of Using Different Measures of Capital Stock

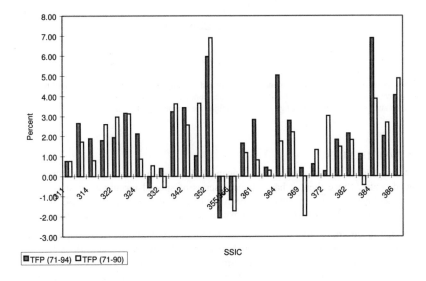

Comparison of Central Banking Policies in Singapore

Soh *Choon San*

&

Dr. Ramin Cooper **Maysami**

Nanyang Business School, Nanyang Technological University, Nanyang Avenue, Singapore 639798
Fax: +(65) 792.4217, Tel: +(65) 799.4900, Email: aramin@ntu.edu.sg

Abstract There is a conflict between monetary stability and exchange rate objectives. The goal of this paper is to find which of the two is and should be of greater concern to the Monetary Authority of Singapore. Regression analysis shows that exchange rate control objective is more significant.

1. INTRODUCTION

In the late 1960s, the government of Singapore decided to develop the country into a financial centre. Since then, it has offered a series of special incentives to stimulate the development process. The results have been gradual but impressive. By 1994, Singapore became the world's fourth largest foreign exchange trading centre despite her small size.

Through its control of monetary policies, the Monetary Authority of Singapore plays a key role in the financial development of Singapore. Before 1971, the various functions related to banking and finance were performed by a number of government departments and agencies. These arrangements worked well until the late 1960s, when it became necessary to bring these bodies under a unified direction and encourage the development of professional expertise.

The purpose of this paper is to study the conflict between monetary stability and exchange rate objectives. More specifically, we aim to find out which policy goal MAS is more interested in -- monetary stability or exchange rate objectives. The next section presents a literature review, followed by a description of the Monetary Authority of Singapore and its functions in Section 3; Section 4 illustrates the circumstances facing Singapore and Section 5 specifies our methodology and data; Section 6 provides the results and Section 7 presents the conclusion.

2. LITERATURE REVIEW

The success of Singapore has been the subject of many studies. Khan (1981) analysed the demand for money in Singapore and found it quite similar to those of other developed countries. He also obtained empirical evidence that the demand functions for narrow money were more stable and hence should be incorporated in predicting money demand. He then ran some simple simulations to 'highlight the difference it makes in the setting of monetary policy when proper attention is paid to the underlying dynamics of the system.' This is especially useful if the government is interested in how the money demand would change over time and hence, the usefulness of monetary policy.

Abeysinghe and Lee (1992) tried to determine if the strong Singapore dollar policy has pushed the Singapore dollar out of its long-run equilibrium path by looking at the relationship of Singapore's dollar with its purchasing power parity. They examined bilateral nominal exchange rates of Singapore with Malaysia, US, UK, Japan and West Germany, and concluded that only the Singapore-US rate was in agreement with the Purchasing Power Parity theorem. Even then, the policy makers seemed to only look at the CPI in targeting the exchange rate rather than the WPI. Assuming that PPP is the long run equilibrium, they showed that Singapore's strong dollar policy had not created a disequilibrium exchange rate. However, the adjustment towards PPP took place more so through price adjustments than exchange rate adjustments.

Simkin (1984) tried to determine if monetarist theory had any impact on Singapore. He performed several simple monetarist tests. One interesting test was that of money supply and the exchange rate. He found that to control the exchange rate, money stocks had to be manipulated to ensure adequate liquidity so as to promote stable growth of real income. This result is, in fact, consistent with the findings of this paper

3. MONETARY AUTHORITY OF SINGAPORE

The MAS was set up in 1971 to perform all the functions of a central bank except issuing currency which, in Singapore, is done by the Board of Commissioners of Currency.

As a statutory board, the MAS is owned and controlled by the government, and its Board of Directors is chaired by the Minister of Finance. As the central bank of Singapore, the MAS promotes stable and non-inflationary growth of the economy as well as a sound and progressive financial services sector. Its main objectives are as follows:

- To conduct monetary and exchange rate policies appropriate for steady and non-inflationary economic growth

- To maintain conditions conducive to a sound financial services sector

- To act as banker to, and financial agent of the government

- To foster sound working relationships with other central banks, international financial institutions, and public and private institutions in Singapore.

To stimulate the growth of Singapore as a financial centre, the MAS has implemented various policies such as encouraging the entry of international institutions to engage in offshore banking and removing exchange controls. Moreover, it has promoted new financial activities by encouraging the establishment of specialised institutions such as merchant banks, money brokers and financial futures dealers.

The MAS has also encouraged the introduction of new financial instruments such as the Singapore dollar NCD, as well as floating rate and fixed rate certificates of deposit. Fiscal measures such as tax incentives have also been implemented to stimulate offshore operations in banking, finance and insurance.

3.1 MONETARY POLICIES AND INSTRUMENTS IN RECENT YEARS

The choice and effectiveness of monetary policy instruments in Singapore have been substantially shaped by the structure and circumstances of the economy. The following are some of the tools used to regulate the economy.

3.1.1 Open Market Operations (OMO)

MAS tries to control the supply of money through monetary base. In an OMO purchase, for example, MAS buys government securities from the public, thus increasing the level of funds in banks and other financial institutions and subsequently increasing the supply of money in the economy.

However, since the money and capital markets in Singapore have not been fully developed yet, open market operations are not the most effective means of regulating the economy. At various times, MAS has found it more suitable to use other instruments to achieve and maintain economic stability.

3.1.2 Cash Reserve Ratio

The MAS requires all commercial banks to hold 6 percent of their liabilities base as a minimum sum balance and another 18 percent as minimum liquid assets. If the reserve ratio increases, banks will have less freedom to lend and money supply will fall. This policy tool is not frequently used in Singapore since the money supply multiplier effect is large and uncertain.

3.1.3 Interest Rate Policy

Another function of the MAS is to make loans to commercial banks to help them meet short-term liquidity shortfalls. The rate of interest charged on such loans is the discount rate and the MAS indirectly influences market interest rates by varying the official discount rates and the volume of Treasury bills tendered. For example, if MAS pursues an expansionary monetary policy, it would reduce the discount rate, thus encouraging banks to borrow more funds. This increases the money supply and reduces interest rates.

3.1.4 Moral Suasion

This is a method of qualitative supervision and the most informal of all the monetary instruments used by MAS. It sets the rules of the game for the financial institutions. Moral suasion can take the form of directives, speeches or press releases and has been quite effective.

4. SINGAPORE'S ECONOMIC CIRCUMSTANCES

Singapore's small land area and population have limited the range of production possibilities and the size of the domestic market. She needs to import even the most basic materials and is dependent on export in order to pay for these materials. The result is an open trade policy with very few trade restrictions. It also shows how vulnerable Singapore is to changes in world prices or exchange rate since its small size limits any influence on world prices. Hence, it is crucial for Singapore to keep her import and export prices as stable as possible.

The openness of the economy also means that domestic monetary instruments like money supply and interest rates do not have as much of a direct influence on domestic inflation as the exchange rate. In addition, the lack of control on capital flows, a small economic base and a high savings rate have all encouraged Singapore's government and private sector to diversify their asset holdings across countries and currencies to spread risk. This makes it difficult to target either the money supply or the interest rates in Singapore.

As a result, MAS can only seek to influence the exchange rate and leave the achievement of domestic objectives to other policies like fiscal policy.

4.1 EXCHANGE RATE POLICY

In principle, the purpose is to achieve an optimum exchange rate which is neither too high so as to hinder exporters, nor too low so as to increase import prices and hence the cost of living. To do so, the MAS manages the exchange rate of the Singapore dollar based on a trade-weighted basket of currencies of major trading partners and competitors. The basket of exchange rates reflects the sources of imported CPI inflation and competitors in export markets. There is no official peg for the value of the currency and MAS can only influence the value of the Singapore dollar by intervening in the exchange market itself.

The Singapore dollar tends to appreciate because the deposition of government budget surpluses with MAS and the institutional arrangement of CPF have the effect of reducing liquidity. Interventions by MAS to buy foreign exchange (largely US dollars) in exchange for new Singapore dollars created by bank reserves is crucial as it re-injects liquidity into the system. This enables the Singapore dollar to float within an undisclosed target band.

5. THE MODEL AND DATA

The main objective of this paper is to study the conflict between monetary stability and exchange rate objectives in Singapore. This section introduces a simple model of the exchange rate to illustrate this conflict. The data is collected from the International Financial Statistics on an annual basis[1] from 1979 to 1993 with 1990 as the base year. Interest rates are money market rates and price of exports are indexed. We assume the foreign country to be the United States of America. Hence, all foreign variables reflect US data.

The relationship between monetary stability and the exchange rate can be studied in the simple monetary model of exchange rate determination. Consider the basic textbook model of money market equilibrium,

$$M/P = m\{r,y\} \tag{1}$$

where M is the money stock, P the deflator, r the interest rate, and y the level of real income. In the long run in a closed economy, one can conclude from this relationship that for a given value of y determined by the real general equilibrium of the economy and r determined by the marginal product of capital, the rate of inflation equals the growth rate of the money supply.

5.1 SMALL AND OPEN ECONOMY WITH ONE-COMMODITY

Following a similar method used by Branson (1981), if there is only one traded commodity and static expectations about exchange rates, we can complement Equation (1) with two other relationships based on the law of one price:

$$P = eP^* \tag{2}$$

and the open-interest arbitrage condition:

$$r = r^* \tag{3}$$

---

[1] Quarterly data found was incomplete. Hence, the use of annual data.

where P* is the world price level, e is the home-country exchange rate (units of home currency per unit of foreign exchange), and r* is the world interest rate. Assuming that P* and r* are exogenous, y is determined by aggregate supply conditions and M is controlled by home monetary institutions, we can convert Equations (2) and (3) into an exchange rate equation:

$$M = eP^*m\{r^*,y\} \tag{4A}$$

Taking natural log on both sides of (4A) gives:

$$\ln(e) = \ln(M) - \ln(P^*) - \ln(m\{r^*,y\}) \tag{4B}$$

Combining natural log of (2) with Equation (4B) yields:

$$\ln(P) = \ln(e) + \ln(P^*) = \ln(M) - \ln(m\{r^*,y\}) \tag{5}$$

We can see that a policy to stabilise the domestic price level would require $de/e = -dP^*/P^*$ and $dM/M = dm/m$. If P* is constant, any policy that set $dM/M=dm/m$ as y and r* varies would hold both e and P constant. If P* varies, as in the case of Singapore, variations in e would hold P constant.

Money market equilibrium requirements will pressure e to offset variation in P* as shown in Equation (4). With variation in M offsetting movement in m, all the movement in the excess demand for money will come from P*. An increase in P* will raise demand for domestic nominal balances. Market participants will start to sell foreign assets to acquire domestic money, causing exchange rate to fall. This fall in e will just offset the rise in P*, hence stabilising P.

So, if the monetary objective is to stabilise the domestic price level, P, the solution would be to vary the nominal money stock, M, so as to offset the variation in real money demand due to movements in r* and y, and to allow the exchange rate to fluctuate so as to offset the variation in P*.

Regardless of what the monetary objectives are, one point is clear from Equation (4): steady money growth is not likely to stabilise either the price level or the exchange rate in an open economy. If the nominal money stock is 'stable', that is $dM/M = 0$, the above stabilisation process would not have been possible since there will be variation in real money demand due to the movements of the exogenous variables r* and y.

5.2 TWO-COMMODITY MODEL

The previous one-commodity model is satisfactory if the objective is to stabilise the domestic price level. If the targets are relative prices of traded and non-traded goods, or exports and imports, we have to consider at least a two-commodity model.

According to the two-commodity model, a more suitable money-market equilibrium is as follows:

$$M/P^{\alpha}(eP^*)^{1-\alpha} = m\{r^*,q\} = M/Q \tag{6}$$

where P is the export price, eP^* the import price, income is the production of the exportable q and the domestic CPI is $Q = P^{\alpha}(eP^*)^{1-\alpha}$.

Variation in Q is given by:

$$dQ/Q = \alpha dP/P + (1-\alpha)[de/e + dP^*/P^*] \tag{7}$$

If the monetary authorities have a target for real exchange rate (eP^*/P), we could express it in the following framework:

$$dP/P = \theta[de/e + dP^*/P^*] \tag{8}$$

Therefore, the resulting variation in Q is then:

$$dQ/Q = [1 - \alpha(1-\theta)][de/e + dP^*/P^*] \tag{9}$$

Together with (6), the monetary variation that will achieve this movement in Q will be:

$$dM/M = [1 - \alpha(1-\theta)][de/e + dP^*/P^*] + dm/m \tag{10}$$

Equation (10) describes the movement in the money stock that will achieve the desired movement in relative price P/eP^*, given exogenous variation in r^*, P^* and q. Given the fluctuation in r^*, P^*, q and M, excess demand for money will be eliminated by movement in e. The main idea is that in an open economy, stabilisation of the money stock will not stabilise the domestic price level or the real exchange rate as P^*, r^*, q or y varies. Whichever model one chooses, one is forced to choose between monetary stability or exchange rate objectives.

5.3 INCLUSION OF EXCHANGE RATE EXPECTATIONS

The inclusion of exchange rate expectations does not really change the basic results. To show how the model works with such expectations, we follow Dornbusch (1976) and combine Equation (1) with the PPP relationship (2) to get:

$$M/eP^* = m\{r,y\} \tag{11}$$

The existence of risk-neutral speculation will transform the open arbitrage condition (3) into:

$$r = r^* + ee \tag{12}$$

where ee is the expected rate of change in the exchange rate. If we assume that the exchange rate will adjust to its long run equilibrium value e':

$$ee = \theta(e' - e) \tag{13}$$

Putting (11) - (13) together, we have the money-market equilibrium condition:

$$M = eP^*m[y, r^* + \theta(e' - e)] \tag{14}$$

Using subscripts to denote partial derivatives, and indexing the initial values of e, P^* and m to unity, the movement in e is given by:

$$de = \{dM - dP^* - [m_y dy + m_r(dr^* + \theta de')]\}/(1 - \theta m_r) \tag{15}$$

This is the same as Equation (4B) except that there is the addition of the expectations 'multiplier' which is less than unity, since $m_r < 0$. Therefore, the addition of exchange rate expectations does not change the results in any significant way.

6. EMPIRICAL EVIDENCE

We begin by estimating the money demand function, (1) and then look at the estimates of the price equations.

6.1 MONEY DEMAND

Equation (1) is the standard money demand function which empirically is frequently estimated in the following form:

$$\ln(M/P)_t = \alpha_0 + \alpha_1\ln(y)_t + \alpha_2 r_t + \varepsilon_t \tag{16}$$

where ε_t is a random disturbance term, α_1 the income-elasticity of demand for real balances and α_2 the 'semi-elasticity' with respect to the interest rate. This equation has been estimated using annual data from 1979 to 1993. M refers to M2, r the interest rate, y the real gross domestic product and P, the GDP deflator.

The results as presented in Table 1 show that the DW statistics were not satisfactory and that there could be serial correlation. Breusch-Godfrey Serial Correlation LM Test was performed and the results are reported in Table 2. We can see that the null hypothesis of no autocorrelation was rejected at 5 percent level of significance since the p-value is 0.0477. Hence, there is serial correlation.

After correcting for serial correlation, the results (with t-ratios in parentheses) are more satisfactory as both the R^2 and DW improved. From Tables 1 and 3, we can see that the income elasticity has dropped from near unity for the period 1967-1978 to 0.36 for the period 1979-1993. In addition, the interest rate coefficient shows that interest rate will reduce money demand by only 0.02 percent instead of 4 percent. The estimates show that money demand for Singapore is normal since the coefficient of interest rate is negative and that of income is positive.

6.2 PRICE AND EXCHANGE RATE

The home-currency price of imports is given by a PPP equation in which the world price is exogenous:

$$P^m = eP^*, \text{ or } \ln(P^m) = \ln(e) + \ln(P^*) \tag{17}$$

Looking at Equation (2), makes it clear that Equation (17) is actually an import-price version of (2). If we further assume that the price of goods produced at home, WPI, depends on the money stock and the import price, then:

$$\ln(P) = \alpha_0 + \alpha_1\ln(M) + \alpha_2\ln(P^m) \tag{18}$$

where WPI is the wholesale price index, P.

Moreover, assuming that the export price index P^x depends on movements in the WPI and on world prices which have been converted into home-currency:

$$\ln(P^x) = \beta_0 + \beta_1\ln(P) + \beta_2\ln(eP^*) \tag{19}$$

Equations (18) and (19) have been estimated by Sumi (1980) using quarterly data from the period 1973 I to 1979 II. . For this paper, annual data has been used from the period 1979 to 1993. A number of lag specifications have been tried on both equations and the results are reported in Tables 4 and 5.

6.2.1 WPI Index Equation

This equation is found to be stationary at 5 percent level of significance. Moving-averages of up to four time periods are used in this equation to find the best fit. From Table 4, it is clear that the effects of both money stock and import price are significant. M1-version of this equation was tested as well, but M2 yielded better results as M2's R^2 and DW values were more acceptable and its variables were more significant.

There is one interesting phenomenon with regards to this equation. We noticed in Table 4 that α_1, the coefficient of money stock, has a negative sign. This is against conventional wisdom. Normally, the money stock moves in the same direction as the price level.

One possible reason to explain this is an initial liquidity drain within the system. The MAS tries to re-inject into the economy through exchange rate intervention by purchasing US dollars. This has the effect of raising the money stock while reducing the domestic price level at the same time.

In addition, even though the Durbin-Watson statistics may not be very satisfactory, as the lag increases from zero to three time periods, the effect of money stock increases. This could be due to policy lags.

Moreover, both R^2 and DW improved as the lag increases. Hence, it is safe to conclude that domestic prices are affected by import prices. This is exactly the same conclusion reached by Sumi.

6.2.2 Export Price Equation

We found Equation (19) to be stationary at the 5 percent level of significance. Table 5 shows the results of this equation.

We tried various lags of moving-average so as to find the best fit, but as with the results of Sumi, the regression which incorporates a Koyck partial-adjustment process (Equation (20)) seems to be the best. Table 6 represents the results of the equation.

$$\ln(P^x)_t = \beta_0 + \beta_1\ln(P)_t + \beta_2\ln(eP^*)_t + \beta_3(P^x)_{t-1} \tag{20}$$

As Table 6 shows, the elasticity of the export price index with respect to WPI is 0.153 and -0.316 with respect to world prices. Both Equations (19) and (20) show a negative relationship between the price of exports and world prices.

For example, in (20), for every unit increase in world prices, our export price falls by about 0.316. This means that exchange rate policy has indeed been effective in keeping domestic prices low by preventing imported inflation. However, is this price reduction sufficient enough such that our exports are not adversely affected by the strong Singapore dollar?

6.3 EFFECTS OF MANAGED FLOATING

Lee (1984), found that Singapore was able to perform well during the devaluation of the UK pound and the subsequent flotation and two devaluations of the US dollar. He concluded that Singapore was able to maintain export competitiveness in the 1970s and 1980s by influencing her inflation rate so as to control appreciation

According to Lee's study, the danger of appreciating Singapore dollar hampering exports had been overstated. Singapore has both high imports and exports and her high exports are possible because she imports a lot of raw materials. In other words, if the exchange rate appreciated, even though exports would become more expensive, imported raw materials are offsetting the higher prices of the exports.

To show that exports of Singapore are still competitive, we rely on the concept of Real Effective Exchange Rate (REER). Following Lee's method, we made use of the Nominal Effective Exchange Rate (NEER) to determine the REER since REER=NEER(P_d/P_f), where P_d is CPI of Singapore and P_f is foreign consumer prices (CPI of US). Table 7 shows the computation of REER using annual data from 1979 to 1993 (1990=100). If domestic inflation rate is less than the foreign inflation, then REER is less than NEER and the negative effect of Singapore dollar's appreciation on export competitiveness would be lessened.

From Figure 1, we can see that over the years, there has not been much loss of export competitiveness. In fact, the REER is less than the NEER after 1990. Even before 1990, the gap between the REER and NEER began to narrow. Hence here, as in Lee's analysis, the appreciation of the exchange rate does not appear to have reduced the competitiveness of Singapore's exports.

7. CONCLUSION

The money demand function seems to fit Singapore's context. In addition, all prices are significantly sensitive to the exchange rate. This conclusion coincides with that of Branson's and Simkin's. According to them, this has two implications: First, we should include the exchange rate in the deflator for the money stock. This is important in deriving the exchange rate equations in the previous sections.

Another implication is that the movements of exchange rate do affect the domestic price level and the terms of trade. This explains MAS's focus on the exchange rate rather than other monetary objectives.

We also found that the domestic price level has an unconventional negative relationship with the money stock. We guessed this to be the result of MAS's efforts on improving Singapore's liquidity situation. When MAS re-injects liquidity into the system, the money stock increases while domestic price level falls due to the abatement of imported inflation.

Yet another interesting result was that the export price has a negative relationship with world prices. This showed that the exchange rate policy has been effective in preventing imported inflation in Singapore.

It is a well known fact that neighbouring countries like China, Vietnam and Malaysia have been doing well recently and that one day, keeping the Singapore dollar strong may no longer be beneficial. Recent studies have shown that Singapore's inflation has been due to the domestic sector rather than overseas factors. Perhaps the MAS should focus on other policies as well, for example wages and fiscal policies, to keep the costs of production low so that Singaporean exports can remain competitive.

REFERENCES

Abeysinghe, T and K. H. Lee (1992): "Singapore's Strong Dollar Policy and Purchasing Power Parity," *Singapore Economic Review*, 37, 70-79.

Branson, W. H. (1981): "Monetary Stability and Exchange Rate Objectives in Singapore," *Papers on Monetary Economics*, 112-122.

International Monetary Fund (1989 and 1985): *International Financial Statistics Yearbook*.

Khan, M. S. (1981): "The Dynamics of Money Demand and Monetary Policy in Singapore," *Papers on Monetary Economics*, 46-76.

Lee, S. Y. (1984): "Some Aspects of Foreign Exchange Management in Singapore," *Asia Pacific Journal of Management*, 1, 207-217.

_____(1990): "Monetary Policy of Singapore," *Monetary and Banking in Singapore and Malaysia*, 133-149.

Simkin, C. (1984): "Does Money Matter in Singapore," *Singapore Economic Review*, 29, 1-15.

Sumi, Y. (1980): *Exchange Rate Policy in Singapore and Its Effect on Trade*.

Teh, K. P., and T. Shanmugaratnam (1992): "Exchange Rate Policy: Philosophy and Conduct Over the Past Decade," *Public Policies in Singapore: Changes in the 1980s and the Future Signposts*, 285-302.

TABLE 1

Demand for Money

	Coefficients			Statistics	
	α_0	α_1	α_2	R^2	DW
1967-1978[a]	0.35	0.94	-0.04	0.988	1.23
	(0.9)	(26.0)	(-2.8)		
1979-1993	-15.849	1.448	-0.005	0.987	0.946
	(-3.538)	(205.706)	(-55.345)		

    a.   From Branson (1981).

TABLE 2

Breusch-Godfrey Serial Correlation Test

	F-statistics	Obs*R^2
Values	3.891	3.920
Probability	0.074	0.048[a]

    a.   Null hypothesis of no serial correlation rejected at 5 percent level of significance.

TABLE 3

Money Demand Equation after Serial Correlation Correction[a]

Coefficients				Statistics	
α_0	α_1	α_2	AR(1)	R^2	DW
13.4819	0.3627	-0.0002	0.9727	0.9940	1.6448
(0.1070)	(2.9298)	(-5.6713)	(853.1532)		

    a.   For the year 1979-1993.

TABLE 4

Estimates of the WPI Equation

Equations		Coefficients			Statistics	
		α_0	α_1	α_2	R^2	DW
(18-1)	No lags	5.101	-0.117	0.457	0.569	1.095
		(2.637)	(-117.102)	(7.759)		
(18-2)	2-period	5.034	-0.117	0.467	0.579	1.085
	average	(2.706)	(-122.791)	(8.098)		
(18-3)	3-peroid	5.031	-0.119	0.473	0.600	1.093
	average	(2.868)	(-132.803)	(8.627)		
(18-4)	4-period	5.068	-0.121	0.476	0.622	1.122
	average	(3.065)	(-143.807)	(9.191)		

Source: International Financial Statistics Yearbook, 1989 and 1995

TABLE 5

Export Price Equation

Coefficients			Statistics	
β_0	β_1	β_2	R^2	DW
6.950	0.532	-0.923	0.629	1.165
(12.246)	(8.323)	(18.403)		

Source: International Financial Statistics Yearbook, 1989 and 1995

TABLE 6

Export Price Equation after Koyck Transformation

Coefficients				Statistics	
β_0	β_1	β_2	β_3	R^2	DW
4.950	0.153	-0.316	0.006	0.826	2.097
(1.105)	(2.219)	(-1.359)	(470.246)		

TABLE 7

Values of Nominal Effective Exchange Rate and Real Effective Exchange Rate

Year	NEER	CPI(S'pore)	CPI(US)	REER
1979	83.3	73.8	55.6	110.6
1980	85.4	80.0	63.1	108.3
1981	91.1	86.6	69.6	113.4
1982	97.1	90.0	73.9	118.3
1983	100.8	91.0	76.2	120.4
1984	103.7	93.4	79.5	121.8
1985	103.8	93.8	82.4	118.2
1986	91.3	92.6	83.9	100.8
1987	87.4	93.0	87.0	93.4
1988	87.0	94.4	90.5	90.7
1989	92.8	96.7	94.9	94.6
1990	100.0	100.0	100.00	100.0
1991	103.8	103.4	104.2	103.0
1992	106.9	105.8	107.4	105.3
1993	106.8	108.3	110.6	104.6

Source: International Financial Statistics Yearbook, 1989 and 1995

FIGURE 1

Plot of Nominal Effective Exchange Rate and Real Effective Exchange Rate

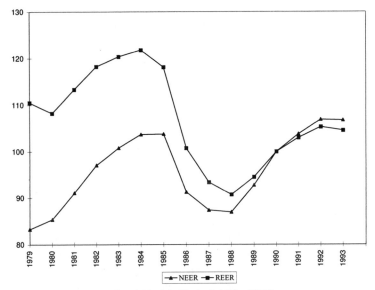

—▲— NEER —■— REER

Source: International Financial Statistics Yearbook, 1989 and 1995

The Effects of Ageing on Saving in Singapore

Tan Ee Ting
&
Soon Lee Ying

Nanyang Business School, Nanyang Technological University, Nanyang Avenue, Singapore 639798
Fax: +(65) 791.3697, Tel: +(65) 799.4778, Email: alysoon@ntu.edu.sg

Abstract Ageing of the population is fast becoming an issue of concern for many countries. Numerous studies have examined the potential economic effects of an ageing population. This paper specifically looks at the impact of ageing on Singapore's private saving. Using cointegration analysis, this study finds strong support for the hypothesis that ageing boosts consumption at the expense of saving. Simulations reveal that increasing the retirement age will moderate the decline in saving in the long run.

1. INTRODUCTION

There are numerous studies on the implications of an ageing population. The ageing phenomenon is occurring not only in industrial countries such as Japan, Germany and the United States but also in Newly Industrialising Economies (NIEs) like Singapore and Hong Kong. In fact, Singapore's rate of ageing is among the top three in the world. The other two top 'ageing countries' are Japan and Hong Kong [Shantakumar (1996)].

Ageing of the population is expected to bring about major changes in the economy, one of which is a decline in saving rates (in particular, private saving rates), as predicted by the Life Cycle model. Specifically, as the population ages, the proportion of people in their prime working age (15-64) declines. This is tantamount to an increase in the average age of the labour force. There are far-reaching implications of a smaller and older workforce for output. Unless offset by technological progress and/or an increase in labour productivity, a smaller workforce is likely to cause a reduction in potential output. This reduction in output in turn would reduce saving. The government has attempted to counter the negative impact of a greying population on the workforce by raising the official retirement age of the workforce. The first adjustment was introduced in April 1993 whereby the previous official retirement age of 55 was raised to 60. Further upward adjustments to 65 can be expected in a few years' time and the retirement age will be raised to 67 in the year 2003 [Bauer (1996)].

Ageing causes an increase in the number of old-age dependants relative to the number of the employed. This measure is known as the old-age or elderly dependency ratio. As defined by Shantakumar (1996), this ratio is equal to the ratio of those aged 60 and above to those aged 15-59. The elderly dependency ratio in Singapore has seen an increase from 7.2 percent to 13.4 percent between 1957 and 1990 and it is projected to increase further to 50.3 percent and 51.9 percent in the years 2030 and 2050 respectively if the current total fertility rate of 1.83 continues throughout the decades to come. Projections by Heller (1989) revealed an elderly dependency ratio of 41.3 percent, 38.5 percent and 34.9 percent for Germany, Japan and the United States respectively in the year 2025. Hence, we can see the severity of Singapore's ageing problem by merely comparing its elderly dependency ratio with that of advanced industrial countries.

1.1 DEMOGRAPHIC CHANGES IN SINGAPORE

The demographic changes of Singapore may be divided into three main phases of concerted action and policies, namely the Pre-policy Phase (before1966), the Anti-natalist Phase (1966-80) and the Post-1980 Phase (1980 onwards) [Shantakumar (1996)].

During the Pre-policy phase, the emphasis was on educating people on the importance of family planning. However, Anti-natalist policies were later implemented by the government due to the growing concern about an excessively rapid fertility increase and its effects on population and labour force growth. Policy measures introduced included incentives and disincentives which explicitly discouraged high parity families. During the 1980s when the Pro-natalist policies came into effect, new tax incentives were introduced to promote large family size, especially among the educated and working women with a minimum level of secondary education. However, poorer families were still encouraged to have small families. The new demographic policies were based on the premise that population and labour resources may be inadequate or depleted as the population ages rapidly.

Despite the change in government policies, the ageing phenomenon has already begun to manifest itself. Since 1970 or so, the proportion of the young population (those below 15) to total population fell sharply. This may be attributed to the secular decline in fertility in the 1960s, 1970s and the early 1980s. Statistics show that while the fertility ratio declined from 42.8 percent in 1957 to 38.8 percent in 1970 and further to 23.2 percent in 1990, the percentage of population aged 60 and above rose from 3.8 percent in 1957 to 5.7 percent in 1970 and 9.1 percent in 1990. Due to improvements in life expectancy[1], the transition from a youthful to an ageing population is even more certain and imminent.

2. LITERATURE REVIEW

The effects of demography on saving have been quantified in a number of studies. Modigliani (1970), in his cross-sectional study involving 36 countries, found not only growth but demographic factors to be of major importance in explaining intercountry differences in private saving rates during 1952-60. More recently, Graham (1987) found that Life Cycle demographic variables explain about two-thirds of the observed variation in the saving rates of OECD nations during the 1970s.

Masson and Tryon (1990), in their simulation of the effects of a shift in dependency ratios over the period 1996-2025 on consumption, found private saving rates in the United States to vary negatively with the dependency ratio. Japan's private saving rate is expected to fall steadily through 2015 as a result of the ageing of its population. Similar effects are also found in Germany, Canada and other industrial countries although the effects of the demographic transition on saving are smaller.

A study by Heller (1989) found that private saving in the group of seven countries (United States, United Kingdom, Japan, Germany, Italy, Canada, and France) as a whole

---

[1] According to the *Yearbook of Statistics*, 1983/84 issue, the expected length of life at birth in 1970 was 65.1 and 70 for males and females respectively. The figures increased to 68.7 and 74 years in 1980. Shantakumar (1996) found that the tremendous improvement in longevity and a continuation of this trend into the next century were expected to lead to male and female life expectancy of 78 and 82 years respectively in the year 2050.

could drop by 1 to 3 percent of GDP from its level in the year 2000 during the period 2000-2010. The decline in saving was higher, 3 to 11 percent of GDP, for the 15 years following 2010, due to the increase in the share of the elderly population, and the impact was likely to be greatest in Canada and the United States. Germany, Japan, and the United Kingdom may also experience large declines. However, for the period 1980-2025, Japan will experience the sharpest fall in saving rate, with saving falling by at least 7 percent of GDP.

As the projections for various countries show, an ageing population can seriously affect a country's saving rate. Despite currently having one of the highest saving rates in the world, Singapore can expect a possible fall in its saving rate as its population ages rapidly. The focus of this study is therefore to examine the implications of Singapore's ageing population on its private saving.

3. DATA AND DETERMINANTS OF SAVING

3.1 DATA

Annual data from 1975 to 1995 are used in the estimation. The figures are obtained from various issues of *Yearbook of Statistics*, *Economic Survey of Singapore*, *Monthly Digest of Statistics*, *Economic and Social Statistics, 1960-1982*, *Profile of the Labour Force of Singapore, 1983-1994* and *International Financial Statistics*. For estimation, we need data for private consumption expenditure, private disposable income, population (incorporating the breakdown of population in various age groups), CPF saving, government saving, gross domestic product (GDP), gross national saving (GNS), saving deposit rate, consumer price index (base year = 1985) as a proxy for inflation, money supply M2, deflator of private consumption expenditure on GDP (base year = 1985) and property price index (base year = 1985). To obtain per capita values, we divide consumption, income and CPF saving by total population.

All income and consumption variables are deflated by the deflator of private consumption expenditures. Private disposable income may be computed as the sum of private consumption (which is directly available from national accounts data) and private saving. The latter is simply the difference between GNS and government saving. Government saving are proxied by the government's consolidated current account surplus. This figure does not include the saving of statutory boards since most statutory boards operate along commercial principles, suggesting that their saving should be regarded as part of private saving instead. CPF saving are measured as total contributions from employees and employers plus accrued interest minus withdrawals on account of retirement, death, medical and educational expenses, or permanent emigration from Singapore. Inflation is measured as the percentage change in the consumer price index while real interest rate is computed as the saving deposit rate less the rate of inflation.

3.2 DETERMINANTS OF SAVING

This section discusses the demographic and non-demographic factors that affect private saving.

3.2.1 Dependency

As emphasised in the earlier sections, demographic factors constitute one of the most important determinants of private saving rates. In particular, most studies have revealed that changes in the dependency ratios affect saving rates negatively. Lahiri (1989) showed in his study of 8 Asian countries, including Singapore, that a 1 percentage point increase in the percentage of the population aged 15-64 results, on average, in a 1.6 percentage point rise in the long run private saving rates in India, Korea, Malaysia, Singapore and Sri Lanka.

In an IMF study, Husain (1995) found that an increase in the ratio of working age population (those between 15-64) to total population by 1 percentage point increased, on average, the private saving rate of Singapore by 1.7 percentage points.

Horioka (1991) used the elderly dependency ratio (defined as the ratio of the population aged 65 and over to the population aged 20 to 64) as well as the young dependency ratio (which is the ratio of the population aged 19 and under to those aged 20 to 64) in his study. He found that a 1 percentage point increase in the elderly and young dependency ratios caused the private saving rate of Japan to decline by 1 and 0.3 percentage points respectively.

3.2.2 Female Labour Force Participation Rate

Sturm (1983) found that the female labour force participation rate is likely to affect the saving behaviour. According to Sturm, *ceteri paribus*, this rate will determine the number of households with two income earners. There exist arguments to the effect that the ratio of households with two income earners tend to have an important impact on household consumption behaviour and most likely so in the direction of reducing saving. Several reasons for this were cited in his paper. First, households with two income earners usually gain increased access to consumer credit. Second, the need for precautionary assets is less pronounced for such households due to a reduction in variability of income.

In view of the significant increase in female labour force participation in Singapore over the last two decades, this study will attempt to examine its impact on private saving.

3.2.3 Economic Growth

Economic growth is one of the main determinants of saving rate in the Life Cycle hypothesis. According to an Asian Development Bank Survey (1990), countries with high growth rates have achieved high domestic saving rates. Lahiri (1989) estimated consumption functions derived from a simple Life Cycle model for eight Asian countries[2] and found that growth in per capita income stimulated private saving. According to his findings, a 1 percentage point increase in the rate of growth of per capita income brings about, on average, an equivalent increase in private saving rate in the long run. In contrast, Husain (1995) found that, on average, a 1 percentage point increase in the rate of growth of private disposable income only results in a 0.3 percentage point increase in the long run private saving rate of Singapore.

3.2.4 Social Security

There are basically two types of social security schemes — funded and pay-as-you-go. The main difference between the two is that under the former, the actuarial value of retirement benefits of an individual is equal to the amount of contributions he/she made

---

[2] The countries include Singapore, Malaysia, Indonesia, Thailand, The Philippines, India, Sri Lanka, and the Republic of Korea.

during his/her working life while in the latter, the working population is taxed to provide income for the retired population [Datta and Shome (1981)]. Empirical evidence on the impact of compulsory saving on other forms of saving has been mixed. Cagan (1965) and Katona (1965) found that private pension schemes stimulated saving in the United States[3]. However, Feldstein (1974) argued that social security schemes reduce saving rates. Barro (1978) challenged Feldstein's views by arguing that the negative impact of social security on saving is fully offset by voluntary private intergenerational transfers.

It is nevertheless interesting to note that Datta and Shome (1981) and Husain (1995) found no significant impact of social security on voluntary private saving and total private saving respectively[4]. Husain's study supports the findings of an earlier study by Loh and Veall (1985) for Singapore. Indeed, given the liberalisation of the guidelines on the use of CPF balances in recent years, it is likely that CPF saving have become a substitute for voluntary private saving.

3.2.5 Government Saving

One view of how changes in government saving can affect private saving is the Ricardian Equivalence Theorem. According to Barro (1974), any change in government saving which is accompanied by a change in future taxation, is exactly offset by private sector dissaving and has no impact on national saving. However, Asilis and Ghosh (1992) noted that a commitment by the government to a higher saving rate is likely to give rise to private sector expectations that overall saving will be high and thereby induce private individuals to save more. However, Husain's (1995) study on Singapore concluded that a dollar's increase in government consumption was offset, on average, by a reduction in private consumption of only 60 cents.

3.2.6 Real Interest Rate

The Life Cycle hypothesis stipulates two opposing effects of a nonzero interest rate on saving. According to the income effect, interest earned on wealth increases income and hence consumption. The substitution effect on the other hand states that a nonzero interest rate increases the opportunity cost of current consumption in terms of future consumption and hence reduces consumption.

The literature on the impact of interest rate on private saving shows mixed evidence. Wong (1986) found that interest rate has a positive impact on private sector saving in Singapore although the coefficient was statistically insignificant. An earlier cross-sectional study by Williamson (1968) revealed a negative correlation between real interest rates and national saving rates. His findings have since been challenged by Fry (1978, 1986), who argued that the national saving rate is responsive to increases in the nominal interest rate although it 'was not large enough to warrant substantial policy significance' [Fry (1986)]. Fry's cross-sectional study included Singapore.

---

[3] The social security system in the United States is pay-as-you-go.

[4] Datta and Shome's study covers five Asian countries. Singapore, Malaysia and India have funded social security systems while Sri Lanka and the Philippines have pay-as-you-go social security systems. However, the social security system for government employees in the Philippines is funded.

3.2.7 Financial Intermediation

Financial intermediation, which is the process of channelling funds from savers to borrowers, tends to raise the levels of saving and investment which contribute to the growth of an economy [Gurley and Shaw (1960)]. While most studies, including a survey paper on saving by Mikesell and Zinzer (1973), found a significant positive relationship between private sector saving ratio and financial intermediation, Dayal-Gulati and Thimann (1996) suggested that the development of financial markets may actually turn out to be a double-edged sword. A more developed financial market increases the availability of saving instruments and most likely the return on saving. At the same time, it also makes it easier for individuals to take loans, thus lowering saving. Since it is difficult to quantify financial market development, we have, as most studies have done, used the degree of monetization of the economy [generally defined as the ratio of broad money (M2) to GDP] to capture the degree of financial development.

3.2.8 Wealth

As pointed out in Bovernberg and Owen (1990), the Life Cycle hypothesis stipulates that individuals reduce their saving if capital gains improve their net wealth positions. Indeed, the overall empirical evidence does suggest that movements in wealth are a major determinant of saving behaviour. For instance, Montgomery (1986) found that increase in wealth was one of the factors that accounted for 40 percent of the fall in personal saving rate during 1975-82 in the United States. While wealth in general is measured by the value of shares and property held by individuals, Summers and Carroll (1987) noted that the adverse effect of housing wealth on saving exceeded that of stock market wealth in the United States.

Property represents a major component of the assets owned by Singaporeans. The sharp appreciation in property prices over the last two decades is expected to have a positive effect on consumption. In this study, we use the property price index as a proxy for wealth[5].

We use a total of eight independent variables to explain the changes in private consumption and hence private saving in the short and long run. These dependent and independent variables are as follows:

1. LC = natural log of per capita private consumption deflated by the deflator of private consumption expenditure (1985 = 100)

2. LY = natural log of per capita private disposable income deflated as above

3. ODR55[6] = ratio of population aged 55 and above to those aged 15-54

4. FLPR = female labour force participation rate (in percentage)

5. LCPF = natural log of per capita CPF saving deflated as above

6. GS = government saving as a percentage of GDP

7. REALR = real interest rate (saving deposit rate less rate of inflation)

---

[5] The correct measure of wealth is the value of net wealth, data for which are not available.

[6] We have assumed in the cointegrating relationship that the minimum retirement age continued to be 55 between July 1993 and December 1995 even though the Retirement Age Act took effect on 1 July 1993.

8. FS = money supply (M2) as a percentage of GDP

9. PPI = property price index (1985 = 100) deflated as above

4. METHODOLOGY

The methodology used in this study is as follows. The variables were all tested for stationarity using the Dickey-Fuller (DF) and Augmented Dickey-Fuller (ADF) unit root tests. Section 5.1 discusses the results of the tests. Section 5.2 describes the results of the Engle and Granger test for cointegration while section 5.3 discusses the findings of the second step of the Engle-Granger-Yoo three step approach using Ordinary Least Squares (OLS). Section 5.4 presents the results of the third step.

5. EMPIRICAL RESULTS

5.1 RESULTS OF UNIT ROOT TESTS

The results of the ADF tests for unit roots on the time series variables indicate that apart from real interest rate, which is stationary or integrated of order zero, the rest of the variables are all random walks or non-stationary with no drift or trend terms, i.e. they are integrated of order one. Note that meaningful conclusions can only be drawn from regressions involving variables with the same order of integration.

5.2 RESULTS OF ENGLE AND GRANGER TEST FOR COINTEGRATION (STEP 1)

The cointegration regression posits a long run relationship between consumption, income, elderly dependency ratio, female labour force participation rate and government saving:

$$LC_t = \alpha_0 + \alpha_1 LY_t + \alpha_2 ODR55_t + \alpha_3 FLPR_t + \alpha_4 GS_t + e_t \tag{1}$$

A preliminary regression shows that the inclusion of the variable, LCPF, in the cointegrating regression changes the sign of the coefficient of ODR55 to negative, suggesting that the inclusion of LCPF might result in a misspecification of the model. REALR has not been included since the Life Cycle hypothesis does not stipulate that real interest rate affects consumption and saving in the long run. FS and PPI have not been included because the former is commonly regarded as a cyclical variable while the latter is only a rough proxy for wealth rather than an accurate measure of wealth.

Table 1 gives the results of the parameter estimates of the variables in equation (1) while Table 2 reports the results of the ADF test for stationarity of the residual, e_t. The reported •-statistic allows us to reject the null hypothesis of a unit root at 5 percent level of significance and confirm the existence of a cointegrating relationship between the variables in equation (1).

5.3 RESULTS OF ERROR CORRECTION EQUATION (STEP 2)

The specification of the error correction equation takes the following form:

$$\Delta LC_t = \beta_1 \Delta LY_t + \beta_2 \Delta ODR55_t + \beta_3 \Delta FLPR_t + \beta_4 \Delta GS_t + \beta_5 \Delta LCPF_t + \beta_6 REALR_t + \beta_7 \Delta FS_t + \beta_8 \Delta PPI_t + \beta_9 e_{t-1} + v_t \tag{2}$$

The results of the estimation of the error correction equation are shown in Table 3. Apart from LCPF, the first difference (Δ) of the other variables not included in the cointegrating regression, namely FS and PPI and the level term, REALR, are statistically insignificant. The results suggest that financial deepening in Singapore has a negative effect on private saving probably because it enhances credit availability, although the impact is insignificant. The negative although statistically insignificant impact of an increase in 'wealth' on private consumption does not support the Life Cycle hypothesis. The findings on real interest rate are consistent with those of Wong (1986). They show that while real interest rates do not affect saving and consumption in a significant manner, the substitution effect is stronger than the income effect.

In view of the low explanatory power of REALR, ΔFS, and ΔPPI, these variables were dropped from the final error correction equation shown in Table 4. In general, the results appear to be satisfactory. Apart from ODR55, the coefficients of the first differences of the other variables are statistically significant at the 10 percent level of significance or better[7]. The results for ΔLCPF suggest that an increase in CPF saving is accompanied by lower private consumption expenditures and hence higher voluntary private saving, which is contrary to the findings of Datta and Shome (1981) and Husain (1995).

The speed of adjustment parameter (e_{t-1}) which represents the gap between last period's per capita real consumption and its long-run value, suggests that 41.2 percent of the disequilibrium in real per capita private consumption in one period is corrected in the next period.

5.4 *RESULTS OF THE THIRD STEP OF ENGLE-GRANGER-YOO THREE STEP APPROACH*

The third step of the Engle-Granger-Yoo three step approach suggests the following long-run relationships between real per capita consumption and the independent variables:

$$LC = 0.325LY + 0.044ODR55 + 0.020FLPR + 3.89E\text{-}06GS \qquad (3)$$

The coefficient of LY implies that for every 1 percent increase in the real per capita private disposable income, real per capita private consumption expenditure increases by 0.325 percent in the long-run. The coefficient of ODR55 suggests that in steady state, a 1 percentage point increase in the elderly dependency ratio will lead to an increase in real per capita consumption of 4.4 percent. The coefficients of FLPR and GS indicate that in the long-run, a 1 percentage point rise in the female labour force participation rate and the ratio of government saving to GDP will reduce real per capita private saving by 2 percent and approximately 0.0004 percent.

6. SIMULATION AND IMPLICATIONS

In this section, we perform two simulation exercises [using the coefficient of ODR55 in equation (3)] to assess the impact of changes in the elderly dependency ratio on private saving. The period of simulation is between the year 2000 and 2030.

---

[7] We have conducted two diagnostic tests on the error correction equation, namely the Breusch-Godfrey serial correlation LM test and White's heteroscedasticity test. The results show no evidence of autocorrelation and heteroscedasticity respectively.

6.1 PART ONE

Simulations were performed on 3 scenarios of age projections put forth by Shantakumar[8]. According to Shantakumar, the population projections (from 1990 to 2050) have been modified to allow for different assumptions regarding fertility over the projected period. In addition, for all three scenarios, nil or age-specified migration rates has been assumed. Furthermore, it is also assumed that life expectancy at birth is the same for all three scenarios, with the male and female life expectancy averaging 72.0 and 78.0 years respectively in 1990 and 78.0 and 82.0 years respectively in the year 2050.

In Scenario 1, it is assumed that there is a gradual increase in the fertility level from the total fertility rate (TFR) of 1.83 in 1990 to the replacement level of 2.10 by the year 2050. In Scenario 2, the 1990 TFR is assumed to remain constant throughout the 1990-2050 period while in Scenario 3, the assumption made is that the TFR will increase gradually from 1.83 in 1990 and rise beyond the replacement level to reach a 3-child norm by the year 2050.

Table 5 reports the results of the simulation. Note that the projected populations for the years 2000, 2005 and 2010 are the same under different assumptions concerning the TFR and that the figures in the later years do not differ substantially. This may be explained by the fact that the effects of changes in fertility are not realised immediately since there is a gestation period of 15 to 20 years before young dependants can grow into working age adults. In addition, the growth in fertility rates (if any) is gradual every year. This implies that increases in fertility and hence their impact on the population structure and private saving will only be apparent in the long run. Hence, we find the largest percentage decline in real per capita private saving under Scenario 2, followed by Scenario 1 and Scenario 3. However, we must remember that per capita income will not remain at their 1995 levels (as assumed in the simulation exercise) but will increase over the next few decades. While a higher TFR may serve to mitigate the effects of ageing on saving, its potential contribution is only minimal. Besides, high fertility levels is a highly unlikely scenario in the next twenty to thirty years in the absence of a substantial influx of young adults [Shantakumar (1994)].

6.2 PART TWO

In this simulation, the mandatory retirement age is raised from 55 to 60 and eventually to 65 under all three scenarios. The underlying assumption is that there are no changes in the consumption patterns of those in the 55-59 and 60-64 age groups since the estimated coefficient for ODR55 specifically denotes the ratio of the population aged 55 and above to those aged 15-54 in the sample period 1975 to 1995. We use the second and third set of population projections, with the assumption of a constant TFR of 1.83 and a rising TFR (from 1.83 to 3 in 2050) respectively, to capture the upper and lower bounds of the results.

Table 6 presents the results of the simulation. The differences are generally pronounced, particularly so for the years 2015 to 2030. For instance, for the case of rising TFR, the impact of the increase in elderly dependency ratio on private saving is almost 2.7 times higher under the assumption of a minimum retirement age of 55 than under the assumption of a retirement age of 65 in 2030. The results confirm the belief that a higher

---

[8] We wish to thank Dr. G. Shantakumar from the Department of Economics and Statistics, National University of Singapore, for providing us with his population projection figures.

retirement age norm is actually a more effective solution for moderating the effects of an ageing population on private saving.

7. CONCLUSION

This paper investigated the impact of the elderly dependency ratio, and other variables, on private saving during the period 1975 to 1995 using an error-correction model of consumption behaviour. The regression results show that demographic factors such as the elderly dependency ratio and female labour force participation rate had a negative effect on private saving in the long run. Other important factors that affected private saving in the long run include private disposable income and government saving. The results of the simulations indicate that the increase in the elderly dependency ratio could reduce private saving by as much as 208 percent in the year 2030 relative to its level in 1995. Finally, a higher mandatory retirement age might serve to significantly mitigate the effects of ageing on private saving.

REFERENCES

Asian Development Bank (1990): *Asian Development Outlook*, Manila.

Asilis, C. and A. R. Ghosh (1992): "The Savings Trap and Economic Take-off," *IMF Working Paper*, 91.

Barro, R. J. (1974): "Are Government Bonds Net Wealth?," *Journal of Political Economy*, 82, 1095-1117.

_____(1978): "The Impact of Social Security on Private Savings: Evidence from the U.S. Time Series, with a Reply by M. Feldstein," Washington D. C.: American Enterprise Institute.

Bauer, J. (1996): "Responses to Labour Scarcity and Ageing in Singapore," *Economic Policy Management in Singapore*, 119-146, ed. by Lim Chong Yah.

Bovernberg, L. and O. Evans (1990): "National and Personal Saving in the United States," *IMF Staff Paper*, 37, 636-669.

Cagan, P. (1965): "The Effect of Pension Plans on Aggregate Savings : Evidence from a Sample Survey," New York : National Bureau of Economic Research.

Datta, G. and P. Shome (1981): "Social Security and Household Savings : Asian Experience," *Developing Economics*, 19, 143-160.

Dayal-Gulati, A. and C. Thimann (1996): "Saving in Southeast Asia and Latin America Compared : Searching for Policy Lessons," Paper Prepared for the Conference on Macroeconomic Issues Facing ASEAN Countries, Jakarta.

Department of Statistics: *Economic and Social Statistics, 1960-1982*, Singapore.

_____: *Monthly Digest of Statistics*, various issues, Singapore.

_____: *Yearbook of Statistics*, various issues, Singapore.

Feldstein, M. (1974): "Social Security, Induced Retirement and Aggregate Capital Accumulation," *Journal of Political Economy*, 82.

Fry, M. (1978): "Monetary Policy and Domestic Saving in Developing ESCAP Countries," *Economic Bulletin for Asia and the Pacific*, 29, 79-99.

_____(1986): "National Saving, Financial Saving and Interest Rate Policy in Asian Developing Economies in United Nations," *Saving for Development*, 29-46.

Graham, J. W. (1987): "International Differences in Saving Rates and the Life Cycle Hypothesis," *European Economic Review*, 31, 1509-1529.

Gurley, J. G. and E. Shaw (1960): "Money in a Theory of Finance," Washington Institution : Brookings Institution.

Heller, P. S. (1989): "Aging, Savings, and Pensions in the Group of Seven Countries," *IMF Working Paper*, 13, 1-35.

Horioka, C. (1991): "Future Trends in Japan's Saving Rate and the Implications Thereof for Japan's External Imbalance," *Japan and the World Economy*, 3, 307-330.

Husain, A. M. (1995): "Determinants of Private Saving in Singapore," *IMF Occasional Paper*, 119, 42-65, ed. by Kenneth Bercuson.

International Monetary Fund: *International Financial Statistics*, various issues.

Katona, G. (1965): "Private Pensions and Individual Saving," University of Michigan : Survey Research Centre, Institute of Social Research.

Lahiri, A. K. (1989): "Dynamics of Asian Savings: The Role of Growth and Age Structure," *IMF Staff Paper*, 36, 228-261.

Loh, C. C. and M. R. Veall (1985): "A Note on Social Security and Private Savings in Singapore," *Public Finance*, 2, 299-304.

Masson, P. R. and R. W. Tryon (1990): "Macroeconomic Effects of Projected Population Aging in Industrial Countries," *IMF Staff Paper*, 37, 568-600.

Mikesell, R. F. and J. E. Zinzer (1973): "The Nature of the Savings Function in Developing Countries : A Survey of the Theoretical and Empirical Literature," *Journal of Economic Literature*, 11, 1-26.

Ministry of Finance: *Economic Survey of Singapore*, various issues, Singapore.

Ministry of Labour: *Profile of the Labour Force of Singapore, 1983-1994*, Singapore.

Modigliani, F. (1970): "The Life-Cycle Hypothesis of Saving and Inter-country Differences in the Saving Ratio," *Induction, Growth and Trade : Essays in Honour of Sir Roy Harrod*, ed. by W. A. Eltis, M. F. G. Scott and J. N. Wolfe.

Montgomery, E. (1986): "Where Did All the Saving Go? A Look at the Recent Decline in the Personal Saving Rate," *Economic Enquiry*, 24, 681-697.

Shantakumar, G. (1994): *The Aged Population of Singapore, Census Monograph No. 1*, Singapore : Ministry of Trade and Industry.

_____(1996): "Population and Labour Supply in Singapore," *Economic Policy Management in Singapore*, 39-82, ed. by. Lim Chong Yah.

Sturm, P. H. (1983): "Determinants of Saving: Theory and Evidence," *OECD Economic Studies*, 1, 147-197.

Summers, L. H. and C. Carroll (1987): "Why is U.S. National Saving So Low?," *Brookings Papers on Economic Activity*, 2, 607-642.

Williamson, J. G. (1968): "Personal Saving in Developing Nations: An Intertemporal Cross-section from Asia," *Economic Record*, 44, 94-209.

Wong, K. P. (1986): "Saving, Capital Inflow and Capital Formation," *Resources and Growth in Singapore*, 45-78, ed. by Lim Chong Yah and Peter Lloyd.

TABLE 1

Results of Estimates of the Cointegrating Regression

Independent Variable	Estimated Coefficient	t-statistic
Constant	4.122	7.454
LY	0.353	3.915
ODR55	0.040	3.807
FLPR	0.016	3.413
GS	6.88E-06	1.667
$R^2 = 0.993$	Adjusted $R^2 = 0.992$	DW = 1.260

Note: Definitions of all variables and notations are given in section 3.

TABLE 2

Results of ADF Test on Residual e_t (Lagged First Difference = 1)

Null Hypothesis	e_t	Critical Value at 5% Level of Significance
No constant, trend		
$(\rho-1) = 0$	-3.74	-1.95

TABLE 3

Results of Estimates of the Error Correction Equation

Independent Variable	Estimated Coefficient	t-statistic
ΔLY	0.558	6.475
ΔODR55	0.015	0.851
ΔFLPR	0.010	1.669
ΔGS	1.00E-05	2.566
ΔLCPF	-0.049	-2.532
REALR	-0.173	-0.562
ΔFS	0.001	0.686
ΔPPI	-1.16E-04	-0.416
e_{t-1}	-0.468	-1.581
$R^2 = 0.802$	Adjusted $R^2 = 0.658$	DW = 2.005

Note: Definitions of all variables and notations are given in section 3.

TABLE 4

Results of Estimates of the Error Correction Equation

Independent Variable	Estimated Coefficient	t-statistic
ΔLY	0.528	8.383
ΔODR55	0.016	1.198
ΔFLPR	0.012	2.540
ΔGS	8.31E-06	2.979
ΔLCPF	-0.050	-2.941
e_{t-1}	-0.412	-1.994
$R^2 = 0.791$	Adjusted $R^2 = 0.717$	DW = 1.979

Note: Definitions of all variables and notations are given in section 3.

TABLE 5

Projected Percentage Decline in Private Saving Relative to its Level in 1995

Year	Scenario 1	Scenario 2	Scenario 3
2000	12.80	12.80	12.80
2005	39.29	39.29	39.29
2010	75.86	75.86	75.86
2015	124.70	124.74	124.48
2020	171.73	172.04	170.81
2025	197.16	197.87	194.74
2030	212.52	214.06	207.59

TABLE 6

Projected Percentage Decline in Private Saving Relative to its Level in 1995 Under Different Settings of Different Minimum Retirement Age

	TFR constant at 1.83			TFR increase gradually from 1.83 to 3 in 2050		
Year	ODR55	ODR60	ODR65	ODR55	ODR60	ODR65
2000	12.80	9.99	6.20	12.80	9.99	6.20
2005	39.29	16.76	12.06	39.29	16.76	12.06
2010	75.86	37.58	16.90	75.86	37.58	16.90
2015	124.74	67.58	33.84	124.48	67.45	33.79
2020	172.04	107.18	58.08	170.81	106.52	57.73
2025	197.87	143.40	88.84	194.74	141.42	87.74
2030	214.06	159.72	114.58	207.59	155.54	111.94

PART III

ASEAN AND EAST ASIAN ECONOMIC ISSUES

Finance and Growth in ASEAN[1]

Lee Boon Keng
&
Chua *Poh Chai*

Nanyang Business School, Nanyang Technological University, Nanyang Avenue, Singapore 639798
Fax: +(65) 792.4217, Tel: +(65) 799.4857, Email: abklee@ntu.edu.sg

Abstract This paper determines the impact of financial development on economic growth. It adopts the basic model generated by King and Levine (1993a) to show financial deepening. We find evidence showing that financial developments are robustly correlated with economic growth in high growth periods. However, there is only weak evidence during periods of low growth. A Granger-causality test (that accounts for preceding developments) showed that finance and growth are causal to each other during high growth periods but not during periods of low growth. Although each country exhibits different characteristics, there is sufficient evidence to support both the 'supply-leading' and 'demand-following' theories.

1. INTRODUCTION

Is finance a precondition or a passive follower of growth? Is financial liberalisation essential for future growth? Development economists, including three Nobel Laureates, have put little emphasis on finance. Lucas (1988) even argues against economists who overstate the importance of finance. Financial deepening merely adheres to the growth in the real sector

In contrast, the pioneer works by Schumpeter (1932), Goldsmith (1969) and McKinnon (1973) laid the foundation to suggest a positive correlation between financial developments and growth. Greenwood and Jovanovic (1990) showed that finance and growth are symbiotic. Growth provides the means for financial intermediaries while presence of financial intermediaries entail economic growth through increasing the efficiency of funds invested due to their abilities to gather and evaluate information at a lower cost. Bencivenga and Smith (1991) and Saint-Paul (1992) demonstrated that intermediaries allow investors to overcome their liquidity constraints and enable risk diversification Although King and Levine (1993a, 1993b) and De Gregorio and Guidotti (1995) found evidence across countries to support their pioneering works, the latter proved that this impact varies according to regions, time periods and income levels. Nevertheless, both found that countries with higher financial development in their initial stages of development provides a catalyst for future growth. However, Chandavarkar (1992) warns against full financial liberalisation unless the macroeconomic conditions are stabilised and a regulatory and prudential framework has been installed. We discovered that initial liberalisation spurs future growth only in high growth period but not when growth is low.

We have chosen to study the ASEAN countries because of the amount of interest that is placed on these financial sectors recently. Moreover, each has a different income level,

---

[1] ASEAN refers to Association of the Southeast Asia Nations. In this paper, we consider 5 of the 7 ASEAN countries namely, Singapore, Malaysia, Thailand, Philippines and Indonesia.

unique financial characteristics and various degrees of development. Sections 2 and 3 of this paper discuss the financial development in the ASEAN countries and individual reforms respectively. Section 4 explains the methodology. Section 5 presents the empirical findings and Section 6 concludes.

2. FINANCIAL LIBERALISATION AND DEVELOPMENT IN ASEAN

The ASEAN countries differ in their economic development and financial sophistication. However, before their financial sectors were liberalised, they had some common features. These included interest rate restriction, domestic credit controls, reserve requirements, segmented financial markets, underdeveloped money and capital markets and controls on international capital funds.

Before liberalisation, monetary authorities imposed ceilings on deposit and loan rates. This was to ensure the availability of low-cost funds that could be employed in investments, especially in priority sectors. In addition, market determined interest rates can be too high to generate a socially optimal level of investment. Nevertheless, these restrictions led to financial disintermediation when depositors and investors sought alternative informal sources of funds. Moreover, banks often bypassed the restrictions by imposing compensating balances and other fees that were not subjected to control, thereby aggravating the distortions of financial services provided. Thus, financial deepening was hindered and resources were not directed to the most productive areas.

In setting credit ceilings, monetary authorities determine the scope for the future lending base on banks' previous share in total loans. This inhibits competition and development. Since banks are unable to extend credit more than their share. Sectoral credit allocation schemes direct bank lending to preferred sectors. These schemes reduce allocative efficiency because directed credit programs in many countries often yield poor returns. This further burden the banks with non-performing debts. Moreover, monetary authorities will be obliged to continue to provide credit to priority sectors, which will disrupt their policy targets. Finally, subsidised credits might not be used for the intended purposes.

High reserve requirements act as additional implicit taxes on financial institutions since no interest is paid on these reserves. This increases the cost to these institutions. Therefore, they will be tempted to bypass the system. Hence, more control is needed. As more control is enforced, this will cause a vicious cycle, which is damaging.

High market segmentation in the financial sector restricts institutions to conduct business within its scope. New entrants are often extensively regulated if allowed to enter. For example, foreign banks are constrained to their prescribed activities. Although this protects domestic investors and maintain confidence, this might lead to inefficiency. Moreover, resources targeted at priority sectors might not be utilised appropriately.

Before 1980, money and capital markets were underdeveloped. Interbank markets were used primarily to ease short-term liquidity needs. Non-bank investors who were precluded, from these markets had to seek alternative means to tap available funds. Consequent long-term funds were difficult to acquire due to poor capital markets. International capital flows were controlled to insulate the domestic economy from external disturbances. Hence, monetary authorities were forced to commit themselves to fixed exchange rate regime.

Financial liberalisation helped to overcome the inefficiency that prevailed in a controlled market. An economy's financial sector must be groomed to prevent any bottlenecks, which could arise in future, from impeding economic growth.

3. INSTITUTIONAL DEVELOPMENTS

3.1 SINGAPORE

As early as the 1970s, Singapore has embarked on a nurtured path to become an international financial centre. In contrast to playing a supporting role, Singapore financial sector has grown, overtaking manufacturing in 1995 to become the nation's leading growth engine (27.4 percent of GDP, Yearbook of Statistics, Singapore, 1995). Policy measures are targeted to enhance Singapore's position as the financial hub to facilitate domestic, regional and international transactions.

The Monetary Authority of Singapore (MAS) was set up in 1971 to ensure monetary stability and a conducive environment for economic growth. MAS supervises and regulates the systems to safeguard investors' interests. In its drive to promote the Asian Dollar Market(ADM) in 1981, MAS offered Asian Currency Unit (ACU) licenses to international financial institutions to participate in ADM. With concessionary tax of 10 percent, ACUs' assets have grown ever since.

In June 1973, MAS shifted from fixing the domestic currency to the US dollars to a managed floating regime. There are no exchange restrictions on current account transactions and capital account transactions. In July 1975, deposit and lending rates were liberalised. Banks could determine their quotation according to market conditions. This deregulation encouraged competition and promoted efficiency in the banking sector.

In 1986, the 5 domestic leading banks (including Post Office Savings Bank) launched the Network for Electronic Transfers (NETS) to facilitate a cashless payment system. With more electronic banking services available, transactions could be completed more efficiently. An example is the application for Initial Public Offerings (IPOs) through automated tellers machines.

The financial sector has flourished since the financial reforms. The ratio of broad money to GDP (see Figure 1) has increased from 66.3 percent in 1970 to 84.5 percent in 1995. In addition, the ratio of deposit money banks' domestic assets to GDP reached 104.2 percent in 1995 from 57.7 percent in 1970.[2] Domestic credit to the private non-financial sector has grown from 45.9 percent of GDP in 1970 to 61.1 percent of GDP in 1995 (see Figure 2). The ratio of domestic credit given by the government to GDP has increased from 25.9 percent in 1970 to 30 percent in 1995. The Singapore government has been a net lender to the domestic credit ever since 1970. Total domestic credit to GDP amounts to 91.1 percent in 1995 from a 20.0 percent in 1970. Investment over GDP has decreased from 38.7 percent in 1970 to 32.2 percent in 1995.

Ever since Singapore's independence, its government has capitalised on its historical and geographical endowments to develop into an international financial centre. In order to attract foreign institutions to set up their operating branches, incentives were given. This created competition and added more depth to the industry. Infrastructure construction was

---

[2] Figures can be found in IMF, *International Financial Statistics 1996.*

high on the list of development. In addition, to facilitate trade and services in the region, it extended its activities across the globe. Lessons learnt from the 1985 Pan-Electric crisis led to more prudent supervision by MAS. Macroeconomic stability like low inflation, high economic growth and strong currency complemented policy measures undertaken to develop the financial sector coincide with the country's long term economic plan.

3.2 MALAYSIA

Since 1973, the Malaysian currency, which was pegged to a composite basket of currencies of its major trading partners, was used by Bank Negara (BN) to stabilise the domestic economy. A new interest rate package was introduced in 1974 to discourage large-scale capital flight by imposing higher interest rates and to control the money supply with credit ceilings.

Formal financial liberalisation was initiated in October 1978 when BN abolished the maximum deposit rates and minimum commercial loan rates. However, Lending rates to priority sectors like the Bumiputra-Malay aborigines, manufacturing and exports sector continued to be regulated. By late 1981, commercial banks are allowed to determine their lending rates according to their cost of funds. Total domestic credit as a ratio of GDP soared from 42.0 percent in 1980 to 52.4 percent in 1981. Nevertheless, government-linked Bank Bumiputra and Malayan Bank continued to set the benchmark for other banks.

It was the second oil shock in 1979 that tested the viability of the deregulated financial system. After the initial liberalisation, markets were highly liquid. The excessive credit and favourable demand conditions generated from heavy government spending led to over-optimism of investors. This induced speculative activities. In 1982, the government was forced to cut spending due to mounting budget deficits. BN reduced access to easy credit to tighten liquidity. With liquidity constraints, firms were forced to dissolve and banks were plagued with nonperforming debts. BN undertook several measures to restore confidence in the financial system. This included more stringent capital adequacy requirements and supervision to ensure solvency of the banks.

The financial sector has evolved rapidly especially in the last five years. The ratio of broad money to GDP increased from 33.9 percent in 1970 to 51.5 percent in 1980 (only 46.8 percent in 1979) to 66.2 percent in 1990 to 89.1 percent in 1994. Deposit money banks' domestic assets as a percentage of GDP grow from 25.3 percent in 1970 to 48.4 percent in 1980 (only 39.8 percent in 1979) to 90.4 percent in 1994. Central banks' domestic assets as a percentage of GDP increased from 1.0 percent in 1970 to 4.2 percent in 1994. The ratio of total domestic credit to GDP rose from 18.7 percent in 1970 to 42.0 percent in 1980 (32.2 percent in 1979) to 86.6 percent in 1994. Non-financial private credit as a percentage to GDP climbed from 18.5 percent in 1970 to 38.2 percent in 1980 (only 31.5 percent in 1979) to 76.9 percent in 1994. Domestic claims on Central Government over GDP dropped from 1.3 percent to 1.0 percent in 1980 (-1.5 percent in 1979) to 0.5 percent in 1994. However, domestic credit to central government over GDP fluctuated -1.5 percent to 7.4 percent between 1970 to 1994. Investment over GDP peaked at 38 percent in 1994 from an initial 20.3 percent in 1970.

Although Malaysia embarked on the road towards complete liberalisation (as indicated in 1991 by the total deregulation of interest rates) the government continue to exert substantial influence in the financial environment. Supervision and regulation are needed to achieve policy targets and maintain stability in the economy. An abrupt deregulated scheme may disrupt the financial infrastructure. In addition, the financial framework may be unable to withstand both internal and external shock if it is left on its own. The development of financial institutions generally lags behind economic needs and the lack of an effective financial infrastructure is constantly one of the inhibiting factors holding back sustained economic expansion.[3]

3.3 THAILAND

In the first oil shock, the economy's stability was threatened. Current account deficits soared while inflation escalated to double digits. Real interest rates were negative. In 1975, commercial banks were forced to set aside 5 percent of their loans for the agricultural sector. The problem of concentrated banks' ownership was overcome after an amended Commercial Banking Act in 1979. During the second oil shock, the Thai financial system was troubled by international financial unrest. The Baht was devalued and pegged to a composite basket of currencies of its major trading partners. In addition, policies were geared to insulate external shock. A more flexible exchange rate regime was administered in November 1984.

Financial infrastructure in Thailand was inadequate; management expertise was scarce. This hindered future needs by the industry. Moreover, the financial scene was dominated by the major 5 commercial banks. To promote competition and inject efficiency, a 3 year financial reform plan was carried out in 1989. This included removing time deposit rates over 1 year ceiling to attract more savings. In May 1990, foreign exchange control was eased. Commercial banks could transact foreign currencies with the public without the need of consulting the authorities. In addition, free repatriation of profits and investments funds were allowed. To enhance domestic banks' competitiveness relative to foreign banks, local banks are encouraged to underwrite government securities and other debt instruments.

Traditionally, Bank of Thailand (BOT) had to ensure that institutions adhered strictly to the legislation. Currently, the supervision has focused on the operation and solvency of institutions. Moreover, the rules of Bank for International Settlements was adopted by BOT to ensure capital adequacy. BOT proposed the use of electronic banking system to increase speed and efficiency of transactions. The system includes check clearing, interbank transfer and data transfusion concerning government securities and banks' reports.

The financial depth improved tremendously especially the most recent periods. Broad money over GDP was only 28.3 percent in 1970 before it climb to 65 percent in 1989 (only 61.3 percent in 1988) and settle at 79.5 percent in 1995. Deposit money banks' domestic assets over GDP started from a mere 23.6 percent in 1970 to a 67.0 percent in 1989 (only 63.3 percent in 1988) to the recent 106.6 percent in 1995. In contrast, central banks' domestic assets over GDP drop from 8.6 percent in 1970 to 5.1 percent in 1989 (7.7 percent in 1988) and further decrease to 2.4 percent in 1995. However, between the period 1979-1987, central bank's domestic assets to GDP average at 12.8 percent. Domestic claims on Government to GDP was 6.1 percent in 1970, 8.2 percent in 1989 (13.5 percent in 1979) and -9.51 percent in 1995. During 1979-1987, domestic claims on Government to GDP average at 13.5 percent. Total domestic credit to GDP was 25.8 percent in 1970 and

---

[3] Lin See Yan(1993) in EDI seminar series.

97.6 percent in 1995 while non-financial private domestic credit to GDP was 18.1 percent in 1970 and 98.3 percent in 1995. Investment to GDP ratio increased from 25.6 percent in 1970 to 40.1 percent in 1995.

The financial reform package has yielded favourable outcomes. Institutions are entrusted with more freedom. This flexibility resulted in more market efficiency. Interest rates are more reflective of both domestic and international and international conditions. Although the reform deregulated the traditional practice, BOT's supervision has not lapsed. In replace, a modern approach was undertaken to subdue any fraudulence arising from the increasing sophisticated operations. BOT superintends institutions' solvency and liquidity management as well as quality of assets. To develop the financial sector, the authorities are committed to enact more infrastructure to meet the demand of tomorrow.

3.4 PHILIPPINES

In the 1970s, all economic activities were under the influence of the Marcos regime. To encourage investments in favoured sectors, the government determined the flow of funds to priority projects. Interest rates were suppressed to become negative. Private banks were forced to adhere to the credit allocation policy. This caused the banks to finance projects that generated below average rates of return. Therefore, banks which tried to reduce risk only allocated funds to firms with political affiliation or adequate collateral. In the early 1980s, world-wide recession was translated to domestic financial crisis. The government had to bail out several major companies. Since investments were not generating sufficient returns, debts could no longer be serviced. Finally in October 1983, Philippines had to declare a debt moratorium-legal authorisation to postpone payment. This shut down access to foreign capital markets.

When the Philippines turned to the International Monetary Fund (IMF) for financial aid, a conditional financial reform was initiated. The reform aimed to liberalise interest gradually. To suppress high inflation by monetary contraction, Central Bank of Philippines (CBP) sold high-yield financial instruments. This lured banks' depositors to relocate their funds. Banks had to compete for funds by bidding at high deposit rates. Moreover, highly-leveraged firms had to uphold a larger burden. This amounted to more unsavoured bad debts when defaults seem inevitable. CBP had to perform its role of last resort to salvage the crisis from antagonising into further damage. This was especially evident in 1986 when the state-owned Philippine National Bank, largest commercial bank, and the Development Bank of Philippines were insolvent. Banks were used to rely on government for its influence on their operations. Many feared of their existence during the crisis. Finally in April 1987, the government launched a rehabilitation program . This helped the economy to recover in the recession years of 1984-1986 which accompanied with political unrest.

In mid 1989, the numbers of weak banks were escalating so much so that higher operating costs hindered the efficiency of the system. The government's attempt to enhance competition failed due to monopolistic behaviour exhibited by cartel-like banks. Moreover, local banks were protected from competition from their foreign counterparts due to prohibition of foreign entry. This barrier was removed only in 1993. Lack of competition resulted in low deposit rates and deterred savings mobilisation. Broad money to GDP dipped from 33.7 percent in 1983 to 27.8 percent in 1984 due to shortage of funds. In 1995, broad money to GDP reached 50.3 percent from a 23.1 percent in 1970. Deposit money banks' domestic assets to GDP started from 24.8 percent in 1970 to 32.3 percent in

1984 (45.3 percent in 1983) to 49.3 percent in 1995. Central bank's domestic assets to GDP was 10.3 percent in 1970 before it settle down from 15.2 percent in 1984 (18.2 percent in 1983) to 12.8 percent in 1995. Domestic private non-financial credit was 19.0 percent in 1970 before it almost doubled to 37.5 percent in 1995. Domestic claims on Government to GDP was 4.6 percent in 1970, 4.6 percent in 1984 (6.5 percent in 1983) and 14.0 percent in 1995. Total domestic credit to GDP was 30.2 percent in 1970, 39.3 percent in 1984 (53.9 percent in 1983) and 54.4 percent in 1995. From 1986 to 1992, total domestic credit was lowest averaging at 21.0 percent. Investment as a percentage to GDP was 21.2 percent in 1970, 20.3 percent in 1984 (29.3 percent in 1983) and 22.3 percent in 1995. Hence, we can see that there was a significant drop in financial deepening in 1984.

To sum up, the financial system in Philippines was under too much influence of the government for loan allocation Furthermore, financial reforms were manifested by economic developments to the extent that its economy's weakness can easily be translated into a financial crisis. The fundamental economic issues of huge current account deficits, budget deficits, inflation, exchange rate depreciation and sustainable growth must be addressed concurrently with the financial reform. When the economic environment is unstable, any disturbances can destroy the whole system. This was evident since there is inadequate supervision which is essential especially when corruption is pervasive.

3.5 INDONESIA
Indonesia's financial system has been influenced directly by the developments of he petroleum sector. The expansion of oil revenue in 1970s enhanced growth of financial services and savings mobilisation. However, when oil prices dropped in 1983, the government undertook measures to boost the competitiveness of the Indonesian economy. Part of the programme was to devalue the rupiah.

Although the move towards a free exchange regime started in the 1970s, the financial reform become more effective after June, 1983 when deposits and lending rates were deregulated. Prior to this reform, the government relied on direct credit control and reserve requirements to manage the money supply. After deregulation, the authorities resorted to indirect measures like open market operations, discounting tools and moral suasion. Credit ceilings were removed. Subsidised credit to banks by Bank Indonesia (BI) was minimised. Banks were told to increase the mobilisation of resources through increased savings from the public and reduce their dependency on BI. In 1984, BI offered Sertificate Bank Indonesia(SBI) and created discount windows to help banks to ease daily liquidity needs. In addition, BI introduced the Syrat Berharga Pasar Uang (SBPU) to facilitate transactions in the money market. In 1991, BI implemented new measures to maintain order in the system.‘These include adopting the BIS capital adequacy standard and ensuring sound management policies.

Broad money to GDP was merely 8.2 percent in 1970 before it reached 20.0 percent in 1984 (18.9 percent in 1983) and 45.8 percent in 1992. Deposit money banks' domestic assets to GDP was 8.6 percent in 1970, 21.2 percent in 1984 (17.5 percent in 1983) and 49.3 percent in 1992. Central bank's domestic assets which were 9.7 percent of GDP in 1970 become 14.0 percent in 1984 (12.9 percent in 1983) but dropped to 9.0 percent in 1992. Domestic non-financial private credit to GDP ratio began at 8.8 percent in 1970 and attained 16.4 percent in 1984 (14.1 percent in 1983) and 47.9 percent in 1992. The government was a net borrower of 0.9 percent of GDP in 1970. However, since 1972, it has become a net lender to the domestic economy. Domestic claims by the government reached 8.9 percent in 1984 (6.4 percent of GDP in 1983) and 5.9 percent in 1992. Total domestic credit to GDP was 11.3 percent in 1970, 13.3 percent in 1984 (14.3 percent in 1983) and 47.4 percent in 1992. Investment as a ratio of GDP was 13.6 percent in 1970, 26.2 percent in 1984 (28.7 percent in 1983) and 41.8 percent in 1995. These figures show that the reform in 1983 failed to produce significant developments in the short run. Recent developments showed that the financial sector has deepened and widened

The government is cautious about the pace of reform. Rapid deregulation may pose adjustment problems. This is evident in most developing countries. Primarily, policy measures will inject more autonomy in the institutions instead of them following blindly central bank's activities. Banks have to be more innovative and enterprising in their operations and activities. Due to the gradual pace of reforms, banks adjusted substantially to adopt new policies. This contrasts with other developing countries where institutions suffered from the need to modify their management objectives to adhere to the abrupt change of policies. Finally, initial reform set the pace for future developments.

4. METHODOLOGY

4.1 KING AND LEVINE

The basic model is adapted from King and Levine (1993a) It consists of 1 growth indicator[4] and 4 financial indicators. All data are obtained from International Financial Statistics.

$$GYP_t = \bullet_0 + \bullet_1 GLLY_t + \bullet_2 GBANK_t + \bullet_3 GPRIVATE_t + \bullet_4 GPRIVY_t + \bullet_t \qquad (1)$$

G denotes the percentage change of that variable.

4.1.1 Growth Indicator

$$GYP = \text{Real per capita GDP growth} \qquad (2)$$

4.1.2 Financial Indicators

$$LLY_t = 0.5*(M2_t + M2_{t-1})/GDP_t \qquad (3)$$

The general measure of financial depth is LLY which is the ratio of liquid liabilities $(M2)^5$ to GDP. M2 consists of currency in circulation, demand deposits, time and saving deposits. The average monetary stock was taken instead of the current money stock in order to make the monetary stock to be comparable to the GDP, which is a flow.

According to the Quantity theory of money, M2 over GDP is inversely proportionate to the velocity of money. However, financial depth does not indicate the type of financial services and efficiency of the financial system.

BANK = (Deposit money banks' domestic assets)/(Domestic assets of deposit money banks and central bank) $\qquad (4)$

---

[4] In the original paper, four growth indicators were examined.

[5] M2=sum of lines 34 and 35 of IFS.

It is believed that commercial banks are able to provide the more efficient financial service through better information and risk sharing management. BANK[6] segregates the importance of deposit money banks from central bank to determine their importance to the economy. However, in most of the ASEAN countries, the central bank might exert significant influence on commercial banks. This can reduce the distinction between commercial banks and central bank. Another deficiency of this variable is that it does not indicate to whom do the commercial banks allocate their credit to.

$$\text{PRIVATE} = (\text{Claims on non-financial private sector})/(\text{Total domestic credit}) \tag{5}$$

$$\text{PRIVY} = (\text{Claims on non-financial private sector})/\text{GDP}. \tag{6}$$

PRIVATE[7] and PRIVY aim to segregate credit to private sector from public sector. Any systems that primarily provide credit to the government will not serve its intended purposes of channelling resources to where the highest returns can be generated.[8] All these financial indicators complement the conclusion that can be drawn by LLY alone.

4.2 GRANGER CAUSALITY TEST

$$GYP_t = \sum_{i=1}^{3} \bullet_i \, GYP_{t-i} + \sum_{j=1}^{3} \bullet_j \, GLLY_{t-j}{}^9 + \mu_t \tag{7}$$

$$GLLY_t = \sum_{n=1}^{3} S_n \, GYP_{t-n} + \sum_{k=1}^{3} V_k \, GLLY_{t-k} + w_t \tag{8}$$

This test determines the significance of preceding developments to the current growth which the King and Levine model does not account for. The autoregressive lags were found by adding iteratively to a maximum of 3 lags and the best model is indicated by the largest adjusted R^2. This is followed by the adding of lags of financial indicators.[10] The sum of the coefficients of the lags of the financial indicators and growth indicators are tested for $\sum \Pi_j = 0$ and $\sum V_k = 0$ respectively. Each country is examined for 2 different periods, namely 1970-1984 and 1985-1995. Average GYP for these periods are different.

5. EMPIRICAL RESULTS

Although different countries exhibit patterns, the general finding is that in periods of average high per capita GDP growth, financial developments are significantly correlated with economic growth. However, there is little evidence to support this during periods of low growth.

---

[6] Central bank's domestic assets is sum of IFS line 12a to 12f. Deposit money banks; domestic assets is the sum of IFS lines 22a to 22f.

[7] Claims on non-financial private sector is IFS line 32d. Total domestic credit(to nonbanks) is the sum of lines32a to 32f excluding 32e.

[8] For Singapore and Indonesia, the government is a net creditor throughout the period.

[9] GBANK, GPRIVATE and GPRIVY are also tested.

[10] This is similar to the method suggested by Darrat, LaBarge and LaBarge (1989) which minimises the FPE-final prediction error. We also tested the opposite direction whereby growth causes financial development.

5.1 SINGAPORE

During 1970-1984 when average GDP per capita growth was 7.8 percent, monetary growth (GLLY) and domestic private non-financial credit (GPRIVY) were important to economic growth. However, in the period 1985-1995, only monetary growth is relevant. We see the inverse velocity of money improves over the years since the economy is more responsive to negative monetary growth.

During the period of high growth, GLLY Granger Cause[11] income growth. Economic growth led to GPRIVY. In periods of lower growth, the growth of private domestic non-financial credit to total domestic credit (GPRIVATE) and income growth was bi-directional. However, GPRIVY preceded GYP.

5.2 MALAYSIA

In the first period when average economic growth was higher relative to the second period, monetary expansion is important to growth of income. In contrast, GLLY is insignificant in the second period. Moreover, there is a relative decrease in the velocity of money. The other financial indicators yield poor results.

In both periods, income growth contributes merely to monetary growth. However, previous financial developments fail to enhance economic growth.

5.3 THAILAND

Financial development had insignificant impact on economic growth. However, GPRIVATE and GPRIVY were influential in the later period. During the later period, average income was 7.3 percent This showed that financial liberalisation in 1989 has indeed helped to spur Thailand's growth to 10.4 percent in 1989 and 9.9 percent in 1990. Although the velocity of money declined, it is insignificant in both periods.

Initially, financial deepening in the form represented by GLLY and GPRIVY helps income growth. In the later period, causation runs from finance (through GBANK, which represents the growth of ratio of deposit money bank's domestic assets to total deposit money banks and central bank's domestics assets, GPRIVATE and GPRIVY) to growth.

5.4 PHILIPPINES

In the first period, financial development in the form of monetary growth, GLLY, deposit money banks' domestic assets expansion, GBANK, and growth of private domestic credit, GPRIVY, are linked to economic growth. Commercial banks' domestic assets are highly responsive to economic growth. However, finance and growth are weakly correlated in the second period. This may be due to several financial crises in the late 1980s. Velocity of money was negatively related to growth. This can be explained by the recession experienced in 1985-86 and 1991-92.

In the first period, GLLY causes income growth while income growth determine GPRIVY. In the second period, finance and growth have no causal relation.

---

[11] Any causal relations mentioned in this paper merely means that the variable precedes another.

5.5 INDONESIA

Finance and growth are insignificantly correlated in both periods. This can be possible since the pace of financial development is rather slow relative to Thailand even though Indonesia deregulated its markets earlier. In addition, the data showed that substantial financial deepening was only realised from 1990.

Although current income growth and current finance are not correlated, previous monetary growth(GLLY) and domestic private non-financial credit growth (GPRIVY) cause current income growth in the first period. In the second period when average income growth was lower, GPRIVATE causes income growth while income merely supports monetary growth.

6. CONCLUSION

To sum up, we showed that finance and growth are closely related to each other. Growth endows the financial sector to develop while finance facilitates growth. The channel to which finance affects growth differs among the countries studied. Nevertheless, during periods of average high-income growth, financial development is more closely related to growth. The causal direction between finance and growth cannot be concluded based on this study due to widespread variations.

Across the ASEAN countries, policy measures undertaken to develop the financial sector have emphasised similar constituents. These include promoting competition to improve efficiency by deregulating markets, increasing supervision by authorities, enacting infrastructure support and managing economic fundamentals. The discernment of the importance of the financial sector is needed to pursue long term economic objectives.

REFERENCES

Atje R. and Jovanovic B. (1992): "Stock Markets and Developments," *European Economic Review*, 37, 632-640.

Bencivenga V. R. and Smith B. D. (1991): "Financial Intermediation and Endogenous Growth," *Review of Economic Studies* 58, 195-209.

Chandavarkar, A. (1992): "Of Finance and Development: Neglected and Unsettled Questions," *World Development*, 20, No.1, 133-142.

Cheng, H S ed,(1986): *Financial Policy and Reform in Pacific Basin Countries*, D C Heath and Company.

Darrat, A., LaBarge, K. P. And LaBarge, R A(1989): "Is Financial Deepening a Reliable Prescription of Economic Growth," *The American Economist*, Fall, 25-33.

De Gregorio, J. and Guidotti, P. E. (1995): "Financial Development and Economic Growth," *World Development*, 23, No 3, 433-448.

Department of Statistics of Singapore, *Yearbook of Statistics*, Singapore , 1995.

Faruqi, S. ed,(1993): "Financial Sector Reforms in Asian and Latin American Countries," *EDI Seminar Series*, World Bank.

Goldsmith, R. W. (1969): *Finance Structure and Development.* Yale University Press

Greenwood J. and Jovanovic B. (1990): "Financial Development, Growth and the Distribution of Income," *Journal of Political Economy*, 98 No. 5, 1076-1107.

IMF, *International Financial Statistics* 1996.

Jappelli T. and Pagano M. (1994): "Saving, Growth, and Liquidity Constraints," *Quarterly Journal of Economics* 109, 83-109.

King, R. G. and Levine, R. (1993a): "Finance and Growth: Schumpeter might be Right," *Quarterly Journal of Economics*, August , 717-735.

King R. G. and Levine R. (1993b): "Finance, Entrepreneurship, and Growth," *Journal of Monetary Economics* 32, 513-542.

Levine, R. And Zervos, S .(1996): "Stock Market Development and Long-Run Growth," *World Bank Economic Review*, 10, No. 2, 323-339.

McKinnon, R. I. (1973): *Money and Capital in Economic Development*. Brookings Institution, Washington

Pagano, M. (1993): "Financial Markets and Growth," *European Economic Review*, 37, 613-622.

Saint-Paul, G. (1992): "Technological Choice, Financial Markets an Economic Development," *European Economic Review*, 36, 763-781.

Schumpeter, J. A. (1932): *The Theory of Economics Development*. Harvard University Press

Tseng, W. And Corker, R. (1991): *Financial Liberalisation, Money Demand, and Monetary Policy in Asian Countries*. International Monetary Fund, Occasional Paper 84.

TABLE 1

Finance and Growth

Country	Period	constant	GLLY	GBANK	GPRIVATE	GPRIVY	R^2	Average GYP
Singapore	1970-1995	0.069***	-0.451***	-	0.0456	0.176*	0.43	6.9%
	1970-1984	0.067***	-0.301*	-	-0.004	0.257**	0.46	7.8%
	1985-1995	0.069***	-0.589**	-	-0.024	-0.125	0.50	5.6%
Malaysia	1971-1994	0.058***	-0.258***	-0.513	0.027	-0.077	0.49	4.4%
	1971-1984	0.059***	-0.389**	0.084	-0.192	0.035	0.62	4.7%
	1985-1995	0.053***	-0.239	-1.610	0.308	-0.137	0.54	4.1%
Thailand	1970-1995	0.051***	-0.163	0.248	0.198	0.144	0.34	5.5%
	1970-1984	0.041***	-0.209	-0.295	-0.021	0.163	0.40	4.2%
	1985-1995	0.046***	-0.175	0.236	0.327*	0.220**	0.88	7.3%
Philippines	1970-1995	0.006	-0.070	0.319**	-0.077	0.142***	0.45	1.1%
	1970-1984	0.016***	-0.133**	0.456***	-0.067	0.221***	0.87	1.7%
	1985-1995	-0.011	0.451**	-0.114	0.113	-0.060	0.76	0.2%
Indonesia	1970-1992	0.046	0.005	0.040	0.033	-0.021	0.18	4.7%
	1970-1984	0.049***	0.008	0.036	0.027	-0.028	0.23	4.9%
	1985-1992	0.050	-0.079	0.004	0.248	0.043	0.31	4.2%

Source: IMF, International Financial Statistics

Note : ***, ** and * refer to 1 percent, 5 percent and 10 percent level of significance respectively.

TABLE 2

Granger Causality Test

Country	Period	Dep.Var.: Growth	Ind.Var.: Finance	$\sum\Pi_j= 0$, F-value	Dep.Var.: Finance	Ind.Var. : Growth	$\sum V_k= 0$, F-value
Singapore	1970-1984	GYP	GLLY	6.602**	GPRIVY	GYP	9.244**
		GYP	GPRIVATE	0.161			
		GYP	GPRIVY	3.085			
	1985-1995	GYP	GPRIVATE	3.650*	GLLY	GYP	1.804
		GYP	GPRIVY	4.286*	GPRIVATE	GYP	13.794***
					GPRIVY	GYP	0.321
Malaysia	1970-1984	GYP	GLLY	2.149	GLLY	GYP	4.249*
		GYP	GPRIVY	0.228	GBANK	GYP	0.354
	1985-1994	GYP	GLLY	0.280	GLLY	GYP	12.769**
		GYP	GBANK	1.237	GBANK	GYP	0.619
					GPRIVATE	GYP	0.092
					GPRIVY	GYP	0.340
Thailand	1970-1984	GYP	GLLY	4.385*	GLLY	GYP	3.068
		GYP	GBANK	2.943	GBANK	GYP	0.206
		GYP	GPRIVATE	0.488	GPRIVATE	GYP	0.074
		GYP	GPRIVY	4.396*	GPRIVY	GYP	2.038
	1985-1995	GYP	GLLY	2.272	GLLY	GYP	3.406
		GYP	GPRIVATE	2.113	GBANK	GYP	8.076**
		GYP	GPRIVY	0.138	GPRIVATE	GYP	3.13*
					GPRIVY	GYP	9.179**
Philippines	1970-1984	GYP	GLLY	8.831**	GLLY	GYP	0.174
		GYP	GBANK	1.819	GPRIVATE	GYP	0.018
		GYP	GPRIVATE	1.160	GPRIVY	GYP	3.587
	1985-1995	GYP	GLLY	0.176	GLLY	GYP	2.924
					GBANK	GYP	0.063
					GPRIVATE	GYP	0.204
					GPRIVY	GYP	0.008
Indonesia	1970-1984	GYP	GLLY	4.492*	GBANK	GYP	3.877*
		GYP	GPRIVATE	0.421	GPRIVATE	GYP	0.379
		GYP	GPRIVY	9.723**	GPRIVY	GYP	5.755**
	1985-1992	GYP	GPRIVATE	6.023*	GLLY	GYP	5.770*
		GYP	GPRIVY	2.006	GBANK	GYP	2.821
					GPRIVATE	GYP	1.432

Source: IMF, International Financial Statistics 1996.

Note :When the dependent variable is growth, we are testing whether finance causes growth.

***,** and * represent 1 percent, 5 percent and 10 percent significance level respectively.

FIGURE 1

Monetary Aggregates as a Percentage of GDP

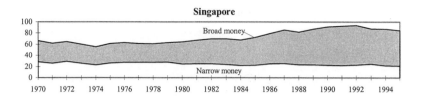

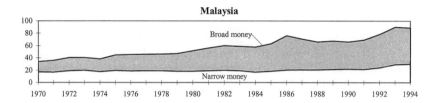

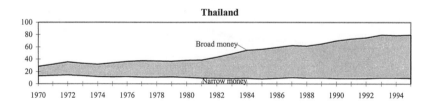

Source : IMF, International Financial Statistics 1996.

FIGURE 2

Domestic Credit as a Percentage to GDP

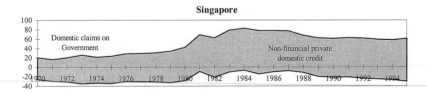

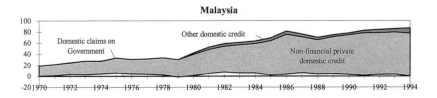

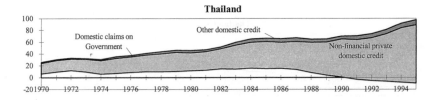

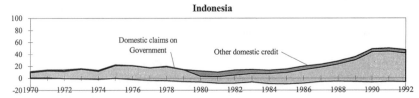

Source : IMF, International Financial Statistics 1996. Note: When Domestic Claims on Government is negative, it means that the government is a net lender to the private non-financial sector. For example, Singapore and Indonesia.

An Econometric Model of China's Sichuan Province

Lau Chin Boon, Daren
&
Chen Kang

Nanyang Business School, Nanyang Technological University, Nanyang Avenue, Singapore 639798
Fax: +(65) 792.4217, Tel: +(65) 799.6431, Email: akachen@ntu.edu.sg

Abstract Sichuan Province is China's chief agricultural base. Construction of the 'Third Front' district in the mid-1960s has turned the province into one of the country's largest industrial bases as well. The experience of Sichuan Province serves as an interesting case in the study of economic growth in China's inland region. In this paper, we build an econometric model to study certain special features of Sichuan's agricultural, state-owned industrial and foreign investment sectors.

1. INTRODUCTION

Sichuan is a big inland province in the south-western part of China. It is located in the upper reaches of the Yangtze River and covers 570,000 square kilometres. It has a population of 110.84 million, which is nearly 10 percent of the national total. The province has long been known as the 'Land of Abundance' due to its mild climate, fertile soil, abundant natural resources and a long history of well-developed agriculture.

Sichuan is China's chief agricultural base and as such, it is of great importance to the national agricultural production. With 6.232 million hectares of cultivated land, Sichuan is the country's largest producer of grain, oil and pig. In 1994, the province produced 116.9 billion yuan worth of agricultural output, which is about 7.42 percent of the national total (1575.1 billion); it also produced 42.3 million tons of grain, which is about 9.50 percent of the national total (445.1 million).

The 'Third Front' district was constructed in the mid-1960s to counter the then Soviet Union's military threat. This has turned Sichuan into one of the largest industrial bases in the country, with a large modern industrial sector in the south-western region. The 'Third Front' has also resulted in a large proportion of the industrial enterprises being state-owned and defence-related. However, the military factories were later encouraged to produce civilian products and since the 1980s, the quantity of civilian products manufactured by these military factories has grown sharply. By the end of 1994, the annual total value of civilian products produced by these military factories has reached 13.25 billion yuan.

In this paper, we build an econometric model of Sichuan Province to study certain special features of Sichuan's agricultural, state-owned industrial and foreign investment sectors. Separate data for military enterprises are unavailable and as a result, they are lumped together with all the other state-owned industrial enterprises in the model.

The organisation of the paper is as follows. Section 2 discusses the specification of the model and the estimation techniques employed. In Section 3, we evaluate the model on the basis of a historical simulation and also run three policy simulations. The fourth section presents the results of the forecast based on the model and Section 5 sets out the conclusion.

2. MODEL SPECIFICATION AND ESTIMATION

The model uses annual data and the period of estimation is from 1985 to 1993. This short period of estimation is due to the relative scarcity of published data. We collected the data from official publications such as the Statistical Yearbook of Sichuan (various years) and the Statistical Yearbook of China (various years).

The accounting system used in the model is the Material Product System (MPS), which is the system adopted by most of the command economies in the world. The MPS is different from the more commonly used System of National Accounting (SNA) in that the MPS does not take into account the non-material sector or the service sector. We reconcile the two systems in Table 1.

The model consists of 20 endogenous variables (Table 2), 7 exogenous variables (Table 3), 13 behavioural equations and 7 identities (Table 4). We model the demand side by looking at consumption, investment, international trade and inter-provincial trade.

We estimate the 13 behavioural equations using the Ordinary Least Squares (OLS) method and put them together with 7 identities to form a model. We then solve the whole model using the Gauss-Seidel procedure. All the computations are performed by the Econometric Views Version 2.0 software produced by Quantitative Micro Software.

3. MODEL EVALUATION AND SIMULATION

We perform a historical simulation for the period 1986 to 1993 to evaluate the model. The evaluation is based on two criteria. The first is to examine how closely the simulated values of the major endogenous variables track their actual values. This is done using the Root Mean Square Percent Error[1] (RMS percent) and the results are presented in Table 5. The RMS percent of the major endogenous variables are relatively small and thus, the model has a good overall statistical fit.

The second criteria is to observe whether the turning points of the major endogenous variables in the simulation follow those of the actual data. A casual observation reveals that most of the turning points are captured by the model. Thus, not only does the model has a good overall statistical fit, but it is also sensitive to variations in turning points.

3.1 POLICY SIMULATIONS

Besides the historical simulation, we run three other simulations to study the impacts of the agricultural, state-owned industrial and foreign investment sectors on Sichuan's GDP. Dynamic elasticities for the various simulations are calculated and presented in Table 6. The dynamic elasticities tell us how the major endogenous variables respond to a one percent change in the policy variables over the period of the simulation.

---

[1] See Pindyck and Rubinfeld (1991) for a discussion of Root Mean Square Percent Error.

3.1.1 Policy Simulation 1: National GDP Deflator (NATDGDP)

Our first policy simulation considers the effects of an increase in the national price level, which is measured by the National GDP deflator (NATDGDP). In this simulation, a 5 percentage point increase in the growth rate is assumed for NATDGDP in the year 1987. NATDGDP affects real rural income in the next period negatively (Table 4 Equation 2). The procurement prices for agricultural output are controlled by the government and it is usually fixed. The result is that procurement prices are not adjusted according to the rising national price level causing real rural income to decrease. The impact of this is great in Sichuan's economy as Sichuan has a large agricultural sector. This, in turn, affects rural consumption negatively which will, in turn, affect Sichuan's GDP (RGDP90) negatively.

The results in Table 6 shows that the NATDGDP dynamic elasticities of RGDP90 are all negative throughout the period from 1988 to 1993. In 1987, the dynamic elasticity is zero as the effect of the increase in the national price level materialises only in 1988. Over the period 1988 to 1993, the dynamic elasticities, in absolute value terms, ranges from a high of 1.120 to a low of 0.535, with an average of 0.887. The negative values of the dynamic elasticities means that an increase in NATDGDP will result in a decrease in RGDP90. Over the period 1988 to 1993, on average, a one percent increase in NATDGDP results in a 0.887 percent decrease in RGDP90.

The policy implication of this simulation is that national inflation is harmful to the economy of Sichuan and that policy makers should make fighting inflation one of their top priorities. Policy makers should also adjust agricultural procurement prices according to the price level. Inflation will adversely affect real rural income and rural consumption. And since the rural sector constitutes a large proportion of Sichuan's economy, a fall in rural consumption will adversely affect the economy.

3.1.2 Policy Simulation 2: Loans to Industry (RINDLOAN90)

Sichuan is one of the largest industrial bases in China and a large proportion of the industrial enterprises are state-owned. Our second simulation simulates an increase of 10 percentage points in the growth rate of RINDLOAN90 in the year 1987 to see how RGDP90 responds to this increase and the consequent increase in the value-added of the state-owned enterprises.

The results presented in Table 6 shows that the RINDLOAN90 dynamic elasticities of RGDP90 ranges from a low of 0.065 to a high of 0.244, with an average of 0.174 over the period 1987 to 1993. The values of the dynamic elasticities are positive, meaning that an increase in RINDLOAN90 will result in an increase in RGDP90. Over the period 1987 to 1993, on average, a one percent increase in RINDLOAN90 results in a 0.174 percent increase in RGDP90.

The policy implication of this simulation is that the provision of more liquidity to the state-owned enterprises will be beneficial. With more liquidity, those enterprises would have more funds for productive investment. This will help to increase their value-added. The end result is a positive impact on urban income and urban consumption, which will help boost Sichuan's GDP.

3.1.3 Policy Simulation 3: Foreign Capital Utilised (FCU)

Foreign investment has not played a significant role in the economy of Sichuan until recent years, when it began to grow at a substantial rate. Our third simulation examines the effect of an increase of 30 percentage points in the growth rate of FCU in the year 1987 on RGDP90.

The results presented in Table 6 shows that the FCU dynamic elasticities of RGDP90 ranges from a low of 0.021 to a high of 0.188, with an average of 0.068 over the period 1987 to 1993. Again, the dynamic elasticities are positive and over the period 1987 to 1993, on average, a one percent increase in FCU results in a 0.068 percent increase in RGDP90.

The policy implication of this simulation is that although foreign investment has not played a significant role in the economy in the earlier years, this sector of the economy deserves attention as it has been growing in importance more recently. The dynamic elasticity for the year 1993, the latest in the simulation period, is 0.188, and this is higher than any other year. Thus, policy makers should adopt a more open approach when it comes to attracting foreign investment and also, should create an environment that is conducive to doing business. With its large population and a huge potential market, Sichuan is already highly attractive to foreign investors.

4. FORECASTING

Forecasting is performed for the period 1994 to 1998. Ex-post forecasting is done for the years 1994 and 1995 and ex-ante forecasting is done for the years 1996 to 1998. The values of the exogenous variables for the years 1994 and 1995 are the actual values wherever possible and if the actual values are not available, we use estimated ones instead.

For the years 1996 to 1998, the values of FERTCONSUM and POWEROFMAC are estimated using ARMA generating processes. The remaining five exogenous variables of FOREX, NATDGDP, SICDGDP, RINDLOAN90 and FCU are estimated using various assumptions of their growth rates. For FOREX, the Renminbi is assumed not to continue depreciating, but to appreciate slightly, due to the building up of China's foreign reserves. And for FCU, foreign investment is assumed to continue to experience high growth rates due to the continual opening up of Sichuan's economy. The projected values of the exogenous variables are presented in Table 7 and the forecast values of the major endogenous variables are presented in Table 8.

The forecast values of Sichuan's GDP for the years 1994 and 1995 are lower than the actual values. It is underestimated by 6.21 percent in 1994 and 8.34 percent in 1995. Forecasts into the years 1997 and 1998 give GDP growth rates of about 12 percent, indicating that the provincial economy of Sichuan will continue to experience strong growth.

5. CONCLUSION

We build this econometric model of Sichuan to study the agricultural, state-owned industrial and foreign investment sectors. We run three policy simulations in Section 3 to study the effects on RGDP90 of a sustained increase in NATDGDP, RINDLOAN90 and FCU variables for the period 1987 to 1993.

Our first simulation has shown that inflation is harmful to the economy of Sichuan and thus, policy makers should make controlling inflation one of their top priorities. Policy makers should also adjust agricultural procurement prices according to the price level. Our second simulation has shown that an increase in loans to industry will increase the value-added of the state-owned enterprises, which will have a positive impact on Sichuan's GDP. And finally, our third simulation has shown that an increase in foreign investment will have positive impact on the economy and thus, Sichuan should adopt more open policies towards foreign investment.

REFERENCES

Chen, K. (1995): The Chinese Economy in Transition: Micro Changes and Macro Implications, Singapore University Press.

Pindyck, R. S. and D. L. Rubinfeld (1991): Econometric Models and Economic Forecasts, McGraw-Hill, Inc.

Sichuan Statistical Bureau (various years): Sichuan Tongji Nianjian (Statistical Yearbook of Sichuan), Beijing: Zhongguo Tongji Chubanshe.

State Statistical Bureau (various years): Zhongguo Tongji Nianjian (Statistical Yearbook of China), Beijing: Zhongguo Tongji Chubanshe.

Watanabe, T. (1996): "Open-door Policy and Economic Development in China: The Possibility of Development in the Inland Provinces," East Asian Economic Perspectives.

Yu, P. K., A. N. Yand and D. Liao (1994): "Sichuan Region: A Balance Sheet on its Status," Chinese Regionalism: The Security Dimension, Westview Press.

TABLE 1

National Income Accounting Table

Demand Side	Supply Side
Rural Consumption	Primary Sector GDP
+ Urban Consumption	(Agricultural)
+ Public Consumption	+ Secondary Sector GDP
= Total Consumption	(Industry and Construction)
	+ Tertiary Sector GDP
+ Investment (Accumulation)	(Transport and Commerce and others)
= National Income Used	= Gross Domestic Product
+ Exports	- Other Tertiary Sector GDP
- Imports	- Depreciation
- Net Regional Inflow	- Statistical Discrepancy
= National Income Produced in MPS	

TABLE 2

Endogenous Variables

RPRIGDP90	Primary GDP	NIMP	Nominal Import
RAGRIN90	Rural Income	RNRO90	Net Regional Flow
RAGRCON90	Rural Consumption	ROGDP90	Other Tertiary GDP
RVASOE90	Value-added of SOE	REXPO90	Real Export
RURBIN90	Urban Income	RIMP90	Real Import
RURBCON90	Urban Consumption	RNIU90	Net Income Used
RPUBLICC90	Public Consumption	RNIP90	Net Income Produce
RFCISO90	SOE Investment	RGDP90	GDP
RACC90	Accumulation	GDP	Nominal GDP
NEXPO	Nominal Export	RPRIVATE90	Private Consumption

Note: All variables are in real terms unless otherwise stated.

TABLE 3

Exogenous Variables

POWEROFMAC	Power of Machinery Used in the Farms
FERTCONSUM	Fertilisers Used in the Farms
RINDLOAN90	Loans to Industry in Real Terms
FCU	Foreign Capital Utilised
FOREX	Foreign Exchange Rate
NATDGDP	National GDP Deflator
SICDGDP	Sichuan GDP Deflator

TABLE 4

Behavioural Equations and Identities

1) RPRIGDP90 $=$ 179.457 + 0.108 POWEROFMAC $R^2 = 0.968$

   (8.848)   (2.457)

   + 0.584 FERTCONSUM

   (2.454)

2) RAGRIN90 $=$ - 210.106 + 2.520 RPRIGDP90 $R^2 = 0.908$

   (-1.687)   (5.077)

   - 3.674 NATDGDP(-1)

   (-3.837)

3) RAGRCON90 $=$ -125.602 + 0.957 RAGRIN90 $R^2 = 0.896$

   (-1.366)   (5.443)

   + 0.237 RAGRCON90(-1)

   (1.730)

4) RVASOE90 $=$ 229.542 + 1.030 RINDLOAN90 $R^2 = 0.881$

   (5.96)   (6.068)

   + 0.635 D(RVASOE90)

   (2.514)

TABLE 4 (CONT)

Behavioural Equations and Identities

5)	RURBIN90	=	8.968 + 0.529 RFCISO90 + 0.218 RVASOE90	$R^2 = 0.927$
			(0.240) (4.064) (2.046)	
6)	RURBCON90	=	54.772 + 0.701 RURBIN90	$R^2 = 0.935$
			(3.594) (10.027)	
7)	RPUBLICC90	=	-3.107 + 0.032 RGDP90	$R^2 = 0.960$
			(-0.482) (2.810)	
			+ 0.478 RPUBLICC90(-1)	
			(2.338)	
8)	RFCISO90	=	38.624 + 0.696 RINDLOAN90(-1)	$R^2 = 0.726$
			(0.952) (3.984)	
9)	RACC90	=	63.578 + 0.154 RGDP90 + 0.002 FCU	$R^2 = 0.977$
			(2.521) (6.251) (4.592)	
10)	NEXPO	=	-37.798 + 14.506 FOREX + 0.588 NEXPO(-1)	$R^2 = 0.999$
			(-8.275) (9.935) (10.892)	
11)	NIMP	=	2.581 - 14.207 FOREX + 0.070 GDP	$R^2 = 0.945$
			(0.205) (-2.509) (5.750)	
12)	RNRO90	=	-49.359 - 0.852 REXPO90 + 1.920 RIMP90	$R^2 = 0.838$
			(-5.614) (-3.119) (5.252)	
13)	ROGDP90	=	-189.925 + 0.432 RNIP90	$R^2 = 0.809$
			(-2.445) (5.448)	
14)	REXPO90	=	NEXPO*100/SICDGDP	
15)	RIMP90	=	NIMP*100/SICDGDP	
16)	RPRIVATE90	=	RAGRCON90 + RURBCON90	
17)	RNIU90	=	RPRIVATE90 + RPUBLICC90 + RACC90	
18)	RNIP90	=	RNIU90 + RNRO90 + REXPO90 - RIMP90	
19)	RGDP90	=	RNIP90 + ROGDP90	
20)	GDP	=	(SICDGDP*RGDP90)/100	

TABLE 5

Results of Historical Simulation

Variable	RMS%	Variable	RMS%
RGDP90	7.51	RACC90	6.75
RNIP90	6.92	RAGRCON90	4.48
RNIU90	7.88	RURBCON90	2.58
RPRIGDP90	1.37	RPUBLICC90	7.53
RVASOE90	3.04	RPRIVATE90	3.51

TABLE 6

Results of Policy Simulations (Dynamic Elasticities)

	1987	1988	1989	1990	1991	1992	1993
RGDP90	0.000	-0.535	-0.769	-0.892	-0.967	-1.039	-1.120
	0.065	0.131	0.170	0.176	0.210	0.222	0.244
	0.021	0.063	0.085	0.025	0.053	0.040	0.188
RACC90	0.000	-0.372	-0.534	-0.620	-0.672	-0.722	-0.779
	0.045	0.091	0.118	0.122	0.146	0.154	0.169
	0.058	0.169	0.227	0.059	0.138	0.101	0.506
RPUBLICC90	0.000	-0.340	-0.651	-0.878	-1.035	-1.155	-1.264
	0.041	0.103	0.157	0.187	0.223	0.247	0.273
	0.013	0.046	0.076	0.052	0.059	0.053	0.145
RAGRCON90	0.000	-0.591	-0.829	-0.946	-1.016	-1.086	-1.169
	0.000	0.000	0.000	0.000	0.000	0.000	0.000
	0.000	0.000	0.000	0.000	0.000	0.000	0.000
RURBCON90	0.000	0.000	0.000	0.000	0.000	0.000	0.000
	0.165	0.328	0.419	0.427	0.508	0.535	0.587
	0.000	0.000	0.000	0.000	0.000	0.000	0.000

Line 1: Simulation 1 (National Price Level)

Line 2: Simulation 2 (Loans to Industry)

Line 3: Simulation 3 (Foreign Capital Utilised)

TABLE 7

Projected Values of Exogenous Variables

Variable Name	1994	1995	1996	1997	1998
FOREX (RMB/US$)	8.61	8.35	8.30	8.29	8.28
FERTCONSUM (10 kiloton)	228.3	244.9	260.7	272.1	283.5
NATDGDP	135.3	139.4	143.6	147.9	152.3
POWEROFMAC (10 megawatt)	1531.4	1595.8	1657.2	1718.2	1778.3
FCU (US$10000)	91426	54855	76798	107517	150523
RINDLOAN90 (RMB 100 million)	555.2	832.9	916.1	1007.8	1108.5
SICDGDP	151.2	174.9	183.6	192.8	202.5

TABLE 8

Forecast Values of Major Endogenous Variables (RMB 100 Million)

Variable Name	1994	1995	1996	1997	1998
RACC90	474.7	436.3	521.9	611.6	725.9
RAGRCON90	482.9	506.2	535.7	560.0	582.3
REXPO90	94.6	95.7	98.6	98.0	95.5
RGDP90	1723.2	1852.6	2181.2	2445.7	2743.0
RIMP90	41.1	63.0	89.4	111.0	134.6
RPRIGDP90	478.5	495.1	511.0	524.2	537.4
RPUBLICC90	92.1	100.0	114.2	129.5	146.2
RURBCON90	284.0	361.2	436.6	472.4	505.2
RVASOE90	814.7	934.2	958.7	1052.6	1112.5

Analysis of the Thailand Baht: Trends and Prospects

Lau Hon Wei

&

*Jon D **Kendall***

Nanyang Business School, Nanyang Technological University, Nanyang Avenue, Singapore 639798
Fax: +(65) 792.4217, Tel: +(65) 799.6232, Email: kendall@pacific.net.sg

Abstract We examine the fundamentals behind the Thailand baht's movements from 1990 to 1996. Specifically, we study key variables underpinning the Thailand baht as well as the influence of major currencies on the Thailand baht basket. We then formulate three models to predict the Thailand baht's daily exchange-rate movements.

1. INTRODUCTION

'Thailand's financial status has been rising in the international arena, especially in Asia. Compared to the other emerging markets, Thailand's performance has been extraordinarily outstanding in the recent years. Today, Thailand's economy stands out clearly amongst the most successful and dynamic economies of the Asia-Pacific region, as evidenced by the continued strong growth performance and a high degree of macroeconomic stability.'[1]

The Bank of Thailand has used the exchange rate as an instrument to ensure economic stability consistent with long-run sustainable growth. This has motivated our interest in studying the operation of the exchange rate mechanism and its currency trend.

The primary objective of this paper is to study short-term (monthly and daily) movements of the Thailand baht relative to economic fundamentals over the period 1990 to 1996. A secondary objective is to develop and test forecasting models for predicting daily currency movements from September 1995 to November 1996.

For the analysis on the exchange rate trend and the currency's movement with key economic variables, we focus on monthly observations as we believe that they are more relevant for the length of period studied. On the other hand, we choose daily data to build our forecasting model as short-term forecasting models will be more relevant for the industry.

We begin with a brief description of Thailand's exchange rate system and its monetary authority, the Bank of Thailand. This is followed by chart studies on the Thai baht's bilateral exchange rate with the currencies of its three major trading partners, namely the US dollar, the Japanese yen and the Deutschmark. Other chart studies include the real exchange rate and the effective exchange rates. The next section focuses on relative movements of the Thailand-US bilateral exchange rate with key indicators. The last section presents an accurate forecasting model of the currency.

---

[1] Excerpt from a speech delivered by Vijit Supint, Governor for Bank of Thailand on 31 March 1993.

2. THE FOREIGN EXCHANGE AUTHORITY OF THAILAND

2.1 THE BANK OF THAILAND

The central bank of Thailand, represented by the Bank of Thailand, was set up in 1942. In its earliest stage of establishment, the Bank of Thailand's functions were primarily to finance government expenditure and issue banknotes. Its roles and functions have since developed into a full-fledged central bank in the conventional sense. Currently, the Bank of Thailand performs three principle functions:

- To formulate and implement the monetary policy;

- To supervise and scrutinise all commercial banks, finance companies and credit companies;

- To develop the financial system.

In addition, the Bank of Thailand also assumes the responsibility of the foreign exchange authority of the economy. The aim of its exchange rate policy is to ensure exchange rate stability is consistent with its long-term growth.

2.2 THE FOREIGN EXCHANGE AUTHORITY OF THAILAND

2.2.1 Evolution Of The Foreign Exchange System Of Thailand

After the Second World War, Thailand adopted a multiple exchange rate system in the midst of economic difficulties and during a serious shortage in supply of foreign exchange. In 1963, Thailand changed to the par value system in which the value of the baht was pegged to the value of gold and hence fixed at the rate of 20.80 baht per US dollar. The Exchange Equalisation Fund (EEF) was set up to maintain the prescribed baht parity and to stabilise exchange rate movements within assigned margins. The parity of the baht has since been maintained for almost two decades.

The role of the EEF and representatives from commercial banks is to determine the dollar exchange rate by taking into account the demand and supply of the US dollar. The EEF would intervene to stabilise the foreign exchange market when necessary. This system of daily fixing went on smoothly until 1981 when problems surfaced due to the strong appreciation of the dollar as relative to other currencies. In an attempt to stabilise the declining baht value against other currencies, twice the Thai authorities in mid-1981 devalued the baht. However, public confidence could not be restored. In July 1981, the EEF abolished the system of daily fixing. The EEF decided upon defining the exchange rate independently and henceforth, the dollar exchange rate was fixed at 23.00 baht from July 1981 to November 1984.

As a result of world economic recession since 1980, domestic economic difficulties and external disequilibrium have prevailed. To prevent the value of baht from unrealistically rising with the rapidly appreciating U.S. dollar, the authorities decided in November 1984 to devalue the baht by almost 15 percent against the US dollar. The dollar-pegging system was also replaced by the system of pegging the baht to a basket of internationally accepted currencies, namely Japanese yen, US dollar and Deutschmark. This exchange rate system has prevailed until the present time.

2.2.2 The Foreign Exchange System Mechanism

Under the basket-pegging system, the EEF acts as the sole agent in establishing the mid-rate for the U.S. dollar exchange rate on a daily basis. The EEF stands ready from

8:30a.m.-12:30p.m.to buy and sell unlimited amounts of US dollars from and to commercial banks at ±0.02 baht from the mid-rate. Hence, this establishes the intervention band for the commercial players. In determining the mid-rate, the following three criteria are considered:

- The average values of the currencies in the basket which would be weighted according to the significance of the trade conducted with Thailand;

- The volume of US dollars traded in the past; and

- The economic conditions, export, import, and domestic price levels.

3. EXCHANGE RATE TRENDS

3.1 *NOMINAL BILATERAL EXCHANGE RATE (THAILAND-US EXCHANGE RATE)*

This section focuses on the Thailand-US exchange rate. As the indirect quotation (Thai baht/US$) is most commonly used in the foreign market, the Thailand-U.S. exchange rate in this paper will be quoted as baht/US$. In Figure 1, the baht showed its weakest point at 26 baht/US$ in May 1990 and hit a record high at 24.6 baht/US$ in May 1995.

For 1990 and 1991, the graph exhibits sharp fluctuations. In the first half of 1990, the dollar appreciated against the baht as the Federal Reserve set in to strengthen the currency as the dollar has been on a downward trend since late 1989 and early 1990. However, in the second half of the year, the linked recession in US and the other major European economies led the dollar to fall from ¥158/US$ in May 1990 to ¥130/US$ in November 1990. The exchange rate dropped 3.6 percent from 26 baht/US$ to 25.07 baht/US$. In 1991, demand for the US dollar as a safe-haven currency was high due to the Gulf War; investors' confidence in the favourable prospects for the US economic growth led to a surge in the dollar, pushing the exchange rate up to its second peak of 25.71 baht/US$ in September 1991.

In 1992 and 1993, the exchange rate experienced small-scale fluctuations of less than 2 percent. There was no significant sign of a breakthrough. However, there was a downward trend of successive troughs in the period. Despite the presidential election in 1992, the dollar was not been able to strengthen as market sentiments remained sceptical on an economic rebound in the United States. In addition to the stagnant economic condition of the country, and with the widening of the trade gap between US and Japan, US Minister for Commerce signalled his move towards reducing trade deficits as his primary goal and this further weakened the U.S. dollar.

In 1994 and early 1995, the exchange rate fell by 2.4 percent from 25.56 baht/US$ to 24.6 baht/US$ because of the continuous weakening of the dollar. This was mainly due to the US trade deficit and the delayed trade talks between US and Japan. The weakening of the dollar thus allowed the strengthening of the baht against the dollar. However, in the second half of 1995 the dollar appreciated due to its expanding growth and the exchange rate showed an upwards trend till November 1996, standing at the month-end of 25.51 baht/US$.

3.2 *JAPAN-US AND GERMANY-US EXCHANGE RATES*

The Thai baht basket is heavily weighted with the dollar; however, the currency also exhibits strong cohesion to the fluctuations of the Japanese yen and the Deutschmark. In Figures 2 and 3, these patterns can be explained by the exchange rate policy of pegging the baht to the yen and the Deutschmark. Figure 2 shows a stronger relationship between the baht/US$ relative to that of Figure 3. This is due to a heavier weight placed on the yen; this reasoning is verified by a quantitative analysis in the later section of the paper.

3.2.1 Japan-US Exchange Rate

The baht/US$ and yen/US$ graphs in Figure 2 show a gradual strengthening trend of the baht and the yen against the dollar from mid-1990 to mid-1995. The dollar appreciated against the Japanese yen since late 1989 until April 1990, hitting an average of ¥158.85/US$ for the month of April 1990. Following a similar trend, the baht/US$ exchange rate recorded a peak of 26 baht/US$, which indicated a nominal depreciation of the baht against the dollar. Off the peak in April 1990, the dollar depreciated against the yen; this can be seen similarly for the baht. This trend of strong appreciation of the yen against the dollar ended in November 1990 when the yen/US$ underwent minor fluctuations due to the continuous adjustment of the bilateral exchange rate to correct the large trade surplus of Japan against US and the trade competitiveness of the Japanese currency.

This trend continued into 1992 and 1993. In 1992, it continued to display minor fluctuations and is still having a downward trend. This gradual appreciation of Japanese yen against the dollar is largely caused by the improvement in the Japanese stock market. Moreover, investors switched to Japanese yen holding on account the Exchange Rate Mechanism (ERM) crisis[2] in September. The trade surplus of Japan still remained the main concern over the yen appreciation in 1993. In 1992 and 1993, both graphs exhibited a closely tied trend movement.

Into 1994 and 1995, the yen appreciated sharply *vis-a-vis* the dollar on account of the strong fundamental of the Japanese economy, low inflation and continued trade surplus. The yen/US$ exchange rate reached a low of 83.5 in May 1995. Since then, the dollar regained its appreciation momentum due to the expanding growth of US. The dollar continues to grow strong against the yen, closing at an average of ¥113.36/US$.

3.2.2 Germany-US Exchange Rate

Referring to Figure 3, from 1990 to 1991, the dollar appreciated slightly against the Deutschmark in the beginning of 1990, reached its first peak in the graph at DM1.72/US$. This is two months ahead of the first peak of the baht/US$ in May 1990. On the contrary, the recorded trough of DM1.4685/US$ came three months later in February 1991 compared to the bottom of the trough of the baht/US$ in November 1990. The substantial lead and lag period of the two graphs imply a strong conflict in the adjustment of Thai baht exchange rate to the Deutschmark movement. This conflict can be explained by the transitional period of unifying Germany. The Deutschmark underwent sharp fluctuations and thus sentiments on the currency movements were rather unstable. The drastic appreciation of the dollar against the Deutschmark occurred from February 1991 to July 1991. In less than half a year, the Germany-US exchange rate shot up from 1.4685 to 1.8275. This weakening trend of the Deutschmark was mainly due to the German government's move to meet fiscal needs for the reconstruction of East Germany in which it raised income tax rates. In addition, Germany's economic fundamentals showed some deterioration, particularly in view of the resurgence of a current account deficit of DM1.2

---

[2] A more detailed discussion of the ERM crisis in 1992 can be found in Bank of Thailand (1992).

billion in January 1991. The Deutschmark strengthened in the second half of 1991, reflecting the slower-than-anticipated economic recovery in the US combined with the Bundesbank's pursuit of a tight monetary policy stance to control inflation.

In 1992 and 1993, despite a gradual downward trend of the baht/US$, the DM/US$ exchange rate exhibits sharp fluctuations. In the first three quarters of 1992, the Deutschmark strengthened, following an attempt by the German authorities to maintain high interest rate level to reduce inflationary pressure. However, from September 1992 to January 1994, the Deutschmark weakened tremendously, due to problems staying within the ERM. The German government continued to cut interest rates to ease pressure on the members of the European Monetary System (EMS). DM/US$ shot from 1.39 in September 1992 to 1.7445 in January 1994. The baht/US$ followed the short-term fluctuations in the DM/US$ though in a broader picture, the baht/US$ showed a falling pattern while the DM/US$ exhibited an unstable picture.

The Deutschmark appreciated against the US dollar in 1994 until mid-1995. This was mainly due to the economic recovery in Germany and a strong favouritism of the of the Thailand investors to turn to the Deutschmark as a safe haven currency due to the political instability in Italy, Spain and France. Since mid-1995, the Deutschmark depreciated against the dollar as the momentum of the economic recovery in US picked up. The DM/US$ closed at a month-end of 1.5135 in November 1996.

3.3 REAL BILATERAL EXCHANGE RATE (THAILAND-US EXCHANGE RATE)

In order to facilitate interpretation of the index, the real bilateral exchange rate is expressed in US$/baht. The real exchange rate was calculated based on the following equation:

$$(US\$/Thai\ baht)_{real} = (US\$/Thai\ baht)_{nominal} * [\ Price_{Thailand}\ /\ Price_{US}\ ] \qquad (1)$$

The wholesale price indices (WPIs) for the two countries are used rather than the consumer price indices (CPIs) since the WPIs are more pertinent to trade competitiveness. Both the nominal and real bilateral exchange rate indices are thus constructed by basing the exchange rate on January 1990. In other words, a unit rise of the indices represents a percent rise in the exchange rate *vis-a-vis* January 1990.

From Figure 4, the two graphs show a wide divergence since January 1990. The real US$/baht index exhibits an upward trend and exhibits sharp fluctuations in the first four years of the 1990s, which then remains rather stable in late 1995. For the first quarter of 1996, it lies between 117 and 119. The nominal Baht/US$ index appears relatively stationary, fluctuating within a 5 percent band.

Thailand has been experiencing high inflation relative to the US in the 1990s. Figure 4 depicts an increasing difference between the two inflation rates. This shows that despite the fact that nominal bilateral exchange rate has kept steady, the increase in the real bilateral exchange rate represents erosion of Thailand's export competitiveness. This may explain the high trade deficit affecting the economy.

3.4 NOMINAL AND REAL EFFECTIVE EXCHANGE RATE

An effective exchange rate measures the overall value of one currency against a basket of other currencies. Changes indicate the average change in one currency relative to all the others. There is no official published measure for baht's effective exchange rate; we therefore discuss both the nominal and real trade-weighted indices constructed by Citibank

NA. The indices use Thailand's trade proportion to the country's total trade as weights for the computation of its effective exchange rate. The indices are based on January 1990=100 and have used the top fifteen major trading partners to weight bilateral exchange rates. To avoid bias, the indices are geometric averages rather than arithmetic averages. The indices are constructed so that rises in the indices represent an appreciation of the baht's effective rate. That is, a unit size represents a percent rise in the collective value of the currency, based on January 1990.

Figure 5 illustrates the nominal and real effective exchange rates. The Thai baht basket is predominantly weighted by the dollar. The dollar was a weak currency in the first four years of the 1990s, so the baht's nominal effective exchange rate (NEER) has generally depreciated, falling sharply in early 1995 from January 1990 to June 1995. Since the dollar began to bounce back against the yen in late 1995, the baht's NEER has appreciated modestly, closing at an average index of 93.68 in November 1996.

The baht's real effective exchange rate has diverged from the NEER. Despite the real effective exchange rate (REER) having tracked the NEER relatively well, the REER shows that inflation is rising in Thailand relative to its other major trading partners.

4. ECONOMIC FUNDAMENTALS

This section examines the trends of certain key variables that fluctuate with the Thailand baht's movement. As advocated by various versions of the monetary model, certain economic variables do display consistent movement with its exchange rate. We focus on three key economic variables that move in accordance with the nominal Thailand-US exchange rate:

- Domestic interest rate
- Relative money supply
- Relative inflation level

4.1 DOMESTIC INTEREST RATE AND NOMINAL THAILAND-US EXCHANGE RATE

The conventional view of the interest rate is that it moves in the opposite direction to that of its currency. A tightening of money supply will appreciate the currency; this is associated with upward pressure on the interest rate. Thus, an upward trend of its interest rate should indicate a strengthening of the currency and vice versa. Figure 6 depicts the bank rate, 3-month interbank rate and the nominal Thailand-US exchange rate from January 1990 to June 1996. The bank rate is the interest rate that the central bank charges under the loan window. It indicates the direction of the monetary policy and carries strong announcement effect. Tracking the 3-month interbank rate, we notice a strong correlation of its movement to that of the bank rate. This shows a strong simultaneous influence of the central bank to control its interest rate policy. The tight tracking of the bank rate to that of the 3-month interbank rate has shown that the central bank has responded similarly to market sentiments.

The bank rate fluctuated between 8 and 12 percent whilst the 3-month interbank displayed greater volatility, moving between 7 and 17.25 percent. The closely-tied inverse relationship between the interest rate and the exchange rate shows that the interest rate had been very responsive to movement of the Thailand baht.

4.2 RELATIVE MONEY SUPPLY AND NOMINAL THAILAND-US EXCHANGE RATE

Money supply measures the level of liquidity in the economy. In our discussion, we use the broadest available supply growth, M2. The conventional view of relative money supply growth indicates that there is a direct relationship with its exchange rate. Whenever the domestic money supply grows relatively faster than its foreign counterpart, we should notice a depreciation of the domestic currency against the foreign currency. The rationale is that an increase in the relative money supply growth will stimulate output growth and push up the price level relative to that of the foreign economy.[3] According to the Purchasing Power Parity (PPP) theory, the domestic currency will thus depreciate against the foreign currency.

In Figure 7, we see an upward trend of the money supply ratio index. The index surged to about 2.5 times of its base in January 1990. The graph is rather linear from 1990 to 1993 but there exists minor fluctuations from 1994 to 1996.

The figure shows that theoretical argument cannot account for the movements of the two graphs. With sharp fluctuations of the exchange rate in the time period, the money supply ratio index depicts a rather linear upward trend. The explanation is that the exchange rate is fixed daily by the central bank; this is done with its main regard to major currencies in the basket, thus the relative money supply does not affect the exchange rate movement.

4.3 THE RELATIVE INFLATION LEVEL AND THE NOMINAL THAILAND-US EXCHANGE RATE

According to the law of one price, identical goods sold in different countries must sell for the same price when their prices are expressed in terms of the same currency. With the law of one price as its building block, the theory of purchasing power parity states that the exchange rate between two countries' currencies equals the ratio of the countries' prices.[4]

Theory predicts that a relative rise in the domestic price level will trigger a demand for foreign goods and thus depreciate the domestic currency against the foreign currency. The converse also applies. However, the argument does not seem to apply to the case of the nominal Thailand-US exchange rate. Generally, Thailand has been suffering from high inflation. In Figure 8, the price ratio index shows two upward trends. From January 1990 to October 1991, the index rose 11 percent. It then hovered and fell slightly until mid-1993. Since then, the price ratio index experienced an upward surge, rising to a level of 118 in November 1996. The exchange rate, on the other hand, experienced several peaks and troughs in the time period studied, and displayed a gradual downward trend from January 1990 to May 1995. It has recovered slightly since then.

The price ratio index does not exercise the same trend as the nominal exchange rate since the exchange rate is fixed daily by the central bank in accordance with major currencies in the trade-weighted basket of currencies. Hence, the price ratio is not a direct determinant of the exchange rate; this explains why the two graphs do not show similar trends. However, we observe that the price ratio index follows the money supply ratio index in Figure 7 more closely.

---

[3] The inverse relationship of the relative money supply and its corresponding exchange rate is implied by the Flexible Price Monetary Model which explains that money stocks determine relative prices which in turn determine the exchange rate via PPP.

[4] Krugman and Obstfeld (1995) discuss the relationship between PPP and the Law of One Price.

5. FORECASTING

We now establish forecast models to predict movements of the daily nominal Thailand-US exchange rate. Section 2.2.2 showed how the Exchange Equalisation Fund (EEF) determines the daily exchange rate for the baht by establishing the mid-rate for the US dollar exchange rate. We have therefore chosen daily 9.00 a.m. (Bangkok time) nominal Thailand-U.S. exchange rate data to build our forecasting model. The time period studied is from 18 September 1995 to 30 November 1996 based on exchange rate data collected on the trade floor.

All holidays and weekends are replaced with values calculated using a natural cubic spline (using the time series database package Dbank). This method allows smoothing of exchange rates over time in order to facilitate more robust estimation.[5]

Each of the three models constructed is based on data from 18 September 1995 to 31 August 1996 (approximately one year). A forecast based on each model is made for the period 1 September 1996 to 30 November 1996.[6] A comparison of the forecasted and actual values is then subjected to root mean squared error, mean absolute error, and mean absolute percentage error tests.

5.1 TESTS FOR STATIONARITY

Many economic variables display the characteristics of non-stationary time-series; this has adverse effects when we perform regression on these time-series. The variances of these series will not be constant over time. Failure to correct for nonstationarity would lead to misleading hypothesis testing later on [Gujarati (1995)].

For our Thailand-U.S. exchange rate time-series, we tested formally for stationarity using the 'Augmented Dickey-Fuller' test [Dickey and Fuller (1979)]:

$$\Delta THB_t = \alpha_0 + \alpha_1 THB_{t-1} + \Sigma_{j=1} \alpha_j \Delta THB_{t-j} + e_t \qquad (2)$$

where THB_t is the nominal Thailand-U.S. exchange rate at time t and e_t is assumed to be Gaussian white noise.

The results of the Augmented Dickey-Fuller test are shown in Table 1. THB contains a unit root. Correction requires transforming THB into D(THB) :

$$D(THB)_t = (THB_t - THB_{t-1}) / THB_{t-1} \qquad (3)$$

This 'rate of change' function transforms the series so that it is stationary. The ADF test statistic in Table 1 for D(THB) indicates a rejection of the hypothesis of a unit root at 99% confidence level. Hence, the exchange rate time-series is run on its 'rate of change' form in our analysis.

5.2 FORECASTING MODELS

5.2.1 Model 1: the 'Naïve' Model

The 'Naïve' model is built based on the economic intuition that the $D(THB)_t$ is highly influenced by its first lag, $D(THB)_{t-1}$. The purpose of setting up this model is two-fold:

---

[5] The authors are grateful to Dr Sam Ouliaris, National University of Singapore, Faculty of Business Administration for his assistance in advising us on the technique for smoothing the data.

[6] A vector autoregression was run on one to four lags on D(THB), D(YEN) and D(DM); the results showed that the lags were not significant; we therefore excluded the vector autoregression model from consideration.

firstly, the tight control of the currency by the central bank signals the rigidity of the exchange rate; the influence of its first lag is a strong and logical argument. Secondly, the model establishes the foundation for testing for additional lags in subsequent forecast models.

The model is built using data from 18 September 1995 to 31 August 1996; a forecast is then made and compared to the actual values from 1 September 1996 to 30 November 1996. The AR(1) model with a constant is presented below:

$$D(THB)_t = 0.0000225 - 0.0497D(THB)_{t-1} \tag{4}$$

$$(0.398) \qquad (-0.783)$$

The values in brackets show t-statistics for the coefficients (See Table 2). The result shows that the coefficients for the constant and $D(THB)_{t-1}$ are insignificant at the 10 percent level of significance. We know that the main consideration for determining the basket is based on the pegged currencies; this shows why the model shows a low R^2. The forecast made is presented graphically in Figure 9.

5.2.2 Model 2: the ARMA Model

Building upon the 'Naïve' model, we further expand the model by adding moving average terms. The ARMA model is based on Box and Jenkins (1976) and is commonly known as the Box-Jenkins methodology. The orders of the autoregression (AR) and the moving average (MA) terms are determined and then the autocorrelation and partial autocorrelation statistics from the correlogram are studied. Several ARMA models are tested and the ARMA(3,3) model is deemed to be the most appropriate model. The ARMA(3,3) model is estimated as shown:

$$D(THB)_t = 0.0000318 - 0.573D(THB)_{t-3} + e_t + 0.0248e_{t-1} - 0.101e_{t-2} + 0.586e_{t-3} \tag{5}$$

$$(0.380) \qquad (-3.54) \qquad\qquad (0.485) \quad (-1.91) \quad (3.59)$$

The values in the brackets are the t-statistics. Diagnostic checking indicates the residuals of the model are white noise.

The results of the regression are presented in Table 2. The table shows that the coefficients of $D(THB)_{t-3}$, e_{t-2} and e_{t-3} are highly significant. Similar to the 'Naïve' model, the ARMA model has a low R^2 but tracks actual values well (see Figure 10).

5.2.3 Model 3 : the 'Weighted Basket' Model

The 'Weighted Basket' model is commonly by the industry for short-term forecasting. It is a linear representation of the major currencies that the Bank of Thailand uses to peg the baht. As was the case for the baht/US exchange rate, the yen/baht and Deutschmark/baht exchange rates exhibit non-stationarity in levels; thus 'rate of change' functions are used for these exchange rates as the differenced forms appear to be stationary. The model is estimated as:

$$D(THB)_t = 0.115D(YEN)_t + 0.0274D(DM)_t \tag{6}$$

$$(21.54) \qquad\qquad (5.34)$$

The values in brackets are t-statistics; results of the regression are shown in Table 2. Results show that the Japanese yen having a heavier weight on the baht than on the Deutschmark, consistent with figures discussed in Section 3.2. The result shows that the coefficients are highly significant; 75.8 percent of the variation in $D(THB)_t$ is explained by

D(YEN)$_t$ and D(DM)$_t$ as indicated by its R^2. However, this model depends on simultaneous data of the yen and Deutschmark in order to forecast the baht. Figure 11 shows that the forecasted values track the actual values relatively well.

Table 3 compares the three forecasting models in terms of their root-mean-squared error, mean absolute error, mean absolute percentage error. The three measurements show that the 'Weighted Basket' model has the smallest variation in its forecasting relative to the actual values.

6. CONCLUSION

The Bank of Thailand tightly controls the movement of the baht. From 1990 to 1996, the nominal Thailand-US exchange rate shows a fluctuation between a band of 5.5 percent with the peak value recorded in May 1990 and the lowest in May 1995. Apart from the sharp fluctuations that occurred in 1990 and 1991, the exchange rate fell gradually from 1992 to mid-1995. This trend is due mainly to the weakening of the dollar due to its slow economic recovery and the huge trade deficits that the economy was suffering. With a rebound on its economic growth in mid-1995, the dollar rose; we see an upward trend in the nominal Thailand-US exchange rate as the dollar appreciated against the baht. Hence, we infer that the economic condition of the US has very great influence on the baht. From chart studies, we also notice that the baht exhibits strong association with the yen and the Deutschmark, with a heavier weight on Japanese yen than on the Deutschmark.

Among the three forecasting models, we can see from Table 3 that the 'Weighted Basket' model shows the lowest root mean squared error, the lowest mean absolute error and the lowest mean absolute percentage error. Moreover, the model also possesses the highest R^2 among the three. Hence, we conclude that the 'Weighted Basket' model is our most appropriate forecasting model. However, the R^2 indicates that although 75.8 percent of the fluctuation of the exchange rate is explained by the major currencies, there are other determinants that the central bank takes into consideration for fixing the daily exchange rate. Hence, other economic issues have to be studied in order to provide a holistic view of the determination of the value of the Thailand baht.

REFERENCES

Bank of Thailand (1990-1995): *Annual Economic Report.*

Box, G. E. P. and G. M. Jenkins (1976): *Time Series Analysis, Forecasting and Control,* revised edition, Holden-Day: San Francisco, Chapter 7.

Citibank (1994): 'Thai Baht Basket,' Working paper.

Dickey D. A., and W. A. Fuller (1979): 'Distribution of the Estimators for Autoregressive Time Series with a Unit Root,' *Journal of the American Statistical Association,* Volume 74, pp.427-431.

Gujarati, N. D. (1995): *Basic Econometrics,* third Edition. New York: McGraw-Hill.

Krugman, P. R. and Obstfeld, M. (1994): *International Economics: Theory and Policy,* 3rd edition, New York: HarperCollins College Publishers.

Ng, E. (1995): *Outlook for the Thai Baht and Philippine Peso and their Economic Implementations,* ASEAN/Singapore Briefing, DBS Bank.

Wibulswasdi, C., and O. Tanvanich (1993): 'Liberalization of the Foreign Exchange Market: Thailand Experience,' *Papers on Policy Analysis and Assessment*, Economic Research Department, Bank of Thailand, 5-18.

Wong, Y.F., and S.L. Tan (1996): "What a Thai Currency Basket may look like," VIEWPOINTS, Area Economics Unit, Standard Chartered.

TABLE 1

Test for Unit Roots: Augmented Dickey-Fuller Test

Variable	ADF Test Statistic	Significant / Insignificant
THB	ADF Test Statistic = -1.40	Insignificant
D(THB)	ADF Test Statistic = -8.14	Significant at 1% level of significance

Rejection Criteria:	1 percent Critical Value	-3.4533
	5 percent Critical Value	-2.8710
	10 percent Critical Value	-2.5718

TABLE 2

Regression Output of the Forecasting Models

Dependent Variable : $D(THB)_t$			Sample : 19th September 95 to 31st August 96	
Model	**Variable**	**Coefficient**	**P-value**	**R-squared**
Model 1	Constant	0.0000225	0.691	0.00249
	$D(THB)_{t-1}$	-0.0450	0.435	
Model 2	constant	0.0000318	0.704	0.0569
	$D(THB)_{t-3}$	-0.573	0.0005	
	e_{t-1}	0.0248	0.628	
	e_{t-2}	-0.101	0.0575	
	e_{t-3}	0.586	0.0004	
Model 3	$D(YEN)_t$	0.115	0.0000	0.758
	$D(DM)_t$	0.0274	0.0000	

TABLE 3

Comparison of the Forecasting Models

Model	Root Mean Squared Error	Mean Absolute Error	Mean Absolute % Error
Model 1	0.0171	0.0126	0.0497
Model 2	0.0173	0.0127	0.0498
Model 3	0.00588	0.00466	0.0184

FIGURE 1

Nominal Thailand-Us Exchange Rate

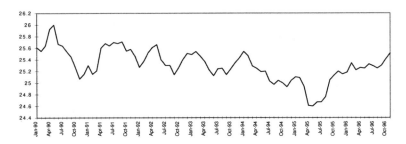

FIGURE 2

Nominal Thailand-US and Japanese-US Exchange Rates

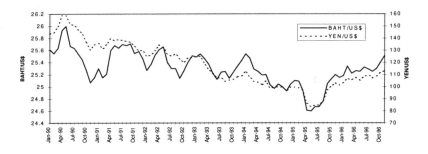

FIGURE 3

Nominal Thailand-US and Germany-US Exchange Rates

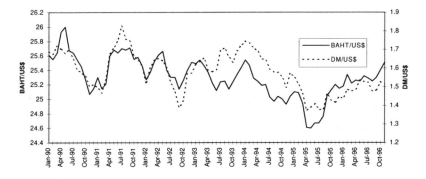

FIGURE 4

Nominal and Real Thailand-US Exchange Rate Indices

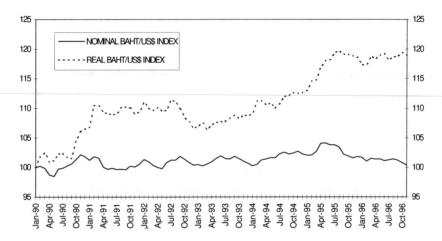

FIGURE 5

Nominal and Real Effective Exchange Rate Indices
(Thailand-US Exchange Rate)

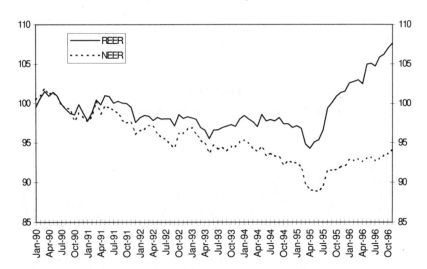

FIGURE 6

Domestic Interest Rate and Nominal Exchange Rate

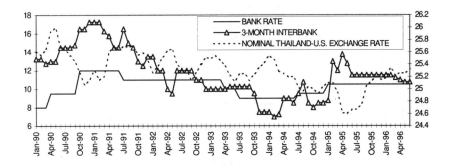

FIGURE 7

Relative Money Supply and Nominal Exchange Rate

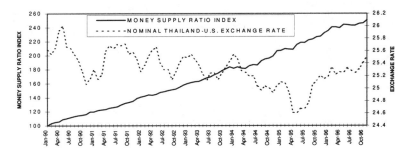

FIGURE 8

Relative Inflation Level and Nominal Exchange Rate

FIGURE 9

Model 1: Actual and Forecasted Thailand Baht Values

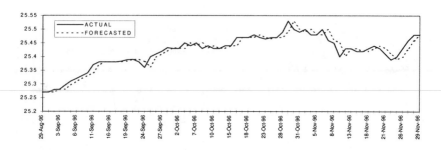

FIGURE 10

Model 2: Actual and Forecasted Thailand Baht Values

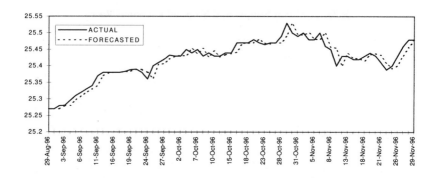

FIGURE 11

Model 3: Actual and Forecasted Thailand Baht Values

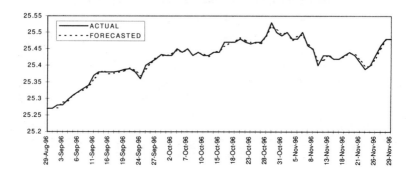

The Natural Rate of Output, Supply Side Potential and the Long Term Sustainable Growth Band for Malaysia

Tan Khee Giap
&
Dennis Lee Wee Keong

Nanyang Business School, Nanyang Technological University, Nanyang Avenue, Singapore 639798
Fax: +(65) 792.4217, Tel: +(65) 799.4832, Email: atankg@ntu.edu.sg

Abstract To achieve a developed country status by 2020, Malaysia aims to achieve real GDP growth at an annual rate of 8 percent from 1990 to 2020. The estimation of this long term sustainable growth is crucial for the formulation of macroeconomic policies so as to prevent overheating and facilitate optimising. Hence, this paper attempts to estimate the natural rate of unemployment and sustainable growth of Malaysia by employing the Lucas-Sargent aggregate supply function, which is observationally equivalent to the Price Expectations Augmented Phillips curve (PEP). A structural approach that integrates the goods, labour and money market and the external trade sector specific to the Malaysian economy, and incorporates rational expectations into the economy, will be used. We aim to establish the initial stage of uncovering this potential growth so that policy makers could tailor the economy along this rate with minimal fluctuations, uncertainty and resource misallocation.

1. INTRODUCTION

1.1 PROJECT MOTIVATION AND EXPECTED CONTRIBUTION

The aim of doubling real GDP every 10 years from 1990 to 2020 through maintaining an annual growth rate of 8 percent, seems to suggests that the Ministry of International Trade and Industry (MITI) estimation of the potential supply side growth is at 8 percent.

In the last few years, for fear of an overheated economy, the continuous implementation of a contractionary monetary policy and prudent fiscal policy by the Malaysian government, imply that a GDP growth of above 9 percent in both 1994 and 1995 is not that desirable after all. As bottlenecks to future growth, such as a tight labour market and wage growth outstripping productivity gains are fast emerging along the highway to 2020, it is crucial to emphasise rapid growth with stability in the Seventh Malaysia Plan.

However, this is feasible only if the long term sustainable growth rate is accurately determined. Over estimation will lead to policies in overheating the economy, and thus resulting in inflationary pressures and over-employment. A lower than estimated equilibrium rate will mean undermining the performance of the economy and hence, not optimising its resources fully. Any misjudgement may lead to frequent shifts in the governments' targeted growth rate over the medium to long term, which will prove too costly for the private sector.

The targeted growth of 8 percent is believed to be able to contain inflation at a low rate, apparently below 4 percent, and keep the labour market at full employment with unemployment rate stabilising at 2.8, also known as the "non-accelerating inflation rate of unemployment" or NAIRU.[1] However, Malaysia's tough anti-inflationary macro-economic policies can be a double-edged sword, having also cast the fear of over-softening the economy.

1.2 PROJECT OBJECTIVE AND RESEARCH SCOPE

This paper aims to provide some guidelines for policy makers to steer the Malaysian economy towards a sustainable growth path with price stability. We will attempt to identify the relevant parameters specific to Malaysia's economic structure, through understanding the macro-transmission mechanism in the economy, particularly with respect to the casual relationship between the labour and goods market, as well as the money market and the external trade sector. Rational expectations will be incorporated weakly into the model.

Previous studies often concern themselves with only the production function while deriving the optimal output, ignoring the concept of natural rate of unemployment. This may be too simplistic a view and thus, a need for an alternative study by adopting the new monetarists' view of the New Classical Aggregate Supply curve derived based on rational expectations, which is observationally equivalent to the PEP curve, but differs in concept.

With the estimated optimal growth rate and its corresponding NAIRU, supply-side factors like the labour market, and the necessary infrastructure could be tailored in advance accordingly to enhance output growth, so as to cater for the forthcoming demand-side conditions. This level of optimal growth rate is believed to be controllable at least in the medium term. Such foresight could help to identify and clear bottlenecks, and has important implications on Malaysia's future macroeconomic policies.

1.3 CHAPTER OUTLINE

Section 2 of the paper provides a brief discussion on the concept of optimal output and the natural rate of unemployment. A critical evaluation is subsequently made on both the Phillips curve and the New Classical Aggregate Supply curve. Section 3 keeps track of the development of the Malaysia economy from 1985 onwards, paying particular attention to its inflationary transmission mechanism and wage price dynamics, as well as the vulnerability of the economy to external factors.

Section 4 discusses the data sources, the methodology adopted and estimated models, followed by reports on the empirical results. Section 5 will give some of the tentative findings and policy implications on macro policy options based on the results drawn from section 4.

2. POTENTIAL OUTPUT, NATURAL RATE OF UNEMPLOYMENT, AND THE NEW CLASSICAL AGGREGATE SUPPLY CURVE. (A CRITICAL EVALUATION)

2.1 POTENTIAL OUTPUT : ISSUES AT STAKE AND MEASUREMENT DIFFICULTIES

Although Malaysia has been experiencing an average 8.5 percent Gross Domestic Product (GDP) growth per annum for the past decade, such rosy economic growth is not without its thorns. After the 1985 recession, the need to contain and avoid inflationary pressure has

---

[1] Figures obtained from 7th Malaysia Plan by *BZW Asia Limited*, p.34 - 36.

constantly been a major concern of the Bank Negara, for fear of overheating Malaysia's economy, yet bearing in mind not to dampen her favourable investment climate.

Defined as the maximum output that can be sustained without risking a rise in inflation and thus, requiring expectations of inflation to be realised (Adams, Paul and Flemming (1987)), it seems that superior knowledge in the economy's potential output, and equating actual output to it will help alleviate the danger of causing an imbalance and subsequent economic instability.

On the contrary, gaps between the actual and potential output, also known as the output gap, will tend to lead to either inflationary or deflationary pressures in the economy, both in the labour and goods market. Thus knowledge of potential output is deemed as crucial for policy makers, in tailoring their macroeconomic policies away from those traumatic consequences of instability. Several measurement of potential output had evolved, some of which will be briefly discussed here.

The Okun's (1962) approach is based on a simple relationship between two gaps, namely the employment gap, which is the gap between the natural and actual rates of unemployment, and the output gap, as represented by the following equation:

$$(Y/Y^* - 1) . 100 = \bullet . (U^* - U) \tag{1}$$

Y and Y^* represents actual and potential output, and U and U^* refers to actual and natural rate of unemployment, while $\bullet$ is known as the Okun's coefficient. A number of weaknesses are present. Firstly, it is dependent on the natural rate of unemployment which is not easily available. Secondly, it does not take into account other structural factors that may affect the potential output and it depends on a consistent Okun's coefficient. However, significant changes in technological advancement and capital utilisation rates may deem it unsuitable to have a fixed coefficient.

An alternative method is the use of the Cobb-Douglas production function which establishes a relationship between the output produced and the input used, namely capital and labour, and estimate the output level if all the inputs are fully employed. Its difficulties are similar to the Okun's approach, being dependent on the definition of full employment of resources, which is difficult to estimate on the surface. The need to classify various types of inputs into capital and labour inputs and the lack of account for changes in the quality of labour and capital over time is also problematic. Most importantly, the production function method ignores the causal relationship between various macroeconomic variables.

Adams and Cole (1990) adopted a systematic approach towards estimating the potential output for the United States. One of their most significant contributions is that estimates of potential output, natural rate of unemployment, wage growth and prices are jointly estimated on a system of simultaneous equations, which systematically integrates wage and price data with real and structural data in the determination of the natural rate of unemployment and potential output. This allows for causality to set in, into the economy.

Two studies on estimates of potential output for Malaysia had been done till date, one by Gan (1993) assuming Hicks neutral technological change, while the other by Zarina and Shariman (1994) who adopted the systematic approach in Adams and Coe (1990).

2.2 NATURAL RATE OF UNEMPLOYMENT, PHILLIPS CURVE AND EXPECTATIONS OF AUGMENTED PHILLIPS CURVE ANALYSIS

2.2.1 Natural Rate of Unemployment

From the labour market's perspective, producing at potential output is equivalent to "full employment", which is itself difficult to define precisely, due to the result of frictional and structural unemployment.

This is known as the natural rate of unemployment, the rate of unemployment which would prevail in equilibrium, when expectations about inflation are realised. Any increase in the output is synonymous with a lower unemployment rate in the market, as represented,

$$(U^* - U) = -\phi(Y^* - Y) \tag{2}$$

with ϕ as the magnitude of change in unemployment associated with change in output. This is observationally similar to the Okun's (1962) law in (1). Thus an unemployment gap in the labour market occurs when actual rate differs from the natural rate. Estimation of the natural rate of unemployment is complex in nature, a result of the difficulty in quantifying the necessary data and in eliminating the cyclical influences, to obtain U^* under stable inflation rate, or alternatively known as NAIRU.

2.2.2 Phillips Curve

Built on the assumption of competitive labour market, A.W. Phillips (1958) provided an important discovery connecting inflation to the level of unemployment, as represented by the famous Phillips curve.

The Phillips curve provided a bridge between the Classical model and the Keynesian model, which was subsequently incorporated by Keynesian economists into their macroeconometric models, and widely used in the analysis of government macroeconomic policies. The Classical model encompassed instantaneous wage adjustment, while the Keynesian model adopted the assumption of inflexible wage rate.

The Phillips curve postulates that when excess or shortage of labour supply conditions prevails, the wage rate is assumed to adjust through time, although the adjustment is not instantaneous, to its new equilibrium level.

$$\Delta w = \tau(U^* - U) \tag{3}$$

Equation (3) represents the basic Phillips curve wage equation, with τ as the effect on the size of wage changes for a given increase in unemployment. The implication to most policy makers is the observed trade-off between unemployment and inflation rate.

2.2.3 Price Expectations Augmented Phillips (PEP) curve

Monetarists critics of the Phillips curve (particularly Milton Friedman (1968) and Phelps (1967)) pointed out two major defects of Phillips analysis; the first being the failure to distinguish nominal wages from real wages in relation to the rate of unemployment, the second being the importance of the long-run relationship between the level of wage rate and the rate of unemployment, and not between changes in the wage rate and the rate of unemployment.

Friedman's first argument was based on the fact that both firms and labour make their decisions from real and not nominal terms. This would require the Phillips curve to be augmented to include the expected inflation rate, Δp^e.

$$\Delta w = \Delta p^e + \tau(U^* - U) \tag{4}$$

Equation (4) , subsequently known as the PEP curve, was developed on the assumption that wage rates are usually fixed for a certain period of time and therefore, limiting the short run flexibility of the wage rate. Thus the expected value of future prices is incorporated in formulating the real wage, highlighting the importance of price expectations in wage determination, with its coefficient at unity to maintain constant real wage rate.

Friedman's second argument indicated his rejection of the trade-off implied by the Phillips curve. Hence, there is no permanent trade-off between inflation and unemployment. Temporary trade-off is only possible through unanticipated inflation in the short run with misperception among the labour force. In the long run, these misperceptions will be corrected when inflation is fully anticipated and markets clear, bringing unemployment back to its natural rate.

Under the acceptance of labour producing according to their marginal product at the microscopic view, labour productivity should be reflected in the wage rate:.

$$\Delta w = \Delta PRODT + \Delta p^e + \tau(U^* - U) \tag{5}$$

To incorporate the price element into the model, most economists used a simple mark-up system to describe a firm's pricing decision. With p as the price, and taking into account the role of imported prices, the price equation will be:

$$\Delta p = \Delta w - \Delta PRODT + \kappa \Delta FP \tag{6}$$

In conclusion, the PEP curve provides an explanation, one that is missing from both Classical and Keynesian models, of how an economic system can simultaneously experience both inflation and unemployment. This resulted in a wage-price two system equation.

2.3 NEW CLASSICAL AGGREGATE SUPPLY CURVE VERSUS THE PHILLIPS CURVE

The New Classical Aggregate Supply curve (or Lucas supply curve), was developed on the combination of the rational expectations hypothesis (REH) and NRH, by Lucas (1972). The common implication of this function is the neutrality of money, which states that only unexpected changes in the price level can affect real output. This function is as follows:

$$Y_t = Y_t^* + e(p_t - p_t^e) + \upsilon \tag{7}$$

υ is a random error and is developed based on 3 assumptions (1) Economic agents optimise; (2) market always clear; and (3) individuals have incomplete information.

Careful observation showed that Equation (7) is observationally equivalent to the combined relationship of the Phillips curve wage-price equation, when we substitute Equation (5) into (6) and assuming zero imported foreign inflation,

$$\Delta p = \Delta PRODT + \Delta p^e + \tau(U^* - U) - \Delta PRODT - \kappa \Delta FP \tag{8}$$

$$\tau(U^* - U) = \Delta p - \Delta p^e \tag{9}$$

Since $U^* - U \approx Y - Y^*$ we have:

$$Y = Y^* + 1/\tau \, (\Delta p - \Delta p^e) \tag{10}$$

Although the New Classical Aggregate Supply curve and the PEP curve are observationally similar, the economic theory and lines of causality used differ.

Friedman employed the hypothesis of adaptive expectations for the PEP curve as in Equation (10),

$$P^e_t = P^e_{t-1} + \delta(P_t - P^e_{t-1}) \tag{11}$$

The above equation implies that expectations adapt to past mistakes and that prices do not instantaneously move to their new equilibrium level. This permits a temporary trade-off between unemployment and inflation in the short run since money is neutral in the long run, resulting in a disequilibrium state which gradually converges through adaptive expectations. Thus the PEP curve cannot be exploited by policy makers in the long run.

In contrast, Lucas's analysis adopted the REH and the assumption of continual market clearing, which does not permit for gradual convergence. As soon as individual agents discover and correct their misperceptions, they would immediately change and correct their perception completely based on all the information available to them. A narrow version of the REH is in the form,

$$P_t = E_{t-1}(P_t / I_{t-1}) + \varepsilon_t \tag{12}$$

Thus public expectations of P_t, conditional on information (I) available at time t-1, differ from P_t only by an error which is pure white noise, ε_t. Any deviations from the natural rate is strictly temporary and that it is re-established as soon as undesirable expectational errors are corrected. This imply absolute money neutrality in all perfect market situations.

The neutrality of anticipated monetary and fiscal policies of the new classical macroeconomics model can be mathematically derived by incorporating the IS and LM curve with Equation (7).

$$\text{IS equation: } Y = aA - bR + \mu \tag{13}$$
$$\text{LM equation: } M-p = cY - dR + v \tag{14}$$

The notation A represents all the exogenous components contained with the IS curve intercept, while M-p denotes real money supply[2], and μ and v are error terms of white noise in nature. Substituting the IS equation into the LM equation, we obtain the aggregate demand curve,

$$p = M - v + ad/b(A) + d/b(\mu) - (c + d/b)Y \tag{15}$$

By solving the aggregate demand equation with the New Classical Aggregate Supply equation and under the assumption of rational expectations, $E(\mu, v, \upsilon) = 0$, we would yield the following result,

$$Y = Y^* + f[(M - M^e) - v + ad/b(A - A^e) + d/b(\mu) + \upsilon/e] \tag{16}$$

where $f = 1 / (1/e + c + d/b)$

---

[2] The variables M-p are expressed in logarithm form.

Equation (16) shed some important implications. Any correctly anticipated monetary policy ($M = M^e$) would be ineffective in affecting the level of real output. Similarly, correctly anticipated fiscal policy ($A = A^e$) will not generate any increase in real demand. Only unanticipated changes in monetary and fiscal policy is capable of affecting real output. Hence, the level of output will be randomly distributed about the potential output.

2.4 A STEADY PATH AND POLICY OPTIONS TO A LONG TERM SUSTAINABLE NON-INFLATIONARY GROWTH.

With the neutrality of both the monetary and fiscal policy, efforts to increase the long term sustainable growth path could only come in the form of improvement in capital, labour and technology. Though capital can be attracted into an economy through various incentives programmes, huge capital flow over a short period of time may not be desirable as it may cause uncertainty, especially in an open economy such as Malaysia. Technological improvement over the short run is very limited and hence, may constrain the potential growth of the economy.

Hence, it is only feasible to increase labour so as to increase the potential supply side growth of an economy. Labour supply could be controlled to a greater extent by the government through its foreign labour policy, and therefore, does not pose as much constraint as compared to capital and technological improvement. As such, the government can introduce a larger pool of foreign workers to help alleviate any tightening signals in the labour, and retrench this pool of foreign labour when the economy shows sign of cooling off. This could open up an option to the government to steer the economy along the optimal output without risking any inflationary effect, which can be quickly corrected. While guiding the economy through its foreign labour policy along the steady path, improvements in technology and labour capability could be implemented concurrently to meet up with the increasing demand of the economy.

3. THE POTENTIAL OUTPUT & NATURAL RATE OF UNEMPLOYMENT FOR MALAYSIA

3.1 INFLATIONARY TRANSMISSION MECHANISM AND WAGE PRICE DYNAMICS

3.1.1 Inflationary Transmission Mechanism

Measurement of inflation in Malaysia takes the form of consumer price index (CPI). Inflation in Malaysia is transmitted through domestic prices, import prices, as well as the level of liquidity in the market which is often influenced by the high level of foreign capital inflow into the money market. Domestic inflation is highly dependent on the level of real aggregate domestic demand of the country, while imported inflation often fluctuates according to global inflation and the Ringgit's exchange rate.

With the current status of expanding economy due to increasing external demand and robust domestic demand, the fear of demand-pull inflation is becoming increasingly visible. Real aggregate domestic demand has remained consistently high for most of the last eight years, with consumers' spending experiencing similar trend as well. Excess liquidity has often lead to ready available bank credit for consumption purposes. Money supply, although not a fundamental cause of inflation, needs to be watched closely.

Inflationary pressure could also be strongly felt from the labour market. Labour constraint has consistently created an upward pressure on wages, which could be translated into higher cost of production and higher end-prices, resulting in cost-push inflation. The problem is particularly strenuous as past experiences had proved that wage increase is more inflation linked rather than productivity linked.

The above findings indicate these three areas of inflationary element need to be kept under control to prevent any inflationary momentum from setting in.

3.1.2 Wage Price Dynamics

With the economy operating near full capacity, labour shortages and rising wage growth have become the major concerns among policy makers. The situation of wage-price spiral phenomenon is now a common question among many, or is it just a trade-off between inflation and low unemployment.

Past experiences of wage inflexibility and institutional rigidities had often resulted in wage growth climbing faster than productivity growth. In Tan and Low (1996), it is found that consumer price index unidirectionally Weiner-Granger caused wages, which is especially obvious in the manufacturing sector, whereby productivity is barely correlated to real wage. Majority of Malaysia's private sectors' wage increase are automatic and its collective agreement often last for at least three years. However, wage increase using CPI as a benchmark, will be more performance based in future. Productivity linked wage adjustment will allow for a more flexible wage mechanism that permits wages to be adjusted accord to the business environment. Incidentally, no feedback from wages to prices is found, indicating that wages may be irrelevant to the determination of inflation and to an evaluation of the monetary policy of Bank Negara.

3.2 EXTERNAL TRADE, CAPITAL MOBILITY AND OPENNESS FOR THE ECONOMY

The expansion of the Malaysian economy has been heavily dependent on the external demand, with the economy plunging into recession when world demand and commodity prices fell significantly in 1985, and recovering strongly in 1987 when world demand and commodity prices improved significantly. Her recovery in the past 8 years of rapid growth had led to a massive increase in the size of the trade sector, deeming her to be more vulnerable to external forces on the economy, especially with the greater import content of its non-resource based manufactured exports goods.

Her degree of openness (calculated as total trade over GNP) had been increasing steadily from an index of 1.10 in 1988 to 1.78 in 1995, significantly higher than the ASEAN average of 1 in 1992. The flow of capital funds has also been highly mobile in the financial market, a result of huge inflow and outflow of foreign capital funds, both long-term and short-term. The further development of a competent service and financial sector will lead us to expect greater capital flows in the future.

Being highly dependent on the external sector has important implications on her potential output and it is important for the economy to accumulate sufficient supply to meet future long term demand, so as to prevent any supply bottlenecks from recurring, and subsequently leading to economic instability.

4. DATA STRUCTURE, METHODOLOGICAL APPROACHES & ECONOMETRIC MODELING ON POTENTIAL OUTPUT

4.1 DATA SOURCES AND METHODOLOGICAL APPROACHES

The majority of the macroeconomic aggregates adopted in this study are quarterly data, but are seasonally unadjusted. The sample size of our studies begins from the period of 1985:1 to 1995:4, accounting for up to 44 observations.

Specific data limitations include the unavailability of quarterly series for our capital stock level, productivity level, real gross domestic product, unemployment rate, labour force and terms of trade. As such, capital stock level was approximated using gross fixed capital formation, with a depreciation rate of 5 percent per annum. Industrial Production Index at 1978 prices is used as a proxy for real output, with the other three series to be interpolated from annual data. Movements in external prices are proxied using exchange rates. Three seasonal dummies are also included in all the estimation.

All the sources of our data include (1) *International Financial Statistics* from the International monetary Fund (CD-ROM); (2) *Monthly & Quarterly Statistical Bulletin* (various issues) from the Bank Negara, Malaysia; and (3) *Economic Report* (various issues) from the Ministry of Finance Malaysia.

Econometric approach

Adams & Coe's (1990) systematic approach based on a two-stage procedure will be used for our subsequent systems estimation. The equations are expressed in the following general form (lowercase variables represent logarithms, while Δx indicates change in x, and is approximated using the first difference) :

$$UNE = \alpha_0 + \alpha_1(y - y^{tr}) + \alpha_2(s - s^e) + \alpha Z^U + \varepsilon_u \tag{17}$$

$$\Delta w = \Delta p^e + \beta_1(UNE - UNE^{NAT}) + \beta_2 \Delta q + (1 - \beta_2) \Delta q^{tr} + \beta Z^w + \varepsilon_w \tag{18}$$

$$y = \gamma_0 + \gamma_1 l + \gamma_2 k + \gamma_3(s - s^e) + \gamma_4 T + \gamma Z^y + \varepsilon_y \tag{19}$$

$$\Delta p = (\Delta w - \Delta q^{tr}) + \delta_1(y - y^{tr}) + \delta Z^p + \varepsilon_p \tag{20}$$

The unemployment equation is represented in Equation (17), with unemployment rate (UNE) explained by the output gap $(y - y^{tr})$, and other relevant variables (Z). The unanticipated shock $(s - s^e)$ is also introduced based on the Lucas supply curve of rational expectations, as adopted from Mishkin (1983). The Phillips curve, is represented in Equation (18), relating wage growth (Δw) to price expectations (Δp^e), the deviation of actual from the natural rate of unemployment (U^{NAT}), and a weighted average among the growth of actual and trend productivity. In addition to labour (l) and capital (k) in the production function, unanticipated shock is also included in the equation. The change in prices (Δp) equation in (20) consist of the growth of normalised unit labour costs $(\Delta w - \Delta q^{tr})$ and output gap.

The first stage of the estimation process will begin with single equation estimate to determine the functional forms of each of the four equations, and specifications to quantify anticipated price and monetary growth so as to arrive at the unanticipated movements

Rational expectations implies that the anticipation of s_t will be formed optimally, using all relevant available information, which takes the form of a forecasting equation like

$$s_t = \lambda D_{t-1} + \mu_t, \tag{21}$$

where

D_{t-1} = a vector of variables used to forecast s_t, which are available at time t-1 and before,

λ = a vector of coefficients,

μ_t = an error term that is serially uncorrelated with any information available at t-1.

Thus the optimal forecast for s_t involves taking the expectations of Equation (21) conditional on information available at t-1, to arrive at Equation (22),

$$s_t^e = \lambda D_{t-1} \tag{22}$$

By substituting this into the Lucas-aggregate supply curve in Equation (13), and including the test on rationality and neutrality hypothesis, the equation will take the general form of

$$y_t = y_t^* + \sum \gamma_i(s_t - s_t^e) + \sum \delta_i s_t^e + \varepsilon_y \tag{23}$$

Estimated separately, rationality of expectation is imposed since the coefficient γ appears in both equation. The neutrality principle, is also imposed if δ is constrained to zero.

The second stage of the approach will involve the derivation of the natural rate of unemployment and the optimal output. These four system equations, with the expectations equation, will be subsequently estimated using non linear three stage least square (NL3LS) to obtain the natural rate of unemployment and optimal output.

4.2 SINGLE EQUATION ESTIMATION: SPECIFICATION AND ESTIMATION RESULTS

Single-equation estimates for trend output and productivity starts from 1985:1 and 1985:2 respectively, while the other equations estimates will cover the period from 1987:2 to 1995:4. All equations were estimated using ordinary least squares. Specifications include lags of up to 4 period, since the inclusion of irrelevant lags will only reduce the power of fit, but omission of relevant variables will result in biased estimates. Both the trend output and trend productivity were estimated by fitting a trend line through its actual values.

4.2.1 Inflation Expectation

The price expectation growth equation consists of the following variable: one lagged government expenditure, one lagged interest rate, two lagged Ringgit against U.S. exchange rate (u.s.), and four lagged values of price growth. Predictors other than its own history are also included as explanatory variables, since this would result in a more superior fit, as in Barro (1977). Government expenditure is expected to have a positive impact on domestic prices, since it represents additional demand in the economy. For fear of over-heating and high inflation, Bank Negara has been maintaining a tight monetary policy, partly through high interest rate policy. Hence, interest rate is believed to have an active role in forming price expectations. The U.S. exchange rate is included, since most exchange rates are pegged to the greenback and U.S. is Malaysia's second largest importer after Japan in 1995.

Finally, the price expectations growth equation also included four lagged values of price growth, to pick up any elements of serial dependence or lagged adjustment that might not been captured by the other explanatory variables.

The estimated price equation is as follows, with standard error in parentheses,

$$\Delta p_t^e = -0.42 + 0.10\Delta p_{t-1} + 0.34\Delta p_{t-2} + 0.23\Delta p_{t-3} - 1.20\Delta p_{t-4} + 0.05govt_{t-1} - 0.14int_{t-1}$$
$$\qquad (0.21) \quad (0.12) \qquad (0.15) \qquad (0.13) \qquad (0.19) \qquad (0.02) \qquad (0.05)$$

$$- 0.17u.s._{t-1} + 0.30u.s._{t-2} - 0.006DUMV1 - 0.0001DUMV2 + 0.001DUMV3. \qquad (24)$$
$$\quad (0.10) \qquad\quad (0.10) \qquad\quad (0.006) \qquad\qquad (0.005) \qquad\qquad (0.006)$$

$R^2 = 0.77$,   SEE = 0.01,   Durbin's h alternative = 0.94.

The historical effect of price growth on expected price growth is significant up to four lag periods. Government expenditure is significantly positive, implying that any increase in it does have an inflationary effect on the economy. The significant negative impact of interest rate on prices proves that the tight monetary policy is indeed effective in controlling inflation. The combined positive effect of the two significant lagged U.S. currency implies that a depreciation of Ringgit against the greenback may result in higher imported inflation and hence, higher domestic prices.

4.2.2 Expected Monetary Growth

The monetary growth ($\Delta m1$) equation includes the following variables: four lagged values of monetary growth, and four lagged interest rate. The historical effects of money supply are tested only up to four lags, with the assumption that lags effects would only amount up to 4 periods.

The expected monetary growth estimated with the above mentioned variables is,

$$\Delta m1_t^e = 0.15 + 0.66\Delta m1_{t-1} + 0.23\Delta m1_{t-2} + 0.08\Delta m1_{t-3} - 0.62\Delta m1_{t-4} + 0.04int_{t-1} + 0.10int_{t-2}$$
$$\qquad (0.18) \quad (0.17) \qquad\quad (0.23) \qquad\quad (0.26) \qquad\quad (0.24) \qquad\quad (0.21) \qquad (0.10)$$

$$+ 0.015.int_{t-3} - 0.19int_{t-4} - 0.003DUMV1 + 0.003DUMV2 + 0.004DUMV3. \qquad (25)$$
$$\quad (0.13) \qquad\quad (0.09) \qquad\quad (0.02) \qquad\qquad (0.02) \qquad\qquad (0.02)$$

$R^2 = 0.80$,   SEE = 0.03,   Durbin's h alternative = 0.67

The equation seems to imply that expected money growth has a significant dependence on its historical value, indicating that there may be some lag adjustment not captured by existing variables. The coefficients of interest rate and its lags are found to be significant. Unanticipated money growth can be derived as the residual of Equation (25), or alternatively, the difference between the actual and fitted values of monetary growth.

4.2.3 Unemployment Rate Equation

Specifications of the unemployment rate (UNE) consist of the current output gap to account for the cyclical movements of the unemployment rate. Both the anticipated (s_t^e) and unanticipated ($s_t - s_t^e$) price growth or monetary growth are also included, to test on the hypothesis of rationality and neutrality. Specifically government expenditure and the Japanese Yen , are also used as additional explanatory in the equation.

The estimated results on the inclusion on either the anticipated and unanticipated price and monetary shock are as follows:

$UNE_t = 15.03 - 0.65(y - y^{tr})_t + 1.20\Delta p_t^e - 0.54(\Delta p_t - \Delta p_t^e) - 2.51gvt_t + 2.34gvt_{t-1} + 0.24gvt_{t-2}$
       (3.13)   (0.65)   (0.70)   (1.17)   (1.12)   (1.55)   (1.14)

$\qquad - 1.49gvt_{t-3} - 0.42yen_t + 0.74yen_{t-1} - 0.22yen_{t-2} + 0.52yen_{t-3} + 1.26UNE_{t-1} - 0.40UNE_{t-2}$
         (0.66)   (0.31)   (0.27)   (0.26)   (0.28)   (0.13)   (0.12)

$\qquad + 0.01DUMV1 - 0.0007DUMV2 - 0.002DUMV3.$ (26)
         (0.02)   (0.02)   (0.02)

$\qquad R^2 = 0.99, \quad SEE = 0.05, \quad \text{Durbin's h alternative} = 1.23$

$UNE_t = 15.03 - 0.78(y - y^{tr})_t - 0.40\Delta m1_t^e - 0.51(\Delta m1_t - \Delta m1_t^e) - 1.48gvt_t + 1.30gvt_{t-1}$
       (2.78)   (0.56)   (0.15)   (0.29)   (0.93)   (1.30)

$\qquad + 0.02gvt_{t-2} - 1.25gvt_{t-3} - 0.19yen_t + 0.58yen_{t-1} - 0.22yen_{t-2} + 0.53yen_{t-3} + 1.20UNE_{t-1}$
         (0.95)   (0.55)   (0.25)   (0.23)   (0.22)   (0.24)   (0.11)

$\qquad - 0.34UNE_{t-2} + 0.02DUMV1 + 0.01DUMV2 + 0.005DUMV3.$ (27)
         (0.10)   (0.02)   (0.02)   (0.02)

$\qquad R^2 = 0.99, \quad SEE = 0.04, \quad \text{Durbin's h alternative} = -1.37.$

It is observed that both the hypothesis of neutrality and hypothesis is rejected in Equation (26) at 95 percent significance level, and that the expected price growth gives the wrong sign. However, in Equation (27), the hypothesis of neutrality and rationality by monetary growth are significantly different from zero at the 95 percent significance level. This could imply that the monetary growth captures the effect of the shock better than the price growth, since money reflects both the nominal and real effect, while price only consists of the nominal effect of the shock. The coefficients of the other variables do not differ much in both equations.

4.2.4 Production Function Equation

The production function equation consists of labour (λ) and capital ($1-\lambda$) contribution towards growth of the economy, with the two coefficients being constrained to sum up to one. A time trend variable is also included as a proxy for technological progress. Government expenditure, which is significant in the unemployment equation, will also be considered. Similarly, with interest rate being an effective tool in stabilising the economy, it is included into the equation estimates as well. The U.S. dollar exchange rate is used as a proxy to account for the effect of the external environment in the Malaysian's market. Both the anticipated and unanticipated shock are estimated as part of the equation as well.

Two sets of estimation results are produced, one set with, λ and ($1-\lambda$) taken as estimated, and the other set with λ constrained to 0.85. The first set of estimated results with the price and monetary growth shock are as follows:

$$y_t = - 9.82 - 0.02T - 0.23l_t + 1.23k_t + 0.03\Delta p_t^e - 0.42(\Delta p_t - \Delta p_t^e) - 0.05gvt_t + 0.28gvt_{t-1}$$
$$\quad (1.84) \quad (0.02) \quad (0.67) \quad (na) \quad (0.23) \quad (0.34) \quad (0.30) \quad (0.22)$$

$$+ 0.13int_t + 0.21int_{t-1} - 0.07int_{t-2} - 0.20int_{t-3} - 0.22u.s._t + 0.50u.s._{t-1} + 0.29y_{t-1}$$
$$\quad (0.08) \quad (0.10) \quad (0.06) \quad (0.07) \quad (0.23) \quad (0.19) \quad (0.15)$$

$$- 0.04DUMV1 - 0.04DUMV2 + 0.02DUMV3. \tag{28}$$
$$\quad (0.009) \quad (0.01) \quad (0.01)$$

$R^2 = 0.96$, SEE = 0.02, Durbin Watson Stat. = 2.12.

$$y_t = - 9.62 - 0.04T - 0.59l_t + 1.59k_t + 0.06\Delta m1_t^e + 0.26(\Delta m1_t - \Delta m1_t^e) - 0.009gvt_t$$
$$\quad (1.63) \quad (0.02) \quad (na) \quad (0.64) \quad (0.07) \quad (0.11) \quad (0.25)$$

$$+ 0.34gvt_{t-1} + 0.14int_t + 0.26int_{t-1} - 0.08int_{t-2} - 0.26int_{t-3} - 0.40u.s._t + 0.67u.s._{t-1} + 0.36y_{t-1}$$
$$\quad (0.20) \quad (0.07) \quad (0.10) \quad (0.05) \quad (0.08) \quad (0.19) \quad (0.15) \quad (0.14)$$

$$- 0.04DUMV1 - 0.04DUMV2 + 0.02DUMV3. \tag{29}$$
$$\quad (0.007) \quad (0.01) \quad (0.01)$$

$R^2 = 0.97$, SEE = 0.01, Durbin-Watson statistic = 2.21.

Similar results with the unemployment rate equation are observed. The hypothesis of neutrality and rationality are both rejected in Equation (28), with price shock giving the incorrect sign as well. In Equation (29), the hypothesis of rationality is not rejected at the 95 percent significance level, while that of neutrality is statistically insignificant,

However, this set of estimates does not give a logical explanation on the time trend (T) and on the contribution of the labour and capital input when they are estimated as part of the equation. Thus the next set of estimates will restrict labour contribution to real output at 85 percent, with capital at 15 percent. The estimated results are as follows:

$$y_t = - 7.71 + 0.009T + 0.85l_t + 0.15k_t + 0.10\Delta p_t^e - 0.36(\Delta p_t - \Delta p_t^e) - 0.30gvt_t + 0.34gvt_{t-1}$$
$$\quad (2.10) \quad (0.003) \quad (na) \quad (na) \quad (0.24) \quad (0.36) \quad (0.24) \quad (0.23)$$

$$+ 0.11int_t + 0.21int_{t-1} - 0.009int_{t-2} - 0.13int_{t-3} - 0.43u.s._t + 0.43u.s._{t-1} + 0.31(y - 0.85\lambda l$$
$$\quad (0.08) \quad (0.10) \quad (0.05) \quad (0.06) \quad (0.20) \quad (0.20) \quad (0.16)$$

$$- 0.15\lambda k)_{t-1} - 0.04DUMV1 - 0.04DUMV2 + 0.02DUMV3. \tag{30}$$
$$\quad (0.009) \quad (0.01) \quad (0.01)$$

$R^2 = 0.99$, SEE = 0.02, Durbin's h alternative = 0.92.

$y_t = -7.37 - 0.008T + 0.85l_t + 0.15k_t - 0.007\Delta m1_t^e + 0.20(\Delta m1_t - \Delta m1_t^e) - 0.32gvt_t$

(2.01)   (0.003)   (na)   (na)   (0.07)   (0.11)   (0.23)

$+ 0.36gvt_{t-1} + 0.10int_t + 0.22int_{t-1} - 0.01int_{t-2} - 0.13int_{t-3} - 0.60u.s._t + 0.58u.s._{t-1}$

(0.22)   (0.08)   (0.11)   (0.05)   (0.06)   (0.19)   (0.17)

$+ 0.34(y - 0.85\lambda l - 0.15\lambda k)_{t-1} - 0.04DUMV1 - 0.04DUMV2 + 0.02DUMV3.$ (31)

(0.16)   (0.008)   (0.01)   (0.01)

$R^2 = 0.99$,   SEE $= 0.02$,   Durbin's h alternative $= 0.65$.

The imposition of the labour share coefficient improves the results significantly. The time trend (T) is significant for both equations, and the fit improved as well. Results on the two hypothesis do not differ much from the earlier set of estimation. The hypothesis of neutrality and rationality are rejected in Equation (30). On the other hand, the hypothesis of rationality using monetary growth is significant, with neutrality being rejected.

4.2.5 Phillips Curve

Based on earlier discussions, the nominal wage growth rate is specified with inflation expectations (Δp^e), the unemployment rate (U), and changes in actual and trend productivity $(\Delta q$ & $\Delta q^{tr})$, and other relevant variables. It is found that changes in palm oil prices has a significant impact on the growth of nominal wages.

In equilibrium, nominal wage growth should grow as a result of the realised price expectations and labour productivity. Malaysia's nominal wage growth is expected to be significantly influenced by price expectations, since it is observed in Tan & Low (1996) that wages in Malaysia are pegged to its consumer price index on the 3 year wage agreement.

$\Delta w_t = 0.69 + 0.57\Delta p_t^e - 0.01UNE_t - 0.07\Delta q_t + 0.02\Delta oil_t - 0.05\Delta oil_{t-1} - 0.09\Delta oil_{t-2}$

(0.02)   (0.29)   (0.003)   (0.18)   (0.05)   (0.05)   (0.04)

$+ 0.006DUMV1 + 0.03DUMV2 + 0.03DUMV3$ (32)

(0.01)   (0.01)   (0.01)

$R^2 = 0.68$,   SEE $= 0.02$,   Durbin-Watson statistic $= 1.62$

The estimated equation shows that nominal wage growth is significantly affected by inflation expectations, with productivity changes wrongly signed and not significant. However, it is observed that the fit of the equation is not relatively high and hence, may not have capture the effect of productivity on wages. The coefficient of unemployment rate is statistically significant, implying that excess demand in labour will lead to tightening of the labour market, and subsequently translated into higher nominal wage growth.

4.2.6 Price Equation

The price equation in Equation (20) imply that in equilibrium, inflation should grow in line with the growth of normalised unit labour costs, and its other relevant variables, with no output gap. The other variables specified in the equation are U.S. exchange rate, interest rate, and government expenditure.

The estimated price growth equation is as follows:

$$\Delta p_t = -0.34 + 0.12(\Delta w - \Delta q^{tr}) - 0.19(y - y^{tr}) + 0.10 u.s._{-t} - 0.35 u.s._{-t-1} + 0.26 u.s._{-t-2} + 0.11 int_t$$

(0.18) (0.16)   (0.24)   (0.18)   (0.24)   (0.15)   (0.06)

$$- 0.16 int_{t-1} + 0.04 govt_t + 0.02 DUMV1 + 0.01 DUMV2 + 0.02 DUMV3. \tag{33}$$

(0.07)   (0.01)   (0.02)   (0.02)   (0.02)

$R^2 = 0.50$, SEE $= 0.02$, Durbin-Watson statistic $= 1.92$.

The estimated price growth equation shows that normalised unit labour costs and output gap do not have any significant impact on inflation. Interest rate is detected to have a negative influence on prices, while both the exchange rate with U.S. and the government expenditure are significantly positive. These existing explanatory variables explain well with the correct expected sign. However, they may not be sufficient in explaining fully the movement in inflation.

5. SOME TENTATIVE FINDINGS AND POLICY IMPLICATIONS OF MACRO POLICY OPTIONS

5.1 INTERPRETATION OF THE ECONOMETRIC FINDINGS

From our empirical results, its indicates that monetary growth is more superior to price growth on capturing the effect of an unanticipated shock in the economy. Following the results using monetary growth, the hypothesis of neutrality and rationality are both not rejected in the unemployment equation. Hence, the theory that only unanticipated monetary growth can affect real economic variables is rejected. Specifically in the labour market, monetary growth can be increased to induce greater employment, and hence reduce unemployment rate.

With reference to the production function equation, only the hypothesis of rationality is not rejected, with the neutrality principle rejected. This is in agreement with the Macro Rational Expectation (MRE) model, which is not rejected in explaining Malaysia's real output. This means that real output cannot be induced through higher monetary growth.

The results imply that there is greater market imperfections in the labour market, while imperfections in the output market is minimal after experiencing consistent high growth in the past decade. Higher government expenditure is found to be capable of reducing unemployment and increasing real output in the economy.

5.2 INTERPRETATION OF MACRO POLICY OPTIONS

Some important policy implications can be derived from our empirical results. Firstly, the government is able to influence the level of unemployment through monetary management, to take advantage of the significant market imperfection in the labour market. At the present level of tight labour market, Bank Negara can adopt a tight monetary policy to prevent any excess demand on labour from increasing further.

Secondly, although the careful regulation of money supply is effective in the labour market, it is ineffective against the output market. In other words, the government may not be able to induce higher growth in the economy through easing its monetary policy. In the long run, the monetary ineffectiveness in sustaining long term growth applies in the Malaysian economy. Thirdly, higher government expenditure is able to drive the economy towards higher growth and lower unemployment. However, this may be at the cost of higher inflation rate. Fourthly, an effective management of the movements in the exchange rate between Rinngit and U.S. dollar can have a significant impact on the economy. This conclusion is not surprising, given the relative openness of the Malaysian's economy and its high level trade and investment with the United States, and Singapore as well, whose currency is also significantly affected by movements of the greenback.

5.3 AGENDA FOR FUTURE RESEARCH AND FURTHER IMPROVEMENT

Due to the data constraints faced in the specification process, further research and improvements in the equation estimates could be done in the following areas:

- Specifications in both the price and wage equation under the proposed system estimate could be improved through the use quarterly export and import price index data, which is currently not available,

- Suitable proxies for structural variables in the unemployment equation could be introduced to account for the structural changes in the Malaysia labour market,

- A joint estimation on the principle of rationality and neutrality can be carried using non linear three stage least square estimation, together with the rest of the system equations, instead of using the Barro's two step approach, given its limited implications,

- Subsequently, the optimal output growth and natural rate of unemployment could be derived from the system estimate and this will have important implications on the policy management of the Malaysian government.

REFERENCES

Adams, C. and D. Coe (1990): "A Systems Approach to Estimating the Natural Rate of Unemployment and Potential Output for the United States," *IMF Staff Papers*, Vol.37, No.2.

Adams, C., Paul R. Fenton., and Flemming Larsen (1987): "Potential Output in Major Industrial Countries," *Staff Studies for the World Economic Outlook,* World Economic and Financial Surveys (Washington: International Monetary Fund, August, 1987), 1-38.

Bank Negara Malaysia, *Annual Report*, various issues from 1985-1995.

Bank Negara Malaysia, *Quarterly Bulletin*, various issues from 1985-1995.

Barro, R.J. (1977b): "Unanticipated Money Growth and Unemployment in the United States", *American Economic Review*, 67, 101-105.

Friedman, Milton (1968): "The Role of Monetary Policy", *American Ecoomic Review* (Nashville, Tennessee), Vol.58.

Gan Wee Beng (1993): "Aggregate Supply and the Wage-Price Mechanism: Some Implications for Inflation Stabilisation in Malaysia", Paper presented at HIDD-ISIS seminar.

Lucas, R.E., Jr. (1972): "Expectations and the Neutrality of Money", *Journal of Economic Theory*, 4, 103-24.

Minford, Patrick and David Peel (1992): *A Rational Expectations Macroeconomics: An Introductory Handbook,* Oxford : Blackwell Publishers.

Ministry of Finance Malaysia, *Economic Report 1996/97,* Kuala Lumpur: National Printing Department.

Mishkin, F.S. (1982): *A Rational Expectations Approach to Macroeconometrics,* Chicago : University of Chicago Press.

National Productivity Corporation Malaysia, *Productivity Report,* 1994.

Okun, Arthur (1962): "Potential GNP: Its Measurement and Significance," *Proceedings of the Business and Economics Section of the American Statistical Association,* Washington, D.C.: American Statistical Association, pp. 98-104.

Phelps, Edmund (1967): "Phillips Curve, Expectations of Inflation and Optimal Unemployment over Time," *Economica,* Vol.34, (August 1967), pp. 254-81.

Phillips, A. William (1958): "The Relation between Unemployment and the Rate of Change of Money Wage Rates in the United Kingdom, 1861-1957," *Economica,* New Series, 25:100, November, 283-299.

Tan, Khee Giap and Cheng, Chee Seng (1995): "The Causal Nexus of Money, Output and Prices in Malaysia," *Applied Economics,* 1995, 27, pp.1245-1251.

Tan, Khee Giap and Low, Linda (1996): "Wage-Employment Relationship in Malaysia.".

Zarina Zainal Abidin and Shariman Alwani (1994): "Growth, Inflation and Potential Output." *Bank Negara Malaysia Discussion Papers No. 33,* Economics Department,Bank Negara Malaysia.

ASEAN—5 and China: Trade Competitors?

Lim Dyi Chang
&
Mike Leu Gwo-Jiun

Nanyang Business School, Nanyang Technological University, Nanyang Avenue, Singapore 639798
Fax: +(65) 792.4217, Tel: +(65) 799.1404, Email: agjleu@ntu.edu.sg

Abstract There is a very strong belief that fast-growing China is overtaking the ASEAN-5 nations, namely Singapore, Malaysia, Indonesia, Thailand and the Philippines, in the international trade arena. In this study, we use Balassa's (1965) revealed comparative advantage (RCA) indices and SITC (revision 2) trade statistics to test this belief. We find that China had largely caught up with the 3 relatively less developed ASEAN-5 countries (Thailand, Indonesia and the Philippines) between 1980 and 1994. However, Singapore and Malaysia are relatively safe from Chinese competition. In addition, product-specific analysis shows that there is indeed competition in many products, and China has wrested the comparative advantage of several export commodities away from the ASEAN-5 countries.

1. INTRODUCTION

The economic issue currently pertaining to China is no longer whether her economy will open up further, but rather, how fast will she continue to open up. Blessed with a vast amount of practically all kinds of resources and a 1.2 billion population, the sky is the limit to her economic growth potential. Since the Chinese economy adopted the open door policy in 1979, her exports have been growing at an average rate of 14.8 percent between 1980 and 1994.[1] With this rate of growth, her exports increased by 6.2 times and her share of world exports reached 2.74 percent in 1994[2] (which in 1980 was only 0.96 percent). Certainly, this phenomenon has stirred great concern, especially among developing countries, about the likelihood of encountering trade competition. In particular, the ASEAN countries have felt the pressure most intensely. Generally considered as the third tier of newly industrialising countries (NICs), the ASEAN-5 nations, namely Malaysia, Thailand, Indonesia, the Philippines and Singapore (which actually belonged to the second tier NICs) also performed exceptionally well. Thailand's exports increased by 6.54 folds and enjoyed an average annual export growth rate of 15 percent over similar period. Singapore and Malaysia quadrupled their exports with an average growth of 12 percent; and the exports of Philippines and Indonesia almost doubled with an average growth of about 5 percent between 1980 and 1994.

The 'four Asian tigers' (Taiwan, South Korea, Hong Kong and Singapore) took the lead in trying to catch up with Japan, followed closely by the ASEAN[3] nations, and then China, India, Vietnam and Cambodia. Conventional wisdom has suggested that due to differences in the economic characteristics (such as wage rates, availability of skilled

---

[1] All further trade related figures are calculated by authors from the World Trade Database by Statistics Canada.

[2] Shares of world exports for USA, Singapore, Malaysia, Thailand, Indonesia and the Philippines are 12.43%, 2.14%, 1.33%, 1.03%, 0.95% and 0.30% respectively.

[3] Unless otherwise stated, ASEAN consists of six countries, including Brunei.

labour and industrial policies adopted by the government) of individual countries, those in the earlier waves of export development could be caught up by the better performers in the subsequent waves. If a country is able to keep pace with an early starter, she is expected to replace the importance of those 'backward' export industries that are forsaken by the 'leader' and also, to compete directly in the more advanced industries. It is thought that the comparative advantage in traditional unskilled labour-intensive product lines will gradually and systematically shift from the relatively more industrialised nation to the economically less developed ones (for example from Japan to the NICs, from the NICs to the ASEAN nations, and from the ASEAN nations to China). In the mean time, the more industrialised nation will push ahead into the territory of relatively higher technology and capital-intensive industries.

The present study attempts to find out whether China's economic development, with her strong growth in exports, poses a threat to the ASEAN-5 countries in the trade arena. In Section 2, we define the methodology of the study. Section 3, examines the empirical findings and eventually in Section 4, we will give a broad summary and conclusion.

2. METHODOLOGY

In an article by Balassa (1965), export-import ratios of similar but not homogeneous goods under the same SITC product category were used to approximate the comparative advantage of a country in producing that category of product. However, the assumptions of uniformity of tastes and uniform incidence of duties are not fulfilled in the real world. In an article by Lutz (1987), shifts of comparative advantage from one country to another was measured by changes in export shares in 3-digit product categories of SITC 8 (miscellaneous manufactures) and SITC 65 (textiles). But concentrating only on the labour-intensive products of the developing countries will not enable us to see the overall comparative advantage positions of the nations. In the present study, the revealed comparative advantage (RCA) method[4] is used. The RCA index is calculated based on the following formula :

$$RCA_{i,j} = (X_{i,j} / X_i) / (M_j / W)$$

where : $X_{i,j}$ =   world's total import of jth good from country i,

X_i =   world's total import from country i,

M_j =   world's total import of jth good,

W =   world's total import of all goods.

This formula incorporates two important concepts that are related to comparative advantage. The first, as shown in the numerator of the equation, is the share of the export commodity in the country's total exports. The second, as shown in the denominator, is the import share of the same good in the world market. The RCA index puts them together and shows the relative importance of the exporting country in that product in the world economy.[5]

---

[4] This method is used in Balassa's 1965 paper concurrently with export-import ratios.

[5] Therefore, if Country A has a higher RCA index for a particular export product than Country B, then A is said to have comparative advantage in that product relative to B.

The period chosen for study is from 1980 to 1994. This time span of 15 years is of particular importance to the countries involved. It is especially so for China, which officially opened her doors to foreign investors, for (mainly) technology imports, and the lucrative global market for her own exports in 1979. The export-led industrialisation of the ASEAN-5 nations (which began in 1960s for Singapore, Malaysia and the Philippines, 1970s for Thailand and Indonesia), was beginning to translate into phenomenal economic growth in the period of study as well.

3-digit SITC product categories, common to all six countries and with export shares of more than 0.01 percent of the total exports, are used to calculate the RCA indices. Filtering out only the common goods exported by all the six countries is a rather important step in this study because it allows for unbiased comparisons of the eventual RCA figures using correlation analysis.[6]

Two important markets are chosen to represent the world market—the United States and European Community (12). The scope is limited to the US and EC-12 markets for several reasons. First, these markets are the two largest import markets of the world which account for 15.34 percent and 36.46 percent (on average over the past 15 years) of the world's total imports respectively. Second, Japan's trade relationships with developing countries are relatively lopsided and her imports are skewed towards standardised products. Her re-imports of electronic products from developing countries after the appreciation of yen following the Plaza Accord in 1985 further complicated the picture. Therefore we drop it from our analysis. Emphasis of the present study will be on the US market because it is one single country, and there is no need to worry about the different trade restrictions imposed by different nations of the EC-12 market on the six countries under study. The imports of US also demonstrated greater diversity than those of the EC-12.

The computed RCA indices of all the common exports among China and the ASEAN-5, and in the two markets over the 15 years, are further analysed using correlation methods to examine the shift in each nation's comparative advantage position.

3. EMPIRICAL FINDINGS AND ECONOMIC IMPLICATIONS

3.1 COMPARISONS OF THE OVERALL RCA INDICES

3.1.1 Year-to-Year Comparisons (US Market)

Since comparative advantage is expected to determine the structure of exports, the extent of export competition between any two countries can be inferred from the similarity of their export structures. One way to examine that relationship is through the comparisons of the Spearman Rank Correlation coefficients of the RCA indices between each of the ASEAN-5 nation with China over the period of interest in each market.[7] The results of the computation are shown in Table 1 of the appendix. An overview of the findings in the US market shows that China's RCA has various degrees of correlation with each of the ASEAN-5 nations. At one extreme, the correlation coefficients are negative and slightly

---

[6] For example, China exports a much larger array of products than Singapore. Entering zeros for those products that Singapore does not export will bias the outcome towards insignificant relationships.

[7] However since Spearman Rank Correlation Coefficients only consider the rankings of the RCA indices, the level of 'similarity' of export structures should be interpreted more cautiously.

significant between China and Singapore. At the other end, the coefficients are strong and positive between both Indonesia and Thailand and China. There appears to be no meaningful relationship between the export structure of Malaysia and China, and in the case of China and the Philippines, the strength and significance of the relationship appears to be fading.

An understanding of the Chinese economy is crucial when interpreting our findings. The Chinese economy, especially at the beginning of market liberalisation (early 1980s), was still very much a command economy. There were a lot of ideological differences about how and how much to open up the economy among the top leaders of the country. It has been documented by J. Howell (1993) that since its opening until 1990, China had experienced a total of six cycles of economic tightening and easing, involving several unexpected reversals of policy decisions and causing various degrees of impacts on the economy. The effects of the power struggles among the top echelon of leaders should not be ignored as well. However, the strength of the 'invisible hand' has proven to be rather unstoppable. In 1978, the conservative Premier Hua Guofeng had used Lenin and Stalin to justify the speed-up in trade . He said China could effectively make use of foreign factors such as foreign loans, machines and experts for further growth, and Deng Xiaoping had displayed even less "self-reliant" sentiments (Jonathan 1989).

In terms of manufactured exports, China was a very slow starter. For 7 years after adoption of the open door policy, the share of manufactured products (SITC 5-8) of her total exports showed marginal increases of only 4 percent (from 67.9 percent in 1980 to 72 percent in 1986). But after that, her manufactured exports experienced robust growth, reaching a high of 95 percent of total exports in 1994! The opening significantly affected the import sector of the economy first when the state empowered provincial authorities to sign import contracts for technology-related (mainly heavy machinery) and intermediate products. Huge trade account deficits were recorded especially in the years 1984-6 mostly with Japan and USA, which consequently, led to a policy that favoured export growth and the judicious use of international borrowing over the 'dangerous' policy of directly clamping down on imports.

While it was advantageous for China to have substantial energy exports, the depressed state of oil prices in the early 1980s reduced foreign exchange income from oil. This drop appears to have forced China both to boost her output of other primary goods (foodstuffs) and to put more effort into expanding machinery and manufactured goods exports. A decade-long decline in the world commodity prices from peaks in the early 1980s has further encouraged China to switch towards higher value-added goods with greater market potential (Jonathan 1989). This is evidenced by export data which shows that the share of SITC 7 (machinery and transport equipment) products of total exports grew from 0.5 percent in 1980 to 2.8 percent in 1986, and then took a great leap to reach 22.6 percent in 1994. Spectacular growth is also observed in the SITC 8 product category (miscellaneous manufactured articles), which include furniture, handbags, clothing accessories and footwear. This product group had a share of 58 percent of total exports in 1994, up from 36 percent in 1980. However, the good performance in SITC 7 and 8 categories was achieved at the expense of declining shares of the SITC 5-6 products (Chemicals and related products, and manufactured goods classified chiefly by materials), which include plastic chemicals, textile, iron and steel, and articles of paper pulp, as well as SITC 0-4 products (generally classified as non-manufactures).[8]

3.1.1.1 Thailand and Indonesia and China

As shown in Table 1 of US market, the complete significance of the correlation coefficients of the RCA indices between both Thailand and Indonesia and China suggests that there is a great similarity of export structures among the three of them. A further investigation of export structures correlation between Thailand and Indonesia confirmed this possibility. The economic implication of this finding is rather displeasing from the viewpoints of both Thailand and Indonesia. Under Balassa's (1983) stage theory of comparative advantage, it shows that China has managed to replicate the export patterns of both these ASEAN-5 nations (in fact more that of Indonesia due to higher coefficients). This suggests that Thailand and Indonesia no longer enjoy a competitive edge in exports over China (at least in the US market).

3.1.1.2 The Philippines and China

The findings are even more ominous for the Philippines. The decrease in similarity of export pattern between her and China in the US market may be interpreted as the comparative advantage position of the Philippines' exports having been surpassed by that of China! Except for the last few years, political and economic mismanagement in the Philippines had prevented her domestic industries from developing along the lines of comparative advantage. The industrialisation effort has been frustrated by inadequate foreign exchange earnings and heavy reliance on imported inputs. Macro economic imbalances (inflation and debt repayment) had also hindered industrialisation, and inconsistent electricity supply had caused serious disruptions to production lines almost everyday (Tan and Low 1996). With a large proportion of her exports in the primary products category (11 percent) and in the category of special transactions (44 percent), it might take the Philippines some effort to close the export comparative advantage gap between herself and China.

3.1.1.3 Singapore and China

In the case of Singapore and China, the correlation coefficients in Table 1 of US market show that China's export structure has never come close to that of Singapore throughout the years of study. Probably due to Singapore's deliberate high wage policy implemented in 1979 to help the economy shift away from unskilled labour-intensive industries to technology and more human capital-intensive industries, China was left even further behind in terms of export performance (as shown by the significant negative correlation from 1982 to 1991). From 1990 onwards, the negative relationships become less significant. This could be an indication that China was slowly trying to replicate Singapore's export path. Also because the Singapore government has been encouraging domestic entrepreneurs to invest in China to tap labour resources, it would increase the exports of Singapore in the labour-intensive product category, and thus closing the disparity of export structure with China[9]. Then again, Singapore has been pushing further into the financial and services industries which, together with manufacturing sector, are presently called the "twin engines" of growth. In so doing, and due to the acute labour

---

[8] In absolute amounts, most of them have not been declining. Rather, their relatively slower growth has led to the decline in their export shares

[9] Note that the exports of a firm that is wholly owned by Singaporeans or a Singapore registered company in China, are still recorded as Singapore's exports.

shortage problem, Singapore will further direct her resources into high value-added manufacturing industries. Singapore is thus well positioned away from the Chinese threat at least in the foreseeable future.

3.1.1.4 Malaysia and China

As for the case of Malaysia and China in the US, we could not make definite conclusions based on the correlation of their RCA figures, except for two years-1986 and 1987. This is consistent with the study by Jomo K. S. and C. Edwards (1993), which indicated that industrialisation in Malaysia since the late 1950s can be divided into four phases. The first phase of import-substituting industrialisation started in the late 1950s to 1960s. The second phase involved export-oriented industrialisation, beginning from the late 1960s. The third stage was a push of import-substitution, involving heavy industrialisation in the first half of the 1980s. The fourth and current phase is a renewed commitment to and growth of export-oriented industrialisation which started in the second half of 1980s. Due to Malaysia's relatively earlier start in export expansion, China has lagged behind Malaysia in export performance by quite a big margin. In fact, since Malaysia and Singapore share a rather similar export structure, Malaysia is instead close on the heels of Singapore in the export sector (with reference to the results of correlation test between them provided in Table 1 also).

3.1.2 Year-to-Year Comparisons (European Community Market)

To substantiate the above findings, similar methodology of correlating RCA indices is applied to the exports of the six countries to the European Community (EC-12) market. It should first be noted that protectionist practices aimed at maintaining higher levels of intra-EC exports, have had a big impart on the exports of developing countries to the EC-12 market. This limit on the shift of comparative advantage in manufactured products away from the EC countries could perhaps have made it more difficult for developing countries to shift production facilities into new product lines, and at the same time, made it more likely that the developing countries would maintain older export productions (Lutz 1987). A look at Table 3 in the appendix, reveals that there are indeed more products belonging to the labour-intensive and non-manufacturing categories imported by the EC-12 than by the US. It could thus be seen in Table 1 of European Community market that due to such restraints, there appears to be more significant correlation relationships between China and the ASEAN-5 nations. This shows more similar export structures, in general, between them and implicitly suggests greater trade competition among them within the EC-12 market.

Specifically, similar extent of export structure similarity is obtained for the case of both Thailand and Indonesia and China in the EC-12 market However Thailand seems to demonstrate a stronger relationship than Indonesia with China in this case. More interestingly, the Philippines shows resemblance of export structure with China throughout the 15 years, and China appears to replicate Malaysia's export pattern in the years 1980-81, and from 1986 onwards. The negative associations between Singapore and China is also less obvious in the EC-12 market. Bearing in mind the above findings by Lutz, this systematic change, pertaining to all ASEAN-5 nations, especially to Malaysia and the Philippines and China, is only to be expected. In other words, the strength of the comparative advantage of exports from China and the ASEAN-5 countries are not fully reflected in the EC-12 market. Those countries exporting relatively more advanced products are 'held back' to compete in similar exports with the rest of the countries. The rather consistent correlation results obtained for Singapore and Malaysia, and Thailand and Indonesia in the US and EC-12 market can further support such arguments.

3.1.3 1994-to-Previous Years Comparisons (US Market)

In order to examine the extent to which the export expansion in China has become more similar with each of the ASEAN-5 nations, a Spearman Rank Correlation test is performed on China's RCA indices in 1994 with the indices of Singapore, Malaysia, Thailand and Indonesia in each year in the previous time period. As for the case of China and the Philippines, the reverse is done by correlating the Philippines' 1994 indices with China's indices in previous years. The results of this operation is reported in Table 2 of the appendix. Once again, as suggested by the stage theory of comparative advantage, if these countries went through similar stages of industrialisation, then the correlation coefficients of the RCA indices between the ASEAN-5 nations and China would indicate the extent to which a country has succeeded in matching the export pattern, and thus the comparative advantage position, of another which is ahead.

Table 2 for the US market shows that in 1980, Malaysia and Singapore were already ahead of China's 1994 export performance. China's 1994 comparative advantage position has only reached that of Thailand's in 1989. As for Indonesia, China's 1994 export structure has been close to hers as early as 1980 (or even earlier) but became even more similar from 1983 onwards. An explanation for this interesting findings could be the Indonesians had, in the late 1970s, penetrated the US market with her full range of exports of labour and low technology-intensive products. But due to her relatively slow growth in export performance, China could continuously match her until 1994.[10] The Philippines' comparative advantage position is only meaningfully similar to China's up to 1983, and occasionally in 1987-8 and 1993. These results has to a large extent confirmed our findings on the degree of identical export characteristics between China and each of the ASEAN-5 nations in Table 1 of US market.

3.1.4 1994-to-Previous Years Comparisons (European Community Market)

The results obtained for the EC-12 market in Table 2, with the caveat that the EC-12 imports more low technology-intensive products, is nonetheless rather predictable. China's 1994 export characteristics have replicated those of Singapore's only in the early years of 1982-3. Sporadic significant relationships are also observed for the years 1988 and 1990-92. There could be two possible reasons for this. First, it may be due to the sluggish world-wide economic performance in those years which adversely affected Singapore's export of skill-intensive products to the EC-12 market. Second, it could be due to the increase in Singapore's investment in China and neighbouring countries like Indonesia and Thailand (which raises her export of standardised products). Nevertheless, the relationship between China's 1994 export performance and that of Singapore's in all the previous years is not very strong. China's 1994 position successfully replicated Malaysia's export structure since 1986 in the EC-12 market, and as for Thailand and Indonesia, their comparative advantage position has long been similar to that of China's 1994 position. As explained in the previous case of China and Indonesia, we can interpret this as being a sign of stagnation in improvements of export performance of Thailand, and to a lesser extent, Indonesia, in the EC-12 market. Lastly, for the similarity of China's

[10] The early significance is mainly due to the similarity of their importance rankings in the labour and low technology-intensive product groups.

export structure with that of the Philippines' in 1994, the result is very similar to what happened between China and both Thailand and Indonesia.

3.2 ANALYSES OF SPECIFIC PRODUCT GROUPS

As suggested by Peter Chow (1990), using the growth rates of the RCA indices (GRRCA) of each specific product (at SITC 3-digit level) to perform a correlation test between two countries over the years of interest will reveal information about any product-specific shift of comparative advantage. In this part of the study, we use the GRRCAs of China to correlate with the GRRCAs of each country of ASEAN-5. It was pointed out that a shift of comparative advantage in any one of these products will be signalled by a significant negative correlation coefficient. On the other hand, a positive correlation coefficient of the GRRCAs indicates complementary growth in that product. In this case, the comparative advantage in that product is either increasing or declining simultaneously in both countries, depending on whether GRRCAs are both positive or negative.

Once again, the methodology is applied to the six countries in the two different markets. The products are classified into seven broad categories following the classification scheme used by Hadi Soesatro (1996) as follows : **non-manufacturing (NM), natural resource-intensive (NRI), unskilled labour-intensive (ULI), human capital-intensive (HCI), physical capital-intensive (PCI), technology-intensive (TI)** and **miscellaneous (M)**[11]. The conventional wisdom is that while the more industrialised country expands its comparative advantage into higher technology-intensive industries, her labour-intensive, standardised exports will be shifted to the less industrialised countries. In this product-specific analysis, that relationship, incidentally, does show up. With the information on the degrees of export expansions from the previous part of the study, we can expect significant coefficients of both signs (suggesting complementary and shift of comparative advantage) in the NM, NRI and ULI groups of products between both Singapore and Malaysia and China. Many significant relationships (both signs) should exist in the first three groups, and some positive ones in the rests, between both Indonesia and Thailand and China. For the case of China and the Philippines, one can expect significant coefficients in all the groups.[12] On the whole, there appears to be some unexpected significant relationships within the seven product classifications, but nonetheless, we can still see the pattern.

Table 3 of US market indicates that Singapore had experienced shift of comparative advantage in two traditional ULI products (SITC 652 and 846). However, strong competition was encountered in product category SITC 899 (ULI), and unexpectedly, in SITC 761 (HCI) and SITC 678 (PCI), as indicated by the strong positive correlation coefficients. Also, as postulated, there are no meaningful relationships in the TI group, illustrating the strength of Singapore's comparative advantage in this area. Malaysia has shown more erratic relationships with China. Her competitive edge in product category SITC 028 (NM), SITC 812 (ULI), SITC 512 (PCI) and SITC 583 and 884 (TI) had been

---

[11] No attempt is made to explain the significant relationships in miscellaneous product group.

[12] The implicit assumption is that two countries have to compete in the product before one can attempt to replace the other. If the product also declines in importance in the second country, then negative growth of that product will be observed in both countries. However, simultaneous decline is only expected in the primary (NM and NRI) sectors in developing countries like China and ASEAN-5.

taken over by China, and furthermore, China had another four products competing with Malaysia : SITC 287 (NM), SITC 665 and 821 (ULI) and SITC 749 (PCI).

For Thailand, complementary products are : SITC 651 and 665 (ULI), SITC 761, 784 and 792 (HCI), and SITC 512 (PCI). She is also losing comparative advantage in five goods to China: SITC 036 (NM), SITC 642 (HCI), SITC 749 (PCI), SITC 871 (TI) and SITC 931 (M). As will be explained later, the unexpected competition encountered and even shift of comparative advantage in the HCI, PCI and TI groups between China and both Malaysia and Thailand could be due to the 'inner strength' of the Chinese economy.

As for Indonesia and China, they share only five significantly related commodities, of which four are competing,: SITC 652 and 845 (ULI) as well as SITC 642 and 775 (HCI). Indonesia has lost her comparative advantage to China in SITC 666 (ULI). This result is not too far out of line with conventional wisdom.

In the case of China and the Philippines, the result shows much support for the initial hypothesis. Between them, three products compete in the upper three groups of the list : SITC 248 (NM), SITC 651 and665 (ULI). One product SITC 761 in HCI group, another SITC 751 in the PCI group, and one in M group : SITC 931. Those products replaced by China are : SITC 847 and 848 (ULI), SITC 897 (HCI), and SITC 776 and 881 (TI). This is pretty much as expected.

One possible explanation for those results that contradict conventional wisdom could be that many have overlooked the fact that China exports a much wider range of products than any of the ASEAN-5 countries due to her abundance of resources. Although China certainly is not an industrialised nation, her available resources range from the cheapest labour to very advanced technology and skilled professionals. This could enable her to produce practically anything so long as government officials permit. Another likely explanation for the 'irrational' relationships in Table 3 could be the foreign direct investments in China which spearheaded the economy's technology exports in all the special economic zones (SEZs). As multinational companies were increasingly responsible for the world-wide movements of resources in their search for the cheapest production methods, they promoted intra-industry specialisations involving the developing countries (Lutz 1987). These factors could serve to answer the puzzle of the concurrent occurrence of both complementary growth as well as shifting of comparative advantage in the HCI, PCI and TI categories between China and the ASEAN-5 nations. Then there is the product-specific development within a country. It may be due to stronger local demand for a particular product, which accelerated the learning curve of that industry, and therefore leads to earlier and better quality exports. Indeed, China's domestic market potential should never be underestimated. As noted by Lutz, competition among developing countries for export markets suggests that export expansion by one developing country often does not result from shifts in comparative advantage of the industrialised nations. Rather, the gain is at the expense of existing exporters. We find supporting evidence for Lutz's argument in this study, as indicated by the many significant positive coefficients between Thailand, Indonesia and the Philippines and China.

Now looking at Table 3 for EC-12 market, one should realise the results reflect two major differences with that for US market. First, there are more significant relationships in the NM, NRI and ULI categories. Second, there are less negative significant coefficients in the HCI, PCI and TI categories. Without going into a detailed analysis, this finding strengthens our conclusions regarding the EC-12 market and the conventional wisdom as spelled out at the beginning of this part of the study

4. CONCLUSION

This study attempts to address two issues in connection with the question of whether ASEAN-5 countries and China are trade competitors. The first is the degree of similarity between the overall export structures of China and individual ASEAN-5 nations. The second is the extent of competition at the product-specific level.

Due to differences in national characteristics and the starting periods of export-oriented industrialisation, there exist a spectrum of export performance levels within the ASEAN-5 nations, with Singapore at the top, followed by Malaysia, Thailand, Indonesia and the Philippines. Under the stage theory of comparative advantage, China will replicate the export pattern of earlier starters as she moves up the industrialisation spectrum. Using USA as the dominant market for analysis, we found that China has successfully replicated the export structure of Thailand and Indonesia; Singapore and Malaysia are clearly exporting more skill-intensive products than China; and as for the Philippines, empirical evidence strongly suggests that China has surpassed her in terms of export performance.

The answer to the second issue supports the general findings of the first. The results of the analysis of the correlation coefficients of the GRRCAs between China and individual countries of ASEAN-5 members have, to a large extent, conformed to conventional wisdom. Reasons for a few unexpected results could be that China has a more diversified export structure, that FDI in the economy was spearheading the exports of the more dynamic technology-intensive industries, and that there is increasing intra-industry specialisation among China and the ASEAN-5 countries.

Though not greatly emphasised throughout the study, the maintenance of trade restrictions by developed countries (USA and EC-12) against developing ones (China and the ASEAN-5 countries) has caused serious distortions in the export performance of the latter. Since developing nations are not allowed to grow along their lines of comparative advantage, such barriers unquestionably undermined the accuracy of any study in this area of economics.

REFERENCES

_____ (1977): "'Revealed' Comparative Advantage Revisited," in *Comparative Advantage Trade Policy and Economic Development*, Balassa, B. New York: Harvester Wheatsheaf.

Balassa, B. (1965): "Trade Liberalisation and 'revealed' Comparative Advantage," *The Manchester School*, 33, 2, 99-123.

Chow, Peter C. Y. (1990): "The Revealed Comparative Advantage of the East Asian NICs," *The International Trade Journal*, Vol. 5, 2, 235-260.

Hadi, S., (1996) : "The Economy: a General Review," in *Indonesia Assessment 1995, Development in the Eastern Indonesia*, ed. by Barlow, C and J. Hardjono. Singapore: ISEAS.

Hiemenz, U., R. J. Langhammer (1988): ASEAN and the EC : Institutions and Strutural Change in the European Community. Singapore : ISEAS

Howell, J. (1993): *China Opens its Doors: the Politics of Economic Transition*. Harvester Wheatsheaf.

Jomo K. S. and C. Edwards (1993): "Malaysian Industrialisation in Historical Perspective," in *Industrialising Malaysia, Policy , Performance, Prospects*, ed. by Jomo K S. London: Routledge

Jonathan R. W. (1989): *China's Economic Opening to the Outside World*. New York: Praeger.

Lim, C. Y. and associates, (1988): *Policy Options for the Singapore Economy*. Singapore: Mcgraw-Hill.

Lutz, J. M. (1987): "Shifting Comparative Advantage, the NICs, and *the Developing Countries,"* The International Trade Journal*, Vol. 1, 4, 340-358.

Tan, T. M., Low, Aik Meng, Williams, J. J. and Calingo, Luis M. R. (1996) : "Investment Potential in the Philippines: An Overview," in *Business Opportunities in the Philippines. Singapore*: Prentice Hall.

World Bank (1994): *China Foreign Trade Reform, a World Bank Country Study*. The World Bank.

TABLE 1

Spearman Rank Correlation Coefficients of RCA
Indices Between ASEAN-5 and China
(US Market)

YEAR	SIN/CHI	MAL/CHI	THA/CHI	IND/CHI	PHI/CHI	SIN/MAL	THA/IND
1980	-0.1459	0.1759	0.5534***	0.6648***	0.5313***	0.3747***	0.3218**
1981	-0.1783	0.1452	0.5460***	0.6463***	0.4605***	0.3070**	0.3232**
1982	-0.2269*	0.0891	0.4945***	0.5528***	0.4054***	0.2658**	0.4110***
1983	-0.3039**	0.0868	0.5291***	0.7008***	0.3689***	0.2958**	0.4269***
1984	-0.3425***	0.1257	0.4052***	0.5628***	0.2736**	0.2811**	0.4012***
1985	-0.4041***	0.1032	0.3424***	0.5805***	0.2772**	0.3017**	0.3730***
1986	-0.3201**	0.2518*	0.3635***	0.7063***	0.3892***	0.2225*	0.3360**
1987	-0.3568***	0.2904**	0.4162***	0.6954***	0.4295***	0.2218*	0.4054***
1988	-0.3248**	0.2453	0.3179**	0.6266***	0.2572*	0.1861	0.3373**
1989	-0.2766**	0.0961	0.2750**	0.5238***	0.2749**	0.2863**	0.3220**
1990	-0.2310*	0.0727	0.2869**	0.4848***	0.1995	0.2689**	0.3074**
1991	-0.2510*	0.0465	0.3623***	0.5726***	0.2444*	0.2870**	0.3256**
1992	-0.1968	0.0452	0.3623***	0.5194***	0.1918	0.3155**	0.3221**
1993	-0.0967	0.1114	0.4644***	0.5029***	0.2128	0.3091**	0.4067***
1994	-0.0817	0.1009	0.4198***	0.3688***	0.2098	0.3772***	0.3794***

a.   *** : Significant at 1 percent   ** : Significant at 5 percent   * : Significant at 10 percent

b.   Source : Calculated by authors from World Trade Database by Statistics Canada

TABLE 1 (CONT)

Spearman Rank Correlation Coefficients of RCA
Indices Between ASEAN-5 and China
(European Community Market)

YEAR	SIN/CHI	MAL/CHI	THA/CHI	IND/CHI	PHI/CHI	SIN/MAL	THA/IND
1980	-0.0629	0.2493*	0.5774***	0.4651***	0.3252**	0.4547***	0.3431***
1981	-0.0344	0.2933**	0.6525***	0.4551***	0.2862**	0.4075***	0.3255**
1982	0.0264	0.2029	0.6048***	0.5256***	0.3424***	0.4515***	0.3692***
1983	0.0646	0.1773	0.6235***	0.5353***	0.3838***	0.3726***	0.5377***
1984	-0.1214	0.0643	0.5943***	0.4811***	0.2523*	0.3523***	0.5051***
1985	-0.2565*	0.0879	0.5601***	0.4982***	0.2597*	0.3241**	0.5336***
1986	-0.2465*	0.2504*	0.5844***	0.5820***	0.3564***	0.3112**	0.5607***
1987	-0.1837	0.3660***	0.6780***	0.5509***	0.4201***	0.3005**	0.5629***
1988	-0.1297	0.3339**	0.5999***	0.5455***	0.3267**	0.3195**	0.4829***
1989	-0.1859	0.3319**	0.6328***	0.5732***	0.3701***	0.3673***	0.5030***
1990	-0.0877	0.3648***	0.5860***	0.5325***	0.4162***	0.4532***	0.4221***
1991	-0.0262	0.3263**	0.5262***	0.6018***	0.4908***	0.4540***	0.4467***
1992	0.0098	0.3589***	0.5536***	0.6196***	0.4251***	0.4662***	0.3978***
1993	0.1015	0.4382***	0.5468***	0.4497***	0.3924***	0.3927***	0.3755***
1994	0.1079	0.2912**	0.5893***	0.3455***	0.3564***	0.3365***	0.2814**

a.   *** : Significant at 1 percent   ** : Significant at 5 percent   * : Significant at 10 percent

b.   Source : Calculated by authors from World Trade Database by Statistics Canada

TABLE 2

Spearman Rank Correlation Coefficients of RCA Indices of ASEAN-5 and China's 1994 Indices (except Philippines)
(US Market)

YEAR	SIN/CHI(94)	MAL/CHI(94)	THA/CHI(94)	IND/CHI(94)	CHI/PHI(94)
1980	-0.0225	-0.1095	0.2147	0.2903**	0.3827***
1981	0.0100	-0.0315	0.2271*	0.2424*	0.3735***
1982	-0.0261	-0.0040	0.2073	0.2550*	0.3391**
1983	-0.1411	0.0078	0.1951	0.3766***	0.3783***
1984	-0.1569	0.0591	0.2144	0.3629***	0.2147
1985	-0.2273*	0.0895	0.1697	0.3266**	0.1934
1986	-0.2129	0.0458	0.1803	0.3811***	0.1980
1987	-0.1710	0.0942	0.1488	0.4054***	0.2996**
1988	-0.1082	0.0678	0.2074	0.4411***	0.2917**
1989	-0.1457	0.0563	0.3494***	0.3756***	0.1809
1990	-0.1382	0.1725	0.3641***	0.4239***	0.1863
1991	-0.1320	0.2177	0.3746***	0.4080***	0.2118
1992	-0.0774	0.1581	0.4158***	0.3435***	0.1757
1993	-0.0839	0.1299	0.4292***	0.4216***	0.2221*
1994	-0.0817	0.1009	0.4198***	0.3688***	0.2098

a.   *** : Significant at 1 percent   ** : Significant at 5 percent   * : Significant at 10 percent

b.   Source : Calculated by authors from World Trade Database by Statistics Canada

TABLE 2 (CONT)

Spearman Rank Correlation Coefficients of RCA Indices of ASEAN-5 and China's 1994 Indices (except Philippines)
(European Community Market)

YEAR	SIN/CHI(94)	MAL/CHI(94)	THA/CHI(94)	IND/CHI(94)	CHI/PHI(94)
1980	0.1625	0.1163	0.3116**	0.2392*	0.2637**
1981	0.2092	0.1702	0.4248***	0.2165	0.3215**
1982	0.2636**	0.1675	0.3991***	0.3245**	0.3179**
1983	0.3176**	0.1602	0.3945***	0.3316**	0.3867***
1984	0.1618	0.1326	0.4037***	0.3339**	0.2262*
1985	0.0294	0.1495	0.3479***	0.3056**	0.2763**
1986	0.1193	0.2300*	0.4206***	0.3724***	0.2833**
1987	0.1543	0.2805**	0.4534***	0.3445***	0.3372***
1988	0.2277*	0.2992**	0.5861***	0.3073**	0.3790***
1989	0.1487	0.3393***	0.6740***	0.3786***	0.3674***
1990	0.2469*	0.4085***	0.6818***	0.3231**	0.3871***
1991	0.2730**	0.4111***	0.6248***	0.4366***	0.3842***
1992	0.2266*	0.3981***	0.6008***	0.4915***	0.3929***
1993	0.1521	0.3779***	0.5784***	0.4093***	0.4199***
1994	0.1079	0.2912**	0.5893***	0.3455***	0.3564***

a.   *** : Significant at 1 percent   ** : Significant at 5 percent   * : Significant at 10 percent

b.   Source : Calculated by authors from World Trade Database by Statistics Canada

TABLE 3

Product Specific Correlation Coefficients of the Growth Rates of RCA (GRRCA) Indices
(US Market)

SITC	PRODUCT NAMES	SIN/CHI	MAL/CHI	THA/CHI	IND/CHI	PHI/CHI
Non-Manufacturing (NM)						
036	Crustaceans and molluscs			-0.5147*		
037	Fish and crustaceans n.e.s.					
058	Fruit preserve					
248	Wood, simply worked		-0.4782*			0.5561**
287	Ores and base metal		0.5698**			
334	Petroleum oils					
424	Vegetable and coconut oil					
Natural Resource-Intensive (NRI)						
635	Wood manufactures n.e.s.					
Unskilled Labour-Intensive (ULI)						
651	Textile yarn			0.4926*		0.4688*
652	Cotton fabrics, woven	-0.6314**			0.4994*	
653	Fabrics of man-made textile					
658	Textile made-up articles n.e.s.					
665	Glassware		0.5153*	0.4894*		0.5186*
666	Pottery				-0.5653**	
812	Sanitary and plumbing fixtures		-0.5247*			
821	Furniture and parts thereof		0.4707*			
831	Carriers and containers of leather.					
842	Women's wearing articles of textile, not					
843	Men's wearing articles of textile					
844	Women's wearing articles of textile.					
845	Articles of apparel n.e.s.				0.5176*	
846	Clothing accessories of textile fabrics	-0.5684**				
847	Clothing accessories of textile fabrics					-0.6136**
848	Articles of apparel non-textile, headgear					-0.4660*
851	Footwear					
893	Articles n.e.s. of plastics					
894	Baby carriages, toys and sporting goods					
899	Miscellaneous manufactured articles	0.6507**				
Human Capital-Intensive (HCI)						
628	Articles of rubber					
642	Paper and paperboard, cut			-0.4964*	0.4595*	
699	Manufactures of base metals					
761	Television receivers	0.6700***		0.5096*		0.8200***
762	Radio-broadcast receivers					
775	Household electrical and non-electrical				0.5289*	
784	Parts and accessories of motor vehicles			0.5820**		
792	Aircraft and associated equipment			0.4999*		
897	Jewelry and other articles of precious					-0.5247*
898	Musical instruments and accessories					
Physical Capital-Intensive (PCI)						
512	Alcohols, phenols, etc		-0.5725**	0.4920*		
678	Wire of iron and steel	0.8679***				
749	Non-electric parts and accessories of		0.5941**	-0.6917***		
751	Office machines					0.6666***
Technology-Intensive (TI)						
583	Monofilament of plastics		-0.5565**			
598	Miscellaneous chemical products n.e.s.					
752	Automatic data processing machines					
764	Telecommunications equipment n.e.s.					
771	Electric power machinery and parts					
772	Electrical apparatus for switching.					
773	Equipment for distributing electricity					
776	Thermionic, cathode valves, diodes, etc					-0.5076*
778	Electrical machinery and apparatus n.e.s.					
871	Optical instruments and apparatus, n.e.s.			-0.5222*		
874	Measuring, checking instruments n.e.s.					
881	Photographic apparatus and equipment					-0.4666*
884	Optical goods n.e.s.		-0.5293*			
Miscellaneous (M)						
931	Special transactions, commodities not			-0.6876***		0.6405**

a. *** : Significant at 1 percent   ** : Significant at 5 percent   * : Significant at 10 percent

b. Product names are shortened for purpose of presentation

c. Source : Calculated by authors from World Trade Database by Statistics Canada.

TABLE 3

Product Specific Correlation Coefficients of the Growth
Rates of RCA Indices
(European Community Market)

SITC	PRODUCT NAME	SIN/CHI	MAL/CHI	THA/CHI	IND/CHI	PHI/CHI
Non-Manufacturing (NM)						
036	Crustaceans and molluscs					0.6721***
037	Fish and crustaceans n.e.s.					
048	Cereal preparations and preparations of	0.5327**		0.4678*		
056	Vegetables, roots and tubers n.e.s.					
057	Fresh and dried fruit and nut					
058	Fruit preserve					
071	Coffee and coffee substitutes		0.4741*			
081	Feeding stuff for animals			0.5475**		
098	Edible products and preparations		-0.5371**			
248	Wood, simply worked					
287	Ores and base metal					
288	Non-ferrous base metal waste and scrap		-0.4756*			
292	Crude vegetables materials n.e.s.					
334	Petroleum oils					-0.5442**
424	Vegetable and coconut oil	-0.6022**			-0.4899*	
431	Animal or vegetable fats or oils					
Natural Resource-Intensive (NRI)						
635	Wood manufactures n.e.s.					
689	Mis. non-ferrous base metals metallurgy		-0.4850*	0.4702*		
Unskilled Labour-Intensive (ULI)						
651	Textile yarn	-0.4985*	-0.5496**			
652	Cotton fabrics, woven					
653	Fabrics of man-made textile			0.6336**		
658	Textile made-up articles n.e.s.					0.4629*
665	Glassware					
666	Pottery					
812	Sanitary and plumbing fixtures					
821	Furniture and parts thereof	0.5953**				
831	Carriers and containers of leather, plastics.					
842	Women's wearing articles of textile, not	0.5091*		0.5081*		
843	Men's wearing articles of textile					
844	Women's wearing articles of textile, knitted					
845	Articles of apparel n.e.s.					
846	Clothing accessories of textile fabrics					
847	Clothing accessories of textile fabrics n.e.s.	0.5241*		0.6104**		
848	Articles of apparel non-textile, headgear					-0.6397**
851	Footwear			0.5687**		
893	Articles n.e.s.of plastics					-0.5546**
894	Baby carriages, toys and sporting goods	0.5746**	0.5518**			
899	Miscellaneous manufactured articles n.e.s.					
Human Capital-Intensive (HCI)						
642	Paper and paperboard, cut					
699	Manufactures of base metals					
761	Television receivers					
762	Radio-broadcast receivers					
784	Parts and accessories of motor vehicles				-0.5322**	
792	Aircraft and associated equipment					
897	Jewellery and other articles of precious					
898	Musical instruments and accessories		0.5150*			
Physical Capital-Intensive (PCI)						
714	Engines and motors, non-electric		0.6056**			-0.5196*
751	Office machines				0.5407**	-0.4768*
Technology-Intensive (TI)						
583	Monofilament of plastics					
598	Miscellaneous chemical products n.e.s.					
752	Authomatic data processing machines					0.5093*
764	Telecommunications equipment n.e.s.					
772	Electrical apparatus for switching.					-0.4696*
778	Electrical machinery and apparatus n.e.s.					
871	Optical instruments and apparatus, n.e.s.				0.5872**	
881	Photographic apparatus and equipment	0.5838**			-0.5070*	
Miscellaneous (M)						
931	Special transactions, commodities not		0.4987*		0.4910*	0.5824**

a. *** : Significant at 1%   ** : Significant at 5%   * : Significant at 10%

b. Product names are shortened for purpose of presentation

c. Source : Calculated by authors from World Trade Database by Statistics Canada.

Economic Links between Hong Kong and China

Lynn Ng Lay Wee
&
Wang Ruifang

Nanyang Business School, Nanyang Technological University, Nanyang Avenue, Singapore 639798
Fax: +(65) 792.4217, Tel: +(65) 799.6400, Email: arfwang@ntu.edu.sg

Abstract We try to establish quantitative links between Hong Kong and China in terms of economic growth, investment and trade, which could facilitate a more comprehensive analysis of economic integration with a Hong Kong - China model in the future. In specifying the equations, special attention has been paid to the main features of the economic relationship between the two economies. Five equations describing the behaviour of Hong Kong's FDI in China, China's GNP growth, Hong Kong's imports from China, Hong Kong's exports to China and Hong Kong's exports to the rest of the world are estimated using annual data. The estimation results reveal the importance of Hong Kong in its outward processing trade with China and as a middleman between China and the rest of the world. Lastly, we speculate on the policy implications of our empirical results.

1. INTRODUCTION

Historically, there has been an intimate relationship between Hong Kong and China. While administratively a British colony since 1842, Hong Kong has been populated by Chinese, with the great majority coming from the Pearl River Delta. To many Chinese residents in Hong Kong, Guangdong province is an immediate hinterland. Since 1979 when China opened up to the world, economic ties between Hong Kong and China have been greatly strengthened. Both economies are now close partners in investment, trade and finance. On the one hand, Hong Kong's sustained economic growth, and its position as an entrepot and a financial centre depend crucially on China's economy that has been growing strongly for nearly two decades. On the other hand, foreign direct investment (FDI) from Hong Kong and Hong Kong's continued prosperity are equally important for China's development and growth. With the return of Hong Kong to China just a few months away, there is a growing worry about the stability of Hong Kong after the 1997. There are many uncertainties, but one thing is certain and that is: economically, Hong Kong and China have been closely tied with each other, and that shall act as a stabiliser.

Under the policy of 'one country, two systems,' it is reasonable to assume that Hong Kong and China will continue to be two different economies. Although economic integration has been taking place for a long time and undoubtedly will speed up after the 1997, immediate economic unification is something beyond horizon. Therefore, policy co-operation and co-ordination between policy makers in Beijing and Hong Kong is vital for maintaining Hong Kong's stability and for mutual benefits. For this purpose, some simulation analysis based on a Hong Kong - China model might be helpful. This paper attempts to establish some key quantitative links between the two economies in the hope that vigorous policy analysis of economic integration can be conducted some time in the future.

This paper is organised in the following manner. The next section provides background for the economic ties between Hong Kong and China, with a focus on the main features of the Hong Kong economy. Section 3 is devoted to model specification and discussions on empirical results. In the concluding section, we concentrate on policy implications.

2. BACKGROUND

Hong Kong is often said to be a goose which lays golden eggs for China. Based on recent statistics, Sung (1991a) finds that trade and capital flows between Hong Kong and China are balanced and multifaceted, reflecting the increasing degree of economic integration between the two economies. However, given the differences in size and economic power, as well as the relationship between the central and local governments after the 1997, Hong Kong is certainly not in a position to bargain or manoeuvre much. The continuation of the present mutually beneficial situation will depend on whether Hong Kong can contribute to the future development of the mainland. In this regard, it is worthwhile to first look at the role of Hong Kong in China's economic reform.

2.1 DIRECT INVESTMENT

The most obvious indicator of the intimate relationship between Hong Kong and China since 1979 is the amount of Hong Kong's FDI in China. At present, Hong Kong is the largest foreign investor in China, accounting for about 60 percent of accumulated FDI in China (Luk, 1994). Not surprisingly, most Hong Kong's FDI is concentrated in Guangdong province, especially the two Special Economic Zones (Shenzhen and Zhuhai). In fact, Guangdong is the largest provincial recipient of foreign capital, particularly FDI, with about 30 to 40 percent of the national total realised intake of FDI (Kueh, 1994).

Hong Kong's FDI in China represents to a large extent the large-scale relocation of manufacturing undertakings from Hong Kong to Guangdong. This 'migration' has been prompted by exorbitant land rental increases and continuous labour shortages in Hong Kong. *Outward processing* [1] started in the early 1980s and accelerated during the last few years, affecting the Hong Kong-China economic relationship and the Hong Kong economic structure greatly within a very short span of time.

The flow of investment is not one-directional. Shen (1993) mentions that China has also actively invested in a wide spectrum of business sectors of Hong Kong, including manufacturing, banking, real estate, construction, transportation and telecommunication. Federation of Hong Kong Industries (1993) reports that the total investment by mainland enterprises has been estimated to exceed US$12 billion, the highest among all sources of overseas investment in Hong Kong. For manufacturing sector alone, China's accumulated investment in Hong Kong by 1991 year-end was HK$3.75 billion (evaluated at original cost). In fact, China was the third largest investor in Hong Kong's manufacturing sector after Japan and the U.S.

---

[1] Outward processing in China is motivated by the high costs of production in Hong Kong. Hong Kong investors inject their capital in, and export raw materials and machinery to China, where the costs of production are very much lower due to abundant land and labour. Like jewellery shops in the past, where the front of the shop is for the sale of finished products while the back is for the production of these products, Hong Kong resembles the salesman at the front of the shop while southern China resembles the workers at the back. In other words, China manufactures goods to be re-imported by Hong Kong for re-export to the rest of the world.

2.2 TRADE

A rapid glance at Guangdong's trade and investment statistics reveals the importance of Hong Kong to the economic development of China, especially Guangdong. Kueh (1994) estimates that some 80 percent of Guangdong exports go to, and 70 percent of its imports come from Hong Kong, and 52.4 percent of Hong Kong's total exports to China were related to outward processing. At present, China is Hong Kong's largest trading partner and vice versa. Hong Kong has contributed tremendously to China's external trade by being an entrepot acting as a trade intermediary between China and the outside world. Moreover, Hong Kong's FDI in China due to the relocation of manufacturing undertakings from Hong Kong to China has resulted in a rapid growth of investment-induced trade. This form of trade, whether domestic export, re-export or import, is known as 'outward processing' to Hong Kong, but 'export processing' to China. In 1993, the share of outward processing trade in Hong Kong's domestic exports and re-exports to China, and overall imports from China were 74 percent, 42 percent and 74 percent respectively (Luk, 1994). Consequently, Guangdong has become a manufacturing base for Hong Kong, while Hong Kong a service-oriented economy.

Other than commodity trade, service trade between China and Hong Kong is also extremely vital. Tourism is an important item in China's foreign exchange. Hong Kong visitors account for two-thirds of tourist arrivals and expenditure in China. Hong Kong is the foremost gateway for China tourists. The percentage of non-Hong Kong residents visiting China via Hong Kong has been rising since 1982. Hong Kong also exports transportation, trading, construction, financial and business services to China, although reliable data for these services is lacking.

2.3 FINANCE

Luk (1994) believes that Hong Kong financial institutions and markets have played a vital part in supplementing the mainland's financial markets and facilitating China's economic development, especially in the banking sector and the stock market.

During the early years of China's reforms, Hong Kong's FDI in China was mostly carried out by relatively small firms, which relied on bank loans from Hong Kong banks for their external financing. Thus the banking sector has indirectly financed the production activities on the mainland, especially in southern China.

Hong Kong's financial sector also contributes directly to China's economic development in the form of foreign loans. When China's financial system was decentralised in 1986, allowing selected provincial governments and enterprises to raise foreign loans without the need to seek approval of the central government in Beijing, the share of China's foreign loans syndicated in Hong Kong increased sharply. As expected, that share fell drastically when China embarked on a retrenchment programme to combat inflation and economic overheating in 1988 by re-centralising the power to borrow foreign loans, and during the Tiananmen Square Incident in June 1989. Nevertheless, loans to China quickly resumed and increased in the 1990s. The share of Hong Kong in China's foreign loan may be small as Hong Kong only extends commercial, and no soft, loans to China. But Hong Kong is the centre for loan syndication, arranging and raising 90 percent of China's syndicated loans.

The Stock Exchange of Hong Kong (SEHK) plays an important role in financing economic activities in China. After being successfully listed on the SEHK, China-owned

Hong Kong firms, known as 'China concept,' use the funds they raised in Hong Kong to acquire assets from their mainland parents so that funds from Hong Kong are actually financing operations on the mainland.

Finally, Hong Kong's financial expertise, which has been acquired through the 50 years of being a free-market British colony, helps to develop China's long-neglected financial markets. For instance, the 'B' shares introduced by China to tap foreign capital are in general underwritten and placed on the stock exchange by mostly Hong Kong financial institutions or foreign institutions with representatives in Hong Kong.

3. HONG KONG-CHINA ECONOMIC LINKAGES: SOME EMPIRICAL EVIDENCE

With a deeper understanding of the umbilical bond between Hong Kong and China from the above discussion, we shall now proceed to establish some quantitative links between the two economies. It is hoped that our empirical findings can be used in setting up a comprehensive Hong Kong-China model. This will allow for a detailed policy simulation analysis to be carried out in the future.

Most of the Hong Kong data are extracted from various issues of the *Hong Kong Annual Digest of Statistics* and the *Hong Kong Monthly Digest of Statistics*, while most of the China data are from various issues of the *Statistical Yearbook of China* and *Almanac of China's Foreign Economic Relations and Trade*.

All the variables presented below are in first-order difference of logarithms; in other words, they are growth variables. The conventional cointegration analysis is not used due to the small sample size. Our growth rate model has an advantage of avoiding spurious regressions with time series data. Table 1 defines the variables appeared in the five equations in Table 2, where the estimation results are displayed. The annual data used basically stretch from 1978 to 1994, though the sample size for each equation differs after adjusting for endpoints.

3.1 HONG KONG'S OUTWARD FDI IN CHINA

Hong Kong's outward FDI in China (FDIHC) is probably the most direct and obvious indicator of the strong economic linkages between Hong Kong and China. FDI involves the transfer of long-term physical investment from one economy to another. Table 3 shows that Hong Kong has been the main source of utilised FDI in China, accounting for an average of 64 percent of the national total throughout the ten-year period. FDIHC in the form of joint ventures normally involves export of machinery and equipment, or raw or semi-finished materials from Hong Kong to China. FDIHC is defined as a function of China's gross national product (GNPCN) and Hong Kong's property price level (HKPPty). In the form of growth rate, we have:

$$DLFDIHC = F(DLGNPCN, DLHKPPty) \qquad (1)$$
$$+ +$$

As China's economic growth accelerates, the domestic demand for goods and services by the Chinese increases as well. Given capital constraints, China will have to attract more inward FDI, especially from neighbouring capitalist Hong Kong due. This rise in demand, coupled with the liberalisation of trade, investment and financial policies ever since 1979, raises the amount of inward FDI.

Moreover, joint ventures requires injection of capital from both the Chinese and the Hong Kong parties. During an economic downturn in China, the Beijing government tends to tighten domestic credit policies, deterring the Chinese investors from obtaining the capital required to finance their joint ventures with the Hong Kong investors. Since one party of the joint venture is unable to inject more capital, the other party will not be willing to do so, otherwise the risk borne by the latter would be too high. In this way, China's domestic investment has a 'crowding in' effect on FDIHC. Therefore, economic growth rate is an important factor determining growth rate of FDIHC. As can be seen from the large size of coefficient of DLGNPCN, growth rate of FDI from Hong Kong is highly sensitive to economic growth rate in China.

HKPPty assesses the notorious soaring property prices and rental costs in land-scarce Hong Kong. Table 4 compares Hong Kong's land costs with those in China and some ASEAN countries. We can easily see that in 1990 Hong Kong's land costs are about 8 times higher than these countries. Land costs form a major part of Hong Kong's manufacturing costs of production. Since the manufacturing sector is more dependent on land costs than the service sector, Hong Kong manufacturers relieve the problem of high costs by simply shifting labour-intensive manufacturing activities to lower-cost southern China. This leads to the recent booming outward processing in China, which Wong (1991) believes pioneers FDIHC. Hence, the more exorbitant the property prices in Hong Kong, the more thriving the outward processing in China and so does FDIHC.

3.2 CHINA'S GNP

Teo and Wang (1996) have found that China's economic growth is mainly investment- and export-driven. Our GNPCN function thus comprises both internal and external factors, namely: FDIHC, China's gross domestic investment(DICN) and her domestic total export of goods and services(TXCN).

$$DLGNPCN=F(DLFDIHC, DLDICN, DLTXCN) \qquad (2)$$
$$+ \qquad\quad + \qquad\quad +$$

FDIHC is found to be positively related to GNPCN. On average a 10 points increase in growth rate of FDI from Hong Kong would lead to a 0.33 point increase in China's economic growth rate. Wong (1991) strongly believes that Guangdong's economic growth is propelled by the increase in light manufactured exports from small and medium non-state-owned (or private) enterprises, which is the result of outward processing by Hong Kong manufacturers in the Pearl River Delta region. On top of the spectacular increase in 1992 of FDIHC, mainly due to the greater provincial autonomy of Guangdong from the central government, Deng's famous South China Tour in January/February 1992 to give his blessings to the open-door policy initiated by him in 1978, had further boosted FDIHC in 1993, which in turn had greatly contributed to improving the economic performance of the Chinese economy.

As shown in Table 2, both DLDICN and DLTXCN also have significant beneficial effects on DLGNPCN, which is a result consistent with the empirical finding by Teo and Wang (1996).

3.3 HONG KONG'S VISIBLE IMPORTS FROM CHINA

Hong Kong's visible imports from China (MHC) is a vital component in China-Hong Kong-Rest of the World (ROW) economic relationship. Two salient features of the present Hong Kong economy can be inferred from our MHC function: (i) the importance of outward processing trade between Hong Kong and China; (ii) the importance of Hong Kong's role as a middleman between China and the ROW. MHC is thus specified as being determined by Hong Kong's visible domestic exports to China (DXHC), Hong Kong's visible exports to ROW (ROWX) and real exchange rate of HK$ against RMB (ERHC). Thus,

$$DLMHC=F(DLROWX, DLDXHC, DLERHC) \qquad (3)$$
$$\qquad\qquad\quad + \qquad\qquad + \qquad\qquad -$$

As shown in Table 5, there has been a high content of outward processing in MHC and China's exports via Hong Kong to the ROW. In 1993, the estimated figures were 74 percent and 81 percent respectively. This indicates that most of MHC are actually processed re-imports from Hong Kong's outward processing in China meant to be re-exported through Hong Kong. The fact that up to 89 percent of MHC for re-export in 1989 were manufactures as shown in Table 6 further proves that these MHC comprise mainly finished goods, and not raw materials, for sale to the ROW by Hong Kong exporters. Therefore, higher foreign demand for Hong Kong exports will induce higher Hong Kong imports from China. In this sense, the Hong Kong-China link is prospered by the Hong Kong-ROW link. 1 point increase in growth of exports to the ROW is found to correspond to roughly 1 point increase in growth of imports from China.

On supply side, an increase in domestic exports from Hong Kong to China, about 75 percent of which are outward processing related, will lead to an increase in imports from China. Sung (1992) states that outward processing has induced Hong Kong manufacturers to export domestic textiles and clothing and a variety of other light industrial goods to China. Moreover, these DXHC are definitely not meant for domestic consumption in China, but as industrial raw materials or intermediate goods for further processing (which takes time and thus account for the lag of the growth rate of DXHC) and then for re-exportation back to Hong Kong for either 'finishing touches' before being re-exported or for immediate re-export to Europe and the U.S.. The more thriving the outward processing in China, the more DXHC, and hence the higher the MHC.

ERHC, defined as units of HK$ per unit of RMB, is consistent with theory in explaining MHC. The lag merely indicates that the impact of the change in the real exchange rate on the change in imports is slower than that on the change in exports due to the lag in implementing an imports contract. The inclusion of this variable emphasises that MHC are cost-driven, that is, the relative prices between the two economies are considered by Hong Kong importers.

3.4 HONG KONG'S VISIBLE EXPORTS TO CHINA

Hong Kong's visible exports to China (XHC) complements Equation (3), exhibiting the two-way economic relations between Hong Kong and China. It is used to further highlight the recent Hong Kong-China trade linkages after almost half a century of stagnation because of the severing of the umbilical economic relationship with China due to the 1952 Korean War and the subsequent United Nations trade embargo on China. From our XHC function, we are able to trace the recent prosperous China-Hong Kong-ROW trade to the two prevalent features of the Hong Kong economy mentioned above. As can be seen in Table 5, almost half of XHC are outward processing related. Hence our XHC function is formulated by the following variables: Hong Kong's import of machinery (MM), ERHC, lagged XHC and 1984 dummy variable (D84).

$$DLXHC = F(DLMM, DLERHC, DLXHC_{-1}, D84) \qquad (4)$$
$$ + \qquad + \qquad + \qquad +$$

MM explains most of the indirect imports of goods via Hong Kong to China. Table 7 shows that more than three-quarters of Hong Kong's re-exports to China are manufactures. This is because according to Wong (1991), the relocation of lower value-added Hong Kong manufacturing base to China results in imports of machinery and parts of appropriate technology and cost from more developed economies such as Taiwan and Korea to China. These imports are then re-exported to China for processing/assembling purposes. The transfer of technology embodied in the machinery exported to China via Hong Kong is especially prominent in more elaborate collaborative arrangements like equity joint ventures between Hong Kong and China investors. The more outward processing in China, the more MM to be exported to China to support the outward processing operations there, and hence, the more XHC.

DLERHC is consistent with theory in explaining DLXHC. It is less significant in the above equation compared to other explanatory variables probably because DLXHC is more investment-driven (reflected in the much more significant MM, whose purpose is to support the outward processing investments in China) than cost-driven. Its relative insignificance can also be due to the 1984 drastic devaluation of RMB by the Chinese government to encourage exports, and this is accounted for by D84.

The inclusion of lagged DLXHC is necessary to account for the 'continuity effect'. This effect depicts the continuous steady flow of investments by Hong Kong investors in the outward processing factories set up in southern China. These investors will not reduce their investments drastically even if exchange rate is unfavourable toward them, because of the large sunk capital costs involved.

3.5 HONG KONG'S VISIBLE EXPORTS TO ROW

ROWX is indispensable when explaining the recent buoyant China-Hong Kong-ROW partnership. Our ROWX function is actually an extension of the MHC function above. It specifically emphasises the vital middleman role played by Hong Kong in this flourishing partnership. We have found that exchange rates do not explain ROWX significantly, but economic growth of the importing country does. Thus ROWX is defined as a function of MHC and gross national product of U.S. (GNPUS) which is treated as a proxy to world demand for Hong Kong exports:

$$DLROWX = F(DLMHC, DLGNPUS) \qquad (5)$$
$$ + \qquad +$$

As mentioned in Section 3.3, an increase in ROWX leads to an increase in MHC. Equation (5) shows that this relationship is not one-way, but two-way. The higher the demand for China's goods by the ROW, the more goods will be imported by Hong Kong from China. These MHC are not for Hong Kong's domestic consumption, but for re-export to the ROW to meet the latter's demand. Hence the more indirect trade between China and the ROW, the more MHC, and the more ROWX.

As the economic growth of the world economy improves, its demand for imports will rise. Hence the positive relationship between GNPUS and ROWX is consistent with theory.

4. LONG TERM IMPLICATIONS AND CONCLUSION

Based on our empirical results, we shall now turn to the implications of the various economic linkages depicting Hong Kong-China trade and investment flows. We shall first summarise the main economic linkages between Hong Kong and China, as well as the linkages among China-Hong Kong-ROW. We then attempt to list the major factors which will most likely affect the current pattern of these linkages.

FDIHC is mostly induced by the boom in outward processing by Hong Kong in China. Equation (1) shows that the success of Hong Kong-China outward processing trade predominantly depends on the economic performance of the Chinese economy. The high domestic cost of production in Hong Kong is the most important domestic economic rationale behind the recent booming outward processing by Hong Kong in China. The shift of lower value-added manufacturing activities to China allows Hong Kong to concentrate her domestic investment on the higher value-added ones. Thus the so-called 'hollowing out' of Hong Kong manufacturing sector is misleading. Moreover, this relocation also allows Hong Kong to further develop her service sector. Therefore, the long term implications of outward processing for Hong Kong are the speeding up of the structural transformation of her economy and the solving of the problem of shifting comparative advantage (due to land scarcity as well as the long run labour shortage generated by Hong Kong's declining fertility rates and an ageing demographic structure).

Equation (2) reveals Hong Kong's contribution to China's economic development and growth by being a major supplier of additional funds for China's capital formation. Moreover, the medium-level technology transferred by Hong Kong to China is more suitable for the latter, and Hong Kong's stage of development is much closer to that of China (compared to that of the developed countries). Therefore, it seems that Hong Kong's FDI in China is especially important in terms of the survival of Hong Kong as a capitalist economy in the long run after her return to China, since China *tolerates* capitalism in the former mainly because she can reap substantial economic benefits from the former, especially investment gains.

Equations (3) and (4) further prove that the trade linkages between Hong Kong and China are mainly investment-driven. Hong Kong manufacturers export and re-export capital and other essential goods to their factories in China and then re-import the processed goods for re-export to the rest of the world. This whole process reflects the stage of international division of labour to which countries at different stages of development such as Japan, Asian NIEs, ASEAN and China have progressed. This trend has resulted in what Maruya (1992) called the 'Asian Extended Economic Circle,' where Hong Kong has an important role to play in linking China with the world economy. Moreover, Sung (1992) finds that the dependence of countries like the U.S., Canada, Indonesia and South Korea on Hong Kong for their trade with China has not faltered even though they have direct commercial and diplomatic relations with China since the 1970s.

In addition, Equation (5) substantiates the strong Hong Kong-China investment-led trade links and the flourishing China-Hong Kong-ROW economic relationship by further emphasising the importance of Hong Kong's middleman role. This importance is accentuated whenever U.S. imposes trade sanctions on China (recently due to human rights issue) or removes China's Most Favoured Nation (MFN) status from China. When such situations occur, one would expect ROWX to decline. Equation (3) shows that a decrease in DLROWX would reduce DLMHC, and slow down the growth of China's visible exports to Hong Kong, which is a component of China's total exports. This, through Equation (2), would lead to a slow down in China's economic growth. This in turn would result in a decrease in the growth of Hong Kong's FDI in China, hence, a deterioration of the Hong Kong economy. Therefore, our empirical findings imply that as Sino-U.S. economic relation turns sour, Hong Kong will be sandwiched in-between and will inevitably be adversely affected as well.

All the above five equations exhibit the adverse effects of China's unfavourable or re-centralisation of export and investment policies or systems on the trade and investment links between Hong Kong and China, as well as their economic relations with ROW.

We can generally conclude that Hong Kong's outward processing in China and its role as a middleman between China and the world economy will continue to be important after the 1997. The China-Hong Kong-ROW economic relations will be strengthened as China becomes more active in the world economy. Through efficient division of labour, China will be transformed into the manufacturing base of the service-oriented Hong Kong. For realisation of this scenario, there must be a continuation of the current practices. The major factors influencing the 'One Country, Two Systems' formula after 1 July this year include the continuation of economic reform in China, the implementations of the economic provisions embedded in the Basic Law, the preservation of Hong Kong's economic vitality and the linked exchange rate system and prudent fiscal policies, and lastly, the Sino-U.S. trade disputes.

We do not believe that full economic integration (hence economic unification) between Hong Kong and China is possible in the near future, since there are even limits to the basic requirements: free mobility of both outputs and inputs across the regions. One such limit is the strict Hong Kong-China immigration policies imposed by the Beijing government. However, the foremost constraints are the difference in the two economic systems and the economic autonomy to which Hong Kong is entitled under the Sino-British Joint Declaration and the Basic Law, which provides only broad guidelines and cannot (and *should not*) specify details in the execution of policies.

There may be hiccups like the 1989 Tiananmen Incident on the path to reunification and after, but we still maintain our optimistic view that Hong Kong's 'competitive edge' or hallmark—resilience, which has been the characteristic of this economy during times of economic turbulence, will pull the country through the critical year 1997 and survive brilliantly under Chinese sovereignty.

REFERENCES

Federation of Hong Kong Industries (1993): *Investment in China: 1993 Survey of Members of the Federation of Hong Kong Industries*, Industry and Research Division.

Hong Kong Census and Statistics Department (various issues): *Hong Kong Annual Digest of Statistics*, Hong Kong.

_____: *Hong Kong Monthly Digest of Statistics*, Hong Kong.

_____: *Almanac of China's Foreign Economic Relations and Trade*, Hong Kong.

Kueh, Y.Y. (1994): "The Fifth Dragon: Aspects of the Economic Take-off in Guangdong Province, China." Centre for Asian Pacific Studies, Working Paper Series No. 15 (8/94 CAPS.

Luk, Y.K. (1994): "Outlook on the Hong Kong Economy," in Choi, Po-King and Ho, Lok-Sang (ed.), *The Other Hong Kong Report 1993*.

Maruya, Toyojiro (1992): "Economic Relations between Hong Kong and Guangdong," in *Guangdong: "Open-Door" Economic Development Strategy*.

Mondejar, Reuben (1994): " Integrating Hong Kong into China: An Organisation Theory Case," in *Hong Kong and Guangdong: a case of organisation integration*. Weltforum Verlag.

Shen, George (1993): "China's Investment in Hong Kong," in Choi, Po-King and Ho, Lok-Sang (ed.), The Other Hong Kong Report 1993.

State Statistics Bureau (various issues): *Statistical Yearbook of China*, Beijing: Zhongguo tongji chubanshe.

Sung, Yun-Wing (1991a): "Hong Kong's Economic Value to China," in Sung, Yun-Wing and Lee, Ming-Kwan (ed.), *The Other Hong Kong Report 1991*.

_____(1991b): *The Hong Kong-China Connection: The Key to China's Open-Door Policy*.

_____(1992): "The Economic Integration of Hong Kong with China in the 1990s: The Impact on Hong Kong." Canada and Hong Kong Research Project, Research Papers No. 1, University of Toronto-York University, Joint Centre for Asia Pacific Studies, Toronto.

Teo, C.H. Jason and Wang, Ruifang (1996): "Modelling the Macro Effects of China's Inward Foreign Direct Investment," in Chew, S.B. and Kendall, Jon D., Regional Issues in Economic, Applied Economics Research Series, Vol. II, Nanyang Business School, Nanyang Technological University.

Wong, John (1991): "Economic Integration of Hong Kong and Guangdong: Hong Kong's Outward Processing in China." IEAPE Internal Study Paper No. 2.

TABLE 1

Variable Definitions

DL*VARIABLE* :		First order difference of logarithm of *Variable*
D84	:	Dummy variable representing China's devaluation of RMB against HK$ for the export-orientation programme in 1984, D84=1 in 1984, 0 in other years
DICN	:	China's domestic investment
DXHC	:	Hong Kong's visible domestic exports to China
FDIHC	:	Hong Kong's outward FDI in China
GNPCN	:	China's GNP
HKPPty	:	Hong Kong's property price level
MHC	:	Hong Kong's visible imports from China
MM	:	Hong Kong's total imports of machinery and equipment
ERHC	:	Real exchange rate of HK$ against RMB
ROWX	:	Hong Kong's visible exports to the Rest of the World
TXCN	:	China's total exports of goods and services
XHC	:	Hong Kong's total visible exports to China
GNPUS	:	United States' gross national product

TABLE 2
Estimation Results (OLS)

1) DLFDIHC = -0.8708 + 9.5262DLGNPCN + 1.6238DLHKPPTY(-1)

          (-4.389)   (5.053)   (3.356)

Adjusted R^2 = 0.788   DW statistic   = 1.837

Sample period   = 1985 - 94

2) DLGNPCN = 0.0551 + 0.0327DLFDIHC + 0.0909DLDICN + 0.0848DLTXCN(-1)

          (8.602)   (2.593)   (2.702)   (2.534)

Adjusted R^2 = 0.848   DW statistic   = 1.980

Sample period   = 1985 - 94

3) DLMHC   = 0.0426 + 1.0433DLROWX + 0.0566DLDXHC(-1) - 0.0846DLERHC(-1)

          (4.045)   (14.177)   (4.903)   (-1.715)

Adjusted R^2 = 0.947   DW statistic   = 1.938

Sample period   = 1980 - 94

4) DLXHC   = -0.0002 + 0.8786DLMM + 0.5774DLERHC + 0.4579DLXHC(-1)

          (-0.002)   (2.210)   (1.337)   (5.540)

          + 0.4816D84

           (1.971)

Adjusted R^2 = 0.756   Durbin's h statistic   = -1.346

Sample period   = 1980 - 94

5) DLROWX = -0.0636 + 0.8837DLMHC + 0.7267DLGNPUS

          (-4.004)   (9.703)   (2.267)

Adjusted R^2 = 0.891   DW statistic   = 1.752

Sample period   = 1979 - 93

TABLE 3

Utilised FDI in China (US$m)

Year	All Sources	From Hong Kong[a]
1984	1,419	748
		(53)
1985	1,956	956
		(49)
1986	2,244	1,329
		(59)
1987	2,6647	1,809
		(68)
1988	3,740	2,428
		(65)
1989	3,773	2,342
		(62)
1990	3,755	2,118
		(56)
1991	4,366	2,487
		(57)
1992	11,008	7,709
		(70)
1993	27,515	17,861
		(65)
Totals	62,423	39,787
		(64)

Source: Luk (1994), Table 4.1.

Note: The figures in ( ) represent Hong Kong's percentage share of the total amount of FDI in China.

a.   The Hong Kong figures include investment from Macao, but the share of the latter has been very small.

TABLE 4

Hong Kong, Guangdong and ASEAN: Comparative Cost Advantage, 1990

Location	Wage Rate per month of Unskilled Workers (US$)	Industrial Rental per month (HK$ per sq. ft.)
Hong Kong	412	8
	(5.5)	(New Kowloon)
Guangdong	75	0.8-1.5
(Shenzhen)	(1.0)	
Thailand	90	1
	(1.2)	(Chon Buri)
Malaysia	110	2
	(1.5)	(Ipoh)
Indonesia	60	2
	(0.8)	(Bonded Zone)
Philippines	—	1
		(Cebu)

Source: Maruya (1992), Table 5.

Note: The figures in ( ) represent the indicator comparing to the base of 1.0 of Shenzhen, Guangdong.

TABLE 5

Hong Kong Trade involving Outward Processing in China (%)

Estimated Content involving Outward Processing in:	1989	1990	1991	1992	1993
Total Exports to China	53.0	58.8	55.5	52.4	47.9
- Domestic exports	76.0	79.0	76.5	74.3	74.0
- Re-exports	43.6	50.3	48.2	46.2	42.1
Imports from China	58.1	67.8	67.6	72.1	73.8
Re-Exports of China Origin	—	—	74.1	78.3	80.8

Source: Luk (1994), Table 4.2.

TABLE 6

Hong Kong's Imports from China for Re-export by Commodity (%)

Year	Food & Crude Materials	Chemicals	Manufactures	Total
1979	25.8	7.1	67.1	100
1981	26.8	7.4	65.8	100
1983	23.1	6.4	70.5	100
1984	20.3	5.6	74.1	100
1985	19.5	5.6	74.9	100
1986	15.6	4.9	79.5	100
1987	13.0	4.6	82.4	100
1988	11.7	3.8	84.5	100
1989	8.4	3.1	88.5	100

Source: Sung (1991b), Table 7.8.

TABLE 7

Hong Kong's Re-exports to China by Commodity (%)

Year	Food & Crude Materials	Chemicals	Manufactures	Total
1979	16.0	7.4	76.6	100
1981	9.8	4.7	85.5	100
1983	14.0	6.7	79.3	100
1984	8.7	5.8	85.5	100
1985	6.7	6.3	87.0	100
1986	10.1	8.5	81.4	100
1987	9.1	10.4	80.5	100
1988	9.2	14.5	76.3	100
1989	11.2	12.0	76.8	100

Source: Sung (1991b), Table 7.9.

NIEs and ASEAN: Trade Competitors?

Poa *Tiong Siaw*
&
Mike **Leu** *Gwo-jiun*

Nanyang Business School, Nanyang Technological University, Nanyang Avenue, Singapore 639798
Fax: +(65) 792.4217, Tel: +(65) 799.1404, Email: agjleu@ntu.edu.sg

Abstract In Asia, the NIEs have been the second tier of countries to undergo rapid industrialisation after Japan while the ASEAN nations have emerged as the third wave in more recent years. An analysis of selected three-digit SITC product categories from 1980-1994 shows evidence of competition between the two groups of countries in the US market. The fact that the export structures of pairs of countries show varying but significant degrees of similarity supports the presence of competition. We also find evidence of shifts in comparative advantage in both traditional and non-traditional products from the NIEs to ASEAN.

1. INTRODUCTION

Following the 'miraculous' growth of the East Asian NIEs in the last three decades, many eyes are now turning toward the third wave of countries in the 'flying-geese' pattern of development in Asia. After Japan and the East Asian NIEs, ASEAN countries have gradually caught up in terms of growth rates. In 1990, the ASEAN countries averaged 7.8 percent growth while the NIEs grew at 6.2 percent.

Export-led strategies have been the proven winning formula in the Asian experience, a golden rule which the ASEAN countries have abided by faithfully. This can be seen from their increasing share of world exports. With rising wage rates in the NIEs in the late 1970s and early 1980s, it is widely believed that their comparative advantage in traditional labour-intensive products has systematically shifted to the ASEAN countries.

In this study, the 'revealed comparative advantage' (RCA) of the NIEs and the ASEAN countries are examined using trade data between 1980 and 1994. We seek to determine if the two groups of countries had been trade competitors in that period. We then seek to study the extent of their competition or the lack of it, as well as the products repsonsible. In the following analysis, Brunei has been excluded so that ASEAN comprises Malaysia, Thailand, Philippines and Indonesia. The variety of Brunei's exports are so limited that if we take it into account, the number of comparable SITC3 products falls to only a handful. Therefore, to make comparisons 1) within only contestable markets and 2) for a reasonable array of products, ASEAN is represented by ASEAN4. The US market is used as the benchmark as in preceding studies.

The present study indicates that in the period of 1980-1994, between the NIEs and ASEAN, there is sufficient evidence that the export structure of several pairs of countries were significantly similar. As suggested by Chow(1990), such a result implies comparative advantage shifting from the former. We believe that it also captures simultaneous growth of exports in similar product categories, implying direct competition at the early stage of the product cycle. This belief is reinforced by an analysis of specific product groups a la Chow(1990). The present study also uncovers substantial evidence of significant negative correlations between the growth rates of RCAs in various product groups. There is strong evidence of shifts in comparative advantage, especially in the more traditional labour-intensive products during the given period.

This paper is organised in the following manner. Section 2 reveals the selection criteria for SITC3 product categories and discusses the methodology of calculating RCAs. Section 3 examines the degree of export structure similarity between pairs of NIEs and ASEAN4 countries by comparing their overall RCA indices. Section 4 tests hypotheses of shifts of comparative advantage by comparing the growth rates of RCA indices for each specific product group. We summarise and conclude in the final section.

2. METHODOLOGY AND PRODUCT SELECTION

This study adopts Balassa's (1965, 1979, 1983) 'Revealed Comparative Advantage' (RCA) to unveil the relative export performances and degree of competition between the NIEs and ASEAN. We calculate the RCA index in each SITC3 product category as follows:

$$RCA_{ij} = (X_{ij} / X_i) / (C_j / W)$$

where W = total US manufactured imports

              C_j = total US imports of the jth product

              X_i = total US imports from the ith country

              X_{ij} = total US imports of the jth product from the ith country

Although we adopt generally the same methodology as Chow(1990) in computation as well as analysis, this study differs in its selection of products for analysis. In his paper, Chow utilised the commodity classification by Haufbauer and Chilas (1974), with 88 fixed SITC3 groups further aggregated into 40 Heckscher-Ohlin and product cycle goods. The present study does away with fixing a specific group of products to compare across countries. We feel that using Chow's selection method introduces bias into correlation studies since not all the 88 SITC3 products might be exported by all the countries under study.

For example, a large country may export all 88 groups while a smaller one may export only 50 groups. Then according to Chow, measuring the degree of competition between the two countries would entail entering zero values for the 38 groups which the smaller country does not export. A correlation exercise on these RCAs would inadvertently understate the degree of competition.

Hence, instead of fixing a basket of products to compare cross-country performance, we let the data decide the appropriate products to be included in any comparison. The selection criteria for a product in this study are the following:

- It must constitute at least 0.01 percent of the total exports of the country under study.
- It must be exported by every country under study.

As such, the basket of products will differ in both the number and type of products included for the analysis of each NIE. We feel this will allow for more meaningful interpretation of the results than in Chow's study.

3. COMPARING THE OVERALL RCA INDICES

To understand the implications of the results in Table 1-4, note that a positive significant Spearman Rank Correlation coefficient implies export structure similarity between two countries. The degree of similarity increases with the magnitude of the coefficients. The asterisks represent the level of statistical significance. The following subsections describe each NIE's export structure similarity with ASEAN4 countries.

3.1 SINGAPORE VS ASEAN4

Table 1 shows that the export structure of Singapore and Malaysia have been largely similar for 1980-1994. This implies strong competition in the product groups concerned in the US market. Malaysia's emulation of Singapore's development pattern has been well documented. So the results come as no surprise and it has implications for Singapore in that the threats from Malaysia's industries are real and have continued for many years. The degree of export similarity had increased in magnitude during the period. This trend is potentially unfavourable to Singapore and should be a cause for concern.

As for the three other ASEAN4 countries, no significant relationship could be found. Compared to Malaysia, Thailand, Philippines and Indonesia have lagged behind somewhat in their industrialisation drives. This fact is reflected in the last three columns. At first glance, the table magnifies the gap between Malaysia and the rest of ASEAN4. However, Singapore differs fundamentally in resource endowment with the rest of ASEAN4 and hence cannot be used as a model to be emulated by them. Rather, the results reflect the closer similarity of resource endowment between Singapore and Malaysia than between Singapore and the rest of ASEAN4. Interestingly, the coefficients, although not statistically significant, are largely negative. This suggests that Singapore has been able to shift away from products in which the three countries have been gaining in comparative advantage.

3.2 HONG KONG VS ASEAN4

The announcement of China's opening up and initiation of reforms in 1978 has had a tremendous impact on Hong Kong's export structure. According to Lai(1994), in the years that followed, Hong Kong's entrepot role re-emerged such that re-exports began to overtake domestic exports by 1988 and accounted for some 68.9 percent of total exports in 1991. Specifically, by the mid-1980s industrialists have come to see Hong Kong and China's economies as one and Hong Kong industry began moving into China to make use of the low land and labour costs.

Table 2 captures this re-emergence of entrepot trade. In particular, Indonesia's export structure has been exceptionally close to Hong Kong's. This does not imply that Indonesia has caught up with Hong Kong in terms of the level of industrialisation. Rather, it shows that Hong Kong's foreign direct investment in China had largely been in industries which were in direct competition with those of Indonesia. These industries are likely to be labour intensive ones. Furthermore, according to Lai(1994), Indonesia received the largest share of Hong Kong's FDI in ASEAN until 1988, further reinforcing their export structure similarity. After 1988, Indonesia received the second largest share of Hong Kong's FDI in ASEAN with a dramatic increase in 1990.

As a hedge against a possibly hostile take-over by China, Hong Kong has internationalised her economy, including making investments in ASEAN. The first three columns of Table 4 reflect the possibly rapid increase in Hong Kong's FDI in Malaysia, Thailand and Philippines after 1986. In particular, Thailand's share of the FDI rocketed to overtake that of Indonesia in 1988 [Lai(1994)]. This could account for increasing export structure similarity in the second column starting from the same year. The same can be said about Hong Kong's relationships with the Philippines and Malaysia.

3.3 *TAIWAN VS ASEAN4*

Table 3 shows only spotty evidence of export structure similarity between Taiwan and ASEAN4. Specifically, Malaysia displayed no similarity at all while elements of competition with Indonesia and Philippines appeared only temporarily from 1980 to 1983.

The surprising finding is in the second column. Apparently, Thailand and Taiwan have been competing in the US market up to 1985. In 1985, however, in view of the rising protectionistic measures in the US, Taiwan started to diversify its exports towards Europe and Asia. This led to a secular decline in US share of Taiwan's total exports ever since. According to Tsay(1994), this policy was to change in later years as the government realised that Taiwan needed to re-concentrate on the US market to realise medium to long term advantages concerning absorption of technology, information and market expansion.

The increasing similarity since 1988 could be a result of Taiwan's rising FDI in Thailand with the former's establishment of the International Economic Co-operation Development Fund (IECDF). The ensuing divergence in export pattern from 1992 may be due to decreasing amount of investment associated with, according to Tsay(1994), Thailand's rising land costs, rising real wages and inadequate infrastructure.

3.4 *KOREA VS ASEAN4*

The second oil shock had derailed Korea's macroeconomic balance by 1979. As a result, the unlimited support for heavy and chemical industry (HCI) in Korea since 1973 was abruptly reversed in 1980. From 1980 to 1987, Korea's economic policy was largely aimed at stabilisation and policies that favoured the HCI sector were abandoned. According to Lee (1996), 1988 to 1994 was a period of transition for the Korean economy. The development of service industries outpaced that of manufacturing so that the latter accounted for only 27.1 percent of GNP in 1993 as compared to 30.3 percent in 1985.

Table 4 shows that any significant competition between Korea and ASEAN4 materialised only after 1987, when the former started to move away from manufacturing. Thailand showed a competitive export pattern from 1987, peaked in 1990 and gradually disappeared by 1994 after Korea had switched to the higher value-added and services sectors. Indonesia was competitive with Korea from 1988 to 1994 while Malaysia displayed irregular patterns and Philippines showed hardly any significant relationship.

3.5 *ALTERNATIVE EXAMINATION OF RCAS*

It is conventional wisdom that comparative advantage in traditional labour intensive products have systematically shifted from Japan to the NIEs and then to ASEAN in the past thirty years. Therefore to further examine the extent to which the export expansions in ASEAN4 countries have become more similar to that of the NIEs, another series of Spearman Rank Correlation Coefficients are developed in Tables 5-8. This time however, the coefficients are between the RCA indices of the four ASEAN countries in 1994 and the indices of the NIEs in each year from 1980 to 1994. Balassa's stage theory of comparative advantage suggests that if these countries go through similar stages of industrialisation, then the coefficients indicate the extent to which the ASEAN4 countries managed to catch up with the NIEs in succeeding years.

Table 5 bears a striking resemblance with Table 1. This result is expected and it further strengthens the conclusion in Section 3.1. Malaysia's export performance in 1994 indicates that its comparative advantage position had reached that of Singapore in the same year. This also reflects both countries' relatively constant export patterns during the given period. The lack of any statistically significant coefficients again illustrates the fundamental dissimilarity between Singapore and the rest of ASEAN4 in export structure.

Table 6 again supports our findings in Section 3.2. In the first column, we find that Malaysia's export composition, like that of Thailand and Indonesia, resembled that of Hong Kong until 1985, after which the similarity starts to diminish. It is interesting to note that for the remaining three ASEAN4 countries, it is in 1985 that their degree of similarity with Hong Kong starts to increase. This again is reflective of the increasing entrepot role of Hong Kong in the mid-80s. Specifically, Malaysia, due to its more advanced export composition, began to deviate from Hong Kong's as the latter increased its re-exports of less sophisticated made-in-China products.

The results in Table 7 show a consistent trend only in the last column. Here, there is clear evidence that Indonesia has managed to follow Taiwan's export path in the US market up to 1988. Taiwan's diversification of markets towards Asia and Europe resulted in the ensuing divergence. The Philippines managed to match Taiwan's export composition in 1983 but the subsequent sporadic relationship is difficult to explain. It is clear that Malaysia and Thailand did not follow Taiwan's export path during this period.

Table 8 shows Thailand's 1994 export structure closely followed Korea's up to 1990 although the similarity disappeared in 1994. This is again due to Korea's moving away from manufactures. The Philippines' export structure seemed to resemble Korea's only in 1983 while Indonesia managed to do the same up to 1993. Finally, as expected, there is no clear relationship at all between Malaysia and Korea.

4. ANALYSES OF SPECIFIC PRODUCT GROUPS

The growth rates of the RCA (GRRCA) of each SITC3 product group are calculated for the period between 1980 and 1994 for each country. We then calculate the simple Pearson correlation coefficients of these GRRCA indices. A significant negative correlation coefficient implies shifting comparative advantage from NIEs to ASEAN4 for the particular product group. A positive correlation coefficient would indicate complementary growth or decline in a product group. Growth or decline would in turn depend on whether the GRRCA indices are both positive or both negative respectively.

In that respect, we must analyse competition in two stages. Firstly, shifting comparative advantage implies the later stage of competition whereby the ASEAN4 countries have competed favourably and have been taking over the exports of the respective products. Secondly, as a positive correlation of positive GRRCA indices implies, competition is taking place at an earlier stage whereby the countries involved have been gaining in comparative advantage. Therefore, we would expect to find more traditional products in the former case and more sophisticated products in the latter.

According to conventional wisdom, comparative advantage in traditional labour intensive products has systematically shifted from the NIEs to ASEAN. However, in his study, Lutz (1987) found little evidence of such shifts between the NICs (including East Asian NIEs) and other developing countries (including ASEAN4) in the years 1968-1982. In that study however, Lutz utilised only 'all three-digit categories of SITC 8 (miscellaneous manufactures) and SITC 65 (textiles)'. The present study provides a useful extension of that study by using 1980-1994 data although we use a different technique of analysis. Since there is no product restriction mentioned in Section 2, we feel that the analysis here will be more comprehensive. The results in Tables 9-12 show substantial shifts in comparative advantage as the following sections will describe.

4.1 SINGAPORE

Table 9 reaffirms the earlier conclusion about Singapore's export pattern relative to ASEAN4. With Malaysia, we observe largely positive and significant correlation coefficients, with particularly strong relationships for the three-digit SITC groups of 058 and 843. The RCAs of these products move in the same direction so we can conclude that Singapore and Malaysia compete rigorously in common exports.

The remaining columns reveal shifts in comparative advantage in various products toward Thailand, the Philippines and Indonesia. For unskilled labour-intensive manufactured goods, the SITC 628 and 652 groups have shifted to Indonesia while the 658, 831, 842 and 848 groups have shifted to the Philippines. Among non-manufactured goods, the 232 group has shifted to Thailand. It is interesting to note that among technology intensive manufactures, Singapore has lost its comparative advantage in automatic data processing machines (SITC 752) to the Philippines and aircraft and associated parts (SITC 792) to Indonesia.

As for early competition, apart from Malaysia, there are competitive threats from the Philippines in the physical capital intensive SITC 749 group. Among technology intensive products, we see extremely strong competition in the telecommunication equipment and parts group (SITC 764). Moreover, the Philippines has also been competing in equipment for distributing electricity, aircraft and associated parts and optical goods (SITC 773, 792 and 884).

4.2 HONG KONG

As suspected, Table 10 shows that shifts in comparative advantage from Hong Kong to Malaysia took place in more sophisticated products which include the technology intensive electrical apparatus and optical goods (SITC 772 and 884) and the human capital intensive household electrical and non-electrical equipment (SITC 775). Shifts toward Thailand and the Philippines have occurred in the more unskilled labour intensive products (SITC 036, 248 and 665). Among technology intensive sectors, Thailand has significantly taken over the measuring, analysing, checking instruments group (SITC 874) while Indonesia had done so in the telecommunication equipment industry (SITC 764).

In terms of early competition, the most notable product group is equipment for distributing electricity (SITC 773) where the comparative advantage of Malaysia, Thailand and the Philippines have shown strong trends of complementary growth with Hong Kong. Thailand displayed more significant positive relationships than the others. These include all labour intensive (SITC 651, 848 and 851), human capital intensive (SITC 697), physical capital intensive (SITC 751) and technology intensive (SITC 752 and 773) industries. The Philippines has competed mainly in the technology intensive SITC 771 and 773. Finally, Malaysia showed the most ambiguous relationship with Hong Kong.

4.3 TAIWAN

Table 11 shows that Taiwan's comparative advantage in many technology industries has shifted to Malaysia and the Philippines. Specifically, equipment for distributing electricity, aircraft and parts, and optical goods (SITC 773, 792 and 884) have shifted to Malaysia while automatic data processing machines, electric power machinery, electrical apparatus, and thermionic, cold and photo-cathode valves and tubes (SITC 752, 771, 772 and 776) have shifted to the Philippines. In both countries though, the same shifts have occurred in largely labour intensive garment products in SITC 844, 845, 846 and 848.

Taiwan's relationship with Thailand was significant in only four product groups. There has been a shift only in the labour intensive garment group SITC 846. Shifts to Indonesia took place primarily in labour intensive garment products (SITC 845, 847 and 893).

There are very few product groups which show complementary growth with ASEAN. With Malaysia, these are SITC 699, 784 and 848, all of which have different factor intensity. With Thailand, SITC 699, 749 and 847 which are also of diverse factor intensity. Taiwan's exports in the relatively sophisticated telecommunication equipment (SITC 764) and radio broadcast receivers (SITC 762) faced fierce competition from the Philippines. Finally, with Indonesia, we observe complementary growth in the aircraft and equipment group (SITC 792) as well as woven fabrics (SITC 653).

4.4 KOREA

As Table 12 shows, shifts of comparative advantage from Korea to ASEAN occurred largely in technology intensive products. These include telecommunication equipment (SITC 764), thermionic, cold and photo-cathode valves, tubes (SITC 776), and aircraft and parts (SITC 792). Other shifts took place in petroleum products (SITC 334), wood manufactures (SITC 635) and articles of plastic (SITC 893). Each of the four ASEAN countries accounted for a fair share of those shifts.

Among technology intensive industries, there is evidence of early competition with Malaysia in electrical apparatus (SITC 772) and with the Philippines in equipment for distributing electricity (SITC 773). Among unskilled labour intensive goods, complementary growth occurred in glassware, pottery and baby goods (SITC 665, 666 and 894). This is also true for non-electrical parts and accessories of machines (SITC 749) and parts and accessories of motor vehicles (SITC 784).

4.5 CAVEATS

The above conclusions are subject to some important qualifications. Firstly, due to our method of product selection, the subsequent export structures of each country were defined strictly in terms of the product basket. Hence, similarities in export structure per se do not imply similar national export structures, let alone equivalent levels of industrialisation. Furthermore, we must remember that the US market is our benchmark for analysis.

Our second qualification concerns trade policies applied by the US government. The history of US trade restrictions on imports from the NIEs stretches back to the early 1970s. These restrictions included quotas on textile/clothing, voluntary export restraints (VERs), orderly marketing arrangements (OMAs) and other non-tariff barriers to check imports from the NIEs. Some VERs were negotiated on a bilateral basis [Chow (1990)]. Hence, the GRRCA indices may not reflect the real comparative advantage of the NIEs.

Thirdly, complementary growth in similar product categories may not necessarily imply direct competition since there are different stages in the product cycle, different levels of technological sophistication and/or product differentiation. As a case in point, the Philippines' apparent comparative advantage in telecommunication equipment (SITC 764) could well be in similar products that are less sophisticated than those exported by Singapore and Taiwan. Our analysis ignores such possibilities.

5. SUMMARY AND CONCLUSION

Our comparison of RCA indices show strong evidence of competition between several pairs of NIEs and ASEAN4 countries in the US market. Singapore has faced fierce competition from Malaysia since 1980. It did not however show any sign of export pattern similarity with the rest of ASEAN. This reflects fundamental differences in resource endowment throughout the period. For Hong Kong, all ASEAN4 countries except Malaysia began to develop similar export patterns since the second half of the 1980s. This result reflects the re-emergence of Hong Kong as an entrepot centre. That is, re-exports of traditional products from China have begun to dominate Hong Kong's export structure. It is of great concern to Hong Kong that its re-entry into less sophisticated manufactures may retard its diversification drive into more technology and knowledge intensive products. Taiwan's export pattern was significantly followed only by Thailand up to 1992. There was little evidence of competition with the remaining three ASEAN4 countries. Finally for Korea, competition from Thailand began in 1987 but disappeared by 1994. The only ASEAN4 country which still competed with it in 1994 was Indonesia.

Another important finding of our study is evidence of shifting comparative advantage from the NIEs to ASEAN4. Interestingly, these shifts were not limited to the traditional labour intensive industries. Instead, we find that such shifts had in fact occurred for many technology intensive products. We see very strong evidence of this in the case of Korea. This goes to show the growing export dynamism of ASEAN4 in the 1980s and early 1990s.

In view of such developments, we can conclude that there exists a certain degree of trade competition between the NIEs as a grouping and ASEAN4 as a region. The elements of competition would however be more obvious when we study the specific inter-country relationships. The evidence found of shifting comparative advantage supports this argument. All these are in spite of the fact that the NIEs have experienced higher export growth than the ASEAN4 countries. The high growth rates of the ASEAN countries led many to believe in their gradual displacement of the NIEs' exports. While this displacement had not been evident in previous studies, we can see in the present one that it is beginning to take shape in the 1980s.

The competitive capabilities of the next tier of developing countries headed by China is then of great interest. Many have dubbed the next century the era of the Asia Pacific and judging from the trends of international trade, that era does not appear to be too far off.

REFERENCES

Balassa, B. (1965): "Trade Liberalisation and 'Revealed' Comparative Advantage," *Manchester School of Economics and Social Studies*, 33, 99-123.

Chow, P.C.Y. (1990): "The Revealed Comparative Advantage of the East Asian NICs", *The International Trade Journal*, 5, 235-262.

Fong, P.E. (1987): "The Asian NICs in the 1980s: Development Strategies and Perspectives," *East Asia : International Review of Economic, Political, and Social Development*, Colorado: Westview Press, 4, 101-129.

Haufbauer, G.C. and J.G. Chilas (1974): "Specialisation by Industrial Countries : Extent and Consequences", *The International Division of Labour: Problems and Prospects.* Tubringen: J.C.B. Mober, 3-38.

Hong, M.S. (1987): "Competition between NICs and ASEAN," *East Asia : International Review of Economic, Political, and Social Development*, Colorado: Westview Press, 4, 130-144.

Kim, K. and D.M. Leipziger (1993): "Korea : a case of government-led development", *The Lessons of East Asia*, Washington: The World Bank.

Kim, W.B. (1994): "The Korean Peninsula and the Future of Northeast Asia," *Economic Interactions and Interdependence in East Asia,* Tokyo : Ushiba Memorial Foundation, 41-84.

Kuo, S.W.K. (1996): "Development of the Asia-Pacific Region, 1960-90," *Development, Trade and the Asia-Pacific: Essays in honour of Professor Lim Chong Yah*, Singapore: Prentice-Hall, 341-357.

Lai, F. (1994): "Prospects for Economic Interactions in the Asian Pacific : The Case of Hong Kong," *Economic Interactions and Interdependence in East Asia,* Tokyo : Ushiba Memorial Foundation, 104-124.

Lee, H.K. (1996): *The Korean Economy : Perspectives for the Twenty-First Century.* New York : State University of New York, 19-34.

Lutz, J.M. (1987): "Shifting Comparative Advantage, the NICs and the Developing Countries," *The International Trade Journal*, 1, 339-358.

Redding, S.G. (1994): "Competitive Advantage in the context of Hong Kong," *The Competitive Advantages of Far Eastern Business*, Oregon: Frank Cass, 71-89.

Tsay, C.L. (1994): "Taiwan and the Prospects for Economic Interactions in East Asia," *Economic Interactions and Interdependence in East Asia,* Tokyo : Ushiba Memorial Foundation, 133-163.

TABLE 1

Spearman Correlation Coefficients of RCA Indices
of Singapore and ASEAN4 in the US Market

Year	Singapore / Malaysia	Singapore / Thailand	Singapore / Philippines	Singapore / Indonesia
1980	0.3869***	0.0707	-0.0704	0.0306
1981	0.3361***	0.1511	-0.0657	0.0068
1982	0.3061***	0.0219	-0.0929	0.0385
1983	0.3326**	-0.0551	-0.0002	-0.0908
1984	0.3159**	-0.1243	-0.0110	-0.0356
1985	0.3331**	-0.1000	-0.0773	-0.0839
1986	0.2513*	-0.1484	-0.1449	-0.1914
1987	0.2594*	-0.0927	-0.1176	-0.1499
1988	0.2214*	-0.1428	-0.0969	-0.1992
1989	0.3227**	-0.0014	-0.0118	-0.1987
1990	0.3025**	-0.0077	-0.0355	-0.1821
1991	0.3262**	-0.0024	-0.0708	-0.1860
1992	0.3331**	-0.0180	-0.0930	-0.1352
1993	0.3278**	-0.0308	-0.1142	-0.1383
1994	0.3709***	-0.0625	-0.1268	-0.2064

TABLE 2

Spearman Correlation Coefficients of RCA Indices
of Hong Kong and ASEAN4 in the US Market

Year	Hong Kong / Malaysia	Hong Kong / Thailand	Hong Kong / Philippines	Hong Kong / Indonesia
1980	0.0935	0.2151	0.2835**	0.3751***
1981	0.0916	0.1723	0.2619*	0.2564*
1982	0.1144	0.2058	0.2963**	0.3551***
1983	0.1234	0.1835	0.2384*	0.3690***
1984	0.1880	0.1714	0.1468	0.3750***
1985	0.2642*	0.1419	0.2142	0.3790***
1986	0.2426*	0.1382	0.1675	0.3998***
1987	0.2764**	0.2020	0.3571***	0.3988***
1988	0.2249*	0.2409*	0.1878	0.4706***
1989	0.2132	0.2932**	0.3294**	0.4093***
1990	0.2985**	0.3070**	0.2746**	0.4636***
1991	0.3526***	0.3394**	0.3154**	0.4461***
1992	0.2571*	0.3703***	0.3036**	0.4043***
1993	0.2279*	0.3890***	0.2359*	0.4633***
1994	0.1650	0.3750***	0.2945**	0.4043***

*** significant at the 1 percent level

** significant at the 5 percent level

* significant at the 10 percent level

Source : Tables generated by author using data from WORLD TRADE DATABASE, Statistics Canada.

TABLE 3

Spearman Correlation Coefficients of RCA Indices
of Taiwan and ASEAN4 in the US Market

Year	Taiwan / Malaysia	Taiwan / Thailand	Taiwan / Philippines	Taiwan / Indonesia
1980	0.0766	0.3051**	0.3321**	0.1473
1981	0.0665	0.3536***	0.3443***	0.2522*
1982	-0.0690	0.4306***	0.3231**	0.2487*
1983	-0.0765	0.4095***	0.2238	0.2726**
1984	-0.1093	0.3614***	0.1286	0.1772
1985	-0.1663	0.3693***	0.1374	0.1357
1986	-0.0709	0.1674	-0.0271	0.0652
1987	0.0215	0.1202	0.0389	0.0385
1988	-0.0047	0.3213**	0.1251	0.1894
1989	-0.0191	0.3315**	0.2043	0.1603
1990	0.0821	0.3742***	0.1835	0.2253*
1991	0.1801	0.3449***	0.2559*	0.1802
1992	0.1245	0.2542**	0.1238	0.0564
1993	0.1483	0.2206	0.0773	0.0833
1994	0.1111	0.1853	0.0752	-0.0154

TABLE 4

Spearman Correlation Coefficients of RCA Indices
of Korea and ASEAN4 in the US Market

Year	Korea / Malaysia	Korea / Thailand	Korea / Philippines	Korea / Indonesia
1980	-0.0983	0.1837	0.1383	0.2453*
1981	0.0149	0.2247*	0.1358	0.1865
1982	0.1065	0.1700	0.1491	0.1762
1983	0.1578	0.1277	0.0923	0.3071**
1984	0.1786	0.1429	-0.0316	0.2819**
1985	0.2510*	0.1019	-0.0124	0.2545*
1986	0.2041	0.1048	-0.0166	0.2083
1987	0.2736**	0.2506*	0.1354	0.2191
1988	0.1692	0.2803**	-0.0006	0.3055**
1989	0.2167	0.3238**	0.2405*	0.3184**
1990	0.2981**	0.3554***	0.1448	0.3137**
1991	0.2670**	0.2823**	0.2369*	0.2684**
1992	0.2554*	0.2799**	0.1141	0.3154**
1993	0.1823	0.2261*	0.0988	0.3048**
1994	0.1157	0.1819	0.0677	0.2310*

*** significant at the 1 percent level

** significant at the 5 percent level

* significant at the 10 percent level

Source : Tables generated by author using data from WORLD TRADE DATABASE, Statistics Canada.

TABLE 5

**Spearman Correlation Coefficients between the RCA Indices of ASEAN4
in 1994 and the RCA Index of Singapore in the Specific Year in the US Market**

Year	Singapore / Malaysia	Singapore / Thailand	Singapore / Philippines	Singapore / Indonesia
1980	0.3776***	0.1663	-0.0471	0.0721
1981	0.3312**	0.1708	-0.1256	0.0413
1982	0.3393***	0.1605	-0.1520	-0.0568
1983	0.3990***	0.0265	-0.1425	-0.0760
1984	0.4328***	-0.0787	-0.0845	-0.0560
1985	0.4306***	-0.0516	-0.0675	-0.1081
1986	0.3757***	-0.0716	-0.0913	-0.1388
1987	0.3846***	0.0153	-0.0865	-0.1229
1988	0.4117***	-0.0073	-0.0766	-0.1206
1989	0.4114***	0.0133	-0.1055	-0.0871
1990	0.4386***	-0.0402	-0.1292	-0.1319
1991	0.3527***	-0.0230	-0.1694	-0.1387
1992	0.3608***	-0.0249	-0.1583	-0.1293
1993	0.3932***	-0.0241	-0.1424	-0.1575
1994	0.3709***	-0.0625	-0.1268	-0.2064

TABLE 6

**Spearman Correlation Coefficients between the RCA Indices of ASEAN4
in 1994 and the RCA Index of Hong Kong in the Specific Year in the US Market**

Year	Hong Kong / Malaysia	Hong Kong / Thailand	Hong Kong / Philippines	Hong Kong / Indonesia
1980	0.1856	0.2283*	0.2470*	0.3135**
1981	0.2316*	0.2498*	0.2170	0.2862**
1982	0.2461*	0.2512*	0.2470*	0.2756**
1983	0.2753**	0.2815**	0.2100	0.3004**
1984	0.2881**	0.2740**	0.2153	0.3129**
1985	0.2753**	0.2971**	0.2182	0.3232**
1986	0.2626*	0.3304**	0.2417*	0.3613***
1987	0.2480*	0.3405**	0.2519*	0.3672***
1988	0.2388*	0.4113***	0.2317*	0.4224***
1989	0.2050	0.3869***	0.2267*	0.4264***
1990	0.1841	0.3717***	0.2553*	0.4408***
1991	0.1763	0.4112***	0.2696**	0.4529***
1992	0.1720	0.3993***	0.2619*	0.4345***
1993	0.1794	0.3937***	0.2682**	0.4229***
1994	0.1650	0.3750***	0.2945**	0.4043***

*** significant at the 1 percent level

** significant at the 5 percent level

* significant at the 10 percent level

Source : Tables generated by author using data from WORLD TRADE DATABASE, Statistics Canada.

TABLE 7

Spearman Correlation Coefficients between the RCA Indices of ASEAN4 in 1994 and the RCA Index of Taiwan in the specific year in the US Market

Year	Taiwan / Malaysia	Taiwan / Thailand	Taiwan / Philippines	Taiwan / Indonesia
1980	-0.0258	0.1156	0.3269**	0.3192**
1981	-0.0450	0.1487	0.3200**	0.3467***
1982	-0.0539	0.1626	0.2898**	0.3250**
1983	-0.0963	0.1362	0.2708**	0.3223**
1984	-0.0685	0.1404	0.1884	0.2525*
1985	-0.1302	0.1139	0.2825**	0.2779**
1986	0.0341	0.0705	0.1820	0.2900**
1987	0.0589	0.1508	0.1646	0.2425*
1988	0.0674	0.2063	0.2713**	0.3094**
1989	0.0636	0.1772	0.1982	0.2356*
1990	0.0719	0.1643	0.1843	0.2264*
1991	0.0758	0.1405	0.2029	0.1981
1992	0.0611	0.1681	0.1258	0.0951
1993	0.0970	0.1939	0.1034	0.0259
1994	0.1111	0.1853	0.0752	-0.0154

TABLE 8

Spearman Correlation Coefficients between the RCA Indices of ASEAN4 in 1994 and the RCA Index of Korea in the Specific Year in the US Market

Year	Korea / Malaysia	Korea / Thailand	Korea / Philippines	Korea / Indonesia
1980	0.2136	0.4509***	0.2496*	0.5171***
1981	0.2096	0.4401***	0.2850**	0.5312***
1982	0.1729	0.4437***	0.3076**	0.5140***
1983	0.1970	0.4460***	0.2416*	0.5187***
1984	0.1683	0.4486***	0.2268*	0.4843***
1985	0.1696	0.4348***	0.2328*	0.4982***
1986	0.2170	0.4587***	0.2164	0.4488***
1987	0.2041	0.4778***	0.2648*	0.4676***
1988	0.2121	0.4669***	0.2534*	0.4499***
1989	0.2178	0.3943***	0.2031	0.4155***
1990	0.2032	0.3849***	0.2024	0.4156***
1991	0.1491	0.3224**	0.2420*	0.3302**
1992	0.1742	0.2967**	0.1515	0.3554***
1993	0.1478	0.2304*	0.1213	0.2985**
1994	0.1157	0.1819	0.1677	0.2310*

*** significant at the 1 percent level

** significant at the 5 percent level

* significant at the 10 percent level

Source : Tables generated by author using data from WORLD TRADE DATABASE, Statistics Canada.

TABLE 9

Correlation Coefficients of Growth Rates of RCA Indices between Singapore and ASEAN4

SITC3	Description	FI[++]	Singapore / Malaysia	Singapore / Thailand	Singapore / Philippines	Singapore / Indonesia
058	Fruit, prepared or preserved	NM	0.7567***			
232	Natural rubber latex	NM		-0.5486**		
628	Articles of rubber	NM				-0.5453**
652	Cotton fabrics	U				-0.5637**
658	Made-up articles of text. materials	U			-0.5818**	
666	Pottery	U	0.5832**			
749	Non-electric parts & access. of machines	P			0.6829***	
752	Automatic data processing machines	T			-0.4871*	
761	Television receivers	H	0.4723*			
764	Telecom. equip. & parts	T			0.8011***	
773	Equipment for distributing electricity	T			0.5327**	
792	Aircraft & associated equipment & parts	T			0.5424**	-0.5966**
831	Travel goods, handbags and similar containers	U			-0.5482**	
842	Outer garments, men's, of textile fabrics	U			-0.4551*	
843	Outer garments, women's, of textile fabrics	U	0.8017***			
844	Under garments of textile fabrics	U				0.6064**
845	Outer garments and other articles, knitted	U				0.5268*
848	Art. of apparel and clothing, no textile	U	0.5683**		-0.4765*	
884	Optical goods	T			0.4589	
893	Articles of materials described in 58	U	0.6456**			
898	Musical instruments, parts & access.	NM	0.4918*			

TABLE 10

Correlation Coefficients of Growth Rates of RCA Indices between Hong Kong and ASEAN4

SITC3	Description	FI[++]	Hong Kong / Malaysia	Hong Kong / Thailand	Hong Kong / Philippines	Hong Kong / Indonesia
036	Crustaceans and molluscs	NM		-0.5024*		
058	Fruit, prepared or preserved	NM	0.4871*		0.5059*	
248	Wood	NM		-0.4546*		
628	Articles of rubber	NM			-0.5457**	
651	Textile yarn	U		0.5239*		
665	Glassware	U		-0.4588*		
697	Household equipment of base metal	H		0.4602*		
751	Office Machines	P		0.5660**		
752	Automatic data processing machines	T		0.4586*		
764	Telecom. equip. & parts	T				-0.7339***
771	Electric power machinery & parts	T			0.4722*	
772	Elec. App. such as switches, relays, fuses, plugs etc	T	-0.5022*			
773	Equipment for distributing eletricity	T	0.7597***	0.7653***	0.6106**	
775	Household type, elect. & non-elect. equipment	H	-0.6222**			
844	Under garments of textile fabrics	U			-0.4694*	
845	Outer garments and other articles, knitted	U	0.5610**			
848	Art. of apparel and clothing, no textile	U	-0.4996*	0.5820**		
851	Footwear	U		0.5008*		
874	Measuring, analysing, checking instruments	T		-0.7456***		
884	Optical goods	T	-0.5833**			
931	Special transactions & commod., not class. to kind	NM			-0.5607**	

*** significant at the 1 percent level

** significant at the 5 percent level

* significant at the 10 percent level

[++] FI stands for Factor Intensity (for manufactured goods) where N: Natural Resource Intensive; P: Physical Capital Intensive; U: Unskilled Labour Intensive; H: Human Capital Intensive; T: Technology Intensive; NM: Non-manufactured good.

Source : Tables generated by author using data from WORLD TRADE DATABASE, Statistics Canada.

TABLE 11

Correlation Coefficients of Growth Rates of RCA Indices between Taiwan and ASEAN4

SITC3	Description	FI[++]	Taiwan / Malaysia	Taiwan / Thailand	Taiwan / Philippines	Taiwan / Indonesia
058	Fruit, prepared or preserved	NM				-0.4722*
512	Alcohols	NM				-0.5073*
653	Fabrics, woven	U				0.5376**
699	Manufactures of base metal	H	0.4865*	0.6002**		
749	Non-electric parts & access. of machines	P		0.6588***		
752	Automatic data processing machines	T			-0.4986*	
762	Radio broadcast receivers	H			0.5513**	
764	Telecom. equip. & parts	H			0.7498***	
771	Electric power machinery & parts	T			-0.6099**	
772	Elec. App. such as switches, relays, fuses, plugs etc	T			-0.6617***	
773	Equipment for distributing electricity	T	-0.6642***			
776	Thermionic, cold & photo-cathode valves, tubes, parts	T			-0.4755*	
784	Parts & access. of 722, 781, 782, 783	H	0.5545**			
792	Aircraft & associated equipment & parts	T	-0.5610**			0.5596**
844	Under garments of textile fabrics	U			-0.5525**	
845	Outer garments and other articles, knitted	U	-0.8150***			-0.5128*
846	Under garments, knitted or crocheted	U		-0.5445**	-0.4799*	
847	Clothing access. of textile fabrics	U		0.4567*		-0.5122*
848	Art. of apparel and clothing, no textile	U	0.5593**		-0.8298***	
884	Optical goods	T	-0.4884*			
893	Articles of materials described in 58	U				-0.5098*
894	Baby carriages, toys, games and sporting goods	U			0.5770**	

TABLE 12

Correlation Coefficients of Growth Rates of RCA Indices between Korea and ASEAN4

SITC3	Description	FI[++]	Korea / Malaysia	Korea / Thailand	Korea / Philippines	Korea / Indonesia
334	Petroleum products	NM	0.4737*		-0.5567**	
512	Alcohols	P				0.4648*
628	Articles of rubber	NM		0.5395**		
635	Wood manufactures	N	-0.4914*			
665	Glassware	U		0.5290*		
666	Pottery	U	0.5103*			
749	Non-electric parts & access. of machines	P			0.5162*	
762	Radio broadcast receivers	H		0.6251**		
764	Telecom. equip. & parts	T		-0.6031**		
772	Elec. App. such as switches, relays, fuses, plugs etc	T	0.7565***			
773	Equipment for distributing electricity	T			0.5827**	
776	Thermionic, cold & photo-cathode valves, tubes, parts	T		-0.4774*	-0.4918*	
784	Parts & access. of 722, 781, 782, 783	H		0.4835*		
792	Aircraft & associated equipment & parts	T				-0.5480**
844	Under garments of textile fabrics	U	-0.4927*			
893	Articles of materials described in 58	U		-0.4566*		
894	Baby carriages, toys, games and sporting goods	U		0.5169*		

*** significant at the 1 percent level

** significant at the 5 percent level

* significant at the 10 percent level

[++] FI stands for Factor Intensity (for manufactured goods) where N: Natural Resource Intensive; P: Physical Capital Intensive; U: Unskilled Labour Intensive; H: Human Capital Intensive; T: Technology Intensive; NM: Non-manufactured good.

Source : Tables generated by author using data from WORLD TRADE DATABASE, Statistics Canada.

An Econometric Model of Shandong Province

Poh Bee Tin
&
Chen Kang

Nanyang Business School, Nanyang Technological University, Nanyang Avenue, Singapore 639798
Fax: +(65) 792.4217, Tel: +(65) 799.6431, Email: akachen@ntu.edu.sg

Abstract Since the economic reform of 1978, Shandong has been one of the fastest growing regions in China. It has one of the highest provincial gross domestic products (GDP) in the country. Its GDP has been growing at 11 percent since 1987 and in 1993, the rate rose to 24 percent. In this paper, we build an econometric model of Shandong and use it to analyse certain special features of the economy in the areas of foreign investment and rural industry development.

1. INTRODUCTION

Since economic reforms began in 1978, China has been experiencing rapid economic development. As coastal provinces have great advantages of global access, the open door policy has resulted in rapid growth in these provinces unmatched by those inland provinces. Economic changes in different regions have resulted in highly differentiated economic geography.

Shandong is a coastal province situated in the eastern part of China. Since the open-door policy and economic reform programme, it has become one of the fastest growing regions in China. The gross domestic products (GDP) has been growing at 11 percent annually since 1987 and in 1993, the rate of growth rose to 24 percent. In 1994, Shandong's GDP was ranked the third highest among all provinces in China.

The open door policy and decentralisation of control has benefited its trade sector. The province is now one of China's leading foreign trade centres with established economic and trade ties with more than 160 countries and regions.

Shandong Provincial Government has been active in encouraging foreign investment in all types of industries. This is reflected in a series of preferential policies that were being introduced in open economic coastal zones, economic and technological development zones and so on. These attempts have opened up many investment opportunities for foreign investors. As such, foreign investment has shown a marked increase in the past few years. The province now receives the fourth largest share of the foreign investment commitment in China.

The Province also has a large base of Township and Village Enterprises (TVEs). Since 1980, Shandong's TVEs ranked after Jiangsu's in the gross output value ranking. The percentage of Shandong's rural gross output value attributed to TVEs has also increased from 24.8 percent in 1980 to 85 percent in 1994. We can thus conclude that the TVEs in Shandong has indeed grown considerably.

Shandong is a province that has one of the highest fixed capital commitments. In 1994, its fixed capital investment was ranked third among all the provinces. From the period

1985-1992, the major share (averaging 54 percent) of this investment was contributed by the state-owned enterprises (SOEs). The rural collectives, being the second largest investing group, contributed approximately 17 percent per annum to the total fixed capital investment.

In this paper, we build an econometric model of Shandong and use the model to analyse the economy in the reform era in the areas of foreign investment and rural industry development.

This paper is organised as follows: Section 2 specifies the model, explains the accounting framework adopted as well as the estimation techniques employed in the modelling exercise. In Section 3, a historical simulation is performed to estimate the model. 2 policy simulations are also performed to examine the impact of variables change in the economy. Section 4 presents the forecasting results for 1993-1998.

2. MODEL SPECIFICATION AND ESTIMATION

This model is based on the National Income Accounting System of China, which follows the Material Production Balance System (MPS). National Income computed by the MPS differs from the System of National Accounting (SNA) in that it does not include the service sector. As the service sector has grown in importance since economic reform in 1978, efforts have now been made to replace the accounting system by SNA. In recent years, China has attempted to publish some value added data series in SNA framework but data based on SNA are only available for the supply side. As such, there is still a need to utilise data series from both systems to build the model. The link between the output series in the two systems is illustrated in Table 1.

All data are from official publications: *Statistical Yearbook of Shandong* and *Statistical Yearbook of China*. The estimation period from 1985 to 1992 is chosen based on the availability of data. Annual observations are utilised in this modelling exercise. The computer software that is used is the 'Econometric Views' package. The regression method used for all regressions is Ordinary Least Squares (OLS).

The model consists of 30 endogenous variables, 18 exogenous variables, 14 behavioural equations and 16 identities. The variables are defined in Tables 2 and 3. The complete model is shown in Table 4.

3. SIMULATIONS AND EVALUATION

A historical simulation is performed from the period of 1987 to 1992. The model is evaluated based on 2 criteria. The first criterion is how closely the simulated values track the historical values. This process is accomplished through the use of Root-Mean-Square Percent Error (RMS%). The formula is

$$RMS\% = \sqrt{\frac{1}{T}\sum_{t=1}^{T}\left[\frac{Y_t^s - Y_t^a}{Y_t^a}\right]^2} \qquad (1)$$

where

Y_t^s = simulated value of Y_t

Y_t^a = actual value

T = number of periods in the simulation

Table 5 shows the Root-Mean-Square Percent errors of major endogenous variables from the historical simulation. Most of the endogenous variables have relatively small RMS %. This shows that the model on the whole has a good statistical fit.

The second criterion is how well the model simulates turning points in the data. The model in this case is able to track most of the turning points in the historical data series. Hence, we can say that this model is both of good fit and sensitive to variation in the data.

2 policy simulations are performed to study the impact of changes in the exogenous variables on the economy. Table 6 provides the dynamic elasticities of various endogenous variables over the simulation period. The impact of the change in exogenous variables is greater in the earlier years when the policy change was just implemented but die down in the later part of the simulation period. Table 7 provides the average elasticities of the various endogenous variables for the first 3 years from 1988 to 1990.

3.1 SIMULATION 1: TOWNSHIP AND VILLAGE ENTERPRISES (TVES)

Shandong is a rural-based province with majority of its population engaged in agricultural production. As a result of low land endowment relative to labour, rural unemployment was very high. The development of the rural industry has been an effective strategy in absorbing the surplus labour from the rural areas. Through its provision of investment funds, the rural industry has also helped in promoting agricultural production. In terms of productive investments, the rural collectives emerge as the second largest investing group after the SOEs.

Simulation 1 studies the impact of rural enterprises, specifically the Township and Village Enterprises (TVEs), on the economy of Shandong. We assume that the growth rate of the value-added of TVEs experienced a sustained 20 percent increase in 1988.

From Table 7, we can see that a 1 percent increase in the value-added of TVEs generates an average increase of 0.49 percent in the rural collective fixed capital investment over the period 1988-1990. Exports increase by an average of 0.29 percent as the TVEs is likely to export more with an increase in production. Since income from TVEs made up approximately 30 percent of the rural income (rural gdp), the increase in production of TVEs will also result in an increase in rural income. In this case, the rural income increases by an average of 0.12 percent for every 1 percent increase in the value-added of TVEs. The average elasticity of GDP with respect to the change in value-added of TVEs is 0.11, implying an increase of 0.11 percent for every 1 percent increase in the production of TVEs.

Summarising the above, we can conclude that TVEs have contributed to Shandong's economic growth in the simulation period. With more liberal policies towards them, they are likely to gain a more significant role in the economy in future.

3.2 SIMULATION 2: FOREIGN INVESTMENT

In the eighties, Shandong received only relatively small amounts of foreign investment. The share of cumulative amount of foreign investment for the period 1979-1987 was only 1.9 percent of the national total. In recent years, there has been a tremendous increase in this source of capital. The average growth rate of foreign investment utilised over the last ten years was approximately 60 percent.

Simulation 2 studies the impact of a sustained doubling of the growth rate of foreign investment in 1988 on Shandong's economy.

Examining the elasticities in Table 7, we can see that the impact of a change in foreign investment on the major endogenous variables is very insignificant. This is due to the fact that foreign investment was not the major source of capital during the simulation period. In fact, the major sources of funds during this period were domestic loans and locally-raised funds. However, given its tremendous growth in recent years, it is likely to have an important role to play in Shandong's economy in the future.

4. FORECASTING

4.1 VALUES AND ASSUMPTIONS OF EXOGENOUS VARIABLES

The model is utilised to make forecasts for the economy of Shandong for the period 1993-1998. The values of exogenous variables used in 1993-1995 where possible are the actual published values. Estimated values are also utilised whenever data are unavailable.

For the period 1996-1998, the projected values of the exogenous variables are based on certain assumptions. We assume that public consumption will grow at an average rate of 15 percent per annum. Foreign investment utilised is projected to grow at 20 percent annually. The annual rate of growth of bank loans to TVEs is assumed to be 24 percent and that of investment loans is expected to be 19 percent per year. For primary sector GDP, we expect that it will grow at 5 percent annually. Finally, the population growth is projected to be 1 percent annually with urban population growing at an annual rate of 10 percent. The actual and projected values of exogenous variables are shown in Table 8.

4.2 FORECAST EVALUATION

Table 9 presents the forecasted results of major endogenous variables for the period 1993-1998. The forecasted values of GDP are lower than the actual for the 3 years from1993 to 1995. This might be due to the fact that the model is unable to capture the strong momentum of the economy as well as the high growth rate of foreign investment. However, the percentage error of the forecast is rather small, averaging at 4.6 percent annually.

From 1996-1998, Shandong's GDP is predicted to grow at a stable rate of 15 percent per annum. This seems reasonable in the light of more intense regional competition especially from upcoming inland provinces whereby labour is cheap and natural resources are abundant. Her exports' growth rate is expected to fall from 10.3 percent to 2.9 percent but TVEs will still remain vibrant in the economy with an average growth rate of 21.2 percent for its value-added.

5. CONCLUSION GLOBAL AND THEORETICAL ISSUES

Summarising the above, the modelling exercise has been satisfactory. The simulated model has good statistical fit and is sensitive to variations in data. In addition, it has been able to provide good representation of Shandong's economy during the estimation period. As such, it can be employed as a guide to the study on the economy of Shandong.

REFERENCE

Pindyck, R.S. and Rubinfeld, D.L. (1976): *Econometric Models and Economic Forecasts*, Tokyo: McGraw Hill.

Chen, K. (1991): "Modelling China's Economy in Transition", *Economic Systems Research*, Vol 3, No 1.

Chen, K. (1995), *The Chinese Economy in Transition: Micro Changes and Micro Implications*, Singapore University Press.

Goodman, D.S.G. (ed) (1989): *China Regional Development*, New York: Routledge for Royal Institute of International Affairs.

Goodman, David S.G. and Segal, G. (eds) (1994): *China Deconstructs*, London: Routledge.

Toh, David and Chai, M. (eds), *Trade and Investment Guide: Shandong*, Singapore: Sinagpore Trade Development Board.

Ho, P.S.S. (1995): "Rural Non-agricultural Development in Post-Reform China: Growth, Development Patterns and Issue", *Pacific Affairs*, Vol 68, No3.

Garnaut, R. and Liu, G. (eds) (1992), *Economic Reform and Internationalisation: China and the Pacific Region*, The Australian National University.

Almanac of Shandong (1989), *Shandong Nianjian*, Shandong Reminin Chubanshe.

Almanac of China Township and Village Enterprises (various years): *Zhongguo Xiangzhen Qiye Nianjian*, Beijing: Nongye Chubanshe.

State Statistical Bureau (1985-1996): *Zhongguo Tongji Nianjian* (Statistical Yearbook of China), Beijing: Zhongguo Tongji Chubanshe.

Shandong Statistical Bureau (1985-1996): *Shandong Tongji Nianjian* (Statistical Yearbook of Shandong), Beijing: Zhongguo Tongji Chubanshe.

TABLE 1

National Income Accounting Table

<u>Demand Side</u>	<u>Supply Side</u>
Consumption	**Primary Sector GDP**
Urban Personal Consumption	(Agriculture)
Rural Personal Consumption	
Institutional Consumption	**+ Secondary Sector GDP**
	(Industry and Construction)
+ Investment (Accumulation)	
Fixed Capital Investment	**+ Tertiary Sector GDP**
Inventory Investment	(Transport, commerce and others)
= National Income Used	**= Gross Domestic Product**
+ Exports	- Other Tertiary Sector GDP
- Imports	- Depreciation
- Net Regional Inflow	- Statistical Discrepancy

=National Income Produced in MPS

TABLE 2

List of Endogenous Variables

Variable	Description	Variable	Description
gdp85	real gdp	vasoedf	change in real value-added of SOEs
rpcdispy	rural per capita disposable income	fci85	real total fixed capital investment
rpcdisp85	real rural per capita disposable income	acc85	real accumulation
rpccon85	real rural per capita consumption	niu85	Real national income used
upcdispy	urban per capita disposable income	x85	real exports
upcdispy85	real urban per capita disposable income	m85	real imports
upccon85	real urban per capita consumption.	inflow85	real net regional inflows
rucon85	real rural consumption	ni85	real national income produced
urcon85	real urban consumption	otgdp85	other tertiary sector real gdp
con85	real total consumption	gdp	nominal gdp
vatve85	real value-added of TVEs	pcgdp	nominal per capita gdp
rucolfci85	real rural collective fixed capital	rgdp85	real rural gdp
vatvedf	change in real value-added of TVEs	rgdp	nominal rural gdp
vasoe85	real value-added of SOEs	pcrgdp	nominal per capita rural gdp
otherfci85	real other fixed capital investment	gdpdf	change in real gdp

TABLE 3
List of Exogenous Variables

Variable	Description	Variable	Description
rucpi	rural consumer price index	pubcon85	real public consumption
urcpi	urban consumer price index	loantve85	real bank loans to TVEs
rupop	rural population	loantvedf	change in real bank loans to TVEs
urpop	urban population	invloan85	real investment loans
pop	total population	invloandf	change in real investment loans
statcon	statistical consumption discrepancy	rdni	Price ratio between Shandong and China (dni/dnni)
stat	statistical discrepancy	dni	national income deflator, Shandong
dgdp	gdp deflator	dnni	national income deflator of China
eus	exchange rate (RMB/US$)	pgdp85	real primary sector gdp
fiu85	foreign investment utilised		

TABLE 4

Behavioural Equations and Identities

1)	rpcdispy = 261.125 + 0.342 pcrgdp	$R^2 = 0.9500$
	(7.596) (10.680)	
2)	rpccon85 = 4.244 + 0.796 rpcdispy85	$R^2 = 0.9073$
	(0.094) (7.661)	
3)	upcdispy = 146.682 + 0.674 pcgdp	$R^2 = 0.9930$
	(3.858) (29.200)	
4)	upccon85 = 229.295 + 0.632 upcdispy85	$R^2 = 0.9290$
	(3.904) (8.860)	
5)	vatve85 = -90.376 +0.233 gdp85(-1) +2.675 fiu85	$R^2 = 0.9997$
	(-3.858) (4.474) (13.859)	
	+ 2.447 loantve85	
	(7.487)	
6)	rucolfci85 = 14.061 + 0.214 vatvedf + 1.831 loantvedf	$R^2 = 0.9591$
	(2.584) (2.546) (2.846)	
7)	vasoe85 = 174.689 + 0.381 otherfci85(-1) + 4.364 fiu85(-1)	$R^2 = 0.9952$
	(15.610) (6.987) (8.122)	
	+ 0.234 gdpdf	
	(5.533)	
8)	otherfci85 = 189.939 + 0.939 vasoedf + 1.265 vasoedf(-1)	$R^2 = 0.9984$
	(101.388) (13.820) (15.908)	
	+ 1.353 invloandf	
	(12.321)	
9)	acc85 = -282.487 + 0.622 gdp85(-1) + 0.416 fci85	$R^2 = 0.9775$
	(-5.378) (8.369) (2.085)	
10)	x85 = -30.635 + 29.862 eus +0.241 vatvedf	$R^2 = 0.9708$
	(-1.792) (6.499) (3.022)	
11)	m85 = -6.849 + 0.311 fiu85 + 0.030 gdp85(-1)	$R^2 = 0.9885$
	(-1.260) (3.989) (4.287)	
	+ 4.291 dum89	
	(2.521)	

TABLE 4 (CONT)

Behavioural Equations and Identities

12)	inflow85 = 763.468 - 748.578 rdni	$R^2 = 0.6708$
	(3.757) (-3.496)	
13)	otgdp85 = 30.539 + 0.117 ni85(-1) + 0.322 x85	$R^2 = 0.9931$
	(4.681) (7.481) (4.975)	
14)	rgdp85 = -127.521 + 0.428 vatve85 + 1.921 pgdp85	$R^2 = 0.9777$
	(-0.825) (3.492) (2.640)	
15)	rpcdispy85 = rpcdispy*100/rucpi	
16)	upcdispy85 = upcdispy*100/urcpi	
17)	rucon85 = rpccon85*rupop/10000	
18)	urcon85 =upccon85*urpop/10000	
19)	con85 = rucon85 + urcon85 + statcon + pubcon85	
20)	vatvedf = vatve85 - vatve85(-1)	
21)	vasoedf = vasoe85 - vasoe85(-1)	
22)	fci85 = rucolfci85 + otherfci85	
23)	niu85 = con85 + acc85	
24)	ni85 = niu85 + x85 - m85 - inflow85	
25)	gdp85 = ni85 + stat + otgdp85	
26)	gdpdf = gdp85 - gdp85(-1)	
27)	gdp = gdp85*dgdp/100	
28)	pcgdp = gdp*10000/pop	
29)	rgdp = rgdp85*dgdp/100	
30)	pcrgdp = rgdp*10000/rupop	

TABLE 5
Root-Mean-Square Percent Error

Variable	RMS%	Variable	RMS%
rucon85	5.1	gdp85	7.0
urcon85	5.6	inflow85	20.5
rucolfci85	10.4	otgdp85	4.8
otherfci85	9.4	x85	5.3
vatve85	4.2	m85	7.9
vasoe85	5.2	rgdp85	3.5
acc85	11.4		

TABLE 6
Dynamic Elasticities of Endogenous Variables

Variables	1988	1989	1990	1991	1992
gdp85	0.061	0.104	0.175	0.102	-0.043
	0.011	0.006	0.008	0.008	-0.014
con85	0.029	0.046	0.096	0.065	-0.027
	0.003	0.002	0.003	0.002	-0.002
rucon85	0.032	0.047	0.103	0.075	-0.030
	0.002	0.002	0.002	0.001	0.001
urcon85	0.035	0.066	0.126	0.076	-0.032
	0.007	0.004	0.006	0.006	-0.011
rucolfci85	0.805	0.274	0.378	-0.492	-0.460
	0.026	0.004	-0.003	-0.009	-0.003
otherfci85	0.057	0.124	0.024	-0.083	-0.288
	0.040	-0.025	0.028	0.027	-0.156
acc85	-0.008	0.148	0.189	0.215	0.044
	0.020	0.010	0.017	0.020	-0.034
x85	0.380	0.138	0.345	-0.173	-0.390
	0.015	0.002	-0.002	-0.006	-0.002
m85	-0.064	0.083	0.140	0.237	0.138
	0.030	0.032	0.031	0.019	0.011

TABLE 6 (CONT)

Dynamic Elasticities of Endogenous Variables

Variables	1988	1989	1990	1991	1992
inflow85	0.000	0.000	0.000	0.000	0.000
	0.000	0.000	0.000	0.000	0.000
otgdp85	0.052	0.067	0.140	0.071	-0.019
	0.006	0.008	0.003	0.004	0.005
vatve85	-	-	-	-	-
	0.016	0.019	0.016	0.009	0.007
vasoe85	0.064	0.049	0.092	-0.043	-0.129
	0.024	0.018	0.052	0.031	-0.086
rgdp85	0.062	0.100	0.199	0.143	-0.058
	0.004	0.005	0.004	0.002	0.002

First Line   : Simulation on value-added of TVEs.

Second Line: Simulation on foreign investment utilised.

TABLE 7

Average Elasticities of Endogenous Variables For 1988-1990

Exogenous/ Endogenous	Value-added of TVEs (vatve85)	Foreign Investment Utilised (fiu85)
gdp85	0.109	0.016
rucon85	0.061	0.002
urcon85	0.076	0.005
con85	0.057	0.003
vatve85	-	0.017
rucolfci85	0.486	0.009
vasoe85	0.068	0.031
otherfci85	0.068	0.014
acc85	0.110	0.016
x85	0.288	0.005
m85	0.053	0.031
inflow85	0.000	0.000
otgdp85	0.086	0.006
rgdp85	0.120	0.004

TABLE 8
Values of Exogenous Variables

Variables	1993	1994	1995	1996	1997	1998
pubcon85	172.436	198.301	228.047	262.253	301.592	346.830
eus	5.760	8.620	8.350	8.400	8.400	8.400
rdni	0.959	0.954	0.949	0.944	0.939	0.935
fiu85	77.547	145.716	119.795	143.753	172.504	207.005
invloan85	148.014	158.796	167.845	199.752	237.724	282.914
loantve85	148.311	224.887	277.743	343.023	423.645	523.216
pgdp85	318.688	341.953	372.533	390.303	408.921	428.427
statcon	-3.903	-3.148	-3.148	-3.148	-3.148	-3.148
stat	34.589	34.589	34.589	34.589	34.589	34.589
rupop	6600	6306	6116	5962	5782	5573
urpop	2020	2347	2585	2847	3136	3455
pop	8620	8653	8701	8809	8918	9028
rucpi	195.6	237.1	279.5	310.4	344.8	383.0
urcpi	216.9	272.0	317.7	357.1	401.4	451.1
dgdp	167.9	201.2	227.7	247.5	269.0	292.4

TABLE 9

Forecasted Values of Major Endogenous Variables (100 million Yuan)

Year	gdp85	rucon85	urcon85	con85	vatve85	rucolfci85
1993	1490.39	265.92	170.05	604.51	796.85	95.00
1994	1897.21	298.66	223.86	717.67	1197.40	239.86
1995	2141.35	306.90	260.95	792.75	1352.32	143.94
1996	2478.09	329.26	309.06	897.42	1633.09	193.58
1997	2861.61	357.61	366.36	1022.41	1985.82	237.05
1998	3300.17	391.66	434.88	1170.23	2411.21	287.27

Year	otherfci85	x85	m85	inflow85	otgdp85	rgdp85
1993	288.42	188.84	58.44	45.82	224.62	825.67
1994	204.53	342.98	83.63	49.44	285.31	1041.79
1995	202.18	285.44	87.91	53.04	307.42	1166.83
1996	233.11	314.97	102.76	56.62	342.97	1321.12
1997	241.31	326.21	121.91	60.18	381.93	1507.85
1998	251.08	335.73	144.26	63.73	425.43	1727.37

PART IV

GLOBAL AND THEORETICAL ISSUES

Competitiveness and Education: An Econometric Viewpoint

*Benjamin **Goh***

&

__Yao Hong__

Nanyang Business School, Nanyang Technological University, Nanyang Avenue, Singapore 639798
Fax: +(65) 792.4217, Tel: +(65) 799.5725, Email: ahyao@ntu.edu.sg

Abstract Scant literature exists with regard to the role education and human capital play in a country's competitiveness although there are many studies on the relationship between education and economic development. By using regression analysis, it is possible to identify the relative importance of education, along with other factors, in a country's competitiveness as ranked by the World Competitiveness Report. Equipped with this knowledge, policymakers can then formulate and implement policies to enhance a country's global competitive standing.

1. INTRODUCTION

1.1 MOTIVATION AND OBJECTIVE

Since the 1970s there has been much excitement in the developed economies regarding the enhancement of trade competitiveness. This has been partly due to the growing balance of payments deficit as well as the slower rate of economic growth the West faces vis-à-vis Japan and later, the dynamic economies of the Pacific Rim.

First published in 1986, *World Competitiveness Report* by the World Economic Forum and the International Institute of Management Development is an annual report used to both measure and compare countries' competitiveness. Now in its eleventh year, the Report provides accurate and impartial assessments of the competitiveness of individual countries and has been used widely by government agencies as a reference for macroeconomic policy.

Eight major factors are used to measure a country's competitiveness. They are the country's domestic economic strength, internationalisation, government, infrastructure, management, science and technology and people. However, the significance and magnitude of these factors need to be analysed in order to determine the impact of the factors on the rank of a country's competitiveness.

The purpose of this study is to analyse the contribution of the various factors on a country's rank of competitiveness within the framework of the World Competitiveness Report. With a special focus on the role of human capital, such as education and skilled labour force, this will then provide a viable means of forecasting the effects on competitiveness of government policy.

1.2 RELATED ISSUES OF HUMAN CAPITAL AND ECONOMIC DEVELOPMENT

Although little work has been done on directly examining the role human capital plays in a country's competitiveness, there have been many studies on human capital issues in general since 1960s. For example, of interest was the rate of return to education as a form of capital and it's profitability vis-à-vis physical capital. Such comparisons would then be used to explain past economic growth rates (Schultz, 1961).

Other issues such as the what priority to give to primary and university education and estimates of profitability between types of curricula (i.e. secondary general vs. secondary technical) were useful in resource allocation decisions (Dougherty and Psacharopoulos, 1977).

Also of interest was whether and by how much the yield on human capital investment would decline following it's expansion if diminishing returns should apply to it and the contrast between the social and private rates of return (Psacharopoulos, 1973, 1985).

Thus far the importance of education, training and investment in human capital with respect to a country's economic well-being is undisputed. However, its contribution to a country's trade competitiveness with the rest of the world remains ambiguous as little research has been done in this respect.

The objective of this research paper then, is to explore that dimension of human capital.

2. RESEARCH METHODOLOGY AND DESIGN

The data used in this paper can be found in the 1994 and 1995 edition of the World Competitiveness Report (WEF and IMD, 1994, 1995). The sample of countries include members from both the OECD as well as non-OECD countries. The statistical methods used for this study focuses on the international comparison and regression approach in order to answer the questions:

- What are the factors that influence a country's competitiveness *vis-à-vis* the rest of the world?

- Specifically, what is the impact (if any) of education, training and investment in human capital on a country's competitiveness?

- How do these factors affect a country's competitiveness?

2.1 VARIABLES

The dependent variable is the country's competitiveness, as ranked by the World Competitiveness Report. A country with the rank of 1 would then signify that it is ranked by the World Competitiveness Report as the most competitive country in the world. Similarly, a rank of 2 would then signify that the country is the second most competitive country in the world, and so on.

Nine independent variables are selected from the eight major factors used to assess a country's competitiveness.

The first independent variable used is the real GDP per capita growth (GDP) which is measured as an annual compound percentage change computed on a local currency basis at 1990 prices. The second independent variable used is the country's balance of trade (BOT) as a percentage of its GDP. The third variable used is total quality management (TQM). This variable is calculated based on the World Competitiveness Report's executive opinion poll on whether "Total quality management either is comprehensively applied in your country or neglected in your country." The fourth variable is enterpreneurship and innovation (INNO) and is also calculated based on the World

Competitiveness Report's executive opinion poll on whether "Managers generally either have a good sense of enterpreneurship and innovation or lack a sense of enterpreneurship and innovation." The fifth variable is the country's labour force (LFORCE) as a percentage of its population. The sixth variable is the growth of labour force (GLFORCE) calculated as an average annual compound percentage rate of growth. The seventh variable is the availability of skilled labour (SKILL) and is also calculated based on the World Competitiveness Report's executive opinion poll on whether "Skilled labour is either easy or hard to get in your country." The eighth variable is the country's pupil-teacher ratio (RATIO) and is simply the number of pupils per teacher in the country. The ninth variable is the country's higher education enrolment (ENR) and is the percentage of 20-24 year-old population enrolled in higher education.

As can be seen, several variables have been selected as proxies for education and human capital. They are Total Quality Management, Enterpreneurship and Innovation, Labour Force, Pupil-Teacher Ratio and rate of Higher Education Enrolment. Several other variables such as education expenditure and illiteracy rate could have been used as proxy independent variables as well but these were discarded as they exhibited high correlation to real GDP growth and some of the other regressors, inevitably giving rise to a sever multicollinearity problem.

2.2 STATISTICAL PROCEDURE

A multivariate linear regression model utilising cross-section analysis with a data set covering the years 1994 and 1995 was used for this study.

The regression equation considered was linear, using the Ordinary Least Squares method.

The problem of heteroskedasticity inherent in a sample of this nature was minimised by using White's heteroskedasticity-consistent standard errors and covariance.

2.3 ANALYSIS AND RESULTS

2.3.1 Results for the Year 1994

For the year 1994, the following regression equation was estimated (with t-statistics in parentheses):

$$\text{RANK} = 96.867 - 0.717\text{GDP} + 0.071\text{BOT} - 7.273\text{TQM} - 2.126\text{INNO} - 0.215\text{LFORCE}$$
$$\qquad (9.812) \quad (-1.471) \quad (0.536) \quad (-4.533) \quad (-1.618) \quad (-0.984)$$
$$+ \; 0.186\text{GLFORCE} - 0.327\text{SKILL} - 0.294\text{RATIO} - 0.162\text{ENR} \qquad\qquad (1)$$
$$\quad (0.246) \qquad\qquad (-0.353) \qquad (-1.708) \qquad (-2.320)$$

$R^2 = 0.869$ F-statistic = 17.017
adj $R^2 = 0.818$ Number of observations, N= 33

From the t-statistics calculated above, it is concluded that the constant, total quality management and higher education enrolment are significant at the 10 percent level of significance. The independent variables pupil-teacher ratio and enterpreneurship and innovation are significant only at the 11 percent and 12 percent level of significance respectively.

As can be seen, the signs of the independent variables total quality management and higher education enrolment are negative. This is indicative that when product quality improves and when the number of people in a country studying for and subsequently possessing graduate degrees increase, it is expected that the competitive standing of that country should improve.

Total quality management is significant since rational consumers are expected to want more goods than less, to demand them at a cheaper price and at a better quality, it is no surprise that improved product quality and consumer satisfaction will enable one country to export more than others.

Higher education enrolment is significant with regards to competitiveness because much beneficial economies and positive externalities exists if a larger proportion of a country's population is relatively more educated and highly trained. Apart from the fact that this will lead to a more productive workforce, an economy whose participants are highly educated would then be in a better position to focus and specialise in highly technical and specialised industries such as the computer and electronics industry as well as the banking and financial services industry. Since the global economy comprise such industries, countries which have a comparative advantage in these industries are naturally expected to enjoy increased exports and consequently, become more competitive.

At the 10 percent level of significance, total quality management and higher education enrolment, both proxy variables for human capital, are statistically significant and contribute to competitiveness, while the variables pupil-teacher ratio and enterpreneurship and innovation do not. Interestingly, pupil-teacher ratio and enterpreneurship and innovation are significant at the 11 percent and 12 percent level respectively. Although these variables are not statistically significant, the fact that they have such large t-statistics and are so close to the 10 percent level of significance indicate that they do contribute somewhat to a country's competitiveness.

The sign of pupil-teacher ratio is negative which means that a higher pupil-teacher ratio will improve a country's competitiveness. This is contrary to popular assumptions that smaller class sizes and the inevitable closer supervision and guidance of students will give rise to better students and subsequently a more productive workforce. Perhaps a lower pupil-teacher ratio is important but what might be equally or even more important is the quality of the teaching staff and relevance of the curriculum.

As for enterpreneurship and innovation, its sign is negative which means that a country is more competitive if it is more enterprising and innovative than its rivals. Intuitively this comes as no surprise as it is these qualities that enable businesses and on a larger scale, countries to compete effectively.

From the 1994 results, it would appear that human capital is important and does in fact contribute to a country's competitiveness.

2.3.2 Results for the Year 1995

For the year 1995, the following regression equation was estimated (with t-statistics in parentheses):

$$RANK = 100.801 - 0.712GDP - 0.055BOT - 5.495TQM - 3.536INNO - 0.453LFORCE$$
$$(6.292) \quad (-1.702) \quad (-0.322) \quad (-5.108) \quad (-2.286) \quad (-1.900)$$
$$+ 0.050GLFORCE + 0.018SKILL + 0.136RATIO - 0.148ENR \qquad (2)$$
$$(0.061) \qquad (0.014) \qquad (0.780) \qquad (-2.308)$$

$R^2 = 0.787$ F-statistic = 13.950

adj R^2 = 0.730   Number of observations, N = 44

From the t-statistics calculated above, it can be seen that the constant, real GDP growth, total quality management, enterpreneurship and innovation, labour force and higher education enrolment are all significant at the 10 percent level of significance

In contrast with the results for the year 1994, real GDP growth is significant at the 10 percent level of significance. The negative sign of its coefficient indicates that a higher rate of real GDP growth will improve a country's competitiveness. This can be explained by the fact that higher economic growth will result in a greater potential for specialisation, division of labour and greater economies of scale which then enable a country to be more competitive.

Total quality management and enterpreneurship and innovation are highly significant and both have negative signs. As with the results for the year 1994, this is testimonial to how important product quality and customer satisfaction as well as business creativity is in order to compete effectively in the global economy.

Higher education enrolment is significant and negative. As already explained above, a more educated workforce will not only lead to increased productivity but will also stimulate the growth of high technology and high value-added industries which will improve a country's competitive edge.

Pupil-teacher ratio is statistically insignificant. As already explained, perhaps the issue is not so much how many students there are in a class but the quality of the teaching staff and relevance of the curriculum.

Interestingly, the coefficients of growth of labour force as well as availability of skilled labour are of the wrong sign but given how insignificant these two variables are, it would be prudent not to put too much emphasis on these variables.

From the 1995 results, it also appears that human capital is important and do contribute to a country's competitiveness.

3. CONCLUDING REMARKS

Knowing which variables are more important as well as in what capacity human capital plays when competitiveness is concerned is instrumental in implementing policies to improve a country's competitiveness.

In this study, we have tried to quantify the contributions of factors such as real GDP growth, balance of trade, total quality management, entrepreneurship and innovation, labour force, growth of labour force, availability of skilled labour, pupil-teacher ratio and the rate of higher education enrolment to a country's competitiveness. We find that variables which serve as proxies for human capital, such as total quality management, enterpreneurship and innovation, labour force, pupil-teacher ratio and higher education enrolment (measuring education), are important and do contribute to a country's competitiveness as ranked by the World Competitiveness Report. In this, how human capital affects a country's competitiveness is crucial as education and training are the sectors in which governments can play a direct and beneficial intervening role.

As an economy grows or the international environment changes, some structural changes may take place in the factors that influence a nation's competitiveness. For example, some variables may become more significant while others less significant to a country's competitiveness. By doing cross-section and time series analysis, we may be able to forecast the future trend of the factors which influence a country's competitiveness over time. This can be done in a future research.

REFERENCES

Dougherty, C. and Psacharopoulos, G. (1977): "Measuring the Cost of Misallocation of Investment in Education," *Journal of Human Resources*, 12, 446-459

Psacharopoulos, G. (1973): *Returns to Education: An International Comparison.* San Francisco: Elsevier-Jossey Bass

_____(1985): "Returns to Education: A Further International Update and Implications," *Journal of Human Resources*, 20, 583-604.

_____(1987): *Economics of Education, Research and Studies.* New York: Pergamon Press.

Schultz, T. W. (1961): "Education and Economic Growth," in *Social Forces Influencing American Education.* Chicago: National Society for the Study of Education.

World Economic Forum and the International Institute of Management Development (1994 and 1995): *World Competitiveness Report.* Switzerland: The Foundation.

Empirical Evidence on Islamic Banking:
Iran, Pakistan and Sudan

__Mong__ Wai Nie
&
Ramin Cooper __Maysami__

Nanyang Business School, Nanyang Technological University, Nanyang Avenue, Singapore 639798
Fax: +(65) 792.4217, Tel: +(65) 799.4900, Email: aramin@ntu.edu.sg

Abstract Recently, there has been a revival of fundamental Islamic values leading to the 'Islamisation' of the financial system in the Islamic Republic of Iran and Pakistan. Under this system, payment of a pre-determined rate of interest is prohibited. The goal of this paper is to empirically examine the stability of financial system after the introduction of non interest-bearing assets. Consequently, we conclude whether the absence of interest-bearing assets would promote or hinder economic development.

1. INTRODUCTION

The general resurgence of fundamental Islamic values in many parts of the world has manifested itself on the economic front as well, with a number of countries moving to transform their economic systems to accord more closely with the precepts of Islam.

1.1 WHAT IS ISLAMIC BANKING?

The basic characteristic of an Islamic banking system is the prohibition of the payment or receipt of a predetermined interest. The Islamic system operates under the general principle of profit-and loss-sharing, which effectively transforms banks into equity-based firms. In other words, the essential feature of Islamic banking is that it is interest-free. Although it is often claimed that there is more to Islamic banking, such as a more equitable distribution of income and increased equity participation in the economy, its specific rationale has to do with the fact that there is no place for the institution of interest in the Islamic order.

1.2 THE BASIS FOR ISLAMIC BANKING

Some scholars have put forward economic reasons to explain why interest is banned in Islam. It has been argued, for instance, that interest, being a pre-determined cost of production, tends to prevent full employment. In the same vein, some have contended that international monetary crises are largely due to the institution of interest and that trade cycles are in no small measure attributable to interest as well. Others, anxious to vindicate the Islamic position on interest, have argued that interest is not very effective as a monetary policy instrument even in the capitalist economies and have questioned the significance of the interest rate as a determinant of savings and investment.[1]

---

[1] A complete introduction to Islamic Banking may be found in "Interest-Free Financial Activities in Indonesia, Malaysia, Bahrain, and Pakistan," by Ramin Cooper Maysami in *Asian Economies*, Vol 24, No.2, 1995.

The Western system is very much based on the institution of interest. It goes without saying that Western economists have questioned the viability of an Islamic banking system. However, Mohsin Khan (1986) demonstrated that an interest-free banking system is quite compatible with both Keynesian and classical economic theories. Henry Simon (1948) and Charles Kindleberger (1985) have also proposed certain economic reforms that were in many ways similar to Islamic banking.

Khan has also questioned the traditional banking practice of paying depositors a fixed and predetermined interest regardless of whether or not the bank is doing well. This may prevent banks from quickly adjusting to any potential asset shocks, and in his opinion, such rigidity could lead to possible financial instability. Islamic banking system can provide cushions against bank failures and financial instability.

It should be noted that these profound and interesting conclusion are based on purely theoretical grounds. Indeed, there are no previous studies which provide any empirical results. Yet, evidence may be the only way to resolve the issues.

2. METHODOLOGY

We aim to empirically test the hypothesis that the financial system is more stable without interest-bearing assets as prescribed in Islamic banking, compared to when such assets exist as in the Western system. To do so, we employ a model originally developed by Ali F. Darrat in 1988.[2]

First, we analyse the historical record of the velocity of interest and non-interest-bearing money in Iran, Pakistan and Sudan over a 30 years period. Next, we estimate the public's demand for interest- and non-interest bearing financial assets, and will subject the resulting demand equation to structural stability tests. Finally, we examine and compare the relative usefulness and effectiveness of both financial aggregates for policy purposes.

Data used were extracted from the IMF's International Financial Statistics for the period 1966 to 1995.

2.1 VELOCITY OF MONEY

The velocity of money, defined as the rate of turnover of money, that is, the average number of times per year that a dollar is spent in buying the total amount of goods and services produced in the economy. It plays a fundamental role in macroeconomics analysis. The quantity theory of money demand developed by Fisher suggests that the demand of money is purely a function of income and interest rates have no effect on the demand for money. The equation is express as $MV = Y$[3]. Hence, the velocity of money has profound implications for general economic stability.

If V is stable, and with M under the control of the monetary authorities, policy actions would be very effective in controlling economic activities. However, if V exhibits violent temporal changes, the link between policy actions and the pace of economic activities will be weakened. An unstable velocity could lead to overall financial and economic instability

---

[2] The model could be found in "The Islamic Interest-fee Banking System:some empirical evidence" by Ali F. Darrat in *Applied Economics,* Vol 20, Iss. 3, 1988.

[3] M is the money demand, V is the velocity of M and Y is the aggregate nominal income.

as the potential for erroneous monetary actions increase, making monetary policy itself a major source of financial and economic disruption. Fisher took the view that the institutional and technological features of the economy would affect velocity only slowly over time, so velocity would normally be reasonably constant in the short run.

A primary goal of monetary authorities is to stabilise the aggregate nominal income -- to achieve a GDP high enough to promote full employment without causing inflation. This study attempts to determine the relative stability of interest-bearing money (MI) and interest-free money (MNI). Figures 1 to 3 represent the velocity of money in the three countries.

2.2 MONEY DEMAND

In order to arrive at a more definite conclusion about the relative stability of the financial system with and without interest-bearing assets, we further perform formal tests of the demand function for money. Since the velocity of money is simply the inverse of the demand for money, it would change only if the public alters their holdings of money relative to their income.

The desired real money demand, $^M/_P$, is assumed to respond positively to real gross domestic product, X, negatively to the yields expected on real assets, P^e_t, and negatively to the yield expected on alternative financial assets. Thus, the general money demand function can be expressed as

$$(^M/_P)_t = f(X^t, P^e_t)$$

where t denotes time. The money demand is cast in real terms because theoretical considerations usually postulate that economic agents are a priori free of money illusions and hence their money demand is a demand for real purchasing power. Applying the usual logarithmic functional form, the equation becomes

$$\log(^{Mj}/_P) = b_0 + b_1\log X_t + b_2 P^e_t + b_3\log(^{Mj}/_P)_{t-1}$$

After obtaining the above, we need to solve two issues. First, we need to approximate expected inflation since this variable is not observable. Assuming static expectations as in Driscoll and Lahiri (1983), among others, the actual inflation rate in any given period is used as a proxy for the inflation rate expected to prevail in the next period. Such an assumption seems reasonable, especially in the context of annual time-series data.

Secondly, we also need to replace desired real money demand - which is also unobersvable- with obersvable real money holdings. One technique which has become quite popular in money demand literature is the Koyck partial adjustment procedure. This procedure assumes that the adjustment of actual real money holdings to the desired level is only a fraction of the gap between the desired level in the current period (t) and the actual level in the previous period ($t-1$). Combining this partial adjustment scheme with the money demand equation above, it can be shown that the entire adjustment process can be approximated by a lagged dependent variable. Thus, the public demand for real balances can be represented by the following equation

$$\log(\frac{M_j}{P})_t = b_0 + b_1 \log X_t + b_2 P^e_t + b_3 \log(\frac{M_j}{P})_{t-1} + U_t \tag{1}$$

where j refers to either interest- or non-interest-bearing money stock. U is the associated error term, assumed to be white noise with zero mean and a constant variance[4]. Interest-bearing money is defined as the public's time and savings deposits with the commercial banks and interest-free money refers to the currency in the hands of the public and demand deposits.

2.3 POLICY CONTROLLABILITY

To further assess the preeminence of the two financial systems, we follow and test Batten and Thornton (1983) argument that any monetary aggregate becomes useful for policy purposes only if it satisfies two prerequisites:

- the aggregate has to be effectively under the control of the monetary authority without being affected by unnecessary non-policy factors.

- there is also a need for a reliable and strong link between the monetary aggregate and the main goals of the authorities. If such a link is weak, then that particular financial aggregate, even if controllable, ceases to be of much use for policy purposes.

3. ANALYSIS OF EMPIRICAL RESULTS

3.1 VELOCITY OF MONEY

We found that the 3 countries show similar patterns: the velocity of interest-bearing money is greater than that of interest-free money. Table 1 shows the standard deviation of the velocity of interest-bearing and non-interest bearing money in the 3 countries.

The results obtained show that the velocities of interest-free money in Pakistan and Sudan are very much stable (8.14, 3.90) compared to the velocity of the interest-bearing money (15.82, 18.72). An unstable velocity could lead to monetary policy itself becoming a major source of financial and economical disruption. The results indicate that the removal of interest could allow for better implementation of monetary policies.

Iran's result was not similar to the other two countries. Although the velocity of interest-bearing money is greater than that of interest-free money, the difference (0.04) is statistically negligible. The results are to be tested further in the next section.

3.2 MONEY DEMAND

In Equation 2, we define M as MNI (non-interest-bearing money stock) and in Equation 3, we define M as MI (interest-bearing money stock):

$$\log(\frac{MNI}{P})_t = \underset{(t_1)}{c_o} + \underset{(t_2)}{b_1} \log X_t + \underset{(t_3)}{b_2} P_t^e + \underset{(t_4)}{b_3} \log(\frac{MNI}{P})_{t-1} \tag{2}$$

$$\log(\frac{MI}{P})_t = \underset{(t_1)}{c_o} + \underset{(t_2)}{b_1} \log X_t + \underset{(t_3)}{b_2} P_t^e + \underset{(t_4)}{b_3} \log(\frac{MI}{P})_{t-1} \tag{3}$$

Table 2 presents the regression results for Equation 2 and 3. The three countries show a positive relationship between money demand and the real gross domestic product, signifying that an increase in the GNP leads to an increase in money demand. Noteworthy

---

[4] This section was adapted from Ali Darrat (1988) to avoid any mistakes in econometric techniques.

is the high significance of the variable X for Pakistan and Sudan. This was not the case for Iran.

However, the coefficients of the expected yields on real assets had the right sign only for Pakistan. Iran and Sudan showed counter-intuitive signs. The coefficients, however, are small in absolute value and are statistically insignificant.

Table 2 also shows the results for Equation 3 where the dependent variable is the interest-bearing money. Again, the three countries show a positive relationship between money demand and the real GNP, X, although the variable is significant only for Pakistan. The variable P^e is not significant in any case.

The purpose of the above regressions is to obtain the demand equation for interest- and non-interest-bearing money. Hence, we would not emphasise the values or significance of the variables. The equations were then subjected to the Chow Test for structural stability.

At the 5 percent level, the critical F-value is 3.01. The respective values for the Chow Test are shown in Table 3. Clearly, the Chow Test does not reject the hypothesis that the public's demand for non-interest money is stable in Pakistan and Sudan. However, the test rejects the stability hypothesis for interest-bearing money in the two countries. In all, a more formal testing of the asset-holding behaviour of the public in Pakistan and Sudan supports our previous historical analysis of the velocity of money.

In the case of Iran, we could not arrive at any conclusive results. The F-statistics, 0.08 and 2.99 for the interest-bearing and non-interest-bearing money demand equations respectively, are below the critical value of 3.01. Hence, we could not draw any conclusions regarding the relative stability of each type of system.

Both tests suggest that the public's demand for non-interest-bearing assets is structurally stable over time for Pakistan and Sudan but the public's demand for interest-bearing assets suffers from structural instability over time. Such a finding renders the presence of interest-bearing money assets a potential source of disruption within the Iranian financial system.

3.3 CORRELATION BETWEEN THE MONETARY BASE AND MONETARY AGGREGATES

As mentioned earlier, we need to ensure that our monetary aggregates are not affected unduly by other factors. Monetary policy is often implemented through the monetary base which is defined as currency held both by the public and banks plus reserve deposits of banks held at the central bank. The issue to be investigated is which monetary aggregate displays stronger links with the monetary base and is thus more controllable.

Since the monetary policy is typically discussed in a growth-rate framework, both the monetary base (MB) and the monetary aggregates (MI and MNI) are expressed in percentage changes (growth rates) denoted by the operator D.

$$DMNI = c_0 + \beta_0 DMB \tag{4}$$

$$DMI = c_1 + \beta_1 DMB \tag{5}$$

Table 4 shows the results for Equation 4 and 5 when the dependent variable is the growth rate of the non-interest-bearing money and interest-bearing money respectively.

When the growth of interest-free money is regressed against the monetary base, Iran showed a negative result. We could not establish a strong relationship between the two variables. Hence, the tool may not be useful in Iran. Although Pakistan and Sudan showed significant changes in the monetary base, the changes may be too small (0.51, 0.59) to be useful for policy purposes.

When the dependent variable is interest-bearing money, relationship with the monetary base is highly significant and positive for Iran and Sudan. The same could not be for with Pakistan. Not only is the coefficient low, it is also insignificant.

3.4 ECONOMIC GOAL LINK

Any actions taken by the monetary authorities must allow for the presence of other economic goals besides the targeted one. Traditionally, price stability is considered to be one of the prime targets of central banks. Therefore, we used regression analysis to examine the impact of the growth rate of the two monetary aggregates on inflation (DP) as measured by the growth rate of the GDP deflator, to check for compatibility with other economic goals.

Because prices usually respond to monetary changes with a lag, we experimented with various lag lengths. Three lags seem appropriate since lags beyond the third year proved insignificant as evident in Equations 6 and 7 and Table 5.

$$DP_t = c_0 + \alpha_1 DMNI_t + \alpha_2 DMNI_{t-1} + \alpha_3 DMNI_{t-2} + \alpha_4 DMNI_{t-3} \tag{6}$$

$$DP_t = c_1 + \beta_1 DMI_t + \beta_2 DMI_{t-1} + \beta_3 DMI_{t-2} + \beta_4 DMI_{t-3} \tag{7}$$

The DP equation with regard to interest-free money explains 21 percent, 28 percent and 89 percent of the variation in inflation in the tested period for Iran, Pakistan and Sudan respectively. Durbin-Watson statistics generally indicated first-order serial correlation.

The DP equation with respect to DMI equation explained 1 percent, 40 percent and 68 percent of the inflation within the tested period. We could conclude the DP/DMI equation better explains the inflation situation in Iran and Sudan but not for Pakistan. But, the DP/DMI equation could still accounts for 28 percent which might not be that bad afterall.

4. ADDITIONAL TESTING

We further test the stability of the systems in different periods within the 30-years time-series.

The regression results for the respective periods are presented in Tables 6 and 7. The money demand equations were again subjected to stability test. I did not use Chow Test in the testing. The 30-years period is divided into 3 smaller periods of 10 years each. Hence, there is not sufficient observations to conduct the Chow Test.

Recursive residuals have been suggested by Brown, Durbin and Evans[5] for testing the stability of regression relationships. For stability analysis purposes, I computed the cumulative sums of square.

The three countries tested stable for the 3 periods which is 1966 to 1975, 1976 to 1985 and finally 1986 to 1995 for both interest-free and interest-bearing moneys. This meant that if the sector tested unstable when using data for 30 years, the 'unstable' elements

---

[5] R. L. Brown, J. Durbin and J. M. Evans, "Techniques for Testing the Constancy of Regression Relationships" (with discussion), *Journal of the Royal Statistical Society, Series B*, Vol 37, 1975.

occur during the 'break period'. That is either between 1975 and 1976 or 1985 and 1986. For example, Pakistan had experienced a change in the economy during either in 1975 or 1985 or both years. We would like to point out that the recent recession years are in 1975 and 1985. In 1975, the world experience a global oil crisis affecting a lot of countries.

5. CONCLUSION

This paper attempts to provide empirical evidence on the feasibility of an Islamic, interest-free financial system. A time-series analysis of Iran, Pakistan and Sudan gives us the following conclusion:

- The results for Iran gives us no support for the feasibility of an Islamic financial system: the standard deviation test indicates a more stable velocity for interest-bearing money; The stability test was inconclusive; the controllability of the system is in doubt since a negative relationship exists between the monetary base and the interest-free aggregate; And the feasibility of achieving economic goals such as controlling inflation is also doubtful.

- The evidence on Pakistan do support the Islamic system. The results indicates that the Islamic system seems to work better in the country. This is best shown in the results of the stability test. In addition, the interest-bearing monetary system seems to explain economic targets, such as monetary inflation

- Sudan proves to be the country that best supports the theory of Islamic banking. The velocity of interest-free money is much lower than that of interest-bearing money. Furthermore, the stability test strongly rejects the stability of an interest-bearing system.

Iran's empirical evidence does not seems to support the Islamic banking system that is in existence now. One of the possible reasons is her steps taken towards Islamizing the financial system. She took an abrupt step to convert the country's financial system. Hence, the act might introduce instability to the system as everything has to take a new view without any cushions for changes overnight.

The Pakistani experience differs from the Itanian one in that Pakistan had opted for a grudual islamisation process which began in 1979. The Pakistani model took care to ensure that the new modes of financing did not upset the basic functioning and structure of the banking system. The gradual pace of transition made it easier for the Pakistani banks to adapt to the new system.

Another reason to explain the weak performance of Islamic banking is that the study may have been influenced by various internal and external factors unique to each country: Iran's 8 year long war with Iraq, and the trade embargo imposed on the country, for example, or political stability and riots in Sudan and Pakistan, as well as frequent dismissal of the Pakistani government on corruption charges. Finally, the inaccuracy of the data of the three developing nations, and the variation between actual and reported data must be acknowledged.

Nevertheless, given the available data, it does appear that the interest-free monetary system has positive merit on financial stability, policy usefulness and economic efficiency.

REFERENCES

Ahmad, I. Iqbal, M and Khan, M. F. (1983), *Money and Banking in Islam*, Institute of Policy Studies, Islamabad, Pakistan

Ali, S. Nazim and Naseem N. Ali, *Information Sources on Islamic Banking and Economics* (TJ Press)

Batten, D. S. and Thornton, D. L. (1983), M1 or M2 : Which is the better monetary target?, *Federal Reserve Bank of St. Louis, Review*

Boughton, J.M. (1981), Recent instability of the demand for money : An international perspective, *Southern Economic Journal*

Chow, G. C. (1960), Test of Equality between sets of coefficients in 2 linear regressions, *Econometrica*

Darrat, Ali F. (1986), *The Islamic Interest-Free Banking System: Some Empirical Evidence* (Applied Economics, 1988)

International Monetary Fund, *International Financial Statistics*

Khan , Mohsin S. (1986), Islamic Interest-free banking : a theoretical Analysis, *IMF, Staff Paper*

Khan , Mohsin S. (1987), *Theoretical Studies in Islamic Banking and Finance* (The Institute for Research and Islamic Studies)

Kindleberger, C.P. (1985), *Bank Failures: the 1930s and 1980s*, paper presented at the conference on the search for financial stability : the past 50 years, San Francisco

Maysami, Ramin Cooper, "Interest-Free Financial Activities in Indonesia, Malaysia, Bahrain, and Pakistan," *Asian Economies*, Vol 24, No.2, 1995.

Thornton, D. L. (1983), Why does velocity matter?, *Federal Reserve Bank of St. Louis, Review*

TABLE 1

Standard Deviation of the Velocity of Interest- and Interest-Free Money

	IRAN	PAKISTAN	SUDAN
STD DEV (VMNI)	99.83	8.14	3.90
STD DEV (VMI)	99.79	15.82	18.72

Source : International Financial Statistics

TABLE 2

Regression Results

EQUATION 2

	C	LOG(X)	PE	LOG(MNIP)	R^2	DW
IRAN	3.00	0.07	0.07	0.82	0.92	2.11
	(0.77)	(0.46)	(0.57)	(11.59)		
PAKISTAN	-3.51	0.94	-0.16	0.15	0.99	1.67
	(-3.99)	(5.69)	(-2.67)	(0.97)		
SUDAN	-4.05	0.38	0.01	0.79	0.98	1.46
	(-3.35)	(4.75)	(2.80)	(17.44)		

EQUATION 3

	C	LOG(X)	PE	LOG(MIP(-1))	R^2	DW
IRAN	-7.92	1.00	0.16	0.22	0.33	2.29
	(-0.52)	(1.65)	(0.35)	(1.00)		
PAKISTAN	-1.55	0.40	-0.02	0.63	0.92	1.19
	(-0.89)	(2.16)	(-0.14)	(3.37)		
SUDAN	-6.04	0.54	0.03	0.73	0.81	2.90
	(-0.90)	(1.35)	(1.34)	(6.37)		

Source : International Financial Statistics

*numbers in parentheses below the coefficient estimates are the absolute values of the t-ratios

TABLE 3

Results For Stability Test

	IRAN	PAKISTAN	SUDAN
F-STATISTIC(LMNIP)	0.08	0.40	2.27
F-STATISTIC(LMIP)	2.99	3.75	8.34

Source : International Financial Statistics

TABLE 4

Regression Results with regard to the Correlation to Monetary Base

EQUATION 4

	C	DBM	R^2	DW
IRAN	0.17	0.01	0.00	0.54
	(2.73)	(0.09)		
PAKISTAN	0.07	0.51	0.28	2.54
	(2.55)	(3.23)		
SUDAN	0.12	0.59	0.71	1.52
	(3.79)	(8.92)		

EQUATION 5

	C	DBM	R^2	DW
IRAN	0.00	2.97	0.61	2.01
	(0.02)	(6.29)		
PAKISTAN	0.13	0.26	0.02	1.44
	(1.95)	(0.65)		
SUDAN	0.18	1.05	0.22	2.06
	(1.07)	(3.02)		

*Dependent variable is the rate of change of interest-bearing money, DMI

TABLE 5

Regression Results with regard to the linkage with Economic Goals

EQUATION 6

	C	DMNI	DMNI(-1)	DMNI(-2)	DMNI(-3)	R^2	DW
IRAN	0.16	0.12	0.12	0.37	-0.42	0.21	1.63
	(1.47)	(0.77)	(0.31)	(0.77)	(-0.82)		
PAKISTAN	-0.24	0.78	-0.09	1.60	-0.65	0.28	1.29
	(-1.17)	(1.29)	(-0.15)	(2.69)	(-1.18)		
SUDAN	-0.17	0.85	0.06	0.87	-0.14	0.89	1.50
	(-3.52)	(4.54)	(0.42)	(3.98)	(-0.46)		

EQUATION 7

	C	DMI	DMI(-1)	DMI(-2)	DMI(-3)	R^2	DW
IRAN	0.18	0.00	0.00	0.00	0.00	0.01	1.26
	(4.05)	(0.33)	(0.22)	(0.24)	(0.89)		
PAKISTAN	0.21	-0.19	0.05	-0.45	-0.63	0.40	1.46
	(2.78)	(-0.84)	(0.21)	(-1.89)	(-2.40)		
SUDAN	0.17	0.42	0.08	-0.13	-0.11	0.68	1.04
	(2.61)	(6.40)	(1.60)	(-2.12)	(-1.85)		

Source : International Financial Statistic

*Dependent variable is the rate of change of interest-free money, DMI

TABLE 6

Regression Results for Different Periods with respect to Equation 1

		C	LOG(X)	PE	LOG(MNIP)	R^2	DW
1966 - 1975	IRAN	10.83	0.93	0.11	-0.37	0.82	2.02
		(1.71)	(2.07)	(0.14)	(1.51)		
	PAKISTAN	8.57	0.42	-0.16	0.21	0.62	1.40
		(0.74)	(0.31)	(-1.21)	(0.02)		
	SUDAN	-2.44	0.28	0.04	0.80	0.97	2.57
		(-1.20)	(1.54)	(2.43)	(3.29)		
1976 - 1985	IRAN	49.36	-0.80	1.00	0.18	0.71	2.23
		(1.53)	(-1.11)	(0.77)	(0.44)		
	PAKISTAN	1.54	0.52	0.32	0.40	0.96	2.43
		(0.66)	(1.76)	(1.31)	(1.54)		
	SUDAN	4.19	0.16	0.01	0.67	0.89	2.67
		(0.92)	(1.03)	(0.94)	(5.37)		
1986 - 1995	IRAN	12.75	0.08	0.06	0.66	0.92	2.64
		(1.10)	(-0.47)	(2.01)	(2.83)		
	PAKISTAN	-0.02	0.91	-0.25	0.04	0.95	2.07
		(-0.00)	(2.00)	(-1.29)	(0.12)		
	SUDAN	-25.84	0.38	0.05	1.90	1.00	3.37
		(-1.15)*	(5.62)**	(1.82)*	(1.09)*		

Source : International Financial Statistic

* multiply by 10^{36}

** multiply by 10^{35}

TABLE 7

Regression Results for Different Periods with respect to Equation 2

		C	LOG(X)	PE	LOG(MIP)	R^2	DW
1966 - 1975	IRAN	-0.47	0.18	-1.20	0.83	0.95	3.05
		(-0.04)	(0.20)	(-1.59)	(1.51)		
	PAKISTAN	19.50	0.18	-0.14	0.01	0.38	2.05
		(1.51)	(0.31)	(-1.20)	(0.02)		
	SUDAN	0.49	0.37	-0.00	0.53	0.90	1.95
		(0.12)	(1.50)	(-0.02)	(1.85)		
1976 - 1985	IRAN	-3.43	-0.42	-6.50	1.56	0.29	0.98
		(-0.02)	(-0.19)	(-1.24)	(0.37)		
	PAKISTAN						
	SUDAN	27.38	-0.89	0.03	0.49	0.84	2.51
		(1.20)	(-1.08)	(1.30)	(1.41)		
1986 - 1995	IRAN	24.21	0.15	-0.03	0.03	0.46	1.48
		(4.15)	(0.80)	(-0.54)	(1.20)		
	PAKISTAN	-13.96	0.66	0.47	0.84	0.73	1.06
		(-1.07)	(1.32)	(0.52)	(2.50)		
	SUDAN	48.91	-6.57	-0.81	6.21	1.00	3.41
		(4.11)*	(-3.07)*	(-2.65)*	(3.08)*		

Source : International Financial Statistic

* multiply by 10^{36}

FIGURE 1

Iran

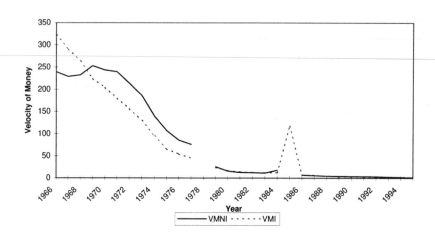

FIGURE 2

Pakistan

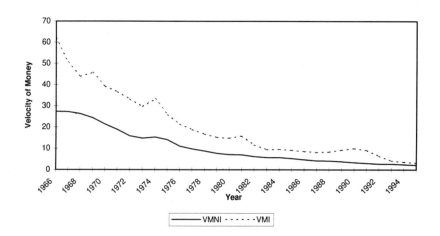

FIGURE 3

Sudan

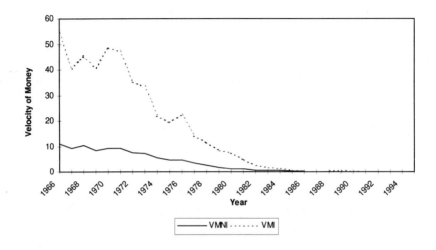

Performance of Johansen's Cointegration Test

Poh Chee Wee

&

Randolph **Tan**

Nanyang Business School, Nanyang Technological University, Nanyang Avenue, Singapore 639798
Fax: +(65) 792.4217, Tel: +(65) 799.4895, Email: arandolph@ntu.edu.sg

Abstract The Johansen cointegration test has a number of obvious advantages over the simpler Engle-Granger test. As the test is designed for a multivariate system, it has the potential of becoming the benchmark for uncovering cointegration. However, uncertainty revolves around its finite sample properties, which is an important issue to the applied economist. Thus the objective of the paper is to assess the relative power and size performance of the trace test. Monte Carlo simulations were used in achieving the cause. The Johansen's trace test appears to be suffering from a positive bias in finite samples. This leads to a higher probability of rejection than is required. The authors recommend working with Johansen's test at higher significance levels.

1. INTRODUCTION

The Engle and Granger (1987) procedure is frequently used for testing the validity of a cointegrating relationship. In this procedure, the choice of the dependent variable is usually random. In a large sample, the choice for normalisation does not make a difference. However, this random selection of variables in a small sample can lead to different conclusions regarding the existence of a cointegrating relationship.[1] More generally, the Engle-Granger approach makes use of a normalisation that would constitute a serious misspecification unless such a normalisation was more than arbitrary. The situation is entirely analogous to that of the two-stage least squares (2SLS) estimator in simultaneous equation theory.[2] Another issue that arises when using the Engle-Granger procedure lies in the absence of a systematic procedure for testing the number of cointegrating vectors and the estimation of these vectors.

The maximum likelihood (ML) approach adopted by Johansen (1988) does not suffer from the above defects. As maximum likelihood estimates (MLE) are invariant to normalisation, there is no ambiguity. On top of that, the Johansen methodology offers a unique way to find the number of cointegrating relationships and estimating these relationships. Unlike the Engle-Granger method which tests for the stationarity of the residual to establish cointegration, the Johansen method rely heavily on the relationship between the rank of a matrix and its characteristic roots. As the Johansen method is more appropriate for a multivariate system, it is gaining popularity over the Engle-Granger procedure.

The authors believe that the critical values for the two test statistics suggested by Johansen and Juselius (1990) might not be universal. The values probably exhibit asymptotic properties. However, most economists are more concerned about the finite

---

[1] See Maddala (1992), pg. 377-382.

[2] See for example Hillier (1990).

sample properties. Incidentally, it is in this area that the application of the Johansen cointegration test appears to be more uncertain.

It is the objective of this paper to have a better understanding of the distribution of the Johansen test statistics. In order to confirm the superiority of the Johansen cointegration test, there must also be sufficient proof that the test offers reasonable, if not better size and power properties. The shift in methodology can then be further justified. As the reader might have already guessed, the authors have used Monte Carlo simulations in tackling the task.

The paper is organised as follows. In Section 2, the methodology of the Johansen framework is examined. Section 3 discusses the specification of the consumption function and elaborates on the Monte Carlo experiment. After this, an analysis of the empirical results is provided in Section 4. Finally, Section 5 ends the paper with a brief comment on the implications of the results as well as its limitations.

2. JOHANSEN METHODOLOGY

An (n×1) vector Z_t is said to be cointegrated if there exists a nonzero (n×1) vector **a** such that **a**'Z_t is stationary. If each individual element in Z_t is I(1), then the system is CI(1,1), and **a** is known as a cointegrating vector. In general, there may be r < n number of linearly independent (n×1) cointegrating vectors (a_1, a_2, ..., a_r). If we let A = (a_1 a_2 ... a_r), then A'Z_t is a stationary (r×1) vector. For any nonzero (r×1) vector **b**, the scalar **b**'A'Z_t is also stationary. Therefore, the (n×1) vector π given by π = Ab is also a cointegrating vector such that the cointegrating vectors are not unique. What is unique is the basis for the space of cointegrating vectors. If the columns of A span the space of cointegrating vectors for Z_t, then for any (n×1) vector **c** which is linearly independent of the columns of A, **c**'Z_t is also nonstationary.

More formally under the Johansen's approach, such a multivariate model can be expressed as an unrestricted vector autoregression (VAR) involving up to k number of lags in n potentially endogenous variables in the form:

$$Z_t = D_1 Z_{t-1} + ... + D_k Z_{t-k} + \mu_t \qquad \mu_t \sim IN(0,\sigma^2) \tag{1}$$

where Z_t is an (n×1) vector of n endogenous variables

D_i is an (n×n) matrix of parameters.

Since economic time series are generally non-stationary processes, (1) has to be reformulated into a vector error-correction (VECM) form:

$$\Delta Z_t = \Gamma_1 \Delta Z_{t-1} + ... + \Gamma_k \Delta Z_{t-k+1} + \Pi Z_{t-k} + v_t \qquad v_t \sim IN(0,\Omega) \tag{2}$$

where $\Gamma_1 = - (I - D_1 - ... - D_i) \qquad i = 1, ..., k-1$

$\Pi = - (I - D_1 - ... - D_k).$

It is expressed as a traditional first difference VAR except for the term ΠZ_{t-k}, which may contain information about the long-run relationships between the variables in the data vector. Specifically,

$$\Pi = \alpha\beta'$$

where α represents the speed of adjustment to disequilibrium β is a matrix of cointegrating vectors that ensure the convergence of Z_t to their long-run steady-state solutions.

There are 3 cases governing the rank of matrix Π:

(i) $\text{Rank}(\Pi) = n$

The matrix Π has full rank and so the vector process Z_t is stationary.

(ii) $\text{Rank}(\Pi) = 0$

The matrix Π is a null matrix and so (2) represents a traditional first difference VAR.

(iii) $0 < \text{Rank}(\Pi)=r < n$

The matrix Π is of reduced rank and there exists r cointegrating relationships in β, where $r \leq n-1$.

Most of the time, matrix Π is of reduced rank. If Z_t is a vector of non-stationary I(1) variables, μ_t will only be stationary if ΠZ_{t-k} is stationary since all the other terms in (2) are I(0). All the three cases satisfy the above condition. However, case (i) indicates an absence of spurious regression and case (ii) corresponds to a system without any long-run relationships. Both cases are trivial in the context of VECM. It is in case (iii) where Π contains up to a maximum of (n-1) cointegration vectors that excites most economists.

In this approach, the MLE of the cointegrating vectors of Π are obtained by computing the canonical correlation between the sample error covariance matrices of the following auxiliary regressions:

$$\Delta Z_t = P_1 \Delta Z_{t-1} + \ldots + P_{k-1} \Delta Z_{t-k+1} + e_{1t} \tag{3}$$

$$Z_{t-k} = T_1 \Delta Z_{t-1} + \ldots + T_{k-1} \Delta Z_{t-k+1} + e_{2t} \tag{4}$$

The MLE of the cointegrating vectors are then computed as the eigenvectors corresponding to the r largest eigenvalues of the canonical correlation matrix. Obviously, the actual number of eigenvectors depends on the rank of Π. This is estimated by the number r of distinct nonzero eigenvalues of the canonical correlation matrix above. Suppose we ordered the n eigenvalues from the matrix Π such that $\lambda_1 > \lambda_2 > \ldots > \lambda_n$. If the variables in Z_t are not cointegrated, the rank of Π will be zero and all the eigenvalues will also be equal to zero. Similarly, the number of non-zero eigenvalues will indicate the rank of matrix Π. The significance of the eigenvalues thus offers a direct way of testing for the number of cointegrating relationships.

In practice, the matrix Π and its corresponding eigenvalues can only be estimated. In order to test for the number of non-zero eigenvalues, we need to employ either one of the following two test statistics:

$$\lambda_{\text{trace}}(r) = -T\Sigma \ln(1 - \lambda_i) \qquad i = r+1, \ldots, n \tag{5}$$

$$\lambda_{\text{max}}(r, r+1) = -T\ln(1 - \lambda_{r+1}) \tag{6}$$

where   r is the number of cointegration vectors assumed by the null hypothesis

T is the number of usable observations

λ_i is the ith largest estimated eigenvalue obtained from the Π matrix.

The first test statistic, better known as the trace statistic, tests the null hypothesis that there are at most r cointegration vectors against a general alternative. The second test statistic is called the maximal eigenvalue or λ_{max} statistic. It tests the null hypothesis of r cointegration vectors against the alternative that r+1 exists.

It is obvious that the λ_{max} test has the sharper alternative hypothesis. Nevertheless, Cheung and Lai (1993) suggested that the trace test shows more robustness and excess kurtosis in the residuals than the λ_{max} test. Since it is not uncommon for the two test statistics to be conflicting, the reader has to be careful in drawing conclusion from the two tests. As a matter of choice, the authors have chosen to focus on the trace test.

3. THE EXPERIMENT

3.1 SPECIFICATION OF THE CONSUMPTION FUNCTION[3]

Economists have always been interested in the factors determining the proportions in which a society divides its income between consumption and saving. As saving is crucial to the development of nations, the division of contemporaneous income between consumption and saving will directly affect the intertemporal welfare of nations. Hence, the consumption function is one of the most widely researched topics in the field of economics.

The earliest form of consumption function proposed by Keynes (1936) is a simple relationship between national consumption and national income. He called this relationship "the propensity to consume" as he believed that a society will divide an increase in income in some regular proportion between an increase in consumption and an increase in saving. Since then, different hypotheses and specifications of the consumption function has sprouted. Better-known ones are Duesenberry (1949) relative income hypothesis, Friedman (1957) permanent income hypothesis and Modigliani and Brumberg (1954) life-cycle hypothesis. Although there were numerous theoretical and empirical developments, few improvements were made. This makes the 'correct' specification of the consumption function a difficult issue.

Since the emphasis of the paper is not on the specification of the consumption function, a simple relationship that takes into account of wealth effect is adopted. The consumption function looks like this:

$$C_t = \gamma Y_t + \delta W_t + \mu_t \tag{7}$$

where C_t denotes the natural logarithm of real consumption

Y_t is the natural logarithm of real disposable income

W_t is the natural logarithm of real wealth holdings.

Non-human wealth is explicitly included in the modelling of the consumption function.[4] Keynes intentionally excluded the variable in his theoretical framework as his emphasis was on a stable relationship between consumption and income. However, wealth was

---

[3] A comprehensive survey of related topics are given in Hadjimatheou (1987).

[4] Human capital/wealth is frequently argued to be an important variable. But it is usually ignored since there is not an objective way of measuring it.

found to be a significant variable in later studies. Real wealth effects were seen as an important channel whereby the inflation rate influences consumer expenditure. Unfortunately, the appropriate definition for non-human wealth is still uncertain. In this paper, non-human wealth is taken to mean real personal financial wealth.

A few problems are associated with a simple regression like (7). First, the stationarity of the variables are ignored. If the variables are indeed non-stationary, then the ordinary least squares (OLS) method will produce inconsistent and biased estimates. Secondly, expressing the consumption function in a single equation form effectively ignores the endogeneity of the income and wealth variable. Most economists will not take the income variable as completely exogenous. Thirdly, past values of all the three variables will undoubtedly provide power in explaining current consumption. If the lags are suppressed with no good reason, serial correlation will become a real problem.

Clearly, estimation has to be done using a system of equations. Expressing all the potentially endogenous variables in the form of a VECM can circumvent the problems mentioned above. Furthermore, the VECM accounts for both the short-run and long-run dynamics, which is extremely appealing theoretically. In fact, Davidson (1978) used VECM to provide a model that could conform to steady-state postulates of economic theory and could also account for previous models and findings.

The data set, which belongs to Holden and Perman, is taken from Rao (1994) and used here.[5] Following the notation given earlier in (2), the data generating process is defined as:[6]

$$\Delta Z_t = \Gamma_1 \Delta Z_{t-1} + \Gamma_2 \Delta Z_{t-2} + \Pi Z_{t-3} + v_t \qquad v_t \sim IN(0,\Omega) \tag{8}$$

where Z_t' is $(C_t\ Y_t\ W_t)$.

The MLE of (8) are obtained through the methodology outlined in Section 2.[7]

3.2   MONTE CARLO SIMULATION[8]

Monte Carlo simulations are often used to study the statistical properties of various forms of test statistics. Whenever the distributions of the appropriate test statistics are non-standard and cannot be analytically evaluated, these simulations are used. The beauty of the method comes from the knowledge of all the important attributes of the constructed sequence. For this reason, it is commonly referred to as an 'experiment'. The only uncertainty comes from the stochastic part of the experiment.

An important limitation of a Monte Carlo simulation is that it is specific to the assumption used to generate the simulated data. For example, if the sample size is changed, or an additional parameter is added to the data generating process, an entirely new simulation needs to be performed. Nevertheless, it is this characteristic that enables

---

[5] Refer to data appendix for the details of the data set.

[6] C, Y and W are all I(1) variables and the VAR system formed by these series is found to have a lag structure of 2.

[7] Refer to data appendix for the estimates of the parameters.

[8] A brief exposition of the method can be found in Enders (1995), pg. 215-216.

the Monte Carlo experiment to study the behaviour of different test statistics in small or finite samples under different specifications.

The first step in a Monte Carlo experiment is to specify the parameters of the data generating process. In step 2, the computer generates a set of random numbers for one replication of the entire $\{v_t\}$ sequence, using the estimated Ω as the variance-covariance matrix. This set of random numbers together with the relevant parameters and initial conditions, are used to construct one sample consisting of the entire $\{Z_t\}$ sequence. Step 3 involves the computation of Johansen's trace test statistics for the sample generated in step 2. As this is just a single outcome of an experiment, steps 2 to 3 are repeated hundreds or even thousands of times to simulate many outcomes.

Using the MLE found earlier in Section 3.1, 1000 samples each of size 100 are generated.[9] Applying the Johansen's test to one particular sample, we would obtain three different test statistics, each representing a different pair of null and alternative hypothesis, namely:

(a) Null hypothesis of rank(Π) = 0 against the alternative of rank(Π) > 0.

(b) Null hypothesis of rank(Π) = 1 against the alternative of rank(Π) > 1.

(c) Null hypothesis of rank(Π) = 2 against the alternative of rank(Π) > 2.

The experiment was constructed in such a way that the maintain hypothesis is of rank(Π) = 1. Consolidating the results from 1000 samples, three sets of test statistics were produced. By analysing the distribution of these three sets of test statistics, we can assess the performance of Johansen's trace test.

4. EMPIRICAL RESULTS

In hypothesis testing, two types of error can be committed. Type I error is committed whenever the null hypothesis (H_0) is rejected when H_0 is in fact true. The probability of committing such an error is the level of significance α that a H_0 is being subjected to. Hence, we always know the chances of committing a type I error. Type II error is committed whenever H_0 is accepted when H_0 is in fact false. The probability of committing such an error is β where it is dependent on α and the true value of that parameter that is being tested. Since we do not usually know the true value of that parameter, there is no easy way to determine β.[10]

An objective way to judge the performance of a test is to find out its size and power properties. Given a particular sample size and α, the power (P) of a test is defined as the probability of rejecting H_0 when H_0 is actually false. In other words, it is the probability of avoiding a type II error. Therefore, P is equal to 1-β.

It would be obvious from the above explanation that a powerful test will have a high value for P. The procedure to determine P is also relatively straightforward. In practice, however, things are not so simple. First, the true value of β might be unknown. As it was mentioned earlier, the true value of the test parameter is unlikely to be known. Hence, a

---

[9] This procedure was repeated for sample sizes of 80, 60 and 40.

[10] See Berenson (1992), pg. 384-396 for a clear explanation of these concepts.

'correct' statistical distribution has to be selected to facilitate comparison. In this case, the critical values given by Johansen were chosen. This is of course based on the assumption that the values provided by Johansen are 'true'.

Secondly, the statistical distribution derived under the maintain hypothesis might suffer a fair amount of discrepancy from the true distribution. This is because finite samples do not enjoy the asymptotic properties that large samples have. If the Johansen's distribution is assumed to be a close approximation of the true distribution, there is likely to be such a discrepancy between the critical values given by the maintain hypothesis and that given by Johansen. As the focus of the paper is on the finite sample properties of the trace test, the magnitude of this discrepancy is also a major concern. This discrepancy can be measured by the probability of making a type II error.

The cumulative frequency distribution of the test statistics for a sample size of 100 can be found in Figure 1. The cumulative frequency curves J100-0, J100-1 and J100-2 represent the test statistics under the null hypothesis of rank(Π) = 0, rank(Π) = 1 and rank(Π) = 2 respectively. Based on the simulations, it is found that the probability of making a type II error is extremely low. At 1 percent significance level, β is roughly 2 percent and this gives a remarkable 98 percent for P. However, the maintain hypothesis is almost always rejected, even at a staggering 80 percent significance level. If the maintain hypothesis is tested at 10 percent significance level, the probability of making a type I error is about 30 percent. This drops to about 20 percent and 8 percent at 5 percent and 1 percent significance level respectively. Fortunately, the trace test does not encourage further rejections thereafter.

In the findings for a smaller sample size, namely 80, 60 and 40, the chances of committing a type II error gets larger as the sample size decreases. This is not a surprise. Intuitively, the power of a statistical test should diminish when sample size decreases. Incidentally, the probability of committing a type I error is also larger when the sample is smaller. This is also consistent with statistical theory. The cumulative frequency distributions of these test statistics can be found in Figures 2 to 4.

5. CONCLUDING REMARKS

It is evident from the empirical results that the trace test is indeed a powerful test. The test still holds considerable power for sample sizes as small as 40. However, judging the performance on just the power of the test is not wise. The other side of the story must come from the risk of running into a type I error. It would be just as bad if we were to reject a correct hypothesis. Since the trade-off seems to be in favour of the type II error, the recommended strategy is to carry out hypothesis testing at high significance levels. Obviously, this strategy will be more appealing to economists who are more conservative.

This study did not examine the issue of misspecification, which has an impact on the performance of the Johansen's trace statistics. Further research could also look into the possibility of tabulating critical values for small sample sizes.

REFERENCES

Berenson, M.L. and D.M. Levine (1992): *Basic Business Statistics: Concepts and Applications (5th Edition)*. New Jersey: Prentice Hall.

Cheung, Y.W. and K.S. Lai (1993): "Finite-Sample Sizes of Johansen's Likelihood Ratio Tests for Cointegration," *Oxford Bulletin of Economics and Statistics*, 55, 313-328.

Davidson, J.E.H., D.F. Hendry, F. Srba and S. Yeo (1978): "Econometric Modelling of the Aggregate Time-Series Relationship between Consumer's Expenditure and Income in the United Kingdom," *The Economic Journal*, 88, 661-692.

Duesenberry, J.S. (1949): *Income, Saving and the Theory of Consumer Behaviour*. Cambridge: Harvard University Press.

Enders, W. (1995): *Applied Econometric Time Series*. New York: John Wiley & Sons, Inc.

Engle, R.F. and C.W.J. Granger (1987): "Co-Integration and Error Correction: Representation, Estimation, and Testing," *Econometrica*, 55, 251-276.

Friedman, M. (1957): *A Theory of the Consumption Function*. New Jersey: Princeton University Press.

Hadjimatheou, G. (1987): *Consumer Economics after Keynes: Theory and Evidence of the Consumption Function*. Great Britain: Wheatsheaf Books.

Harris, R.I.D. (1995): *Using Cointegration Analysis in Econometric Modelling*. Harvester Wheatsheaf: Prentice Hall.

Hillier, G.H. (1990): "On the Normalization of Structural Equations: Properties of Direction Estimators," *Econometrica*, 58, 1181-1194.

Johansen, S. (1988): "Statistical Analysis of Cointegration Vectors," *Journal of Economic Dynamics and Control*, 12, 231-254.

Johansen, S. and K. Juselius (1990): "Maximum Likelihood Estimation and Inference on Cointegration – With Applications to the Demand for Money," *Oxford Bulletin of Economics and Statistics*, 52, 169-210.

Keynes, J.M. (1936): *The General Theory of Employment, Interest and Money*. London: Macmillan.

Maddala, G.S. (1992): *Introduction to Econometrics (Second Edition)*. New Jersey: Prentice Hall.

Modigliani, F. and R. Brumberg (1954): "Utility Analysis and the Consumption Function: An Interpretation of Cross-Section Data," *Post-Keynesian Economics*, 19, 99-124.

Rao, B.B. (1994): *Cointegration for the Applied Economist*. New York: St. Martin's Press. Holden, D. and R.J. Perman: "Unit Roots and Cointegration for the Economist".

Tobin, J. (1987): *Essays in Economics (Volume 2): Consumption and Econometrics*. Cambridge: MIT Press.

von Ungern-Sternberg, T. (1981): "Inflation and Savings: International Evidence on Inflation-Induced Income Losses," *The Economic Journal*, 91, 961-976.

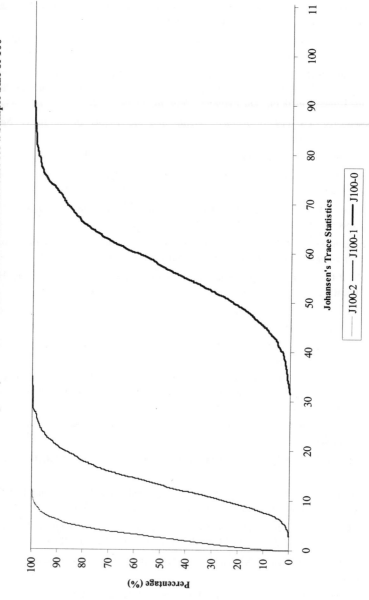

FIGURE 1

Cumulative Frequency Distribution of Johansen's Trace Statistics for a Sample Size of 100

FIGURE 2

Cumulative Frequency Distribution of Johansen's Trace Statistics for a Sample Size of 80

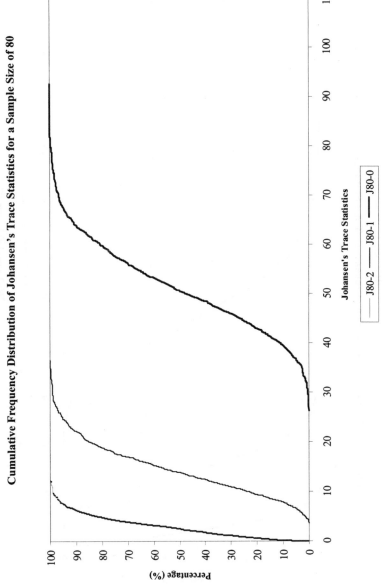

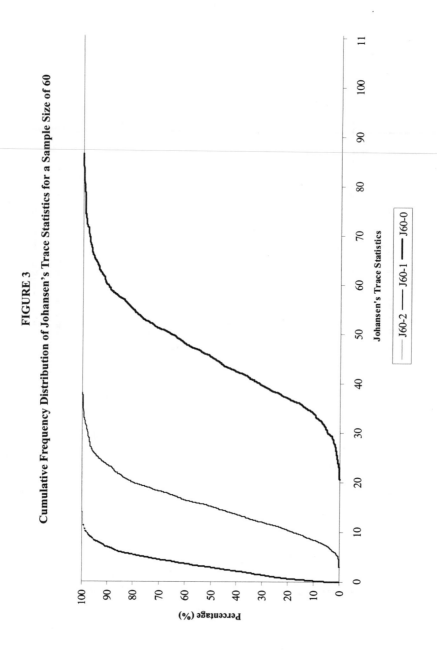

FIGURE 3

Cumulative Frequency Distribution of Johansen's Trace Statistics for a Sample Size of 60

FIGURE 4

Cumulative Frequency Distribution of Johansen's Trace Statistics for a Sample Size of 40

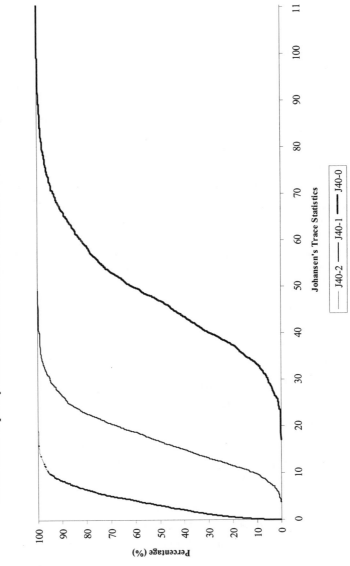

DATA APPENDIX[11]

DATA SOURCE

The U.K. quarterly data used in this paper is the same set of data adopted by Holden and Perman in their estimation of the consumption function. Three time series variables, namely consumption, income and wealth are used. These series are derived from the following original series:

(i)   CAAB – seasonally adjusted real consumers' expenditure in millions of pounds, 1985 prices.

(ii)   AIIX – seasonally adjusted nominal consumers' expenditure in millions of pounds, current prices.

(iii)   AIIW – seasonally adjusted nominal personal disposable income in millions of pounds, current prices.

These series can be found in Table 5 of *Economic Trends Annual Supplement* (1992).

The wealth series is defined as seasonally adjusted gross personal financial wealth in millions of pounds, current prices, and is compiled from several editions of *Financial Statistics* in order to obtain a consistent series.

Constant (1985) price series for income and wealth were obtained from the current price series using the implicit consumers' expenditure deflator (AIIX/CAAB). C, Y and W are the natural logarithms of the constant price consumption, income and wealth series.

PARAMETER ESTIMATES

$$\Gamma_1 = \begin{pmatrix} -0.401472 & 0.357848 & 0.081489 \\ 0.005820 & -0.154310 & 0.033510 \\ -0.356483 & 0.219360 & 0.193978 \end{pmatrix}$$

$$\Gamma_2 = \begin{pmatrix} 0.016794 & 0.064204 & 0.046832 \\ 0.264473 & -0.073391 & 0.017407 \\ 0.062981 & 0.099582 & 0.034108 \end{pmatrix}$$

$$\Pi = \alpha\beta' = \begin{pmatrix} 0.206272 \\ 0.363515 \\ 0.299067 \end{pmatrix} \begin{pmatrix} 1 & -0.928365 & -0.050390 \end{pmatrix}$$

$$\Omega = \begin{pmatrix} 0.000156 & 7.79\text{E}-05 & 5.71\text{E}-06 \\ 7.79\text{E}-05 & 0.000242 & -1.11\text{E}-05 \\ 5.71\text{E}-06 & -1.11\text{E}-05 & 0.001702 \end{pmatrix}$$

---

[11] Adapted from the data appendix in Rao (1994).

Trends in the Global Distribution of Income: 1960-1990

Tan Siew Hwee, Alice
&
Park Donghyun

Nanyang Business School, Nanyang Technological University, Nanyang Avenue, Singapore 639798
Fax: +(65) 792.4217, Tel: +(65) 799.6130, Email: adpark@ntu.edu.sg

Abstract In this paper, we use data from the Penn World Tables to examine whether the global distribution of income became more equal over the period 1960-1990. The evidence strongly indicates that it did not.

1. INTRODUCTION

Widespread poverty seems to persist in some developing countries while others are growing rapidly. The overall effect of such diverse performances on global income equality is unclear. Using data from the Penn World Table, this paper examines trends in the global distribution of income over the period 1960 - 1990. We assume the world to be one economy and all the people of the world to be members of this economy. We also assume that there is perfect income equality among the citizens of each country. Under those assumptions, we address our central question of whether there has been a global convergence of income. That is, whether global income inequality has been decreasing.

Theoretically, the question of convergence revolves around economic growth theories. Some growth theories, especially those assuming diminishing returns to scale, predict that international income inequality will decline over time. Others such as endogenous growth models do not. We discuss the various growth theories and their theoretical implications for convergence.

2. GROWTH THEORIES AND CONVERGENCE

For international convergence to take place, poor countries must catch up economically with rich ones over time. This will be possible only if poor countries experience higher growth rates than rich ones. Different theories of economic growth generate different predictions about the pattern of economic growth across countries over time. In this section, we shall examine a number of growth theories.

2.1 NEOCLASSICAL APPROACH

The neoclassical approach to growth theory is the most widely used by economists working in this field. It consists of two distinct strands : theories based on the Solow model and theories based on endogenous growth models.

2.1.1 Solow Model

The Solow model is the most basic neoclassical model of economic growth. Solow(1956, 1957) combined the usual two-factor neoclassical production function with a simple model of capital accumulation in which a constant proportion of output is saved and devoted to increasing the stock of capital.

The assumption of diminishing marginal productivity in Solow's basic model means that in steady-state capital and labour must be growing at the same rate. Therefore, the capital-labour ratio is constant. However, this model could not explain the stylised fact of rising per capita incomes. Solow introduced exogenous technological progress to overcome this problem. Per capita output growth can then be attributed to growth in the capita-labour ratio and growth in technology. According to Solow, the latter was the more important source of economic growth .

The Solow model itself does not give much insight as to whether convergence will take place. However, this is a basic model and the point of departure for other, more sophisticated models. We now discuss a particularly significant variant of such models-the MRW model.

2.1.1.1 MRW Model

In an empirically-oriented 1992 paper, Mankiw, Romer and Weil (henceforth MRW) extend the Solow model by incorporating human capital. A critical assumption of MRW is that the level of technology is the same across all countries since most important technological information are freely available to all countries, through sources such as scientific journals and the media.

Relative to the Solow model, a higher share of output goes to capital, which now consists of human as well as physical capital. However, capital is still subject to diminishing marginal productivity. Consequently, like the basic Solow model, the MRW model implies that per capita income growth is unsustainable in the absence of technological progress.

2.1.1.2 Implications for Convergence:

Whether there is convergence in the MRW model depends crucially on assumptions concerning capital mobility. If there is no mobility, then each country converges to the steady-state, which grows at the uniform rate of technological progress. As a result, there is no tendency for international incomes to converge. Countries growing the fastest are simply those furthest from their steady-state. Over time, all countries will grow at the same rate.

However, if we assume capital mobility, investors allocate their funds around the world so as to obtain the highest return. Since capital is subject to diminishing marginal productivity, countries with high capital-labour ratios and hence high per capita incomes must have low returns to capital relative to countries with low capital-labour ratios and hence low per capita incomes. As such, funds will flow from the rich countries to poor countries. Consequently, poor countries will catch up with rich ones over time, leading to international convergence.

2.1.2 Endogenous Growth

Romer(1986) and Lucas(1988) sought to explain economic growth as the result of an endogenous process of rational economic activity. This school of thought downplays the importance of exogenous technological progress as a cause of economic growth. The two main endogenous growth models are the AK model and the extended AK model which allows for human capital.

2.1.2.1 The AK Model
The AK model assumes that there are always constant returns to physical capital. The consumption and accumulation paths are determined by the representative agent's utility maximisation. In this model, growth is endogenous and requires no technical progress to be sustainable. Rather, the rate of capital accumulation alone determines the rate of growth since there is no diminishing marginal productivity. An increase in the private rate of return on capital, a reduction in the representative agent's discount rate or any other event which affects the decision to accumulate physical capital will permanently change the rate of economic growth.

2.1.2.2 Adding Human Capital
The model developed by Barro and Sala-i-Martin(1994) discards the notion of technical progress altogether. They assume that all output growth which cannot be attributed to physical capital is due to human capital and completely ignore unskilled labour as a factor of production. This make sense if we define human capital as describing the full range of human capacities. Both human and physical capital are characterised by constant returns. Economic growth does not require exogenous technological progress to be sustainable since neither type of capital is subject to diminishing marginal returns. Consumption and accumulable paths are determined as in the basic AK model.

2.1.2.3 Implications for Convergence:
In the AK model, if there are no policies which affect the representative agent's discount rate or the private rate of return on capital, there is no tendency for countries with different income levels to experience different rates of growth. Hence, there is no convergence.

The two-factor model predicts that capital mobility will lead to identical growth rates and returns to both types of capital, but not necessarily incomes. A poor country will remain poor despite an inflow of physical capital from abroad if it is poorly endowed with human capital. Thus, a pre-condition for international convergence is that poor countries must be relatively well-endowed with human capital.

3. INCOME INEQUALITY AND MEASURING INCOME INEQUALITY

Income inequality denotes the dispersion aspect of income distribution. It refers to the extent of income disparity between the rich and the poor. The simplest definition is to state that there is inequality whenever one person has more resources than some other person. The greater the disparity, the more unequal is income distribution. There are various measures of inequality that we can use to empirically examine the issue of convergence.

3.1 INEQUALITY MEASURES

A good income inequality index should have three basic properties: (1) mean or scale independence, that is, the index remains invariant if everyone's income is changed by the same proportion; (2) population size independence, that is, the index remains invariant if the number of the people at each income level is changed by the same proportion; and (3) the Pigou-Dalton condition, that is, any transfer from a rich person to a poorer person which does not reverse their relative ranks reduces the value of the index.

Measures of inequality can be classified into two groups : positive measures and normative measures. A positive measure reflects a purely statistical measurement of the deviation of a given income distribution from perfect equality. It makes no explicit use of any concept of social welfare. Positive indices can be further divided into those which make specific assumptions about the probability distribution of income and those which do not. A normative measure, in contrast, does incorporate value judgements about the distribution. It is thus based on some explicit formulation of a social welfare function.

In this paper, we will make use of three positive indices - the coefficient of variation, the Theil index and the Gini coefficient. Of the positive indices, only the Theil index is based on specific assumptions about the income distribution. More precisely, it assumes income to be lognormally distributed.

4. DATA DESCRIPTION AND METHODOLOGY

The data we use are from the Penn World Tables(PWT), version 5.6. Its unique feature is that all economic variables are denominated in a common set of prices and in a common currency. This enables us to make meaningful international comparisons of economic variables [see Summers and Heston (1991), Kravis (1976), Kravis (1986)].

Where data is not available in the Penn World Tables, we use estimates from either the Tables themselves or an alternative source, the World Development Report. Since we are interested in trends in global inequality, it is important to try to include as many countries as possible so that our data set encompasses as much of the world as possible.

Our actual sample consists of 137 countries and territories, and covers well over 95 percent of the world population. Our variables of interest are population(POP in PWT) and real GDP per capita (RGDPC in PWT) of each economic entity. We examine the data at 5-year intervals from 1960 to 1990.

We do not make use of information about income distribution in individual countries, which are available only on a limited basis in any case. The reason is that we are interested in inequality among the nations of the world rather than among the individuals of the world. That is, since we are analysing inequality among countries rather than inequality among individuals, we do not need country data on income distribution.

Table 1 shows the trends in global population, income and per capita income implied by our data set. We obtain global population and global income by summing up all the populations and national incomes in our data set respectively, while we calculate global per capita income by dividing global income by global population.

4.1 PURCHASING POWER PARITY

Before we proceed to discuss our findings, we shall first briefly touch on the concept of purchasing power parity. The Penn World Tables are derived from the benchmark studies of the ICP(International Comparison Program). The best known of the ICP's empirical results is the documentation of the difference between a country's exchange rate and its purchasing power parity, defined below. The ICP method of estimating national incomes is based on purchasing power parity and gives a much more accurate picture of incomes and their dispersion relative to the traditional method, which is based on exchange rate and exaggerates the dispersion of incomes by systematically understating those of poorer countries.

Exchange rate is the price of a currency and is affected by the demand and supply of the currency which, in turn depends on the flows of goods and services between countries. That is to say, only flows of traded goods and services affect the exchange rate. Thus, the use of the exchange rate to estimate economic variables will introduce a bias in cross-country comparisons since non-traded goods are omitted. More precisely, using exchange rates to convert the GDP of all the countries in the world into a common currency will greatly understate the incomes and living standards of the poor countries. This is because non-tradable goods and services tend to be cheaper in poor countries than in rich countries.

On the other hand, purchasing power parity is the ratio of the prices of both tradable and non-tradable in a country relative to those of another. As such, it allows for a more accurate comparison of price levels and hence real incomes across countries than exchange rates. RGDPC has been estimated on the basis of international prices which embody purchasing power parity so it is free from the biases associated with using exchange rates.

4.2 METHODOLOGY

We will make use of three inequality measures to analyse trends in international income inequality from 1960 to 1990. We divide the global population or, more accurately, the total population of the countries and territories in our sample, into fifths. We first rank the economic entities by their per capita income in ascending order. For example, in 1960, we have Ethiopia on one end and United States at the other.

And then, we divide the world population by five. For example, if there are four billion people in the world, each fifth would consist of 800 million. In constructing the poorest fifth, we would include all Ethiopians and the populations of the next poorest countries until 800 million people living in the poorest countries are included. We do the same for the other 4 fifths. Countries at the cut-off points will have a part of their population included in one fifth and another part in another fifth. We can obviously repeat this exercise for tenths of the world population rather than fifths.

5. EMPIRICAL EVIDENCE

In Table 2, Q1 represents the share of global income accruing to the poorest fifth of the global population while Q5 refers to the share of the richest fifth. The gap between the rich countries and the poor ones does not seem to have narrowed over time. From Figure 1, we can see that the share of global income accruing to each fifth has been fairly constant.

Next we re-examine the data after dividing the global population into tenths. As Table 3 and Figure 2 show, the trend for tenths of the global population closely follows that of fifths. The proportion of income attributing to each tenth is also fairly constant. There is no evidence that the poor are catching up with the rich.

5.1 GINI COEFFICIENT

Gini coefficient is the most well-known and widely used measure of inequality. It bears a closest relationship to the Lorenz curve, which plots the cumulative share of total income against the cumulative share of the total population. A Gini coefficient value of zero means perfect equality while a value of one denotes perfect inequality. There are various formulations of the Gini coefficient.

Let us denote the income of the ith person as y_i and assume there are n individuals. Then with individuals labelled in ascending order of income so that $y_1 \leq y_2 \leq \dots\dots \leq y_n$, Sen (1973) formulates the Gini coefficient as

$$G = 1 + \frac{1}{n} - \frac{2}{n^2 y}[ny_1 + (n-1)y_2 + \ldots\ldots+2y_{n-1} + y_n]$$

$$= \frac{n+1}{n} - \frac{2}{n^2 y} \sum_{i=1}^{n}(n+1-i)'y_i \tag{1}$$

To derive the values of the Gini coefficients from fifths and tenths of the global population, we can re-express the above formula as

$$G = 1 + \frac{1}{n} - \frac{2}{n^2 Q}[nQ_1 + (n-1)Q_2 + \ldots\ldots+2Q_{n-1} + Q_n]$$

$$= \frac{n+1}{n} - \frac{2}{n^2 Q} \sum_{i=1}^{n}(n+1-i)Q_i \tag{2}$$

where Q_i is the income share of the ith fraction of global population, $\overline{Q}$ is the average income share and $Q_1 \leq Q_2 \leq \ldots\ldots \leq Q_n$.

As Table 4 and Figure 3 show, for both fifths and tenths of the global population, the pattern is similar. Inequality rises, falls and then rises again over the period 1960 to 1990. The values of the Gini coefficient in 1990 do not differ substantially from those of 1960.

5.2 COEFFICIENT OF VARIATION

Coefficient of variation is defined as the standard deviation divided by the mean. It is a measure of relative dispersion and is unit free.

$$C = \frac{\sqrt{V}}{\overline{y}} \tag{3}$$

where V is the variance of income :

$$V = \frac{1}{n} \sum_{i=1}^{n}(\overline{y} - y_i)^2 \tag{4}$$

$\overline{y}$ is the average income and y_i is the income of individual i. The coefficient of variation is equally sensitive to transfer of income at all income levels. That is, it attaches equal weights to transfer at different income levels.

Again, since we are using fractions of the global population, we can re-express the above as

$$V = \frac{1}{n} \sum_{i=1}^{n}(\overline{Q} - Q_i)^2 \tag{5}$$

As Table 5 and Figure 4 show, for both fifths and tenths of the global population, the movement of the coefficient of variation during 1960 - 1990 mirrors that of the Gini coefficient.

5.3 THEIL INDEX

Theil index [see Theil (1967)] is based on the notion of entropy in information theory. The fundamental idea of information entropy is that occurrences which differ greatly from what was expected should receive more weight than events which conform with prior expectations.

The Theil index of income inequality(T) builds on this concept of entropy. Formally, it is the expected information of the message that transforms population shares into income shares. The algebraic formula is:

$$T = \log n - \sum_{i=1}^{n} \frac{y_i}{Y} \log\left(\frac{Y}{y_i}\right)$$

$$= \sum_{i=1}^{n} \frac{y_i}{Y} \log\left(\frac{y_i n}{Y}\right) \tag{6}$$

where Y is total income.

We can transform the above equation into

$$T = \sum_{i=1}^{n} Q_i \log(Q_i n) \tag{7}$$

The value of the Theil index ranges from a minimum of zero when there is perfect equality to a maximum of log n when there is perfect inequality.

Table 6 and Figure 5 show that the trend is similar to that of the Gini coefficient and the coefficient of variation. The value of the Theil index has not changed much over the period under study.

We shall now take a closer look at inequality between developed and developing countries. Developed nations include all members of the OECD except Turkey and Mexico while developing countries comprise all the other countries in our sample.

Table 7 shows that the proportion of the world income accruing to the OECD countries has been declining over the years. However, it is important to note that, as we can see in Table 8, the proportion of the world population living in those countries has also been falling. Therefore, the ratio of the average per capita income of developed countries to that of developing countries might be a more appropriate index. As we can see from Table 9 and Figure 6, this ratio is slightly higher, not lower, in 1990 than in 1960.

Among developing nations, there is a wide variation in growth rates. For instance, East Asia is growing at such a quick rate such that the growth of the area is often considered a miracle. On the other hand, many African countries have experienced stagnation, with some even experiencing negative growth. We now examine convergence among developing countries during 1960 - 1990. We make use of the same inequality measures.

As can be seen from Tables 10 - 12 and Figures 7 - 9, all three measures of inequality show identical trends. Inequality among developing nations rose during the 1960s and 1970s, and then fell slightly during the 1980s. It should also be noted that inequality among developing countries does not appear to have changed greatly over the past 3 decades.

6. CONCLUSION

In this paper, we address the question of whether international convergence has taken place both at the global level and among developing countries. In both cases, we do not find any evidence of decreasing inequality among countries. In fact, according to all three indices of inequality we use, inequality has increased slightly both the global level and among developing nations during the period under study.

The rapid growth of some developing nations, particularly in East Asia, has not been significant enough to close the gap between developed and developing nations. However, with the rapid growth of China and to a lesser extent India, two nations with enormous populations, we can expect greater convergence in the near future.

REFERENCES

Barro, R. J. and X. Sala-i-Martin (1994): *Economic Growth, manuscript.* Harvard University.

Cowell, F. A. (1977): *Measuring Inequality*, John Wiley and Son, New York.

Kravis, I. B. (1976): "A Survey of International Comparisons of Productivity", *The Economic Journal*, 86, 1 - 44.

_____ (1986): "The Three Faces of the International Comparison Project", *The World Bank Observer*, 1(1):3-26, January.

Lucas, R. (1988): " On the Mechanics of Economic Development," *Journal of Monetary Economics,* 22, 3 - 42.

Mankiw, N., D. Romer and D. N. Weil (1992): "A Contribution to the Empirics of Economic Growth," *Quarterly Journal of Economics,* May, 407 - 437.

Romer, P. M. (1986): "Increasing Returns and Long-Run Growth", *Journal of Political Economy,* 94, 1002 - 1037.

Sen, A. K. (1973): *On Economic Inequality*, Clarendon Press, Oxford.

Solow, R. M. (1956): "A Contribution to the Theory of Economic Growth", *Quarterly Journal of Economics*, 70, 65 - 95.

_____ (1957): " Technical Change and Aggregate Production Function", *Review of Economics and Statistics*, 39, 312 - 320.

Summers, R. and Heston, A. (1991): "The Penn World Table(Mark 5): An Expanded Set of International Comparisons, 1950 - 1988", *Quarterly Journal of Economics*, 327 - 368.

Theil, H. (1967): *Economic and Information Theory*, North Holland, Amsterdam.

World Development Report, Oxford University Press, New York, various issues.

TABLE 1

Trends in Global Population and Income

	Population (in millions)	Total Income (in billions US$)	Per Capita Income (in US$)
1960	2,954.411	6,598.285546	2,233.37
1965	3,240.819	8,490.020219	2,619.71
1970	3,592.903	11,047.673070	3,074.86
1975	3,949.484	13,417.011560	3,394.16
1980	4,308.683	16,379.097390	3,801.42
1985	4,693.626	18,788.784040	4,003.04
1990	5,117.167	22,111.545520	4,321.05

TABLE 2

Percentile Shares of Global Income by Fifths

	1960	1965	1970	1975	1980	1985	1990
Q1	0.0475854	0.0418971	0.0423303	0.0417265	0.0419646	0.0445986	0.0458686
Q2	0.0575732	0.0501591	0.0485554	0.0468382	0.0507529	0.0599941	0.0603034
Q3	0.0834905	0.0765536	0.0703238	0.0655364	0.0677054	0.0716750	0.0704533
Q4	0.2028410	0.2119243	0.2199805	0.2429323	0.2378837	0.2205088	0.2042437
Q5	0.6085098	0.6194658	0.6188100	0.6029666	0.6016933	0.6032235	0.6191310

TABLE 3

Percentile Shares of Global Income by Tenths

	1960	1965	1970	1975	1980	1985	1990
Q1	0.0221978	0.0198718	0.0196951	0.0191782	0.0187627	0.0183685	0.0166576
Q2	0.0253877	0.0220253	0.0226352	0.0225483	0.0232019	0.0262300	0.0292110
Q3	0.0258597	0.0225602	0.0228120	0.0228475	0.0251835	0.0284681	0.0296628
Q4	0.0317136	0.0275989	0.0257435	0.0239907	0.0255694	0.0315260	0.0306407
Q5	0.0343966	0.0298069	0.0267681	0.0261108	0.0272003	0.0315260	0.0307539
Q6	0.0490939	0.0467467	0.0435556	0.0394256	0.0405051	0.0401490	0.0396994
Q7	0.0862464	0.0855370	0.0845730	0.0927292	0.0887566	0.0821678	0.0731740
Q8	0.1165946	0.1263872	0.1354075	0.1502030	0.1491271	0.1383409	0.1310696
Q9	0.2130185	0.2248058	0.2408552	0.2371631	0.2344140	0.2342061	0.2404249
Q10	0.3954913	0.3946601	0.3779548	0.3658035	0.3672793	0.3690174	0.3787060

TABLE 4

Gini Coefficient, 1960 to 1990

	1960	1965	1970	1975	1980	1985	1990
10%	0.530508	0.550245	0.550813	0.547824	0.543772	0.532159	0.538051
20%	0.506847	0.526761	0.529754	0.527430	0.522635	0.511106	0.516186

TABLE 5

Coefficient of Variation, 1960 to 1990

	1960	1965	1970	1975	1980	1985	1990
10%	1.136785	1.161072	1.144753	1.119947	1.115883	1.106127	1.136782
20%	1.058250	1.092661	1.096385	1.074278	1.066641	1.056476	1.085686

TABLE 6

Theil Index, 1960 to 1990

	1960	1965	1970	1975	1980	1985	1990
10%	0.518549	0.552973	0.554438	0.547424	0.539260	0.518708	0.537158
20%	0.466995	0.504222	0.511911	0.506138	0.495525	0.474753	0.490555

TABLE 7

Proportion of Income Accruing to Developed and Developing Countries

	1960	1965	1970	1975	1980	1985	1990
Developed countries	0.60508	0.61005	0.59223	0.55905	0.54046	0.527726	0.52596
Developing countries	0.39492	0.38995	0.40777	0.44095	0.45954	0.472274	0.47404

TABLE 8

Proportion of Global Population

	1960	1965	1970	1975	1980	1985	1990
Developed countries	0.20761	0.20039	0.18922	0.17992	0.17072	0.16148	0.15267
Developing countries	0.79239	0.79961	0.81078	0.82008	0.82929	0.83852	0.84733

TABLE 9

Ratio of average income of developed nations to that of developing nations

1960	1965	1970	1975	1980	1985	1990
5.847881	6.242668	5.328912	5.778799	5.713142	5.802467	6.158004

TABLE 10

Gini Coefficient for Developing Countries, 1960 to 1990

	1960	1965	1970	1975	1980	1985	1990
10%	0.347563	0.388918	0.407257	0.438316	0.435849	0.407797	0.404538
20%	0.333423	0.375537	0.392925	0.422023	0.418638	0.387896	0.383178

TABLE 11

Coefficient of Variation for Developing Nations, 1960 to 1990

	1960	1965	1970	1975	1980	1985	1990
10%	0.705359	0.799410	0.852395	0.928125	0.922052	0.863657	0.875947
20%	0.675246	0.772490	0.823921	0.897000	0.886285	0.811841	0.809264

TABLE 12

Theil Index for Developing Countries, 1960 to 1990

	1960	1965	1970	1975	1980	1985	1990
10%	0.209822	0.264944	0.297592	0.350603	0.343577	0.298527	0.300320
20%	0.1966582	0.253271	0.283975	0.332033	0.324719	0.274562	0.271432

FIGURE 1

The Share of Global Income Accruing to each Fifth of Global Population

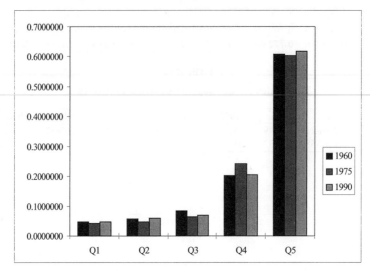

FIGURE 2

The Share of Global Income Accruing to each Tenth of Global Population

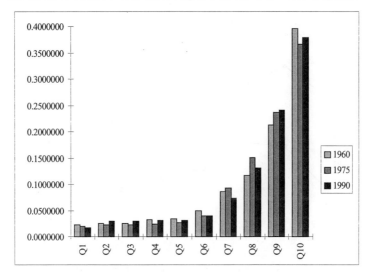

FIGURE 3

Gini Coefficient Trends, 1960 - 1990

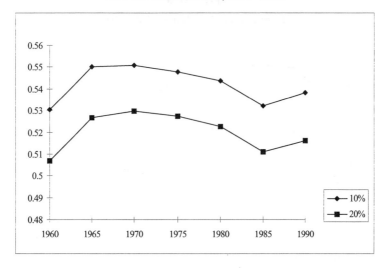

FIGURE 4

Trends in Coefficient of Variation, 1960 - 1990

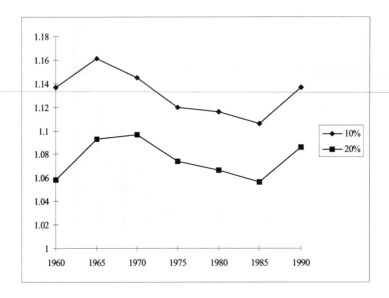

FIGURE 5

Trends in the Theil Index, 1960 - 1990

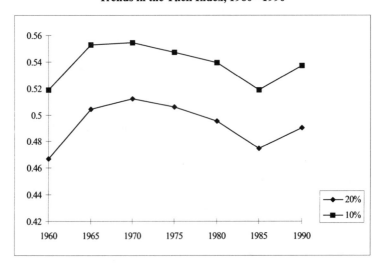

FIGURE 6

The Ratio of Average Per Capita Income of Developed Countries to the Average Per Capita Income of Developing Countries

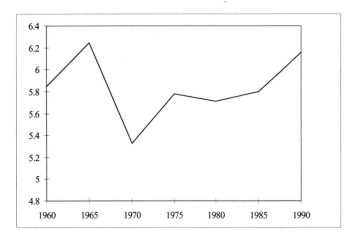

FIGURE 7

Trends in Gini Coefficient for Developing Countries, 1960 - 1990

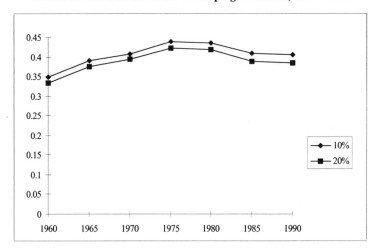

FIGURE 8

Trends in Coefficient of Variation for Developing Countries, 1960 - 1990

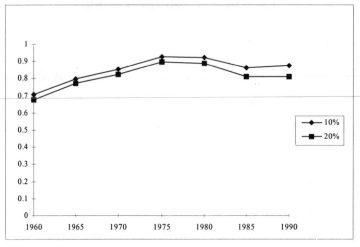

FIGURE 9

Trends in Theil Index for Developing Countries, 1960 - 1990

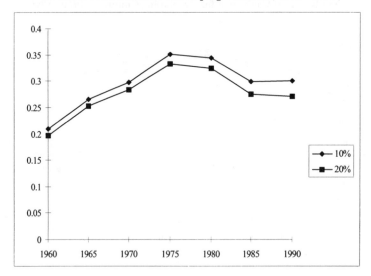